Music Education Research

Music Education Research

An Introduction

PETER MIKSZA,
JULIA T. SHAW,
LAUREN KAPALKA RICHERME,
PHILLIP M. HASH, AND
DONALD A. HODGES

with a contribution by
ELIZABETH CASSIDY PARKER

Oxford University Press is a department of the University of Oxford. It furthers the University's objective of excellence in research, scholarship, and education by publishing worldwide. Oxford is a registered trade mark of Oxford University Press in the UK and certain other countries.

Published in the United States of America by Oxford University Press
198 Madison Avenue, New York, NY 10016, United States of America.

© Oxford University Press 2023

All rights reserved. No part of this publication may be reproduced, stored in a retrieval system, or transmitted, in any form or by any means, without the prior permission in writing of Oxford University Press, or as expressly permitted by law, by license, or under terms agreed with the appropriate reproduction rights organization. Inquiries concerning reproduction outside the scope of the above should be sent to the Rights Department, Oxford University Press, at the address above.

You must not circulate this work in any other form
and you must impose this same condition on any acquirer.

Library of Congress Cataloging-in-Publication Data
Names: Miksza, Peter, author. | Shaw, Julia T., author. |
Richerme, Lauren Kapalka, author. | Hash, Phillip M., author. |
Hodges, Donald A., author. | Parker, Elizabeth Cassidy, contributor.
Title: Music education research : an introduction / Peter Miksza, Julia T. Shaw,
Lauren Kapalka Richerme, Phillip M. Hash, Donald A. Hodges ;
with a contribution by Elizabeth Cassidy Parker.
Description: [1.] | New York, NY : Oxford University Press, 2023. |
Includes bibliographical references and index.
Identifiers: LCCN 2022038429 (print) | LCCN 2022038430 (ebook) |
ISBN 9780197639757 (hardback) | ISBN 9780197639764 (paperback) |
ISBN 9780197639788 (epub)
Subjects: LCSH: Music—Instruction and study—Research.
Classification: LCC MT1.M98244 2023 (print) | LCC MT1 (ebook) |
DDC 780.71—dc23/eng/20220811
LC record available at https://lccn.loc.gov/2022038429
LC ebook record available at https://lccn.loc.gov/2022038430

DOI: 10.1093/oso/9780197639757.001.0001

"This fresh, new book captures the remarkable diversification and advancement of music education research that has taken place over the last several years. Concise yet comprehensive, Miksza et al.'s resource should be required reading for each and every one of our graduate students."

—Martin J. Bergee, Professor of Music Education, University of Kansas

"*Music Education Research: An Introduction* is the perfect text for music educators interested in studying the important issues of teaching and learning in their classrooms. Authors in the text write in an accessible way and highlight the key concepts that relate to research design when referencing music education studies. I can't wait to use it as a text with my summers-only Master of Music Education students who are curious and want to know more, in practitioner terms, about how to design, implement, and interpret their own research projects as well as understand the research of others."

—Colleen Conway, Professor of Music Education, University of Michigan–Ann Arbor

"This comprehensive and approachable volume promises to be the 'household text' for the next generation of music education researchers. The book is rich with recent examples of music education scholarship from a wide range of methods and perspectives. Complex topics are presented thoughtfully and pedagogically, with ample practical applications and how-to steps for students who are new to the world of research. At the same time, the text provides such a thorough and thoughtful treatment of more recent trends in music education scholarship that it deserves a place on the bookshelf of every active music education researcher."

—Karin S. Hendricks, Associate Professor and Chair of Music Education, Boston University

"As the authors suggest, research moves a profession forward, but without a solid background in research methodologies, no aspiring researcher will ever be equipped to undertake studies of lasting value. *Music Education Research: An Introduction* provides a timely, comprehensive, and authoritative resource upon which to hone one's craft as a researcher, as well as a resource that will inspire the next generation of music education researchers."

—Gary E. McPherson, Professor of Music, Ormond Chair of Music, Melbourne Conservatorium of Music, University of Melbourne

"I have been teaching an introductory music education research class for over 30 years, and finally my 30-year search for an ideal text is over! The authors of this excellent book clearly understand the needs of students who are learning to consume, conduct, and disseminate research. Students will benefit from the balanced approach to various research paradigms, clear explanations of complex ideas, valuable sections with definitions of terms, and excellent use of examples drawn from pertinent music education literature. Instructors will appreciate the action-oriented activities suggested at the end of each chapter. This text was written by a team of first-rate scholars, each with an impressive record of engagement in producing exemplary music education research, as well as mentoring others through their roles as teachers and as reviewers/editors for professional journals. Thus, it is no wonder that this is a high-quality book that makes a much-needed contribution to the profession. I look forward to using it for my music education research course!"

—Wendy Sims, Curators' Distinguished Teaching Professor of Music Education, University of Missouri

Contents

Preface ix
About the Companion Website xiii

1. The Role of Research in Music Education — 1
2. The Typical Components of Music Education Research — 19
3. Conducting a Review of Related Literature — 39
4. Historical Research — 59
5. Philosophical Researchers' Aims and Processes — 83
6. Conducting Philosophical Research: Additional Considerations — 97
7. Characteristics of Qualitative Inquiry — 115
8. Common Elements of Qualitative Research Reports — 129
9. Qualitative Case Study Research — 157
10. Additional Qualitative Approaches: Ethnography, Grounded Theory, Narrative, and Phenomenology — 183
11. Considerations of Quality in Qualitative Research — 217
12. Quantitative Descriptive and Correlational Research — 241
13. Experimental Research — 263
14. Designing Experimental Research — 283
15. Measurement — 309
16. Descriptive Statistics — 325
17. Correlational Statistics — 347
18. Determining Differences with Inferential Statistics — 371
19. Action Research — 403
20. Scholarly Writing: Practice, Patience, and Passion — 417
21. Disseminating Research — 431

viii CONTENTS

*Appendix A: Selected Online Resources for Primary Source Material on
the History of Music Education* 451
Appendix B: Data Entry 455
Appendix C: Research Journals Related to Music Education 459

Index 461

Preface

We have come to realize that music teachers cannot help but be curious about the teaching and learning phenomena they observe each day on the job. In fact, we are certain that the rich experiences you have had as a teacher in communities, schools, classrooms, rehearsal halls, lesson studios, concert venues, and elsewhere have led you to your own unique and fascinating questions about music education. Oftentimes it is the pursuit of answers to these questions that drives teachers to become leaders in the field, introducing innovative and insightful new ideas and practices for the benefit of all.

In this book, we invite you to consider how conducting research can serve to satisfy your curiosity while also contributing to our collective professional knowledge. The chapters that follow will introduce you to what systematic research in music education is as well as provide an overview of how a variety of research approaches can be applied to address a wide range of research questions. Our aim is that this book can serve as a resource for you as you begin to explore the scholarly world of music education.

We are aware that some readers may find the systematic approaches to research described in this book to be unfamiliar to them. We imagine this could especially be the case for those who have dedicated their professional lives to keeping up with and adjusting to the challenges their students face on a daily basis. For example, when teachers notice a student struggling, they will want an immediate solution to apply. In contrast, conducting research is a drawn-out, gradual process, and research results must be vetted through peer review before they will be accepted into the collective knowledge base of the profession. Moreover, for some, an introduction to research can appear to be intimidating. Most new scholars will encounter a vast number of new terms, and many will find that the specificity and precision that scholars seek to achieve through academic styles of writing can be challenging to digest at first.

As such, we have crafted the materials in this book to be as straightforward as possible. We do not wish to stifle your interests by including too much jargon and detail; rather, we took special care to include only information and examples that could reveal key principles and concepts. By doing so, we hope that you can, instead, focus your energies on how you might begin to incorporate research into your professional work as well as how you might begin to engage in scholarly research of your own. Ultimately, what we are offering you in this book are simply additional avenues for learning more about what music education is and can be and another method for helping the profession grow.

Compared to other areas of investigation, music education research has a fairly short history. The *Journal of Research in Music Education* was the first journal aimed specifically at addressing topics of music teaching and learning, and its first issue appeared in 1953. Since then, many new journals have come on the scene, and these publications, along with opportunities to present research at conferences and symposia, have enormously increased the quantity of music education research available. Quality has improved exponentially, too, as each new generation of music education researchers reaps the benefit of the work of those who have gone before. This book should be considered an introduction to music education research, but be aware that there are many advanced sources one can access for additional information.

As a prelude to what you are about to read, we have three suggestions:

1. In addition to taking a course or reading a book on music education research, one of the best things you can do to become a researcher is to read published research studies. Many examples are presented throughout this book. Although it is not necessary to read every one of these examples, reading quite a few, especially in one's area of interest, is highly recommended.
2. Early in the process, even before one has a solid grasp on all the fine points, it can be very helpful to engage in research. Initial attempts can be small, informal projects that give you—as a beginning researcher—some experience in collecting and analyzing data or constructing philosophical ideas. Please note, however, that before engaging children in any research project, it is important to gain the approval of parents, administrators, and other authorities.
3. Be inquisitive. It is important to be curious about music teaching and learning. Most successful researchers are passionate about unlocking mysteries that surround our profession. Some of these "unknowns" are relatively practical matters that music teachers face on a daily basis. Others are concerned with the deepest, most profound aspects of the human musical experience, such as Why are we musical? and Why do human beings respond so strongly and emotionally to music? Find the questions that motivate you.

The core value of research is that it can help us continuously move the profession forward. What does this mean? It means that far too often music educators rely on their own experiences or on the advice or opinion of others. For example, whether we wish to identify evidence-based practices, explore the intersection of music and culture, critically reflect on the state of the profession, learn from our history, or imagine new paradigms to shape music teaching and learning, research can help.

Knowledge derived from research assumes critical importance in most serious professions. For example, although doctors must certainly have their own opinions, the practice of their craft depends to a great extent on what researchers have learned and disseminated to the world. Physicians do not prescribe a drug unless scientific research has demonstrated that it will be effective for the symptoms presented by the patient. Likewise, a judge must rule on the factual evidence presented by lawyers at a trial, not on personal whim.

Of course, teaching is much different from the practice of medicine or law. However, when we are able to base our understanding of music education on research, we can move closer to effective and meaningful practices. Ideally, over time, more and more of our work will be based on research. The purpose of this book, then, is to introduce music educators to the basic principles that undergird music education research. It is our hope that after reading it, students will be prepared to begin their journey toward becoming music education scholars.

While all five authors had the opportunity to review and contribute to this entire text, one or two individuals served as the sole or primary writers for each chapter. Hash authored Chapter 4 ("Historical Research") and Hash and Hodges wrote Chapter 21 ("Disseminating Research"). Richerme wrote Chapters 5 and 6, which address philosophical research, and she was the primary author for Chapter 20 ("Scholarly Writing"), which included ideas from Hodges. Shaw authored the chapters describing qualitative research practices (Chapters 7, 8, 9, 10, and 11). Hodges and Miksza served as the primary authors for Chapters 1 and 2, although Hash, Richerme, and Shaw also made contributions to these chapters. Hodges and Miksza wrote the information on conducting a literature review (Chapter 3) and the quantitative research chapters (Chapters 12, 13, 14, 15, 16, 17, and 18). Also, Elizabeth Parker participated in this collaboration as a contributing author and wrote Chapter 19 ("Action Research").

About the Companion Website

Oxford has created a website to accompany *Music Education Research*. Material that cannot be made available in a book is provided here. We encourage you to consult this resource in conjunction with the chapters. Examples available online are indicated in the text with Oxford's symbol ⏵. These materials are available at https://global.oup.com/us/companion.websites/9780197639764/

1
The Role of Research in Music Education

Chapter Preview

In this chapter we will examine the role that research plays in the music education profession and introduce several ways to categorize different types of research. Research in music education includes quantitative, qualitative, historical, philosophical, and action approaches to systematic inquiry. Each of these types of research has a unique contribution to make concerning music teaching and learning. Quantitative researchers gather numerical information to answer descriptive questions (e.g., What is . . . ?), questions of associations (e.g., How is variable x related to variable y?), and questions pertaining to cause and effect (e.g., What causes variable y to be the way that it is?). Qualitative researchers explore complex phenomena within naturalistic settings, foregrounding participants' perspectives. The researcher generates text-based data sources such as interview transcripts, field notes, and artifacts, and analyzes them to illuminate themes that emerge from the data. The resulting research report provides a detailed description of and supports theorization about the phenomenon of interest. Historical researchers examine original documents, artifacts, and testimony to answer questions, uncover facts, and draw meaningful conclusions related to the past and its effect on present conditions. Philosophical researchers use logical arguments and examples to investigate the assumptions underlying current music education practices and to imagine how attitudes and actions within the profession might be. Action researchers typically study their local contexts in order to take action within and as a result of their inquiries.

Introduction

Music educators are faced with the need to solve problems, answer questions, and make decisions on a daily or even hourly basis. The ways in which we find solutions to problems not only affect individual students and programs, but collectively they shape the profession. Music education as a formal process is primarily concerned with music teaching and learning. As a professional discipline, it is important that we continually examine our practices critically and work to gather new information to support what we do. The systematic inquiry that scholars engage in to move our profession forward is called research. The purpose of this book is to introduce music educators to the basic principles and most common practices of music education research.

Many professions (e.g., medicine, counseling, engineering) are what might be called "research-driven." People working within such professions are more likely to refer to knowledge gained through research when making decisions and steering their work into the future. This is not to deny, of course, that those working in research-driven professions may have varying opinions about a certain protocol. However, most often their practice will follow accumulated, scholarly evidence. Other professions—like teaching—may tend to be more opinion-based. Despite the existence of educational research, teachers have historically relied more on personal judgments or experience.

The point is not that research-driven disciplines are better than those that are driven by other types of knowledge, but rather that each discipline should take advantage of the benefits of several approaches to gathering knowledge and find a balance that is most appropriate for that particular discipline. Consider a musical example to see how knowledge derived from research and other means might complement each other. Suppose we wanted to know what tempo to choose when leading a big band group through Duke Ellington's piece *Caravan*. We could gather evidence about what Ellington intended. Metronome markings in the original score, Ellington's correspondence with his colleagues, and contemporary accounts of early performances he led might give us clues. We could listen to recordings made by well-known artists. We could try out different tempos to determine which sound better. However, any decision about the "best" tempo that does not take into account characteristics of the ensemble, the performing space, or the inspiration of the performing artists might lead to a less than thrilling performance.

When we have questions, we may find answers in the following ways:

1. By using *common sense*. Some problems can be solved simply by doing what seems to be the most reasonable thing. For example, it is common sense to have young, beginning piano students learn by playing age-appropriate pieces rather than attempting advanced literature. Unfortunately, we have many questions for which common sense cannot supply the answers.
2. From the *opinions of experts*. Sometimes, we simply need to ask someone who has a great deal of expertise in our area of concern. For example, we might ask an experienced choral director for their opinion on how best to position singers on risers. In a university setting, often the experts are faculty members from whom you take classes. Other experts can be the authors of textbooks you are using or guest speakers who come to give a lecture. Teachers in the public schools who have many years of experience or who have been quite successful are also a good source of answers to many questions.

    Unfortunately, sometimes experts do not have good answers to our questions. Sometimes their answers are wrong, are suitable only to a particular context, or are biased toward a personal preference. Experts can also disagree. Therefore, while we do not want to dismiss the advice of experts, we do not want to rely on them totally for all the answers to our questions about music teaching and learning.

3. Through *informal reasoning*. We can solve many problems or answer many questions by reasoning our way to a good answer. We can organize our thoughts in a series of statements and decide which ones are true and which are false or arrange the answers in a way that leads to a good answer. For example, let us suppose a parent has asked us whether their child should begin violin lessons. We might ask questions such as "How old is the child?," "Does the child want to play the violin?," "Does the child have the maturity to pay attention to the instructor and to practice daily?," and so on. Depending on the answers to questions such as these, we may agree that the child is ready to begin, or we may recommend that the child wait until they are more mature physically and mentally.

Many concerns can be addressed through logical thinking. Sometimes, however, such reasoning may not lead us to an appropriate answer. We may use faulty logic. Or we may have incomplete information on which to make a decision.

4. Through *authority*. There are times when authority figures or agencies have determined that a specific policy should be followed. Thus, a principal, superintendent, school board, district supervisor, or state or other governmental agency may provide the solution to a problem by insisting that this textbook should be used, this curriculum should be followed, and so on. Sometimes these policies have the advantage of providing uniformity across different schools or districts. However, at other times the authority figure may not be in a position to make the best decision for a particular situation.

5. By *trial and error*. Experience is often a very good teacher, and by trying various ways of doing things, teachers can often arrive at a good solution to a problem. However, what works for one teacher in one situation may not work for another teacher in a different situation. Although trial and error can result in improved pedagogy, it may be an ineffective use of time and can omit other, potentially beneficial solutions.

6. By *research*. Research has unlimited potential for yielding important insights and discoveries for music education. As we will discuss throughout this book, systematic inquiry in music education can take many forms. For example, quantitative researchers may conduct experiments to compare the relative impact of various instructional conditions, whereas a qualitative researcher might conduct a case study of a music program to learn about the relationships that students form in their learning community. A historical researcher could be interested in investigating how particular educational policies came about, while a philosophical researcher might problematize the sociopolitical assumptions underlying such policies. In contrast, a teacher-researcher may wish to study a curricular innovation in their own school to determine if it is meeting their students' needs.

Familiarizing ourselves with these foundational paradigmatic approaches to inquiry—quantitative, qualitative, historical, philosophical, and action research—can provide us with tools and methods for conducting research studies that can address an amazingly diverse range of critical questions about music teaching and learning. Throughout this book, this is what we mean when we use the word "research."

At this point, let us assume that all six ways of solving problems or finding answers to questions are important and useful, but each in their own way and only for certain problems or questions. Research is not necessarily better than the other means of arriving at answers or solutions, but it is critical for the growth of the profession. If music education relies only on common sense, the opinions of experts, informal reasoning, authority, or trial and error, it will not continue to develop to its full potential. Consider medicine, for example. It was recently announced that researchers have developed a new way of using stem cells to regenerate the lens of the eye following cataract removal (Lin et al., 2016). It is hard to believe that they could have achieved this marvelous breakthrough, described as one of the most outstanding achievements in the field of regenerative medicine until now, by common sense, trial and error, or in any other way than through research.

We could also consider how each of the approaches for finding answers to questions or solving problems that were described above could be applied to issues relevant to music education. For example, music teachers often have many questions when it comes to pedagogical methods appropriate for accommodating children's developing voices. Indeed, teachers have come up with many ingenious ways to deal with the myriad challenges that young singers face using all of the problem-solving methods described above. We're sure you can think of several instances from your own experience. Moreover, sometimes pedagogues share the methods they've found to be successful via journals which aim to provide practical ideas for music teachers such as *The Music Educators Journal*, *The Instrumentalist*, *The Choral Journal*, *The Journal of General Music Education*, and so on.

Searching out solutions to problems in practitioner periodicals or other secondary sources (e.g., textbooks, blogs, peer groups) is often described colloquially as a kind of research. However, while beneficial, this is not what we are referring to when we use the term "research" in this book. Instead, we restrict our use of the term to mean the careful, systematic, and reflective pursuit of understanding that adds to our collective knowledge. The key elements of the definition we are using which distinguishes it from broader and colloquial uses of the term are that (a) the process of knowledge generation is carried out via studies that employ a systematic method and (b) it is crucial that the knowledge generated be disseminated so that it can contribute to a collective understanding of an issue in the field. Here are some examples of how researchers working in various paradigms have contributed critical knowledge on the topic of children's singing:

- *Quantitative research*: Killian (1999) measured the vocal characteristics of fifth and sixth grade boys and found that voices may change earlier than was previously thought.
- *Qualitative research*: Kennedy's (2004) investigation of the culture at the American Boychoir School depicted the uniqueness of each boy's experience, revealing how powerful emotional reactions can shape the students' experiences.
- *Historical research*: Rutkowski (1985) conducted a study of how music educators have characterized the "child voice" and documented the various pedagogical methods and techniques that scholars and practitioners have developed over time.
- *Philosophical research*: Pascale (2005) interrogated what we might mean when we use the term "nonsinger" via philosophical inquiry. In her work, she discussed how cultural and societal assumptions about musicianship can impact our perceptions and teaching practices.
- *Action research:* Parker (2010) explored how students' in a high school choral program developed feelings of belonging. Her study was an action research project conducted with her own students.

Our goal in this introduction has been to demonstrate that while research is not the only way to solve problems or answer questions, it is a vital aspect of the growth and development of the music education profession. To continue our discussion of research, we will examine some different ways of classifying music education research: (a) according to the relationship between research and practice and (b) according to the methodological paradigm that informs a study's design (i.e., quantitative, qualitative, historical, philosophical, or action research).

Relationships between Research and Practice

Music educators approaching research for the first time may be surprised when studies do not provide clear applications for practice. Some research is designed to investigate general background information on a topic and, while beneficial for the development of theory, does not typically lead directly to specific applications for music teaching and learning. Ray and Hendricks's (2019) study of collective efficacy beliefs, that is, a group's belief in their ability to successfully execute a task, is an example of basic research. The researchers collected data from musicians within 18 different ensembles and examined whether the ensemble members' sense of collective efficacy would be related to their degree of within-group agreement as well as their performance quality. Indeed, significant relationships were found for both cases. Members of ensembles that felt more collectively efficacious were more likely to agree with each other in their efficacy assessments than members of ensembles that tended to feel less collectively efficacious. In addition, ensemble groups that had relatively stronger collective efficacy beliefs tended to score relatively higher at festivals. Although we might speculate about potential applications of these findings for practice, the research study itself was mainly geared toward generally furthering our understanding about how the theoretical construct of collective efficacy operates among music ensemble members.

At the other end of this continuum, research can be focused on methods for solving particular practical problems. For example, researchers might investigate pedagogical techniques to identify teaching methods that would be particularly beneficial for specific circumstances. In contrast with more general or theoretical research, research grounded in specific practical problems often leads to classroom applications that can be put into immediate use. As an example, consider a study by Lily Chen-Hafteck (2007), who investigated whether teaching Chinese music to elementary school students would influence their attitudes toward multicultural musical experiences. She examined the impact of a program called the *Sounds of Silk*, involving three schools, six teachers, and 250 fifth- and sixth-grade students in New York City. The 10-week project involved live demonstrations by professional Chinese musicians and dancers, lessons integrating music and culture, students' hands-on creative projects, and a final concert. Results indicated that the students' experiences with Chinese music motivated learning; they became interested in music with which they were previously unfamiliar; they were captivated and the music maintained their interest; they were excited and eager to learn about Chinese culture; and for Chinese students it boosted their confidence and cultural pride.

Similarly, researchers interested in education policy might investigate both policy texts, which can range from institutional mission statements to course offerings and standardized graduation requirements, and policy actions, such as which music standards educators routinely address. Using various methodological designs, researchers can interrogate the nature of these policies and how they play out in practice, including their benefits and limitations. When offering implications of such research, authors might consider ideas for teachers and teacher educators as well as administrators, arts organization leaders, various levels of appointed and elected policymakers, and other policy stakeholders (Graham et al., 2022).

Often findings from more general or theoretical studies can also inform research addressing particular practical problems, despite not being overtly practical by design. Findings providing general background information or a theoretical framework can allow us to understand a situation more fully. Such frameworks could then be used to inform the design of research emphasizing specific practical issues in music teaching and learning. For example, in the more general research example given previously, Ray and Hendricks (2019) found that ensembles with members who had similar perceptions of their collective efficacy tended to perform better than those who did not. Knowing this theoretical information, a researcher might further investigate what kinds of practical communications training could help to increase within-group agreement among ensemble members.

Methodological Paradigms

Scholars choose research designs according to the particular questions about music teaching and learning that they have. Research methods, therefore, are tools for music education inquiry—a means for gathering/generating information and extracting meaning from that information, rather than an end in and of themselves. Throughout this book we refer to the methodological paradigms of quantitative, qualitative, historical, philosophical, and action research. We use the term "paradigm" because we are talking about general categories or archetypes of research methodologies that, in some cases, have emerged from different disciplinary traditions. Given the introductory nature of this book, the descriptions of each methodological type that we offer in this chapter as well as those that follow in later chapters are limited and not exhaustive of all approaches to research that you may encounter in the music education literature. However, we believe that a basic understanding of some of the most foundational elements of these five diverse approaches to inquiry will serve as an excellent starting point for your first forays into systematic research.

Certain types of questions are better suited to certain methodological approaches. Sometimes the best match between a research question and a research design is fairly straightforward. For example, it's hard to imagine making much progress answering questions pertaining to music education history without using historical research methods. Similarly, answering a philosophical question would necessitate actually doing philosophy. However, at other times the best match between a research question and a design is less obvious. Consider, for example, the question "How do teachers motivate students?"—the way a researcher might approach this topic could depend on many things. This particular topic could be addressed using quantitative and/or qualitative designs. Which approach a researcher might ultimately commit to would depend on the sorts of information that they believe would be most meaningful to gather, which could, in turn, depend upon their assumptions about knowledge and the world in general.

Scholars often refer to assumptions about knowledge and the world as "epistemological" and "ontological" perspectives, respectively. Broadly speaking, epistemology[1] is the branch of philosophy concerned with knowledge, and therefore, one's epistemological perspective has to do with how one might conceptualize what it means to know something. For example, quantitative research designs (e.g., surveys, experiments) typically gather information via relatively objective "empirical" observations (e.g., measurements) which can be externally verified or corroborated, as is typical within the tradition of the scientific method. In contrast, qualitative research designs (e.g., case studies, ethnographies) tend to prioritize the nuance and richness that might emerge from relatively subjective sources of

---

[1] From the Greek *episteme* and *logos*, roughly translated to English as "knowledge" and "understanding," respectively.

information about human experience (e.g., individuals' accounts), similar to those that have historically been employed in disciplines like anthropology.

Ontology[2] generally refers to the philosophical study of being, and one's ontological perspective can involve one's thoughts on the nature of reality. To continue our comparison of generic quantitative and qualitative paradigms, quantitative researchers are typically concerned with describing and explaining phenomena such that they could then generalize the knowledge they acquire to multiple contexts, whereas qualitative researchers are more likely to emphasize how individuals and social systems play a role in constructing what might be considered "multiple" possible realities, while being less concerned with whether their research findings are generalizable to other contexts.

These descriptions of epistemological and ontological perspectives above are necessarily limited to only a few very brief examples. Our goal here is not to communicate all of the different sorts of philosophical assumptions that could impact a researcher's choices. Rather, we hope that now you might begin to imagine how approaching the question "How do teachers motivate students?" could look different to researchers with different assumptions about knowledge and the world. For example, a quantitative approach to this question might involve administering questionnaires to a large group of students from many teachers' classes to determine what sorts of motivational beliefs typically energize them, whereas a qualitative approach might involve spending a substantial amount of time embedded in a classroom in which the teacher and students have an excellent sense of rapport in order to gather information via observations, interviews, and artifacts.

As you may have deduced by now, research conducted within different methodological paradigms can be mutually beneficial and complementary. Investigating a topic from multiple methodological perspectives will only enrich our understanding. As such, methodological paradigms should not be considered hierarchically, such that one is perceived as better or more valid than another. Research from each paradigmatic approach is capable of bringing valuable insights to our field, and the field is better off with inquiry conducted from multiple perspectives. Each research approach will be presented with more depth and detail later in the book; at this point we are going to present examples of research to help familiarize you with the sorts of research that could be conducted within each paradigm.

Quantitative Research

Researchers taking a scientific approach when investigating music teaching and learning often employ *quantitative research* methods. Quantitative research designs are built upon the scientific method and are used to answer descriptive questions (e.g., What is . . . ?), questions of association (e.g., How is variable x related to

---

[2] From the Greek *ontos* and *logos*, roughly translated to English as "being" and "understanding," respectively.

variable y?), and questions pertaining to cause and effect (e.g., What causes variable y to be the way that it is?). The term "quantitative" refers to the fact that researchers working in this paradigm gather information in the form of numerical measurements, which are then subjected to statistical analyses to identify meaningful tendencies, patterns, and/or trends in the data.

Gary McPherson and Susan O'Neill's (2010) investigation of students' motivation to study music as compared to other school subjects is an excellent example of descriptive quantitative research. They gathered data from 24,143 children in Brazil, China, Finland, Hong Kong, Israel, Korea, Mexico, and the United States. The authors wanted to know what value elementary and secondary students placed on their studies in art, mother-tongue language, physical education, mathematics, science, and music. Results indicated that students valued music as a school subject less than all the other subjects except art. Unfortunately, the value the students placed on music declined across the school years in every country except Brazil.

Qualitative Research

Qualitative research is ideal for exploring phenomena involving many interrelated variables that may be challenging to isolate for the purposes of investigation or for situations in which the precise variables of interest have not yet been identified. Characteristics of qualitative research include exploring those phenomena within naturalistic settings, foregrounding participants' perspectives, and addressing the researcher's subjectivity. Data generation typically involves text-based sources (e.g., interview transcripts, field notes, artifacts), which converge in a triangulating fashion to permit more in-depth analysis than a single data source might yield. Data analysis features recursive cycles through which the researcher identifies patterns, categories, and themes that emerge from the data. The resulting research report describes, interprets, and supports theorization about the central phenomenon.

Kelly-McHale's (2011, 2013) collective case study exploring the dynamic interactions between one elementary general music teacher and four of her students exemplifies characteristics that are typical of qualitative studies. The teacher strongly identified as a Kodaly-inspired educator, with a conceptual sequence associated with that approach driving much of her curricular decision-making. All four student participants were second-generation Mexican immigrants, meaning that they were born in the United States to parents who had emigrated from Mexico. Research questions focused on ways in which the teacher's curricular beliefs and pedagogical practices influenced the students' cultural identities, musical identities, and possible intersections between the two. The central phenomenon at the heart of the inquiry, cultural identity, is acknowledged to be complex, encompassing many interrelated variables such as an individual's age, gender, race, ethnicity, nationality, religion, sexual orientation, immigration status, and (dis)ability, as well as interactions and intersections between these facets of identity. This is an example of the type of phenomenon for which qualitative designs are well-suited: those for which an emphasis on depth and particularity would be useful for answering the research questions.

Typical of qualitative research, data generation included a rotating schedule of individual and group interviews, classroom observations, and a collection of classroom artifacts such as curriculum documents, lesson plans, and musical scores. Findings indicated that the music classroom environment successfully met the teacher's expressed goals of developing students' singing proficiency and notational literacy. However, the teacher's rigid adherence to a Eurocentric framework and sequence-centered instructional approach "resulted in an isolated musical experience that did not support the integration of cultural, linguistic, and popular music experiences, and largely ignored issues of cultural responsiveness" (Kelly-McHale, 2011, p. 3). Findings further revealed a cultural gulf between students' musical experiences inside and outside of the school music domain. Given the complex nature of phenomena such as culture and identity, the intent of this study was not to generalize broadly about the educational experiences or needs of students who identify as Mexican immigrants. To do so would risk promoting stereotypical or essentialist thinking. Rather, an in-depth analysis of the particularities of these specific participants' experiences supported theorization about the central phenomenon and crystalized implications for practice.

Mixed Methods Research

Quantitative and qualitative approaches to research can be conceptualized as endpoints along a continuum, with mixed methods inquiry positioned in the center as an approach that substantively incorporates elements of both paradigms (Creswell & Gutterman, 2019). In a mixed methods study, the combination of quantitative and qualitative data yields a more comprehensive understanding of a research problem than either might permit on its own. Rather than connoting a single method, the term "mixed methods" can refer to multiple designs that differ from one another in terms of the priority given to each type of data, whether quantitative and qualitative phases occur concurrently or sequentially, and precisely how the two are combined in order to support analysis pertinent to the research questions (see Creswell & Plano Clark, 2018).

Fitzpatrick's (2008, 2011) investigation of how instrumental music teachers navigate teaching within urban educational contexts offers one example of how mixed methods designs have been used in music education scholarship. Research questions focused on the knowledge, skills, and attitudes upon which these educators relied, as well as their perceptions of challenges and rewards associated with teaching in urban contexts. A quantitative data collection phase involved conducting a survey of instrumental music educators employed in the Chicago Public Schools ($N = 90$). A qualitative phase resembled a collective case study design, with the researcher conducting interviews and classroom observations with four selected teachers. The survey offered a broad view of urban music teaching, supporting generalization to a broader population, while the collective case study supported in-depth analysis of the particularities of four specific teachers' experiences working within a complex sociocultural landscape. The researcher analyzed the complete data corpus with an eye toward how the quantitative and qualitative data aligned with or contradicted one another.

Findings revealed the extensive knowledge base and specialized skills upon which teachers relied to teach effectively within urban schools, as well as their asset-based views of urban students and communities. The convergence of survey results and case study findings revealed several intriguing patterns. For example, one theme that emerged from qualitative analysis described teachers' experiences of "struggle between frustration and reward" (Fitzpatrick, 2008, p. 221). While the qualitative data evidenced teachers' experiences of highs and lows through which they cycled while undertaking routine teaching responsibilities, survey results indicated a moderately positive mean level of job satisfaction. The author noted that participants experienced

> extremes of frustration because of the constant challenges that they face. However, participants also perceive a high level of reward from working with their students. These two factors, rather than "averaging out" to produce a level of contentment with urban instrumental music teaching, are constant, daily, and polarizing presences in the lives of participants. (p. 277)

Considering the two types of data in tandem revealed that job satisfaction is a more complex issue than the survey data alone demonstrated. Fitzpatrick reported positive correlations between teachers' job satisfaction and their perceptions of program success, administrative and collegial support, and school and community safety. These results hold implications for teacher retention, an issue of particular concern within urban contexts. Fitzpatrick's study illustrates how the convergence of quantitative and qualitative data in mixed methods designs can support appropriately nuanced analyses of complex educational issues.

Historical Research

Historical research involves an examination of past events, institutions, conditions, or phenomena related to music education or the lives and work of former music educators. Historians seek to answer questions about the past by studying primary source material, such as letters, diaries, newspaper or journal articles, personal interviews, and so on. Matthew Thibeault (2018), for example, studied the use of sound recordings in the pedagogy of Shinichi Suzuki, a prominent violin teacher in Japan. Suzuki developed his method beginning in the 1930s through experiments that established central ideas related to the importance of repetition, the recording as teacher, the involvement of mothers in the learning process, and the teachability of talent. John Kendall at Southern Illinois University–Edwardsville introduced Suzuki's pedagogy to the United States in the 1960s through an English translation of his work and other publications. The use of audio recording evolved in the 1970s with the introduction of the cassette tape, which allowed for the convenient recording of student performances. In addition to people, facts, and events, Thibeault examined the differing cultural values surrounding the use of recordings in Japanese and American contexts.

Philosophical Research

Philosophical research investigates the assumptions underlying current music education practices and imagines how attitudes and actions within the profession ought to be. Using logical arguments and examples to build on other writers' ideas, philosophical researchers address questions related to the nature and value of music making, teaching and learning, and music education-society relationships. For example, Koza (2008) used critical race theory to examine the nature of collegiate admission auditions at schools of music. She argued that by valuing classical music and its associated musical characteristics and devaluing musical styles (e.g., gospel, R&B, hip-hop) that tend to be preferred by non-Whites, admissions processes play a role in systematically excluding non-White individuals from collegiate music study without ever referencing "race." In considering what ought to be, Koza proposed purposefully listening for Whiteness in music admissions practices and then troubling its role in these and other institutional processes. She added, "Substantive discussions of race can help interrogate the explicit and implicit purposes of school music" (p. 154). Like most philosophers, Koza proposes ideas with which readers might wrestle rather than clear directives or answers.

Action Research

Action research refers to a variety of approaches to inquiry that can be used to investigate topics for the sake of improving practices in specific professional contexts. The researchers and participants involved in action research are often individuals with a personal stake in the development and success of music education endeavors in such contexts (e.g., music teachers, students, administrators, community members). The action research process involves iterative cycles of looking, thinking, and acting (Stringer & Ortiz Aragon, 2021). Regarding methods, action researchers tend to incorporate tools from the qualitative and quantitative paradigms when carrying out their work.

Miller (1996) conducted an action research study to explore how music instruction could be integrated with a first-grade whole-language curriculum. Miller was herself a full-time elementary music educator in the setting of the research project at the time of the inquiry. She described several possible models of curricular integration she was interested in exploring (webbed, integrated, and threaded; see Fogarty, 1991), and engaged in many iterative cycles of inquiry with her collaborator, the first-grade classroom teacher. The methods for this study included both qualitative (e.g., interview, observation) and quantitative (e.g., questionnaire, tests of student knowledge) data generation techniques. The findings of this study were multifaceted, with Miller (1996) providing a discussion of pedagogical lessons learned as well as her reflections on the action research process in general.

Recognizing the Potential Impact of Personal and Structural Biases

Research is often intended to be *value-free* by excluding researchers' own values to make the observations and interpretations as unbiased as possible. However, one could argue that no research is truly value-free (Kent, 2006). According to Mantie (2021, p. 8), "The choice to study this rather than that is a political decision, in effect if not also in intent." Research and researchers are, of course, susceptible to all of the varieties of personal and structural biases that exist in our world and likely hold some preconceptions of which they are not aware. As a researcher, it is important to recognize that everyone holds biases of some type based on their background, race, gender identity, sexual orientation, political affiliation, socioeconomic status, education, religious beliefs, and many other factors. It is also important for researchers to be cognizant of their own biases and interrogate how their worldviews and preconceptions can impact their work.

Biases can cause a researcher to expect a certain outcome or unwittingly manipulate the study to favor a particular result. In education, assumptions and anecdotal evidence about effective teaching can cloud judgments and keep us from making objective appraisals based on evidence from systematic research (Suter, 2012). Therefore, researchers must be skeptical of their own work and constantly apply critical thinking to data, interpretations, and the conclusions that follow.

A researcher's background has the potential to influence many decisions related to a study. An author's experience as a White middle-class individual might inform the types of research questions they ask or create bias about a topic in general. For example, when designing a quantitative study centered on student or teacher behaviors, a researcher could assume that a classroom consisting of students who are Black, Brown, Indigenous, or Asian (BBIA) should look and sound the same as a predominantly White classroom. A historian who is White might select topics that involve only White teachers and students, contributing to erasure of BBIA individuals' histories, presence, and contributions. A researcher designing and administering a survey might inadvertently exclude certain individuals, such as those who do not want to identify their race or sexual orientation, who possess limited English-language skills, or who lack reliable internet access. Strategies for attenuating bias or managing researcher subjectivity could involve asking colleagues for feedback and criticism that question findings and implications discussed by the author. Through processes called "member checking" (Creswell & Poth, 2018) or "member reflections" (Tracy, 2010), participants can be invited to review raw data, findings and interpretations, and/or disseminable products and provide feedback about the extent to which these faithfully represent their contributions to the research (see Chapter 11).

Summary

There are many ways for music educators to solve problems and answer questions. We can use common sense, rely on the opinions of experts, follow informal reasoning, obey the directions of authoritative figures, employ trial and error, and conduct research studies. While all of these are good ways in particular circumstances, research is necessary for the profession to grow and develop to its full potential.

To structure our thinking about music education research, we can characterize much of the research that appears in the music education literature according to the methodological paradigm from which it stems: quantitative, qualitative, historical, philosophical, or action research. Each methodological approach is suited for addressing particular kinds of music teaching and learning questions and can yield insights critical for the profession.

As we proceed through the remaining chapters of this book, we will be revisiting all of these topics and providing additional details. In the meantime, you might wish to write down your responses to the following prompts as a way of clarifying your understanding:

1. Provide your own examples for each of the ways (e.g., common sense, opinions of experts) we can solve problems or answer questions in music education.
2. Give some examples outside music education where quantitative, qualitative, historical, philosophical, or action research has been conducted in an effort to solve a problem or answer a question. Consider current news articles, blog sites, and popular books as well as research articles.
3. Imagine a three-year sequence in which you conduct a quantitative study in year 1, a qualitative study in year 2, and a philosophical or historical study in year 3—all addressing a single research topic. Write one paragraph describing the general topics that could be addressed by each study.

4. Provide an example of each of the following types of research by searching for music education research using Google Scholar (https://scholar.google.com):
   - Quantitative research.
   - Qualitative research.
   - Historical research.
   - Philosophical research.
   - Action research.
6. Write a letter to a school administrator explaining why research is necessary for the continuing development of music education.

Important Terms for Review

Research is the careful, systematic, and reflective pursuit of understanding that adds to our collective knowledge.

Methodological paradigm refers to a general category of research methods (e.g., quantitative, qualitative, historical, philosophical, action research).

Epistemology is the branch of philosophy devoted to the study of knowledge.

Ontology is a branch of philosophy nested within the general category of metaphysics that is devoted to the study of being.

Quantitative research includes scientific investigations wherein observations are made via measurements. These measurements yield numerical data that are subjected to statistical analyses to derive meaningful conclusions.

Qualitative research explores complex phenomena within naturalistic settings, foregrounding participants' perspectives. The researcher generates text-based data sources such as interview transcripts, field notes, and artifacts and analyzes them to illuminate themes that emerge from the data. The resulting research report provides a detailed description of and supports theorization about the phenomenon of interest.

Historical research refers to investigations that examine original documents, artifacts, and testimony to answer questions, uncover facts, and draw meaningful conclusions related to the past and its effect on present conditions.

Philosophical research uses logical arguments and examples to investigate the assumptions underlying current music education practices and to imagine how attitudes and actions within the profession might be.

Action research refers to a variety of approaches to inquiry that can be used to investigate topics for the sake of improving practices in specific professional contexts. Action researchers tend to incorporate tools from the qualitative and quantitative paradigms when carrying out their work.

References

Chen-Hafteck, L. (2007). Contextual analyses of children's responses to an integrated Chinese music and culture experience. *Music Education Research, 9*, 337–353. https://doi.org/10.1080/14613800701587688

Creswell, J. W., & Gutterman, T. C. (2019). *Educational research: Planning, conducting, and evaluating quantitative and qualitative research* (6th ed.). Pearson.

Creswell, J. W., & Plano Clark, V. L. (2018). *Designing and conducting mixed methods research* (3rd ed.). Sage.

Creswell, J. W., & Poth, C. N. (2018). *Qualitative inquiry and research design: Choosing among five approaches* (4th ed.). Sage.

Fitzpatrick, K. R. (2008). *A mixed methods portrait of urban instrumental music teaching* (Publication No. 3303647) [Doctoral dissertation, Northwestern University]. ProQuest Dissertations and Theses Global.

Fitzpatrick, K. R. (2011). A mixed methods portrait of urban instrumental music teaching. *Journal of Research in Music Education, 59*(3), 229–256. https://doi.org/10.1177/0022429411414912

Fogarty, R. (1991). Ten ways to integrate curriculum. *Educational Leadership, 49*(2), 61–65.

Graham, M., Overby, L., Richerme, L. K., Wager, A. C., & Conway, C. (2022). Writing for Arts Education Policy Review. *Arts Education Policy Review, 123*(2), 110–114. https://doi.org/10.1080/10632913.2020.1813231

Kelly-McHale, J. (2011). *The relationship between children's musical identities and music teacher beliefs and practices in an elementary general music classroom* (Publication No. 3456672) [Doctoral dissertation, Northwestern University]. ProQuest Dissertations and Theses Global.

Kelly-McHale, J. (2013). The influence of music teacher beliefs and practices on the expression of musical identity in an elementary general music classroom. *Journal of Research in Music Education, 61*(2), 195–216. https://doi.org/10.1177/0022429413485439

Kennedy, M. C. (2004). "It's a metamorphosis": Guiding the voice change at the American Boychoir School. *Journal of Research in Music Education, 52*, 246–280. https://doi.org/10.2307/3345859

Kent, M. (2006). *Oxford dictionary of sports science & medicine* (3rd ed.). Oxford.

Killian, J. (1999). A description of vocal maturation among fifth- and sixth-grade boys. *Journal of Research in Music Education, 47*, 357–369. https://doi.org/10.2307/3345490

Koza, J. E. (2008). Listening for whiteness: Hearing racial politics in undergraduate school music. *Philosophy of Music Education Review, 16*(2), 145–155.

Lin, H., Ouyang, H., Zhu, J., Huang, S., Liu, Z., Chen, S., Cao, G., Li, G., Signer, R., Xu, Y., Chung, C., Zhang, Y., Lin, D., Patel, S., Wu, F., Cai, H., Hou, J., Wen, C., Jafari, M., . . . Liu, Y. (2016). Lens regeneration using endogenous stem cells with gain of visual function. *Nature, 531*(7594), 323–328. https://doi.org/10.1038/nature17181

Mantie, R. (2021). Struggling with good intentions: Music education research in a "post" world. *Research Studies in Music Education, 44*(1), 21–33. https://doi.org/10.1177/1321103X211056466

McPherson, G. E., & O'Neill, S. A. (2010). Students' motivation to study music as compared to other school subjects: A comparison of eight countries. *Research Studies in Music Education, 32*, 101–137. https://doi.org/10.1177/1321103x10384202

Miller, B. A. (1996). Integrating elementary general music: A collaborative action research study. *Bulletin of the Council for Research in Music Education, 130*, 100–115. https://www.jstor.org/stable/40318815

Parker, E. C. (2010). Exploring student experiences of belonging within an urban high school choral ensemble: An action research study. *Music Education Research, 12*(4), 339–352. http://dx.doi.org/10.1080/14613808.2010.519379

Pascale, L. M. (2005). Dispelling the myth of the non-singer: Embracing two aesthetics for singing. *Philosophy of Music Education Review, 13*, 165–175. https://doi.org/10.1353/pme.2005.0039

Ray, J., & Hendricks, K. S. (2019). Collective efficacy belief, within-group agreement, and performance quality among instrumental chamber ensembles. *Journal of Research in Music Education, 66*, 449–464. https://doi.org/10.1177/0022429418805090

Rutkowski, J. (1985). The child voice: An historical perspective. *The Bulletin of the Council for Research in Music Education, 6*, 1–15. https://doi.org/10.1177/153660068500600101

Stringer, E., & Ortiz Aragon, A. (2021). *Action research* (5th ed.). Sage.

Suter, W. N. (2012). *An introduction to educational research: A critical thinking approach* (2nd ed.). Sage.

Thibeault M. D. (2018). Learning with sound recordings: A history of Suzuki's mediated pedagogy. *Journal of Research in Music Education, 66*, 6–30. https://doi.org/10.1177/0022429418756879

Tracy, S. J. (2010). Qualitative quality: Eight "big-tent" criteria for excellent qualitative research. *Qualitative Inquiry, 16*(10), 837–851. https://doi.org/10.1177/1077800410383121

2
The Typical Components of Music Education Research

Chapter Preview

In this chapter we will introduce the typical components of a music education research article. Typically, researchers aim to (a) convince readers that the topic under study is important and relevant to music educators; (b) describe the conceptual or theoretical framework that informs their perspective on the problem; (c) persuade the readers that their research will fill a gap in the current literature and further our understanding of the topic; (d) specify the particular purpose, questions, and/or hypotheses that their study will address; (e) explain the methodological steps taken to conduct their research; (f) present the findings of their inquiry; and (g) describe how their research has contributed to and/or extended our collective knowledge on the topic at hand. Often, a research project begins with the description of a problem or a broad area of concern relevant to music teaching and learning. Opening sections of the paper would then typically shape the problem toward a specific purpose statement and set of research questions. Quantitative, qualitative, and action research articles often include a review of related literature, that is, a synthesis of the research studies that have already been published on the problem at hand. Method sections identify the participants and the context of the study, the data being collected and analyzed, and the specific procedures followed. Results are reported, and a discussion or conclusion section places the findings into a broader context. Historical and philosophical research studies may contain some but not all of these sections.

Introduction

Research studies are most often reported via articles in peer-reviewed journals. Our intentions in this chapter are threefold: (a) to familiarize you with the typical components of a research article so that they will be easier for you to comprehend, (b) to provide brief insights about each section so that you can begin to approach reading research with a critical eye, and (c) to introduce you to the kinds of writing that will be expected of you should you conduct your own research. However, it is important to note that—try as we might—neatly categorizing the typical components of a research article such that each paradigmatic approach to research is covered in depth

Music Education Research. Peter Miksza, Julia T. Shaw, Lauren Kapalka Richerme, Phillip M. Hash, and Donald A. Hodges,
Oxford University Press. © Oxford University Press 2023. DOI: 10.1093/oso/9780197639757.003.0002

is not possible in a single chapter. The extent to which scholars use a preset format and consistently label article components varies based on the research paradigm.

Quantitative research articles have an extremely predictable arrangement of sections—introduction, method, results, and discussion—and each of these sections serves nearly the same purpose and includes similar types of content regardless of author, topic, or design (e.g., observational study, survey, experiment). Qualitative research and action research articles tend to include similarly labeled sections; however, that is not always the case. In addition to resting upon different assumptions than quantitative research, approaches to research designs that fall within the category of qualitative research and action research can be quite different from each other as well. For example, some qualitative approaches (e.g., grounded theory) are more emergent than others; that is, the purpose, questions, and methods are not necessarily predetermined. Other approaches rely more on literary construction (e.g., narrative research) and may not include sections like those that are found in quantitative research. Consequently, the ways in which such studies are introduced, explained, and interpreted can look different from studies employing other design types.

Historical and philosophical research articles are even less consistent in their components than qualitative research articles. The structure of a historical research article will often begin with a section that provides background and context for the topic, followed by a relatively brief purpose statement and rationale. The study itself will consist of sections organized according to the primary topics and themes that comprise the findings. Philosophical research articles are the least formulaic in presentation. Indeed, as you will learn in our later chapters, the notion of philosophical research methods is a frequently debated topic in and of itself. Approaches that philosophers take to tackle their subjects can vary tremendously. As such, philosophical authors will most likely choose to construct their papers according to the idiosyncratic needs of their arguments rather than according to prescribed forms.

Given that the organizational structure of quantitative and qualitative research articles can be somewhat similar and rather formulaic, and that action research will typically take on the conventions of one or both paradigms, we have organized this chapter according to the functions of the major sections of quantitative and qualitative articles. Because of the different types of research, as discussed in Chapter 1, the current discussion is only a generic overview; specific details pertaining to all four research paradigms will be presented in subsequent chapters.

Opening Section

Researchers typically strive to achieve four aims in an introductory section of a research article: (a) to convince the reader that the topic of their study is an important and relevant problem to address within the field, (b) to describe the conceptual or theoretical framework that informs their perspective on the problem, (c) to

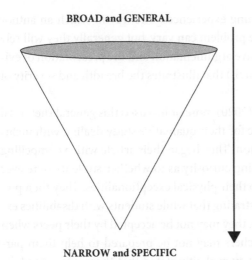

Figure 2.1 Often a research project begins with a problem, a broad area of concern. Opening sections of the paper would then typically shape the problem toward a specific purpose statement and set of research questions.

describe how the research they wish to conduct can fill a gap in the current literature and further our understanding of the topic, and (d) to specify the particular purpose, questions, and/or hypotheses that their study will address.

Article introductions are often crafted such that they begin rather broadly, outlining a pressing need for research that addresses a particular problem in the field. This is combined with or sometimes followed by a discussion of selected previous literature on the topic that is positioned such that the need for the author's study is even more evident. The introduction may or may not include the presentation of a theoretical framework or conceptual model that has informed the author's perspective on the problem at hand. Once the rationale and context for the study is established, the author will then narrow the discussion to the specific purpose of their study and present research questions or hypotheses that informed the design, analysis, and interpretation of findings that the reader will encounter in the rest of the article. This "funneling-down" process, from general rationale to specific questions or hypotheses, is depicted in Figure 2.1. Although it is a common rhetorical structure employed by authors, it is important to note that it is not the only way that research article introductions are formulated.

Research Problem and Rationale

A researcher will typically begin an article by identifying an important problem that must be addressed. The problem is a broad area of concern within the profession. Music education scholars often derive problems from concerns that arise out of their own teaching and learning experiences. The way in which an author presents a rationale for studying the problem can vary, but generally they will rely on a combination of logical, persuasive argumentation and the presentation of evidence (i.e., citation of previous research) that illustrates the breadth and severity of the problem.

For example, Thornton and Culp (2020) more or less used this general rhetorical strategy when presenting a rationale for their qualitative study dealing with inclusivity in instrumental music education. They began their article with a compelling quote from a music teacher expressing curiosity as to whether students were ever denied opportunities to learn due to their physical exceptionalities. They then pivoted to citing prior research demonstrating that while students with disabilities express interest in instrumental music, they may not be accepted by their peers when actually participating and their teachers may not be prepared to help them participate. Later in the introduction they explicitly stated that there was a need for researching effective inclusive teaching strategies from the perspective of students with exceptionalities. By the end of the introduction, Thornton and Culp had clearly introduced a problem in the field that needed to be addressed and had convincingly argued that researching this problem was important and worthwhile.

Research Framework

Research frameworks refer to the theoretical assumptions or conceptual model that informs an author's perspective on a topic. A research framework can be thought of as a metaphorical skeletal structure upon which the rest of a study can be built. Frameworks are valuable for many reasons (e.g., Miksza & Berg, 2013). Researchers use them to highlight the key ideas and conceptual processes that serve as explanations for the phenomena most critical to their research problems. More practically, frameworks help researchers prioritize and delimit their research questions and methods, allowing them to allocate their resources and attention to the most important aspects of the phenomena they are studying. Frameworks are also helpful for interpreting findings, since researchers can compare what they've learned from their investigation to preexisting explanations described by the framework.

You will find that some authors employ established, formal theoretical frameworks, whereas others might develop their own conceptual model to help justify and direct their study. In contrast, some may not include any discussion of a framework whatsoever. Miksza and Johnson (2012) found that only about one-third of the authors of articles in the *Journal of Research in Music Education* from 1979 to 2009 specified a framework.

Eisenhart (1991, p. 205) described a theoretical framework as a "structure that guides research by relying on a formal theory; that is, the framework is constructed by using an established, coherent explanation of a certain phenomenon and relationships." One such framework that has been applied to studies of music teacher development is Berliner's (1986) theory of teacher expertise. Drawing upon ideas relevant to cognitive psychology, educational psychology, and cognitive science, Berliner's theory depicts key concepts and processes that can explain differences between novice and expert teachers as well as how novices may develop into expert teachers. Standley and Madsen (1991) used Berliner's theory to frame their study of the difference between music teaching experience and music teaching expertise, since years of experience accrued does not necessarily translate to expertise accrued. Standley and Madsen built their study upon Berliner's theoretical claim that expert teachers are able to draw subtle and sophisticated inferences about student learning when observing educational situations, whereas novices are typically able only to interpret situations literally. Using this as their starting point, Standley and Madsen were able to devise a method to distinguish teachers with relatively more expertise from others, despite having similar levels of experience.

Conceptual models that authors build themselves can serve the same or similar purposes as theoretical frameworks. We use the term "conceptual model" instead of "conceptual framework" to indicate the relatively provisional nature of a conceptual model compared to a theory. Admittedly, the semantic difference between words like "theory," "framework," and "model" is subtle, and it's important to recognize that these terms are not necessarily used consistently throughout the research literature. However, we specifically use the term "model" here to signify that conceptual models typically consist of relatively conjectural descriptions of concepts and processes when compared to theoretical frameworks.

McKoy (2013) employed a conceptual model in her study of music learning and teaching processes influenced by race, ethnicity, and culture (see Butler et al., 2007 for a thorough description of the model). The model illustrates how race, ethnicity, and school community settings can influence whether teachers develop cross-cultural competence. It highlights how issues pertaining to race, ethnicity, and community contexts can influence teachers, students, instructional content, instructional methods, and social contexts to thwart or support student learning. McKoy (2013) developed research questions that reflected key aspects of the model. Among several interesting findings, McKoy learned that students who identified as racial/ethnic minorities reported more cross-cultural experiences as well as being more willing to teach in a multicultural environment.

Purpose Statement

The opening section of an article will often culminate in a purpose statement. Purpose statements are often quite explicit, taking on the form: "The purpose of this study was to. . . ." A purpose statement will typically highlight the particular aspects of a broader research problem that the researcher plans to focus on in their study as well as the context in which they will investigate the problem. The purpose statement is a critical component of a study since all of the other components operate with respect to it. An introductory section should prepare the reader for recognizing the salience of the purpose, whereas methods are chosen in service of the purpose, and analyses and the interpretation of findings should be pursued to satisfy the purpose.

Here are some examples of purpose statements from recent articles:

> *Quantitative research:* "The purpose of this study was to examine the effect of a music improvisation and composition professional development workshop on teachers' perceptions and frequency of teaching music improvisation and composition in their music classes." (Hickey & Schmidt, 2019, p. 31)
>
> *Qualitative research:* "Accordingly, the purpose of this study was to explore how successful urban choral music educators use contextual knowledge to inform pedagogical practice." (Shaw, 2015, p. 199)
>
> *Historical research:* "The purpose of this study was to explore music instruction in selected public normal schools of the United States during the nineteenth century." (Hash, 2020, p. 415)
>
> *Philosophical research:* "Given the ambiguous meaning of 'diversity' in contemporary music education rhetoric, the purpose of this inquiry is to explore the assumptions underlying such understandings." (Richerme, 2019, p. 156)
>
> *Action research:* "The purpose of this social constructivist inquiry was to examine the experiences of three elementary music teachers and me, the researcher, involved in a collaborative teacher study group (CTSG) designed specifically to focus on student collaboration in elementary music classrooms." (Stanley, 2012, p. 56)

Research Questions and Hypotheses

Immediately following the statement of purpose, most authors of quantitative, qualitative, action research, and historical research will present a series of research questions. Research questions help to translate the purpose of a study into actionable steps. That is, authors use research questions to express exactly what they hope to achieve in their study in a manner even more specific than that communicated via the purpose statement. These questions often foreshadow the methodological choices made, the kinds of analyses that are performed, and the organization of the study findings. Readers should not necessarily encounter new information when reading research questions. The contents and contexts specified by the research questions should have been introduced throughout the introductory section of the article. While philosophical researchers rarely provide specific research questions, they will sometimes express what they hope to achieve in their study by explaining the structure of their argument (see below).

The following are examples of research questions that are drawn from the same articles as the purpose statements presented above.

Quantitative research (from Hickey & Schmidt, 2019, p. 31):

- "What was the immediate and long-term effect of improvisation and composition professional development on teachers' perceptions about teaching improvisation and composition?"
- "Did professional development relating to improvisation and composition impact teachers' intent on implementing these activities in their classes?"
- "Was there a change in the amount of improvisation and composition activities teachers offered in their classes following professional development? And did time since intervention impact the effect of professional development on these practices?"

Qualitative research (from Shaw, 2015, p. 200):

- "What contextual knowledge do successful urban choral music teachers hold about their students and about the communities in which they teach?"
- "How do urban choral music educators use contextual knowledge to inform their pedagogical practice?"
- "What experiences do effective urban choral educators consider to be essential preparation for teaching in an urban environment?"

Historical research (from Hash, 2020, p. 415):

- "What were the responsibilities and working conditions of music faculty in nineteenth-century state normal schools?"
- "What constituted music curricula at state normal schools during this period, and how did these develop through the turn of the twentieth century?"
- "How did music diploma and degree programs evolve in state normal schools?"
- "How did nineteenth-century music instruction at state normal schools influence the music teaching profession, the preservice teachers they served, and society at large in the United States?"

Philosophical research (from Richerme, 2019, p. 156) (outline of an argument):

- "First, I use the legal history of diversity in education to examine the NAfME's [National Association for Music Education] statements on equity, access, inclusivity, and diversity."
- "Second, drawing on Thomas Green's educational systems framework, I analyze the political arguments surrounding diversity and equity."
- "Third, I investigate the advantages and limitations of what Natasha Warikoo calls the "diversity bargain.""
- "Finally, I consider implications for practice."

Action research (from Stanley, 2012, p. 56):

- "How do the participants describe their experience in the CTSG?"
- "How has the focus on collaboration in the CTSG changed their teaching practice?"
- "What can these music teachers tell other music educators about collaboration?"

Hypotheses are sometimes included in place of or in addition to research questions in quantitative research articles. Hypotheses are less open-ended than research questions. A hypothesis is a prediction that a particular outcome will occur. Researchers investigating relationships among variables or conducting experiments to examine potential causal effects would be those most likely to offer hypotheses rather than research questions. Hypotheses are typically derived from theoretical frameworks or conceptual models. Here is an example of hypotheses from a recent article by Stambaugh (2011, pp. 370–371), who examined the relative efficacy of blocked versus random repetition strategies for clarinet practice:

- "Students in the blocked condition will perform more accurately, faster, and more steadily than students in the random condition at the end of practice (acquisition)."
- "Students in the random condition will perform more accurately, faster, and more steadily than students in the blocked condition at 24-hour retention and transfer testing."

Research findings are then used to determine whether the hypotheses are supported by the data or if, instead, the hypotheses should be rejected.

Delimitations and Operational Definitions

Although more common in theses and dissertations, authors may also include a brief mention of delimitations and/or a presentation of operational definitions at the end of the introductory section to the article. You will tend to find these in quantitative research articles more often than in those from other paradigmatic approaches. The delimitations of a study have to do with the scope of the research, the context in which it was conducted, and the potential generalizability of the findings of the study. Essentially, an author is acknowledging that their study is able to address only certain aspects of a research problem (as is the case for any single study) and, consequently, that there are limitations regarding what can be learned from their study.

Some terms authors use in articles may be understood in different ways by different people, or they may be confusing or unclear. Researchers may wish to clarify such terms early on by offering a list of operational definitions at the end of the introductory section. This is especially true if you are inventing new terms or using familiar terms in exceptional or highly restricted ways. An operational definition explains how a term will be used or understood in the context of the article. For example, Miksza (2006) was interested in the practice effectiveness of college musicians. Because there is no standard definition of practice effectiveness, Miksza needed to define it specifically as it was used in his study: "Practice effectiveness was operationally defined as the amount of change in performance achievement across a 23-minute, researcher-controlled practice session" (p. 311). Practice sessions in which a considerable amount of change in performance achievement occurred were considered more effective practice sessions than those in which little change occurred. Quantitative researchers will also often provide operational definitions to explain how important elements of their study (e.g., variables, constructs) will be represented as measurements. Terms that are commonly understood or that are routinely used in consistent ways do not need to be operationally defined.

Review of Related Literature

An important part of a typical quantitative or qualitative article introduction is a review of related literature, that is, a synthesis of the research studies that have already been published on the problem at hand. A review of related literature can be more or less integrated with the rationale and description of the research problem in general or set apart under its own heading, depending on the author's preferred style. However, in quantitative and qualitative research it is most often presented prior to the statement of the research purpose and the research questions. In historical research, primary and secondary sources are often used together in the introduction to describe context and background rather than strictly as a review of previous studies. In philosophical research, relevant literature is referenced throughout the article.

A review of related literature presents background information on the research problem, while simultaneously providing a context for the rationale for the study. One of the author's goals in this section of an article is to articulate how their study will fit within and extend our accumulated knowledge about the research problem. An effective review will also typically be written from a critical perspective. An author will mention the shortcomings, limitations, and/or gaps in the previous literature in an effort to bolster the rationale and need for their study. As such the author will typically present the previous literature to position their study as either (a) a replication of previous work for the sake of challenging or corroborating previous findings, (b) an extension of previous work that will examine a problem with a new method or from a novel theoretical perspective, or (c) an examination of some aspect of the problem that has yet to be studied.

In a dissertation or thesis, in which there are no page limitations, the related literature section may run for many pages. In journal articles, which have strict page limitations, the related literature section may range from a few paragraphs to several pages. Given the economy of space that authors must attend to, an article literature review will tend to devote the most space to those previous studies which are most similar to the current study and relevant to supporting the rationale for the current study. The collection of studies synthesized can include older research on the problem but must include the most recent studies the author is able to locate.

A well-written review of related literature will not consist of a series of paragraphs, each one containing an abstract of a single study. This would force the reader to make connections among the various studies cited as well as to the author's study. Instead, the author should present the previous literature via topical syntheses. As such, a literature review can often be organized with subheadings that address themes that have emerged in the previous research. Paragraphs should be organized with clear topic sentences that highlight salient points of synthesis. For example, a literature review of research on the topic of adolescents' preferences for popular music might include paragraphs organized around their age, grade level, years of musical training, and so on. See the paragraph below from the same article by Shaw (2015) referenced above. Notice how the author establishes a topic in the first sentence (e.g., challenges associated with urban education) and how the citations to previous research are used to elaborate upon that central topic:

> The practical realities of teaching in urban settings can present a myriad of obstacles that reinforce negative perceptions of urban education. The property tax–based system of public-school funding distributes resources unequally between neighborhoods, solidifying existing social boundaries (Erickson, 2008). These dynamics can particularly disadvantage urban schools situated in underserved communities where teachers are challenged to provide quality educational experiences but given inadequate resources (Calloway, 2009; Costa-Giomi, 2008). Federal policy emphasizing high-stakes testing has reduced funding and instructional time for arts education in many urban schools (Hazelette, 2006). An extreme emphasis on standardization, in which teachers are required to adhere strictly to prescriptive curricula, reduces teachers' ability to exercise creativity and deprofessionalizes teaching (Achinstein & Ogawa, 2012; Delpit, 2003). Seasoned veterans as well as novice teachers might experience frustration stemming from these issues. (Shaw, 2015, p. 199)

Method

Authors will describe the design elements of their study and the data collection processes—if data are indeed collected—in the method section of an article. The author aims for transparency in their method so that readers can critically evaluate the robustness of the procedural elements of the study and, therefore, the interpretations of the findings for themselves. One rule of thumb is that the method section should include enough detail that others could replicate the study if they wished. Method sections are most often found in quantitative and qualitative research, are sometimes included in historical research, and are only rarely included in philosophical research.

Participants and Contexts

Most of the research conducted in music education deals with information collected from or about people in some manner. Accordingly, the first part of a method section for such studies is most often a description of the study *participants*; in older studies the demeaning term "subjects" was used to refer to study participants. Authors will provide all the information they can about the participants of their studies. Possible information could include number of participants, self-identified gender, age or grade, experience, instrument or voice type, socioeconomic status, race, ethnicity, abilities, and so on.

Descriptions of participants will tend to be much shorter in quantitative research compared to qualitative research. For example, it is extremely important to describe the participants in great detail when conducting a qualitative case study of an individual or a group of people. Quantitative researchers are concerned with generalizing findings of their studies to broader populations and, as such, often strive to gather information from a large sampling of individuals. Consequently, the descriptions of participants in quantitative studies usually consist of simple, statistical summaries of group characteristics. In contrast, qualitative researchers are not necessarily concerned with generalization and will typically select only enough participants to gather information about the key elements of their research questions. This approach of purposeful sampling of key individuals combined with the need to provide a rich sense of context for the data analyses and interpretation of the individuals' experiences later in the article calls for a highly detailed description of each participant. Given that qualitative studies are often bound to specific, naturalistic settings, qualitative researchers will tend to provide very detailed descriptions of the contexts and settings surrounding their studies as well.

As music education research continues to mature, researchers need to be sensitive to issues of diversity, equity, and inclusion as represented in sampling practices and procedures. Increasingly, behavioral researchers are aware of and concerned about sampling bias on a large scale. That is, in fields such as psychology and sociology and, specifically for our interests, music education, the vast majority of research participants are from WEIRD countries: Western, educated, industrialized, rich, and democratic (Henrich et al., 2010). However, as Ghai (2021) argued, dichotomizing research participants into WEIRD and non-WEIRD categories glosses over many additional aspects of human diversity. Within the 8% of the world's population that come from WEIRD countries and the overwhelming 92% of people who come from non-WEIRD countries are a host of varying characteristics and behaviors. Music education researchers should be aware of and interested in these concerns from both "across" and "within" perspectives. An "across" perspective relates to music education research that includes a diversity of cultural perspectives, as seen in Machado et al.'s (2021) article "Popular Education and Music Education: Lessons from a Strings Program in Erechim, Brazil." Some examples of a "within" perspective might include the following research articles:

- *Issues of gender*: "Pursuing Diversity from the Podium: Insights from Australia for Wind Band Conductors and Educators on Achieving Gender Parity for Women Composers" (Howley, 2021)
- *Issues of cultural orientation*: " 'He Didn't Know What He Was Doin' ": Student Perspectives of a White Teacher's Hip-Hop Class" (Kruse, 2020)
- *Issues of disability*: "Academy of Music and Arts for Special Education (AMASE): An Ethnography of an Individual Music Instruction Program for Students with Disabilities" (Draper & Bartolome, 2021)
- *Issues of geography*: "Music Education and Educators in Missouri, Iowa, and Illinois" (Prendergast, 2021)
- *Issues of sexual orientation*: "Experiences of LGBTQ Students in Music Education Programs across Texas" (Taylor et al., 2020)

While these few examples do not begin to cover all of the possible topics, perhaps they can serve as examples of how researchers can address issues of diversity, equity, and inclusion.

Data Sources

Authors will also go to lengths to describe the ways they've gathered their data for their studies and any tools they used. For example, a method section of an article will usually include descriptions of questionnaires, tests, devices, musical examples, observation protocols, interview protocols, a researcher's field notes, methods for acquiring artifacts from a setting, recordings, and so on. It is important that the author provide clear enough descriptions of their data-gathering methods that readers can independently evaluate their integrity. However, beyond being extremely clear, authors should also describe why their data-gathering methods are valid and appropriate for the study at hand. It is especially helpful when authors provide examples of their data-gathering methods or even samples of entire data collection tools either within their article or as supplemental appendices. Quantitative, qualitative, and historical researchers will argue for the appropriateness of their data collection methods on somewhat different grounds. This will be explored in the subsequent chapters dealing with each paradigmatic approach.

Procedural Detail

An author will also attempt to describe the design details of their study in a method section. Lengthy descriptions of procedural details may be provided in theses and dissertations in which page limits are not an issue. However, in most articles, authors do the best they can to explain as much as they can as succinctly as they can. In this section of an article, authors may also discuss data analysis methods they used. The sorts of design and analysis information that would be reported in this section vary so widely across the four paradigmatic approaches to research described in this book that it would not be productive to discuss them here. Instead, we provide more information on various research design types and analysis methods in subsequent chapters.

Institutional Review Board

Nearly every institution that sponsors research has an Institutional Review Board (IRB) to assist researchers with the conduct of studies involving human participants. This body might also be called an ethical review board or research ethics board. Regardless, an IRB's primary responsibility is "to review research to assure the protection of the rights and welfare of the human subjects" (U. S. Food and Drug Administration, 1998). The agency must follow guidelines established by the state and/or federal government when making approval decisions.

Researchers undergo training—often through online modules—and then fill out approval forms to submit to the IRB for each research project. IRB staff members review the proposal and work with researchers to complete all requirements before approval. Before you begin collecting data for any research study that involves interacting with people, you will need to submit a proposal to the appropriate IRB. Even when research is being conducted primarily by a college student, a university faculty member will often need to serve as the primary investigator for the study. The student then will serve as a co-investigator. If an institution does not have its own IRB, it may refer proposals to an IRB at another institution. For projects conducted through a university and involving public schools, you may need approval from both entities. A researcher working in a public school or an institution other than a college or university might not have an IRB or a similar agency from which to seek approval. Regardless, it is important to consider ethical issues related to what they are asking participants to do and to follow self-imposed standards to ensure the well-being of everyone involved. Music education research articles should include a clear declaration (i.e., a sentence) that IRB approval was achieved. Although that is usually the extent to which it is mentioned in an article, issues pertaining to the ethical conduct of research are critical. Therefore, we will briefly elaborate upon some of them here.

To protect the rights of participants in a research study, informed consent must be obtained from each person. Where minors are concerned, informed consent must be given by parents or legally responsible parties. To obtain informed consent, you will prepare a brief statement that includes at least the following (University of Michigan Office of Research, n.d.):

- A statement that participation in this research project is voluntary and that the participant can withdraw from the study at any time without penalty.
- A summary of the research, including purpose, duration, and list of procedures.
- A list of reasonable, foreseeable risks or discomforts.
- A list of reasonable, expected benefits.

Each potential participant and parent/guardian should be given the opportunity to ask questions about the study. To preserve privacy and anonymity, records and data must be preserved in a safe and secure environment. Different governmental agencies or universities may have additional requirements beyond those described above.

Many music research proposals receive an expedited review or are labeled "exempt" by the chair of the IRB. This is because a determination has been made that participants will not be facing any reasonable or foreseeable risks or discomforts by participating in the study. Even if an exempt status is expected, however, you are still required to submit a proposal for IRB approval and will likely need to obtain informed consent in some form. In some cases, consent can be as simple as providing an introductory statement that participation in the activities connected to a study indicates consent. An exception may also occur when the researcher is utilizing data that already exists, such as standardized test scores archived within a school district or data available on the internet or through various channels, such as the National Center for Education Statistics.

Consider three examples:

- Austin and Berg (2020) assessed the reliability, validity, and utility of Educative Teacher Performance Assessment (edTPA) scores for three academic year cohorts of music student teachers ($N = 60$). The study involved comparisons of edTPA scores with candidate's high school and college GPAs, ACT, or SAT scores, music education and licensure program admission interview outcomes, and college course grades. Although not stated directly in the article, it is likely that the IRB granted exempt status for this study because it focused on preexisting data collected by the institution.
- Rawlings (2019) utilized a series of interviews to create an oral history of the life and work of E. Daniel Long, a prominent American school orchestra teacher during the second half of the 20th century. Because this study involved asking the subject of the research to share personal thoughts and memories through live interviews, the author had to obtain consent and seek approval

from the IRB. Due to the nature of the research, the IRB granted the study exempt status.
- Vaughn et al. (2013) examined laryngeal tension in adolescent choral singing. In contrast, to the Rawlings study, Vaughn and her colleagues went through a rigorous IRB review process because their study required adolescents to undergo videostroboscopy, which involved threading a fiberoptic scope through nasal passages to take images of vocal folds in action. Because there are risks attached to this procedure and the participants were minors, the reviewing committee was particularly concerned about safety. Approval was eventually gained because the procedure was being conducted by a professional speech-language pathologist who was a nationally recognized expert. Informed consent was obtained from parents and guardians.

Any study that involves human participants or an analysis of preexisting data should undergo an IRB review. To reiterate, a short statement somewhere in the method section should indicate compliance with an IRB. For example, "Permission to conduct this research was granted by the university institutional review board through exempted review" (Fisher et al., 2020, p. 56).

Results or Findings

The outcomes of any data analyses conducted in a study are usually presented in a section titled "Results" or "Findings." As in other sections, the style in which data analyses outcomes are presented can depend on the paradigmatic approach used. When it comes to reporting findings, there are some similarities between typical quantitative and qualitative articles. Again, action research articles are likely to follow the conventions of either (or both) quantitative and qualitative articles. However, historical and philosophical research articles are not likely to have a findings or results section.

In quantitative research, a results section would typically include statistical summaries of trends in the data and the results of statistical tests that address the research questions and/or hypotheses. A written description of the statistical summaries and test results would also be accompanied by tables and figures that help depict the important aspects of the data. The results section in a quantitative study is usually organized according to the research questions and/or hypotheses. Quantitative researchers traditionally restrict this section to presenting the results of data analyses, with no or perhaps only minimal commentary on the results or interpretation of the results within broader contexts.

In contrast, qualitative researchers are less likely to use "Results" as a heading for this section and may instead be more likely to use "Findings." Given that the primary data source for qualitative research is often verbal- or text-based data, this section is typically organized according to the themes, categories, and/or codes that emerge from the analyses of data. In contrast to quantitative research, the style in which the findings are presented can vary quite a bit. For example, for some studies authors may move in a rather linear way, presenting primary themes, then secondary themes, and so on; for other studies authors may choose to present their findings via vignettes or more abstract means. In addition, sometimes a qualitative study is itself an emergent enterprise. That is, some of the questions and methods qualitative researchers choose to use may emerge only once data analysis has begun. In contrast to quantitative researchers, qualitative researchers often interpret their findings in this section of an article and will often discuss how their findings relate to previous research along with the presentation of their findings. Obviously, statistical summaries are rarely presented in qualitative research.

Discussion and Conclusions

The final section of a quantitative, qualitative, or historical research article will typically include a restatement of the purpose and research questions/hypotheses of the study. This will be followed by a summary of answers to each question along with a description of how the findings of the study fit those from the previous literature (e.g., contradict, corroborate, extend). Authors may speculate a bit about why they found what they found as well. The extent of this discussion will depend on how much space the author has already devoted to interpreting their findings in the previous section. As mentioned above, qualitative researchers may have already covered some of this ground in the previous section. Other typical features of this last section include discussions of any practical implications of the research, the limitations of the research, and ideas for further research on the topic.

Summary

This chapter has provided an overview of structural features commonly used in research reports. It is important to note that there are many, many variations on this general outline of a research study. Each of the various research paradigms you learned about in the first chapter has its own structure and style. In subsequent chapters, we will provide an in-depth look at each specific approach (e.g., quantitative, qualitative, historical, philosophical, action). Also, in these discussions of specific research approaches, we will be revisiting the major themes of this chapter. Thus, if some concepts are not completely clear in your mind, you will have many opportunities to review them as we proceed. Finally, one of the best ways to become familiar with all the different aspects of research is to read original studies as they appear in research journals. The more of these you read, the more you will encounter not only the basic parts of a research study but also many of the possible variations.

Here are some study prompts that will help you clarify your understanding of the topics presented in this chapter:

1. Drawing from your own expertise, think of problems in the field that you are really interested in or even passionate about. If you can't think of something off the top of your head, then browse in the literature (e.g., music education research journals). At first, just getting some general ideas of what others have done can be very helpful.
2. Identify a research article that addresses the topic that you are interested in.
   a. Look for the purpose statement of the study and see if you can identify any specific research questions or hypotheses the author addressed.
   b. Do you feel that the author's rationale is strong? Do they present a logical argument? Do they establish a need for their study given the previous literature that exists?
3. Think of a topic that you might want to research yourself—perhaps it is the same topic from items 1 and 2 above.
   a. Write a purpose statement for your hypothetical research.
   b. Follow this with several research questions or hypotheses that you might want to answer.
4. Using your own words, write a paragraph that explains what an author hopes to achieve in a method section of an article. Aim your writing so that it will be useful for someone who is not familiar with research.
5. Why is it necessary to obtain IRB approval before data collection begins?
6. Explain the differences between the section of an article that emphasizes the findings of a study and the discussion section of an article.

Important Terms for Review

A *research problem* is the particular problem being addressed in a given study. Authors must provide a rationale describing why the problem is important to address and why the way they propose to address it is valuable.

A *research framework* in general refers to the theoretical assumptions or conceptual model that informs a researcher's perspective when conducting a study.

The *purpose* is the specific intent of a particular research study that is often explicitly stated by an author (e.g., "The purpose of this study was to . . .").

Research questions focus and delimit the objective(s) of a study even further than the purpose statement. Research questions establish what an author specifically hopes to learn about from a given study and inform methodological and analytical choices researchers make.

A *hypothesis* is a prediction about an outcome of a study derived from a theoretical proposition.

A *literature review* is a section of a manuscript in which previous research on a topic is synthesized and rhetorically positioned to support and provide context for the research questions, design, and or analysis methods chosen.

The term *design* refers to the type of research being conducted (e.g., case study, survey, oral history), the methodological details of the study, and the analysis approaches chosen.

References

Achinstein, B., & Ogawa, R. T. (2012). New teachers of color and culturally responsive teaching in an era of educational accountability: Caught in a double bind. *Journal of Educational Change, 13*(1), 1–39. https://doi.org/10.1007/s10833-011-9165-y

Austin, J. R., & Berg, M. H. (2020). A within-program analysis of edTPA score reliability, validity, and utility. *Bulletin of the Council for Research in Music Education, 226,* 46–65. https://doi.org/10.5406/bulcouresmusedu.226.0046

Berliner, D. C. (1986). In pursuit of the expert pedagogue. *Journal of Teacher Education, 36*(6), 2–8. https://doi.org/10.3102/0013189x015007007

Butler, A., Lind, V. L., & McKoy, C. L. (2007) Equity and access in music education: Conceptualizing culture as barriers to and supports for music learning. *Music Education Research, 9,* 241–253. https://doi.org/10.1080/14613800701384375

Calloway, J. (2009). *In search of music equity in an urban middle school* (Publication No. 3362521) [Doctoral dissertation, University of San Francisco]. ProQuest Dissertations & Theses Global.

Costa-Giomi, E. (2008). Characteristics of elementary music programs in urban schools: What money can buy. *Bulletin of the Council for Research in Music Education, 177,* 19–28. https://www.jstor.org/stable/40319449

Delpit, L. D. (2003). Educators as "seed people" growing a new future. *Educational Researcher, 32*(7), 14–21. https://doi.org/10.3102/0013189X032007014

Draper, A. R., & Bartolome, S. J. (2021). Academy of music and arts for special education (AMASE): An ethnography of an individual music instruction program for students with disabilities. *Journal of Research in Music Education, 69*(3), 258–283. http://dx.doi.org/10.1177/0022429421990337

Eisenhart, M. A. (1991). Conceptual frameworks for research circa 1991: Ideas from a cultural anthropologist; implications for mathematics education researchers. In R. G. Underhill (Ed.), *13th Annual Psychology of Mathematics Education–North America meeting* (pp. 202–220). Christiansburg Printing.

Erickson, B. (2008). The crisis in culture and inequality. In S. J. Tepper & B. J. Ivey (Eds.), *Engaging art: The next great transformation of America's cultural life* (pp. 343–362). Routledge.

Fisher, R. A., Hoult, A. R., & Tucker, W. S. (2020). A comparison of facial muscle activation for vocalists and instrumentalists. *Journal of Music Teacher Education, 30*(1), 53–64. https://doi.org/10.1177/1057083720947412

Ghai, S. (2021). It's time to reimagine sample diversity and retire the WEIRD dichotomy. *Nature Human Behaviour, 5,* 1–2. doi.org/10.1038/s41562-021-01175-9

Hash, P. M. (2020). Music instruction at selected state normal schools during the nineteenth century. *Journal of Research in Music Education, 67,* 413–439. https://doi.org/10.1177/0022429419888740

Hazelette, E. N. (2006). Surviving the first year of teaching music in an urban school district: The music administrator's perspective. In C. Frierson-Campbell (Ed.), *Teaching music in the urban classroom* (Vol. 2, pp. 13–22). Rowman & Littlefield.

Henrich, J., Heine, S. J., & Norenzayan, A. (2010). Most people are not WEIRD. *Nature, 466*(7302), 29–29. https://doi.org/10.1038/466029a

Hickey, M., & Schmidt, C. (2019). The effect of professional development on music teachers' improvisation and composition activities. *Bulletin of the Council for Research in Music Education, 222*, 27–43. https://doi.org/10.5406/bulcouresmusedu.222.0027

Howley, R. (2021). Pursuing diversity from the podium: Insights from Australia for wind band conductors and educators on achieving gender parity for women composers. *International Journal of Music Education, 39*(2), 247–259. https://doi.org/10.1177/0255761420928627

Kruse, A. J. (2020). "He didn't know what he was doin'": Student perspectives of a White teacher's hip-hop class. *International Journal of Music Education, 38*(4), 495–512. https://doi.org/10.1177/0255761420924316

Machado, J., Ody, L. C., & Ilari, B. (2021). Popular education and music education: Lessons from a strings program in Erechim, Brazil. *International Journal of Music Education, 39*(1), 80–92. https://doi.org/10.1177/0255761420946937

McKoy, C. L. (2013). Effects of selected demographic variables on music student teachers' self-reported cross-cultural competence. *Journal of Research in Music Education, 60*(4), 375–394. https://doi.org/10.1177/0022429412463398

Miksza, P. (2006). Relationships among impulsiveness, locus of control, sex, and music practice. *Journal of Research in Music Education, 54*(4), 308–323. https://doi.org/10.1177/002242940605400404

Miksza, P., & Berg, M. H. (2013). Transition from student to teacher: Frameworks for understanding preservice music teacher development. *Journal of Music Teacher Education, 23*, 10–27. https://doi.org/10.1177/1057083713480888

Miksza, P., & Johnson, E. (2012). Theoretical frameworks applied in music education research: A content analysis of the *Journal of Research in Music Education*, 1979 to 2009. *Bulletin of the Council for Research in Music Education, 193*, 7–30. https://doi.org/10.5406/bulcouresmusedu.193.0007

Prendergast, J. S. (2021). Music education and educators in Missouri, Iowa, and Illinois. *Journal of Research in Music Education, 69*(2), 228–243. http://dx.doi.org/10.1177/0022429420961501

Rawlings, J. R. (2019). "Don't keep it a secret": E. Daniel Long and his career in music education. *Journal of Historical Research in Music Education, 42*(2), 159–179. https://doi.org/10.1177/1536600619893067

Richerme, L. K. (2019). The diversity bargain and the discourse dance of equitable and best. *Philosophy of Music Education Review, 27*, 154–170. https://doi.org/10.2979/philmusieducrevi.27.2.04

Shaw, J. T. (2015). "Knowing their world": Urban choral music educators' knowledge of context. *Journal of Research in Music Education, 63*, 198–223. https://doi.org/10.1177/0022429415584377

Stambaugh, L. A. (2011). When repetition isn't the best practice strategy: Effects of blocked and random practice schedules. *Journal of Research in Music Education, 58*, 368–383. https://doi.org/10.1177/0022429410385945

Standley, J. M., & Madsen, C. K. (1991). An observation protocol to differentiate teaching experience and expertise in music education. *Journal of Research in Music Education, 39*, 5–11. https://doi.org/10.2307/3344604

Stanley, A. M. (2012). The experiences of elementary music teachers in a collaborative teacher study group. *Bulletin of the Council for Research in Music Education, 192*, 53–74. https://www.jstor.org/stable/10.5406/bulcouresmusedu.192.0053

Taylor, D. M., Talbot, B. C., Holmes, E. J., & Petrie, T. (2020). Experiences of LGBTQ students in music education programs across Texas. *Journal of Music Teacher Education, 30*(1), 11–23. https://doi.org/10.1177/1057083720935610

Thornton, L., & Culp, M. E. (2020). Instrumental opportunities: Music for all. *Update: Applications of Research in Music Education, 38*, 48–57. https://doi.org/10.1177/8755123320907140

University of Michigan Office of Research. (n.d.). *Informed consent guidelines and templates.* https://bit.ly/3iPqout

U.S. Food and Drug Administration. (1998). *Institutional review boards frequently asked questions: Guidance for institutional review boards and clinical investigators*. https://bit.ly/2KOyB5y

Vaughn, B., Hooper, C., & Hodges, D. (2013). Laryngeal tension in adolescent choral singing. *Journal of Singing, 69*, 403–412.

3
Conducting a Review of Related Literature

Chapter Preview

In this chapter we explore ways of reviewing literature in order to provide a context within which to place your own study. A literature review can provide background information necessary for a reader to understand your study. Furthermore, syntheses of findings from related literature will reveal what is known about your topic and allow you to identify the gaps or weaknesses in the knowledge base, which will help you establish a rationale for your study. Quantitative, qualitative, and action research studies always include a review of related literature; historical and philosophical studies may not. Modern search engines make finding related literature easy but correspondingly difficult in that they return so many possibilities that it can take considerable time and effort to sort through and identify the most relevant sources. Using a reference management system can save many hours of labor in organizing and formatting your references. Organizing information under various headings based on important elements of your study will help the reader understand how these studies relate to your own. A literature review should also entail critique, as you are expected to point out weaknesses in data collection or analysis or discrepancies among various findings. Most important, you will need to demonstrate how previous research is connected to your own. Perhaps you are attempting to fill in gaps in the literature, extend previous findings, or contradict prevailing notions.

Introduction

In the previous chapter, you were introduced to the concept of a review of related literature. All quantitative, qualitative, and action research articles will have a section devoted to a review of related literature, and while historical and philosophical studies may not typically include a distinct literature review section, they will still be grounded in relevant literature in one manner or another. The purpose of this chapter is to expand on your understanding of the role of a literature review and to provide some practical advice on how to effectively write your own review. You may wish to reread the corresponding section in the previous chapter before continuing with this one; however, here are two main points worth repeating:

- The purpose of a review of related literature is to provide a context within which to place your study. It presents background information necessary for a reader to understand your study.
- A review of related literature allows you to present a rationale for your study by revealing what is known about your topic and what gaps or weaknesses there may be in the knowledge base.

Constructing a review of related literature involves a great deal of reading, and experienced researchers are likely to be avid readers. They have developed a habit of reading broadly on a wide variety of subjects and deeply on specific topics of relevance for research problems of interest. For example, eminent music education researcher Richard Colwell set himself a self-imposed task of reading *all* the funded research and *every* doctoral dissertation in music education, in addition to all his other professional reading (personal communication, 2009).

As you read, develop a system of keeping track of two important things. One is major conclusions. A simple way to do this is to copy an abstract of the study and keep it with the citation information. Beyond that, notes that help you remember main conclusions from the study are helpful. The other is bibliographic citation information. Nothing is more frustrating than spending hours looking for a year of publication or page numbers for a source that you identified months previously. Relevant citation information for articles includes author(s), title, journal, year, issue, volume, page numbers, and the permanent digital object identifier (doi) if one is available for the source. Be meticulous in your record-keeping. Keeping electronic copies of the full papers when available will save you many late nights at the library or hunting online, and it is very easy to keep your files in a series of nested folders on your computer. An uncomplicated way to organize the sources you identify in your searches in the early stages would be to create three folders: "Not useful," "May be useful," and "Useful." Although it may seem unnecessary to keep documentation of those studies you deem not useful, you may change your mind as you progress in your study. It can be very frustrating and time-consuming trying to track down something you read months ago because you have only just then decided it may be pertinent.

Another alternative for organizing the sources you find is to use reference management software. For example, many universities endorse and/or provide technical support for popular applications, such as Endnote (https://endnote.com/), Zotero (https://www.zotero.org/), and Mendeley (https://www.mendeley.com/). These applications can automatically create records of the bibliographic information of a digital source if the publisher included the necessary metadata in the file—which is the case for most contemporary publications that have an online presence. For some, simply dragging a pdf into an open window of the program is all that you would need to do to trigger the application to extract the relevant metadata and create an entry cataloguing the source in a database on your computer. Conveniently, digital files of the sources you locate can also be stored and organized within folder hierarchies directly in reference management software. Most programs allow you to write notes for each entry as well.

Furthermore, these applications have the capability of being integrated with other kinds of software. For example, Mendeley's web browser extension gives you the capability of adding items to your account with a click while searching databases in Google Chrome online. In addition, each of the programs mentioned above work relatively seamlessly with word processing software (e.g., Microsoft Word). You could use the reference management program to insert citations and the respective additions to your reference list in your documents, and these can be automatically formatted according to any style guide you tell the software to use. This can be very helpful, since remembering all of the particulars of how to format citations for different style guides can be challenging and frustrating. One additional benefit of using reference management software is that you can create a personal account and then sync your database on your personal computer with the cloud. This allows you to add to or access your files, notes, and bibliographic information from any device connected to the internet at any time.

As mentioned, an important function of the section on related literature is to provide the reader with context. By analogy, think of it as a travel guide for a trip you are about to take. If you were going to Paris, say, you would likely want to take along a book or travel guide app that provides a broad overview of the city and its history. You would also want the travel guide to provide specific information on sites of interest, such as the Eiffel Tower, Notre Dame Cathedral, or the Louvre. Another feature of a good travel guide is maps. The related literature section of your article is like a good travel guide: it provides context for your study and maps for how you are going to arrive at the purpose of your study.

It is important to keep in mind that a literature review is different from a research framework. While a literature review involves a synthesis of the research studies that have already been published on the problem at hand, a research framework refers to the theoretical assumptions or conceptual model that informs an author's perspective on a topic. For more information about research frameworks, see Chapter 2.

Finding Relevant Sources

Before you begin conducting your literature review, it is crucial to decide on the specific topic or construct under investigation. For example, while the topics of culturally responsive teaching and multicultural music pedagogy may initially seem similar, they involve different assumptions and practices. Likewise, there is a marked contrast between such practices as informal learning, constructivism, and problem-based learning, and most studies will focus on only one of these pedagogies. Determining the exact wording of one's problem statement and research questions prior to starting the literature review can avoid wasting time while examining literature not directly related to one's study.

Prior to the advent of widespread internet use, researchers had to spend hours in the library searching through card indexes and roaming library stacks in dogged pursuit of their quarry (i.e., relevant studies). Although library searches could be enjoyable (no interrupting phone calls or texts, etc.), it was difficult to locate all the pertinent research and researchers were often too dependent upon any given library's holdings. Now, although internet searches make the job much easier in many ways, the problem may be that too much literature can be instantly available. As an example, suppose your study concerns ways to improve intonation in a concert band. A recent search in Google Scholar on the term "band intonation" turned up 56,900 results in only 0.11 seconds. Obviously, not all of these would be pertinent to your study, so the chore of sifting through all these entries would be exceedingly time-consuming. (We'll offer some suggestions for refining your searches subsequently.) The reason for this brief discussion is simply to point out that conducting a thorough search for useful sources is not quickly nor easily done, no matter whether you search with or without computers. One skill efficient researchers develop is the ability to skim articles; focus on the abstract and the conclusions at the first reading to determine whether the study is relevant to your own. Of course, careful, thorough reading will be necessary as you proceed.

In the next chapter, you will see that for some studies, visits to the library to access archives and repositories are necessary. However, for the moment, let's assume that the bulk of your search for relevant literature is going to be via the internet. Google Scholar (https://scholar.google.com) is an excellent way to begin. Google Scholar is a search engine for scholarly literature that indexes a broad array of disciplines. Because of that, you will need to refine or tweak the words you choose. For example, staying with the previous topic, suppose you enter "tuning for band" into Google Scholar. The search will return titles such as "Tuning the Band Gap in Silicene by Oxidation" (Du et al., 2014). Making the slight adjustment of "tuning for wind band" retrieves many more useful sources. In fact, before you begin to search for relevant sources, make a list of as many pertinent variables as you can and use those as key words to guide your searches.

Google Scholar has many helpful features. For example, items returned in a search also come with reference entries formatted according to APA, Chicago, Harvard, MLA, and Vancouver styles. You can also restrict your search to specific date ranges. Often, you will see "[PDF]" in the right-hand column, indicating that you can download a full-text pdf of the article. At most universities, it is possible to link your university library to your Google account by entering your university information in the "library link" field within the settings options in Google Scholar. Once you link your university library, any items you can get full-text access to via your library will also be available straight from the search results. Google Scholar has limited options for using Boolean operators ("and," "or," "not") because it searches in the full text of publications. However, you can conduct an advanced search to look for a particular phrase or a particular author in a particular journal by following options that appear after clicking on the three lines in the upper left-hand corner. It is also possible to use quotation marks around search terms to search for specific phrases. See Google Scholar search hints for more information (https://scholar.google.com/intl/en/scholar/help.html).

If a full-text pdf is not available in Google Scholar and you are not able to link to your university library within Google Scholar, try the following approaches: (a) Using your library's online collections, find the catalogue entry for the specific journal in which the article you are looking for is published and try to download a full-text document; (b) if your library does not have this journal in its collection, go to the authors' websites (often a university faculty page) and see if they have posted a copy of the article on their personal pages; more and more scholars are doing this; or (c) explore the interlibrary loan options at your institution. In some cases, making a request for an item that is not available in your library can result in a digital interlibrary loan delivery on the same day.

Google Books (books.google.com) is another wonderful search engine. Suppose you want to confirm a quotation you hastily scribbled down in the library without marking the page number or the year of publication. As an example, suppose that you have the following quote, along with the author, title, and publisher, but the date of publication you scribbled down is not clear and you forgot to indicate the page number:

> Wind instruments are manufactured to play in tune at an external temperature of 72 degrees Fahrenheit, after proper warm up. (Garofalo, year?, p.?)

Looking the book up in Google Books, you could confirm that the year of publication is 1996 and that the quotation is found on p. 10.

There are many other search engines in addition to Google Scholar and Google Books, including:

- ProQuest Dissertations & Theses Global (https://about.proquest.com/products-services/pqdtglobal.html) is a repository of over 5 million works from nearly 100 countries. To access documents, you will need to go through a university library or purchase your own account. Most documents are available in full text as a pdf. Alternatively, you can order a hard copy.
- JSTOR "provides access to more than 12 million academic journal articles, books, and primary sources in 75 disciplines" (about.jstor.org). Using the same search on "tuning" or "intonation" and "band" resulted in 24,238 hits. If you have access through a library, you can download full-text pdfs of articles. For example, on our selected topic, you could download the article "Wind Instrument Intonation: A Research Synthesis" by Powell (2010). You can also copy citation information already formatted in APA, Chicago, or MLA style or export to several reference management systems.

- Education Resources Information Center (ERIC) (https://eric.ed.gov) is a digital library of education research and information. Most of the published research studies are not available in full-text format, but with the abstract you can determine a publication's relevancy to your project, and with the citation information you can search for full-text options through your library.
- Répertoire International de Littérature Musicale (RILM) (rilm.org) contains 1,509,986 abstracts and 432,027 full-text articles; it requires an annual subscription but may be available through your university library while you are affiliated as student, faculty, or staff. A search on "tuning" or "intonation" and "band" resulted in 10,024 hits. One advantage of RILM is that it includes dissertations and theses. You can export citations to EndNote, RefWorks, or EasyBib.

Of course, there are many other search engines that might be useful. A faculty mentor or librarian can direct you to the appropriate ones beyond these few. In addition, it is often very helpful to "tree back" or examine the reference sections of the sources you locate to identify other potentially relevant articles. Considering the sources other authors have cited in their studies of topics similar to yours can sometimes easily reveal important papers that might otherwise be obscured within long lists of search engine results.

What about Wikipedia? Because Wikipedia's articles are not peer-reviewed, it is not considered a suitable source of scholarly information. In other words, you would not want to cite a Wikipedia entry in an academic paper. However, Wikipedia may play a useful role, especially early in the process when you are just beginning to explore your topic. The sources listed at the end of the entry might direct you to a few published sources to help you get started.

How Many Related Literature References Should You Have?

There is, as you might have guessed, no clear answer to this question. Some topics may necessitate extensive references because the published literature is quite voluminous. Other topics may have a much smaller library of relevant research. A general rule of thumb is that the related literature section should reflect the published literature. It is inappropriate to "cherry-pick" the studies that support your thesis. As stated previously, one purpose of a related literature section is to provide the reader with the context to understand your study. In that sense, the related literature section must fairly and accurately represent what previous scholars have discovered. Note that the phrase "published literature" does not mean that unpublished studies such as theses and dissertations are necessarily excluded. However, studies that have been published reflect the process of peer review, a process critical to ensuring quality. (For more information on peer review, see Chapter 21.)

Knowing when to stop searching for relevant literature is difficult. One way to determine whether your list of sources is relatively complete is to take note of when the same citations begin to appear repeatedly across various searches and when treeing back through references of published works no longer reveals new sources. Another good way to gain a sense of the completeness of your set of references is to examine the reference list in the most recently published literature review you can find—whether it be a stand-alone article or a section within a recent article. Powell (2010) and Springer (2020), who both reviewed articles of wind band tuning, are good examples. As you peruse the reference lists in other articles, you can easily tell whether or not you have already identified most or all of the studies. In most cases, there is no need to be exhaustive.

Furthermore, not every study you have uncovered needs to be included. The litmus test should be whether a study contributes to the discussion at hand. Suppose, for example, you have identified six articles with the following publication dates: 2019, 2018, 2018, 2016, 1954, and 1948. The latter two may certainly provide pertinent information that argues for their inclusion. However, let us suppose that in this case, the oldest references have been superseded by the newer studies in such a way that they no longer make a relevant contribution. In this instance, they may be safely omitted, particularly if space (i.e., word count) is an issue. A counterexample is that works even as old as those from Plato and Aristotle can still have relevance for scholars today. Therefore, date of publication is not necessarily a reason for exclusion.

As mentioned previously, space or word count is often a factor that restricts the number of references cited. Institutional dissertations and theses guidelines commonly have minimal or no restrictions on word count, whereas journals can have fairly strict limitations. Therefore, it is not unusual for a dissertation to have many more pages devoted to a related literature section than the few paragraphs that may be found in a published study. To bring an end to this discussion of "how many" references, consider that a dissertation by Davis (2019) concerned with pedagogical approaches to intonational instruction included 140 references. By contrast, in the first issue of 2021, the *Journal of Research in Music Education* published seven articles; the average number of references was 48, with a range of 31 to 57. These numbers should only be taken as "snapshots"; certainly, a detailed study of both published and unpublished studies in music education research would provide more accurate information. Table 3.1 provides some information on word count and page length for articles published in various journals. It is these restrictions that often require authors to condense their related literature section considerably from what might appear in a dissertation.

Table 3.1 Style manuals in selected music education research journals

Journal	Style Manual	Page or Word Limitations
ACTME	CMS w. exceptions	No restrictions on length
BCRME	APA	About 20 pp. (6,000 words)
BJME	*	About 5,000 words
IJMER	APA	Will not exceed 6,000 words including tables, references, and captions of figures
JHRME	CMS	No more than 8,000 words, excl. footnotes
JRME	APA, CMS, Tur.	About 20–25 pp. (at 300 words per page = 6,000–7,500 words)
PMER	CMS	No more than 8,000 words, incl. endnotes and abstract
RSME	APA	About 6,000 words, excl. abstract and refs.

ACTME: *Action, Criticism, and Theory for Music Education*
BCRME: *Bulletin of the Council for Research in Music Education*
BJME: *British Journal of Music Education.* *No style manual is specified for BJME; examples of how to format quotations and references are given.
IJMER: *International Journal of Music Education Research*
JHRME: *Journal of Historical Research in Music Education*
JRME: *Journal of Research in Music Education*
PMER: *Philosophy of Music Education Review*
RSME: *Research Studies in Music Education*
CMS: *Chicago Manual of Style* (2017)
APA: *Publication Manual of the American Psychological Association* (2019)
Tur.: *A Manual for Writers of Term Papers, Theses, and Dissertations* (Turabian, 2007)

Formatting Your Sources

Each university publishes requirements for formatting dissertations and theses. Likewise, each journal publishes its own requirements for formatting manuscript submissions. For this discussion, we will focus primarily on style manuals used to format in-text citations and reference lists and will not cover other formatting issues such as headings, page margins, and so on.

As is evident in Table 3.1, APA and CMS are the most frequently used style manuals for music education research. If given a choice, say with JRME, the decision of which style manual to use may be a preference for foot/endnotes rather than in-text citations. For example, authors of historical or philosophical papers that commonly use a more literary writing style may prefer not to interrupt the flow of the text with numerous in-text citations and, therefore, choose CMS.

At first it may seem very fussy to worry about whether the date comes at the beginning after the author—in APA: Springer, D. G. (2020) . . .—or at the end—CMS: Springer, D. Gregory . . . (2020). But remember, the primary reasons for this are consistency and accuracy. Scholars rely on finding accurate information in a consistent format; this expedites their research activities immensely. Fortunately, you have citation management systems to help (see previous discussion), and there are also some excellent online sources available to provide examples and answer questions. The Purdue Online Writing Lab (https://owl.purdue.edu) is just one useful resource among many.

Another important point to recognize is the difference between a bibliography and a reference list. A bibliography allows you to include sources you may have used in preparing your manuscript but did not cite. A reference list requires an exact match between works cited in the test and the reference list at the end. Most journals follow a reference list style. When using a reference list approach, make certain you go through your paper to determine that information in the text matches exactly the information in the reference list. It is not uncommon for copyeditors to find names spelled differently or publication dates that do not match. Fortunately, if you use reference management software, the reference list it can generate for you automatically will include only the literature you cite.

Summarizing and Organizing Your Sources in Preparation for Writing

Once you have identified your sources, you are then left with the energy-intensive task of reading it all! It's important to recognize that academic writing can be dense and will often take more time to digest than popular forms of writing would (e.g., news stories, blogs, novels). Fortunately, reading research will become easier over time as you gain familiarity with the stylistic conventions and idiomatic features that are common to each of the major research paradigms.

One goal to strive for when reading your sources is to develop a general sense of what previous scholars have learned about your topic of interest thus far. However, you also need to be able to imagine whether and how each source you read might inform the rationale, design, and interpretation of the potential findings for your study. Reading each source and noting the gaps or weaknesses present within each as well as across the literature is also important since a critique of previous literature can often lead to a more robust rationale for new studies that can address previous limitations. Moreover, at some point you will want to be able to think across the literature you've identified so that you can synthesize and summarize the work when writing the review of literature for your own paper. (Approaches for writing about the information you extract from your sources are described later in this chapter.)

The typical strategies students tend to use for close reading and note taking such as highlighting key passages and writing notes in the margins of papers can be helpful for maintaining attention while reading and may also help you retain information. However, such methods may not be as effective when the ultimate goal is being able to synthesize information across a large body of sources. For example, you would have to go back to each individual document to refresh your memory of the most salient aspects of each source when using such methods. This would be very time-consuming, and toggling back and forth between papers is likely to make it difficult to think across papers and synthesize their content.

In contrast to traditional note-taking methods, summarizing the key components of the literature you read and collating that information in a spreadsheet can be particularly helpful for managing such large amounts of information. Consider the typical components of a music education research article, presented in Chapter 2. Some of the major components of a research article could be used as column headings in a spreadsheet to organize your notes, and each row could represent a different source. For example, columns could be created for notating information about (a) the purpose of the study, (b) the framework employed, (c) the participants, (d) procedural information, (e) findings, and (d) discussion points made by the author. These column headings could be particularly well-suited to qualitative and quantitative research. However, you could imagine including other headings or perhaps consolidating headings if you were aiming to synthesize historical or philosophical papers. It could also be helpful to include additional columns, such as a column devoted to notes about how what you've read may be relevant to your study (or not) as well as a column in which you mention any critiques that arose as you read. You could populate the relevant cells in the spreadsheet as you read your sources. You could then simply scan the spreadsheet to remind yourself of the key aspects of each source without having to toggle back and forth across files or notes. Such a spreadsheet would also allow you to find commonalities or discrepancies across your sources more easily.

Two of the authors of this text, Lauren Richerme and Peter Miksza (2020), created a literature summary spreadsheet for use when synthesizing literature for their article titled "Constructive Controversy in an Instrumental Music Classroom: An Exploratory Case Study." Table 3.2 shows the column headings and just one of the article entries for illustrative purposes. The complete literature summary spreadsheet is available among the online supplemental materials for this book (see item 1, Chapter 3 on the Companion website ▶).

As you start finding studies that might be relevant to your own work, you can think of organizing them around the center of a target (Figure 3.1). A study that is almost exactly like yours would be at the center. A study that is similar, but with some slight differences, would be at the next circle, and so on. Generally speaking, you can plan to provide more detail for and devote more space to those studies that are nearest the center. In other words, studies that are most relevant to your own work should typically receive the most attention in your review. If you have a large number of studies clustered around the center, you may not need to go so far out in your search. If you can find little around the center, you will need to range to circles farther out. Seeking sources outside of the music education discipline (e.g., in general education, psychology, sociology) may be necessary when researching topics that have received relatively little attention among music education scholars to date. In fact, making interdisciplinary connections can usually be beneficial for both disciplines.

When it comes time to organize these studies for the section of your paper titled "Review of Related Literature," avoid writing only a series of paragraphs in which

Table 3.2 An example of a literature summary spreadsheet

Author (Year)	Theoretical Framework	Purpose	Sample	Stimuli/ Task Measures	Procedure/ Conditions	Results/ Findings	Notable Discussion Points	Other
Santicola (2015)	Johnson & Johnson's (1993) five-step model (see notes on Johnson & Johnson, 1993 in this spreadsheet)	To examine effect of constructive controversy (i.e., active learning processes) vs. passive lecture in collegiate economics courses	$N = 34$, freshman, sophomore, continuing levels, full- and part-time	Test of Understanding in College Economics (TUCE)	Constructive controversy group = 8 lessons, one every two weeks, students in groups of 4 with 2 assigned to each position Control = traditional lecture Intact sections as group assignment	No differences on TUCE at pretest Difference in posttest favoring controversy group	Suggests that conceptual conflict increases epistemic curiosity (e.g., Piaget, Kohlberg)	Beneficial for knowledge acquisition among college students

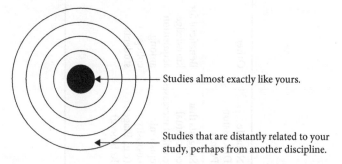

Figure 3.1 Imagine that your research topic is at the center of the target. The closer a published research article is to the center, the more relevant it is. If you find many studies near the center or the first few rings away (i.e., similar to yours), you have less need to search for articles that are farther away. In contrast, if you do not find articles that are close to your proposed study, you may need to range farther away.

each one contains an abstract of a single study (see Table 3.3). Occasionally, it will be convenient to spend an entire paragraph or so on a single study—especially if that study is particularly informative for or very close to your own. However, doing so too often would force the reader to spend too much energy making connections among the various studies and to your study.

Table 3.3 An ineffective way of presenting related literature

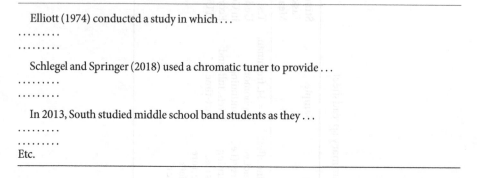

A more effective way of writing your review of related literature is to organize the content you have read according to subheadings representing the topics or synthesis points that are most informative with regard to the rationale, design, and interpretation of your study. If possible, it could also be helpful to the reader if you order these in some degree of priority, that is, according to which topics or synthesis points are most intimately connected to the purpose of your study, followed by the next most closely related topic, and so on. For example, consider how a Council for Research in Music Education Outstanding Dissertation Award winner from 2015, Cara Bernard, organized the literature review for her qualitative dissertation,

Ensemble Educators, Administrators, and Evaluation: Support, Survival, and Navigating Change in a High-Stakes Environment:

> The literature review presented in this chapter is organized into five sections. Section one describes the history of education reform in the United States and teacher quality over the past 30 years, leading to current teacher evaluation policies and practices. Section two provides a more in-depth look at teacher quality and evaluation, examining the value-added model and looking at a prominent evaluation system used nationwide. Section three narrows the umbrella of evaluation to music, describing music teacher quality, evaluation, and policy both nationwide and at the state level. Section four serves as an overview of teacher identity and mid-career teaching, as the participants of this study were mid-career teachers; also, during this shift into high-stakes evaluation, these mid-career teachers may feel like new teachers, having to rethink and reflect on their current practices and pedagogies. A background of teacher identity, through new and mid-career levels, may help to better understand the participants' words in the data. Lastly, section five discusses the relationships between the age of education accountability and stress in the workplace. (Bernard, 2015, pp. 29–30)

In contrast, an approach for organizing literature when conducting quantitative research could involve synthesizing research according to the particular variables that have been addressed in relation to the topic. For example, returning to our topic of band intonation, consider the list of selected studies and their variables presented in Table 3.4. Dependent variables indicate an outcome that was measured in a study, which, in this example, are measures of musical abilities related to intonation: pitch discrimination (PD), playing in tune (PiT), or pitch matching (PM). The independent variables are the things manipulated by the researcher to determine what effect, if any, they might have on the dependent variables; these included:

- Melodic context (MC): monitoring intonation within a melody rather than a single pitch.
- Visual feedback (VF) from a chromatic tuner.
- The instrument sounding the tuning note (IST), whether an oboe, clarinet, tuba, or other.
- Vocalization (V): singing pitches before playing them.
- Timbre (T): asking students to tune while using a "bright" or "dark" tone, for example.

Undoubtedly, more variables than are presented in Table 3.4 have been examined in these studies and others not listed. However, even based on this table, you can begin to see potential approaches for organizing and synthesizing the literature. For example, subheadings and/or paragraphs could be created around the topics of (a) the impact of vocalization on intonation, (b) the impact of timbral characteristics

Table 3.4 Variables used in selected articles on wind band intonation

Author	Year	Independent Variables					Dependent Variables		
		MC	VF	IST	V	T	PD	PiT	PM
Bennett	1994				X			X	X
Byo & Schlegel	2016		X				X		
Byo et al.	2011			X					
Elliott	1974				X		X		
Geringer & Worthy	1999					X	X		
Jones	2003				X		X		
Morrison	2000	X						X	
Schlegel & Springer	2018		X					X	
Silvey et al.	2019				X			X	X
South	2003				X				
Springer et al.	2020					X		X	
Wapnik & Freeman	1980					X	X		
Worthy	2000					X	X		

MC: melodic context; VF: visual feedback; IST: instrument sounding the tuning note; V: vocalization; T: timbre; PD: pitch discrimination; PiT: playing in tune; PM: pitch matching.

on intonation, or (c) the variety of ways that intonation has been measured in the literature. Or, taking a different perspective, it seems that it would also be possible to synthesize according to what has or hasn't received substantial attention in the literature. For example, one synthesis point could be that the ability to play in tune within a melodic context has not received the attention that other variables such as vocalization or timbre have.

Whenever possible, paragraphs in a review of related literature should be written according to topic sentences that summarize what you have learned from reading a collection of studies. For example, when synthesizing research on how vocalization may influence the ability to "play in tune," you could combine the findings of the five studies out of the 13 identified in Table 3.4 that included vocalization as an independent variable: Bennett (1994), Elliott (1974), Jones (2003), Silvey et al. (2019), and South (2013). Here is how Springer (2020, p. 5) synthesized the relatively inconclusive findings that emerged from those studies:

> Previous research has demonstrated mixed results concerning the effects of vocalization (e.g., singing) on intonation, with some results indicating that it provided positive effects on pitch discrimination (e.g., Elliott, 1974; Jones, 2003) and others indicating that it had no effect on pitch matching (e.g., Bennett, 1994; South, 2013). Silvey et al. (2019) tested for the effects of two types of vocalization—singing and humming—on wind instrumentalists' tuning accuracy while performing concert B-flat tuning notes. Participants completed a tuning task three times. In each case,

they heard an oboe stimulus tone, then they were asked either to (a) sing the pitch, (b) hum the pitch, or (c) wait in silence before playing. There were no significant differences in tuning accuracy across those three conditions.

Consider next a paragraph from the literature review of Blackwell et al.'s (2020) study of studio music instruction. This paragraph begins with a topic sentence orienting the reader to previous research that has emphasized how teachers use their time with students, which is then followed by a description of the relatively clear conclusions that can be drawn from the literature. The paragraph ends with a statement that shifts the reader to consider how this extant research could serve as a foundation for future work (e.g., the authors' own study):

> Much of the research aimed at investigating studio music instruction expertise to date has been focused on categorizing teachers' time usage (Sogin & Vallentine, 1992; Siebenaler, 1997; Colprit, 2000; Creech, 2012), identifying a taxonomy of teacher behaviors that contribute to students' skill acquisition by observing renowned pedagogues (Duke & Simmons, 2006; Duke & Chapman, 2011; Parkes & Wexler, 2012; Blackwell, 2018), and exploring the nature of interpersonal relationships between students and teachers (Nerland & Hanken, 2002; Gaunt, 2008, 2011; Montemayor, 2008; Clemmons, 2009/2010; Hyry-Beihammer, 2010; Creech, 2012; Schiavio et al., 2019). Studies categorizing time usage during studio music instruction have found that most of the time was spent on student and teacher performance, followed closely by teacher verbalizations (Sogin & Vallentine, 1992; Colprit, 2000; Creech, 2012). These studies are instructive in understanding how teachers use their time, and provide a basis for exploring why teachers might make those decisions, and in particular their impact on student outcomes. (p. 2)

It could also be valuable to follow synthesis paragraphs with a few sentences of amplification and/or elaboration on what you learned by providing additional details, highlighting specific studies, or including commentary on the nature of any dissenting views or contradictions. Additional sentences that make a direct connection to the purpose and rationale of your own study are also important. Such sentences could reinforce the need for your own study or support the methodological choices you have made (e.g., frameworks, design, materials). Consider the following example from Hickey and Schmidt's (2019) study of whether professional development activities could encourage music teachers to incorporate improvisation and composition activities in their teaching. The last sentence of this excerpt positions a lack of research on the topic as a direct statement supporting the rationale for their own study

> Although there has been some research on teacher creative experiences and the relationship to instructional practice (Chan & Yuen, 2014; Koutsoupidou, 2005;

Odena & Welch, 2007, 2009) and some research on what constitutes meaningful professional development to enact change in teacher practice (Guskey, 2002; Hookey, 2002; Penuel et al., 2007; Richardson, 1990), there seems to be none regarding the impact of professional development on specific perceptions and the practice of music composition and improvisation over time. While studies show that teachers desire to learn through professional development (e.g., Bell, 2003; Madura, 2000; Ward-Steinman, 2007), there has not been any research to investigate the effectiveness of professional development specifically addressing composition and improvisation on changing teacher perceptions and practice over time. (p. 31)

Once you have laid out an organizational structure for your review of literature and have chosen the sources that could be included in each section, you can simply work step by step through each topic until you feel you have captured the relevant information with sufficient detail. When you are finished with one topic or subheading, place all the studies relevant to the next topic together and repeat. Continue this process, creating synthesis paragraphs and so on for all the topics that you wish to represent in your review. It is important to recognize that each study can appear under as many subheadings for which it contains a relevant topic or variable. For example, some articles may end up being cited numerous times and in numerous places, whereas others may be cited only once.

It is also important to approach the sources you read with a critical eye. In other words, don't just parrot authors' conclusions; instead, diplomatically point out potential limitations or even errors or flaws in the studies you read that might have influenced the findings. These might come in the design of the study, in data collection or analysis, or in interpretation (e.g., drawing conclusions that are not supported by the data analysis).

If individual subsections of the related literature are quite lengthy, a summary at the end of each subheading may be very helpful for the reader. Likewise, if the entire related literature section is quite long, or if there are numerous subsections, an overall summary at the end is often necessary. Remember, your main responsibility is to help readers understand the context of your study, not to confuse them. Also, if the related literature section is quite lengthy, you may wish to restate the purpose of your study, along with the research questions. Alternatively, this may be done at the beginning of the next section.

Summary

Developing and writing a clear and accurate review of related literature is a key component of a successful research project. It is by this means that you provide a context for your study and support for various aspects of it. Modern search engines make finding related literature easy but correspondingly difficult in that they return so many possibilities that it can take considerable time and effort to sort through and identify the most relevant sources. Using a reference management system can save many hours of labor in organizing and formatting your references.

Once you have collected your sources, presenting them to the reader in coherent fashion is necessary. Organizing them under various headings based on topics important to your study will help the reader understand how these studies relate to your own. Just writing raw, unfiltered information is insufficient. Rather, you will want to provide a critique of the literature and point out limitations of the studies you review. Most important, you will need to demonstrate how previous research is connected to your own. Perhaps you are attempting to fill in gaps in the literature, extend previous findings, or contradict prevailing notions. If you have done this job properly, the remainder of your study will be solidly nestled in the context of existing scholarly research.

References

Bell, C. L. (2003). Beginning the dialogue: Teachers respond to the national standards in music. *Bulletin of the Council for Research in Music Education, 156*, 31–42. https://www.jstor.org/stable/40319172

Bennett, S. J. (1994). *Can simple vocalization help improve the intonation of wind players?* (Publication No. 9514867) [Doctoral dissertation, Arizona State University]. ProQuest Dissertations and Theses Global.

Bernard, C. F. (2015). *Ensemble educators, administrators, and evaluation: Support, survival, and navigating change in a high-stakes environment.* (Publication No. 3704455) [Doctoral dissertation, Teachers College, Columbia University]. ProQuest Dissertations and Theses Global.

Blackwell, J. A. (2018). *Pedagogical preparation and expertise in pre-college applied music teaching.* (Publication No. 10841344) [Doctoral dissertation, Indiana University]. ProQuest Dissertations and Theses.

Blackwell, J., Miksza, P., Evans, P., & McPherson, G. E. (2020). Student vitality, engagement, and rapport in studio music instruction. *Frontiers in Psychology, 11*, 1007. https://doi.org/10.3389/fpsyg.2020.01007

Byo, J. L., & Schlegel, A. L. (2016). Effects of stimulus octave and timbre on the tuning accuracy of advanced college instrumentalists. *Journal of Research in Music Education, 64*(3), 344–359.

Byo, J. L., Schlegel, A. L., & Clark, N. A. (2011). Effects of stimulus octave and timbre on the tuning accuracy of secondary school instrumentalists. *Journal of Research in Music Education, 58*(4), 316–328. https://doi.org/10.1177/0022429410386230

Chan, S., & Yuen, M. (2014). Personal and environmental factors affecting teachers' creativity fostering practices in Hong Kong. *Thinking Skills and Creativity, 12*, 69–77. https://doi.org/10.1016/j.tsc.2014.02.003

Chicago manual of style. (2017). 17th ed. University of Chicago Press.

Clemmons, J. (2009/2010). The importance of being earnest: Rapport in the applied studio. *College Music Symposium, 49*, 257–264.

Colprit, E. J. (2000). Observation and analysis of Suzuki string teaching. *Journal of Research in Music Education, 48*, 206–221. https://doi.org/10.2307/3345394

Creech, A. (2012). Interpersonal behaviour in one-to-one instrumental lessons: An observational analysis. *British Journal of Music Education, 29*, 387–407. https://doi.org/10.1017/S0265051712 00006X

Davis, J. M. (2019). *Expert middle school band directors' pedagogical approaches to intonation instruction* (Publication No. 22618712) [Doctoral dissertation, University of Florida]. ProQuest and Theses Global.

Du, Y., Zhuang, J., Liu, H., Xu, X., Eilers, S., Wu, K., Cheng, P., Zhao, J., Pi, X., See, W. K., Peleckis, G., Wang, X., & Dou, S. X. (2014). Tuning the band gap in silicene by oxidation. *ACS Nano, 8*(10), 10019–10025. https://doi.org/10.1021/nn504451t

Duke, R. A., & Chapman, D. (2011). Changing learners: The nature of expertise in music teaching. In P. Madura Ward-Steinman (Ed.), *Advances in social-psychology and music education research* (pp. 29–38). Ashgate.

Duke, R. A., & Simmons, A. L. (2006). The nature of expertise: Narrative descriptions of 19 common elements observed in the lessons of three renowned artist-teachers. *Bulletin of the Council for Research in Music Education, 170*, 7–19. https://www.jstor.org/stable/40319345

Elliott, C. A. (1974). Effect of vocalization on the sense of pitch of beginning band class students. *Journal of Research in Music Education, 22*(2), 120–128. https://doi.org/10.2307/3345312

Garofalo, R. (1996). *Improving intonation in band and orchestra performance*. Meredith Music.

Gaunt, H. (2008). One-to-one tuition in a conservatoire: The perceptions of instrumental and vocal teachers. *Psychology of Music, 36*(2), 215–245. https://doi.org/10.1177/030573560 7080827

Gaunt, H. (2011). Understanding the one-to-one relationship in instrumental/vocal tuition in higher education: Comparing student and teacher perceptions. *British Journal of Music Education, 28*(2), 159–179. https://doi.org/10.1017/S0265051711000052

Geringer, J. M., & Worthy, M. D. (1999). Effects of tone-quality changes on intonation and tone-quality ratings of high school and college instrumentalists. *Journal of Research in Music Education, 47*(2), 135–149. https://doi.org/10.2307/3345719

Guskey, T. R. (2002). Professional development and teacher change. *Teachers and Teaching: Theory and Practice, 8*(3), 381–391. https://doi.org/10.1080/135406002100000512

Hickey, M., & Schmidt, C. (2019). The effect of professional development on music teachers' improvisation and composition activities. *Bulletin of the Council for Research in Music Education, 222*, 27–43. https://doi.org/10.5406/bulcouresmusedu.222.0027

Hookey, M. R. (2002). Professional development. In R. Colwell & C. Richardson (Eds.), *The new handbook of research on music teaching and learning* (pp. 887–902). Oxford University Press.

Hyry-Beihammer, E. K. (2010). Master-apprentice relation in music teaching: From a secret garden to a transparent modelling. *Nordic Research in Music Education, 12*, 161–178.

Johnson, D. & Johnson, R. (1993). Creative and critical thinking through academic controversy. *The American Behavioral Scientist, 37*(1), 40–53.

Johnson, D., & Johnson, R. (2000). Cooperative Jones, S. A. (2003). *The effect of vocalization on pitch discrimination among high school instrumentalists* (Publication No. 3092752) [Doctoral dissertation, University of Minnesota]. ProQuest Dissertations and Theses Global.

Koutsoupidou, T. (2005). Improvisation in the English primary music classroom: Teachers' perception and practices. *Music Education Research, 7*(3), 363–381. https://doi.org/10.1080/14613800500324432

Madura, P. D. (2000). Vocal music directors' confidence in teaching improvisation as specified by the National Standards for Arts Education: A pilot study. *Jazz Research Proceedings Yearbook 2000*, 31–37.

Montemayor, M. (2008). Flauto: an ethnographic study of a highly successful private studio. *International Journal of Music Education, 26*, 286–301. doi: 10.1177/0255761408096071

Morrison, S. J. (2000). Effect of melodic context, tuning behaviors, and experience on the intonation accuracy of wind players. *Journal of Research in Music Education, 48*(1), 39–51. https://doi.org/10.2307/3345455

Nerland, M., & Hanken, I. M. (2002). Academies of music as arenas for education: Some reflections on the institutional construction of teacher student relationships. In M. Hanken,

S. G. Nielsen, & M. Nerland (Eds.), *Research in and for higher education* (pp. 167–186). Norges musikkhgskole.

Odena, O., & Welch, G. F. (2007). The influence of teachers' backgrounds on their perceptions of musical creativity: A qualitative study with secondary school music teachers. *Research Studies in Music Education, 28*(1), 71–81. https://doi.org/10.1177/1321103X070280010206

Odena, O., & Welch, G. (2009). A generative model of teachers' thinking on musical creativity. *Psychology of Music, 37*(4), 416–442. https://doi.org/10.1177/0305735608100374

Parkes, K. A., & Wexler, M. (2012). The nature of applied music teaching expertise: Common elements observed in the lessons of three applied teachers. *Bulletin of the Council for Research in Music Education, 193*, 45–62. https://doi.org/10.5406/bulcouresmusedu.193.0045

Penuel, W. R., Fishman, B. J., Yamaguchi, R., & Gallagher, L. P. (2007). What makes professional development effective? Strategies that foster curriculum implementation. *American Educational Research Journal, 44*(4), 921–958. https://doi.org/10.3102/0002831207308221

Powell, S. (2010). Wind instrument intonation: A research synthesis. *Bulletin of the Council for Research in Music Education, 184*, 79–96. https://www.jstor.org/stable/27861484

Publication manual of the American Psychological Association. (2020). 7th ed. American Psychological Association.

Richardson, V. (1990). Significant and worthwhile change in teaching practice. *Educational Researcher, 19*(7), 10–18. https://doi.org/10.3102/0013189X019007010

Richerme, L. K., & Miksza, P. (2020). Constructive controversy in an instrumental methods classroom: An exploratory case study. *Bulletin of the Council for Research in Music Education, 226*, 27–45. https://doi.org/10.5406/bulcouresmusedu.226.0027

Schiavio, A., van der Schyff, D., Biasutti, M., Moran, N., & Parncutt, R. (2019). Instrumental technique, expressivity, and communication: A qualitative study on learning music in individual and collective settings. *Frontiers in Psychology, 10*, 737. https://doi.org/10.3389/fpsyg.2019.00737

Schlegel, A. L., & Springer, D. G. (2018). Effects of accurate and inaccurate visual feedback on the tuning accuracy of high school and college trombonists. *International Journal of Music Education, 36*(3), 394–406. https://doi.org/10.1177/0255761418763914

Siebenaler, D. J. (1997). Analysis of teacher-student interactions in the piano lessons of adults and children. *Journal of Research in Music Education, 45*, 6–20. https://doi.org/10.2307/3345462

Silvey, B. A., Nápoles, J., & Springer, D. G. (2019). Effects of pre-tuning vocalization behaviors on the tuning accuracy of college instrumentalists. *Journal of Research in Music Education, 66*(4), 392–407. https://doi.org/10.1177/0022429418806304

Sogin, D. W., & Vallentine, J. F. (1992). Use of instructional time and repertoire diversity in university applied music lessons. *Quarterly Journal of Music Teaching and Learning, 3*, 32–36.

South, A. L. (2013). *An examination of middle school band students' ability to match pitch following short-term vocal technique training* [Unpublished master's thesis, Louisiana State University, Baton Rouge].

Springer, D. G. (2020). Research to resource: Evidence-based strategies for improving wind intonation. *Update: Applications of Research in Music Education, 39*(1), 4–7. https://doi.org/10.1177/8755123320930483

Springer, D. G., Schlegel, A. L., & Lewis, A. J. (2020). Effects of dark and bright timbral instructions on the production of pitch and timbre. *Journal of Research in Music Education, 68*(4), 482–498. https://doi.org/10.1177/0022429420944347

Turabian, K. (2007). *A manual for writers of terms papers, theses, and dissertations,* 7th ed. Rev. by W. Booth, G. Colomb, J. Williams, and the University of Chicago Press Editorial Staff. University of Chicago Press.

Wapnick, J., & Freeman, P. (1980). Effects of dark-bright timbral variation on the perception of flatness and sharpness. *Journal of Research in Music Education, 28*(3), 176–184. https://doi.org/10.2307/3345235

Ward-Steinman, P. (2007). Confidence in teaching improvisation according to the K–12 achievement standards: Surveys of vocal jazz workshop participants and undergraduates. *Bulletin of the Council for Research in Music Education, 172*, 25–40. https://www.jstor.org/stable/40319363

Worthy, M. D. (2000). Effects of tone-quality conditions on perception and performance of pitch among selected wind instrumentalists. *Journal of Research in Music Education, 48*(3), 222–236. https://doi.org/10.2307/3345395

4
Historical Research

Chapter Preview

In this chapter we introduce historical research, the study of people (e.g., biographies), pedagogy (e.g., curriculum), places (e.g., schools), organizations (e.g., state music associations), events (e.g., contests), and less tangible phenomena (e.g., philosophical perspectives) of the past and their effect on the present and future in music education (see Box 4.1). Historical researchers use various frameworks, including narrative history (organizing material into chronological order), comparative history (comparing phenomena across different times and places), quantitative history (using numerical data to study the past), content analysis (examining materials over a long period), historical sociology (investigating social structures and processes over time), anthropology and ethnohistory (focusing on the ordinary and everyday life of people without documented histories), gender history (studying relationships between males and females), and public history (examining history in the public sphere).

Introduction

As defined in Chapter 1, historical research concerns the past. More specifically, history may be defined as a "[contextual] narrative or description of past events, written in the spirit of critical inquiry, to find the whole truth and report it" (Good, 1963, p. 180). Historians find, analyze, document, and interpret historical information to explain causes and effects of previous and present conditions and phenomena.

Topics and Frameworks

Topics that music education historians typically pursue center on people (e.g., biographies, sociological studies), pedagogy (e.g., methods, curriculum), places (e.g., schools, communities, regions), organizations (e.g., state music associations, National Association for Music Education, Music Teachers National Association, individual ensembles), events (e.g., contests, festivals, professional conferences), and less tangible phenomena (e.g., philosophical perspectives, progressive education) of the past and their effect on the present and future. Several frameworks can provide the researcher with a lens through "which evidence is selected, filtered, and understood"

> **Box 4.1 Research to Practice: Historical Research**
>
> With all the challenges of education in general and music education specifically, it might be difficult to see why a researcher would focus on the past rather than work to solve current problems. However, historical research can contribute to the field today by providing (a) a basis for understanding the past, (b) perspectives for decision-making and policy formulation, (c) context for understanding current conditions or practices, and (d) information to formulate solutions to modern problems and avoid repeating previous mistakes. Historical research can also (e) assist in identifying past trends and applying these to current and future trends and (f) function as a storehouse of great ideas that serve as a basis for progressive ideas (Heller, 1985, 1998).

(Green & Troup, 2016, p. vi). The most common in music education is *narrative history*, in which the author organizes material in a chronologically sequential order to tell a single coherent story. Narratives often follow an empiricist method, which involves "(a) rigorous examination and knowledge of historical evidence; (b) verification of references; (c) a drive for impartiality in research; (d) the use of the inductive method of reasoning; and (e) the valuing of coherence" (McCarthy, 2019, p. 97).

Narrative histories might furthermore be characterized as small-scale or large-scale humanistic studies (Volk, 2003). A small-scale humanistic study focuses on how one person or a select group experienced the past. A biography of Joseph Mainzer, for instance, examined the life and work of a pioneer music educator who was active in Europe and the United Kingdom during the first half of the 19th century. Mainzer's work contributed to the development of singing classes for children and adults, much like that of Lowell Mason in the United States. The author described how Mainzer's efforts intersected with societal issues surrounding the democratization of music education and improving the lives of the working class (Southcott, 2020). Ward-Steinman (2020) documented the music education faculty at Indiana University from the early 1900s to the present day. The study presented a comprehensive list of faculty names and years of service and identified important publications, leadership roles, curriculum development, and biographical insights related to these individuals.

Large-scale humanistic studies piece together numerous sources of evidence to construct a narrative describing the experiences of a sizable group or people. Sondra Wieland Howe (2014), for instance, used hundreds of sources to construct a history of female music educators in the United States. Her book complements that of earlier historians who often omitted the contributions of females in the profession.

Historical studies in music education might intersect with larger social, political, and religious issues. Two separate studies, for example, examined how the child study (Humphreys, 1985) and social efficiency (Humphreys, 1988) movements associated with progressive education influenced school music during the late 19th and early 20th centuries. Miller (2019) described how religious politics might have contributed to the dismissal of Lowell Mason from the Boston Public Schools in 1845. Research on the Austin High School Girls' Band of Chicago investigated the activities of this ensemble in relation to changing gender norms before, during, and after World War II (Hash, 2018).

All historical research involves narrative to some degree. However, other frameworks can focus the narrative on a particular aspect of the topic. *Comparative history*, for example, is an examination of phenomena across different times and places. Learning how others teach and learn music in different regions of the world and comparing their approaches with our own can be very informative. In such a study, it is imperative that the researcher has a firm grasp on the broader context of the countries or regions involved, as well as the aspects under investigation, such as music and politics. Gruhn (2001) compared the assimilation of Pestalozzian ideas into music education in Germany and the United States during the early 19th century. The author concluded that Pestalozzi's approach as implemented by Lowell Mason lost its original connection to the European concept of *Bildung*—a powerful means of self-realization and individual growth—and reduced the philosophy to a formal technique of instruction. However, Mason also integrated his own thinking, methods, and materials to enhance the method's effectiveness within the U.S. educational context. Likewise, research into the development of elementary music education in the United Kingdom, the United States, and Australia compared similarities and differences in practices among these countries in relation to cultural and philosophical beliefs, singing pedagogy, technologies, methodologies, faculty, and curricula (Groulx, 2013).

Quantitative history uses numerical data, statistical analyses, computer programs, and other quantitative tools to study the past. A few examples exist in music education. Humphreys and Schmidt (1998) examined demographic and economic data of the membership of Music Supervisors National Conference /Music Educators National Conference (MSNC/MENC) from 1912 to 1938. Data included membership lists, census files, annual state education expenditure tables, and information on teachers' salaries and gender from the U.S. Bureau (later Office) of Education. Based on these data, the author concluded that MENC membership (a) increased more rapidly than the general population, (b) differed significantly between MENC divisions, (c) correlated with average teacher salaries and per capita state spending on education, and (d) correlated only slightly with geographical distance to convention sites. In addition, (e) women comprised a significant majority of the membership in each division but a smaller majority than in the nation's teaching profession as a whole and (f) implementation of MENC s biennial convention plan did not affect membership totals significantly. In another example of quantitative research Groulx (2021) compared contest ratings of Black high school bands with White high school bands the year before (1965–1966) and after (1966–1967) integration of the all-White Florida Bandmasters Association and the all-Black Florida Association of

Band Directors. Results indicated significant differences between ratings awarded to Black and White bands. However, there was no evidence to support racial bias as a cause of these differences.

Content analysis examines materials, sometimes over a long period, to determine trends, patterns, or changing philosophies or values. Examples of material a researcher might examine are songbooks, textbooks, concert programs, curricula, university catalogues, and articles in periodicals. Dunbar (2016), for example, explored mainstreaming practices in music education through an analysis of articles published from 1960 to 1989 in the *Music Educators Journal*, the *Journal of Research in Music Education*, and the *Bulletin of the Council for Research in Music Education*. Research questions examined (a) increases in pedagogical and research articles at the time or immediately after particular disability legislation became law in 1975, (b) the ratio of research articles to pedagogical articles as related to proportions within the special education populations, (c) the disabilities addressed in the articles, (d) institutional affiliations, and (e) geographical regions of the primary authors. Results indicated that over the three-decade period, only 49 articles related to mainstreaming appeared in the selected journals. Most of the articles were authored by faculty in higher education, were pedagogical in nature, and explained various disabilities.

In another example of content analysis, Sanders (2017) examined temperance songs found in 76 school music textbooks published between 1865 and 1900. Reformers hoped that these songs would indoctrinate children to temperance ideology and that the children would, in turn, convey the message to their parents and other adults. This study noted common themes and tactics employed by temperance lyricists over the 35-year period.

Other frameworks also exist for historical research. *The Houses of History: A Critical Reader in History and Theory* by Anna Green and Kathleen Troup (2016) offers 14 different lenses through which to examine the past. Several of these frameworks, besides the narrative and empiricist approaches discussed previously, are relevant to music education historians. *Historical sociology* examines social structures and processes over time to determine how outcomes unfolded in individual lives and society and to determine characteristics of social structures and patterns of change. An examination of the papers and proceedings of the Music Teachers National Association from 1906 to 1930, for example, determined the changing demographic characteristics of the membership and important topics in music education (Cooper & Bayless, 2008). Likewise, *anthropology and ethnohistory* focus on the ordinary and everyday life of people without documented histories. Dunbar-Hall (2008), for instance, synthesized and interpreted writings by several mid-20th-century scholars on the teaching of music and dance in Bali in the 1930s and compared what was discovered from that context with current practices.

Gender history seeks to examine occurrences in the past resulting from behaviors of and relationships between individuals of different genders. Although these studies often focus on women's perspectives, the field has expanded in recent years to include studies in masculinity and sextual identity. Sondra Weiland Howe (e.g., 2014) and Jill M. Sullivan (e.g., 2017) have each published multiple studies related to gender and the history of music education.

Public history focuses on the use of history in the public sphere through restoration, preservation, building monuments, museum exhibitions, heritage studies, television programs, and film. Examples include the Lowell Mason House in Medfield, Massachusetts, the Sousa Archives and Center for American Music at the University of Illinois at Urbana-Champaign, and the film series *Jazz* and *Country Music* by Ken Burns (2001, 2019). Although only a few examples of public history, quantitative history, historical sociology, and gender history currently exist in music education literature, all have the potential to contribute to the field and deserve consideration by future researchers.

Historical Method

Choosing a Topic

The first step in historical research is to select a topic. Think about what aspects of music teaching and learning interest you. Perhaps you are thinking of a particular method, an influential educator or pedagogue, a model school music program, or an event of some type. You should also consider the extent to which the topic is of interest to others and the value it will hold for the profession. It is not enough for you to be interested in a particular topic. You will need to demonstrate why it should be of interest to others and what value and significance the topic has to the field of music education.

Some topics, such as a biography of a long-serving music supervisor, might be of interest mainly to a local audience. This research could be presented at a county historical society or a state music education conference or appear in a state history journal or music education association periodical. Other topics will have wider appeal to the profession at large. These are appropriate for both state and national presentation and for consideration in top-tier music education research journals. The extent to which the people and events under investigation affected, influenced, or exemplified music teaching and learning will determine whether a study has local, state, or national appeal.

After you settle on a potential topic, it is important to do a considerable amount of reading to determine its viability. If other authors have already produced articles or dissertations on your topic, you might want to look at investigating something else unless you believe your work will result in new knowledge on the subject. Duplicating someone else's work will not contribute to the field. You should also do a preliminary search of original historical materials to ascertain whether the extent and viability of sources is sufficient to answer your research questions. If you have trouble finding information on a given topic, it may not be a good one for you to pursue. Contrarily, if there are many sources, you may be able to identify some gaps or missing pieces of information that you could fill in. You might also determine the need to narrow your research topic in some way, such as by examining only a certain timeframe or location. Once you succeed in identifying a topic that is of interest to you and relevant for other music educators, you are ready to proceed.

Research Questions

Historians should begin a study with an idea of what they want to know about their topic and develop research questions around these themes. Research questions can be both narrow and broad. Sullivan (2019), for example, examined music teaching and learning in the U.S. Navy band program at the Great Lakes Naval Training Station near Chicago during World War I, as led by Lieutenant John Philip Sousa. Although a great deal of research already existed on Sousa and the U.S. Navy Band at the time of this study, Sullivan was able to add to the historical record by providing additional information on these topics. Questions narrower in nature included "(a) What were the benefits for Sousa to volunteer for this work near the end of his career? (b) How did Sousa organize the Navy band program? (c) What were the details of teaching the enlisted bandsmen? (d) What other music ensembles and experiences were provided for the sailors?" Broader questions included "(e) How did the bandsmen's work benefit the Navy and U.S. government? (f) Which of the military band experiences likely influenced teaching and learning of instrumental music education after the war?" (p. 147).

Research questions in historical studies often evolve during the project as you find and examine evidence. However, it is important to begin with an idea of what you hope to discover. A good place to start in determining preliminary research questions is to consider the biographical (*Who?*), geographical (*Where?*), chronological (*When?*), and functional (*What?*) (Gottschalk, 1963) aspects of the topic. The biographical aspect concerns people important to the story. The researcher may be interested in teachers, administrators, performers, composers, or anyone who played a salient role. Geographical aspects concern the role of location. The researcher may want to investigate programs or events that occurred in a particular country, region, city, or school district. Chronological aspects involve the timeframe in which events or phenomena occurred. The functional aspect deals with what happened in a certain place and time.

Gathering Evidence

Historians find and interpret evidence from a wide variety of primary and secondary sources. *Primary sources* consist of materials connected with the topic that originated either during the period or at a later date through a participant directly involved in the events under investigation (e.g., memoirs). These may include letters, diaries, newspaper articles, institutional reports, school yearbooks, conference proceedings, pedagogical materials, concert programs, school board minutes, handwritten documents, and so on. Although most information will likely come from text-based materials, artifacts such as photographs, audio or video recordings, instruments, clothing, and other objects related to the topic can yield valuable information or raise additional questions. Living human informants directly connected to the topic can also serve as primary sources. Researchers typically collect data from these individuals through oral history interviews, discussed below.

Secondary sources consist of materials that aid in interpreting or analyzing historical events or phenomena. They are typically (a) based on primary sources, (b) produced by someone not directly involved in the events under investigation, and (c) created after the period of the study. Examples include journal articles, dissertations, history texts, reference books, and interviews with informants who have secondhand knowledge (e.g., siblings or children or principal players in the narrative). Historians should rely mainly on primary sources for the main body of their study. However, secondary sources are useful for creating context around the topic and filling in information not available from primary materials. They might also help identify primary sources unknown to the author.

There are several texts on the history of music education that authors use as secondary sources. Birge's (1937) *History of Public School Music in the United States* was the first book to document music education in the U.S. This text remains an often-cited source today. Other texts focused on the United States include *Historical Foundations of Music Education in the United States* (Sunderman, 1971); *Music in American Education: Past and Present* (Tellstrom, 1971), *A History of American Music Education* (Mark & Gary, 2007), and *A History of Music Education in the United States* (Keene, 2009).

Each of these books offers a unique perspective on the history of music education in the United States. Birge (1937), Tellstrom (1971), and Mark and Gary (2007) organized their narratives chronologically, while Sunderman (1971) and Keene (2009) presented chapters around specific topics. All these works offer valuable insight into the history of the field. However, they have been criticized for a lack of analysis, a narrow focus on in-school versus out-of-school music, an emphasis on white males, and limited geographical representation (Humphreys, 2015). Howe's (2014) *Women Music Educators in the United States: A History* has helped fill this gap by telling the stories of female music teachers in America. International authors have also contributed texts on music education in England (Cox, 2017; Rainbow & Cox, 2006), Ireland (McCarthy, 1999), and elsewhere (e.g., Whitwell, 2011). Historians certainly have much work to do in adding to this story throughout the world. Future research will hopefully include a greater representation of music teaching and learning among currently underrepresented populations, including females, people of color, the LGBTQIA+ community, and individuals with cognitive and physical differences.

The line between primary and secondary sources is not always clear. For example, *A History of Public School Music in the United States* (Birge, 1937) could be considered both a primary and a secondary source. Birge, a music supervisor in Indianapolis, Indiana, and later a professor at Indiana University, was present and directly involved in many of the events in the early 1900s reported in the book. However, he relied on secondary sources to construct the history of music education during the 18th and 19th centuries. Likewise, obituaries, books on local history, and other materials may contain characteristics of both primary and secondary sources.

Historical research often seems like an attempt to assemble many small pieces of a very large puzzle. Furthermore, pieces are always missing, and the resultant image can change depending on who is putting the puzzle together (Southcott & Sell, 2014). Researchers should exhaust all avenues for locating primary and secondary sources. Volk (2003) described this process using the terms "immersion" and "saturation," borrowed from qualitative research. Immersion refers to the process of collecting and examining everything possible on the topic until the historian has a complete understanding of the historical context and the people or events under investigation. Saturation occurs when searches result in duplicate findings or unrelated data.

Archives and Repositories

Most primary sources will likely come from archives, repositories, or libraries, which may be located online or in a physical structure. Archives exist for the purpose of preserving the past by storing historical documents, records, or other materials. Government agencies at all levels as well as universities, historical societies, and commercial entities often preserve their past in various archives. Repositories serve as central locations for housing similar items, but not necessarily to preserve the past. Public school districts, for example, might store student records, personnel files, and other materials at a central repository. These records contribute to the day-to-day operation of the district and might be destroyed once they are no longer needed. Public, private, and institutional libraries serve a broader mission and house numerous books and other materials. However, they can often be of use in finding sources. Many public libraries, for example, maintain a local history section that contains primary and secondary sources, including newspapers preserved on microfilm, city directories, school yearbooks, family memoires, and various other materials. University libraries often keep items for extensive periods and might have useful primary sources listed in their main catalogue or a special collection.

Online Archives

The advent of the internet and subsequent efforts by archivists, librarians, and others interested in preserving history have resulted in numerous primary sources available on the web. Several online archives preserve millions of materials dating back hundreds of years, including census and military records, newspapers, books, periodicals, and institutional reports, just to name a few. Many are available free of charge (see Appendix A for an extensive listing). The Hathi Trust (https://www.hathitrust.org/), for example, "is a not-for-profit partnership of academic and research libraries that houses 17+ million digitized items." Likewise, Internet Archive (https://archive.org/) is a 501(c)(3) nonprofit dedicated to digitizing cultural artifacts for use by researchers, historians, scholars, and the general public. Contents include millions of books and other text-based materials, audio recordings, videos, and images.

Many sources are available from online databases at no cost. However, some materials might be accessible only through sites that charge a fee for their use. Nonetheless, the materials, searchability, and user services offered by these sites are often worth the fee. Most sites list what sources are available and will let you do a preliminary search before you commit to a short-term or long-term subscription. Examples include GenealogyBank (https://www.genealogybank.com), Ancestry (https://www.ancestry.com), and e-Yearbook (https://www.e-yearbook.com).

Before subscribing to a pay site, make sure they have what you need and that the source is not available on a free database. For example, Classmates.com (https://www.classmates.com), a social media site for connecting with school alumni, has made school yearbooks dating to the late 1800s available to users. Likewise, FamilySearch (https://www.familysearch.org), operated by the Church of Jesus Christ of Latter-day Saints, contains census, military, and other records from around the world. Both sites require users to sign up for an account but do not charge for their services. Pay sites might also be available through your local public or university library. Check their holdings before making the financial commitment.

Historical research today should begin with an online search for primary and secondary sources. Due to the volume of material available, it will be more efficient to find everything you can online before searching in physical archives. Search engines allow for numerous keyword combinations. Make a list of possible terms and word combinations prior to beginning your search. Incorporate Boolean search techniques by combining keywords with operators (or modifiers) such as "and," "not," and "or" to increase the quantity and relevance of results. For example, a Boolean search could be "singing and public schools." This combination would limit the search results to only those documents containing the two keywords. Sometimes users can select a "phrase search" to bring up sources that contain only combinations of words together. For all materials you find online, either (a) print physical copies for later reference, (b) save a pdf file or an image of the document, and/or (c) create a list that includes a brief description and a link to each item.

Physical Archives

Despite the quantity of material available online, most historical studies will require at least one visit to an archive, repository, or library. These places might be large and well established, with regular operating hours and a knowledgeable staff of experienced archivists. They might be smaller entities overseen by one or two people and without regular operating procedures. Regardless, the researcher should follow some basic steps before accessing the facility. After identifying an archive that might house relevant material, conduct a search online to verify what is available. Some archives and most libraries allow researchers to search their holdings through an online database. Archives sometimes include special collections that contain related sources. A *finding aid* will often list materials held in these collections. The A. A. Harding Papers at the University of Illinois, for example, maintains letters, documents, and other items connected with the first band director at that institution. Researchers can access the finding aid online (https://archon.library.illinois.edu/?p=collections/findingaid&id=2117&q=) to search its contents and determine whether a visit to the archive is warranted.

Many research centers have very specific rules for accessing and using the facility. Typically, the researcher will need to do the following:

1. Make an appointment. Many archives will not accept walk-in visitors.
2. Request the materials you want to access at least a week prior to your visit, since materials might be stored off-site and require a few days for their retrieval. If you are unsure whether a particular item or folder of documents is relevant, request them anyway.
3. Once you arrive, check in at the front desk. You might need to complete some forms and sign user agreements before you begin. Be aware that some research centers charge a fee for their use.
4. You might be allowed to take only a notebook and pencil (not a pen) into the reading room; your jacket, backpack, purse, and other items might have to be stored in a locker. A cell phone and/or laptop computer might be allowed, but with permission. Food and drinks are prohibited.
5. Follow rules for handling materials. Some archives, for example, will require that you sit in a particular place, wear white gloves, and/or use a book cradle when examining materials. Regulations might also limit the number of items you can examine at one time. You may need to complete work with one item and return it to the archivist before requesting another.
6. You will likely want to make photocopies of relevant material you find. Know that some items might have restrictions due to binding, size, fragility, or copyright. Make sure you obtain complete copies, including all the information you will need to create a reference citation. Copying the title page to a book or periodical or other identifying markings is necessary. It is very frustrating to get home and realize that you are missing page numbers, publication dates, and so on.

Some archives will allow you to make copies on your own at the facility or request the staff to make copies for you. However, do not expect them to do it immediately. You will likely need to complete a request form and provide an address where they can send copies. There will be a fee for this service. You will either pay before leaving or once the staff makes the copies, in which case they will notify you of the cost and await payment before sending. Instead of photocopies, you can sometimes photograph documents and other materials. There are also free apps such as Adobe Scan that allow you to create pdfs using the camera feature of your smartphone. Compared to photocopying, this process is faster, less expensive, and sometimes safer due to the size or condition of certain items.

7. The facility might ask you to stop at the desk before exiting. Sometimes staff will inspect notes, photocopies, books, and so on to ensure proper use.
8. If you hope to reproduce a photograph, video, or audio recording that you acquired from an archive in your research, understand that you might need to obtain approval and pay an additional fee. You should also acknowledge the research center in your final paper, thesis, dissertation, or article.

Oral History

In addition to digital or physical materials, a researcher might want to include oral history gleaned directly from a person or people with firsthand knowledge of the topic. *Oral history* involves the use of human informants to provide details on the past through live interviews. The extent to which an individual identifies as a primary or secondary source depends on their relationship to the story. Someone present and directly involved with the topic would be a primary source. Family members, former students, or colleagues of that person should be classified as secondary sources.

The researcher should examine as many physical sources as possible prior to the interview(s) so that they understand the topic and have a basis for relevant questions. Participants will then be able to confirm or refute information you have thus far. You should prepare a structured interview that includes a list of questions you will ask your interviewee(s). Also allow for unstructured portions of the interview, as your participant(s) may lead you to unanticipated questions.

The following sample questions come from an oral history interview conducted by Michael Sanchez (2007) with two founding members of the Portland, Oregon, Gay Men's Chorus. This interview is stored in the Gay and Lesbian Archives of the Pacific Northwest Oral Histories, housed in the digital collections of the Oregon Historical Society. Notice the informal and conversational nature of the questions.

1. We are here with two founding members of the Portland Gay Men's Chorus [PGMC]. My name is Michael Sanchez. I will be conducting the interview and I will have both gentlemen introduce themselves. [Participants introduce themselves.]

2. We're going to start at the very, very beginning. Steve and Gary, what events inspired you to be a part of PGMC from the very beginning? What parts did you both have in starting the organization?
3. Do either of you recall what the message of the ad [soliciting members] was?
4. Do you recall how long Pride had been going on by that point in time? Was it just a couple of years?
5. Gary, would you like to talk about some of the other first key players? How about your accompanist for the first rehearsal?
6. Why don't you describe your first performance for us after all those rehearsals? How many rehearsals were there? A couple of weeks? A couple of months?
7. Steve, how about you? Any recollections [of the first performance]?
8. I'd like to go back to the first rehearsals. After the very first rehearsal and in the subsequent rehearsals until the first performance, how did you see the mood of people evolve and change? Was there still that excitement, or... how did it change?
9. What can you tell me about the funding for the first season? Paying for, you know, whatever things that you needed: music printing, accompanists... was that all donated or did you have some means of raising funds for that?

Interviews should be audio- or videotaped. This process will require permission in writing from your interviewee as well as approval from your IRB (see Chapter 2). You will need to decide what you plan to do with the recordings after you complete the study. If all parties agree and IRB approves, arrange to preserve interview recordings for posterity in an archive or your personal files. Otherwise, you will likely need to destroy them. In some cases, a researcher might be able to utilize recorded or transcribed interviews from the past stored in a library or other facility. In this case you would not need written permission or IRB approval, since the interview already exists in a public forum. The Performing Arts Library at the University of Maryland, College Park, for example, houses numerous interviews with important performers, composers, and educators.

You should take notes during the interview that can include observations you make that might not be apparent from the recording, such as body posture or gestures, eye movement or lack of eye contact, and so on. The audio portion of all recorded interviews should be transcribed and double-checked for accuracy. Online applications such as Otter.ai (https://otter.ai/home) can quickly convert audio and video files into text. Statements made by an interview participant should be verified by independent sources whenever possible. Even individuals directly involved with historical events might not remember clearly or accurately or have full knowledge of what happened.

Verifying the Sources

A central concern of historical researchers is the verification of primary and secondary sources through *external criticism* and *internal criticism*. External criticism focuses on the authenticity of a particular source: How do we know the person of interest wrote this document? Could it be a forgery? Is the document an original or a copy? What is the provenance; by this, we mean where did the document come from, how did it come to be in your possession? Fortunately, there is not a lot of fraud that occurs in the study of music education history. However, a researcher might encounter challenges with external criticism when, for example, a date is missing from a newspaper clipping in a scrapbook or the authorship of a handwritten document is unclear, perhaps due to missing pages.

Once a document has been determined to be authentic, the historian must examine its accuracy and credibility through internal criticism. Are opinions or suppositions couched as facts? For whom was a particular document intended; could the audience have shaped the content? Is there a chance that a person's recollections provided in a memoir or interview have changed or diminished through the passage of time? If possible, the researcher will want to verify statements of fact through a process known as *triangulation*, which involves comparing similar information provided by multiple sources. For example, a historian might reconcile concert repertoire listed in a newspaper article with that provided on a program distributed at the event. They might also compare statements from an interview with a former music teacher's son or daughter with information provided in a high school yearbook from the time of the events in question.

Internal criticism is equally important for primary and secondary sources. A comparison of two accounts of the founding of the National Music Camp (now Interlochen Center for the Arts) illustrates the need for internal criticism with secondary sources. In *Joe Maddy of Interlochen*, an undocumented and somewhat romanticized narrative, Browning (1963) stated that the idea for the camp originated from students performing in the 1927 National High School Orchestra at a meeting of the Department of Superintendence in Dallas, Texas. At a party held in a local school gymnasium following the group's final performance, students were despondent that their experience in the orchestra had come to an end:

> Consolation... was in vain. Overwrought, and feeling a sense of inexplicable privation, the group found the sobs of its youngest and most emotional members becoming contagious. Finally[,] an older boy in the back of the room called out urgently, "Mr Maddy, why can't we get together *somewhere* this summer and play all the music we want to play—all day long?"
>
> The boys shouted and whistled. The girls clapped and crowded pleadingly around Joe Maddy. All eyes were fixed on him eagerly demanding an answer.
>
> Joe climbed one of the gymnasium ladders affixed to the wall and hanging there by his elbows, looked out on the sea of young faces. He understood their spirit, and he knew in that instant that his answer could not be a hasty "no." He made a rash promise—he would try to find for them a place where they could come together and play—"all day long," if that was their wish.

The gymnasium resounded with cries of joy. The pall lifted from the farewell party, but Joe, still hanging on the ladder by his elbows and mobbed by the excited throng felt panic. *What* had he left himself in for?

"When?" they cried. "How soon?" "Where?" "How long?"

Grasping at memories of his own boyhood in Wellington with its summer camping trips, he told the youngsters that he would find them a "summer music camp." He didn't know yet exactly where or when, but it would be as soon as possible. He carefully refrained from telling them that he didn't know exactly how, either. (pp. 187–188)

In a later history, *Interlochen: A Home for the Arts*, Boal (1998) cites primary sources to describe how Maddy conceived the idea for a summer camp a year before the Department of Superintendence meeting in March 1927. According to Boal, Maddy thought of the idea after the first National High School Orchestra in 1926 and considered making an offer to purchase land for the camp in Maine in December of that same year. He proposed organization of a camp in the March 1927 issue of *Music Supervisors' Journal*, just before the Department of Superintendence meeting. He also spoke about his proposal at a civic dinner in Detroit a week before the National High School Orchestra convened in Dallas, and used the event to generate enthusiasm among members of the ensemble:

The Dallas performance of the NHSO was a triumph that, along with Maddy's article in the *MSJ*, stimulated great interest in the orchestra camp. The concert aroused students' passions and inspired the audience. Maddy now needed to translate student emotions into attendance at the camp. After the concert, he climbed a ladder backstage and yelled, "How would you like to come to a summer camp to continue playing together?" Students responded with a boisterous chorus of support. Shrewdly, Maddy began to nurture the feeling of elation that the students experienced while playing with talented peers. In the next days, he referred to the students' enthusiasm whenever building support for the camp. The ploy was so successful that, many years later, Maddy turned the story around and ascribed the original camp idea to the students in Dallas, though Charles Warren had originated the idea several months earlier. (pp. 34–35)

Internal criticism should involve triangulation of multiple sources whenever possible. Documents, articles, and books written by supporters or advocates of a particular organization, ensemble, or person might skew or exaggerate facts in a positive direction, due to either bias or the desire to shape the historical record. The historian must seek to create a balanced, objective, and complete narrative rather than simply a tribute to the people involved. It is inappropriate to manipulate the data to support a particular viewpoint.

Writing a Historical Study

Format and Organization

The format of historical papers differs from that of other research methods. Although some journals will accept a historical submission in APA (American Psychological Association) format, historians typically follow the *Chicago Manual of Style* and use footnotes or endnotes rather than parenthetical citations. Likewise, the paper might be longer than an experimental or descriptive study due to reliance on narrative rather than numerical data to convey information. Most journals will accept a historical submission a bit longer than the page limit specified in their manuscript guidelines, provided the content is necessary and relevant. That said, it is up to the researcher to determine what information is necessary. The most effective historical studies are those that tell an important and compelling story through direct and concise writing that avoids unnecessary detours and superfluous details. Sometimes an author can include brief content that provides further explanation in the notes along with appropriate citations. This strategy is appropriate when the information will improve the reader's understanding but does not seem to fit into the narrative. Note the following endnote example from Thibeault (2020):

> 42. Scholars have productively engaged Dewey's notion of rhythm: Felicia Kruse, "Vital Rhythm and Temporal Form in Langer and Dewey," *The Journal of Speculative Philosophy* 21, no. 1 (2007): 16–26, https://doi.org/10.1353/jsp.2007.0023; Mihaly Csikszentmihalyi et al., "What Have We Learned? James and Dewey: A Context for the Study of Experience," in *Talented Teenagers: The Roots of Success and Failure* (Cambridge: Cambridge University Press, 1993), 256–261; Sushil K. Saxena, "Hindustani Rhythm and John Dewey's Aesthetics," *Sangeet Natak* 95 (1990): 1–25. Dewey had also previously engaged in discussion of rhythm, such as this: "To say that food is agreeable, means that food satisfies an organic function. Music is pleasant because by it certain capacities or demands of the person with respect to rhythm of hearing are fulfilled; a landscape is beautiful because it carries to fulfillment the visual possibilities of the spectator." John Dewey, *The Middle Works of John Dewey, 1899–1924: Ethics 1908* (Carbondale: SIU Press, 2008) 257.

The example above also demonstrates that notes can contain multiple citations. Often the historian will utilize multiple sources to assemble information for just one sentence. It is not unusual for a note to be longer than the information it supports.

The organization of a historical research paper will vary depending on the topic and focus. Authors should read historical articles on topics similar to their own study to determine how best to arrange the narrative. Regardless, all historical papers should begin broadly with an introduction that provides general information, move to details of the main topic, and end with general conclusions, implications, and influences on music education during the period under consideration and, if applicable, the field today.

Throughout the process, the historian should go beyond reporting the facts. They must also interpret the findings by speculating on potential causes and effects and by making connections between various aspects of the topic and the larger social-historical perspective. Interpretation is not simply an author's opinion but rather inferences based on a thorough understanding of the context, people, places, and events under investigation. What does this information mean? Has our understanding of these facts changed over time as political and cultural changes have occurred? Are there different ways to interpret the primary sources? Have the data been skewed out of personal or cultural bias? The facts as they are, but also why they are and what they mean, are the responsibility of the researcher to determine in a fair and accurate manner.

Abstracts and Keywords

The abstract provides a summary of the study in anywhere from 150 to 500 words, depending on format. Abstracts are included at the beginning of a thesis, dissertation, or article and may also appear in online databases. An abstract for a thesis or dissertation will tend to be longer than that of an article. An abstract does not contain citations and should function as a stand-alone document. A reader should be able to determine whether a study is of interest simply from the abstract. At minimum, it should clearly state the main topic and provide a summary of the findings. The abstract might also contain information related to research questions and method. In addition to an abstract, most studies will also include keywords provided by the author. These terms are intended to facilitate indexing and increase the visibility of a study to online search engines. Keywords generally repeat important terms found in the text, title, or abstract, but might also include synonyms or variations.

Example 1. Howe, S. W. (2021). Western music on Commodore Perry's "black ships" in Japan, 1853–1854. *Journal of Historical Research in Music Education, 42*(2), 102–116. https://doi.org/10.1177/1536600619877917

Commodore Perry and his "Black Ships" opened Japanese harbors for foreign shipping in 1853 and 1854. Music was important for this Japan Expedition that obtained a treaty between the United States and Japan. Bands and singers performed music for parades, impressive ceremonies, religious services, and entertainment for the sailors and foreign audiences. This article examines the styles of Western music, instrumentation, and performance venues of Perry's musicians as they traveled to harbors in China, Okinawa, and Japan. Since the large bands from Perry's ships were impressive with their fancy uniforms, swords, and loud music, the Japanese associated band music with American military power. The performances on Perry's ships were some of the first performances of Western music in Japan, before the Westernization of the Japanese school music curriculum in the 1880s. Primary sources for this research include contemporary narrative accounts, printed programs, nineteenth-century prints, and songbooks. Secondary sources include websites, articles, and books to put the material in a historical context.

Keywords: Commodore Perry, Japan, bands, minstrel music, music education

Example 2. Hash, P. M. (2015a). Music education at the New York Institution for the Blind: 1832–1863. *Journal of Research in Music Education, 62,* 362–388. https://doi.org/10.1177%2F0022429414555983

The purpose of this study was to document the history of music education at the New York Institution for the Blind (NYIB) from the opening of the school in 1832 through the tenure of the facility's first music director, Anthony Reiff. Research questions pertained to the school's origin and operation and to its music curriculum, pedagogy, faculty, ensembles, and resources. The NYIB provided a home and education for students ages eight to twenty-five. The music program served as recreation and vocational training and as a means of promoting the school. Reiff joined the faculty in 1835 and established a band and choir that performed throughout the city and surrounding states. In 1847, the board of managers hired George F. Root as head of vocal music and named Reiff director of the instrumental division. Sigismund Laser replaced Root in 1855 and remained at the NYIB until 1863, when both he and Reiff left the school. The faculty at the NYIB developed and promoted effective methods for teaching music to people with blindness and prepared graduates to serve as church musicians, piano tuners, and music educators. Findings from this study might serve to remind music educators of past pedagogical methods and principles applicable in teaching students who are blind today.

Keywords: music education, blind, exceptional learners, history, New York

Introduction

The introduction of a historical study should provide social, cultural, and historical context as well as other background information necessary to understand the main topic. A master's thesis or doctoral dissertation will likely include this information in the first two chapters, which will typically consist of the introduction and a review of literature. In a manuscript intended for a journal, however, this section should be integrated into the narrative. Hash (2015b), for example, examined the life and work of Solomon W. Straub, a music leader in the Midwest United States during the late 19th century. The introduction begins with a general description of the multiple roles that music educators assumed during this time and the education they received in preparation for their work, followed by a description of the need and purpose of the study, research questions, and methodology. Depending on content and length, the introduction might benefit from subheadings.

The author will likely call on several secondary sources in the introduction, such as books and journal articles that provide information regarding context and background related to the main topic. However, a researcher might also consult primary materials when they are available and/or secondary sources are lacking. Hash (2011), for example, examined the first heterogeneous instrumental method book, the *Universal Teacher* by J. E. Maddy and T. P. Giddings (1923). In the introduction, Hash utilized didactic materials and several articles from music education periodicals of the early 20th century, in addition to secondary sources, to describe the state of education in general and class instrumental instruction specifically prior to publication of the *Universal Teacher*.

Main Body

The main body of the paper will focus on telling the story as related to your topic. This section will be the longest of the study and should be based mostly on primary source material. It is acceptable to use secondary sources to fill in missing information or add context. However, if you find yourself citing mostly secondary sources, it is likely that you are replicating someone else's work rather than adding new knowledge to the field.

The main body of a historical study will likely be arranged chronologically and/or by subtopics, depending on which structure will allow the narrative to flow in a logical manner. One strategy might be to organize the paper around the research questions or important benchmarks in the story. Authors will benefit from creating an outline before they begin writing and using headings and subheading within the paper.

Conclusion

The final section of the paper should begin with a restatement of the topic (e.g., "This study examined . . .") and perhaps a summary or overview of the findings. In subsequent paragraphs, the author should discuss the conclusions drawn from the study as related to the research questions. In addition, consider how past events shaped subsequent events and practices, including those in contemporary times. If appropriate, you might also examine how past practices could be utilized today in either their original or modified form. Hash (2011), for example, discussed how the *Universal Teacher* incorporated methods from elementary music into instrumental pedagogy during the early 20th century and how band and orchestra instruction might benefit from this connection today.

The conclusion of any study should recommend avenues for future research. No study covers all aspects of a particular topic, especially when we consider that topic from a broader perspective. For example, a biographical study of an important early 20th-century music educator might suggest the need for research on other professionals of the time. Likewise, a study on the use of the Suzuki method for teaching violin in Japan might be followed up with research into the application of this pedagogy for other instruments or in other countries.

Summary

Historical research in music education is an important component of the literature. These studies may utilize one or more frameworks to tell a coherent story that illuminates the past. In choosing a topic, researchers typically focus on biographical (*Who?*), geographical (*Where?*), chronological (*When?*), or functional (*What?*) aspects of the subject. Reading in the literature, both broadly and specifically, is an important prelude to choosing a research topic. Once you determine a focus, make certain it is of interest to you and to others, and that it has importance for the profession.

As you continue to develop your ideas, you will need to gain a solid understanding of the broader context in which your topic fits. Place and time are not independent; even if you emphasize a particular place, such as the city of Boston, you cannot do so without considering a period of time as well. If you are interested in a particular group, individual, or event, you must remember these do not exist in a vacuum.

When you gather evidence for your study, you will need to be aware of differences between primary and secondary sources. You will also need to apply external and internal criticism to verify your sources to make certain they are both authentic and credible. Finally, even after you have gathered all the sources available on your topic, you will need to interpret this information. Make certain your own biases have not colored your opinion of facts. If there are differing opinions about how to understand certain events or the contributions of certain individuals, you need to alert your readers to these discrepancies. If you have compelling arguments in favor of one view over another, make certain they are fair, accurate, and based on the data. As a final point, read a great deal of historical research before you begin to search for a viable topic.

Here are a few prompts to help you solidify your understanding of this material:

1. Write a purpose statement, along with a few research questions for each of the following:
    a. A study with a focus on a person or group.
    b. A study with a focus on a specific place or places.
    c. A study with a focus on one or more specific periods of time.

d. A study with a focus on a particular event or events.
2. Describe why each of the studies you identified in question 1 is important to the music education profession. If you cannot do so, select a different topic.
3. What frameworks might be appropriate lenses for examining each of the topics you chose in question 1? Why?
4. What is the difference between primary and secondary sources? Give some examples.

Figure 4.1 Photograph from *Music Appreciation for Little Children* (Clark, 1920, p. 38).

5. Examine the photograph in Figure 4.1. What can you determine about the students and other contextual details from the photograph? For example, how old are the children? When do you suspect the photo was taken? In what activity might they be engaged? What role might the phonograph play? What questions does the photo raise?
6. Suppose you are preparing to interview someone as part of an oral history. Describe how you would prepare for and conduct the interview.
7. Why is it important for the researcher to interpret historical facts? What concerns must the researcher keep in mind while writing a report?

Important Terms for Review

Historical research is a systematic process of describing, analyzing, and interpreting the past based on information from selected sources as they relate to the topic under study.

Narrative history describes the process of organizing material into a chronologically sequential order to tell a single coherent story.

Primary sources are materials that originated either during the period or at a later date through a participant directly involved (e.g., memoires).

Secondary sources are materials that interpret or analyze historical events or phenomena.

Immersion refers to the process of collecting and examining everything possible on the topic until the researcher has a complete understanding of the context and the people and events under investigation.

Saturation occurs when searches for source material results in duplicate findings or unrelated data.

Oral history involves the use of human informants to provide information on the past through live or recorded interviews.

External criticism involves determining authenticity of a particular source.

Internal criticism involves determining the accuracy of information within a given source.

References

Birge, E. B. (1937). *History of public school music in the United States* (Rev. ed.). Oliver Ditson. (Full text available at www.archive.org. Reprint available from Roman & Littlefield)
Boal, D. (1998). *Interlochen: A home for the Arts*. University of Michigan Press.
Browning, N. L. (1963). *Joe Maddy of Interlochen*. H. Regnery.
Burns, K. (Director). (2001). *Jazz: A film by Ken Burns* [Film]. PBS.
Burns, K. (Director). (2019). *Country music: A film by Ken Burns* [Film]. PBS.
Clark, F. E. (1920. *Music appreciation for little children: In the home, kindergarten, and primary schools*. Victor Talking Machine Company.
Cooper, S., & Bayless, R. (2008). Examining the Music Teachers National Association papers and proceedings 1906 to 1930. *Journal of Historical Research in Music Education, 29*(2), 129–144. https://doi.org/10.1177/153660060802900205
Cox, G. (2017). *Living music in schools 1923–1999: Studies in the history of music education in England*. Routledge. (Original work published 2002)
Dunbar, L. L. (2016). Mainstreaming in American music education journals (1960–1989): An analysis. *Journal of Historical Research in Music Education, 37*(2), 150–161. https://doi.org/10.1177/1536600616641821
Dunbar-Hall, P. (2008). "Good legong dancers were given an arduous program of training": Music education in Bali in the 1930s. *Journal of Historical Research in Music Education, 30*(1), 50–63. https://doi.org/10.1177/153660060803000106
Good, C. V. (1963). *Introduction to educational research: Methodology of design in the behavioral and social sciences* (2nd ed). Appleton-Century-Crofts.
Gottschalk, L. (1963). *Generalization in the writing of history: A report of the Committee on Historical Analysis of the Social Science Research Council*. University of Chicago Press.
Green, A., & Troup, K. (2016). *The houses of history: A critical reader in history and theory* (2nd ed.). Manchester University Press.
Groulx, T. J. (2013). Three nations, one common root: A historical comparison of elementary music education in the United Kingdom, the United States, and Australia. *Journal of Historical Research in Music Education, 34*(2), 137–153. https://doi.org/10.1177/153660061303400205
Groulx, T. (2021). Segregated and superior, integrated and inferior: Effects of integrated band festivals on ratings of Black high school bands. *Journal of Band Research, 57*(1), 41–53.

Gruhn, W. (2001). European "methods" for American nineteenth-century singing instruction: A cross-cultural perspective on historical research. *Journal of Historical Research in Music Education, 23*(1), 3–18. https://doi.org/10.1177/153660060102300102

Hash, P. M. (2011). *The universal teacher*, by J. E. Maddy and T. P. Giddings (1923) [Review]. *Journal of Research in Music Education, 58*(4), 384–410. https://doi.org/10.1177/0022429410385869

Hash, P. M. (2015a). Music education at the New York Institution for the Blind: 1832–1863. *Journal of Research in Music Education, 62*, 362–388. https://doi.org/10.1177%2F0022429414555983

Hash, P. M. (2015b). Solomon W. Straub (1842–1899): A self-made music educator on the prairie. *Journal of Historical Research in Music Education, 37*, 51–74. https://doi.org/10.1177%2F1536600615608462

Hash, P. M. (2018). The Austin High School girls' band of Chicago, Illinois: 1925–1956. *Journal of Research in Music Education, 66*(1), 31–52. https://doi.org/10.1177%2F0022429418755501

Heller, G. N. (1985). On the meaning and value of historical research in music education. *Journal of Research in Music Education, 33*(1), 4–6. https://doi.org/10.2307/3344753

Heller, G. N. (1998). Historical research in music education: Definitions and defenses. *Philosophy of Music Education Review, 61*, 84–85. https://www.jstor.org/stable/40327119

Howe, S. W. (2014). *Women music educators in the United States: A history.* Scarecrow Press.

Howe, S. W. (2021). Western music on Commodore Perry's "black ships" in Japan, 1853–1854. *Journal of Historical Research in Music Education, 42*(2), 102–116. https://doi.org/10.1177/1536600619877917

Humphreys, J. T. (1985). The child-study movement and public school music education. *Journal of Research in Music Education, 33*(2), 79–86. https://doi.org/10.2307/3344728

Humphreys, J. T. (1988). Applications of science: The age of standardization and efficiency in music education. *Bulletin of Historical Research in Music Education, 9*(1), 1–21. https://doi.org/10.1177/153660068800900101

Humphreys, J. T. (2015). Energizing the "Birge story" of public school music in the United States: Some ideas on how to amp it up. *Journal of Historical Research in Music Education, 36*(2), 91–109. https://doi.org/10.1177%2F153660061503600202

Humphreys, J., & Schmidt, C. (1998). Membership of the Music Educators National Conference from 1912–1938: A demographic and economic analysis. *Bulletin of the Council for Research in Music Education,* (137), 16–31. http://www.jstor.org.libproxy.lib.ilstu.edu/stable/40318929

Keene, J. A. (2009). *A history of music education in the United States.* Glenbridge Publishing.

Maddy, J. E., & Giddings, T. P. (1923). *The universal teacher.* C. G. Conn.

Mark, M. L., & Gary, C. (2007). *A history of American music education* (3rd ed.). Roman & Littlefield.

McCarthy, M. (1999). *Passing it on: The transmission of music in Irish culture.* Cork University.

McCarthy, M. (2019). Book review: The houses of history: A critical reader in history and theory, by Anna Green and Kathleen Troup. *Journal of Historical Research in Music Education, 41*(1), 96–98. https://doi.org/10.1177/1536600619865807

Miller, D. M. (2019). The role of religious politics in the dismissal of Lowell Mason from the Boston public schools in 1845. *Journal of Historical Research in Music Education, 40*(2), 105–124. https://doi.org/10.1177/1536600617737062

Rainbow, B., & Cox, G. (2006). *Music educational thought and practice.* Boydell.

Sanchez, M. (2007, May 19). *Oral history interview with Gary Coleman and Steve Fulmer: Founding members of the Portland, Oregon, Gay Men's Chorus* [Sound recording 01]. Gay and Lesbian Archives of the Pacific Northwest Oral Histories; Oregon Historical Society Research Library. https://digitalcollections.ohs.org/sr-11123-oral-history-interview-with-gary-coleman-steve-fulmer-by-michael-sanchez

Sanders, P. D. (2017). Temperance songs in American school songbooks, 1865–1899. *Journal of Historical Research in Music Education, 38*(2), 178–208. https://doi.org/10.1177/1536600616667602

Southcott, J. (2020). Egalitarian music education in the nineteenth century: Joseph Mainzer and singing for the million. *Journal of Historical Research in Music Education, 42*(1), 29–45. https://doi.org/10.1177/1536600619848104

Southcott, J. E., & Sell, D. (2014). Introduction to historical research in music education. In K. A. Hartwig (Ed.), *Research methodologies in music education* (pp. 9–34). Cambridge Scholars.

Sullivan, J. M. (2017). Women music teachers as military band directors during World War II. *Journal of Historical Research in Music Education, 39*(1), 78–105. https://doi.org/10.1177/1536600616665625

Sullivan, J. M. (2019). John Philip Sousa as music educator and fundraiser during World War I. *Journal of Historical Research in Music Education, 40*(2), 143–169. https://doi.org/10.1177/1536600617743013

Sunderman, L. F. (1971). *Historical foundations of music education in the United States.* Scarecrow Press.

Tellstrom, A. T. (1971). *Music in American education: Past and present.* Holt, Rinehart & Winston.

Thibeault, M. D. (2020). Dewey's musical allergy and the philosophy of music education. *Journal of Research in Music Education, 68*(1), 31–52. https://doi.org/10.1177/0022429419896792

Volk, T. M. (2003). Looking back in time: On being a music education historian. *Journal of Historical Research in Music Education, 25*(1), 49–59. https://doi.org/10.1177/153660060302500106

Ward-Steinman, P. M. (2020). "Be true to your school": A 100-year legacy of music education faculty at the Indiana University school of music. *Journal of Historical Research in Music Education, 44*(1). https://doi.org/10.1177/1536600620955133

Whitwell, D. (2011). *Foundations of music education.* Whitwell Books.

5
Philosophical Researchers' Aims and Processes

Chapter Preview

In this chapter, you will learn the primary aims of philosophical research and the key processes that philosophical researchers may use when developing their arguments. A typical process includes constructing a philosophical problem; building an argument through critique, extension, creation, and/or defining terms; and aiming to guide practice. Philosophical researchers aim to illuminate and investigate individuals' unconscious beliefs, principles, values, and assumptions in order to imagine what could be. Such action necessitates identifying and describing a problem within present music teaching and learning practices. High-quality philosophical research addresses problems that are sufficiently narrow (focusing on a limited aspect of a single complex topic), realistic (resonating with many music educators' past and present encounters), and significant (dealing with a pervasive and timely topic). Philosophical researchers might start their problem construction process with the question "What are currently the most pressing problems within the profession?" Philosophical researchers can explain and justify these problems through real or hypothetical narratives as well as texts. Having detailed a problem, philosophical researchers often build their arguments through combinations of critique, extension, and creation. Importantly, philosophical researchers define and clarify terms central to their inquiry. While philosophical researchers aim to guide practice, they typically avoid proposing prescribed solutions (See Box 5.1).

Introduction

Philosophical research studies can take a far wider variety of forms than historical, quantitative, or qualitative articles. This is because the content under investigation determines a philosopher's precise methods (Reichling, 1996; Ruitenberg, 2010). For example, a philosophical researcher predominantly relying on Greek philosophical sources would argue differently from one drawing on Confucian texts or one extending contemporary feminist writings. Likewise, a philosopher problematizing the role of whiteness in secondary instrumental ensembles would construct their arguments differently from one proposing the value of play within an elementary general music classroom.

Given that philosophical researchers rarely include references to methods texts or explanations of their philosophical process in their articles, the philosophical research process may at first seem mysterious and daunting. Yet, despite the variability of their end products, philosophical researchers often rely on a shared set of thinking and writing practices. Understanding the nonlinear processes in which philosophical researchers typically engage can partly demystify such work. Eventually, researchers may even find the absence of a prescribed, sequential research process freeing and empowering.

In this chapter, we explain key processes that can facilitate conducting high-quality philosophical research. These include constructing a philosophical problem; building an argument through critique, extension, creation, and defining terms; and aiming to guide practice. Understanding these processes and identifying them within philosophical research articles can also assist readers in following an author's arguments. Before addressing key considerations for reading and doing philosophy, we examine the importance of philosophical research.

Box 5.1 Research to Practice: Philosophical Research

Philosophical research can inform music teaching and learning by both illuminating the limits of current actions and providing ideas about alternative practices and values. For example, Abramo's (2007) critical investigation of multicultural music reveals that when educators program pieces that treat Indigenous music making as mysterious and primitive (e.g., a repeated, simple drum pattern comes to signify the music making in all of Africa), they further stereotypes and racist attitudes. In terms of changing practices, Abramo offers that, instead of avoiding such repertoire, teachers might use it to facilitate discussions about racism and stereotyping. Importantly, students' prior experiences and unique, place-specific contexts should inform how a teacher alters their practices.

When imagining how philosophical research could inform practice, teachers might consider their language, pedagogical content, and assessment practices as well as student-teacher interactions, student-student interactions, and school-community interactions. Focusing on how a philosophical researcher defines their terms and the details of their argument, as opposed to the general concept under investigation, can illuminate specific implications. For example, imagine a study about democracy and music education. In order to consider the multiple aspects listed above, teachers might ponder questions such as the following: Does the philosopher define democracy in terms of majority rule, an egalitarian respect for one's peers, or an alternative definition? How might teachers change their democratic practices as students mature? What is the relationship between democratic interactions within a classroom and civic engagement, ranging from voting to political protests, outside of the classroom?

Aiming to Make Trouble

Humans are habitual beings. Much of our lives consists of processes that we have not fully examined or imagined could be otherwise. One might pour a bowl of wheat cereal each morning without contemplating the possibilities of a Nutella-filled croissant or a fished-based breakfast, or vice versa. Likewise, music teachers and students often rely on certain pedagogical practices, types of music making, goals, and values without having contemplated why they do so or considered possible alternatives. Enter philosophical research.

Philosophical research illuminates and investigates individuals' unconscious beliefs, principles, values, and assumptions. Through their inquiries, philosophical researchers consider what could or perhaps even should be rather than what is. In contrast to historical researchers, who typically examine what has been, and quantitative, qualitative, and action researchers, who typically examine what currently exists, philosophical researchers imagine how teaching and learning could be otherwise. Teachers and students often feel attached to their current practices, and they may find reconsidering them and imagining alternative possibilities an uncomfortable, frustrating process. As such, philosophical researchers make trouble by unsettling previously unquestioned thinking and action. Through this troublemaking, philosophical researchers can play a key role in the profession's ongoing development.

The joy of reading and discussing philosophical research typically comes from temporarily imagining and engaging with new possibilities. Since philosophical researchers ultimately aim to inform practice (Elliott, 1995; Reimer, 2003), readers might consider how specific philosophical ideas could play out within their own unique teaching and learning settings. Additionally, given that no music education philosophy is ever complete or beyond critique, readers might also consider what is problematic or absent from an author's arguments. Dialoguing about both the problems and the possibilities of a philosophical argument with readers having different backgrounds and life experiences can add to the richness of one's philosophical insights.

While reading and discussing philosophy can contribute much to music education practices, conducting philosophical research enables one to think even more deeply about important issues in the field. Grappling with explaining a topic to others, including possible changes to practice, often reveals its complexities and complications. In order to make trouble in a meaningful and productive manner, philosophical researchers need to identify and explain the specific problem under investigation.

Constructing a Philosophical Problem

In contrast with other research methodologies, philosophers rarely include a clear problem statement in their studies. Yet, convincing readers about the importance of alternatives to present practices necessitates exposing the limitations of current thinking and action within music education. As such, philosophical research studies necessitate clear explanations of specific problems. While philosophical researchers often revise and refine their understanding of the problem under investigation over the course of a study, extended attention to the central problem early in the research process can inform one's main arguments.

Qualities of Well-Constructed Philosophical Problems

High-quality philosophical writing often involves problems that possess three qualities. First, the problem is sufficiently narrow. Just as empirical researchers augment existing research with a single set of results or findings on a limited topic, philosophers add a single set of arguments to the field's existing philosophical discourse on a particular issue. While philosophers address big-picture issues, such as the overarching purposes of music education, each philosophical research study investigates only a narrow aspect of a single complex topic. For example, a philosopher cannot address all potential purposes of music education in a single book, let alone a single article; instead, an article or chapter might address one purpose of music education.

In addition to focusing on a single topic, such as vulnerability, race, or improvisation, philosophers can narrow their arguments by considering one category of philosophical question. This might be centering a question related to ethics, value, the nature of beauty, or what it means to know. (For more information about types of philosophical questions, see Chapter 6.) Another way to narrow the scope of the problem is to consider under what circumstances the issue often arises: Does it occur most often in P–12 school, collegiate, community, informal, or professional music-making settings? For example, Benedict (2009) applies Marx's ideas, including production, exchange value, and alienation, specifically to Orff and Kodály methodologies within elementary general music education.

Second, the problem is realistic, meaning that it resonates with many music educators' past and present encounters. Given that problems within the profession are often complex, such action typically necessitates detailed description. (Tactics for creating realistic descriptions are explained subsequently.) A key part of this realism is honoring the generally good intentions of teachers, students, and other stakeholders. Although it is important to approach issues in the field critically, it would be problematic to state or imply that music educators are woefully uninformed, dictatorial, lazy, or highly resistant to change when describing a particular problem. Such assertions also obscure numerous other subtle factors, ranging from music educator associations' activities to pressure from parents and other stakeholders, that foster and perpetuate current practices.

Third, a problem should be significant, meaning that it is a pervasive and timely topic. Philosophical researchers might start their problem construction process with the question "What are currently the most pressing problems within the profession?" Both long-standing practices and new trends can constitute significant problems. For example, philosophers might address ongoing concerns related to the value of music competitions or more recent issues involving equity-centered practices.

Significant problems generally affect a sizable proportion of music educators. For instance, although a handful of music teachers might self-identify as White Nationalists, the profession at large does not overtly support, and in many instances directly condemns, such thinking. The existence of any self-identified White Nationalist music educators is a significant problem for those teachers' colleagues and students. Yet, given the minimal scope of this problem, it may not be particularly significant for philosophical researchers to address.

Since music educators and the profession's leaders constitute the primary audience for philosophical research, significant problems tend to involve issues that these individuals possess some agency to address. Conversely, consider the realistic problem that public schools rarely cover the costs of private music lessons. Schools have not historically covered these costs, and this idea currently has minimal broader political support. Moreover, many P–12 music educators would likely happily augment their programs with such resources if they were available. It follows that few readers would find the problem that schools do not provide universal private music lessons controversial. Alternatively, since music educators typically have some control over recruiting and goal-setting within their programs, a related, more significant philosophical problem might involve inequitable music education access, enrollment, or outcomes within a single type of school or community setting.

Lessons from Comedy

Examining differences between failed and successful comic routines can further illuminate how to construct sufficiently narrow, realistic, and significant philosophical problems. Have you ever seen a comedian tell a joke that did not quite land with the audience? I once saw a comedian hurl a list of insults about New Jersey without much setup or explanation. Many of the audience members had ties to New Jersey, and the observations did not seem to resonate with their everyday experiences. Without buy-in for the initial premises underlying the subsequent jokes, the routine quickly fell flat. While philosophical arguments clearly necessitate much more depth and nuance than typical comedy sketches, they can flounder for similar reasons.

For example, consider a philosophical argument that began with the assertion "Band, choir, and orchestra directors enact racist practices." A philosophical researcher could potentially construct an argument that eventually justified such an assertion. However, it does not make for a convincing initial problem statement for several reasons.

First, beginning with a characterization of teachers' practices as "racist" often puts readers on the defensive. Philosophers can and should call out problematic practices, but such action necessitates careful, gradual, and comprehensive reasoning. Readers offended by initial broad, unsupported assertions will likely resist subsequent arguments, regardless of their logic and detail.

Second, the assertion assumes that the majority of band, choir, and orchestra directors at all levels and in all places enact similar practices. In this way, it parallels a comedian who problematically combines all New Jersey residents into a single category. Yet, the practices enacted by a Midwestern, urban, middle school choir director likely differ from those of a beginning band educator in the rural Southwest.

A third related concern is that the statement addresses "practices" without naming specific actions. This ambiguity leaves the audience without a clear understanding of the author's point, thus limiting potential resonances with the argument. Had the statement instead addressed favoring White composers or minimizing the aural learning found in much traditional Black music making, readers may observe greater alignment between the argument and their common experiences.

In contrast with the aforementioned comedian, examine how Gary Gulman spends over four minutes explaining how he had a "meltdown" at a Trader Joe's grocery store (https://www.youtube.com/watch?v=j5BZvV1ZTyE). Gulman begins by honoring those he eventually critiques: "I love that place; I love Trader Joe's. They are so thoughtful there. They're nice." By starting with a compliment and empathy rather than an insult, Gulman better enables the audience to accept the subsequent series of jokes about his experience. While philosophical researchers need not pander to their audience or provide false praise, they typically balance and integrate respect for teachers and students with critique. Yet, even repeated compliments or empathy will not save a comedian who makes generalizations that counter many audience members' personal experiences.

Gulman narrows his problem and enhances its realism by limiting his joke to those shopping at Trader Joe's stores in New York City. He thus leaves open the possibility that his story will not directly resonate with those who shop at a Trader Joe's in other locations. Additionally, Gulman's vivid descriptions of employees, fellow customers, and items in his shopping cart enable audience members to visualize his far-fetched scenario. This is particularly key for those who have never visited a Trader Joe's. Likewise, philosophical researchers who narrow their problem scenarios and describe them in significant detail can draw in readers unfamiliar with the topic under investigation. For example, an alternative to the aforementioned problem statement might read "When middle and high school jazz band directors emphasize Western music notation and minimize aural learning and improvisation, they omit what Sarath (2018) explains as key qualities of the Black music traditions central to the founding and evolution of jazz."

Possible Problem Construction Processes

There are many ways to set up a philosophical problem that is sufficiently narrow, realistic, and significant. Like Gulman, philosophical researchers sometimes draw on personal experiences. The initial impetus for philosophical research may come from one's everyday endeavors.

A researcher might experience a puzzling teaching and learning interaction, overhear a colleague's troubling statement, feel moved by a news story, or not know how to engage with a student's question. Even when a philosophical text serves as the primary source of inspiration for a study, a researcher's understanding of that text necessarily evolves with their daily experiences.

When researchers remain open to the philosophical potential of commonplace experiences, those events can provide a ready source of detail that facilitates the construction of a realistic problem. For example, Gould (2007) explained her embodied experiences of oppression and marginalization as a lesbian music educator in a heteronormative profession. Alternatively, O'Toole (2005) details how, as the leader of an adult volunteer choir, she regretfully undermined participants' autonomy and joy.

O'Toole's (2005) story, like Gulman's, portrays the narrator as imperfect and vulnerable. By critiquing oneself, as opposed to other teachers, personal narratives can illuminate problems while not demonizing music educators at large. They can also demonstrate that rethinking and revising one's current practices is an important, ongoing part of professional development. When a researcher has not directly experienced a problematic practice, hypothetical scenarios, in which they imagine a specific, detailed teaching and learning scenario, can serve a purpose similar to that of personal narratives. Importantly, real or hypothetical narratives acknowledge the complicated, complex nature of music teaching and learning endeavors.

Another way of constructing and demonstrating the significance of a philosophical problem is with documents and texts. These can involve policy documents, such as national or state music standards, and practitioner resources, such as beginning instrumental methods texts and general music software. For example, Bradley (2011) centered her argument on the Wisconsin Department of Public Instruction Guidelines for Music Teacher Education. Alternatively, Allsup and Benedict (2008) quoted from a text entitled "The Quantum Conductor" by college band director Eugene Corporon.

Philosophical researchers can also describe and justify their problems through carefully selected language from online sources, including organizations' websites and social media. For instance, Kertz-Welzel (2016) grounded her problem description in both community music leaders' statements and a description from the Community Music Activity Commission. Such references can also assist philosophical researchers in demonstrating the realistic and timely nature of their problems. When reading descriptions of problems within philosophical research, it can be helpful to see which tactics you personally find most convincing and to experiment with them in your own writing.

Building Philosophical Arguments: Beyond Summarizing

In addition to deciding on a sufficiently narrow, realistic, and significant problem, philosophical researchers need to consider how they will craft their main argument. A philosophy-based practitioner article, such as that which a reader might find in the *Music Educators Journal*, can involve summarizing other philosophers' arguments and applying them to practice. Authors of such work need not build a unique, logical argument or interpretation. In contrast, philosophical research necessitates putting forward a genuinely new line of thinking. While philosophical researchers might summarize another philosopher's ideas, their arguments cannot be solely reduced to those ideas. In other words, absent a unique line of argument, summaries of one or more philosophers' writings do not constitute philosophical research.

Three common, potentially overlapping tactics that philosophers can use to build their unique arguments are critique, extension, and creation. In the process of constructing a philosophical problem (see previous section), most philosophical researchers begin their studies by providing or implying a critique of current music education practices. Sometimes philosophical researchers continue this critique throughout their study. In other words, the majority of a philosophical study can involve critiquing specific music education practices. One prominent example of a critique-based philosophical research study is Allsup and Benedict's (2008) critique of band. In their article, they problematized an overreliance on certain traditions, efficiency-based teaching methods, oppressive teacher-student relationships, and the unquestioned reproduction of past practices.

A second kind of philosophical argument is an extension. This occurs when a philosopher builds upon or further develops another author's main ideas. For example, Mantie (2012) used Foucault's work to extend Allsup and Benedict's (2008) critique of band. A variation on an extension argument is a synthesis, in which an author combines the work of two or more philosophers in order to form a unique argument. Tan (2016), for instance, constructed a transcultural theory of thinking for instrumental music education by combining the works of Confucius and Dewey.

A third type of philosophical argument involves creating a new idea or term. Philosophical researchers might invent a completely new term, such as Small (1998) did with "musicking," to refer to the combination of all human musical endeavors, including composing, performing, rehearsing, practicing, and listening. Alternatively, philosophical researchers might uniquely define existing words or phrases. For example, Elliott et al. (2016) put forward the new term "artistic citizenship." They wrote, "'Artistic citizenship' is a concept with which we hope to encapsulate our belief that artistry involves civic-social-humanistic-emancipatory responsibilities, obligations to engage in art making that advances social 'goods'" (p. 7). In some instances, such as Gould's (2009) article addressing "performative literacy," philosophical researchers devote most of an article to defining a new term.

Defining terms also plays an important role in studies mainly involving critique or extension. Since philosophical researchers are "vitally concerned with the meaning of words because words are the vehicles for communicating ideas," they work "to ensure the greatest possible precision in meaning" (Jorgensen, 1992, p. 91). Take, for example, the word "creativity." Whether a philosophical researcher uses "creativity" to mean a skill, disposition, or process will impact the nature and limits of their arguments. A high-quality piece of philosophical research that addresses creativity would therefore include a clear definition of the term early in the study. Likewise, words that music educators might not explain in everyday speech, such as "musical technique," "democracy," and "power," necessitate definitions when used in philosophical research studies.

Philosophical researchers may define terms using a standard dictionary. However, since definitions provided by philosophical or empirical researchers typically rely on more nuanced and scholarly understandings, authors may find them preferable to dictionary-based definitions. Philosophical researchers may also draw on a variety of definitions in order to construct their own. Importantly, philosophical researchers should avoid definitions that contradict prevailing scholarly or public conceptions of a term. For instance, any definition of jazz would need to encompass music making ranging from Louis Armstrong to Charlie Parker to Esperanza Spalding. Having developed their own unique line of argument, philosophical researchers then consider how those ideas might apply to music teaching and learning practices.

Aiming to Guide Practice: Living in the Gray

When music educators first read a philosophical research article or book, they might be surprised or even frustrated that the author does not provide concrete answers or suggestions. Music education philosophers generally aim for their writings to inform practice (Elliott, 1995; Reimer, 2003). However, philosophical researchers usually intentionally avoid offering explicit answers or prescribing specific practices (Bowman & Frega, 2012). Why, you might wonder, would someone spend dozens or hundreds of pages providing logical arguments only to refrain from telling teachers how they should alter their teaching practices? The reason is threefold.

First, since music educators work in a wide variety of settings and with very different types of learners, more specific suggestions would have only limited applicability. What constitutes more democratic teaching and learning in a downtown kindergarten music class in Los Angeles will almost certainly differ from that of a middle school popular music class in rural Wisconsin or a selective high school choir in suburban Connecticut. Philosophical researchers who focus on overarching ideas rather than specific directives can encourage a wide variety of readers to consider possible applications of their arguments.

Second, giving specific directives or ways forward limits alternative possibilities. While a philosophical researcher might have one set of thoughts about how a kindergarten music educator in downtown Los Angeles could implement their ideas, the teacher may have other, equally valuable insights and imaginings. Moreover, leaving philosophical research open-ended encourages music educators to grapple with the underlying ideas. If a music educator passively adopts ideas from a prescribed list absent understanding a philosopher's guiding rationale, they may implement the ideas in problematic ways or find themselves unable to apply them in new contexts.

Similarly, a third reason philosophical researchers typically do not prescribe specific practices is that they want to honor music educators' agency. Providing music educators with definitive answers would place the philosophical researcher in a position of power and authority over the teacher, thus disempowering teachers and undermining their professional knowledge and experiences. Instead, teachers can build on their expertise in order to implement open-ended philosophical research in ways most meaningful for their specific scenarios. Stated differently, avoiding prescriptive practices encourages readers to think and act philosophically.

While philosophical researchers rarely prescribe specific practices, they may still include examples of possible ways forward within their work. For example, Tan (2016) detailed actions and questions that a hypothetical teacher ("Ms. Livingston") drawing on his ideas might use. Importantly, well-constructed philosophical examples go beyond relatively commonplace or vague suggestions. Broad, previously proposed ideas, like focusing on creativity or incorporating more popular or multicultural music, lack the sufficient detail needed to guide new practices. Detailing how a philosophical researcher's arguments might alter or extend previously proposed or currently enacted practices can assist readers in understanding the newness of those ideas.

Philosophical researchers might also offer specific changes to language or focus on concepts or questions that could guide practice. For example, Richerme (2016) argued that because words like "measure" and "assess" transfer action away from an unchanged teacher, they problematically neglect how teachers and students transform through those processes. She suggested complementing those terms "with language such as *grow*, *develop*, and *become*" (p. 287). Richerme also posited that music educators might consider such questions as "To what extent do these evaluations reflect the values of music makers in our multiple communities? How might we evaluate these measured quantities differently?" (p. 287).

Philosophical researchers might also reveal a previously unexamined tension between two or more practices. Reimer (2003), for instance, encouraged readers to decide how they will balance and combine understanding music as form, as practice, and as social agency. Regardless of their tactics, philosophical researchers typically honor teachers' agency by using words like "might" and "could," as opposed to "must" or "should," throughout their work.

Summary

Philosophical researchers aim to illuminate and investigate individuals' unconscious beliefs, principles, values, and assumptions in order to imagine what could be. Such action necessitates identifying and describing a problem within present music teaching and learning practices. High-quality philosophical research addresses problems that are sufficiently narrow, realistic, and significant. Philosophical researchers can explain and justify these problems through real or hypothetical narratives as well as texts, including practitioner resources, policy documents, and online sources. Having detailed a problem, philosophical researchers often build their arguments with a combination of critique, extension, and creation. Importantly, philosophical researchers define and clarify terms central to their inquiry. While philosophical researchers aim to guide practice, they typically avoid proposing prescribed solutions. The following chapter addresses additional considerations, including types of philosophical questions, reasoning skills, philosophical sources, and fallacies, as well as provides a few additional tips for conducting a philosophical research study.

Here are some study prompts that will help you clarify your understanding of the topics presented in this chapter:

1. Looking through issues of either *Philosophy of Music Education Review* or *Action, Criticism, and Theory for Music Education,* find an article on a topic of interest. Answer the following:
   a. What problem is the author addressing?
   b. How does the author narrow the scope of the topic?
   c. How does the author ground the problem in realistic teaching and learning scenarios (e.g., do they cite certain texts or provide specific examples)?
   d. How and to what extent does the author convince you of the problem's significance?
2. Using the same article, explain how the author seeks to guide music educators' practices without prescribing clear directives. (Do they offer examples of reimagined practices? Do they provide key ideas or questions with which music educators might grapple? To what extent do they include open language like "might" and "could"?)
3. Considering a music education topic of interest, imagine how you might construct a related philosophical:
   a. Critique.
   b. Extension.
   c. Newly created term or concept.

4. Find a philosophy-based article in the *Music Educators Journal* (e.g., one by Allsup, Elliott, Hess, Jorgensen, or Richerme) or another practitioner journal. Find a philosophical research article by the same author from a research journal such as *Philosophy of Music Education Review*. Explain similarities and differences between the two articles.

Important Terms for Review

Philosophical research uses logical arguments and examples to investigate the assumptions underlying current music education practices and to imagine how attitudes and actions within the profession might be.

Critique involves a prolonged exploration of problems or limitations with either contemporary teaching and learning practices or another philosopher's arguments.

Extension involves building on or further developing another philosopher's main ideas.

Creation involves introducing new ideas and/or terms.

Synthesis involves combining the work of two or more philosophers in order to form a unique argument.

Defining terms involves clarifying and delimiting how a researcher will use a specific term throughout their study.

References

Abramo, J. (2007). Mystery, fire and intrigue: Representation and commodification of race in band literature. *Visions of Research in Music Education, 9*(10), 1–23. http://www-usr.rider.edu/~vrme/v9n1/vision/AbramoFinal.5.29.07.pdf

Allsup, R. E., & Benedict, C. (2008). The problems of band: An inquiry in the future of instrumental music education. *Philosophy of Music Education Review, 16*, 156–173. https://www.jstor.org/stable/40327299

Benedict, C. (2009). Processes of alienation: Marx, Orff and Kodaly. *British Journal of Music Education, 26*, 213–224. https://doi.org/10.1017/S0265051709008444

Bowman, W., & Frega, A. (2012). Introduction. In W. Bowman & A. Frega (Eds.), *The Oxford handbook of philosophy in music education* (pp. 3–14). Oxford University Press.

Bradley, D. (2011). In the space between the rock and the hard place: State teacher certification guidelines and music education for social justice. *Journal of Aesthetic Education, 45*, 79–96. https://doi.org/10.5406/jaesteduc.45.4.0079

Elliott, D. J. (1995). *Music matters: A new philosophy of music education*. Oxford University Press.

Elliott, D., Silverman, M., & Bowman, W. (2016). Artistic citizenship: Introduction, aims, and overview. In D. Elliott, M. Silverman, & W. Bowman (Eds.), *Artistic citizenship: Artistry, social responsibility, and ethical praxis* (pp. 3–22). Oxford University Press.

Gould, E. (2007). Legible bodies in music education: Becoming-matter. *Action, Criticism, and Theory for Music Education, 6*(4), 201–223. http://act.maydaygroup.org/articles/Gould6_4.pdf

Gould, E. (2009). Music education desire(ing): Language, literacy, and lieder. *Philosophy of Music Education Review, 17*, 41–55. https://www.jstor.org/stable/40327309

Jorgensen, E. R. (1992). On philosophical method. In R. Colwell (Ed.), *Handbook of research on music teaching and learning* (pp. 91–114). Schirmer Books.

Kertz-Welzel, A. (2016). Daring to question: A philosophical critique of community music. *Philosophy of Music Education Review, 24*, 113–130. https://www.jstor.org/stable/10.2979/philmusieducrevi.24.2.01

Mantie, R. (2012). Bands and/as music education: Antinomies and the struggle for legitimacy. *Philosophy of Music Education Review, 20*, 63–81. https://www.jstor.org/stable/10.2979/philmusieducrevi.20.1.63

O'Toole, P. (2005). I sing in a choir but "I have no voice!" *Visions of Research in Music Education, 6*(1), 1–26. http://www-usr.rider.edu/~vrme/v6n1/visions/O%27Toole%20I%20Sing%20In%20A%20Choir.pdf

Reichling, M. (1996). On the question of method in philosophical research. *Philosophy of Music Education Review, 4*, 117–127. https://www.jstor.org/stable/40495423

Reimer, B. (2003). *A philosophy of music education: Advancing the vision* (3rd ed.). Prentice Hall.

Richerme, L. K. (2016). Measuring music education: A philosophical investigation of the Model Cornerstone Assessments. *Journal of Research in Music Education, 63*, 274–293. https://doi.org/10.1177/0022429416659250

Ruitenberg, C. (2010). Introduction: The question of method in philosophy of education. In C. Ruitenberg (Ed.), *What do philosophers of education do? (And how do they do it?)* (pp. 1–9). Wiley-Blackwell Publishers.

Sarath, E. (2018). *Black music matters: Jazz and the transformation of music studies*. Rowman & Littlefield.

Small, C. (1998). *Musicking: The meanings of performing and listening*. University Press of New England.

Tan, L. (2016). A transcultural theory of thinking for instrumental music education: Philosophical insights from Confucius and Dewey. *Philosophy of Music Education Review, 24*, 151–169. https://www.jstor.org/stable/10.2979/philmusieducrevi.24.2.03

6
Conducting Philosophical Research
Additional Considerations

Chapter Preview

In this chapter you will learn about categories of philosophical questions, sources to support philosophical arguments, reasoning processes, and philosophical fallacies. *Ontological questions* address the nature of being and reality. This might include the nature of music making, for example. *Epistemological questions* address the nature of understanding and knowing. For example, does mastering a musical skill, such as playing a B-flat scale, mean that a student understands music? *Axiological questions* address issues related to valuation. For example, should some forms of music making (e.g., art music or jazz) or pedagogical practices be valued over others? *Aesthetic questions* address matters related to beauty. Researchers addressing aesthetic questions consider what *should be* considered beautiful rather than what currently *is* considered beautiful. *Ethical questions* address issues of right and wrong. Are some teaching practices or musical experiences more ethical than others? More recently, issues related to social justice, such as LGBTQIA+ concerns and antiracist pedagogy, have informed key ethical questions within the profession. *Political questions* address matters related to governance and social order. For example, a philosophical researcher might consider how current music teaching and learning settings prepare students for future civic participation.

Introduction

After a philosophical researcher decides on a problem and considers potential forms of argument (e.g., critique, extension), they can then draw upon a variety of processes to develop and refine their thinking. In this chapter, you will learn how considering specific philosophical questions, sources of support, reasoning practices, and philosophical fallacies can inform the philosophical inquiry process. The chapter concludes with a list of tips that may assist researchers when they feel overwhelmed by the uncertainties inherent in conducting philosophical research.

Categories of Philosophical Questions

Philosophical researchers typically address certain categories of questions. According to Jorgensen (1992), these include ontological, epistemological, axiological, aesthetic, ethical, and political questions. Importantly, these questions differ from those explored through quantitative, qualitative, and historical methodologies. Philosophical researchers can refine and clarify their work by determining what category of philosophical question they are investigating. While a philosophical research study may address multiple categories of questions, beginning researchers may find it helpful to focus on a single category.

Ontological and Epistemological Questions

Ontological questions address the nature of being and reality. For music educators, this might include the nature of music making, of specific musical experiences (e.g., listening or composing), of different genres of music, or of education. For example, a researcher might ask whether music making is primarily an intellectual, emotional, or social experience, or they might question to what extent educational experiences are constructive, chaotic, or creative.

Epistemological questions address the nature of understanding and knowing. Examples of music education epistemological questions include "Does mastering a musical skill, such as playing a B-flat scale, mean that a student understands music?" "How is the nature of knowledge in artistic disciplines different from that in scientific ones?"

Philosophical researchers should not address questions answerable through empirical (e.g., qualitative or quantitative) research. For instance, the efficiency of certain teaching techniques and how a specific practice affects skill retention are best addressed through empirical rather than philosophical inquiry. Additionally, philosophical researchers investigating ontological and epistemological questions should consider findings from neuroscience and other empirical disciplines that might be relevant to their research. For example, since neuroscientist Antonio Damasio (1999) has demonstrated that human thinking and feeling function inseparably, a philosophical researcher should avoid making arguments suggesting otherwise. Yet, a philosophical researcher could build on Damasio's work by reasoning how cognition integrates with feeling during specific musical experiences.

Axiological and Aesthetic Questions

Axiological questions address issues of valuation. Music education philosophers might ask what forms of music making or pedagogical practices should be valued over others. Examples of such questions include "Is jazz more valuable for American students than European art music?" "Is popular music more valuable than less prevalent musical genres?" "Are Kodály teaching methods more valuable than Eurhythmics-centered ones?" "Are constructivist education practices more valuable than behaviorist ones?"

Importantly, axiological questions focus on what teachers and students *should* value rather than on what they currently *do* value. Asking whether more music educators value constructivist or behaviorist teaching practices is an empirical question best answered through quantitative methods. Regardless of whether more teachers value constructivist or behaviorist teaching practices, a philosopher would reason why they *should* value one practice over the other. Similarly, arguing that popular music is valuable because many people like it is not sound reasoning (see the "Appeal to People" fallacy below).

Aesthetic questions address matters related to beauty. Music education philosophers might ask what makes a piece of music or musical performance beautiful. They might also question to what extent the nature of beauty is universal versus culturally specific, or how certain criteria traditionally used to evaluate beauty hide cultural, racial, gender, or other biases. While Western philosophers from Aristotle to Kant have treated ideas related to beauty separately from other issues, these questions can also be understood as subsets of ontology (e.g., What is the nature of beauty?) and axiology (e.g., Why should one value certain forms of beauty?). As with axiological questions, researchers addressing aesthetic questions consider what *should be* considered beautiful rather than what currently *is* considered beautiful.

As indicated previously, philosophical researchers may want to peruse neuroscience research as there is now, for example, an emerging field called neuroaesthetics (e.g., Brattico, 2019; Hodges, 2016). Rather than continuing to operate in separate spheres, it might be useful if there were greater dialogue between music philosophers and neuroscientists interested in neuroaesthetics; unfortunately, it is all too common for each to work on related topics with no interchange occurring between them.

Ethical and Political Questions

Ethical questions address issues of right and wrong, including moral norms within societies. Broadly speaking, music education philosophers typically address subsets of the questions "What teaching practices are more ethical than others?" "What musical experiences are more ethical than others?" Traditional ethical schools of thought include virtue ethics, deontological or duty-based ethics, and consequentialist ethics (for more information, see Regelski, 2012). More recently, issues related to social justice, such as LGBTQIA+ concerns and antiracist pedagogy, have informed key ethical questions within the profession.

Political questions address matters related to governance and social order. Rather than focusing on the values of certain political party platforms (an axiological question), political inquiries consider relationships between forms of governance and music teaching and learning. For example, researchers might consider how current music teaching and learning settings prepare students for future civic participation.

They could also ask to what extent classroom order and governance should parallel governing structures (e.g., participatory democracy) beyond the classroom. More broadly, music education philosophers might consider when educators should prepare students to replicate the existing socioeconomic-political order versus to challenge contemporary governing institutions for the sake of improvement.

Supporting Sources

Beginning philosophical researchers may feel overwhelmed by the sheer number of citations used by seasoned authors. However, as readers become familiar with a single music education philosopher's work, they will likely observe the reuse of sources, which then become integrated with new sources across multiple studies. In other words, most philosophical researchers develop deep familiarity with only a limited number of thinkers and schools of philosophical thought. This familiar material can serve as the main supporting sources for inquiries centered on different philosophical questions and topics.

Advanced philosophical researchers continually deepen their understanding of their philosophical area of focus. They also often develop a basic understanding of many philosophical traditions and may expand their areas of emphasis over time. However, they rarely become experts in multiple, drastically different schools of thought. For instance, an author researching contemporary feminist philosophy would rarely suddenly switch to researching ancient Greek philosophy, and vice versa. Likewise, beginning philosophical researchers need not have a comprehensive understanding of diverse philosophical subsets before they can make a unique philosophical contribution.

While the ways in which advanced philosophical researchers use texts to support their work can vary greatly, beginning researchers might think about a study as necessitating two types of source material. First, philosophical researchers typically ground their work in one or more significant philosophical texts (e.g., *Democracy and Education* by John Dewey) or subsets of thought (e.g., antiracist pedagogy). Philosophical researchers drawing on one or more key texts need a basic understanding of that author's overall output and their relationship to larger schools of thought (e.g., education philosophy, pragmatism, political philosophy), but they need not have read all of their texts in depth. Likewise, those grounding their study in a particular subset of thought need a basic understanding of the key thinkers in that area, but they can focus their study on a couple of key authors and texts. Researchers also typically consult secondary sources, including summaries and critiques, related to their chosen text or subset of thought.

Second, philosophical researchers need an understanding of the music education philosophy literature related to their study. This includes research addressing their primary authors and schools of thought as well as other key components of their argument. For example, consider a researcher using poststructuralist philosopher Michele Foucault's work to investigate the nature of music improvisation practices. The scholar would want to gain a deep understanding about music education philosophical research grounded in Foucault's work and a basic understanding about music education philosophical research grounded in poststructuralism more broadly. They would also want to understand how various music education philosophers working from perspectives outside of poststructuralism have addressed improvisation.

Beginning researchers feeling overwhelmed by the diversity of philosophical thought may feel tempted to dive into one philosophical subset without considering other options. This can lead to a mismatch between one's problem, questions, and topic and the philosophical sources that could best inform one's investigation. The following brief overview of philosophical subsets prevalent in contemporary music education research may assist beginning researchers in finding the sources most relevant for their work. Many of these subsets are fluid and overlapping, and philosophical researchers do not necessarily agree about how to construct and label these categories.

Each category includes the names of a few prominent authors outside of music education. General online searches of these categories will reveal many more key thinkers. Researchers can find the music education philosophers currently engaged with these categories by searching our field's many research journals, particularly those focused on philosophy, such as *Action, Criticism, and Theory for Music Education* and *Philosophy of Music Education Review*. Since the music education philosophy community would benefit from a more diverse knowledge base, the following information should be understood as a starting point in need of further expansion.

Traditional Western Philosophical Thought

In his book *A Concise Survey of Music Philosophy*, Hodges (2017) offers a comprehensive, accessible summary of many key ideas from the Western philosophical canon. His historical overview begins with a chapter on ancient Greek philosophy, including sections on mathematics, imitation, and Aristotle. In the following chapter, "From Classical Antiquity to the Renaissance," Hodges addresses topics such as the role of the early Christian Church, Boethius, and Martin Luther. While contemporary music education philosophers continue to draw on these thinkers, they also cite more recent philosophers who have further developed these lines of thought. For example, those interested in Aristotle's virtue ethics might also engage with Alasdair MacIntyre's work.

Next, Hodges (2017) covers the 18th- and 19th-century ideas of rationalism, empiricism, and idealism along with the associated key thinkers Immanuel Kant, Friedrich Schiller, Georg Wilhelm Friedrich Hegel, and Arthur Schopenhauer. Hodges then includes a chapter on formalism, whose adherents value relationships among musical elements and emphasize the intellectual aspects of musical experiences. Key thinkers of this philosophy include Eduard Hanslick, Edmund Gurney, and Leonard Meyer.

Hodges (2017) also references a variety of 20th-century thinkers who examine expressive or emotional aspects of music. This includes Susanne Langer's assertion that music symbolizes the forms of feeling as well as emotion-related arguments made by Stephen Davies, Peter Kivy, and Jenefer Robinson. While these philosophers primarily focus on musical works, philosophical researchers interested in phenomenology emphasize the fleeting, embodied nature of music-making experiences. Important phenomenologist thinkers include Edmund Husserl, Maurice Merleau-Ponty, and Mark Johnson.

Many collegiate philosophy departments remain centered on the works of the authors listed in this section. However, music education philosophers increasingly draw on philosophical and theoretical writings utilized by humanities disciplines outside of philosophy, ranging from gender studies to history and literature. Key subsets of such thinking are described below.

Education Philosophy

Music education philosophers continue to find inspiration in the writings of education philosophers not primarily concerned with music. Pragmatist philosopher John Dewey remains one of the most cited authors within music education. Maxine Greene's imagination-based philosophies, bell hooks's examination of transgressive teaching practices, and Nel Noddings's conceptualizations of care and happiness have also received marked attention. European philosophers have emphasized the long-standing education-related concept of *Bildung*, which has no direct English translation.[1] Conferences and publications associated with groups like the Philosophy of Education Society can provide researchers information about trends within the education philosophy field.

Critical Theory

Founded in early 20th-century Germany, the Frankfurt School is typically understood as the birthplace of critical theory research. Perhaps most notably for music educators, Theodor Adorno wrote scathing critiques of the culture industry, including popular music and what he deemed passive consumerism. Later in the 20th century, Paulo Freire applied critical techniques to expose how education practices can propagate existing oppressive social hierarchies. Today philosophical

---

[1] For example, Varkøy (2010, pp. 87–90) explains three aspects of *Bildung*: culturally inherited products and processes, a metaphor of "the journey," and a critique of instrumentalism.

researchers frequently address critical theory–inspired philosophies related to social justice, including subsets such as ableism, antiracism, and heteronormativity. Authors have also drawn on postcolonialist theory, including the works of Edward Said and Gayatri Spivak.

Political Philosophy

Closely related to critical theory is the subset of political philosophy. Schools and arts organizations exist in integration with politics and policies, including educational, cultural, social, and economic ones. Political philosophers utilized by music education researchers include Hannah Arendt, Karl Marx, and Jacques Rancière. Political topics, such as capitalism, class antagonisms, democracy, globalization, and neoliberalism, also appear regularly in the music education philosophy literature.

Poststructuralist Philosophy

Poststructuralist philosophers, many of whom also address politics, challenge the structured view of existence that undergirds philosophical writings ranging from Aristotle to Langer. Music education philosophical researchers have drawn on Foucault's writings about power, surveillance, and the construction of norms. They have also attended to Gilles Deleuze's emphasis on differing and divergent possibilities and to Jacques Derrida's concept of *différence* and practices of deconstruction.

Feminist Philosophy

Often drawing on poststructuralist ideas, key contemporary feminist philosophers include Sara Ahmed, Rosi Braidotti, Judith Butler, and Donna Haraway. In addition to examining the construction of gender and sexuality, these authors considered how the favoring of male, heterosexual norms excluded and minimalized other possible ways of being in the world. Rather than aiming for equality within male, heterosexual structures, feminist authors typically call for a reimagining of life through female and queer sensibilities.

Eastern Philosophies and Beyond

The music education philosophical community increasingly recognizes the importance of looking beyond European and American philosophical traditions.

In particular, Buddhism, Confucianism, and Daoism have received attention. Research emphasizing philosophical traditions and contemporary writings from different parts of the world would be a welcome addition to the community.

Empirical and Historical Research

As noted above, philosophical researchers often draw on expertise, such as neuroscience research, outside of philosophy. Particularly when addressing ontological and epistemological questions, philosophical researchers might use the latest scientific research to support their arguments. Empirical research in areas such as happiness, trauma, wellness, and beyond can also inform philosophical research.

Likewise, philosophical researchers can draw on historical research. For example, historical research can be used to situate philosophical sources or to provide background for the contemporary teaching, learning, and music-making practices under investigation in a philosophical inquiry. Drawing on historical research, philosophical researchers may also critique previously unquestioned historical ideas and actions. Philosophical researchers have much to offer empirical researchers, and the two groups might benefit from greater dialogue (Hodges, 2013).

Careful Reasoning

When philosophical researchers engage in the processes of critique, extension, and creation (see previous chapter for descriptions of these processes), they rely on reasoning and examples. Philosophers may not consciously acknowledge the type of reasoning that they use at any given instance. However, understanding the processes of deduction and induction may assist researchers in developing their argumentation skills.

Deduction, Induction, and Counterarguments

Deduction involves a conclusion that relies on a logical sequence of true statements. In Baggini and Fosl's words (2020, p. 6), deduction occurs when "the move from premises to conclusions is such that if the premises are true, then the conclusion *must* be true." For example, one might argue that (a) Katie is a DJ and (b) DJs are musicians, so it follows that (c) Katie is a musician. In order for the example of deduction to be sound, the two premises must be true.

While many readers might deem the premise that a DJ is a musician true, I could improve the soundness of this argument by defining the term "musician." If I defined a musician as someone who engages in what Small (1998) terms "musicking," then I could argue that (a) since "musicking" encompasses all musical activity from creating to listening to rehearsing, and (b) a DJ listens to and creates music, it follows that (c) a DJ is musicking and therefore a musician. This sort of detail might seem unnecessary for those who already accepted the initial premise as true. However, since philosophical researchers need to consider how readers coming from different perspectives will engage with their arguments, this sort of detailed deductive reasoning can strengthen arguments not widely accepted within the profession.

Philosophical researchers often address issues beyond a single teaching and learning scenario. The complexities of individual teachers, students, and contexts can make it difficult to construct the true premises needed for deductive reasoning. As such, inductive reasoning often plays a central role in philosophical research that examines educational topics.

Induction involves arguing based on the probable, rather than the necessary.[2] Through induction, philosophical researchers use evidence, "be it example, analogy, predictive quality, or the like," to accept or reject a given proposition (Jorgensen, 1992, p. 98). Take, for instance, the proposition that high school choir directors in a given location do not value ethnically and racially diverse music. A philosophical researcher might support this proposition with the observation that one choir performed music predominantly written by White composers at their previous three concerts. They might then use inductive reasoning to infer that the choir director's programming practices will continue for future concerts or to generalize that neighboring choir directors perform similar repertoire. Yet, given that the director's next concert could feature all Black composers or that neighboring choir directors could have programmed more diverse music throughout the year, inductive reasoning may not provide a sound argument. Remaining aware that inductive reasoning involves the probable rather than the necessary enables philosophical researchers to couch their inductive arguments in those terms and to look for and acknowledge potential limitations in their inferences and generalizations.

Philosophical researchers can build on their deductive and inductive arguments by anticipating potential obvious objections to their arguments. They can then respond to these potential objections through counterarguments. In addition to fending off possible critique, the inclusion of counterarguments can assist researchers in clarifying and refining their central argument. For example, recall the DJ argument. A philosophical researcher might acknowledge the potential objection that Small's (1998) definition of musicking is too broad, and thus a definition of musician based on that argument is also too broad. They might develop a counterargument regarding why a broader definition of a musician is preferable to a narrower one.

---

[2] Deductive and inductive reasoning denote quite general concepts that researchers may use differently depending on the context. Philosophical researchers typically use these terms in the ways described in this chapter. See Chapter 13 to learn how researchers might employ deductive and inductive reasoning in the context of the scientific method.

Developing Reasoning Skills

Since philosophical research fundamentally involves constructing arguments, debating with thoughtful, critically minded others, including individuals outside of music education, can assist researchers in developing their reasoning skills. Philosophical researchers often test out and clarify their initial ideas with friends. Receiving feedback about gaps in logic, points that need further clarity, and potential objections early in the research process enables scholars to improve their work.

Another way of developing one's reasoning skills is by joining or starting a regular philosophy reading group. Even a small group of three to five people can provide plentiful opportunities for dialogue. Participating in such groups can also deepen and expand one's knowledge about potential sources of support for one's arguments.

The formats of music education conferences focused primarily on philosophical research, including the MayDay Group Colloquia and the International Society for the Philosophy of Music Education Symposia, specifically allow for responses and extended dialogue that can assist philosophical researchers in developing their arguments. Additionally, while digesting substantial feedback from anonymous journal reviewers is rarely easy, if viewed like an in-depth exchange with a critically minded friend, thoughtfully and graciously engaging with and responding to reviewers' observations and concerns has the potential to improve one's future philosophical research practices.

Philosophical Fallacies

Philosophical researchers can also develop their reasoning skills by recognizing and naming potential problems with their logic. A philosophical fallacy occurs when a researcher uses faulty or invalid reasoning to support their argument. While a quick online search will reveal dozens of philosophical fallacies, this section addresses the ones most applicable to philosophical research within music education.

Ad Hominem

Latin for "against the man," ad hominem arguments involve personal attacks. Stated differently, an ad hominem fallacy occurs when a philosophical researcher critiques a person's background or other features not relevant to the argument under consideration. For example, a philosophical researcher might call another author unpopular or attack their insufficient teaching or musical experiences. While one's experiences inform how one constructs one's arguments, the focus should remain on problems with the author's premises and conclusions.

Ambiguous Argument or Equivocation

Ambiguous arguments occur when a researcher uses a word or phrase to mean two different things, with the result of confusing readers. For example, using "community music" to mean only participatory ensembles in one argument and to include selective community bands and choirs in another argument creates an ambiguous argument. Philosophical researchers can avoid the ambiguous argument fallacy by clearly defining their key terms and checking for consistency of word usage throughout their studies.

Appeal to Authority

Much philosophical research involves appealing to authority in a logical way. For example, in a research study on consequentialist ethics, one can appeal to a philosophical authority on that topic. Appealing to authority becomes a fallacy when the person is not an authority on the matter at hand. For example, an award-winning band director might be an authority on efficient ensemble rehearsal techniques. However, that qualification alone does not make them an authority on programming culturally responsive repertoire or including students with exceptionalities in an ensemble. Using the band director's statements or actions to support arguments related to areas outside of their recognized expertise would involve the appeal to authority fallacy.

Bandwagon and Appeal to People

The bandwagon fallacy occurs when an author assumes the correctness of an argument based on how many people are coming to believe it (jumping on the bandwagon). For example, claiming that social emotional learning is good or correct because more and more music educators are teaching it is an example of the bandwagon fallacy. Similarly, the appeal to the people fallacy involves assuming that what is popular is right or truthful. An example of this fallacy could involve arguing that since most choir teachers incorporate popular music into their curriculum, such action is necessarily good or right.

Circular Reasoning and Begging the Question

Circular reasoning involves a logical loop in which one begins and ends with the same argument. For example, defining a musician as someone who makes music is a circular argument. Begging the question involves circular reasoning in which a conclusion merely repeats the premises rather than extends logically from them. An example of begging the question is "Dead white men have written the best music, so teachers should mostly perform their music." Rather than a logical progression, this reasoning starts by assuming what is "best" and then ends in the same place. Researchers can check to see if their argument is circular by switching the conclusion and its premise. Since "Teachers should mostly perform the music of dead white men because they have written the best music" has the same meaning as the initial statement, the argument relies on circular reasoning.

False Dilemma/False Dichotomy

A false dilemma or false dichotomy occurs when a researcher incorrectly assumes that there are only two, mutually exclusive options. For example, the argument "Teachers must choose either a social justice–oriented curriculum or a curriculum centered on competitions" omits the fact that a curriculum (a) could involve aspects of social justice and competition and (b) could center on ideas, such as social emotional learning, not directly related to either social justice or competition.

Hasty Generalization

As noted above, music education philosophical research often relies on inductive reasoning. The hasty generalization fallacy occurs when this inductive reasoning lacks rigor. For example, a researcher might draw on their experiences with two shy Brazilian students to assume that all Brazilian students are shy. In order to avoid making hasty generalizations, researchers might clarify the reach of their examples (e.g., "I have personally encountered...") and seek out more evidence (e.g., research on the relationship between shyness and culture).

Red Herring

A red herring fallacy involves incorporating irrelevant information that deviates or distracts from one's main argument. For example, imagine an argument centered on how using Western notation to teach an oral music tradition, such as Javanese gamelan, is a problematic colonialist practice. A red herring fallacy might occur if the researcher argues that Western notation can exclude students who have certain reading disabilities. While the topic of inclusion within music classrooms is important, it distracts from the main argument about colonialism.

Slippery Slope

A slippery slope argument involves assuming, rather than arguing, that a single step will set off a chain of causes and effects. For example, one might argue that a student who values winning a music competition will come to value winning at all costs, which will result in cheating at competitions and then in overtly exploiting future coworkers and employees in order to get ahead. This is fallacious reasoning because one value, winning a competition, does not necessarily result in the second value, winning at all costs, and so forth. A slippery slope argument can also occur when one assumes that a single positive action will automatically result in substantial life changes. For instance, it does not follow that a White student who learned about the racist history of a folk song will automatically understand their own racial privilege or internalize the key principles of the Black Lives Matter movement. Avoiding the slippery slope fallacy involves explaining and justifying each causal step of one's argument.

Straw Man

Since philosophical research involves engaging with other writers' arguments, almost every study necessitates some summarization of prior work. The straw man fallacy occurs when researchers do not honor the depth and complexity of another writer's argument. The researcher then refutes the misrepresented position (the straw man) rather than the original argument. Philosophical researchers might avoid the straw man argument by imagining the reaction of the author being cited reading the researcher's statements. If the author would not agree with how the researcher characterized their work, then the researcher should add further depth and clarity.

Clarity through Confusion: Philosophical Research Tips

As explained in the previous chapter, neither the philosophical research process nor the end product follows a set framework. When philosophical researchers find themselves wedded to any one idea or line of reasoning, they may neglect more convincing or logical lines of argument. As such, it is important that philosophical researchers remain open to revising their arguments throughout the research process.

This variability means that philosophical researchers constantly restructure their writing in order to refine and clarify their points. This includes both reordering sections and restructuring arguments within sections. It also often involves deleting whole paragraphs or sections or realizing that the original idea for a single paper may turn into two or more studies. In short, the initial draft of a philosophy paper will rarely resemble the final draft.

Given this unpredictability and ongoing revision, the philosophical research process can often feel frustrating. However, part of the joy of conducting philosophical research is that the author's own views and understandings develop over the course of the study. As a graduate student in the middle of conducting philosophical research explained:

> I have recognized that even when I save the document or send it for a deadline, I know that there is so much that is still unclear to me; however, I remind myself that I am as clear as I can be in the moment and that I'll glean clarity in the future. The beauty of philosophical research, to me, is allowing yourself to sit with uncertainty knowing that your thoughts will still develop through that uncertain process. (I. Cicco, personal communication, August 17, 2020)

The following seven tips might assist scholars feeling stuck in the confused curiosity that constitutes much of the philosophical research process.

Narrow, narrow, narrow

Contributing genuinely new ideas to the music education philosophy literature necessitates narrow, well-defined, and well-defended arguments. Avoid studies and even sentences within studies that attempt to address multiple big ideas (e.g., "though freedom, love, and empathy...").

Steal!

One of the best ways to improve one's own writing is to steal from those whose writing one admires. When readers come across a piece of philosophical research that they find particularly well-constructed, they might take the time to think through the author's tactics. Modeling another author's argument style using one's own unique arguments can assist emerging scholars in expanding their argument construction repertoire and ultimately in finding their own philosophical writing style.

Outline Repeatedly

Since a clear line of argument is key to high-quality philosophical research, authors may find it helpful to outline both their entire study and each section of their study early in the writing process. As a study develops further, researchers can create reverse outlines of completed sections. Since philosophical research arguments often evolve during the writing process, reducing sections of text to outline form enables researchers to see their argument more clearly, including potential omissions or fallacious arguments. Reading all of the topic sentences, that is, the first sentence in each paragraph, within each section aloud can also give researchers a sense of potential gaps or inconsistencies in their argument.

One Sentence to One Paragraph

Arguments that a philosophical researcher finds clear and logical may necessitate much more explanation for those unfamiliar with a given topic. Often, ideas that a philosophical researcher thinks needs only a single sentence could benefit from a full paragraph of detail. Looking for places throughout a study where one sentence could potentially become a full paragraph can add depth and clarity to the argument.

Talk Aloud

Simply reading their work aloud or talking through in-process ideas aloud to themselves can cause a researcher to hear an argument differently. Similarly, brainstorming about a troubling issue with friends, including those outside of music education, can reveal new insights.

Step Away

Researchers might benefit from regularly scheduled thinking and writing time, but it is important to acknowledge that one cannot force philosophical insights. When the variability and uncertainty of philosophical research feels overwhelming, researchers may find it helpful to physically step away from their work. Philosophical researchers may even observe that their best inspiration comes when they are doing other activities, such as walking outside or doing housework. When paired with patience and persistence, time away from one's study can enhance the end product.

It Is YOUR Argument and Voice

This chapter ends where the previous one began: There is no one method for doing philosophical research. Each philosophical researcher necessarily develops their own individual style of argument. In addition to philosophical texts, researchers might find their writing style inspired by news articles, blogs, podcasts, poetry, fiction, and other works. They can also honor how their personal life experiences shape their aims and voice. Through ongoing reading, reflection, and experimentation, researchers can create their own unique philosophical voice.

Summary

This chapter addressed processes that can assist philosophical researchers in developing and refining their arguments. Researchers might consider whether they plan to address an ontological, epistemological, axiological, aesthetic, ethical, or political question. They might also consider the wide range of possible sources, from ancient Greek texts to contemporary political critiques, that might best inform their arguments. Understanding how to use inductive and deductive reasoning, construct counterarguments, and avoid common philosophical fallacies can facilitate high-quality research studies. These tips might assist researchers in navigating frustrating moments and further refining their work. Yet, philosophical inquiry almost always involves prolonged uncertainty and substantial revision.

Here are some study prompts that will help you clarify your understanding of the topics presented in this chapter:

1. Pick three abstracts for philosophical articles in either *Philosophy of Music Education Review* or *Action, Criticism, and Theory for Music Education*. For each abstract, explain which category(s) of philosophical questions (e.g., ontology, epistemology, axiology, aesthetics, ethics, or politics) the author addresses.
2. Pick a music education topic of your choice. Write three different philosophical questions, each from a different category of philosophical question (e.g., ontology, epistemology, axiology, aesthetics, ethics, or politics), related to that topic. Explain why each question belongs in that category.
3. Using the articles from question 1:
   a. List the four most used sources within the article. (You do not need to count every citation; estimate which ones appear to be used most often or in the most depth. These sources may be from the same or different authors.)
   b. After conducting an online search for these author(s), explain to what philosophical subsets (traditional Western thought, education, critical theory, and so on) they belong.
4. Provide your own examples of three different philosophical fallacies. Explain how each example demonstrates the selected fallacy.
5. Explain which two of the seven philosophical research tips you find most helpful and why. (For example, have you used them in other settings? How could you imagine yourself using them when doing scholarly writing or other endeavors?)

Important Terms for Review

Ontological questions address the nature of being and reality.
Epistemological questions address the nature of understanding and knowing.
Axiological questions address issues related to valuation.
Aesthetic questions address matters related to beauty.
Deduction involves a conclusion that relies on a logical sequence of true statements.

Induction involves arguing based on the probable rather than the necessary. *Counterargument* is a reply to a potential objection to one's premise or argument. *Philosophical fallacies* occur when researchers use faulty or invalid reasoning to support their arguments.

References

Baggini, J., & Fosl, P. S. (2020). *The philosopher's toolkit* (3rd ed.). Blackwell Publishing.

Brattico, E. (2019). The neuroaesthetics of music: A research agenda coming of age. In M. Thaut & D. Hodges (Eds.), *The Oxford handbook of music and the brain* (pp. 364–390). Oxford University Press.

Damasio, A. R. (1999). *The feeling of what happens: Body and emotion in the making of consciousness*. Harcourt.

Hodges, D. (2013). Music listeners, philosophers, and researchers. *Physics of Life Reviews, 10*(3), 275–276. https://doi.org/10.1016/j.plrev.2013.06.003

Hodges, D. (2016). The neuroaesthetics of music. In S. Hallan, I. Cross, & M. Thaut (Eds.), *Oxford handbook of music psychology* (2nd ed., pp. 247–262). Oxford University Press.

Hodges, D. A. (2017). *A concise survey of music philosophy*. Taylor & Francis.

Jorgensen, E. R. (1992). On philosophical method. In R. Colwell (Ed.), *Handbook of research on music teaching and learning* (pp. 91–114). Schirmer Books.

Regelski, T. A. (2012). Musicianism and the ethics of school music. *Action, Criticism, and Theory for Music Education, 11*(1), 7–42. http://act.maydaygroup.org/articles/Regelski11_1.pdf

Small, C. (1998). *Musicking: The meanings of performing and listening*. University Press of New England.

Varkøy, O. (2010). The concept of "Bildung." *Philosophy of Music Education Review, 18*(1), 85–96. https://doi.org/10.2979/pme.2010.18.1.85

7
Characteristics of Qualitative Inquiry

Chapter Preview

This chapter includes a description of the types of research questions for which qualitative approaches to inquiry are well suited and provides an overview of characteristics that typify qualitative research studies. Qualitative approaches are appropriate for investigating research questions that are broad and open-ended, as well as for pursuing underexplored questions for which the precise variables of interest remain unclear. The central phenomenon, or main focus, of a qualitative study is likely to include complex webs of interrelated variables that may be challenging to operationalize or disentangle from one another, making a holistic view desirable. Accordingly, qualitative researchers investigate a few cases of a phenomenon in order to explore the many variables encompassed therein in depth. Qualitative research most often occurs in naturalistic settings (e.g., a music classroom) rather than in a laboratory, affording an opportunity to delve deeply into contextual features surrounding a phenomenon. Another distinguishing feature of qualitative studies is an emphasis on participants' perspectives and experiences. Qualitative research designs, and the research questions themselves, may evolve as the researcher engages in fieldwork and learns from participants. The research report offers a holistic view of, and supports theorization about, the phenomenon of interest.

Introduction

This chapter provides an overview of some typical characteristics of qualitative approaches to inquiry. A definition of qualitative research offered in Chapter 1 is restated here for ease of reference, and the rest of the chapter will describe elements of this definition in further detail.

> Qualitative research is ideal for exploring phenomena involving many interrelated variables that may be challenging to isolate for the purposes of investigation, or for situations in which the precise variables of interest have not yet been identified. Characteristics of qualitative research include exploring those phenomena within naturalistic settings, foregrounding participants' perspectives, and addressing the researcher's subjectivity. Data generation typically involves multiple sources (e.g., interview transcripts, field notes, and artifacts), which converge in a triangulating

fashion to permit more in-depth analysis than a single data source might yield. Data analysis features recursive cycles through which the researcher identifies patterns, categories, and themes that emerge from the data. The resulting research report describes, interprets, and supports theorization about the central phenomenon.

There are manifold approaches to conducting qualitative research, which differ in terms of the philosophical assumptions on which they rest as well as the interpretive frameworks that inform the inquiry. Moving from broader to more narrow levels of abstraction, qualitative researchers take distinctive approaches to research that are shaped by their philosophical orientations, the interpretive frames through which they view the subjects of their research, and the methodological approach they then use to conduct the inquiry. Among the most commonly used qualitative research designs in the scholarship on music teaching and learning are case study, grounded theory, ethnography, narrative, and phenomenology. While subsequent chapters will treat those five methodological approaches in detail, using examples drawn from music education research to illustrate their features, this chapter focuses on broad characteristics that apply across the proliferation of approaches to qualitative inquiry.

Investigating a Central Phenomenon

Ragin's (1987) observation that quantitative researchers work with a few variables and many cases, while qualitative researchers investigate a few cases and many variables, offers one way to conceptualize a key distinction between these two approaches to conducting research. The central phenomenon, or main focus, of a qualitative study is complex, multifaceted, context-dependent, and/or idiosyncratic. This phenomenon is likely to include complex webs of interrelated variables that may be challenging to operationalize or disentangle from one another for the purposes of investigation, making a holistic view desirable. Some examples of central phenomena that qualitative researchers in music education have explored include student engagement (Gurgel, 2013), musical enjoyment (Koops, 2017; Yackley, 2019), creativity (Hickey, 1995), and musical identity (Kelly-McHale, 2011, 2013). If one were to generate a list of variables pertaining to any one of these phenomena and contemplate possible relationships between those variables, the complexity that typifies the central phenomena of qualitative studies would quickly become apparent.

Teachers' professional growth offers an example of a central phenomenon well-suited for qualitative investigation that is likely to be of interest to music educators (see Conway & Edgar, 2014, for a review of qualitative studies investigating professional development for in-service music teachers). Teachers' processes of professional growth involve many elements, such as attitudes, beliefs, aspects of their personal biographies, prior experiences with professional development, the context in which they teach, and their perceptions of outcomes that are consequential for their students (Barrett, 2006; Clarke & Hollingsworth, 2002; Richardson & Placier,

2001). Further, a teacher's professional growth unfolds through processes that are nonlinear and that do not follow a prescribed sequence. For example, a changed attitude might lead a teacher to change some aspect of their practice, or a changed practice might lead to a changed attitude only after teachers observe the outcomes of that changed practice for their students (Clarke & Hollingsworth, 2002). Because of the idiosyncratic and context-dependent nature of teachers' professional growth, a qualitative approach would offer advantages for engaging with complexities inherent in the central phenomenon. An emphasis on depth and particularity, for which qualitative designs are well suited, would be useful for drawing implications about teacher education programming that accounts for individual difference and context specificity.

Owing to the complex, multifaceted nature of phenomena at the heart of qualitative inquiry, the aim is not to generalize to a broader population based on the study participants' views or experiences. Qualitative designs are useful for situations in which such generalizations would be inappropriate or inadvisable. For example, suggesting that all teachers' professional growth unfolds according to a prescribed sequence could result in a one-size-fits-all approach to professional development that fails to account for individual teachers' needs. As another example, making broad generalizations about students who identify with a particular cultural group could prompt teachers to act on misguided assumptions about students' identities. However, a detailed understanding of a particular person's or group's experience with a phenomenon, as well as how that experience unfolded under specific contextual circumstances, can support theorization about that phenomenon and suggest implications for practice. Theorization, rather than generalization to a broader population, is one chief contribution that qualitative studies can make to the professional knowledge base.

Research Questions for Which Qualitative Approaches are Well Suited

Qualitative approaches are well suited for investigating research questions that are broad and open-ended. They afford an appropriate fit for situations in which the central phenomenon has been underexplored and the variables of interest remain unclear, making an exploratory approach desirable. Following are sample research questions excerpted from qualitative studies in music education. Not every question from each study is listed, so interested readers are encouraged to consult the research reports. Note how the questions focus on investigating complex, multifaceted phenomena as well as the general, open-ended manner in which they are written.

From Conway's (2000) "Gender and Musical Instrument Choice: A Phenomenological Investigation":

- Did these high school students recognize gender stereotypes (as defined in previous research) associated with musical instruments? Were these stereotypes apparent in their discussions of instruments and gender? [From] where did they think these stereotypes derived?
- What were the self-stated personal characteristics of those who broke gender stereotypes in instrument choice? What were the self-stated personal characteristics of those who did not break gender stereotypes in instrument choice?
- What did students report as parent reactions to instrument choice? (p. 3)

From Sweet and Parker's (2019) "Female Vocal Identity Development: A Phenomenology":

- What is the lived experience of female vocal identity?
- What influences on vocal identity development do female vocalists cite? (p. 65)

From Thompson's (2016) *The Role of Rap Music Composition in the Experience of Incarceration for African American Youth:*

- How do detained youth perceive their experience of incarceration?
- What role, if any, does creating rap music have in how detained youth experience their incarceration? (p. 25)

From Woodward's (2013) *Shaping Perceptions of Musical Identity: An Ethnography of Non-Music Majors' Experiences in an Undergraduate Music Course Focused on Cultivating Creativity:*

- What does being a musician mean in *MUS 2022*, a course for non-music majors, in which improvisation is the primary strategy for developing creative thinking?
- What meanings do students in *MUS 2022* make of their experiences with music? (p. 8)

Foregrounding Participants' Views

Reviewing the research question exemplars above reveals another distinguishing feature of qualitative studies: an emphasis on participants' perspectives and experiences. Qualitative researchers are interested in "the meanings individuals or groups ascribe to a social or human problem" (Creswell & Poth, 2018, p. 42), as opposed to meaning made by the researcher or advanced in prior literature. Research questions are worded in ways that avoid presuming possible answers, leaving room for participants' views to take primacy in response to the questions. Qualitative research questions often incorporate phrases such as "How do participants describe . . . ," "What is the lived experience of . . . ," "What meanings do participants ascribe to ...," or "What are participants' perspectives on ..." To support prioritization of participants' views, many researchers attempt to redress power differentials in researcher-participant relationships and to engage participants as co-creators of meaning in the study. They may consult with participants about the research questions and engage them collaboratively in the design, analysis, interpretation, and dissemination phases of the study.

Naturalistic Settings

Qualitative researchers recognize that the control emphasized in laboratory settings, while ideal for answering certain types of research questions, may compromise understanding of what occurs in more naturalistic settings such as the real-life context of the music classroom. A laboratory setting affords a precise look at specific variables of interest and an opportunity to rule out plausible alternative explanations by controlling for possible confounding variables. The principle of experimental control is valuable for answering many questions of interest to educators, yet teachers will also recognize that the dynamic environments of their music classrooms bear little resemblance to the more controlled environment achievable in a lab setting. Therefore, qualitative researchers conduct fieldwork in locations where participants experience the central phenomenon, and they interact directly with participants in order to understand their perspectives and experiences.

Context Specificity

Conducting research within naturalistic settings provides an opportunity to delve deeply into contextual features surrounding a phenomenon of interest. Processes of music teaching and learning unfold variously, depending on the classroom, school, community, and broader cultural context in which learners are situated. Qualitative researchers take contextual factors into account, with the aim of understanding "how events, actions, and meaning are shaped by the unique circumstances in which they occur" (Maxwell, 2013, p. 30). They investigate ways in which historical, social, cultural, political, and other contextual factors influence how the central phenomenon manifests in a specific research setting.

Emergent Research Designs

Because qualitative inquiry is often exploratory in nature, and because of its emphasis on participants' perspectives and contextual elements, the research process itself may be emergent. It is often not possible to prescribe the most suitable research plan prior to entering the field and interacting with participants. A researcher's questions, interpretive frame, and design might evolve as they undertake work in the field and begin to learn from participants. The emergent nature of the research process is one characteristic of qualitative research that distinguishes it from other approaches to research. For instance, changes to design elements mid-study would compromise the experimental control that is one hallmark of experimental designs. Whether a research plan is tightly prescribed at the outset or planned intentionally to be more emergent in nature offers different advantages for answering various types of research questions. Emergent designs are well-suited for situations such as the following: the phenomenon of interest is particularly context-dependent, making it desirable to enter the field before finalizing design choices; the precise variables of interest are unclear, making an exploratory approach appropriate; or an emergent design will allow participants to provide input into the research design, offering one way to redress power differentials in the researcher-participant relationship.

Multiple Methods for Data Generation

In qualitative research, the term "data generation" is often preferred to "data collection" to emphasize the researcher's role as a key instrument in the research process. Rather than collecting data from activities undertaken independently by participants (e.g., responding to an instrument, participating in a lab-based procedure), qualitative researchers are active agents in generating data through processes such as contributing to interview conversations and authoring observational field notes. Because of the priority qualitative researchers place on learning from participants' perspectives and experiences, they rely less frequently on preexisting instruments authored by others. When they do use instruments such as interview or observational protocols, they are usually researcher-designed and open-ended enough to provide space for participants' views.

Among the most frequently used data generation techniques are interviewing (see Brinkmann & Kvale, 2015; Roulston, 2010), observing in the field (see Angrosino, 2007; Emerson et al., 2011), and collecting documents, audiovisual materials, or physical artifacts (see Bauer & Gaskell, 2007; Warren & Karner, 2015). Qualitative researchers will often consult multiple data sources with an eye toward how they corroborate or possibly contradict one another, permitting deeper analysis of the phenomenon than any single data source might offer alone. This is called triangulation of data sources (Denzin, 1978; Patton, 1999), a strategy for enhancing a study's credibility that is described further in Chapter 11.

Recursive Cycles of Thematic Analysis

Qualitative data analysis features both inductive and deductive reasoning, with the balance between these varying according to the design used. While a multitude of qualitative data analysis strategies exist, some of which are associated with particular designs, the majority of approaches involve coding data. Codes are descriptive labels that researchers apply to segments of raw data in order to signify their analytic significance in some way. Qualitative data analysis also typically involves thematic analysis, a process for which Roulston (2010) offered the following concise overview:

> This approach generally entails some form of *data reduction*, through applying codes to the data (for example, as described in grounded theory analysis) or elimination of repetitive or irrelevant data (for example, as described in phenomenological reduction) in order to define conceptual categories; *categorization of data*, through sorting and classification of the codes or data into thematic groupings or clusters, and then finally, *reorganization of the data into thematic representations* of findings through a series of assertions and interpretations. (pp. 150–151)

Data generation, analysis, and interpretation are not distinct steps that occur independently of one another, but are processes that can overlap and inform one another. Because researchers frequently engage in iterative cycles of data generation, data analysis, and interpretation, the process of qualitative data analysis is often depicted as a cycle or spiral. See, for example, Creswell and Poth's (2018) "data analysis spiral" (p. 186).

Interpretive Frameworks

Scholars have characterized the process of research as flowing from broad philosophical assumptions to interpretive frameworks, and then to the methodological procedures guiding the study's conduct. At the broadest level, the researcher's ontological, epistemological, and axiological orientations inform the design and conduct of each study. Interpretive frameworks may take the form of a paradigm, which is defined as "a basic set of beliefs that guides action," or a theory, which is "found in the literature and provide[s] a general explanation of what the researcher hopes to find in a study or a lens through which to view the needs of participants and communities in a study" (Creswell & Poth, 2018, p. 18). Examples of interpretive frameworks employed in qualitative studies include postpositivism, social constructivism, postmodernism, pragmatism, feminist theory, critical theory, queer theory, and disability theory.[1]

Accordingly, it is not only the main subject that is of interest in a qualitative study (e.g., a teacher, group of students, classroom, professional development program, rock band) but also the interpretive framework through which the subject is analyzed

---

[1] Readers are encouraged to consult Creswell and Poth (2018) and Roulston (2010) for overviews of interpretive frameworks frequently used by qualitative inquirers.

and interpreted. For instance, Vasil (2015) framed her analysis of secondary music teachers' processes of integrating popular and informal music learning practices in light of theoretical literature on teacher change (Richardson & Placier, 2001; Thiessen & Barrett, 2002), specifically Randles's (2013) *Conceptual Model of Change in Music Education*. As a second example, McCall (2015) used Bourdieu's (1986, 1993) cultural capital theory and Yosso's (2005) community cultural wealth theory as interpretive lenses for illuminating the experiences of African American undergraduate and graduate students who had transitioned from attending a historically Black college and university to a predominantly White institution. Many qualitative reports include a section titled "Conceptual Framework," "Theoretical Framework," "Theoretical Perspective," or "Interpretive Framework" that describes the study's conceptual and theoretical underpinnings.

Because qualitative research often uses emergent designs, it is not uncommon for authors' research questions and theoretical perspectives to evolve as the research unfolds. It may be strategic to enter the field with at least one possible interpretive framework that is expected to offer a useful lens through which to analyze and interpret the data. However, researchers are advised not to adhere so rigidly to a priori theoretical commitments that they miss opportunities to pursue unanticipated directions for data generation and analysis that arise after the study has begun. Once the data are in hand, it may become apparent that a different interpretive framework would be better suited for making sense of the data. Qualitative approaches afford flexibility for researchers to adjust their theoretical perspective over the course of the study. Further, in some qualitative approaches, such as grounded theory, the intended product of the inquiry is newly developed theory. In such cases, a theoretical perspective or interpretive framework may not be specified at the outset because the very purpose of the study is to generate theory.

Researcher Subjectivity

Each researcher occupies multiple social locations relating to age, cultural background, (dis)ability or exceptionality, educational background, ethnicity, gender, nationality, race, religion, sexual orientation, socioeconomic status, and so forth. They are further "positioned" in relation to their research topics according to their personal histories and prior experiences. Qualitative researchers work to understand and explicitly acknowledge their "positionality," taking into account ways that the social locations they occupy motivate their interest in particular research topics and influence their approach to generating knowledge about those topics (Thomas, 2021, p. 73).

The term "researcher subjectivity" refers to "a researcher's personal assumptions and presuppositions" (Roulston, 2010, p. 58). As Peshkin (1988) elaborated, subjectivity can further be described as the particular subset of personal qualities that contact with their research phenomenon has released. These qualities have the capacity to filter, skew, shape, block, transform, construe, and misconstrue what transpires from the outset of a research project to its culmination in a written statement. If researchers are informed about the qualities that have emerged during their research, they can at least disclose to their readers where self and subject became joined. They can at best be enabled to write unshackled from orientations that they did not realize were intervening in their research process. (p. 17)

Rather than viewing "bias" as a source of error that poses threats to a study's validity, qualitative researchers acknowledge and address how their subjectivity unavoidably influences each stage of the research process, from initially posing research questions to disseminating the findings of the research. Many qualitative researchers have moved away from a dichotomous view of objectivity versus subjectivity and have challenged the notion that bias can be "controlled for" or eliminated from a study. Roulston and Shelton (2015), for example, proposed reconceptualizing bias for qualitative inquiry as "a characteristic quality unique to a particular researcher" (p. 337). Authors describe how their subjectivity presents both assets and potential liabilities during the research process, and describe practices in which they have engaged in order to recognize and manage their subjectivity.

So far, we have considered the importance of researchers understanding and theorizing their subject position in relation to the research topic. It is also important to consider the subject positions held by both the researcher and the participant, the dynamic interactions between these, and resulting power differentials in the researcher-participant relationship. The term "reflexivity" refers to "thoughtful, self-aware analysis of the intersubjective dynamics between researcher and the researched. Reflexivity requires critical self-reflection of the ways in which researchers' social background, assumptions, positioning, and behavior impact on the research process" (Finlay & Gough, 2003, p. ix). While reflexivity may involve reflection, these two terms are distinct from one another and are not interchangeable. Reflexivity involves more than self-awareness or self-reflection and is concerned with the dynamics involved in a social relationship—in this case, the researcher-participant relationship. One aspect of reflexive practice is being thoughtful and deliberate with regard to which voices are foregrounded and how participants are represented in research reports (Roulston, 2010).

Professional debate continues in the methodological literature regarding how terms such as "objectivity," "subjectivity," "reflexivity," and "bias" are best defined and theorized (interested readers can consult Roulston & Shelton, 2015, who trace these debates and their paradigmatic associations). Terms such as "subjectivity" and "reflexivity" are generally accepted as being more consistent with the lexicon of qualitative research than is the term "bias," which tends to be more closely associated with quantitative approaches to research. Authors are encouraged to be precise in how these terms are defined and used in their research reports and to use language consistent with their chosen approach to inquiry.

Summary

This chapter has provided an overview of characteristics that typify qualitative approaches to research. Qualitative studies explore complex phenomena involving many interrelated variables that may be challenging to disentangle for the purposes of investigation. Rather than seeking a large number of study participants to promote statistical generalization to a wider population, qualitative researchers study a comparatively smaller number of cases in order to focus on depth, complexity, and particularity. Priorities in qualitative research include exploring phenomena within naturalistic settings, attending to contextual features, foregrounding participants' views, and recognizing and managing the researcher's subjectivity. Because of the emphasis on participants' views and context specificity, qualitative researchers may use emergent designs that evolve over the course of the study rather than tightly prescribing the study's procedures prior to entering the field. Data generation usually involves multiple sources such as interviews, observational field notes, and documents or other artifacts, which are analyzed in a process that emphasizes thematic analysis. The research report offers a holistic view of, and supports theorization about, the phenomenon of interest.

The following questions will assist you with making connections between concepts explored in this chapter and your own potential research interests:

1. Review some exemplar qualitative studies referenced in this chapter or recommended by your instructor. For each study, identify:
   a. The central phenomenon.
   b. The main subject of the study that illuminates the phenomenon (e.g., a teacher, student, classroom, program, event).
   c. The interpretive framework through which the subject and phenomenon are analyzed and interpreted (look for a particular theory, a set of conceptual underpinnings, or a paradigm such as postpositivism, social constructivism, transformative frameworks, postmodern perspectives, etc.).
2. Locate several qualitative studies that examine a phenomenon in which you are interested and compile the purpose statements and research questions into a single document for ease of comparison. Examine how the authors phrased their purpose statements and questions and identify trends in their specific wording. What kinds of constructions do authors use to accomplish the following:
   a. Phrase their questions in a general and open-ended way, leaving room for an emergent design or participants' perspectives.
   b. Emphasize the primacy of participants' views in seeking answers to these questions.
   c. Signal to readers that they have used a qualitative approach to inquiry.

3. Brainstorm six topics of interest that have arisen organically from your professional experiences. Of the six, choose one that would be well-suited for exploration using a qualitative approach. Taking note of trends you identified in qualitative purpose statements and research questions in response to question 2 above, write a purpose statement and set of research questions for a qualitative investigation of your selected topic.

Important Terms for Review

Qualitative research explores complex phenomena within naturalistic settings, foregrounding participants' perspectives. The researcher generates data sources such as interview transcripts, field notes, and collections of documents or artifacts, and analyzes them to illuminate themes that emerge from the data. The resulting research report provides a holistic view of, and supports theorization about, the phenomenon of interest.

A *central phenomenon* is the main focus of a qualitative study and is typically chosen for its complex, multifaceted, context-dependent, and/or idiosyncratic nature.

Data generation is an alternative term for "data collection" that is preferred by some qualitative researchers because of its emphasis on the researcher's active role in producing data.

Triangulation refers to a process of corroborating evidence from multiple data sources, methods of generating data, investigators, or theories to enhance a study's credibility (Patton, 1999).

Thematic analysis is a frequently used approach to qualitative data analysis that involves data reduction, categorization, and reorganization into thematic representations (Roulston, 2010).

Subjectivity refers to "a researcher's personal assumptions and presuppositions" (Roulston, 2010, p. 58).

Reflexivity describes "thoughtful, self-aware analysis of the intersubjective dynamics between researcher and the researched" (Finlay & Gough, 2003, p. ix).

References

Angrosino, M. V. (2007). *Doing ethnographic and observational research*. Sage.
Barrett, J. R. (2006). Recasting professional development for music teachers in an era of reform. *Arts Education Policy Review, 107*(6), 19–28. https://doi.org/10.3200/AEPR.107.6.19-28
Bauer, W. M., & Gaskell, G. D. (Eds.). (2007). *Qualitative research with text, image and sound: A practical handbook*. Sage.
Bourdieu, P. (1986). The forms of capital. In J. Richardson (Ed.), *Handbook of theory and research for the sociology of education* (pp. 241–258). Greenwood Press.
Bourdieu, P. (1993). *The field of cultural production*. Columbia University Press.

Brinkmann, S., & Kvale, S. (2015). *InterViews: Learning the craft of qualitative research interviewing* (3rd ed.). Sage.

Clarke, D., & Hollingsworth, H. (2002). Elaborating a model of teacher professional growth. *Teaching and Teacher Education, 18*(8), 947–967. https://doi.org/10.1016/S0742-051X(02)00053-7

Conway, C. M. (2000). Gender and musical instrument choice: A phenomenological investigation. *Bulletin of the Council for Research in Music Education, 146*, 1–17. https://www.jstor.org/stable/40319030

Conway, C. M., & Edgar, S. (2014). Inservice music teacher professional development. In C. M. Conway (Ed.), *Oxford handbook of qualitative research in music education* (pp. 479–500). Oxford University Press.

Creswell, J. W., & Poth, C. N. (2018). *Qualitative inquiry and research design: Choosing among five approaches* (4th ed.). Sage.

Denzin, N. K. (1978). *Sociological methods: A sourcebook*. McGraw-Hill.

Emerson, R. M., Fretz, R. I., & Shaw, L. L. (2011). *Writing ethnographic fieldnotes* (2nd ed.). University of Chicago Press.

Finlay, L., & Gough, B. (Eds.). (2003). *Reflexivity: A practical guide for researchers in health and social sciences*. Blackwell Science.

Gurgel, R. E. (2013). *Levels of engagement in a racially diverse 7th grade choir class: Perceptions of "feeling it" and "blanked out"* (Document No. 3589385) [Doctoral dissertation, University of Wisconsin–Madison]. ProQuest Dissertations & Theses Global.

Hickey, M. (1995). *Qualitative and quantitative relationships between children's creative musical thinking processes and products* (Document No. 9614754) [Doctoral dissertation, Northwestern University]. ProQuest Dissertations & Theses Global.

Kelly-McHale, J. (2011). *The relationship between children's musical identities and music teacher beliefs and practices in an elementary general music classroom* (Document No. 3456672) [Doctoral dissertation, Northwestern University]. ProQuest Dissertations & Theses Global.

Kelly-McHale, J. (2013). The influence of music teacher beliefs and practices on the expression of musical identity in an elementary general music classroom. *Journal of Research in Music Education, 61*(2), 195–216. https://doi.org/10.1177/0022429413485439

Koops, L. H. (2017). The enjoyment cycle: A phenomenology of musical enjoyment of 4- to 7-year-olds during musical play. *Journal of Research in Music Education, 65*(3), 360–380. https://doi.org/10.1177/0022429417716921

Maxwell, J. A. (2013). *Qualitative research design: An interactive approach* (3rd ed.). Sage.

McCall, J. M. (2015). *Degree perseverance among African Americans transitioning from historically Black colleges and universities (HBCUs) to predominantly White institutions (PWIs)* (Document No. 3702142) [Doctoral dissertation, Arizona State University]. ProQuest Dissertations & Theses Global.

Patton, M. Q. (1999). Enhancing the quality and credibility of qualitative analysis. *Health Sciences Research, 34*, 1189–1208.

Peshkin, A. (1988). In search of subjectivity: One's own. *Educational Researcher, 17*(7), 17–21.

Ragin, C. C. (1987). *The comparative method: Moving beyond qualitative and quantitative strategies*. University of California Press.

Randles, C. (2013). A theory of change in music education. *Music Education Research, 15*(4), 471–485. https://doi.org/10.1080/14613808.2013.813926

Richardson, V., & Placier, P. (2001). Teacher change. In V. Richardson (Ed.), *Handbook of research on teaching* (4th ed., pp. 905–947). American Educational Research Association.

Roulston, K. (2010). *Reflective interviewing: A guide to theory and practice*. Sage.

Roulston, K., & Shelton, S. A. (2015). Reconceptualizing bias in teaching qualitative research methods. *Qualitative Inquiry, 21*(4), 332–342. https://doi.org/10.1177/1077800414563803

Sweet, B., & Parker, E. C. (2019). Female vocal identity development: A phenomenology. *Journal of Research in Music Education, 67*(1), 62–82. https://doi.org/10.1177/0022429418809981

Thiessen, D., & Barrett, J. R. (2002). Reform-minded music teachers: A more comprehensive image of teaching for music teacher education. In R. Colwell & C. P. Richardson (Eds.), *The new handbook of research on music teaching and learning* (pp. 759–785). Schirmer Books.

Thomas, G. (2021). *How to do your case study* (3rd ed.). Sage.

Thompson, J. T. (2016). *The role of rap music composition in the experience of incarceration for African American youth* (Document No. 10160696) [Doctoral dissertation, Northwestern University]. ProQuest Dissertations & Theses Global.

Vasil, M. (2015). *Integrating popular music and informal music learning practices: A multiple case study of secondary school music teachers enacting change in music education* (Document No. 3743553) [Doctoral dissertation, West Virginia University]. ProQuest Dissertations & Theses Global.

Warren, C. A., & Karner, X. (2015). *Discovering qualitative methods: Ethnography, interviews, documents, and images* (3rd ed.). Oxford University Press.

Woodward, R. S. (2013). *Shaping perceptions of musical identity: An ethnography of non-music majors' experiences in an undergraduate music course focused on cultivating creativity* (Document No. 3592850) [Doctoral dissertation, University of North Carolina at Greensboro]. ProQuest Dissertations & Theses Global.

Yackley, A. (2019). *Enjoyment of music by non-participants in school music* (Document No. 27712035) [Doctoral dissertation, Ohio State University]. ProQuest Dissertations & Theses Global.

Yosso, T. J. (2005). Whose culture has capital? A critical race theory discussion of community cultural wealth. *Race, Ethnicity, and Education, 8*(1), 69–91. https://doi.org/10.1080/1361332052000341006

8
Common Elements of Qualitative Research Reports

Chapter Preview

This chapter provides an overview of key methodological decisions to be made when undertaking a qualitative study, as well as ways that researchers commonly describe the methodological approaches they have taken in their published research reports. Participant selection in qualitative research is often accomplished through purposeful sampling, with individuals selected for their perspective on or experience with the central phenomenon. Among the most commonly used data generation techniques are interviewing, observing, and collecting documents and other artifacts. Qualitative data analysis features both inductive and deductive reasoning, with the balance between these varying according to the design used. The majority of approaches entail coding data; organizing codes into broader categories, themes, or second-order constructs; visually representing themes that emerge from analysis; and developing thematic representations. The process of interpretation, involving the extraction of larger meanings from codes and themes, is not a discrete step but underlies every phase of the research process. Rather than purporting to conduct their studies objectively, qualitative researchers recognize and manage their subjectivity through a variety of means. The chapter concludes with a discussion of possible rhetorical structures for presenting and discussing findings of a qualitative study.

Introduction

While qualitative research reports can vary widely in terms of their style and presentation, many follow a predictable sequence and structure as they describe the methodological decisions that guided the study's design and conduct. Becoming acquainted with elements that many qualitative studies share is useful for becoming a more informed consumer of research reports and for understanding key decisions to be made when designing qualitative studies. Qualitative research reports often begin with an introduction and literature review, topics that have been addressed in Chapters 2 and 3. This chapter will detail commonly encountered components of a qualitative study's method section and address ways that authors may approach presenting and discussing the findings of their studies.

Music Education Research. Peter Miksza, Julia T. Shaw, Lauren Kapalka Richerme, Phillip M. Hash, and Donald A. Hodges,
Oxford University Press. © Oxford University Press 2023. DOI: 10.1093/oso/9780197639757.003.0008

Elements of a Qualitative Method Section

A qualitative study's method section will often open by identifying the research design used, with case study, ethnography, grounded theory, narrative, and phenomenology among the most frequently used designs in music education research. Authors will cite one or more methodological experts whose work has informed their approach to that design. They often include a concise definition of that design, reference its key characteristics, and explain why that design offers an appropriate methodological fit for investigating the central phenomenon. Essential components of the design will be succinctly described so that readers have a clear sense of study elements, such as the central phenomenon, main subject (e.g., an individual person, a culture-sharing group, or a case of an event, decision, policy, institution, etc.), and interpretive frame. Box 8.1 presents the introductory paragraph of a methodological overview from Kelly-McHale's (2011) dissertation, which illustrates these conventions.

Data generation and analysis procedures described subsequently in the report's method section will cohere with the specific research design chosen, and the research questions themselves are often encoded with language consistent with the lexicon of that design. Referencing a specific qualitative design also signals to readers the intended product of the inquiry, such as detailed case description(s), a theory grounded in participants' experiences, a description of the essence of an experience shared by participants, a narrative account, and so forth. Specifying the methodological approach then gives readers a sense of the form the report may take as they read on. More information about procedures and vocabulary associated with each of five primary qualitative designs follows in Chapters 9 and 10.

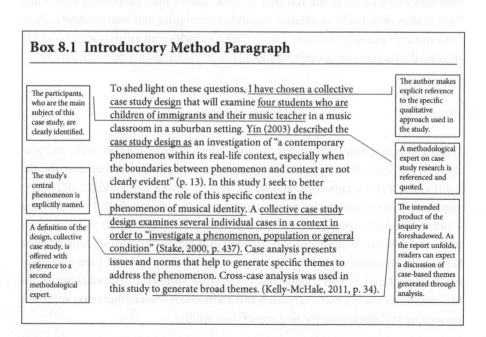

Research Context

Because qualitative researchers prioritize investigating context-dependent phenomena within naturalistic settings, reports offer detailed description of the research context and how it was selected. Authors describe features of the research context that made it particularly well-suited for illuminating the central phenomenon. For example, Kennedy's (2004) ethnographic study focused on the phenomenon of the adolescent male changing voice. The research context was the American Boychoir School, an educational institution structured entirely around adolescent singers who identified as male. The author provided detailed information about this specific school context and how its structure and organization were ideal for affording an in-depth view of how male-identifying singers experienced the adolescent voice change, as well as how their teachers guided them through this process. The article's method section opens with the following description of the research context:

> The American Boychoir School was selected for the study for the following reasons: (a) it was accessible, (b) its population of boys in Grades 5–8 provided informants with a variety of voice ranges, (c) the fact that the school consciously embraced the changing voice and included SATB [soprano, alto, tenor, and bass] repertoire sets it apart from other residential boy-choir schools in the area, and (d) few researchers to date have examined the voice change process from the perspective of boys situated in such a privileged environment. (pp. 264–265)

The author goes on to describe additional features of the research context, including historical information about the school's founding, the curriculum, aspects of the residential program, the faculty and staff, and the organization of the choirs.

Participants

A discussion of the study's participants and how they were selected often flows logically from the section describing the research context. Participant selection in qualitative research is accomplished through purposeful sampling strategies, in which individuals are selected because their perspective on or experience with the central phenomenon positions them well to generate data in response to specific research questions. Researchers have three key decisions to make with regard to sampling, and they will explain each in the report: how many participants took part in the study, who they were, and how they were selected.

Sample sizes in qualitative research vary widely across design frames but are often intentionally kept small in order to promote depth and richness of data generation.

> **Box 8.2 Research to Practice: Qualitative Research**
>
> Kennedy's (2004) investigation of teachers' and singers' experiences at the American Boychoir School offers an example of a qualitative study with clear implications for teaching practice. The researcher's analysis illuminates ways that singers' experiences of the adolescent voice change are idiosyncratic to the extent that generalizing findings to a broad population would be ill-advised. By presenting participant quotes and field note passages and interpreting them in light of extant literature, the researcher illustrated:
>
> - That the voice change may unfold very gradually (e.g., over the course of an entire academic year) or occur rapidly and dramatically (e.g., during a single summer break).
> - That the voice change may begin as early as fifth or sixth grade or still be unfolding during the high school years.
> - That singers' comfortable singing ranges vary widely between individuals, as well as within the same individual from week to week or even day to day.
> - That singers vary widely in terms of their dispositions toward singing during this process.
>
> A reader contemplating the implications of this study for their choral pedagogy would not come away with a collection of discrete strategies assumed to be appropriate for every adolescent singer (i.e., "best practices"). Rather, they would encounter vivid portraits of singers' varying experiences and examples of possible teacher responses to specific situations. Collectively, participants' experiences reveal broad principles and raise questions for teachers' consideration as they guide particular singers through the voice change. Findings suggest a need for teachers to differentiate instruction for each individual, to engage in frequent assessment of singers' vocal characteristics and dispositions toward singing, and to take an asset-based approach to teaching adolescents during a crucial stage in their development.

Sample size considerations for each of five primary approaches to qualitative research are addressed in Chapters 9 and 10, but the following are two examples that illustrate the extent of variability in qualitative sample sizes. In narrative research, it is not unusual to present the story of a single individual in order to illuminate a phenomenon, as introducing additional individuals might compromise the depth and richness with which each story can be presented. For example, Nichols (2013) collaborated closely with one gender-expansive student, Rie, to present a narrative account of her educational and musical experiences as she progressed through middle and high school. The report is focused on this single narrative account, presenting Rie's story in depth and with vivid detail. In contrast, one classic phenomenological study explored 325 high school students' experiences of "really feeling understood" (van Kaam, 1969). Here, the perspectives of many students who had experienced the phenomenon supported analysis aimed at understanding the essence of that experience. Since the aim of qualitative inquiry is not generalization to a broader population, a large sample size would be obtained not in order to reduce sampling error but instead to support exploration of and theorization about a phenomenon.

Because of the priority placed on foregrounding participants' views, an introductory portrait describing each participant may be offered in the "Participants" portion of a method section. Alternatively, detailed description of the participants may be integrated throughout the research report. Authors provide readers with rich descriptions of pertinent elements of the participants' backgrounds and identities, foregrounding participants' self-descriptions and self-identifying language. For studies engaging a larger number of participants, background characteristics may be summarized in a table. For example, a table summarizing characteristics of inservice music teachers might provide details such as years of teaching experience, the number of years in their present position, educational background, grades taught, specialty within music education (instrumental, choral, general music, early childhood, etc.), school demographic information, and so forth.

In addition to specifying the number of participants and describing their personal characteristics, authors will identify the specific qualitative sampling strategy they have used to select participants and explain their reasoning for selecting that strategy. A number of qualitative sampling strategies exist that have precise names and definitions, some of which are summarized in Table 8.1. In one frequently used approach, criterion-based sampling, cases are selected because they meet specific criteria developed by the researcher (LeCompte & Preissle, 1993). In another commonly used strategy, researchers seek "maximum variation" among individuals or sites that differ from one another along several dimensions. Additional sampling strategies include "typical case sampling," in which cases represent what is "normal" or "average"; "extreme or deviant case sampling," in which cases represent "highly unusual manifestations of the phenomenon"; and "intensity case sampling," in which cases "manifest the phenomenon intensely but not extremely" (Miles & Huberman, 1994, p. 28).

Sampling occurs at multiple levels: the site, the event or process, and the participant (Creswell & Poth, 2018). It is possible to use more than one sampling strategy in combination, drawing upon different strategies at each level of sampling. For example, a researcher might use maximum variation sampling to select schools that differ from one another along a range of demographic characteristics, such as self-reported race and ethnicity of students attending, percentage of students receiving free or reduced lunch, and percentage of students enrolled in English as a New Language programs. The researcher might then use criterion-based sampling to select teacher participants from each school who meet certain criteria, such as

Table 8.1 Sampling Strategies in Qualitative Inquiry

Type of Sampling	Purpose
Maximum variation	Documents diverse variations of individuals or sites based on specific characteristics
Homogeneous	Focuses, reduces, simplifies, and facilitates group interviewing
Critical case	Permits logical generalization and maximum application of information to other cases
Theory-based	Elaborates on and examines a construct of a theory or the entire theory
Confirming and disconfirming cases	Elaborates on initial analysis, seeks exceptions, and looks for variation
Snowball or chain	Identifies cases of interest from people who know people who know what cases are information-rich
Extreme or deviant case	Learns from highly unusual manifestations of the phenomenon of interest
Typical case	Highlights what is normal or average
Intensity	Seeks information-rich cases that manifest the phenomenon intensely but not extremely
Politically important	Attracts desired attention or avoids attracting undesired attention
Random purposeful	Adds credibility to sample when potential purposeful sample is too large
Stratified purposeful	Illustrates subgroups and facilitates comparisons
Criterion	Seeks cases that meet some criterion; useful for quality assurance
Opportunistic	Follows new leads, taking advantage of the unexpected
Combination or mixed	Meets multiple interests and needs through triangulation, flexibility
Convenience	Saves time, money, and effort, but at the expense of information and credibility

Note: From *Qualitative Data Analysis: An Expanded Sourcebook* (2nd ed., p. 28), by M. B. Miles and A. M. Huberman, 1994, SAGE. Copyright 1994 by Matthew B. Miles and A. Michael Huberman. Adapted with permission from SAGE.

years of teaching experience, experience with a particular approach to teaching, or attendance at a particular professional development program. Authors will detail the specific strategy or strategies used at each applicable level of sampling, citing methodological sources that support their decisions.

Data Generation

Authors devote a portion of the report's method section to detailing the specific data generation processes in which they have engaged, once again citing methodological sources from which they have received procedural advice. Among the most commonly used data generation techniques are interviewing, observing, and collecting documents and other artifacts. Beyond merely listing the types of data they have generated, authors provide thorough details about the purpose of each type, the extensiveness of data collected, specialized procedures they have used, and the appropriateness of these approaches for generating data in response to the research questions. For example, in describing their approach to interviewing, a researcher might detail the number and duration of interviews conducted, how and when these were scheduled (e.g., biweekly over the course of a calendar year), whether the interviews were conducted individually or in groups, general topics each interview covered, examples of representative interview questions, procedures for audio- or video-recording the interviews, noteworthy decisions made when developing transcripts, and provisions for protecting participants' privacy and maintaining confidentiality during the interviews. Some authors provide a table summarizing the number of interviews and observations conducted and their duration, the extensiveness of documents collected (e.g., 500 pages of lesson plan documents contributed by participating teachers), and the grand total for each type of data generated over the course of the study. Such tables are helpful for providing evidence of "prolonged engagement" in the field, which is one indicator of a study's trustworthiness (Creswell & Poth, 2018; Lincoln & Guba, 1985, p. 301).

The following section provides a broad overview of frequently used data generation strategies in qualitative research. This discussion is not intended to serve as an exhaustive treatment of how to engage in these processes. Methodological sources that provide procedural guidance for each of these types of data generation are recommended in Box 8.3. While it is possible for a study to rely on only one technique for data generation, as in an entirely interview-based study, qualitative researchers often consult multiple data sources to determine whether and how they corroborate one another. This is called triangulation of data sources (Denzin, 1978; Patton, 1999), and is another commonly used strategy for bolstering a study's credibility (Creswell & Poth, 2018; Tracy, 2010).

Interviews

Interviews can be as simple as "a social interaction based on a conversation" (Creswell & Poth, 2018, p. 163). They exist in many forms, such as job interviews and those featured in the media, but qualitative research interviews are specifically defined as conversations "in which an interviewer generates talk with an interviewee or interviewees for the purposes of eliciting spoken, rather than written data to examine research problems" (Roulston, 2010, p. 10). Qualitative research interviews have also been characterized as a knowledge construction process undertaken by the interviewer and interviewee in order "to understand the world from the subjects' point of view, to unfold the meaning of their experience, [and] to uncover their lived world" (Brinkmann & Kvale, 2015, p. 3). While interviews are perhaps most commonly conducted in person, they may also occur by telephone, via synchronous or asynchronous online interaction, or by corresponding through text messages or chat functions.

> **Box 8.3 Selected Methodological Resources**
>
> Recommended resources for procedural guidance about frequently used data generation techniques:
>
> **Interviewing**
>
> Brinkmann, S., & Kvale, S. (2015). *InterViews: Learning the craft of qualitative research interviewing* (3rd ed.). Sage.
>
> Krueger, R. A., & Casey, M. A. (2015). *Focus groups: A practical guide for applied research* (5th ed.). Sage.
>
> Roulston, K. (2010). *Reflective interviewing: A guide to theory and practice.* Sage.
>
> **Observing and Taking Field Notes**
>
> Angrosino, M. V. (2007). *Doing ethnographic and observational research.* Sage.
>
> Emerson, R. M., Fretz, R. I., & Shaw, L. L. (2011). *Writing ethnographic fieldnotes* (2nd ed.). University of Chicago Press.
>
> **Documents and Artifacts**
>
> Bauer, W. M., & Gaskell, G. D. (Eds.). (2007). *Qualitative research with text, image and sound: A practical handbook.* Sage.
>
> Warren, C. A., & Karner, X. (2015). *Discovering qualitative methods: Ethnography, interviews, documents, and images* (3rd ed.). Oxford University Press.

Research interviews vary in terms of their degree of structure, ranging from structured interviews at one end of a continuum to unstructured conversations at the opposite end. Structured interviews rely on predetermined questions in a prescribed sequence, which are presented to participants in a consistent manner. Potential advantages of a structured approach to interviewing include ease and efficiency of administration, increased likelihood that data generated will be germane to the research questions, and a straightforward approach to analyzing the resulting data set. However, a potential drawback is that there is little to no opportunity for participants to raise topics for exploration that the researcher has not anticipated.

An unstructured interview more closely resembles a conversation that arises organically and does not rely on a sequence of predetermined questions. In this approach, interviewees "determine the direction of the interview and the topics that emerge. As the researcher, you go in with an open mind and just try to listen and facilitate" (Thomas, 2021, p. 205). Such an approach can be useful in combination with additional forms of data generation such as participant observation, during which the researcher is interested in gaining participants' perspectives on events that unfold or topics that arise during fieldwork.

One possible facilitation challenge is the potential for unstructured interview conversations to veer off topic. Interviewers may use probes or prompts to guide conversations back to topics pertinent to the research questions. Understanding how and when to redirect interview conversations can be challenging because as participants bring new perspectives to light, their relevance may not be immediately clear to the interviewer. To redirect the conversation too quickly might prematurely shut down a productive pathway for data generation and thwart the goal of prioritizing participants' views.

Positioned toward the center of a continuum ranging from structured to unstructured is a semi-structured approach to interviewing. A semi-structured interview protocol typically includes some predetermined questions but also affords flexibility for the interviewer to pursue topics that arise spontaneously during the conversation (Fontana & Frey, 1994; Roulston, 2010). Or, rather than predetermined questions, the protocol may consist of a list of general issues to explore during the conversation. There is no expectation that a semi-structured interview will follow a prescribed sequence. Instead, the conversation unfolds more organically as the interviewer follows the interviewee's lead with regard to the topics and direction of discussion.

Another key consideration when incorporating interviews into data generation plans is whether to interview participants individually or in groups. Because participants discuss topics differently one-on-one as opposed to with a group, each format offers potential advantages. If the research topic requires participants to make sensitive disclosures, conducting individual interviews can be advantageous for protecting participants' privacy and maintaining confidentiality. One potential drawback of individual interviews is that power differentials between researcher and participant may be experienced more acutely in one-on-one interactions, which may lead participants to position interview comments in particular ways based on their perceptions of roles the researcher occupies. For instance, a music educator discussing their teaching practice with an interviewer who is a teacher educator may highlight certain practices over others based on what they anticipate the researcher would like to hear.

Group interviews are advantageous for situations in which "the group psychology itself has some impact on the situation that is of interest" (Thomas, 2021, p. 210). For example, a group of music educators may discuss teaching practice differently among colleagues than they would one-on-one with a researcher, offering different insights than those that might be supplied in individual interviews on the same topics. As another example, prior research has illustrated ways in which children contribute differently to discussions of their musical preferences depending upon the presence of peers and sociocultural characteristics of peer groups (Alden, 1998; McCrary, 2000). A child might report different musical preferences when speaking to an adult who is a music teacher than they would when speaking with a group of their peers. Both individual and group interviews can be incorporated in a data generation schedule when it is expected that each format will yield different insights, supporting a more robust analysis.

While the terms "group interview" and "focus group" are often used interchangeably, one key distinction relates to the researcher's role in facilitating each type of interview. In a group interview, the researcher takes a more active role in leading discussion and posing questions to participants. In a focus group interview, the group more actively dictates the purpose, direction, and flow of conversation. The researcher occupies the role of facilitator or moderator, prompting conversation among participants as opposed to between themselves and participants. The researcher may use verbal comments to prompt discussion. Alternatively, they may present materials such as concert programs, lesson plans, curriculum guides, musical scores, photos, or audio or video recordings to spark conversation. This data generation strategy is called "artifact elicitation."

One potential advantage of facilitating focus groups is that the group may suggest productive directions for inquiry that the researcher may not otherwise have identified or pursued. Focus group interviews are also useful for illuminating the group's shared vocabulary, knowledge, and experiences, revealing insiders' perspectives on the phenomenon of interest. On the other hand, navigating the social dynamics surrounding group conversation can present facilitation challenges to interviewers. Some individuals may tend to dominate group conversations, while others may be content to primarily listen to others' perspectives. Members of the group may have existing relationships and a shared history of which the researcher is not a part. Strategies for navigating interpersonal dynamics such as these, and for guiding productive focus group interviews more generally, have been discussed by Barbour (2007), Krueger and Casey (2015), and Roulston and Liljestrom (2010).

Observation

Qualitative researchers also generate data through observation, which has been defined as "the act of perceiving the activities and interrelationships of people in the field setting through the five senses of the researcher" (Angrosino, 2007, p. 37). They translate their observations into detailed field notes and add these to the study's data record (Emerson et al., 2011). Foci for observations may include the physical landscape, participants' actions and interactions, and conversations. Observation can also be used to support additional data generation techniques, as when observational notes are composed during the process of interviewing in order to capture nonverbal elements or contextual detail surrounding the conversation.

Thomas (2021) has drawn distinctions between structured and unstructured observations. Structured observations are those in which researchers systematically record occurrences of specific types of behavior. This approach entails assumptions that the social world can be fractured into elements that can be quantified through means such as duration recording, frequency-count recording, or interval recording. In contrast, unstructured observations are those in which researchers "watch informally (but methodically), recording important facets of what is happening" (p. 215). Yin (2009) similarly distinguishes between formal observations, which use instruments to "document the occurrence of particular behaviors of interest across a specified period of time," and casual observations, in which researchers document features of a phenomenon or research context less formally, perhaps while undertaking additional data generation activities (p. 109).

Researchers put observational data through multiple processes of transformation, translating what they observe in the field into a formal data record. In one frequently used approach, researchers engage in a process of taking informal field jottings while they observe in the field. Some observers like to create a visual representation of the layout of the physical landscape, then move to describing observable characteristics of people present in the field. Then they progress to describing the flow of activities as they unfold in real time. The sheer volume of information that can be observed in a lively social setting can be overwhelming. Recognizing the practical impossibility of writing everything down, researchers engage in a process of selective filtering, attending to information that is most germane to answering the research questions. To capture as much detail as possible while continuing to actively observe, informal field jottings are often written in a personalized shorthand.

A two-column format for composing informal field jottings is a commonly recommended approach, using the left-hand column for descriptive notes and the right-hand column for reflective notes (see Creswell & Poth, 2018, p. 171). In the "descriptive notes" column, the observer describes events that unfold in chronological order. In the "reflective notes" column, they record personal reflections, preliminary analytical insights (e.g., hunches, questions), and potential theoretical connections. Having a place to record personal reactions and reflections separately from descriptive accounts of what is occurring in the field is one strategy for managing subjectivity during the process of data generation.

The researcher will next transform their informal jottings into a more formal field record. At this stage, researchers construct field notes in more formal prose, fleshing out their shorthand jottings with as much rich, descriptive detail as possible. Because memories decay quickly, it is best to undertake this process within as short a timeframe as possible after concluding the observation. When translating jottings into more formal field notes, many authors continue to document their personal reflections and preliminary analytic insights. One way to accomplish this in a more formal field record is to embed "observer's commentary" into the notes, offsetting that commentary by indenting it similarly to a block quotation and designating the entries "O.C." (Merriam, 1998).

Authors have a number of writing-related decisions to make as they compose formal field notes, which relate to their stance as authors, the intended audience, approaches to organizing notes (e.g., chronologically, thematically, retrospectively), and how best to represent participants' meanings.[1] When transforming

---

[1] Readers are encouraged to consult Emerson et al. (2011) for detailed treatment of these matters.

field observations into formalized field notes, researchers aim for "thick description," which captures rich detail, contextual nuance, and layer upon layer of locally informed meanings (see Geertz, 1973). Denzin (2001) characterized "thick description" as that which "presents detail, context, emotion, and the webs of social relationships... [and] evokes emotionality and self-feelings.... The voices, feelings, actions, and meanings of interacting individuals are heard" (p. 100). To further illustrate, he contrasted a musical example of thick description with his own thin description:

> Sitting at the piano and moving into the production of a chord, the chord as a whole was prepared for as the hand moved toward the keyboard, and the terrain was seen as a field relative to the task.... There was chord A and chord B, separated from one another.... A's production entailed a tightly compressed hand, and B's ... an open and extended spread.... The beginner gets from A to B disjointly. (Sudnow, 1978, pp. 9–10)

> I had trouble learning the piano keyboard. (Denzin, 2001, p. 201)

Offering thick descriptions of vibrant social settings is not only a hallmark of well-constructed field notes but is also one means of enhancing the verisimilitude of research reports more generally (Creswell & Poth, 2018; Tracy, 2010).

Documents and Additional Artifacts

Additional sources of evidence used to round out a data set could include documents, archival records, audiovisual materials, and physical artifacts. Documents include curriculum guides, lesson plans, concert programs, musical scores, diary or journal entries, personal correspondence (letters or emails), and transcripts of meetings (e.g., school board, booster organizations, teachers' professional development). Archival records, usually in the form of computer files and records, could also be pertinent data sources (Yin, 2009). These might include secondary data from the U.S. Census Bureau or a state's Department of Education, or organizational records such as personnel records, budget information, or repertoire databases. Audiovisual materials could be recordings of musical performances, recordings of students' practice sessions, recordings of students' musical compositions, or videos of teachers' instruction. Additional artifacts, such as drawings, photos, or digital music files students have created, may also be consulted.

Materials such as these may serve as primary data sources in a study. For instance, Stanley (2009, 2012) explored collaborative teacher study groups as a context for elementary music educators' professional development. Transcripts of teachers' biweekly study group meetings served as a primary data source, shedding light on teachers' experiences of collaboration. Hickey (1995) collected digital scraps students generated as they composed music in her study exploring the phenomenon of creativity. The software students used was able to save musical ideas that students generated, revised, adopted, and discarded, offering insight into their processes of creating musical compositions.

Alternatively, documents, audiovisual materials, and artifacts may function primarily to support triangulation of data sources. In those cases, the materials are consulted in an effort to corroborate evidence provided by other data sources, typically interview and observational data. For instance, if teacher participants in a research study discuss upholding certain philosophical beliefs and using particular teaching strategies during interviews, lesson plans and videos of their teaching may corroborate evidence supplied in interview transcripts. When data sources fail to corroborate one another, investigating incongruities between sources may yield analytic insights and suggest directions for additional data generation (Yin, 2009).

Documents, audiovisual materials, and artifacts may also be used to support additional data generation techniques such as artifact-elicited or stimulated-recall interviews. In artifact-elicited interviews, researchers use materials such as photos, concert programs, musical scores, or musical recordings to prompt interview conversations. Participants may provide different insights through relatively informal conversations prompted by artifacts than if responding to more formal, highly structured interviews. Providing opportunities for participants to select the artifacts that will be discussed can assist in redressing power differentials between the interviewer and interviewee in that participants have agency over what will be discussed.

While artifact elicitation can be a productive data generation technique with participants of any age, researchers have noted the usefulness of this approach for generating data with children (Mayall, 2012; Morrow & Richards, 1996; Punch, 2002). Researcher-participant power differentials are particularly salient when engaging children as research participants due to differences in age, social status, authority, physical maturity, and expectations for social responsibility. Children may also have had few experiences speaking one-on-one with adults who were sincerely interested in learning from them. Sitting across a table from an adult researcher who is equipped with a notepad and recording device ready to pose a series of questions may be a daunting proposition for some children. Generating informal interview conversations around items such as drawings, pictures, recordings, and so on may be more conducive to generating meaningful data in such situations.

As one example from music education, Shaw (2014) used a range of materials to elicit adolescents' perceptions of the "terms of engagement" operating in choral rehearsals and performances (Joyce, 2003, p. 1). In a series of artifact-elicited interviews, she used concert programs, audio recordings of singers that teachers and students selected as representing ideal vocal models, and video recordings of their choral performances to spark conversations about musical experiences the students did and did not consider relevant to their cultural identities. Petersen's (2018) dissertation offers an additional example of artifact-elicited interviews in music education research. In this study, the researcher used recordings of orchestra students' independent practice sessions to prompt discussion about their idiosyncratic processes for practicing music.

Stimulated recall interviews, in which teaching videos are used to prompt educators' reflection on practice, highlight the naturalistic setting of the classroom for teachers' comment in particularly vivid ways (Calderhead, 1981; Sherin, 2004). For example, Ankney (2014) used an innovative stimulated recall approach in her study of teachers' processes of teaching musical improvisation. She equipped teachers with point-of-view cameras that were affixed to the top of a baseball cap, recording a view of the classroom similar to the teacher's own perspective. During the process of teaching, participants "tagged" moments in which they noticed something noteworthy about students' improvisations by pressing a button that produced a timestamp within the continuous video file. In subsequent interviews, the researcher and participants reviewed the timestamped moments, using those video-recorded episodes to prompt teachers' discussion. Interviews revolved around moments teachers identified as being salient rather than topics and questions chosen solely by the researcher.

Data Analysis

Yet another portion of a qualitative method section is devoted to detailing the researcher's approach to data analysis. Given the proliferation of approaches to qualitative inquiry, it is perhaps no surprise that a multitude of qualitative data analysis strategies exist. Qualitative data analysis features both inductive and deductive reasoning, with the balance between these varying according to the design used. The majority of approaches entail coding data; organizing codes into broader categories, themes, or second-order constructs; visually representing themes that emerge from analysis; and developing "thematic representations of findings through a series of assertions and interpretations" (Roulston, 2010, p. 151). Authors provide specific details about their engagement with each of these processes in their reports. The following section introduces some overarching principles of qualitative analysis, while subsequent chapters describe analysis strategies associated with particular qualitative designs.

The constant comparative method (Glaser, 1965, 1978; Strauss, 1987; Strauss & Corbin, 1994) is one foundational approach underlying many qualitative analysis processes, leading one author to characterize this method as the "curry sauce," or "basic substrate," of qualitative data analysis (Thomas, 2021, p. 224). The term "constant" refers to an iterative process of making multiple analytic passes through the data, while the term "comparison" refers to comparing data excerpts against one another to identify patterns, categories, and themes. In the constant comparative method

> the researcher simultaneously codes and analyzes the data in order to develop concepts. By continually comparing specific incidents in the data, the researcher

refines these concepts, identifies their properties, explores their relationships to one another, and integrates them into a coherent theory. (Taylor et al., 2016, p. 164)

Drawing upon Glaser (1978), who is credited as one of the originators of the constant comparative method, Bogdan and Biklen (2007) identified six steps in the process:

1. Begin collecting data.
2. Look for key issues, recurrent events, or activities in the data that become categories of focus.
3. Collect data that provide many incidents of the categories of focus with an eye to seeing the diversity of the dimensions under the categories.
4. Write about the categories you are exploring, attempting to describe and account for all the incidents you have in your data while continually searching for new incidents.
5. Work with the data and emerging models to discover basic social processes and relationships.
6. Engage in sampling, coding, and writing as the analysis focuses on the core categories. (p. 75)

Although it is possible to go through these steps in a linear fashion, these overlap in practice as researchers engage in constant comparison.

It is important to note that data generation, analysis, and interpretation are not distinct steps that occur independently of one another but are processes that can overlap and inform one another. Preliminary data analysis often occurs simultaneously with data generation, resulting in iterative cycles of data generation, analysis, and interpretation. Owing to its recursive nature, qualitative data analysis is often depicted as a spiral or cycle. Creswell and Poth's (2018) data analysis spiral is one often-cited representation, and encompasses five recommended steps: (a) managing and organizing the data, (b) reading and memoing emergent ideas, (c) describing and classifying codes into themes, (d) developing and assessing interpretations, and (e) representing and visualizing the data.

Qualitative data sets often include vast quantities of interview transcripts, field notes, documents, audiovisual materials, and additional artifacts. It is therefore essential to develop a system for naming, organizing, and securely storing files for easy access and retrieval. Decisions made during this first step in the cycle hold consequences for later stages of analysis. Researchers might plan to undertake direct comparisons across time or types of data—matters that have implications for how files are organized and managed. In addition, maintaining a formal, presentable database that can be made available to other researchers who would like to review the raw data supporting conclusions articulated in the research report is increasingly recognized as a hallmark of a well-conducted study (Yin, 2009).

Early in the analysis process, researchers engage in an initial reading of the data corpus. During this second stage of the data analysis spiral, inquirers read with an eye toward gaining a sense of the data set as a whole without becoming bogged down in a detailed process of coding. Early explorations of the data record are enhanced by memoing about preliminary analytic insights in the margins of field notes or interview transcripts. Memos are "not just descriptive summaries of data but attempts to synthesize them into higher level analytic meanings" (Miles et al., 2020, p. 88). Memoing offers a way to document analytic decision-making over the course of a study, creating an "audit trail" that can enhance the credibility of a research report (Silver & Lewins, 2014).

The third step, describing and classifying codes into themes, is a core process that typifies qualitative data analysis. Coding has been described as "aggregating the text or visual data into small categories of information, seeking evidence for the code from different databases being used in a study, and then assigning a label to the code" (Creswell & Poth, 2018, p. 190). A code, then, is a short descriptive label that researchers apply to segments of raw data in order to signify their analytic significance. A code could specify a conceptual category to which the data excerpt belongs, adopt the verbatim language participants use to describe a phenomenon (these are called "in vivo codes") or be derived from constructs from an interpretive framework or the extant literature base.

Researchers may approach coding inductively, entering the process with no preconceived notions of what codes or categories may best apply and allowing that information to emerge from the data. Or, they may approach coding deductively, examining the data for its coherence with a priori constructs related to the study's interpretive framework. Analysis often features a blend of inductive and deductive reasoning, with researchers investigating the applicability of some a priori propositions while making every effort to remain open to new, unexpected insights that present themselves in the data.

Making multiple analytical passes through the data, the researcher will refine the coding scheme by expanding or refining codes to reflect differences between instances of each and collapsing or eliminating redundant codes. Researchers develop a codebook, which contains a comprehensive list of codes used in the study with definitions specifying the types of instances to which each applies. The codebook may also provide criteria for applying the codes and examples of data excerpts to which the codes apply. Such information is essential for situations in which multiple researchers work collaboratively to analyze a qualitative data set and would like to maintain a consistent approach to coding the data. As refinements in the coding scheme are made, researchers code and recode the data corpus using the revised coding scheme.

In subsequent rounds of analysis, researchers progress from coding to classifying data. At this stage, analysts note relationships between codes, dimensions of codes, categories into which codes can be organized, secondary constructs, and broader themes that codes illuminate. The term "category" refers to an "abstract concept that analysts use to organize codes that have been generated through examination of a data set" (Roulston, 2010, p. 153).

Themes are defined as "broad units of information that consist of several codes aggregated to form a common idea" (Creswell & Poth, 2018, p. 194). Typically, researchers will identify five to seven broad themes that can be detailed and discussed in the research report. Processes of theoretical and reflective memoing continue to support the process of identifying themes. In theoretical memos, researchers document their analytic hunches, making connections between their data, interpretive frameworks, and extant literature. Or, they might compose memos about their process of generating new theory that is grounded in participants' experiences as evidenced in the data record. As researchers themselves are key instruments in the analysis and interpretation processes, reflective memos are useful for documenting the researcher's sense-making over the course of the study and reflecting on how their subjectivity may enter into this process.

The fourth step in Creswell and Poth's (2018) data analysis spiral concerns the process of interpretation, which "involves abstracting out beyond the codes and themes to the larger meaning of the data" (p. 195). After reviewing the completed data record, refined coding scheme, categories, and themes, researchers develop a series of assertions that can be presented in the research report, supported with illustrative data excerpts. Interpretation involves interweaving raw data excerpts, the author's own interpretive insights, and connections to an interpretive framework in order to put forth broad assertions about "lessons learned" (Lincoln & Guba, 1985) from the data corpus. Although interpretation is highlighted as a fourth step in Creswell and Poth's (2018) data analysis spiral, other authors emphasize that the process of interpretation is not a discrete step but underlies every phase of the research process (Peshkin, 2000).

As the researcher is engaged as a primary sense-making agent, the researcher's subjectivity is inherently involved in the process of interpretation (Peshkin, 2000). For this reason, researchers are frequently advised to challenge their own interpretations and remain alert to the possibility of alternative understandings. Strategies for managing subjectivity with respect to data analysis and interpretation include consulting with an external reviewer who can serve as "devil's advocate" (Lincoln & Guba, 1985), maintaining an "audit trail" that documents the researcher's analytic and interpretive sense-making processes (Silver & Lewins, 2014), and engaging in a process of peer debriefing (Spall, 1998).

The final phase in the data analysis spiral entails "representing and visualizing the data," a process that Thomas (2021) cautions is often underexplored by new researchers. At this stage, researchers create visual representations that elucidate relationships between themes, codes, and illustrative data excerpts. Some common formats for data visualization are comparison tables (Spradley, 1980), matrices (Miles et al., 2020), and hierarchical tree diagrams (Angrosino, 2007). Readers are encouraged to refer to Lehmberg (2008) as an example of a music education dissertation with many strong examples of data visualization.

Researcher's Role

When conducting fieldwork, a number of roles are possible for researchers to occupy, each of which has potential advantages and disadvantages for the types of data that can be generated and the interpretive sense the researcher will make of that data. The roles researchers adopt may affect participants' impression management strategies, disclosures, and willingness to grant researchers access to particular settings and interactions. Making intentional choices with regard to positioning one's role as researcher can also assist in managing subjectivity and enhancing reflexivity.

Creswell and Poth (2018) outlined four ways in which observers may position their role, ranging from complete participant to nonparticipant. A "complete participant" holds insider status within the group being studied and is fully engaged in activities alongside people in the field while generating data. In a "participant as observer" role, the researcher is not a member of the group being studied but is an active participant in the field while simultaneously generating data. These roles may be advantageous for building rapport with participants that encourages disclosure and for obtaining or maintaining an insider perspective. These roles may present challenges if the process of generating data interrupts the flow of activity in ways that are socially awkward or logistically challenging.

A third possible role is that of "nonparticipant observer," in which the researcher is present in the field, but generates data without being directly involved in activities undertaken by participants. Music education researchers frequently cite Campbell's (2010) characterization of a "nonreactive observer" role as "an anthropological fly on the wall perspective" (p. 15). This role supports researchers' ability to filter observations through the lens of a researcher rather than from the perspective of additional roles they may occupy, such as musician, teacher, or teacher educator. Researchers may also position their role as a "complete observer," generating data without being seen or noticed by research participants. It is important to note that the researcher's role may not remain consistent, but may shift and evolve throughout the process of conducting fieldwork.

Researchers are encouraged to remain alert to ways in which professional roles they occupy or have occupied in the past may enter into and influence the research process and to be strategic about the manner in which they position their role as researcher. For instance, many music education researchers have themselves been music educators in school settings. When conducting research in music classrooms, temptation to participate musically, assist students with classroom logistics, or support instruction by behaving in teacher-like ways may lead researchers to filter observations through the lens of a teacher rather than a researcher. As a former elementary music specialist conducting research in a fifth-grade music classroom, Kelly-McHale (2011) wrote:

> As a music teacher, the desire to teach is strong; the urge to get up and sing with the students is undeniable. I felt that if I became a part of the music classroom as a participant–observer ... my identity as a music teacher would begin to influence how I viewed the actions and reactions in the music classroom. (p. 136)

For these reasons, she strategically positioned her role as a "nonreactive observer" and provided readers her rationale for doing so.

Graue and Walsh (1998) coined the term "readily accessible identity" to describe a phenomenon whereby if a researcher does not deliberately take steps to orient participants to the role they desire to occupy in that setting, participants will assign them a role that makes the most sense in light of prior experiences with similar individuals in that context (p. 101). For instance, children encountering a new adult presence in a school setting may be likely to assign them the "readily accessible identity" of teacher, administrator, or other authority figure, as most of the adults with whom they interact in that setting occupy those roles. Participants' perceptions of role positions may be difficult to alter once initial impressions have formed. Therefore, if the researcher desires to occupy a role different from "teacher," or any other readily accessible identity, they will need to take strategic action to position their role in a way that will best serve the goals of the research. By not carefully planning the role of the researcher and the manner in which it will be introduced to participants, researchers risk having this crucial decision made for them upon arrival in the field.

The manner in which the researcher's role is positioned holds implications for gaining access to particular research sites; navigating power differentials in researcher-participant relationships; developing rapport with participants; and generating, analyzing, and interpreting data. Accordingly, this study element should be deliberately planned rather than left to chance. The method section of a qualitative research report will describe the role the researcher adopted, their reasons for adopting that role in relation to the aims of the inquiry, and how they went about positioning their role. This information may appear under a section heading such as "Researcher's Role" or may be integrated within a broader discussion of strategies for enhancing reflexivity and managing subjectivity.

Researcher Subjectivity

As one strategy for recognizing and managing their subjectivity, authors of qualitative reports often include a subjectivity statement (Preissle, 2008), in which they describe their positionality (see Thomas, 2021) discuss potential advantages and liabilities associated with their subjectivity, and describe practices in which they engaged to account for and manage their subjectivity (see Roulston, 2010; Roulston & Shelton, 2015). Such a statement may be presented within the method section of a research report in its own separately headed section. Authors may also integrate autobiographical notes or reflective commentary throughout the manuscript in order to offer readers insight into the subject positions they occupy, the perspective from which they write, and how their subjectivity may have influenced various stages of conducting the research.

While recognizing the impossibility of eliminating subjectivity from the research process entirely, researchers can take steps to recognize and manage their subjectivity. Strategies researchers frequently use to manage subjectivity include maintaining a researcher's journal, being interviewed using protocols they have developed themselves in order to understand their own experiences with the central phenomenon, and analyzing their own contributions to data generation (Roulston, 2010). Readers are encouraged to consult Roulston (2010) for in-depth discussion of how researchers can subject their contributions to data generation to methodological analysis. Roulston and Shelton's (2015) article, in which a research pedagogue and graduate student illustrate this process with data excerpts drawn from the student's project, offers another excellent treatment of this topic. Authors describe the specific strategies and reflexive practices in which they have engaged in their research reports, details that enhance the study's credibility (Creswell & Poth, 2018; Tracy, 2010).

Limitations

Any piece of empirical research will have limitations that should be considered when drawing conclusions from the study's results or findings. Kelly-McHale's (2011) dissertation, which explored the phenomena of adolescents' musical and cultural identities, offers an informative model of a qualitative limitations section. There are many potential influences on students' identities, not all of which may be possible to explore in a single study, no matter how well-designed. The limitations portion of Kelly-McHale's manuscript describes the scope and boundaries of her study and informs readers of factors that limit conclusions that can reasonably be drawn from the study's findings. She reminds readers, "The choice of a collective case study in one research setting prevents generalization; however, the goal of the study is to examine a unique case in a broad construct, not to generalize to a broad population" (p. 40). She then explains that the study's findings have applicability primarily for one teacher and four students within one specific classroom context:

> This study is limited to the perspectives of the four students and the music teacher involved. Although there are influences outside of the music classroom that

contribute to identity formation, I am focusing on the impact of the school music experience, so global influences such as the media will not be emphasized. (p. 41)

She further emphasizes that findings pertaining to the teacher's beliefs and practices may not readily extend to teachers who appear to share commonalities in their approach to teaching:

> I focused this study on a bound case where the teacher uses a Kodály approach. The specifics of the manner in which Karen employs Kodály-based pedagogy is not meant to be read as an example of the Kodály approach; therefore, I cannot extend my findings in this study to any group of teachers who share similar beliefs or demographics. (p. 274)

She concludes by reiterating that instead of promoting generalization, the study supports theorization about the phenomenon of musical identity for students who are second-generation immigrants:

> Despite the limitations . . . the in-depth examination of the musical experiences of the students in the school context, as bounded by the general music class experience . . . provide a clearer understanding of the influence of elementary general music on the development of identity for students who are not members of the dominant culture. (p. 275)

Too often, authors discuss limitations of qualitative studies using terms drawn from quantitative approaches such as "threats to validity" or "lack of generalizability." A common pitfall is for authors to take an apologetic tone when explaining that their study will not support generalization to a broader population, even though the decision to adopt a qualitative approach was warranted given the research questions of interest. It bears repeating that statistical generalization to a larger population is not the intent or purpose of qualitative designs, which are better suited for emphasizing depth, particularity, and context specificity. The choice to explore a complex phenomenon in rich detail is made deliberately, often because generalizing to a broader population would be inappropriate given the nature of the phenomenon studied.

Instead of describing a study's limitations with a statement such as "Unfortunately, a serious limitation of this research is the fact that results cannot be generalized to populations other than the one studied," a qualitative researcher might state, "Findings of this study have applicability primarily for [this specific group of participants] in [this particular context]." The author might then explain why an intentional decision was made not to generalize findings beyond the study population. For example, the author might emphasize that the intent of the study is not to assert that all students belonging to a particular sociocultural group learn music in the same way or that professional growth necessarily proceeds in a predictable manner for broad populations of teachers. If exploring the phenomenon with additional participants in different contexts would be desirable, the author could discuss those matters as a recommendation for future research.

Findings and Discussion

Once the methodological decisions guiding the study's conduct have been detailed, the author presents and discusses the study's findings. The findings and discussion section(s) take different forms according to the methodological approach taken by the author. For instance, findings of a case study often take the form of detailed case descriptions and a discussion of case-based themes. In a narrative study, findings are presented in the literary form of a story or narrative account. In a grounded theory study, the product of inquiry is a newly generated theory that is "grounded" in the research participants' experiences rather than taken "off the shelf" (Strauss & Corbin, 1998). The theory might be presented as a model or a set of propositions.

Regardless of which design-specific conventions an article's findings section may follow, the author will interweave illustrative data excerpts, interpretative commentary, and connections to extant literature. Here, a distinction between "data" and "evidence" may be instructive. While "data" might be used synonymously with "information," such as that contained in interview transcripts and field notes, evidence refers to "data in support of some proposition" (Thomas, 2021, p. 203). When presenting findings, authors put forth a number of assertions using data excerpts as evidence in support of those assertions. They select data excerpts, such as vibrant interview quotes or richly descriptive passages from field notes, that "let readers see for themselves the 'grounds' for analytic or interpretive claims" (Emerson et al., 2011, p. 181). Data excerpts may be selected for a number of reasons: they may highlight patterns in the data record, illuminate key contrasts or distinctions, represent what is typical or commonplace, exemplify analytic themes, or be evocative because they are unusual.

Emerson et al.'s (2011) notion of "excerpt-commentary units" offers a useful conceptualization of building blocks from which findings sections of qualitative reports can be constructed. In these units, the author's analytic commentary "focuses attention through an *analytic point*; illustrates and persuades through a *descriptive excerpt* introduced by relevant *orienting information*; and explores and develops ideas through *commentary grounded in the details of the excerpt*" (p. 182). Authors may compose excerpt-commentary units through an "excerpt strategy," in which the data excerpt is clearly offset from the author's interpretive commentary by indenting and spacing. This visual demarcation on the page signals to the reader, "Here is what I heard and observed, and here is the sense that I *now* make of it" (p. 181). Alternatively, the author may compose excerpt-commentary units through an "integrative strategy" that more fully interweaves data excerpts with interpretation, using minimal visual indicators of transitions between these elements. The author instead uses phrases such as "one illustrative episode" or "for instance" to transition between data excerpts and interpretive commentary. The author will organize multiple except-commentary units into a logical sequence with the goal of presenting a coherent, compelling presentation of the study's findings. As Atkinson (1990) summarized, "the persuasive force of an ethnographic text derives from the interplay of concrete exemplification and discursive commentary" (p. 103).

When discussing the findings, authors bring participants' views and themes that emerge from analysis back into conversation with extant literature to help readers understand how the study fits within a broader body of work in the field. As in additional research traditions, it is typical to suggest practical implications of the study's findings and recommend possible directions for future research. As a whole, a qualitative research report foregrounds the voices of participants, addresses the researcher's subjectivity, offers a holistic view and rich description of the phenomenon of interest, and supports theorization about that phenomenon.

Summary

This chapter has provided an overview of some of the most common design features of qualitative research studies. Due to the proliferation of qualitative approaches to inquiry, not all of the components described in this chapter will be present in every qualitative study. Rather, these elements will be emphasized to varying degrees according to the goals of each study and particular research questions investigated. The next two chapters delve into design features associated with specific qualitative designs: case study in Chapter 9, and ethnography, grounded theory, narrative, and phenomenology in Chapter 10.

Following are some études, or short exercises, through which you can gain hands-on experience with data generation and analysis techniques introduced in this chapter. While a full research investigation would involve more extensive involvement with these processes, these activities are useful for gaining a sense of what each entails:

1. Identify a vibrant social setting such as a coffee shop, swing dance class, train station, community music organization, or another location related to one of your research interests. Visit that setting with a partner and practice taking field notes for 30 minutes. Delay consulting with one another until after you have composed field notes as described below.
    a. While you are in the field, take informal jottings using the two-column format described in this chapter (see also Creswell & Poth, 2018, p. 171).
    b. As soon as possible after visiting the field, translate your informal jottings into a more formal field record. Use complete, formal prose to fully flesh

out the shorthand notes from your jottings. Describe what you observed using the most vivid, richly descriptive language possible.
   c. Exchange field notes with your partner and compare your two accounts of the same events.
      i. What do you notice about your respective processes of selective filtering? Which events or instances stood out as being salient to each of you? Of all that could have been observed, on what did you choose to focus and for what reasons?
      ii. What do you notice about effective writing strategies for achieving richly descriptive accounts? Which specific words, sentences, or paragraphs facilitate your recollection of the observation, transporting you back to the field? What writing strategies can you identify that contribute to rich description?
      iii. What do you notice about effective strategies for organizing field notes? Did you and your partner organize your notes chronologically? Were notes organized thematically or around key incidents?
2. Reread your field notes from the above activity and experiment with coding your data.
   a. Highlight some passages in your data that strike you as being salient, and create codes that you can use to label those passages and any similar instances to which the labels would also apply.
   b. Reread your codes with an eye toward whether they group into categories or highlight broader themes.
   c. If you were to design a study about what you observed in this single visit, what might be the central phenomenon? What research questions would be interesting to pursue? Can you think of any extant literature that might be useful for helping you make sense of the data?
3. Choose one person who was present when you visited the field that you would like to interview. To inform your decision, consider the phenomenon you identified as being of interest in prompt 2c. Then identify an individual who would be well positioned to provide their perspective on or experience with that phenomenon.
   a. For each research question you developed in response to prompt 2c, brainstorm some interview questions that could spark conversations useful for answering the research questions. As you do so, keep the differences between research and interview questions in mind. Research questions are not easily answered due to their breadth and are therefore not usually posed directly to interview participants. An interview question is more focused on an aspect of the central phenomenon, and its comparatively narrow scope makes it easier for participants to answer extemporaneously. The resources about interviewing recommended in Box 8.3 can help you to develop a protocol.

b. If possible, practice actually conducting the interview. With the participant's permission, record the interview so that you can create a text transcript for further exploration.
c. Create a text transcript for the interview. You will notice that you have decisions to make with regard to how best to represent the conversation in writing. For instance, will you preserve disfluencies in participants' responses? Will you note pauses, silences, and nonverbal elements of the conversation?
d. Examine your own speech as represented in the interview transcript.
  i. In what ways did you formulate questions that led to productive data generation?
  ii. Can you identify any trends in your approach to interviewing that shut down potentially productive avenues for conversation? For example, did you interrupt your participant? Did you move on quickly to the next question when they might have had more to say?
  iii. Do you recognize any ways that your subjectivity comes through in your interview commentary? For example, do you feel a need to affirm what participants are saying or empathize with them? Do you feel compelled to talk about your own experiences, and for what reasons?
  iv. What can you learn from examining your own contributions to the interview that will inform your approach to conducting interviews in the future?

Important Terms for Review

Purposeful sampling is an approach through which individuals are selected for research participation because their perspective on or experience with the study's central phenomenon positions them well to generate data in response to the specific research questions.

Qualitative research interviews are those "in which an interviewer generates talk with an interviewee or interviewees for the purposes of eliciting spoken, rather than written data to examine research problems" (Roulston, 2010, p. 10).

Observation, as a qualitative data generation technique, is defined as "the act of perceiving the activities and interrelationships of people in the field setting through the five senses of the researcher" (Angrosino, 2007, p. 37).

The *constant comparative method* is an approach to qualitative data analysis that entails making multiple analytic passes through the data while comparing data excerpts against one another to identify patterns, categories, and themes.

A *code* is a short descriptive label that researchers apply to segments of raw data to signify their analytic significance.

The term *category* refers to an "abstract concept that analysts use to organize codes that have been generated through examination of a data set" (Roulston, 2010, p. 153).

Themes are defined as "broad units of information that consist of several codes aggregated to form a common idea" (Creswell & Poth, 2018, p. 194).

In *subjectivity statements,* researchers describe the social locations that they occupy in relation to their research topic and participants, discuss potential advantages and liabilities associated with these positions, and describe practices in which they have engaged to account for and manage their subjectivity.

References

Alden, A. (1998). *What does it all mean? The National Curriculum for Music in a multi-cultural society* [Unpublished master's thesis, London University Institute of Education].

Angrosino, M. V. (2007). *Doing ethnographic and observational research.* Sage.

Ankney, K. L. (2014). *Master jazz teachers' noticing and responses to students during improvisation activities* (Publication No. 3669190) [Doctoral dissertation, Northwestern University]. ProQuest Dissertations & Theses Global.

Atkinson, P. (1990). *The ethnographic imagination: Textual constructions of reality.* Routledge.

Barbour, R. S. (2007). *Doing focus groups.* Sage.

Bauer, W. M., & Gaskell, G. D. (Eds.). (2007). *Qualitative research with text, image and sound: A practical handbook.* Sage.

Bogdan, R. C., & Biklen, S. K. (2007). *Qualitative research for education: An introduction to theory and methods* (5th ed.). Pearson/Allyn and Bacon.

Brinkmann, S., & Kvale, S. (2015). *InterViews: Learning the craft of qualitative research interviewing* (3rd ed.). Sage.

Calderhead, J. (1981). Stimulated recall: A method for research on teaching. *British Journal of Educational Psychology, 51*(2), 211–217. https://doi.org/10.1111/j.2044-8279.1981.tb02474.x

Campbell, P. S. (2010). *Songs in their heads* (2nd ed.). Oxford University Press.

Creswell, J. W., & Poth, C. N. (2018). *Qualitative inquiry and research design: Choosing among five approaches* (4th ed.). Sage.

Denzin, N. K. (1978). *Sociological methods: A sourcebook.* McGraw-Hill.

Denzin, N. K. (2001). *Interpretive interactionism* (2nd ed.). Sage.

Emerson, R. M., Fretz, R. I., & Shaw, L. L. (2011). *Writing ethnographic fieldnotes* (2nd ed.). University of Chicago Press.

Fontana, A., & Frey, J. (1994). Interviewing: The art of science. In N. K. Denzin & Y. S. Lincoln (Eds.), *Handbook of qualitative research* (pp. 361–376). Sage.

Geertz, C. (1973). Thick description: Toward an interpretive theory of culture. In C. Geertz (Ed.), *The interpretation of cultures* (pp. 3–30). Basic Books.

Glaser, B. G. (1965). The constant comparative method of qualitative analysis. *Social Problems, 12,* 436–445. https://doi.org/10.2307/798843

Glaser, B. G. (1978). *Theoretical sensitivity: Advances in the methodology of grounded theory.* Sociology Press.

Graue, M. E., & Walsh, D. J. (1998). *Studying children in context: Theories, methods, and ethics.* Sage.

Hickey, M. (1995). *Qualitative and quantitative relationships between children's creative musical thinking processes and products* (Document No. 9614754) [Doctoral dissertation, Northwestern University]. ProQuest Dissertations & Theses Global.

Joyce, V. M. (2003). *Bodies that sing: The formation of singing subjects* (Document No. NQ78458) [Doctoral dissertation, University of Toronto]. ProQuest Dissertations & Theses Global.

Kelly-McHale, J. (2011). *The relationship between children's musical identities and music teacher beliefs and practices in an elementary general music classroom* (Document No. 3456672) [Doctoral dissertation, Northwestern University]. ProQuest Dissertations & Theses Global.

Kennedy, M. C. (2004). "It's a metamorphosis": Guiding the voice change at the American Boychoir School. *Journal of Research in Music Education, 52*(3), 264–280. https://doi.org/10.2307/3345859

Krueger, R. A., & Casey, M. A. (2015). *Focus groups: A practical guide for applied research* (5th ed.). Sage.

LeCompte, M. D., & Preissle, J. (1993). *Ethnography and qualitative design in educational research* (2nd ed.). Academic Press.

Lehmberg, L. J. (2008). *Perceptions of effective teaching and pre-service preparation for urban elementary general music classrooms: A study of teachers of different cultural backgrounds in various cultural settings* (Document No. 3326036) [Doctoral dissertation, University of South Florida]. ProQuest Dissertations & Theses Global.

Lincoln, Y. S., & Guba, E. G. (1985). *Naturalistic inquiry*. Sage.

Mayall, B. (2012). Conversations with children: Working with generational issues. In P. Christensen & A. James (Eds.), *Research with children: Perspectives and practices* (3rd ed., pp. 120–135). Taylor & Francis.

McCrary, J. (2000). Ethnic majority/minority status: Children's interactions and affective responses to music. *Journal of Research in Music Education, 48*(3), 249–261. https://doi.org/10.2307/3345397

Merriam, S. B. (1998). *Qualitative research and case study applications in education*. Jossey-Bass Publications.

Miles, M. B., & Huberman, A. M. (1994). *Qualitative data analysis: An expanded sourcebook*. Sage.

Miles, M. B., Huberman, A. M., & Saldaña, J. (2020). *Qualitative data analysis: A methods sourcebook* (4th ed.). Sage.

Morrow, V., & Richards, M. (1996). The ethics of social research with children: An overview. *Children & Society, 10*(2), 90–105. https://doi.org/10.1111/j.1099-0860.1996.tb00461.x

Nichols, J. (2013). Rie's story, Ryan's journey: Music in the life of a transgender student. *Journal of Research in Music Education, 61*(3), 262–279. https://doi.org/10.1177/0022429413498259

Patton, M. Q. (1999). Enhancing the quality and credibility of qualitative analysis. *Health Sciences Research, 34*, 1189–1208.

Peshkin, A. (2000). The nature of interpretation in qualitative research. *Educational Researcher, 29*(9), 5–9. https://doi.org/10.3102/0013189X029009005

Petersen, E. A. (2018). *"Find what works best for you": Learning to practice in a large ensemble* (Document No. 13856107) [Doctoral dissertation, The Ohio State University]. ProQuest Dissertations & Theses Global.

Preissle, J. (2008). Subjectivity statement. In L. M. Given (Ed.), *The Sage encyclopedia of qualitative research methods* (Vol. 2, pp. 844–845). Sage.

Punch, S. (2002). Research with children: The same or different from research with adults? *Childhood, 9*(3), 321–341. https://doi.org/10.1177/0907568202009003005

Roulston, K. (2010). *Reflective interviewing: A guide to theory and practice*. Sage.

Roulston, K., & Liljestrom, A. (2010). Interviews with groups. In K. Roulston (Ed.), *Reflective interviewing: A guide to theory and practice* (pp. 33–50). Sage.

Roulston, K., & Shelton, S. A. (2015). Reconceptualizing bias in teaching qualitative research methods. *Qualitative Inquiry, 21*(4), 332–342. https://doi.org/10.1177/1077800414563803

Shaw, J. T. (2014). *"The music I was meant to sing": Adolescent choral students' perceptions of culturally responsive pedagogy* (Publication No. 3627141) [Doctoral dissertation, Northwestern University]. ProQuest Dissertations & Theses Global.

Sherin, M. G. (2004). New perspectives on the role of video in teacher education. In J. Brophy (Ed.), *Advances in research on teaching: Using video in teacher education* (Vol. 10, pp. 1–27). Elsevier.

Silver, C., & Lewins, A. (2014). *Using software in qualitative research: A step-by-step guide* (2nd ed.). Sage.
Spall, S. (1998). Peer debriefing in qualitative research: Emerging operational models. *Qualitative Inquiry, 4*(2), 280–292. https://doi.org/10.1177/107780049800400208
Spradley, J. P. (1980). *Participant observation*. Holt, Rhinehart & Winston.
Stanley, A. M. (2009). *The experiences of elementary music teachers in a collaborative teacher study group* (Publication No. 3354182) [Doctoral dissertation, University of Michigan]. ProQuest Dissertations & Theses Global.
Stanley, A. M. (2012). What is collaboration in elementary music education? A social constructivist inquiry within a collaborative teacher study group (CTSG). *Bulletin of the Council for Research in Music Education, 192*, 53–74. https://doi.org/10.5406/bulcouresmusedu.192.0053
Strauss, A. (1987). *Qualitative analysis for social scientists*. Cambridge University Press.
Strauss, A., & Corbin, J. (1994). Grounded theory methodology: An overview. In N. K. Denzin & Y. S. Lincoln (Eds.), *Handbook of qualitative research* (pp. 273–285). Sage.
Strauss, A., & Corbin, J. (1998). *Basics of qualitative research: Techniques and procedures for developing grounded theory* (2nd ed.). Sage.
Sudnow, D. (1978). *Ways of the hand*. Knopf.
Taylor, S. J., Bogdan, R. C., & DeVault, M. L. (2016). *Introduction to qualitative research methods: A guidebook and resource* (4th ed.). Wiley.
Thomas, G. (2021). *How to do your case study* (3rd ed.). Sage.
Tracy, S. J. (2010). Qualitative inquiry: Eight "big tent" criteria for excellent qualitative research. *Qualitative Inquiry, 16*(10), 837–851. https://doi.org/10.1177/1077800410383121
van Kaam, A. (1969). *Existential foundation of psychology*. Image Books.
Warren, C. A., & Karner, X. (2015). *Discovering qualitative methods: Ethnography, interviews, documents, and images* (3rd ed.). Oxford University Press.
Yin, R. K. (2009). *Case study research: Design and methods* (4th ed.). Sage.

9
Qualitative Case Study Research

Chapter Preview

Case study research is an approach defined by its focus on a single bounded system, or case, rather than a prescribed set of methodological procedures. Because of the case study's ubiquity in music education research and its accessibility to new researchers undertaking their first studies, this chapter is devoted to treating case study approaches in detail. We begin by presenting definitions from several methodological experts that collectively illuminate characteristic features of case studies. Given that a diversity of procedures can be adopted in a case study, the chapter does not put forth a definitive method for conducting one. Instead, we use examples from music education research to illustrate an array of possible case study types. As with all qualitative research, case studies do not aim to promote statistical generalization, nor are cases intended to be representative of a broader population. Rather, case studies provide rich illustration, promote vicarious experience, afford a view of a case's uniqueness, illuminate a broader issue or phenomenon, and/or support theorization about that phenomenon.

Introduction

Conducting a case study involves a decision to focus on a single entity as the main subject of the study, examining it in depth and from multiple perspectives. That entity is termed a "case" and could take the form of an individual, group, project, program, organization, community, decision-making process, or event. A case is a bounded system, meaning that researchers establish clear boundaries to delineate what is and is not contained within the case. These boundaries are most often defined with regard to time and place, but may also clarify which individuals will be included in or excluded from the case. Cases comprising the focal point of a study may be single or multiple, may be a holistic unity or contain nested elements, and may be situated historically or reflect contemporary phenomena (Barrett, 2014). The flexibility with which researchers can select their case and establish its boundaries makes case studies attractive to educational researchers.

Another type of flexibility afforded by case study designs is the multiplicity of disciplinary perspectives from which researchers can analyze and interpret their case(s). Case studies have historical roots in many disciplines, including those from which educational researchers frequently draw, such as psychology, anthropology, and sociology. As Barrett (2014) observed, "Case studies lend themselves to multiple scholarly orientations such as ethnography, phenomenology, social constructivism, and critical perspectives, where the types of questions and the stances toward inquiry are steeped in interdependent networks of thought and practice" (p. 115).

Some methodological experts use the term "case study" to refer to a design, method, or approach to conducting research. Others insist that the defining feature of a case study is its *focus* on a case as the study's main subject rather than its adherence to a prescribed method or set of procedures. For example, Stake (2005) emphasized:

> Case study is not a methodological choice but a choice of what is to be studied.... By whatever methods, we choose to study *the case*. We could study it analytically or holistically, entirely by repeated measures or hermeneutically, organically or culturally, and by mixed methods—but we concentrate, at least for the time being, on the case. (p. 443)

Thomas (2021) concurred, asserting that the case study "is like an umbrella: it covers a range of ways of doing research.... [I]t is about a focus rather than an approach" (p. 45). Case study researchers draw from an eclectic array of data generation and analysis techniques as they describe, analyze, and interpret their case(s).

Case studies, then, afford researchers flexibility along several dimensions: in selecting and delimiting the case, in adopting varied methodological procedures to explore the case, and in bringing a diversity of scholarly perspectives to bear on analysis and interpretation of the case. These are among the reasons that case studies are prevalent within educational research broadly and within music education scholarship specifically. Further, for researchers undertaking their first qualitative studies, a case study's scope and boundaries can be defined in such a way that the inquiry can be carried out in a practically manageable fashion without sacrificing substance or methodological rigor. Considering the ubiquity of case studies within music education research and their accessibility as an entry point for new qualitative researchers, this chapter is devoted to treating qualitative case study designs in depth.

Definitions and Features of a Case Study

Multiple definitions of "case study" exist in the literature. As VanWynsberghe and Khan (2014) noted, "The past three decades of scholarship on case study research have produced more than 25 different definitions of case study, each with its own particular emphasis and direction for research" (p. 81). This section presents definitions advanced by methodological experts on case study research. Readers interested in conducting a case study are encouraged to refer to resources authored by these scholars for more detailed procedural advice (see Box 9.1).

Stake's (1995) definition offers a useful point of departure: "Case study is the study of the particularity and complexity of a single case, coming to understand

> **Box 9.1 Selected Methodological Resources for Case Study**
>
> **Recommended Methodological Sources**
>
> Stake, R. E. (1995). *The art of case study research* (2nd ed.). Sage.
> Thomas, G. (2021). *How to do your case study* (3rd ed.). Sage.
> Yin, R. K. (2009). *Case study research: Design and methods* (4th ed.). Sage.
>
> **A Look at Case Studies in Music Education**
>
> Barrett, J. R. (2014). Case study in music education. In C. M. Conway (Ed.), *The Oxford handbook of qualitative research in American music education* (pp. 113–132). Oxford University Press.

its activity within important circumstances" (p. xi). The emphasis on singularity in this definition is noteworthy because in focusing on a single case, researchers are able to treat the particularity and complexity of that case in depth and from many angles. Additionally, Stake's definition stresses that case studies account for the contextual conditions, or "important circumstances," under which each case must be understood.

According to Thomas (2011), a case study encompasses two elements:

1. A "practical, historical unity," which [is] the *subject* of the case study, and
2. An analytical or theoretical frame, which [is] the *object* of the study. (p. 513)

While Stake's (1995) definition focuses primarily on a case study's subject, Thomas's (2011) definition turns attention toward the analytical or theoretical frame through which the subject can be described and interpreted:

> Case studies are analyses of persons, events, decisions, periods, projects, policies, or other systems that are studied holistically by one or more methods. The case that is the subject of the inquiry will be an instance of a class or phenomena that provides an analytical frame—an object—within which the study is conducted and which the case illuminates and explicates. (p. 513)

This definition emphasizes that cases are instances *of* some larger class or phenomenon. For example, Brenner and Strand (2013) collaborated with five teachers with varied musical specialties (violin, cello, piano, guitar, voice, and musical theater) to illuminate the phenomenon of musical expressivity. Each teacher served as a case of a personalized approach to teaching musical expression. As another example, Gerrard (2021) examined a middle school band program with robust patterns of enrollment and engagement among Latinx students as a case of barrio-based epistemologies and ontologies (Irizarry &

Raible, 2011). Her analysis demonstrated how this band program exemplified an approach to teaching that builds on sociocultural assets present in specific Latinx communities or barrios (neighborhoods). Each of these studies goes beyond merely describing a case to illuminate a broader class or phenomenon of which it is an instance. Given the emergent nature of many qualitative designs, a case study's analytical focus "crystallizes, thickens, or develops as the study proceeds" (Thomas, 2011, p. 514), a process Barrett (2014) characterized as a "dramatic unfolding" (p. 117).

Yin (2009), another widely recognized expert on case study research, offered a twofold definition:

1. A case study is an empirical inquiry that
   - Investigates a contemporary phenomenon in depth and within its real-life context, especially when
   - The boundaries between phenomenon and context are not clearly evident. (p. 18)

This definition stresses the suitability of case studies for investigating situations in which the central phenomenon and research context are inexorably intertwined. The second part of Yin's definition pivots toward features of data generation and analysis:

2. The case study inquiry
   - Copes with the technically distinctive situation in which there will be many more variables of interest than data points, and as one result
   - Relies on multiple sources of evidence, with data needing to converge in a triangulating fashion, and as another result
   - Benefits from the prior development of theoretical propositions to guide data collection and analysis. (p. 18)

This definition again references trade-offs that researchers make with regard to depth versus breadth, emphasizing that conducting case studies involves investigating a small number of cases in order to explore many intertwining variables in depth. Although considerable variability exists in the techniques for data generation used in case studies, Yin's definition highlights the use of multiple converging data sources as a prototypical feature.

Because having at least a preliminary sense of how a case can be framed theoretically carries downstream implications for generating, analyzing, and presenting data, Yin's (2009) definition emphasizes that case studies benefit from *prior* development of theoretical propositions. Theories used for these purposes can be drawn from existing literature or may be developed during the process of conducting the study as a scaffold for emerging constructs (Barrett, 2014). Bourdieu's characterization of theory as a "thinking tool" describes the latter possibility well:

There is no doubt a theory in my work, or, better, a set of *thinking tools* visible through the results they yield, but it is not built as such. . . . It is a temporary construct which takes shape for and by empirical work. (Quoted in Wacquant, 1989, p. 50)

Thus, theorization in case studies can provide a "temporary conceptual framework" that evolves from and advances the study rather than contributing toward "grand theory" (Thomas, 2021, p. 161).

Collectively, these authors' definitions illuminate several prototypical characteristics of case studies:

- Adoption of a *single* case, or limited number of cases, as the subject of the study.
- Establishment of an *object* for the study, meaning an analytical or theoretical frame through which the case is viewed. The object can also be described as a broader class or phenomenon of which the case is an instance.
- An emphasis on *depth* and *particularity* rather than generality.
- Clear establishment of the case's *boundedness* with regard to time and place.
- Examination of cases within *naturalistic settings*, taking *contextual conditions* into account.
- Use of *multiple methods* of data generation to promote a multidimensional view of the case.
- *Theorization* about a phenomenon of interest supported by examination of specific manifestations (i.e., cases) of that phenomenon in depth and from many perspectives.

The Issue of Generalizability in Case Studies

As in qualitative research more broadly, case studies do not aim to promote statistical generalization, nor are cases intended to be representative of a broader population. As such, terms such as "reliability" and "validity" are less germane to discussions of the scholarly contributions that case studies can make. As Thomas (2021) explained, "where there is no probability sample and we may have no idea at all about what we expect to find out from the research, the idea of validity is less meaningful" (p. 69). Further:

In a case study, where there is one case, expectations about reliability drop away. They drop away because with just one case, there can be no assumption from the outset that, if the inquiry were to be repeated by different people at a different time, similar findings would result. (p. 68)

Researchers have developed alternative terms, as well as nuanced shadings of the term "generalizability," for describing ways in which a case study's findings might have applicability beyond the case itself. Instead of external validity, defined in this context as an ability to generalize findings across different settings, Lincoln and Guba (1985) recommended using the term "transferability" to refer to the applicability of findings beyond the original research context. Researchers support transferability by providing thick description to the extent that readers can assess the potential transferability of findings to additional contexts. The term "case-to-case transfer" describes this precise type of transferability within case study research (Onwuegbuzie & Leech, 2010).

While acknowledging that "single cases are not as strong a base for generalizing to a population of cases as other research designs," Stake (1995) asserted that

> people can learn much that is general from single cases. They do that partly because they are familiar with other cases and they add this one in, thus making a slightly new group from which to generalize, a new opportunity to modify old generalizations. (p. 85)

With co-author Trumbull, he coined the term "naturalistic generalization" to refer to "conclusions arrived at through personal engagement in life's affairs or by vicarious experience so well constructed that the person feels as if it happened to themselves" (Stake & Trumbull, 1982, p. 85). This differs from "explicated generalizations," which people receive from experts, authorities, authors, and teachers. Stake (1995) maintained that research reports can both provide the author's explicated generalizations and leave space for readers to form their own naturalistic generalizations. He listed several "rich ingredients for vicarious experience" which can support naturalistic generalization: narrative accounts, stories, chronological presentations, personalistic descriptions, and an emphasis on time and place (pp. 86–87).

Yin's (2009) notion of "analytic generalization" is yet another reconceptualization for qualitative research. As he explained, case studies are

> generalizable to theoretical propositions and not to populations or universes. In this sense, the case study . . . does not represent a "sample," and in doing a case study, your goal will be to expand and generalize theories (analytic generalization) and not to enumerate frequencies (statistical generalization). (p. 15)

Barrett (2014) also described the potential for case studies to support theoretical extension. Building on Thomas's (2021, 2011) conception of a study's object, or analytical frame, she noted that

> clear conceptualization of a study's object is crucial for informing selection of the case(s) that comprise the study's subject as well as for relating the findings to larger issues that arise *from* the study of the case. Thus—and this is a crucial distinction for those who maintain that case studies are not generalizable—the particularistic

nature of case studies can extend to instances of the phenomenon beyond the case itself. (Barrett, 2014, p. 117)

Note that the "extension" to which she refers is a function of theorization about broader issues and phenomena rather than an attempt to extend findings to a broader population.

Rather than statistical generalization, the scholarly contribution of a well-executed case study can be described in terms of providing rich illustration, promoting vicarious experience, affording a view of a case's uniqueness, using a case to illuminate a broader issue or phenomenon, and/or supporting theorization about that phenomenon. As Stake (1995) aptly summarized:

> The real business of case study is particularization, not generalization. We take a particular case and come to know it well, not primarily as to how it is different from others but what it is, what it does.... [T]he first emphasis is on understanding the case itself. (p. 8)

Purpose Statements and Research Questions in Case Studies

Purpose statements and research questions can be encoded with vocabulary that is aligned with the specific qualitative approach taken, the researcher's chief activities, and the focus of the research. Toward those ends, Creswell and Poth (2018) have provided a useful "script" that can guide formulation of a purpose statement:

> The purpose of this _____ (narrative, grounded theory, ethnographic, case) study (was? will be?) to _____ (understand? describe? develop? discover?) the _____ (central phenomenon of the study) for _____ (the participants) at _____ (the site). At this stage in the research, the _____ (central phenomenon) will be generally defined as _____ (a general definition of the central phenomenon). (p. 132)

This chapter and the next discuss how purpose statements can be embedded with language that signals to readers the methodological approach that has been taken. For a case study, authors often use the script's first open space to specify a type of case study using terms such as the following: single, collective, or multiple; embedded or nested; parallel or sequential; bounded; intrinsic or instrumental. These terms are defined and explained subsequently in this chapter. The second space calls for a verb describing researcher activity, with verbs such as "explore," "describe," and "discover" offering some appropriate options for a case study. Not all published purpose statements are presented as formulaically as this, but articulation of a case study's purpose, subject, and object is an essential component of a clearly presented case study report.

Case studies are well-suited for answering general, open-ended research questions that often begin with words such as "what" and "how." Case studies tend to be less useful for exploring questions that ask "why?," which suggests possible cause-and-effect language. Approaches other than case studies, such as experimental or quasi-experimental designs, are better suited for supporting causal inferences. Research questions in a case study might focus on different elements within a bounded system or might revolve around issues that the researcher seeks to illuminate via the case.

A case study researcher's questions often evolve over the course of their study. Movement through various design phases—formulating the purpose and research questions, conducting a literature review, making methodological decisions about the type of case study to conduct and its procedures—is a recursive rather than a linear process. Thomas (2016) indicated that this process "needs to go backwards and forwards, with twists and turns; there will be a toing and froing as you find out new things and refine your questions and your decisions about your approach in the light of these revisions" (p. 26). While all of this "toing and froing" can initially be disconcerting, periodic wrestling with one's research questions and methodological choices usually indicates productive progress. As Stake (1995) suggested, "The researcher's greatest contribution perhaps is in working the research questions until they are just right" (pp. 19–20), advice that is broadly applicable.

Types of Case Studies

Methodological authors have used different terms to categorize the various types of case studies. One typology developed by Thomas (2011) integrates contributions from several case study experts (e.g., Bassey, 1999; de Vaus, 2001; Merriam, 1988; Stake, 1995; Yin, 2009) and provides a useful heuristic for considering which of the various types would best serve a particular research purpose (see Figure 9.1). Thomas categorized case studies according to how the *subject* is selected, the researcher's *purpose* for examining that subject, their *approach* to establishing the

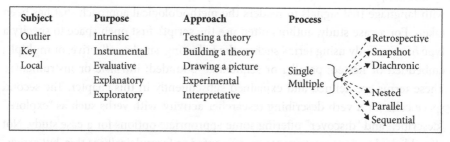

Figure 9.1 Thomas's case study typology.

Note: From *How to Do Your Case Study* (2nd ed., p. 117), by G. Thomas, 2016, SAGE. Copyright 2016 by Gary Thomas. Adapted with permission from SAGE.

study's object, and their *process* for structuring the inquiry. The following section provides an overview of the typology, using examples from music education research to illustrate an array of possible case study types.

Case Studies Categorized According to Subject

A first step in conducting a case study is selecting the case(s) that will comprise the subject and establishing the boundedness of each, a process that Ragin (1992) termed "casing" (p. 218). Following are some types of subjects that researchers might select for in-depth exploration:

- A *key case* is selected because it is a clear exemplar of a larger class.
- An *outlier case* is chosen because it is exceptional in some way and represents an intriguing deviation from what is typical.
- A *local knowledge case* is one in which the researcher's personal experience with the case informs its selection.

One point of scholarly disagreement concerns whether typicality offers a good rationale for selecting a case. Yin (2009) included "representative or typical cases" among several possible types of viable case study subjects. Other authors maintained that since the intent of case studies is not to make assertions about representativeness, typicality is a less informative feature to consider when selecting cases (e.g., Stake, 1995; Thomas, 2021).

Case Studies Categorized According to Purpose

Case studies can further be categorized according to their purpose. A key distinction, attributed to Stake (2005), is that between *intrinsic case studies*, in which the case is inherently interesting, and *instrumental case studies*, in which a case is used to provide insight into a broader issue. Additionally, case studies can be classified according to evaluative, explanatory, and exploratory purposes (Thomas, 2021).

Intrinsic

A case study has an intrinsic purpose

> if the study is undertaken because, first and last, one wants better understanding of this particular case. It is not undertaken primarily because the case represents other cases or because it illustrates a particular trait or problem, but instead because, in all its particularity and ordinariness, the case itself is of interest. (Stake, 2005, p. 445)

For example, Parker (2016) conducted an intrinsic case study in which four public school choral programs illuminated the phenomenon of community as theorized by Buber (2000), Noddings (2003, 2005), and Turner (2012). Four themes emerged from inductive analysis: "support and care, fostering a sense of belonging and acceptance, quality creates and inhibits community, and program legacy and vision" (Parker, 2016, p. 220). Parker designated her inquiry an intrinsic case study because these particular choral communities were of analytic interest in and of themselves.

Instrumental

In an instrumental case study, the case is "examined mainly to provide insight into an issue or to redraw a generalization. The case is of secondary interest, it plays a supportive role, and it facilitates the understanding of something else" (Stake, 2005, p. 445). Thomas (2021) clarified: "With an instrumental case study, the inquiry is serving a particular purpose. So, the case study is acting as an instrument—a tool" (p. 129). For example, the participants in Fitzpatrick et al.'s (2014) study were six undergraduates who self-identified as members of one or more traditionally marginalized populations within university music education programs: students who identified as BBIA, LGBTQIA+ students, and first-generation college students. The cases served the instrumental purpose of shedding light on issues of access, admission, and retention of marginalized groups in university music education programs. The study supported theorization about power structures operating within institutions of higher education and the social and cultural capital required for students to navigate them.

Explanatory

An explanatory case study is one in which "the phenomenon in which you are interested needs 'unpacking,' the connections between different parts of the issue need unravelling, and the case study offers a route to explanation" (Thomas, 2021, p. 142). For example, Major's (2013) case study sought to explain "the decision-making procedures concerning music education in one school district that sustained its music program during a time of tough economic challenge" (p. 8). Findings revealed that decision-makers' choices to fiscally support music education in this district revolved around the following:

> (a) their personal values and philosophies of music education, (b) the values and demands of the community, (c) the quality of teaching that [the school district] could afford and provide, (d) the aesthetic and utilitarian purposes of keeping music education in the curriculum, (e) the economic value that music added, and (f) how the program contributed to the overall image of the school district. (p. 17)

By focusing in depth on this single case, Major's report unraveled and explained a complex decision-making process involving multiple stakeholders and myriad intertwining variables.

Evaluative

An evaluative case study is conducted to "find out how well something is working or whether it has worked as expected" (Thomas, 2021, p. 141). In such studies, a change or new idea has been introduced, and a case study can be used to explore constellations of variables surrounding that change within a naturalistic setting. For example, while prior literature has suggested that collaborative communities of teachers can effectively promote teachers' professional growth, Bell-Robertson (2013) evaluated the extent to which a group meeting exclusively online would serve as effective professional development for early career teachers. After interviewing participants and observing their interactions in the virtual space, the researcher found that this online community addressed early career teachers' personal and affective needs more than it promoted their professional growth with regard to curriculum and instruction. In discussing the study's implications, the author underscored a need for professional development experiences that are specifically focused on curriculum and pedagogy as part of a comprehensive approach to new teacher induction.

Exploratory

An exploratory case study is conducted when "little is known and the principal purpose is to establish the 'shape' of the problem or issue" (Thomas, 2021, p. 142). For instance, Hickey (2015) explored the pedagogy of free improvisation, defined as "improvised music without any rules beyond the logic or inclination of the musician(s) involved" (p. 427). Given the freedom and idiosyncrasy inherent in this central phenomenon, specifying variables of interest at the outset of the study would have proven challenging. Hickey noted the dearth of empirical studies on free improvisation and "scarcity of pedagogical understanding of this art form" (p. 426), warranting an exploratory approach. She interviewed four university-based master pedagogues, observed their teaching, and reviewed documents such as their course syllabi. Findings illuminated the instructors' "array of unique teaching exercises, facility with nontraditional vocabulary, establishment of a safe and egalitarian teaching space . . . [and] comfort with spontaneity" (p. 425). Additional themes described the role of the pedagogue as a performer/improviser and characterized the pedagogues' leadership role as that of a guide.

Categorizing According to Approach

Theory Building and Theory Testing

Case studies can further be categorized according to the approach the researcher has taken to establish the study's object or analytical frame. Thomas (2021) positions "building a theory" and "testing a theory" at opposing ends of a continuum, explaining that researchers may emphasize either of these approaches or blend them in varying combinations. Here, "theory" refers to a framework of ideas that provides some explanation about the subject of the case study. A researcher engaged primarily in building theory brings few preconceived notions to their work, generating new theory from scratch and allowing it to emerge inductively from the data. At the other end of the continuum, a researcher engaged in theory testing would bring a preexisting framework to bear on analysis and interpretation of the case, examining the appropriateness of that theory for making sense of the phenomenon studied.

Langston and Barrett's (2008) case study exemplified both theory testing and theory building. The study's subject and object can be discerned from its purpose statement: "This article examines the manifestation of social capital in a community choir in order to contribute to our understanding of the ways in which community music engagement and participation may shape community" (p. 199). While 27 members of the choir served as participants who informed analysis and interpretation, the unit of analysis (i.e., case) was the choir rather than the individual singers within it.

In their "Theoretical Framework" section, the authors synthesized extant literature pertaining to eight distinct indicators of social capital, each with its own section heading: "participation, interaction, and civic involvement; networks and connections; families and friends; reciprocity and obligations; trust; norms and values; learning; and membership of faith-based organizations" (Langston & Barrett, 2008, p. 120). They offered evidence of the presence of each indicator in the case of this specific community choir, interweaving raw data excerpts, interpretative commentary, and connections to prior literature. In examining their data for its coherence with an existing framework, the authors took a theory testing approach. However, they also engaged in theory building, remaining open to the possibility that new or unexpected information could emerge inductively from their data. One of the study's standout findings was the authors' discovery of a ninth "previously unemphasized" indicator of social capital: "fellowship" (p. 118). With this addition and concrete exemplification of a previously unidentified indicator, the study exemplifies one of the chief scholarly contributions case studies can make: theoretical extension.

Illustration

Another way to establish a compelling analytic frame is to use a case study's subject to provide a rich illustration of its object. Thomas (2021) elaborated on the contribution that case studies providing illustration can make:

> The case study is not a proxy, an alternative for real experience, but incorporates its ingredients. It illustrates and provides metaphors by which the learner can "get inside" the problem, thinking about it and empathizing with the characters of the story being told. It enables readers or inquirers to share the experience, using their own reserves of knowledge and experience... (p. 154)

Carlow's (2006) "Diva Irina: An English Language Learner in High School Choir" exemplifies the way that a richly illustrative case study can promote vicarious experience. The participant after whom the article was titled, Irina Choi, was a 16-year-old Russian immigrant of Korean ancestry who was enrolled in a high school choral program in the United States. The article focuses on this single singer's experiences in order to illustrate "tension between the socio-cultural institution of traditional American programs and ELL [English-language learner's] previous and current experiences with singing" (p. 63). Through vignettes, the author provided snapshots of Irina's musical engagement in contrasting scenarios: a routine sight-reading exercise during one of the school's choral rehearsals and a solo performance of a Russian pop song at the school's International Night event. During in-class rhythmic sight-reading, Irina slumped in her chair, frequently checked her phone, and appeared to be generally disengaged. When extended an opportunity to perform a solo that she had selected, in a language in which she was fluent and a musical genre in which she was skilled, she performed with such confidence and finesse that the researcher described her as a "diva."

Sociocultural "discourse norms," defined in this study as cultural meaning systems (including curricular traits and instructional practices) that apply to the culture of high school choir, provided a useful lens through which to interpret Irina's experiences. Some curricular and pedagogical "norms" that have historically typified the institution of choral music education in the United States include repertoire drawn from the Western classical tradition, the bel canto tradition of singing, learning music primarily by reading notation as opposed to via aural tradition, and large ensembles as a predominant curricular offering. Irina's International Night performance emphasized different norms: repertoire drawn from vernacular music rather than the classical canon, vocal timbre and style appropriate for pop music as opposed to those emphasized in the bel canto tradition, a language in which the singer was fluent, and an individualist rather than collectivist orientation. Were a teacher to encounter Irina only in the classroom context, they might inappropriately assume that she lacked interest or skill in music. Yet, the rich description of her International Night performance vividly illustrates the high level of musical engagement that was possible for Irina when discourse norms were better aligned with her prior singing experiences and present musical interests.

This study exemplifies the utility of case study designs for illuminating a case's *uniqueness*. Irina's cultural identity, experiences of immigration, and musical background were distinctive to her as an individual. Few teachers will encounter students with facets of cultural and musical identity that correspond exactly to Irina's, making generalizations from this case less informative. Rather than revealing a set of discrete practices that may translate elsewhere, this study supports theoretical understanding of how discourse norms operate in school music organizations. Carlow (2006) integrated interview quotes, interpretive commentary, and concepts drawn from existing literature to construct a portrait of Irina through which readers can vicariously experience school music from Irina's perspective.

Taking us inside Irina's experience, the author opens space for readers to form or redraw naturalistic generalizations they may hold about English-language learners or students who appear to be disengaged during class more generally.

Interpretation

Case study researchers often situate their work within a broader interpretivist tradition characterized by particular epistemological and ontological orientations. Thomas (2021) considers interpretivism to be "the 'classic' approach to doing a case study" and describes it as "a particular approach to answering questions—an approach that assumes an in-depth understanding and deep immersion in the environment of the subject" (p. 159). Interpretivism grew in the 1920s and 1930s as an alternative to positivist orientations then prevalent in the natural sciences. Interpretivists challenged the view that it is possible to perceive a single "objective" reality, instead taking interest in the differing ways that individuals perceive the world, build meaning, and construct understandings of complex social situations. An interpretive case study often shares core characteristics of an ethnographic approach to research: conducting fieldwork *with* participants rather than purporting to conduct objective study *of* them, embracing a participant observer role in order to interact closely with participants in the field, and recognizing the inevitable presence of subjectivity rather than pursuing objectivity. In an interpretive case study, the analytic frame is established "[b]y interpreting people's words and behavior ... building theory out of the naked, raw data that are available" (p. 161).

Carlow's (2006) case study with "Diva Irina" also exemplifies an interpretivist approach. Figure 9.2 highlights some characteristic elements of that approach.

Experimental

That the word "experiment" would appear in a typology of case studies may come as a surprise to some readers. While a classic experiment involves systematically

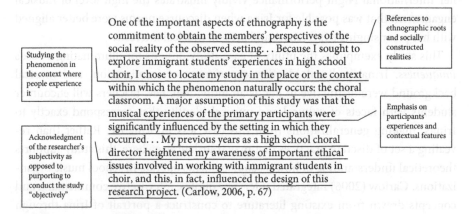

Figure 9.2 A passage exemplifying an interpretivist approach.

manipulating variables under controlled circumstances, Thomas (2021) notes the difficulty of doing so in naturalistic settings such as schools: "[T]he classroom is like an ecology: you cannot change one aspect of it without some unexpected consequence.... Playing with variables in a social situation is a bit like squeezing a balloon—it will bulge somewhere else" (p. 167). A case study in this scenario would retain its focus on the balloon more holistically, observing the bulging of the system as a whole rather than attempting to isolate or control variables for investigation. Here, the term "experimental" does not refer to a specific quantitative research design, as described elsewhere in this book. Rather, a more colloquial use of "experimentation," meaning trying something out and observing what unfolds, can describe a case study's approach.

Menard's (2015) research illustrates how elements of experimentation can be used within a case study design. She examined the cases of two contrasting high school music classrooms in which a researcher-designed composition curriculum was introduced: a general music classroom for students identified as "gifted musicians" and "a typical performance-based band program" (p. 114). Rather than comparing outcomes for groups who experienced the curriculum with those who did not, Menard introduced the curriculum and explored what unfolded within these two specific bounded systems, engaging with many intertwining variables in depth and accounting for contextual circumstances. Along with data sources typical of qualitative studies (interviews with teachers and students, observation of classroom sessions, and participant journals), this study incorporated a pre- and posttest survey assessing teachers' and students' attitudes and numerical rankings of students' compositions using Amabile's (1996) consensual assessment technique. These quantitative design elements were used to explore attitudinal shifts and features of students' creative products within each class as opposed to facilitating comparisons between treatment and control groups. The quantitative data provided analytic insight into the cases of these two classrooms, and interviews, classroom observations, and journals further contributed toward a multidimensional view of each.

Categorizing According to Process

Having decided upon the type of case adopted as the study's subject, the purpose for studying that type of case, and the approach for establishing an analytical frame, researchers will be well positioned to make additional decisions about the process they will use to conduct the study. Thomas (2021) refers to these elements as the "nuts and bolts" of the study (p. 174), and they include the number of cases, the relationships between cases, and the treatment of time within the study.

Singularity or Multiplicity

While the classic form of a case study involves focusing on a single case, another option is to focus on a limited number of cases: "When there is even less interest in one particular case, a number of cases may be studied jointly in order to investigate a phenomenon, population, or general condition. I call this a multiple case study or collective case study" (Stake, 2005, p. 445).

In a multiple case study, the main thrust of the analysis comes from comparing multiple cases that are clearly distinct from one another, with those comparisons illuminating or supporting theorization about a broader phenomenon. Each individual case is typically first analyzed through a process called *within-case analysis*. Codes, categories, and themes generated during within-case analysis represent the unique attributes of each case. In a subsequent phase of analysis, *cross-case analysis*, the researcher compares and contrasts the collection of cases in order to generate additional themes. The study's object is therefore established through cross-case comparison, leading some authors to use the term "cross-case analysis" not only to describe a phase of data analysis but also to designate this type of case study. In an embedded (Yin, 2009) or nested (Thomas, 2021) case study, some cases are situated within a larger case and the analytical frame is established by "contrasting the units *as part of the wider case*" (Thomas, 2021, p. 192). See Figure 9.3 for a graphic depiction of multiple and nested case study designs.

As examples of collective and nested case studies within music education, we offer two of the studies by Shaw (2015, 2020), one of the authors of this book. Shaw (2015) was interested in the specialized knowledge teachers held about specific urban contexts in which they taught and how that knowledge informed their practice. Using maximum variation sampling, she invited four teachers with differing cultural backgrounds who taught in demographically contrasting classrooms to participate in the study. What counted as "good teaching" in each of these settings depended not only on the nature of the subject to be taught but also the specific urban classroom, school, and community in which the learning would unfold,

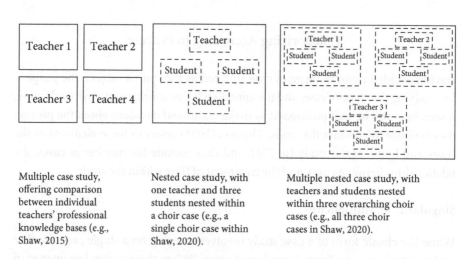

Figure 9.3 Examples of multiple and nested case study designs.

reflecting the entanglement of phenomenon and context that typifies case studies (Yin, 2009). This study is an example of a collective case study, with the four teachers providing illustrative cases of context-specific teacher knowledge in action. Because the central phenomenon involved teachers' knowledge of and responses to differing urban educational contexts, cross-case comparisons were essential to establishing the analytic frame.

A key finding from Shaw (2015) was that teachers drew on context-specific knowledge as they engaged in culturally responsive pedagogy (CRP), leading her to conduct a second study with these teachers that would explore CRP as the central phenomenon (Shaw, 2020). CRP is defined as an asset-based approach to teaching that honors and builds upon the strengths, knowledge, perspectives, and experiences of culturally diverse learners to make learning more relevant to and effective for them (Gay, 2010). Because teachers design CRP in response to particular students, and because it unfolds differently according to the classroom, school, and community contexts in which it is practiced, a research design would ideally afford a view of all of those elements. Shaw (2020) selected a multiple nested case study design in which three demographically contrasting choir classrooms served as the overarching cases. One teacher and three students were "nested" within each choir case and informed the analysis. This design then supported several layers of within- and cross-case analysis:

- Within-case analysis of the nested cases illuminated facets of children's cultural backgrounds and identities that served as bases for CRP and distinctive aspects of teachers' knowledge, skills, and dispositions that supported CRP.
- Cross-case analysis between the nested cases illuminated how CRP unfolded through the dynamic interactions between teachers and learners.
- Analysis focused on how the nested cases (i.e., teachers and students) fit within the overarching case was essential in this study, because CRP must be interpreted in light of the particular classroom and community context in which it unfolds.
- Cross-case analysis of how CRP unfolded in each of the three choir cases supported broader theorization about how CRP can be designed for particular learners who are situated within specific classrooms and communities.

Multiple case studies can further be classified as parallel or sequential. In a parallel study, all of the cases are studied simultaneously and there is no expectation that what occurs with one case will affect any other. Shaw's (2015, 2020) studies both qualify as parallel case studies. In contrast, a sequential case study examines cases one after another because "there is an assumption that what has happened in one or in an intervening period will in some way affect the next" (Thomas, 2021, p. 195).

The treatment of time is another key consideration in case study design. Accordingly, Thomas (2021) offers three additional terms used to categorize case studies:

- A *retrospective* study involves "the collection of data relating to the past phenomenon, situation, or event" (p. 178). Because the case is situated in the past, data generation revolves around documents or archival records as well as interviews with individuals who experienced the phenomenon in the past.
- In a *snapshot* study, a specified increment of time (e.g., a day, a week, a month) plays a primary role in establishing the boundedness of the study. The analytical frame will be established through temporal juxtaposition within a precise timeframe.
- In a *diachronic* study, the passage of time is an important dimension of the study's object. It is distinct from a sequential study, in which two or more studies are conducted one after the other, by showing how the central phenomenon manifests over a passage of time.

Data Generation, Analysis, and Presentation in Case Studies

As Thomas (2021) elaborates, case studies can draw upon an eclectic array of data generation and analysis procedures:

> [T]he case study has broad and capacious arms: it loves all methods. . . . [W]ith different elements of the case study, you may use other design frames under the umbrella of the case study. . . . The important thing is that you are using a case study to examine your case in detail. In doing this, you choose whatever methods and subsidiary design frames you can think of to help answer questions about your singular case. (p. 47)

Because case studies are defined more in terms of their focus on one or more cases than by a prescribed set of procedures, we next describe some frequently used approaches to data generation, analysis, and presentation in case studies rather than offering a definitive how-to guide.

Data Generation

When generating data, case study researchers amass plentiful evidence in pursuit of two goals: permitting in-depth analysis of the case(s) and promoting exploration of the case(s) from multiple perspectives. Thomas (2021) advises that researchers "must 'drill down' as deep as we possibly can to get evidence, penetrating into every nook and cranny, and squeezing out every little bit that can be found" (p. 5). Multiplicity of data sources is another hallmark of data generation in case studies. Researchers corroborate evidence from multiple data sources such as interviews, observations, and documents in order to facilitate triangulation of data and promote a multidimensional view of the case. An eclectic array of data sources is used in case studies, which could include individual interviews, group or focus group interviews, diaries or journals, documents, archival records, physical artifacts, questionnaires, observations, images, and audiovisual materials. Quantitative data such as measurements, statistics, and other numerical information may also be used under a case study's "umbrella."

Data Analysis

As with data generation, case study researchers draw upon a multiplicity of data analysis procedures. Broadly speaking, many researchers use a process of thematic analysis involving data reduction (through coding), categorization, and reorganization into thematic representations (Roulston, 2010). Analysis techniques may be adopted from a different design frame, in which case researchers will use specific terms and cite methodological authorities associated with that particular technique.

Decisions made about the type of case study to pursue will have implications for the process through which analysis proceeds. For intrinsic case studies, the primary goal of analysis will be to understand the case itself, while for instrumental case studies, analysis will be oriented toward issues and relationships identified in the research questions. In a multiple case study, researchers often first conduct within-case analysis, then progress to cross-case analysis.

Stake (1995) describes four forms of data analysis and interpretation that are prominent in case study research: categorical aggregation, direct interpretation, correspondence and pattern, and naturalistic generalizations. In categorical aggregation, the researcher "seeks a collection of instances, expecting that, from the aggregate, issue-relevant meanings will emerge" (p. 75). Case study researchers also recognize that a single occurrence can be just as analytically salient as a collection of instances. Therefore, they sometimes directly interpret a single instance, "trying to pull it apart and put it back together again more meaningfully" (p. 75). Both of these processes, categorical aggregation and direct interpretation, involve seeking correspondences and patterns throughout the data corpus. Stake's notion of naturalistic generalization suggests that readers themselves participate in analytic sense making, a process that authors can strategically promote in the way they present evidence. In addition to considering the researcher's explicated generalizations, readers may form or redraw their own naturalistic generalizations based on analyses presented in the report.

Presentation of Findings

Presentation of data in a case study report often takes the form of a detailed case description followed by discussion of case-based themes. The article's findings and discussion sections present broad assertions about the "facts" of the case or "lessons learned" from the inquiry (Lincoln & Guba, 1985). Researchers provide a rich description of the case(s) and research context in order to enhance the study's credibility and to support the reader's ability to assess potential transferability to additional instances of the phenomenon that share contextual commonalities.

In a classic single-case study, reporting takes the form of a single narrative, which may be complemented with tables, figures, or additional visual displays of data. A multiple case study report will often include multiple narratives for each of the individual cases, each presented in its own chapter or section. Following treatment of the individual cases, an additional chapter or section will present cross-case themes that are applicable to the collection of cases. When cross-case comparison is central to establishing the study's object, the report may not provide narrative descriptions of individual cases, instead presenting solely the cross-case analysis. In this format, discussion may be organized around cross-case themes or research questions, with information pertaining to individual cases dispersed throughout. Exemplar studies referenced throughout this chapter illustrate an array of possible reporting structures for case studies, including a theory-building structure (e.g., Langston & Barrett, 2008), thematically organized case descriptions (e.g., Parker, 2016), and vignettes that promote readers' vicarious experience (e.g., Carlow, 2006). For more detailed advice about composing case study reports, readers are encouraged to consult Stake (1995) and Yin (2009).

Challenges to Address Proactively

Confusion Over the Study's Unit of Analysis

One challenge that may arise in case study research is confusion or indecision regarding the study's unit of analysis, meaning precisely what constitutes the case and its boundaries. Within music education, case studies tend to focus on individuals such as teachers, students, or organizational leaders, who are often nested within classrooms, organizations, or programs that could either comprise cases or serve as the research context for the study. A challenge that researchers new to case study often encounter is focusing data generation and analysis at one level (e.g., focusing on an ensemble as the case) when research questions are focused at a different level (e.g., individuals' experiences within the ensemble).

Because casing decisions are consequential for a researcher's approach to data generation, analysis, and presentation, time invested in making well-informed choices pays significant dividends. Following are some questions that merit repeated consideration throughout the process of conducting a case study:

- What comprises my study's case(s)?
- What elements establish the scope and boundaries of my case?
- Are my data generation and analysis plans aligned with my answers to the above two questions?

Defining the case and establishing its boundaries similarly to the way that researchers have approached these matters previously may help to position your study within a coordinated line of inquiry. As Yin (2009) advised, "the key definitions used in your study should not be idiosyncratic. Each case study and unit of analysis either should be similar to those previously studied by others or should innovate in clear, operationally defined ways" (p. 33).

Failure to Establish an Object or Analytic Frame

Another potential pitfall in case study research is failing to establish an object or analytic frame for the study. For Thomas (2011), this element distinguishes a piece of empirical research from mere description:

> The ostensible looseness of the case study as a form of inquiry and the conspicuous primacy given to the case (the subject) is perhaps a reason for inexperienced social inquirers, especially students, to neglect to establish any kind of object (literally and technically) for their inquiries. Identifying only a subject, they fail to seek to explain anything, providing instead, therefore, a simple description in place of a piece of research. For the study to constitute research, there has to be something to be explained (an object) and something potentially to offer explanation (the analysis of the circumstances of the subject). (p. 513)

Barrett (2014) concurred: "[the] concept of the analytical or theoretical frame is well worth pursuing, as the underdevelopment of this frame fuels many criticisms of case studies, and often plagues work in music education particularly" (p. 117). Even with the understanding that a case study's object might change, "firm up," "thicken," or "dramatically unfold" as the study proceeds, it is advisable to identify one or two theoretical frames at the outset that are expected to inform the inquiry. The following questions may be useful for guiding considerations of the study's object:

- Of what broader class is my case an instance?
- Of what phenomenon does my case offer a concrete example?
- Through what theoretical frame(s) can my case be analyzed or interpreted?

Referencing "Generalization" in the Findings and Implications Sections

Ongwebuzie and Leech (2010) warned that "some qualitative researchers find it difficult to resist the temptation to generalize their findings (e.g., thematic representations) to some population" (p. 883). Even as researchers articulate in their reports that case studies do not rely on probabilistic samples, they sometimes use phrases in their findings and implications sections that nevertheless hint at generalization. For example, terms such as "best practices" can imply widespread application of findings to additional settings. Onwuegbuzie and Leech (2007) further advised, "If generalization is not the goal, then [researchers] should only outline a theory in terms of the particular participant(s), setting, context, location, time, event, incident, activity, experience, and/or processes" (p. 115).

In order to describe a case study's contributions in terms other than generalizability, researchers are encouraged to keep assertions focused on what can be learned from the particular case(s). Discussion could appropriately focus on how the case provides exemplification (as opposed to dealing with generality), promotes "vicarious experience" through vivid illustration, or supports theorization. Another way to navigate this challenge is to use qualitatively oriented terms to describe a study's contribution, such as "case to case transfer" (Onwuegbuzie & Leech, 2010), "analytic generalization" (Yin, 2009), or "naturalistic generalization" (Stake & Trumbull, 1982) and to cite methodological sources for those specific meanings.

Summary

This chapter has provided an introduction to case study research, an approach defined by its focus on a single bounded system, or case, rather than a prescribed set of methodological procedures. Given that a diverse array of data generation and analysis techniques can be adopted in a case study, the chapter did not put forth a definitive method for conducting one. Instead, we used examples from music education research to illustrate an array of possible case study types. The following questions will assist you with reviewing key concepts from this chapter and applying them to your own research interests:

1. Review some exemplar case studies drawn from music education research that are either cited in this chapter or recommended by your instructor. Identify the subject, object, and theoretical framework (if one can be discerned) for each study.
2. Choose a research topic that you would like to undertake and outline how it could be explored using a case study.

a. Determine a potential subject and object for your study. Be able to answer the question "Of what broader class or phenomenon is your subject a case?"
b. Identify a theoretical framework that could possibly inform your analysis and interpretation, knowing that this would be subject to change. For example, if the object for your study is identity, through what theoretical lens could you view identity for the purposes of the study?
c. Using Creswell and Poth's (2018) script for formulating a research purpose, draft a purpose statement for your study.
d. Develop some a priori research questions for your study, understanding that these might evolve if you were to undertake the study.
3. Using Figure 9.1, which represents Thomas's (2016) case study typology graphically, draw arrows from one category to the next to show a possible investigative path for your case study. More than one descriptor in each category might apply (e.g., a case study could involve both theory testing and explanatory purposes), so feel free to draw multiple arrows within a category as needed.

Important Terms for Review

Case studies are "analyses of persons, events, decisions, periods, projects, policies, or other systems that are studied holistically by one or more methods. The case that is the subject of the inquiry will be an instance of a class or phenomena that provides an analytical frame—an object—within which the study is conducted and which the case illuminates and explicates" (Thomas, 2011b, p. 513).

A *case* is a bounded system that comprises the main subject, or focal point, of a case study. This could take the form of an individual, small group, project, program, organization, community, decision-making process, or event.

In this chapter, the term *subject* refers to a case study's focal center rather than serving as an outmoded label for a participant in a research study.

An *object* is an analytical or theoretical frame through which a case study's subject is viewed. The object can also be described as a broader class or phenomenon of which the case is an instance.

An *intrinsic case study* is a type of case study in which analysis focuses on the case itself because it is inherently of interest (Stake, 1995).

An *instrumental case study* is a type of case study in which analysis focuses on a specific issue that the case serves to illuminate or explicate (Stake, 1995).

A *multiple* or *collective case study* is a type of case study that uses more than one case to illuminate a central phenomenon. Comparisons between cases play a key role in establishing the study's analytic frame.

A *nested case study* is a type of case study in which one or more cases fit within a larger case. Analysis of relationships between the overarching case and its nested units plays a central role in establishing the study's analytic frame.

Within-case analysis is a process through which a researcher analyzes individual cases for themes.

Cross-case analysis is a process through which a researcher generates themes by comparing cases with one another. This type of analysis occurs in multiple case studies, typically following within-case analysis.

References

Amabile, T. M. (1996). *Creativity in context: Update to the social psychology of creativity*. Westview Press.

Barrett, J. R. (2014). Case study in music education. In C. M. Conway (Ed.), *The Oxford handbook of qualitative research in American music education* (pp. 113–132). Oxford University Press.

Bassey, M. (1999). *Case study research in educational settings*. Open University Press.

Bell-Robertson, C. G. (2013). "Staying on our feet": Novice music teachers' sharing of emotions and experiences within an online community. *Journal of Research in Music Education, 61*(4), 431–451. https://doi.org/10.1177/0022429413508410

Brenner, B., & Strand, K. (2013). A case study of teaching musical expression to young performers. *Journal of Research in Music Education, 61*(1), 80–96. https://doi.org/10.1177/0022429412474826

Buber, M. (2000). *I and thou* (R. G. Smith, Trans.). Schirmer.

Carlow, R. (2006). Diva Irina: An English language learner in high school choir. *Bulletin of the Council for Research in Music Education, 170*, 63–77. https://www.jstor.org/stable/40319349

Creswell, J. W., & Poth, C. N. (2018). *Qualitative inquiry and research design: Choosing among five approaches* (4th ed.). Sage.

de Vaus, D. A. (2001). *Research design in social research*. Sage.

Fitzpatrick, K. R., Henninger, J. C., & Taylor, D. M. (2014). Access and retention of marginalized populations within undergraduate music education degree programs. *Journal of Research in Music Education, 62*(2), 105–127. https://doi.org/10.1177/0022429414530760

Gay, G. (2010). *Culturally responsive teaching: Theory, research, and practice* (2nd ed.). Teachers College Press.

Gerrard, C. L. (2021). "It's more than playing music": Exploring band in a predominantly Latinx community. *Bulletin of the Council for Research in Music Education, 227*, 66–85. https://www.jstor.org/stable/10.5406/bulcouresmusedu.227.0066

Hickey, M. (2015). Learning from the experts: A study of free-improvisation pedagogues in university settings. *Journal of Research in Music Education, 62*(4), 425–445. https://doi.org/10.1177/0022429414556319

Irizarry, J. G., & Raible, J. (2011). Beginning with *el barrio*: Learning from exemplary teachers of Latino students. *Journal of Latinos and Education, 10*(3), 186–203. https://doi.org/10.1080/15348431.2011.581102

Langston, T. W., & Barrett, M. S. (2008). Capitalizing on community music: A case study of the manifestation of social capital in a community choir. *Research Studies in Music Education, 30*, 118–138. https://doi.org/10.1177/1321103X08097503

Lincoln, Y. S., & Guba, E. G. (1985). *Naturalistic inquiry*. Sage.

Major, M. L. (2013). How they decide: A case study examining the decision-making process for keeping or cutting music in a K–12 public school district. *Journal of Research in Music Education, 61*(1), 5–25. https://doi.org/10.1177/0022429412474313

Menard, E. A. (2015). Music composition in the high school curriculum: A multiple case study. *Journal of Research in Music Education*, 63(1), 114–136. https://doi.org/10.1177/0022429415574310

Merriam, S. B. (1988). *Case study research in education: A qualitative approach*. Jossey-Bass.

Noddings, N. (2003). *Caring: A feminine approach to ethics and moral education*. University of California Press.

Noddings, N. (2005). *The challenge to care in schools: An alternative approach to education* (2nd ed.). Teachers College Press.

Onwuegbuzie, A. J., & Leech, N. L. (2007). A call for qualitative power analyses. *Quality and Quantity International Journal of Methodology*, 41, 105–121. https://doi.org/10.1007/s11135-005-1098-1

Onwuegbuzie, A. J., & Leech, N. L. (2010). Generalization practices in qualitative research: A mixed methods case study. *Quality and Quantity International Journal of Methodology*, 44, 881–892. https://doi.org/10.1007/s11135-009-9241-z

Parker, E. C. (2016). The experience of creating community: An intrinsic case study of four midwestern public school choral teachers. *Journal of Research in Music Education*, 64(2), 220–237. https://doi.org/10.1177/0022429416648292

Ragin, C. C. (1992). "Casing" and the process of social inquiry. In C. C. Ragin & H. S. Becker (Eds.), *What is a case? Exploring the foundations of social inquiry* (pp. 217–226). Cambridge University Press.

Roulston, K. (2010). *Reflective interviewing: A guide to theory and practice*. Sage.

Shaw, J. T. (2015). "Knowing their world": Urban choral music educators' knowledge of context. *Journal of Research in Music Education*, 63(2), 198–223. https://doi.org/10.1177/0022429415584377

Shaw, J. T. (2020). *Culturally responsive choral music education: What teachers can learn from nine students' experiences in three choirs*. Routledge.

Stake, R. E. (1995). *The art of case study research* (2nd ed.). Sage.

Stake, R. E. (2005). Qualitative case studies. In N. K. Denzin & Y. S. Lincoln (Eds.), *The Sage handbook of qualitative research* (pp. 443–466). Sage.

Stake, R. E., & Trumbull, D. (1982). Naturalistic generalizations. *Review Journal of Philosophy and Social Science*, 7(1), 1–12.

Thomas, G. (2011). A typology for the case study in social science following a review of definition, discourse, and structure. *Qualitative Inquiry*, 17(6), 511–521. https://doi.org/10.1177/1077800411409884

Thomas, G. (2016). *How to do your case study* (2nd ed.). Sage.

Thomas, G. (2021). *How to do your case study* (3rd ed.). Sage.

Turner, E. (2012). *Communitas: The anthropology of collective joy*. Palgrave Macmillan.

VanWynsberghe, R., & Khan, S. (2007). Redefining case study. *International Journal of Qualitative Methods*, 6(2), 80–94. https://doi.org/10.1177/160940690700600208

Wacquant, L. D. (1989). Towards a reflexive sociology: A workshop with Pierre Bourdieu. *Sociological Theory*, 7(1), 26–63. https://doi.org/10.2307/202061

Yin, R. K. (2009). *Case study research: Design and methods* (4th ed.). Sage.

10
Additional Qualitative Approaches
Ethnography, Grounded Theory, Narrative, and Phenomenology

Chapter Preview

This chapter introduces four approaches to inquiry—grounded theory, narrative, phenomenology, and ethnography—that, together with case study, comprise five primary qualitative research designs. The purpose of grounded theory is to develop a unified theoretical explanation for a process, action, or interaction such as professional growth or identity development. The theory is "grounded" in data generated with participants who have experienced that process, as opposed to being borrowed "off the shelf" from existing literature. "Stories lived and told" are the focal point of narrative inquiry. Inquirers elicit, interpret, and report detailed stories of individuals' life experiences in order to illuminate phenomena or raise questions for readers' consideration. In phenomenological research, the study's central phenomenon will be some kind of human experience such as grief, belonging, enjoyment, competition, and so forth. Analysis focuses on identifying the essence, or invariant structure, of that phenomenon for individuals who have experienced it. In ethnography, a culture-sharing group with a history of direct interaction is the focal point of the research. The researcher describes, analyzes, and interprets patterns in the group's social organization, behaviors, and ideational systems. The product of inquiry is a rich, complex description of the culture-sharing group at the heart of the study. Exemplar studies drawn from music education illustrate key features of each design.

Introduction

In this chapter, we provide an introduction to four approaches to inquiry that, together with case study, comprise five primary qualitative research designs: ethnography, grounded theory, narrative, and phenomenology. For each, we describe characteristic features, identify research purposes and questions for which the design is appropriate, and provide an overview of associated methodological procedures. Exemplar studies drawn from music education research illustrate key features of each design. While this chapter will acquaint readers with features of these designs, it does not in and of itself offer sufficient procedural guidance for conducting a study using one of these approaches. Readers interested in conducting a study using one of these designs are urged to consult additional sources authored by methodological experts on that specific design, such as those recommended in Box 10.1.

Throughout this chapter, we have used a consistent set of section headings to facilitate ease of reference. However, the phases of conducting research are often not as distinct as these headings might imply. As discussed in previous chapters, the processes of qualitative data generation, analysis, and interpretation often overlap, intersect, and inform one another over the course of conducting a study.

Box 10.1 Key Methodological Readings

Following are some recommended resources that offer detailed procedural advice pertaining to primary qualitative research designs.

Grounded Theory

Charmaz, K. (2014). *Constructing grounded theory* (2nd ed.). Sage.

Clarke, A. E. (2005). *Situational analysis: Grounded theory after the postmodern turn*. Sage.

Corbin, J., & Strauss, A. (2015). *Basics of qualitative research: Techniques and procedures for developing grounded theory* (4th ed.). Sage.

Narrative Inquiry

Clandinin, D. J. (2013). *Engaging in narrative inquiry*. Left Coast Press.

Clandinin, D. J., & Connelly, F. M. (2000). *Narrative inquiry: Experience and story in qualitative research*. Jossey-Bass.

Czarniawska, B. (2004). *Narratives in social science research*. Sage.

Daiute, C. (2014). *Narrative inquiry: A dynamic approach*. Sage.

Reissman, C. K. (2008). *Narrative methods for the human sciences*. Sage.

Phenomenology

Giorgi, A. (2009). *The descriptive phenomenological method in psychology: A modified Husserlian approach*. Duquesne University Press.

Moustakas, C. (1994). *Phenomenological research methods*. Sage.

van Manen, M. (1990). *Researching lived experience: Human science for an action sensitive pedagogy*. State University of New York Press.

van Manen, M. (2014). *Phenomenology of practice: Meaning-giving methods in phenomenological research and writing*. Left Coast Press.

Ethnography

Atkinson, P. (2015). *For ethnography*. Sage.

Fetterman, D. M. (2020). *Ethnography: Step-by-step* (4th ed.). Sage.

Wolcott, H. F. (2008). *Ethnography: A way of seeing* (2nd ed.). AltaMira Press.

Grounded Theory

The purpose of a grounded theory study is to develop a "unified theoretical explanation" for a process or action (Corbin & Strauss, 2008, p. 107). The focal point of the study will be a process with identifiable phases or steps that unfold over time. In this way, "a grounded theory study has 'movement'" that a researcher seeks to explain (Creswell & Poth, 2018, p. 83). For example, music education researchers have conducted grounded theory studies to explore the processes of developing social identity in high school choir (Parker, 2014), acquiring musical independence in concert band (Weidner, 2020), and planning for instruction as preservice music educators (Parker et al., 2017). The product of inquiry is a theory that is "grounded" in data contributed by participants who have experienced that process or action as opposed to being taken "off the shelf" from existing frameworks or literature (Strauss & Corbin, 1998).

Types of Grounded Theory

Sociologists Barney Glaser and Anselm Strauss are credited with developing this approach to research in 1967 and have contributed several seminal texts on the design (Corbin & Strauss, 2008, 2015; Glaser, 1978; Glaser & Strauss, 1967; Strauss, 1987; Strauss & Corbin, 1990, 1998). Presently, two approaches to grounded theory are featured prominently in the literature: a systematic approach developed by Corbin and Strauss (2015) and a constructivist approach advanced by Charmaz (2014). For researchers first becoming acquainted with grounded theory, Strauss and Corbin's approach is useful in that it is highly structured, with a codified set of procedures. For this reason, we rely substantively on their procedural advice as we introduce methodological features associated with grounded theory. Examples of music education studies that draw upon Strauss and Corbin's procedures include Parker (2014) and West (2020).

The systematic procedures of Strauss and Corbin have been critiqued as being too prescriptive for some researchers and situations. One leading alternative approach is that developed by Charmaz (2014), which reflects a social constructivist and interpretivist orientation toward grounded theory. She views theory development as a co-construction process that unfolds through dynamic interactions between researchers and participants in the field. Hallmarks of constructivism discernable in her approach include reflecting multiple realities, representing complexities inherent in participants' views and actions, accounting for context-specific conditions in particular locales, and making power hierarchies that affect the process of theory development visible. Distinguishing features of Charmaz's approach are apparent in her approach to analysis, as reflected in her recommendation that analysts should "avoid imposing a forced framework" (p. 155). Her analysis process entails an initial coding process followed by a more focused round of coding, through which she "piec[es] together implicit meanings" about categories that emerge inductively from analysis (p. 146). Charmaz (2005) maintains that the conclusions at which grounded theorists arrive are ultimately provisional, incomplete, and inconclusive. Examples of music education studies aligned with Charmaz's (2014) constructivist approach include Salvador et al. (2020) and Weidner (2020).

Purpose Statements and Research Questions in Grounded Theory

This research design is appropriate for situations in which there are no available theories to explain a process or for when existing theories are inadequate because they do not yet account for variables or categories that the researcher anticipates would be salient. Researchers might also choose this design when available theories have been developed or tested empirically only with populations other than those that are of interest. Purpose statements in grounded theory studies often incorporate language such as "generate," "develop," "propositions," "process," and "substantive theory" (Creswell & Poth, 2018, p. 135). The following purpose statement and research questions, drawn from Parker (2014), offer one representative example:

> The purpose of this grounded theory study was to describe the process of adolescent choral singers' social identity development within three mid-sized, midwestern high school mixed choirs. Research questions included how high school students describe their social identity development, what actions or interactions influence their development, what strategies they use to develop social identity, what intervening conditions get in the way, and what consequences result from high school students' social identity development. (p. 20)

Embedded within these research questions are the terms "actions," "interactions," "strategies," and "intervening conditions," each of which are elements of Corbin and Strauss's (2015) approach that are emblematic of grounded theory.

Methodological Procedures Associated with Grounded Theory

Sampling

Grounded theory draws upon a process of "theoretical sampling," the purpose of which is "to collect data from places, people, and events that will maximize opportunities to develop concepts in terms of their properties and dimensions, uncover variations, and identify relationships between concepts" (Corbin & Strauss, 2008, p. 143). Unlike approaches in which sampling is completed prior to data generation, theoretical sampling continues while data generation and analysis are underway:

Data collection leads to analysis. Analysis leads to concepts. Concepts generate questions. Questions lead to more data collection so that the researcher might learn more about those concepts. This circular process continues until the research reaches the point of saturation; that is, the point in the research when all the concepts are well defined and explained. (pp. 144–145)

Participant sampling in grounded theory research may progress through a two-phase process involving theoretical and discriminant sampling (Creswell & Poth, 2018). First, through theoretical sampling, the researcher will select individuals who have all experienced the process or action. Data generated with these individuals will inform early stages of the analysis process. Having completed preliminary analysis and begun to develop the theory, the researcher may use discriminant sampling to select participants other than those originally sampled in order to investigate whether the theory also holds true for these additional participants. This second group of participants will be a heterogeneous sample, allowing the researcher to explore conditions under which the theory holds. Considerations of sample size are driven by the number of participants needed to achieve "theoretical saturation," a point at which adding participants and generating additional data no longer contributes fresh insights toward the developing theory (Corbin & Strauss, 2008, p. 143). Creswell and Poth (2018) recommend engaging 20 to 30 participants in a grounded theory study, though the number required to achieve saturation could be larger (Charmaz, 2014).

Data Generation

The image of "zigzagging" depicts data generation and analysis in grounded theory, with researchers interviewing participants, using preliminary analysis to inform theory development, returning to the field to conduct additional interviews, and returning to the evolving theory to flesh it out more fully (Creswell & Poth, 2018, p. 85). Data generation and analysis are therefore not distinct phases that proceed in a linear fashion but instead occur simultaneously and inform one another. Throughout the simultaneous processes of data generation and analysis, researchers engage in theoretical memoing and develop conceptual diagrams to document developments in their thinking about the process being investigated (Corbin & Strauss, 2015).

Data generation in grounded theory studies primarily revolves around interviews with individuals who have experienced the process. Additional data sources may be consulted, including observations, journals, focus groups, and documents or audiovisual materials, but these usually play a role secondary to interviews. Earlier in the interview process, questions might focus on how participants experienced the process and steps that the process entailed. Subsequent interviews, scheduled after the researcher has undertaken preliminary analysis, might focus on questions such as the following: "What was central to the process (the core phenomenon)? What influenced or caused this phenomenon to occur (causal conditions)? What strategies were employed during the process (strategies)? What effect occurred (consequences)?" (Creswell & Poth, 2018, p. 87). As a general heuristic, the process of developing a well-saturated theory requires approximately 20 to 60 interviews.

Data Analysis

In Corbin and Strauss's (2008, 2015; Strauss & Corbin, 1990) approach to grounded theory, inductive analysis proceeds through three phases: open coding, axial coding, and selective coding. The first phase, open coding, is a "brainstorming approach" through which analysts "open up the data to all potentials and possibilities contained within them" (Corbin & Strauss 2008, p. 160). The researcher examines the data record with an eye toward how the information can be segmented into categories. The constant comparative method (Glaser, 1965) is central to this process, with researchers engaged in continual comparison between data excerpts and emerging categories. For each category, the researcher will continue to aggregate instances through the constant comparative method and to generate new pertinent data (via ongoing interviewing) until that category is "saturated."

Researchers also identify subcategories within each category called "properties," which are "characteristics that define and describe concepts" (Corbin & Strauss, 2008, p. 159). They identify data excerpts that illustrate varying degrees of each property that participants have experienced and arrange these along a continuum, a process called "dimensionalizing" the properties (Strauss & Corbin, 1990, p. 71). Overall, the process of open coding reduces a data record to a smaller number of categories that characterize the process or action that the developing theory seeks to explain.

Strauss and Corbin (1990) specify particular subcategories to develop at a second phase of coding, axial coding, which involves "making connections between a category and its subcategories":

> In axial coding our focus is on specifying a category (*phenomenon*) in terms of the *conditions* that give rise to it; the *context* (its specific set of properties) in which it is embedded; the *action/interactional strategies* by which it is handled, managed, carried out; and the *consequences* of those strategies. (p. 97)

Researchers organize these categories into a figure, called a "coding paradigm," that presents a theoretical model of the process being studied.

The next stage, selective coding, involves "selecting the core category, systematically relating it to other categories, validating those relationships, and filling in categories that need further refinement and development" (Strauss & Corbin, 1990, p. 116). The process begins with identifying one category that figured prominently in participants' interview conversations or otherwise seems central to the process being studied. The researcher positions this category as the theory's "central phenomenon" and conducts another round of analysis focused on how additional categories relate to this core feature of the theory. The researcher may develop a storyline, articulate propositions, or put forth hypotheses that explain relationships between categories that have emerged from analysis. The resulting theory might be presented as a visual diagram or model, a discussion, or a collection of formal propositions. Strauss and Corbin recommend a possible additional step of developing a conditional matrix that supports analysis of the micro (e.g., individual, group, and organization) and macro (e.g., regional, national, and global) conditions that influence the phenomenon. However, conditional matrices are seldom found in practice, as most grounded theorists conclude their theory development at the selective coding stage with a substantive, low-level theory as opposed to a contribution to grand theory (Creswell & Poth, 2018).

Data Presentation in Grounded Theory

The findings section of a grounded theory report presents the theory the researcher has developed as a result of the inquiry: "In strict terms, the findings are the theory itself, i.e., a set of concepts and propositions which link them" (May, 1986, p. 148). Researchers interweave description of the theory with data excerpts and connections to extant literature. Raw data excerpts, such as direct quotes from interviews, illustrate how the theory is grounded in participants' experiences while references to existing literature provide external support for the theory (May, 1986). Authors may present the theory in one of several ways: as a visual model with accompanying description and discussion, as a hypothesis presented in discursive form, or as a formalized set of theoretical propositions.

A Grounded Theory Example from Music Education

West (2020) was curious about the processes of change in which music teachers engaged after they attended a professional conference. With its emphasis on theorizing about a process, his study's purpose statement is readily identifiable as one drawn from grounded theory:

> I sought to explore how music teachers engaged the change process following participation in a large-scale conference. Specifically, I theorized how music teachers considered, realized, and made decisions on conference-derived changes to their professional practice in the near term—a process I conceptualized as *proximate change*. (pp. 67–68)

The research questions also include language consistent with grounded theory, with the first focused on explaining a process and the third inquiring into causal and contextual conditions:

1. What process explains music teachers' engagement with proximate change via large-scale conference PD [professional development]?
2. How do music teachers identify conference-derived practices/perspectives, implement them in classroom settings, and evaluate their efficacy?
3. In what way(s) do personal dispositions and school contexts constrain and afford music teachers' professional growth via conference PD? (p. 68)

Three prominent music education conferences served as the research context: the National Association for Music Education National In-Service Conference, the Midwest Clinic, and the Texas Music Educators Association Clinic/Convention. Through theoretical sampling, West (2020) invited 32 practicing music educators who had attended one of these conferences to participate in the study. Through maximum-variation sampling, he selected educators who taught in varying demographic and socioeconomic contexts as well as teachers with varying subspecialties within music education (e.g., choir, band, orchestra, and general music) to support development of a theory that would apply to a range of conditions and contexts. Data generation was primarily interview-based, with the researcher conducting 60 semi-structured interviews in three waves that corresponded with the timing of the three conferences. Periods of data generation at each conference alternated with data analysis such that earlier stages of analysis informed participant selection and data generation for subsequent waves.

Analysis procedures aligned with Corbin and Strauss's (2015) recommended processes for open, axial, and selective coding, and West (2020) provided examples of codes generated during each phase. He described his process for identifying properties and dimensions of each category and presented examples of participants' dimensionalized quotes in a table (pp. 78–79). For example, one category was "deterrent factors/contingencies" and described reasons teachers may not implement a new practice learned at a conference. Within that category, the property "performance pressures" referred to the way that participants' openness toward implementing a new practice related to perceived pressures stemming from performance expectations. Participants' quotes ranged from "contests [are] coming up" and "feeling the pressure" at one extreme to being "willing to give up time away from concert music" at the other (p. 79).

The product of this inquiry was a theoretical model of proximate teacher change that progressed in three phases. During the consideration phase, participants assessed their needs, envisioned change while attending sessions, and then made concrete commitments to change. After deciding which new practices and perspectives to implement, some participants encountered deterrents such as performance demands, which led them to either postpone or forgo implementation. Barring deterrents, participants adapted and implemented new practices and perspectives during the realization phase. Ultimately, in the decision phase, participants evaluated new practices based on student outcomes. They continued practices they deemed effective and discontinued or deferred those deemed ineffective (West, 2020, p. 77). Permeating all three phases was the core category of "convergence," which described participants' perceptions "that their conference PD experiences meet with, or converge on, their classroom teaching experiences to the greatest extent possible" (pp. 77, 80).

West (2020) presented his theoretical model as an integrative diagram and set of nine theoretical propositions (p. 88). For instance, the ninth proposition asserted that "performance demands were a potent consideration for music teachers as they determined the utility and feasibility of new practices/perspectives within their local context" (p. 88). The organizational structure for the research report's findings section was informed by the theory's constituent parts, with section headings corresponding to the model's core category, phases, properties, and dimensions. Participant quotes embedded throughout the findings and discussion sections illustrate how the theory is grounded in participants' experiences. Findings of this study have implications for researchers, clinicians, and conference organizers who endeavor to make conference experiences as meaningful and useful for educators as possible.

Narrative Inquiry

In narrative inquiry, "stories lived and told" are the focal point of the research (Clandinin & Connelly, 2000, p. 20). Inquirers elicit, interpret, and report detailed stories of individuals' life experiences. However, the process of collecting stories for the purposes of empirical research is not necessarily simple or straightforward:

> Narrative inquiry . . . might appear to be simply a matter of getting someone's story, writing it up, and putting some explanatory text around it. Done. But not so fast. What counts as a narrative? . . . Why was a particular story told in the first place? Would the teller change the story depending when or to whom the story was told? Does that matter? Is it ethical to "get" stories and write them up?. . . . These questions (and more) matter to narrative researchers, and all of them may be answered somewhat differently, depending on one's approach to narrative and purposes for choosing narrative as a research mode. (Stauffer, 2014, pp. 166–167)

The term "narrative" can refer to either the central phenomenon explored in a study (i.e., narratives of something) or a methodological approach to analyzing stories (i.e., narrative inquiry).

Narrative studies focus on individual experience, often illuminating facets of participants' identities. Relationality is another hallmark of narrative inquiry, as stories are "shared between teller and listener, and told in different ways depending on time and context as well as the relationship between speaker and listener"

(Stauffer, 2014, p. 177). Attention to contextual details surrounding individuals' stories is then another characteristic feature of narrative research. Clandinin (2013) stresses that narrative inquiry "is not only valorizing individuals' experience, but is also an exploration of the social, cultural, familial, linguistic, and institutional narratives within which individuals' experiences were, and are, constituted, shaped, expressed and enacted" (p. 18). In their reports, narrative inquirers embed plentiful details about the personal, relational, cultural, social, and temporal contexts within which stories unfold.

Temporality is emphasized in narrative inquiry, leading some researchers to assert that the element of chronology distinguishes narrative from other approaches to research (e.g., Cortazzi, 1993). As individuals discuss their lives and experiences, they often convey a sense of temporal change as they describe the past, present, and future (Clandinin & Connelly, 2000). Stories will also often include what Denzin (1989) called "turning points," or specific tensions or transitions that researchers may highlight in a narrative account (p. 40). The researcher reshapes the story into a chronology that may differ from how participants originally shared it as part of a process called restorying.

The retelling of individuals' personal experiences, often for an academic audience, raises ethical questions such as the following: "Who owns the story? Who can tell it? Who can change it? . . . Whose version is convincing? What happens when narratives compete? . . . What do stories do among us [as a community]?" (Pinnegar & Daynes, 2007, p. 30). Many narrative studies feature a strong collaborative element with participants engaged as more equal partners in shaping data generation, analysis, and the products of inquiry that are eventually disseminated. Extensive member checking, and close collaboration between researcher and participant as they "negotiate the meaning of the story," bolster the credibility of narrative studies (Creswell & Poth, 2018, p. 73). Many narrative inquirers view the researcher-participant relationship as one in which both will learn and change through the process of conducting the study. Researchers often embed their own story of personal insights gleaned through the research process within the telling of the participant's story.

Types of Narrative Studies

In a comprehensive handbook chapter addressing narrative inquiry within music education, Stauffer (2014) identified three pathways to narrative most commonly pursued by researchers in music education: narrative knowing, as described by Bruner (1986, 1991, 2004); narrative inquiry, as conceptualized by Clandinin and Connelly (2000); and critical storytelling, as advanced by Barone (2000a, 2000b). Bruner's work evolved within the field of psychology, and researchers who approach their inquiry from a Brunerian perspective are interested in how narrative "operates as an instrument of the mind in the construction of reality" (Bruner, 1991, p. 6). Contributed over a period of three decades, Bruner's seminal writings position narrative as a way of knowing, of making sense of experience, of constructing a sense of self, and of constituting and reconstituting culture.

Another frequently encountered approach is that developed by Clandinin and Connelly (2000), whose work emanates from the fields of teacher education, education, and curriculum studies. Rooted in the work of John Dewey, their approach emphasizes relationships between stories, experience, and meaning:

> People shape their daily lives by stories of who they and others are and they interpret their past in terms of these stories. Story, in the current idiom, is a portal through which a person enters the world and by which his or her experience of the world is interpreted and made personally meaningful. . . . Narrative inquiry, the study of experience as story, then, is first and foremost a way of thinking about experience. . . . To use narrative inquiry methodology is to adopt a particular view of experience as phenomena under study. (Connelly & Clandinin, 2006, p. 477)

Clandinin and Connelly's approach therefore focuses on how people use stories to interpret and derive meaning from their experiences.

A third pathway to narrative inquiry is Barone's (2000a, 2000b) approach to critical storytelling, which has been described as "a symbiotic relationship . . . between the qualities of artful writing, depth of inquiry, and faith in the reader" (Stauffer, 2014, p. 175). Within a literary presentation of a narrative account, researchers embed details of a rigorous methodological approach. Researchers provide space for readers to interpret the story and wrestle with questions it raises. Barone (2007) asserts that the narrative inquirer's purpose "is not to seek certainty about correct perspectives on educational phenomena but to raise significant questions about prevailing policy and practice that enrich an ongoing conversation" about teaching and learning (p. 466).

Purpose Statements and Research Questions in Narrative Inquiry

Purpose statements and research questions in narrative studies are often recognizable by their inclusion of such terms as "narrative," "stories," "epiphanies," "lived experiences," "chronology," and "re-story(ing)" (Creswell & Poth, 2018, p. 135). The following purpose statements, drawn from music education research, draw upon vocabulary that is consistent with narrative inquiry:

> The purpose of this narrative inquiry was to re-story the student teaching experience of two preservice music education majors who are visually impaired or blind. (Parker & Draves, 2017, p. 385)

> The purpose of this narrative inquiry was to re-story the experiences of a first-year music teacher with regard to race and class. Johny was a first-year high school guitar teacher in the southwestern United States who identified as Hispanic and was raised

in a family with a lower income. He was also a first-generation college student whose path to university study was atypical because of his major instrument, musical background, little high school music class participation, and entrance to postsecondary music study at a community college. (Draves & Vargas, 2022, p. 4)

Each of these statements reflects the goal of providing detailed stories of individuals' experiences. Each also reflects an emphasis on facets of participants' identities (e.g., race, class, gender, exceptionality, and first-generation college student status), which can also be characteristic of narrative inquiry.

Methodological Procedures Associated with Narrative Inquiry

Rather than following a prescriptive method, narrative researchers generally adopt a flexible approach and draw from a diverse array of procedures as they conduct their inquiries. Clandinin (2013) characterized narrative research "as a fluid inquiry, not as a set of procedures or linear steps to be followed" (p. 33). This section describes possible approaches for conducting narrative inquiry but does not offer an exhaustive treatment.

Sampling

The number of participants in a narrative study is typically kept small so that an individual's story (or a small number of individuals' stories) can be presented in vivid detail. Studies typically engage one to two research participants, though a larger group may be sought in order to develop a collective story (Creswell & Poth, 2018). Sampling in narrative studies can focus on individuals who have illustrative stories to share (Plummer, 1983), on stories themselves, or on considerations of time and space (Daiute, 2014).

Data Generation

Data generation in narrative studies features a multiplicity of data sources. Researchers interact with participants over a prolonged period of time to elicit their stories and translate them into "field texts." This term emphasizes that data are "created, neither found nor discovered, by participants and researchers in order to represent aspects of field experience" (Clandinin & Connelly, 2000, p. 92). Interviews are often a primary data source, but additional sources could include observations detailed in field notes, stories supplied by individuals who know the participant well, or "personal-family-social artifacts" such as journals, diaries, letters, emails, photographs, memory boxes, and so forth (Creswell & Poth, 2018, p. 71). Considering that stories emerge within and are shaped by a speaker-listener relationship, researchers invest effort into developing "relational and conversational conditions that invite the participants' stories" (Stauffer, 2014, p. 178). Inquirers often embrace a flexible, less-structured approach to interviewing so that interviews resemble conversations as opposed to interrogations (Chase, 1995).

Data Analysis

Polkinghorne's (1995) distinction between "analysis of narratives" and "narrative analysis" offers one point of departure for understanding key debates about interpretive processes among narrative researchers (Stauffer, 2014). According to Polkinghorne (1995), "analysis of narratives" involves "paradigmatic analysis [that] results in descriptions of themes that hold across the stories or in taxonomies of types of stories, characters, or settings" (p. 12). This process typically entails coding data and identifying themes that emerge inductively from analysis. Critics of this approach consider it to be "a reductionist treatment of narrative data that serves the researcher's interests only and may render the participants' meanings and even their stories invisible" (Stauffer, 2014, p. 178). In contrast, "narrative analysis" involves a process of restorying data "by means of a plot into a story or stories" (Polkinghorne, 1995, p. 12). The process involves recursive cycles of reading data, composing narrative texts, and rewriting those texts as the researcher's interpretation evolves. This approach can be characterized as a "writing-as-analysis process which sometimes occurs *with* the participants instead of apart from them" (Stauffer, 2014, p. 178).

Methodological experts have described a multitude of approaches to analysis and interpretation from varying positions within this debate, resulting in numerous and sometimes conflicting uses of the term "narrative analysis." Some narrative inquirers prefer to entirely avoid the term "analysis." Additional possible approaches to interpreting narrative texts may feature a literary orientation (e.g., Clandinin & Connelly, 2000), may center on chronology (e.g., Denzin, 1989), or may be oriented toward the manner in which the story is composed (e.g., Reissman, 2008).

Data Presentation in Narrative Inquiry

Just as narrative inquirers adopt a multiplicity of possible approaches to data analysis, they embrace a flexible approach to composing research reports (Clandinin, 2013; Clandinin & Connelly, 2000; Stauffer, 2014). These range from the typical architecture for an empirical research article, with separately headed sections for literature review, method, discussion, and so on, to more free-flowing presentations without section headings. Stauffer (2014) emphasized, "To be clear, there is no standard narrative article, chapter, or dissertation structure" (p. 179). Passages conveying stories are often complemented with ones written more in the style of an essay, which prompt readers to consider questions raised by the stories. Authors interweave participants' voices, their own interpretations, and connections to existing theory and literature, but not in a prescribed or standardized format. Because narrative inquiry may aim to raise questions rather than present definitive conclusions, sections offering "conclusions" or "recommendations" may be intentionally absent from narrative reports. Regardless of one's approach to reporting, a narrative study ultimately "tells the story of individuals unfolding in a chronology of their experiences, set within their personal, social, and historical context, and including the important themes in those lived experiences" (Creswell & Poth, 2018, p. 73).

A Narrative Example from Music Education

Nichols's (2013) narrative study exemplifies the critical storytelling pathway within music education research. This narrative "account introduces Ryan, a gender-variant[1] student, and offers the story of his journey through middle and high school and his experiences learning music" (p. 264). Because of the care and precision with which the researcher and participant presented this account, it is worth quoting Nichols at length:

> Ryan has always known two things about himself—he is musical and he is unapologetically "Rie." Friends and family struggle to describe this artistic, free spirit who dresses in short skirts and tight halter tops that reveal both an ornate chest tattoo and an Adam's apple. Faltering in their explanations, they typically fall back to "He's just Ryan." Ryan hates the all-too-human practice of categorizing and labeling, but suffers my "how do you identify yourself" question patiently and answers,
>
> I consider myself transgender, though I call myself a cross-dresser because I have never taken hormones. I have never considered SRS [sexual reassignment surgery]. It took me a long time to be comfortable in my skin, and now I am. I have always loved the saying, "If it ain't broke don't fix it," and that is kind of how I feel.
>
> I met Rie in the course of my professional life as a conductor. Rie played the flute in a band I directed, but she was not my student. She projected a funny, fearless persona and I noted her acceptance and popularity with the other band members. I wondered how difficult the gender transition process had been for her, how she navigated the rural midwestern school system in her hometown, and if she had been supported by family, friends, and teachers. I was particularly interested in her experiences with school music, and so I asked her if she would be willing to tell me her story. (p. 266)

These paragraphs introduce details about the participant, context, researcher, and impetus for conducting the study with rich description that continues throughout the report, all while foregrounding the participant's perspective through plentiful direct quotes. As is often the case in narrative reports, the story includes a key turning point, when "Ryan was eventually forced out of public education, ending his participation in the school's accomplished band and choir program" (Nichols, 2013, p. 262). Yet, the account illuminates ways in which music continued to play a role in Rie's life as she embraced songwriting as an emotional outlet and means

---

[1] While the term "gender-variant" appears in this quoted passage, terms for describing gender identity continue to evolve. One respectful alternative in today's parlance is "gender-expansive."

of self-expression. Data generation consisted primarily of in-depth interviews. Rie contributed a range of artifacts such as photo albums, scrapbooks, concert programs, school records, and original songs that prompted interview conversations.

This exemplar illustrates several noteworthy writing features. As this study centers on gender identity, the treatment of personal names and pronouns merited thoughtful attention when crafting the report. After repeated consultation about this matter, Nichols and Rie decided to alternate personal names and pronouns as a way "to create a useful tension that kept Rie's transgender status present in the mind of the reader" (Nichols, 2016, p. 477).[2] A second interesting writing feature is that song lyrics drawn from Rie's compositions are incorporated throughout the account, providing a unique window into her perspective and experiences.

The resulting account is organized into two broad sections, one titled "Rie's Story, Ryan's Journey," which foregrounds the participant's voice, and another titled "Commentary," in which Nichols offers her perspective on what the field of music education might learn from this account. Nichols (2013) explained:

> By separating Ryan's story from my discussion of the possible issues the story raises for music educators, I mean to provide readers with "interpretive space," textual room in which to contemplate Ryan's experiences, construct their own meanings, and consider ways in which Ryan's story might illuminate their own experiences. (p. 265)

This passage exemplifies the notion of "having faith in the reader" (Stauffer, 2014, p. 175) by raising questions for consideration rather than offering definitive answers. The report exemplifies Barone's approach to critical storytelling, reflecting balance between artful writing, methodological detail, and space for the reader to contemplate questions raised by Rie's story. Through a vivid presentation of this account, the researcher "prick[s] the consciences of readers by inviting a reexamination of the values and interests undergirding certain discourses, practices, and institutional arrangements in today's schools" (Barone, 2000b, p. 193).

Phenomenology

In phenomenological research, the study's central phenomenon will be some kind of human experience, such as grief, anger, a caring relationship, or a sense of belonging. Phenomenology can then be defined as the study of the "meaning, structure, and essence of the lived experience of this phenomenon for [a] person or group of people" (Patton, 2002, p. 132). Participants will be individuals who

---

[2] Nichols (2016) noted, "In the present, Rie fully identifies as female, and the main text of this article is written accordingly" (p. 452), and we have treated personal names and pronouns accordingly in our own summary. When quoting passages from the 2013 article, we have preserved the author's intentional use of alternating personal names and pronouns.

can provide detailed descriptions of their lived experiences of the phenomenon. Analysis involves eliminating redundant or superfluous information in individuals' descriptions of their experiences in order to identify the "essence" of that experience. The term "essence" refers to "the very nature of a phenomenon ... that which makes a some-'thing' what it is—and without which it could not be what it is" (van Manen, 1990, p. 10). As a product of a phenomenological inquiry, the researcher generates a composite description of the essence of the experience that details "what" participants experienced and "how" they experienced it (Moustakas, 1994).

Because a central goal of a phenomenology is to explore meanings that individuals collectively ascribe to experiences, the inquiry rests upon philosophical assumptions about the very nature of reality, consciousness, and experience. The writings of German mathematician Edmund Husserl (1859–1938; 1970) were influential in the development of this research tradition, as were the writings of authors who built upon and extended his ideas, including Heidegger, Sartre, and Merleau-Ponty (Spiegelberg, 1982). Phenomenological reports offer substantive treatment of their philosophical underpinnings along with discussion of the methodological decisions that guided the study, often referencing this particular lineage of philosophers.

One helpful resource for familiarizing oneself with this foundational literature is Stewart and Mickunas's (1990) text, which offers a helpful distillation of prominent themes in phenomenological philosophy. One central theme is the notion of "a philosophy without presuppositions" (p. 6). Phenomenologists attempt to suspend their preconceived notions about what can be considered real "until they can be founded on a more certain basis" (p. 7). Husserl termed this suspension of preconceived beliefs "epoche," which derives from a Greek word that refers to "abstention of belief" (p. 7). Husserl also drew upon the metaphor of "bracketing" one's preconceived notions about a phenomenon: "By bracketing the equation, the mathematician does not eliminate it, but merely places it out of question for the present, while the larger context of the equation is investigated" (p. 26). Therefore, phenomenologists temporarily suspend their presuppositions about a phenomenon in order to focus on participants' experiences. Husserl further described this process as "phenomenological reduction," which involves narrowing one's attention to that which is essential about a phenomenon:

> What [the phenomenologist] ignores [or reduces] when performing the phenomenological reduction is his previous prejudice about the world. By narrowing his attention to what is essential, he hopefully will discover the rational principles necessary for understanding of the thing (or phenomenon) under investigation. ("Stewart & Mickunas, 1990, p. 26)

Types of Phenomenology

Two major approaches to phenomenology are found within the literature, each of which is associated with a widely recognized methodological expert: hermeneutical phenomenology (van Manen, 1990, 2014) and transcendental phenomenology (Moustakas, 1994). The term "hermeneutical phenomenology" incorporates *phenomenology* to emphasize an orientation toward lived experience and *hermeneutics* to emphasize a process of interpretation. Thus, van Manen (1990) characterized his approach to research as "textual reflection on the lived experiences and practical actions of everyday life" (p. 4). Rather than putting forth a prescriptive method, he described hermeneutical phenomenology as "a dynamic interplay among six research activities":

1. turning to a phenomenon which seriously interests us and commits us to the world;
2. investigating experience as we live it rather than as we conceptualize it;
3. reflecting on the essential themes which characterize the phenomenon;
4. describing the phenomenon through the art of writing and rewriting;
5. maintaining a strong and oriented pedagogical relation to the phenomenon;
6. balancing the research context by considering parts and whole. (pp. 30–31)

The research process begins with a researcher identifying a phenomenon, or "abiding concern" (p. 31) to study. The inquiry proceeds with identifying significant themes and reflecting on precisely what constitutes the lived experience of that phenomenon. The process culminates in a written description of the phenomenon. In hermeneutical phenomenology, the researcher's interpretation of the meaning of the lived experiences for participants is recognized as an essential element of the research process.

In contrast, transcendental phenomenology de-emphasizes the role of researcher interpretation in order to give primacy to the experiences of participants in the study. Husserl's processes of epoche, bracketing, and phenomenological reduction are central to this approach. Through these processes, researchers suspend their presuppositions and prior experiences to the fullest extent possible in order to approach the phenomenon from a fresh perspective. The term "transcendental" then refers to an approach "in which everything is perceived freshly, as if for the first time," an ideal that may not be possible to achieve fully in practice (Moustakas, 1994, p. 34). A transcendental approach to phenomenology is further characterized by use of specific methodological procedures informed by the Duquesne Studies in Phenomenological Psychology (Giorgi, 2009) as well as the data analysis procedures of Van Kaam (1966) and Colaizzi (1978), which are described subsequently.

Purpose Statements and Research Questions

Research questions in phenomenological studies inquire about "the lived meaning of a human phenomenon that is . . . experientially accessible" (van Manen, 2014, p. 297). Van Manen cautioned:

> Questions that are abstract, theoretical, conceptual, or that ask for explanations, perceptions, views, or interpretations will not lend themselves for phenomenological exploration and reflection.... Instead, phenomenology explores the meanings of phenomena or events as lived through. In simple terms, phenomenology asks: "What is this or that phenomenon or event like?" (pp. 297–298)

Within music education, researchers have inquired into lived experiences of instrument-related gender stereotyping (Conway, 2000), competition in high school band (O'Leary, 2019), and the adolescent voice change (Kennedy, 2004; Sweet, 2015), to name just a few examples.

Purpose statements and research questions in phenomenological studies are often recognizable by their inclusion of such terms as "phenomenology," "describe," "experiences," "meaning," and "essence" (Creswell & Poth, 2018, p. 135). The following excerpt from Sweet's (2015) investigation of the adolescent female voice change offers one representative example:

> The purpose of this phenomenological study was to investigate the experience of female voice change from the perspective of female middle and high school choral students. The study was guided by two questions: How do adolescent female choir students experience voice change? What is the essence of the experience of voice change for middle school and high school females in choir? (p. 70)

Methodological Procedures Associated with Phenomenology

Sampling

Participants in a phenomenological research study will be individuals who have experienced the phenomenon. Sample sizes can range in number from a single participant (e.g., Padilla, 2003) to a group as large as 325 (e.g., van Kaam, 1966). This variability stems from the fact that phenomena under study might be very commonly experienced (e.g., anger, belonging) or might be specific to a smaller group of people, as in McCall's (2015) research with African American instrumental music education majors who transitioned from undergraduate music programs at historically Black colleges and universities to graduate music programs at predominantly White institutions. Sampling for a phenomenological study entails inviting a heterogeneous group of participants who can articulate varying experiences with the phenomenon (Polkinghorne, 1989). As a general heuristic, sample sizes in phenomenological studies often range from 3 to 4 individuals to 10–15 (Creswell & Poth, 2018).

Data Generation

Data generation in phenomenological studies consists primarily of multiple, in-depth interviews with individuals who have experienced the phenomenon in order to elicit "lived experience descriptions (LEDs)" (van Manen, 1990, pp. 253–254). Although interviews lend themselves well to gathering such descriptions, additional forms of data can serve as sources of LEDs: observations, biographies, journals, diaries, logs, and art forms such as poetry and music (van Manen, 1990). Phenomenological interviews are often semi-structured or unstructured, using open-ended questions to seek participants' detailed descriptions of their experiences. Many experts emphasize that the purpose of phenomenological interviews is to elicit participants' descriptions of their experiences, but not their interpretations, explanations, or analyses of those experiences (Kvale, 1983; Polkinghorne, 1989; van Manen, 2014). Further, it is not the researcher's responsibility to determine whether participants' descriptions "correspond to an independent reality" (Polkinghorne, 1989, p. 50).

Seidman (2019) developed an approach to phenomenological interviewing that unfolds through a series of three interviews, each with a precise focus:

> The first interview establishes the context of the participants' experience. The second allows participants to reconstruct the details of their experience within the context in which it occurs. And the third encourages the participants to reflect on the meaning their experience holds for them. (p. 21)

Seidman's text on phenomenological interviewing is recommended for its procedural advice, as the clear three-part structure and logic of this approach make it attractive to many researchers who are undertaking their first phenomenological studies.

Data Analysis

Moustakas's (1994) approach to data analysis draws upon structured methods adapted from van Kaam (1966) and the Stevick-Colaizzi-Keen approach as well as a specialized vocabulary for describing steps in the analysis process (see Moustakas, 1994, pp. 121–122). While this approach may be too prescriptive for some researchers and situations, its structured nature offers a useful guide for individuals making their first forays into phenomenological research. The process begins with the researcher engaging in Husserl's processes of epoche, bracketing, and phenomenological reduction in order to achieve a state in which they can perceive the phenomenon through fresh eyes (pp. 85–97).

When turning attention to data generated with participants, the researcher begins by identifying significant statements about how individuals experienced the phenomenon in the data record. They compile these statements into a nonrepetitive, nonoverlapping list and treat each statement as having equal worth, a process Moustakas (1994) referred to as "horizonalization":

> [E]very statement [contributed by participants] initially is treated as having equal value. Later, statements irrelevant to the topic and question as well as those that

are repetitive or overlapping are deleted, leaving only the *Horizons* (the textural meanings and invariant constituents of the phenomenon). (p. 97)

Next, the researcher groups the significant statements into broader themes or "invariant meaning units," a process that eliminates redundancies and creates "meaning clusters" (Moustakas, 1994, p. 122).

At this stage, the researcher develops two descriptions of participants' experiences of the phenomenon: a "textural description" of what the participants experienced and a "structural description" of how they experienced it (p. 121). The structural description addresses elements of context, conditions, and circumstances surrounding participants' experiences. Finally, the researcher develops a composite description of the phenomenon that incorporates both the textual and structural descriptions. This passage often appears as a single well-crafted paragraph that conveys the "essence" of the experience for the participants (p. 121).

For van Manen (1990), data analysis is an act of "phenomenological reflection," the goal of which is to "grasp the essential meaning of something" (p. 77). The process entails thorough examination of the data record on multiple levels: as a whole ("the holistic reading approach"), at the level of statements or phrases ("the selective reading approach"), and at the level of individual sentences ("the detailed reading approach"). At each of these levels, researchers contemplate questions such as "What statement(s) or phrase(s) seem particularly essential or revealing about the phenomenon or experience being described?" (p. 93). The analytic process is not yet complete once themes have been identified, as the researcher will also develop an interpretive description of the phenomenon's essence that is informed by the themes. To aid in this process, van Manen (2014) recommended reflecting on the themes with respect to five "existentials" or universal aspects of experiences: "lived relation (relationality), lived body (corporeality), lived space (spatiality), lived time (temporality), and lived things and technology (materiality)" (p. 302). Through the processes of identifying themes and reflecting on these five existentials, the researcher ultimately develops a description of the essence of the experience.

Data Presentation in Phenomenology

The analysis procedures adopted in phenomenological research may lead logically to a rhetorical structure for the written research report. For example, as researchers who have adopted Moustakas's (1994) procedures present their findings, they will incorporate significant statements made by participants and describe how these related to broader meaning units or clustered themes. Textural and structural descriptions of the phenomenon will be readily recognizable in the research report. An explicit statement of the phenomenon's essence is yet another hallmark, the presence of which distinguishes a phenomenological report from those developed in other research traditions. The essence is often presented as a single paragraph and may be enclosed within a figure.

Van Manen (1990) described an array of possibilities for composing the report, or "working the text" (p. 167). Authors might present their findings thematically, exploring essential features of the phenomenon. Or, they could begin with a description of the essence, then offer examples of how the essence manifested. Another option is to organize the presentation of findings in relation to the five aforementioned existentials: relationality, corporeality, spatiality, temporality, and materiality (van Manen, 2014). Regardless of the writing approach selected, the goal of phenomenological reporting is to "[p]roduce a research report that gives an accurate, clear, and articulate description of an experience. The reader of the report should come away with the feeling that 'I understand better what it is like for someone to experience that'" (Polkinghorne, 1989, p. 46).

A Phenomenology Example from Music Education

For many professionals working in the field of music, the question of how people experience musical enjoyment is of interest as they plan performances, rehearsals, lessons, or other musical experiences. Koops (2017) explored this question with four- to seven-year-olds in a study that exemplifies how Moustakas's (1994) approach to phenomenology has been applied within music education research. The context for this study was a researcher-led class called the Music Play Zone (MPZ) that engaged children and their parents in weekly 45-minute sessions at a public library. The purpose of the study was "to describe children's lived experience of enjoyment during musical play" (Koops, 2017, p. 364). The first research question asked, "What did children's musical enjoyment look like in the MPZ?" (p. 367), while the second inquired about "how children's musical enjoyment functions" (p. 375). Note how these research questions were phrased so that data generated in response to them would lead to a textural description (concerning what participants experienced) and structural description (concerning how they experienced it) of musical enjoyment. The study's participants included 12 children and four of their parents. While data generation in phenomenological studies often centers on extensive interviews, Koops combined multiple methods for generating data because her primary participants were young children. Data sources included interviews with parents and children, participant observation during class sessions, video-recorded class sessions, and video recordings of children making music at home that were captured by parents.

Within Moustakas's (1994) approach to data analysis, preliminary steps include epoche and bracketing. Accordingly, Koops (2017) described her approach to recognizing elements of her subjectivity and suspending them to the extent possible in order to focus analysis on participants' experiences of musical enjoyment. In the following description of subsequent steps in Koops's analysis process, terms associated with Moustakas's recommended procedures make the passage readily identifiable as one drawn from a phenomenology (e.g., horizonalizing, clustering, textural description, structural description, and essence):

> During bracketing, I considered this initial coding and set aside the data that were not related to my research questions on children's musical enjoyment. . . . For horizonalizing, I searched the data for significant statements arising from interview transcripts and video transcription. This led to clustering, gathering the horizons into themes. Themes provided the organization for my textural description, or what children's musical enjoyment looked like, as well as the structural description, or how enjoyment occurred and how it interacted with other elements of the music play experience. These analytical steps provided the groundwork for the essence, a synthesis of this particular set of data from my perspective. (p. 366)

The "results and interpretations" section of the research report offers a textural description, a structural description, and a discussion of the essence of the experience for the participants, each of which is emblematic of Moustaka's (1994) approach to phenomenology. In this study, the textural description encompassed five "hallmarks" of children's enjoyment: "active musical engagement, signs of physical engagement, a balance of familiarity and novelty, inclusion of activities allowing for student control or choice, and a safe and playful environment" (Koops, 2017, pp. 366–367). In the structural description, Koops identified four ways in which the children's musical enjoyment occurred: "within a balance of structure and freedom, within a balance of community and individual expression, as a cycle between children's musical enjoyment and participation, and as a springboard to musical risk-taking and musical agency" (p. 360).

The culminating element of a phenomenological study is a description of the "essence" of the phenomenon that synthesizes the textural and structural descriptions to create a composite description of the "essential invariant structure" of the phenomenon for the participants (Creswell & Poth, 2018, p. 80). Koops (2017) described the essence in this way: "Children's musical enjoyment occurred when there was a balance of structure and freedom, novelty and familiarity, and individual expression within an established community. Musical enjoyment is a cycle that involves social, personal, kinesthetic, and musical experiences" (p. 373). An interesting feature of this report is that the author presented both a paragraph expressing the essence from her perspective as the researcher and a diagram depicting "the enjoyment cycle" developed by one of the study's child participants (p. 374).

Ethnography

Ethnography is "a qualitative design in which the researcher describes and interprets the shared and learned patterns of values, behaviors, beliefs, and language of a culture-sharing group" (Creswell & Poth, 2018, p. 90). That a culture-sharing group serves as the focal point for a study distinguishes ethnography from other approaches to qualitative research. A culture-sharing group is one with a shared history of interacting together so that discernible patterns of social organization, behaviors, and ideational systems can be explored. While other research designs engage multiple participants (e.g., grounded theory and phenomenology), those individuals are not always located in the same place and may not interact frequently enough to develop the shared patterns that are of interest in an ethnography.

Ethnography aims to look "into the effects of a particular setting as a whole upon the meanings and interpretations of a particular population and culture, with the intent of disturbing the natural setting as little as possible" (Krueger, 2014, p. 134). Analysis focuses on patterns in the culture-sharing group's mental activities, which can be discerned from how the group uses language to convey ideas and beliefs, as well as their physical activities, which can be identified from the group's observable actions and behaviors. The product of inquiry is a rich, complex description of the culture-sharing group at the heart of the study. The term "ethnography" can refer to both a process for studying a culture-sharing group and the written report that serves as the product of such research.

One challenge associated with ethnography is that the construct of culture can be amorphous and challenging to define. Ethnographers often use the term "culture" as an abstraction, referring to something that cannot be studied directly. Rather, it can be inferred from the group's behaviors, language, and artifacts (Spradley, 1980). Within educational research, ethnography can be used to explore the culture of schools:

> Ethnography of schooling refers to educational and enculturative processes that are related to schools and intentional schooling, though this concept leaves room for studies of playgrounds, play groups, peer groups, patterns of violence in schools, and other aspects of school-related life. (Spindler, 1982, p. 2)

Through observing and interacting with a culture-sharing group, an ethnographer "can see 'culture at work' and provide a description and interpretation of it" (Creswell & Poth, 2018, p. 319; see also Wolcott, 2010).

Types of Ethnographies

Ethnography has roots in cultural anthropology and was inspired by the efforts of early 20th-century anthropologists who departed from traditional models then prevalent in the natural sciences by emphasizing firsthand data collection from cultural groups. Currently, a proliferation of subtypes, or "schools," of ethnography exist, each with different theoretical orientations and goals. Some of these include symbolic interactionism, cultural and cognitive anthropology, ethnomethodology, critical theory, and postmodernism (Atkinson & Hammersley, 1994). Two of the most commonly encountered types are the realist ethnography and the critical ethnography.

Realist ethnography is a traditional approach developed by cultural anthropologists in which the researcher positions themselves as a purportedly "objective" observer (Van Maanen, 2011). Realist ethnographies often report on mundane details of a culture-sharing group's routine activities, providing an account of "the taken for granted and common activities" of "common denominator people" (p. 49). The writing style features third-person narration from a dispassionate, omniscient stance so that the author's presence "vanishes" from the text:

> Fieldworkers rarely say very much about precisely what experience in the field consists of, letting the representation stand for itself (i.e., "The X do this," not "I saw the X do this"). Thus realist tales swallow up the fieldworker, and by convention the text focuses almost solely on the saying, doings, and supposed thinkings of the people studied. (p. 47)

Realist ethnographers report factual information, endeavoring to suspend personal subjectivity, political views, and judgments to the fullest extent possible. They often use standard categories for cultural description, such as "family life, work life, social networks, authority relations, kinship patterns, status systems, interaction orders, etc." (p. 48). Realist reports are further characterized by an implied sense of "interpretive authority" or "interpretive omnipotence" in which "the ethnographer has the final word on how the culture is to be interpreted and presented" (p. 51).

Critical ethnography is "a type of ethnographic research in which the authors advocate for the emancipation of groups marginalized in society" (Creswell & Poth, 2018, p. 92; see also Thomas, 1993). Critical ethnographers embrace a value-laden approach to research in which their aims include speaking against inequity and advocating for the needs of research participants. These studies often interrogate unequal distributions of power in society, examining systems of inequality, inequity, hegemony, privilege, prestige, authority, and so forth.

Purpose Statements and Research Questions in Ethnography

Purpose statements and research questions in ethnography are directed toward elucidating patterns in the values, behaviors, beliefs, and language of a culture-sharing group. They may be encoded with such language as "ethnography," "culture-sharing group," "cultural behavior and language," "cultural portrait," and "cultural themes" (Creswell & Poth, 2018, p. 135). The purpose and questions from Lum's (2007) ethnography offer one representative example:

The purpose of this ethnographic study is to examine the musical culture of a group of Singaporean children to determine its influences and meanings in their daily lives. The primary guiding questions of the ethnographic study of children in school and within their families include the following:

1) What are the musical cultures of Singaporean children? How are the musical cultures determined and generated by social, cultural, historical, and political influences?

2) What part do globalization, technology and the media play in the shaping of the musical cultures of these children? Are there ethnic differentiations in the music of these children?

3) What are the implications of research on children's musical cultures for the policies and practices of music education? (pp. 9–10)

Methodological Procedures Associated with Ethnography

Sampling

Sampling in an ethnography is distinctive, in that it occurs at the level of the group rather than the individual. Ethnographers seek an intact group with a sufficiently long history of interaction for their shared values, beliefs, behaviors, and language to have evolved into discernable patterns. In the case of critical ethnography, the culture-sharing group will often be one that has been marginalized by society, with researchers infusing a "critical" perspective into their work by advocating for the needs of the participants. When a researcher is proposing a prolonged research collaboration with a group, it is often helpful to work with a gatekeeper or key participant who can assist with navigating entry to the field.

Considerable variability exists in the kinds of culture-sharing groups that can serve as the focal point for an ethnography. Music education researchers have conducted ethnographies of the cast of a fifth-grade musical (Feahy-Shaw, 2001), "girl choir culture" as experienced by members of a community-based choral organization (Bartolome, 2010, 2013), and "historic jazz culture" as experienced by members of a high school jazz band (Goodrich, 2008). Several ethnographies in the music education literature have focused on children's musical cultures, recognizing "children as members of a cross-national, international 'culture' all their own, separated from adult culture" (Campbell, 2010, p. 8; see also Koops, 2010; Lum, 2007; Lum & Campbell, 2007).

Data Generation

Ethnography is characterized by extensive fieldwork conducted over prolonged periods of time, with researchers generating data in the places where people live and work. Ethnographers generate data through varied means, including observations, interviews, surveys, tests and measures, content analysis, elicitation methods, and audiovisual methods. They may position their role as a participant observer, immersing themselves in the daily lives and activities of group members in order to understand their culture from within. Alternatively, they may position their role as a nonparticipant observer in order to be as unobtrusive to the culture-sharing group as possible. Regardless of the role adopted, "[r]ecognizing and documenting the effects of one's presence . . . remains important. . . . [T]he researcher must describe roles clearly so that the reader can understand the influences of both non-participant and participant observers" (Krueger, 2014, p. 138).

The lengthy immersion of researchers in the contexts where participants live and work requires their sensitivity to a number of potential field issues. Ethnographers thoughtfully plan the manner in which they enter and exit the field and how they navigate relationships with members of the culture-sharing group. Many embrace a principle of scholarly reciprocity, contributing something of value back to participants with whom they have collaborated. Additional ethical questions concern who "owns" the data and who determines how it will be presented, matters that ethnographers endeavor to navigate honestly and respectfully.

Data Analysis

Broadly speaking, data analysis in ethnography involves analyzing patterns across multiple sources of data that will then inform an overall interpretation of the culture-sharing group. Wolcott (1994) describes the process of organizing and reporting qualitative data as unfolding through three phases: description, analysis, and interpretation of the culture-sharing group. For Wolcott (1990), ethnographic analysis begins with description:

> Description is the foundation upon which qualitative research is built. . . . Here you become the storyteller, inviting the reader to see through your eyes what you have seen. . . . Start by presenting a straightforward description of the setting and events. No footnotes, no intrusive analysis—just the facts, carefully presented and interestingly related at an appropriate level of detail. (pp. 27–28)

Wolcott (1994) recommends 10 approaches to composing ethnographic descriptions, among which are highlighting events in chronological order, centering description upon a key event, and presenting contrasting perspectives through the views of different participants (see pp. 17–23 for discussion of all 10 approaches). Descriptions might take on a more literary character, weaving a storyline complete with characters and a plot or presenting a "mystery" to readers. Alternatively, a theoretical framework might inform the style and structure of description.

During the second phase, analysis, the researcher sorts through the data record in order to identify "patterned regularities" (Wolcott, 1994, p. 33). This may be accomplished by reorganizing information from the descriptive phase into tables, charts, diagrams, and figures. Methodologists such as Spradley (1979, 1980) have advanced systematized procedures for developing taxonomies, comparison tables, and semantic tables that may be useful at this stage. Analysis strategies such as developing charts, matrices, and even statistical analysis to examine frequency and magnitude have led authors to characterize this phase as "the quantitative side of qualitative research" (Wolcott, 1994, p. 26). To situate the analysis within a broader context, ethnographers may draw comparisons between the culture-sharing group they have studied and additional ones or bring existing theoretical frameworks to bear on the analysis.

The final phase, interpretation, extends beyond examining the data to consider "what is to be made of them" (Wolcott, 1994, p. 36). At this stage, the ethnographer draws inferences directly from the data or uses existing theory to guide interpretation. The researcher's etic perspective (i.e., their views as an outsider to the culture-sharing group) comes forth as they explain "This is what I make of it all" or "This is how the research experience affected me" (p. 44).

Data Presentation in Ethnographies

The culminating product of an ethnography is a holistic cultural portrait that describes in rich detail the group's way of life as well as pervasive patterns in its social organization, values, beliefs, language, behaviors, and ideational systems. The report synthesizes participants' perspectives and the researcher's interpretation, which might include advocating for needed societal changes in light of the group's experiences. Authors present the patterns or themes that emerged from analysis in written form, perhaps as a working set of generalizations, or in a performance format, such as a theatrical production or poem. Rather than representing a distinct phase in the research process, the process of writing frequently overlaps and intersects with data generation and analysis.

Thick description is valued in ethnographic writing, as emphasized by Fetterman (2020): "Ideally the ethnographer shares the participant's understanding of the situation with the reader. Thick description is a written record of cultural interpretation" (p. 134). Throughout the process of data analysis, interpretation, and presentation, ethnographers strive for balance between emic views, which reflect the participants' insider perspectives, and etic views, which reflect the researcher's outsider perspective. Embedding illustrative verbatim quotes from participants throughout the report is one way to advance emic perspectives.

Emerson et al. (2011) characterize an ethnographic research report as "analytically thematized, but often in relatively loose ways . . . constructed out of a series of thematically organized units of fieldnote excerpts and analytic commentary" (p. 202). They advance the concept of "excerpt-commentary units," introduced in

Chapter 8 of this text, which serve as building blocks from which an ethnographic report can be constructed. Wolcott's (1994) three phases of data transformation (description, analysis, and interpretation) also lead logically to a possible rhetorical structure for an ethnographic report. The author would first offer "description" of the culture oriented toward answering the question "What is going on here?" (p. 12). The researcher would then present "analysis" in order to show "how things work" by displaying findings in tables, charts, or figures or otherwise highlighting "patterned regularities" in the data. Finally, the author would offer an interpretation oriented toward answering "What is to be made of it all?" (p. 12). This could include bringing the findings into conversation with existing theory or literature or contextualizing the findings within the researcher's experiences.

An Ethnography Example from Music Education

Music educators may relate to the idea that a musical ensemble can develop a "culture" of its own, with shared language, thought patterns, and behaviors among its members. Bartolome explored one such musical culture-sharing group in her ethnography of the Seattle Girls' Choir (SGC), reporting findings in both a dissertation (2010) and an article-length research report (2013). She described the manner in which this community-based choral organization functioned as a culture-sharing group, characterizing it as a

> community of youth singers, a music society of girls supported by a dedicated network of music faculty and parent volunteers intent on facilitating the choristers' evolution into musicians and young women. When I first joined the SGC faculty, it struck me as a rich, multifaceted culture, replete with a distinct social system and an attendant collection of shared beliefs, values, and practices. (2013, p. 396)

The above paragraph reveals the author's dual role as a researcher and a member of the organization's artistic staff. As conductor for one of the organization's four choirs, she conducted some fieldwork as a participant observer with her own ensemble and additional fieldwork with choirs for which she was not concurrently engaged as a teacher. By positioning her role in this way, she was able to obtain emic and etic perspectives and represent both in the resulting report.

The study's purpose is expressed as "ascertain[ing] the cultural elements comprising the SGC as an institution" (Bartolome, 2010, p. 22) and is thus encoded with language associated with ethnography. The research questions are also aligned with the purposes of ethnography, with their emphasis on discernible patterns in members' shared values and observable behaviors:

(1) What do various participants consider to be the values and benefits of their participation in the SGC community?

(2) How do the values of the organization manifest themselves in action during rehearsals, performances, classes, meetings, and other SGC events? (Bartolome, 2013, p. 398)

Data generation unfolded across the timeframe of one year and included observations that were documented in extensive field notes, semi-structured interviews with various members of the choir community, parent surveys, and a collection of documents and artifacts. The extensive array of artifacts consulted in this study included 26 years' worth of concert programs, recruiting materials, audition packets, mission statements, and the organization's website.

Several features of Bartolome's approach to data generation are characteristic of ethnography. She generated data with many members of the choral community, including the artistic director, conductors, accompanists, singers in each of the organization's four choirs, parents, and the choir office manager. The emphasis was on understanding a culture-sharing group with a history of direct interaction as opposed to individual's or a select group of participants' experiences. Bartolome's prolonged engagement in the field and the extensiveness of her data generation further typify an ethnographic approach. Over the period of one year, she conducted 150 hours of formal nonparticipant observation and 200 hours of participant observation. The interviews she conducted resulted in 200 single-spaced pages of text data. Embedding such details about the extensiveness of data generation is one way to provide evidence of prolonged engagement in the field, which is an indicator of well-conducted qualitative research in general but also a hallmark of ethnography in particular.

Bartolome (2010) approached data analysis through a recursive, inductive process: "Fieldnotes, interview texts, survey responses, and material culture were repeatedly read and re-read for emergent patterns and themes related to the culture and social system of the SGC and participant values and benefits" (p. 27). Through this process, "the full extent of the data were pieced together to create a picture of the culture and social system of the Seattle Girls' Choir experience as perceived by various members" (p. 27). The 2013 article is organized thematically, with data excerpts and the author's interpretive commentary presented for themes in each of the four broad categories: "musical benefits," "personal benefits," "social benefits," and "external and community benefits" (Bartolome, 2013, pp. 402–412). The author also represented these themes graphically in a figure depicting "an integrated model of the chorister experience" (p. 414). Among many salient findings were participants' perceptions of choir as a constant and as an emotional outlet during adolescent development, choir as a space that valued diversity and upheld diverse role models for adolescents to emulate, and choir as a place to experience a sense of social belonging with like-minded individuals—as reflected in the participant quote selected for the article's title, a six-year-old's exclamation that choir was "like a whole bunch of *me*!" The space afforded in the 2010 dissertation permitted extensive treatment of the organization's distinctive culture and social system, with vignettes helping to "locate the reader in the world of the Seattle Girls' Choir and bring to life the people and places that provided the inspiration for this analysis" (Bartolome, 2010, p. 29).

Summary

This chapter has provided an introduction to four approaches to inquiry—ethnography, grounded theory, narrative, and phenomenology—that, together with case study, comprise five primary qualitative research designs. Reading exemplar studies such as those cited in this chapter offers one way to become better acquainted with the distinguishing features of each of these approaches to qualitative research. While the scope of this chapter precluded exhaustive treatment of how to conduct a study using any of these approaches, the resources recommended in Box 10.1 provide further procedural guidance. Following are some questions that will support your review of content presented in this chapter:

1. Create a table, mind map, or other graphic organizer comparing features of the five primary approaches to qualitative research: case study, ethnography, grounded theory, narrative, and phenomenology. For each research approach, summarize the following: research purpose, focal point or unit of analysis, approach to sampling, methods of data generation, strategies for analysis, and frequently cited methodological experts.
2. Read abstracts drawn from qualitative research studies and highlight specific words or phrases from which the research design can be identified.
3. Choose a phenomenon that you would be interested in researching using a qualitative approach and sketch some ideas for how you could explore that phenomenon using each of the five primary qualitative designs. Consider:
   a. How you would formulate a purpose statement and research questions using language consistent with the purposes of each design.
   b. The focal point for your study in each approach (e.g., a culture-sharing group? an individual's storied account? detailed descriptions of participants' lived experiences?).
   c. The types of data you might generate for each approach.
   d. Strategies you might use to analyze data in each approach.
   e. How the written report might be structured for each approach.
4. Having generated ideas for using each of the five approaches for the preceding question, you will likely find that one or two of the approaches offer the best fit for your specific research questions. Write a brief paragraph explaining why one of the approaches offers an appropriate methodological fit for exploring your chosen phenomenon.

Important Terms for Review

Grounded theory: an approach to qualitative research in which the researcher develops a "unified theoretical explanation" for a process or action (Corbin & Strauss, 2008, p. 107).

Narrative inquiry: an approach to research in which inquirers elicit, interpret, and report detailed stories of individuals' life experiences.

Phenomenology: the study of the "meaning, structure, and essence of the lived experience of [a] phenomenon for [a] person or group of people" (Patton, 2002, p. 132).

Essence: "the very nature of a phenomenon ... that which makes a some-'thing' what it is—and without which it could not be what it is" (van Manen, 1990, p. 10).

Ethnography: "a qualitative design in which the researcher describes and interprets the shared and learned patterns of values, behaviors, beliefs, and language of a culture-sharing group" (Creswell & Poth, 2018, p. 90).

Culture-sharing group: the focal point of an ethnography; an intact group with a shared history of interaction to the extent that discernible patterns of social organization, behaviors, and ideational systems can be explored.

References

Atkinson, P. (2015). *For ethnography*. Sage.

Atkinson, P., & Hammersley, M. (1994). Ethnography and participant observation. In N. K. Denzin & Y. S. Lincoln (Eds.), *Handbook of qualitative research* (pp. 248–261). Sage.

Barone, T. (2000a). Beyond theory and method: A case of critical storytelling. In T. Barone (Ed.), *Aesthetics, politics, and educational inquiry: Essays and examples* (pp. 191–200). Peter Lang.

Barone, T. (2000b). Using the narrative text as an occasion for conspiracy. In T. Barone (Ed.), *Aesthetics, politics, and educational inquiry: Essays and examples* (pp. 137–160). Peter Lang.

Barone, T. (2007). A return to the gold standard? Questioning the future of narrative construction as educational research. *Qualitative Inquiry, 13*, 454–470. https://doi.org/10.1177/1077800406297667

Bartolome, S. J. (2010). *Girl choir culture: An ethnography of the Seattle Girls' Choir* (Publication No. 3406114) [Doctoral dissertation, University of Washington]. ProQuest Dissertations & Theses Global.

Bartolome, S. J. (2013). "It's like a whole bunch of me!": The perceived values and benefits of the Seattle Girls' Choir experience. *Journal of Research in Music Education, 60*(4), 395–418. https://doi.org/10.1177/0022429412464054

Bruner, J. S. (1986). *Actual minds, possible worlds*. Harvard University Press.

Bruner, J. S. (1991). The narrative construction of reality. *Critical Inquiry, 18*(1), 1–21. https://doi.org/10.1086/448619

Bruner, J. S. (2004). Life as narrative. *Social Research, 71*(3), 691–710. https://www.jstor.org/stable/40970444

Campbell, P. S. (2010). *Songs in their heads: Music and its meaning in children's lives* (2nd ed.). Oxford University Press.

Charmaz, K. (2005). Grounded theory in the 21st century: Applications for advancing social justice studies. In N. K. Denzin & Y. S. Lincoln (Eds.), *The Sage handbook of qualitative research* (3rd ed., pp. 507–535). Sage.

Charmaz, K. (2014). *Constructing grounded theory* (2nd ed.). Sage.

Chase, S. (1995). Taking narrative seriously: Consequences for method and theory in interview studies. In R. Josselson & A. Lieblich (Eds.), *Interpreting experience: The narrative study of lives* (Vol. 3, pp. 1–26). Sage.

Clandinin, D. J. (2013). *Engaging in narrative inquiry*. Left Coast Press.

Clandinin, D. J., & Connelly, F. M. (2000). *Narrative inquiry: Experience and story in qualitative research*. Jossey-Bass.

Clarke, A. E. (2005). *Situational analysis: Grounded theory after the postmodern turn*. Sage.

Colaizzi, P. F. (1978). Psychological research as the phenomenologist views it. In R. Vaile & M. King (Eds.), *Existential phenomenological alternatives for psychology* (pp. 48–71). Oxford University Press.

Connelly, F. M., & Clandinin, D. J. (2006). Narrative inquiry. In J. L. Green, G. Camilli, & P. B. Elmore (Eds.), *Handbook of complementary methods in education research* (pp. 477–487). Lawrence Erlbaum Associates.

Conway, C. M. (2000). Gender and musical instrument choice: A phenomenological investigation. *Bulletin of the Council for Research in Music Education, 146*, 1–17. https://www.jstor.org/stable/40319030

Corbin, J., & Strauss, A. (2008). *Basics of qualitative research: Techniques and procedures for developing grounded theory* (3rd ed.). Sage.

Corbin, J., & Strauss, A. (2015). *Basics of qualitative research: Techniques and procedures for developing grounded theory* (4th ed.). Sage.

Cortazzi, M. (1993). *Narrative analysis*. Falmer Press.

Creswell, J. W., & Poth, C. N. (2018). *Qualitative inquiry and research design: Choosing among five approaches* (4th ed.). Sage.

Czarniawska, B. (2004). *Narratives in social science research*. Sage.

Daiute, C. (2014). *Narrative inquiry: A dynamic approach*. Sage.

Denzin, N. K. (1989). *Interpretive biography*. Sage.

Draves, T. J., & Vargas, J. E. (2022). "I made myself fit in": Johny's story. *Journal of Research in Music Education, 70*(1), 4–21. https://doi.org/10.1177/00224294211001876

Emerson, R. M., Fretz, R. I., & Shaw, L. L. (2011). *Writing ethnographic fieldnotes* (2nd ed.). University of Chicago Press.

Feahy-Shaw, S. (2001). The view through the lunchroom window: An ethnography of a fifth-grade musical. *Bulletin of the Council for Research in Music Education, 150*, 37–51. https://www.jstor.org/stable/40319098

Fetterman, D. M. (2020). *Ethnography: Step-by-step* (4th ed.). Sage.

Giorgi, A. (2009). *The descriptive phenomenological method in psychology: A modified Husserlian approach*. Duquesne University Press.

Glaser, B. G. (1965). The constant comparative method of qualitative analysis. *Social Problems, 12*, 436–445. https://doi.org/10.2307/798843

Glaser, B. G. (1978). *Theoretical sensitivity: Advances in the methodology of grounded theory*. Sociology Press.

Glaser, B. G., & Strauss, A. (1967). *The discovery of grounded theory*. Aldine.

Goodrich, A. (2008). Utilizing elements of the historic jazz culture in a high school setting. *Bulletin for the Council of Research in Music Education, 175*, 11–30. https://www.jstor.org/stable/40319410

Husserl, E. (1970). *The crisis of European sciences and transcendental phenomenology* (D. Carr, Trans.). Northwestern University Press.

Kennedy, M. C. (2004). "It's a metamorphosis": Guiding the voice change at the American Boychoir School. *Journal of Research in Music Education, 52*(3), 264–280. https://doi.org/10.2307/3345859

Koops, L. H. (2010). "Deñuy jàngal seen bopp" (they teach themselves): Children's music learning in The Gambia. *Journal of Research in Music Education*, 58(1), 20–36. https://doi.org/10.1177/0022429409361000

Koops, L. H. (2017). The enjoyment cycle: A phenomenology of musical enjoyment of 4- to 7-year-olds during musical play. *Journal of Research in Music Education*, 65(3), 360–380. https://doi.org/10.1177/0022429417716921

Krueger, P. J. (2014). Doing ethnography in music education. In C. M. Conway (Ed.), *The Oxford handbook of qualitative research in American music education* (pp. 133–147). Oxford University Press.

Kvale, S. (1983). The qualitative research interview: A phenomenological and hermeneutical mode of understanding. *Phenomenological Psychology*, 14, 171–196.

Lum, C.-H. (2007). *Musical networks of children: An ethnography of elementary school children in Singapore* (Publication No. 3265372) [Doctoral dissertation, University of Washington]. ProQuest Dissertations & Theses Global.

Lum, C.-H., & Campbell, P. S. (2007). The sonic surrounds of an elementary school. *Journal of Research in Music Education*, 55(1), 31–47. https://doi.org/10.1177/002242940705500104

May, K. A. (1986). Writing and evaluating the grounded theory research report. In W. C. Chenitz & J. M. Swanson (Eds.), *From practice to grounded theory* (pp. 146–154). Addison-Wesley.

McCall, J. M. (2015). *Degree perserverance among African Americans transitioning from historically Black colleges and universities (HBCUs) to predominantly White institutions (PWIs)* (Publication No. 3702142) [Doctoral dissertation, Arizona State University]. ProQuest Dissertations & Theses Global.

Moustakas, C. (1994). *Phenomenological research methods*. Sage.

Nichols, J. (2013). Rie's story, Ryan's journey: Music in the life of a transgender student. *Journal of Research in Music Education*, 61(3), 262–279. https://doi.org/10.1177/0022429413498259

Nichols, J. (2016). Sharing the stage: Ethical dimensions of narrative inquiry in music education. *Journal of Research in Music Education*, 63(4), 439–454. https://doi.org/10.1177/0022429415617745

O'Leary, E. J. (2019). A phenomenological study of competition in high school bands. *Bulletin for the Council of Research in Music Education*, 220, 43–61. https://doi.org/10.5406/bulcouresmusedu.220.0043

Padilla, R. (2003). Clara: A phenomenology of disability. *The American Journal of Occupational Therapy*, 57(4), 413–423. https://doi.org/10.5014/ajot.57.4.413

Parker, E. C. (2014). The process of social identity development in adolescent high school choral singers: A grounded theory. *Journal of Research in Music Education*, 62(1), 18–32. https://doi.org/10.1177/0022429413520009

Parker, E. C., Bond, V. L., & Powell, S. R. (2017). A grounded theory of preservice music educators' lesson planning processes within field experience methods courses. *Journal of Research in Music Education*, 65(3), 287–308. https://doi.org/10.1177/0022429417730035

Parker, E. C., & Draves, T. J. (2017). A narrative of two preservice music teachers with visual impairment. *Journal of Research in Music Education*, 64(4), 385–404. https://doi.org/10.1177/0022429416674704

Patton, M. Q. (2002). Two decades of developments in qualitative inquiry: A personal, experiential perspective. *Qualitative Social Work*, 1, 261–283. https://doi.org/10.1177/1473325002001003636

Pinnegar, S., & Daynes, J. (2007). Locating narrative inquiry historically: Thematics in the turn to narrative. In D. J. Clandinin (Ed.), *Handbook of narrative inquiry: Mapping a methodology* (pp. 3–34). Sage.

Plummer, K. (1983). *Documents of life: An introduction to the problems and literature of a humanistic method*. George Allen & Unwin.

Polkinghorne, D. E. (1989). Phenomenological research methods. In R. S. Valle & S. Halling (Eds.), *Existential-phenomenological perspectives in psychology* (pp. 41–60). Plenum Press.

Polkinghorne, D. E. (1995). Narrative configuration in qualitative analysis. *International Journal of Qualitative Studies*, 8, 5–23. https://doi.org/10.1080/0951839950080103

Reissman, C. K. (2008). *Narrative methods for the human sciences*. Sage.

Salvador, K., Paetz, A. M., & Tippetts, M. M. (2020). "We all have a little more homework to do": A constructivist grounded theory of transformative learning processes for practicing music teachers. *Journal of Research in Music Education, 68*(2), 193–215. https://doi.org/10.1177/0022429420920630

Seidman, I. (2019). *Interviewing as qualitative research: A guide for researchers in education and the social sciences* (5th ed.). Teachers College Press.

Spiegelberg, H. (1982). *The phenomenological movement*. Martinus Nijhoff.

Spindler, G. (1982). Introduction. In G. Spindler (Ed.), *Doing the ethnography of schooling* (pp. 1–13). Holt, Rinehart, & Wilson.

Spradley, J. P. (1979). *The ethnographic interview*. Holt, Rinehart, & Wilson.

Spradley, J. P. (1980). *Participant observation*. Holt, Rinehart & Winston.

Stauffer, S. L. (2014). Narrative inquiry and the uses of narrative in music education research. In C. M. Conway (Ed.), *The Oxford handbook of qualitative research in American music education* (pp. 163–185). Oxford University Press.

Stewart, D., & Mickunas, A. (1990). *Exploring phenomenology: A guide to the field and its literature* (2nd ed.). Ohio University Press.

Strauss, A. (1987). *Qualitative analysis for social scientists*. Cambridge University Press.

Strauss, A., & Corbin, J. (1990). *Basics of qualitative research: Grounded theory procedures and techniques*. Sage.

Strauss, A., & Corbin, J. (1998). *Basics of qualitative research: Techniques and procedures for developing grounded theory* (2nd ed.). Sage.

Sweet, B. (2015). The adolescent female changing voice: A phenomenological investigation. *Journal of Research in Music Education, 63*(1), 70–88. https://doi.org/10.1177/0022429415570755

Thomas, J. (1993). *Doing critical ethnography*. Sage.

van Kaam, A. (1966). *Existential foundations of psychology*. Duquesne University Press.

Van Maanen, J. (2011). *Tales of the field: On writing ethnography* (2nd ed.). University of Chicago Press.

van Manen, M. (1990). *Researching lived experience: Human science for an action sensitive pedagogy*. State University of New York Press.

van Manen, M. (2014). *Phenomenology of practice: Meaning-giving methods in phenomenological research and writing*. Left Coast Press.

Weidner, B. L. (2020). A grounded theory of musical independence in the concert band. *Journal of Research in Music Education, 68*(1), 53–77. https://doi.org/10.1177/0022429419897616

West, J. J. (2020). Understanding the process of proximate change following music teachers' participation in large-scale conferences: A grounded theory. *Bulletin of the Council for Research in Music Education, 225*, 67–94. https://doi.org/10.5406/bulcouresmusedu.225.0067

Wolcott, H. F. (1990). *Writing up qualitative research*. Sage.

Wolcott, H. F. (1994). *Transforming qualitative data: Description, analysis, and interpretation*. Sage.

Wolcott, H. F. (2008). *Ethnography: A way of seeing* (2nd ed.). AltaMira Press.

Wolcott, H. F. (2010). *Ethnography lessons: A primer*. Left Coast Press.

11

Considerations of Quality in Qualitative Research

Chapter Preview

The purpose of this chapter is to describe how excellence and quality can be demonstrated in qualitative research and to provide criteria for discerning these qualities as a consumer of qualitative reports. We begin by familiarizing readers with professional dialogue that has transpired to date concerning the appropriateness of terms such as "validation," "verification," "credibility," and "trustworthiness" for describing qualitative inquiry. We then provide an overview of validation strategies that researchers can use to enhance the credibility of their research. Strategic actions that researchers can take include pursuing triangulation or crystallization, presenting negative case analysis, engaging in reflexive practices, and taking steps to recognize and manage their own subjectivity. Participants can be actively engaged in validation through member reflections, by interacting with the researcher in the field over a prolonged period of time, or through more intense collaboration with researchers in various phases of the research. Additional validation strategies call for external reviewers to audit the research process and products and for readers to assess the potential transferability of research findings based on thick description provided by the researcher. We conclude the chapter with guiding questions readers can use to discern quality in the research reports they consume.

Introduction

This chapter considers how qualitative researchers can demonstrate qualities such as merit or excellence in their research, as well as how consumers can discern these qualities as they review qualitative reports. It is intended to help answer the following questions:

> How can an inquirer persuade his or her audiences (including self) that the findings of an inquiry are worth paying attention to, worth taking account of? (Lincoln & Guba, 1985, p. 290)

> Is the account valid, and by whose standards? How do we evaluate the quality of qualitative research? (Creswell & Poth, 2018, p. 253)

> Are these findings sufficiently authentic ... that I may trust myself in acting on their implications? More to the point, would I feel sufficiently secure about these findings to construct social policy or legislation based on them? (Guba & Lincoln, 2005, p. 205)

As qualitative research became more prominent in the social sciences, early attempts at answering such questions were often couched in language consistent with quantitative and positivist approaches to research. For example, in considering how "validity" could be evidenced in qualitative research, LeCompte and Goetz (1982) translated the concept of threats to internal and external validity from the experimental research tradition to ethnographic research. However, researchers soon began to assert that positivist conceptions of "validity" were incongruent with the aims of qualitative research and consequently sought out ways to describe qualitative inquiry in its own terms.

In one landmark publication, Lincoln and Guba (1985) put forth "naturalistic equivalents" of the quantitatively oriented constructs of internal validity, external validity, reliability, and objectivity. As an alternative to the term "internal validity," they proposed that qualitative researchers use "credibility" to refer to the extent to which the researcher has represented multiple realities adequately (p. 296). Instead of "external validity," they recommended using the term "transferability" to refer to the degree of similarity between the original research context and the setting or situation to which it is translated (p. 297). Rather than "reliability," they proposed that "dependability" could be demonstrated through an audit establishing the consistency of a research process and its findings. Finally, as an alternative to "objectivity," they suggested that naturalistic inquirers seek "confirmability" of their data (p. 300). While many researchers have moved away from asserting the "quality" of qualitative research through direct comparison to quantitative standards, these "naturalistic equivalents" were a seminal contribution that has shaped the field's use of many terms today. For instance, Lincoln and Guba's use of "trustworthiness" to describe whether research has been conducted in such a way as to give the reader confidence in the findings continues to be referenced.

In the years that have elapsed since Lincoln and Guba (1985) put forth their naturalistic equivalents, considerable debate has unfolded within the community of qualitative researchers concerning terms best aligned with the purpose and goals of qualitative research. Some authors have eschewed the term "validation" (Eisner, 1991; Wolcott, 1990), while others have recast the term to be better aligned with the interpretivist orientation of qualitative research (e.g., Angen, 2000; Lather, 1991, 1993). Qualitatively oriented conceptualizations of validation are characterized by the goal of representing multiple, possible realities as opposed to a single, definitive version of truth that can be "verified"; acknowledgment of the researcher's instrumental role in interpretive sense making; engagement of participants in negotiating the meaning of the study; and recognition that interpretations are temporally and contextually situated and therefore subject to reinterpretation (Angen, 2000; Creswell & Poth, 2018). Around the turn of the century, Patton (2002) opined:

The validity of experimental methods and quantitative measurement, appropriately used, was never in doubt. Now, qualitative methods have ascended to a level of parallel respectability. That ascendance was not without struggle and sometimes acrimonious debate and, to be sure, there are still backwaters where the debate lingers, but among serious methodologists and practitioners, the debate is, for all practical purposes, over. (p. 265)

Nevertheless, researchers new to qualitative inquiry can benefit from understanding professional debates that have occurred to date about terms such as "validation," "verification," "credibility," and "trustworthiness." Creswell and Poth (2018) trace such dialogue from early writings with positivist orientations (e.g., LeCompte & Goetz, 1982) to contemporary perspectives more closely aligned with the interpretive orientation of qualitative research (e.g., Angen, 2000). Robinson (2014) tracked parallel developments in music education research, using excerpts from published scholarship to illustrate how authors' lexicon for describing and evidencing quality has evolved to one better aligned with the ontological and epistemological underpinnings of qualitative inquiry. As he aptly summarized:

The words we use to describe our actions and intentions as researchers are powerful tools. These words do more than provide information about content and structure; they offer clues as to our beliefs about the profession, our research, and our view of the world. (p. 95)

Accordingly, researchers are advised to make carefully considered choices about the terms they adopt for describing "excellence" or "quality," and to define and use these terms with precision.

Validation Strategies

Having considered various terms that can be used to describe the "quality" of qualitative research, we now turn to techniques researchers can use to demonstrate quality in their work. Creswell and Poth (2018) recommend nine "validation strategies," which represent a synthesis of several seminal sources (e.g., Creswell & Miller, 2000; Lincoln & Guba, 1985; Merriam & Tisdell, 2015; Miles & Huberman, 1994). Qualitative researchers frequently include a section documenting validation strategies they have used in their reports, and these nine are among the most frequently cited. Although the term "validation" has been contested, Creswell and Poth (2018) specify their particular use:

We consider "validation" in qualitative research to be an attempt to assess the "accuracy" of the findings, as best described by the researcher, the participants, and the readers (or reviewers).... We use the term validation to emphasize a process (see Angen, 2000), rather than *verification* (which has quantitative overtones) or historical words such as *trustworthiness* and *authenticity* (recognizing that many qualitative writers do return to these words, suggesting the "staying power" of Lincoln and Guba's, 1985, standards). (p. 259)

The following section describes each of Creswell and Poth's (2018) validation strategies and provides examples of their use in music education research. Following Creswell and Poth, the strategies are grouped according to the perspective from which validation is approached: the researcher's lens, the participant's lens, and the reader's or reviewer's lens.

Validation Strategies Pursued by the Researcher

Corroborating Evidence Through Triangulation or Crystallization

Triangulation refers to a process of corroborating evidence from multiple data sources, methods of generating data, investigators, or theories to enhance a study's credibility (Denzin, 1978; Patton, 1999). When researchers use the term "triangulation," they are often referring to the first of these four types: comparing multiple and different data sources (e.g., focus group vs. individual interview transcripts, observational field notes, and documents or other artifacts). This strategy evolved as a response to the inherently subjective nature of data generation in qualitative research, with the assumption that "findings may be judged valid when different and contrasting methods of data collection yield identical findings on the same research subjects; a case of replication within the same setting" (Bloor, 2001, p. 384).

However, this conceptualization of triangulation suggests that it is possible to converge on a single, accurate version of reality when qualitative researchers are often interested in presenting multiple possible realities. As Tracy (2010) explained:

> [T]riangulation does not lay neatly over research from interpretive, critical, or post-modern paradigms that view reality as multiple, fractured, contested, or socially constructed. Researchers from these paradigms would argue that just because data all converge on the same conclusion, this does not assure that this specified reality is correct. (p. 843)

As an alternative, Richardson (2000b) suggested that researchers envision a process of "crystallization":

> I propose that the central imaginary for "validation" for postmodern texts is not the triangle—a rigid, fixed, two-dimensional object. Rather the central imaginary is the crystal, which combines symmetry and substances with an infinite variety of shapes, substances, transmutations, multidimensionalities, and angles of approach. Crystals grow, change, and are altered, but they are not amorphous. Crystals are prisms that

reflect externalities and refract within themselves, creating different colors, patterns, and arrays casting off in different directions. What we see depends on our angle of repose—not triangulation but rather crystallization. (p. 963)

This image leaves open the possibility of representing multiple realities within a research report, exploring a phenomenon from many angles. Although Creswell and Poth titled this first strategy "corroborating evidence through triangulation of multiple data sources," we broaden our description to encompass Denzin's (1978) four types of triangulation and Richardson's (2000b) notion of crystallization.

Cape and Nichols's (2012) narrative study with two women who had been military band members during the Second World War offers an excellent example of crystallization. The authors first interpreted participants' stories as contributing a metanarrative "of women in the twentieth century demanding more of society and claiming new ground" (p. 30). Yet, upon reexamining unused portions of interview transcripts, the researchers found quotes suggesting additional possible interpretations. For instance, in response to an interview question about her experience as one of the first women in the military, participant Doris responded, "Well, of course we didn't think of it so much ... at the time, we didn't know we were being women's liberation at all" (p. 29). The researchers explained:

> As we reexamined the transcripts it became clear that while each woman recognized the socio-historical significance of her experiences, neither woman emphasized this perspective. They may indeed have broken new ground, but the women pointed to a more personal understanding of what it all meant.
>
> We had focused on issues of power in Doris and Pat's narratives, but were suddenly made uncomfortably aware of the issues of power playing out in our own story. Entrusted with some of the most meaningful stories of these women's lives, we had assumed the power to weave their words into something else—to identify themes, to draw conclusions, and to present our "findings" to a larger audience. Doris's observation alerted us to alternative horizons. We wanted to tell the women's stories in an ethical way, being faithful to their intentions. . . . We began again. (pp. 29–30)

The authors then presented the narrative a second time, endeavoring to faithfully convey the views of their participants. Representing multiple possible realities in this way exemplifies the principle of crystallization, with readers becoming aware that the meaning of the story depends on the angle from which it is viewed.

Negative Case Analysis

In the process of conducting a qualitative study, some evidence will arise that is contrary to a developing coding scheme or set of emerging themes. This is because "in real life, not all evidence is either positive or negative; it is some of both" (Creswell

& Poth, 2018, p. 261). Researchers can enhance the credibility of their reports by presenting negative or rival evidence that surfaces in the process of conducting the study, as well as how their hunches, hypotheses, analyses, or interpretations evolved in light of this disconfirming evidence. In the research report, a researcher using this technique might describe early developments in their thinking about the phenomenon or data, present evidence that is contrary to those preliminary understandings, and then present refined analysis and interpretation that better accounts for the rival evidence. This approach differs from solely presenting a refined interpretation and its associated confirming evidence, a presentation that may lead readers to wonder whether the analysis is too "neat and tidy" given the complexity of phenomena that are typically studied qualitatively. By transparently describing "points of intrigue" that arise throughout a study, researchers can present appropriately complex and nuanced reports, which in turn may enhance their credibility (p. 261).

Managing Subjectivity or Engaging in Reflexive Practices

The crucial importance of engaging in reflexive practices and managing researcher subjectivity was introduced in Chapter 8. While Creswell and Poth (2018) titled this strategy "clarifying researcher bias," we instead use "managing researcher subjectivity" in light of ways that the construct of "bias" has been reconceptualized for qualitative inquiry (see Roulston & Shelton, 2015). Researchers may use this validation strategy by composing a subjectivity statement in which they describe the social locations they occupy in relation to their research topic and participants, discuss potential advantages and liabilities associated with these positions, and describe practices in which they have engaged to manage their subjectivity. Methodological experts have cautioned that "an absence of subjectivity statements in research reports can be a cause for suspicion on the part of readers" (Roulston, 2010, p. 119; see also Preissle, 2008).

Subjectivity statements often begin with the researcher describing subject positions they occupy so that readers can understand the position from which they write. However, feminist philosopher Harding (2007) cautioned against merely providing a list of subject positions:

> I, the author, am a woman of European descent, a middle-class academic trained as a philosopher, who has lived all her life in the U.S. . . . . [F]or the researcher to stop her analysis of her social location here, with just the confession, is to leave all the work up to the reader. (p. 54)

Therefore, in addition to transparently acknowledging pertinent elements of subjectivity, it is important for researchers to explain *how* these may have influenced the research process.

Qualitative researchers often detail specific efforts they have made to manage their subjectivity. These might include maintaining a researcher's journal (Roulston,

2010), composing autobiographical notes (Glesne, 2006), or participating in "bracketing interviews" in which researchers are interviewed using protocols they have themselves authored in order to better understand their preconceptions of and prior experiences with a phenomenon they are studying (Roulston, 2010). Beyond merely stating that one has used a particular strategy, researchers ideally embed some evidence of the strategy's use within the report itself. For example, an author who has composed autobiographical notes might incorporate excerpts from them throughout the report. The notes would then serve two purposes: helping readers understand the perspective from which the author writes and providing evidence of one technique the author has used to manage subjectivity.

In phenomenology, the processes of epoche, bracketing, and phenomenological reduction assist researchers with managing subjectivity. Authors will often compose a passage describing their own presuppositions about the phenomenon being investigated. This process assists the researcher in temporarily suspending their preconceived notions so that they can view the phenomenon with fresh eyes and focus on participants' experiences. For example, Sweet (2015) incorporated excerpts from her written epoche in her study of the adolescent female voice change:

> I had a good ear for harmony and was placed in the alto section and never left. I was, and am, a classic case of the "adolescent alto" and in hindsight, it makes me sad because the upper part of my vocal range was never developed and I never learned how to properly sing high notes.... [B]y the time I reached college I was convinced that I was an alto and could not sing high.... As a choral music teacher educator, I work to ... prevent future adolescent choir students from suffering from the same doubts and uncertainties about their singing voice that I will always have about mine: that I can physically sing high notes, but I will forever be self-conscious about singing high notes in front of other people. (pp. 75–76)

A passage such as this clarifies the author's vantage point for readers, enhancing the credibility of a report. Another informative example can be found in Sindberg's (2006) dissertation focused on students' experiences with the Comprehensive Musicianship through Performance (CMP) approach, which afforded space for a more expansive presentation of a written epoche.

Another approach to managing subjectivity entails analyzing one's own contributions to data generation, including ways that interview questions are formulated and the perspective from which field notes are written (Roulston, 2010). An instructive illustration of this process is offered by Roulston and Shelton (2015). Roulston, a research pedagogue, and Shelton, a graduate student at the time of publication, detailed their processes of analyzing researchers' interview talk. Shelton discussed one key insight that emerged from this process:

> I found in Miranda's interviews ... that I was overly complimentary of her responses. When she described her classroom environment, I responded, "I think

it's a good answer." Following her description of her efforts to get students' buy-in, I responded, "Well said" and "I like it. I like it a lot." While responding to and encouraging her were not necessarily problematic, I cannot help but feel like I was treating her as if I was the teacher and she was the student (which had been our relationship prior to the study), as she told me about her experiences as a teacher with her students. I certainly still want to be attentive and affirming, but I want to try to limit the number of times that I compliment the participants, so that when I offer such comments, they will be sincere, and not automatic. (p. 337)

Shelton's tendency to offer affirming comments during interviews, related to her subjectivity as a former instructor of the participant, had potential to influence the content and quality of data generation as well as the interpretive sense she would later make of interview conversations. Taking time to analyze and reflect on issues such as these supports researchers in approaching data generation, analysis, and interpretation in ways that are more optimally aligned with their theoretical, methodological, and ethical commitments. Roulston (2010) offers procedural advice for researchers interested in analyzing their data generation contributions methodologically.

Tsugawa (2009) described a technique for managing researcher subjectivity that combines strategic role positioning with analyzing one's own contributions to data generation. For music education researchers who also occupy the professional role of teacher educator, it may be all too easy to slip into the familiar role of evaluator when conducting classroom observations. Tsugawa used a technique for managing these dual roles that other researchers may find instructive. Using qualitative data analysis software, he applied the code "TA," or "teacher adjudicator," to field note passages written in a style and tone more consistent with the purpose of teacher evaluation (e.g., field notes that read like a student-teaching observation report). The software then permitted running a report of any such instances, separating them from the broader data set for closer examination. Detailing such efforts for readers, and providing examples of insights gleaned through these processes, is a powerful way to bolster the credibility of a research report.

Validation Strategies That Directly Engage Participants

Member Reflections

Creswell and Poth (2018) titled this strategy "member checking" to refer to opportunities for participants to provide input into whether the data record, analysis, interpretations, or disseminable products accurately represent their contributions to the research. However, Tracy (2010) observed that the term "member *checks*" suggests that a single truth or reality can be discerned from a research process. Therefore, we have adopted the term "member reflections" as one that may be relevant to a broader array of paradigmatic perspectives.

Opportunities for member reflection arise throughout various phases of conducting a study. One common approach involves providing participants with copies of raw data (e.g., interview transcripts) and inviting them to suggest modifications to, clarifications about, or deletions from the record. Some researchers establish routines whereby each data generation session begins with a review of the previous in order to facilitate member reflection. For example, in her research with fifth-grade students, Kelly-McHale (2013) "was careful to begin each interview session with a review of the previous interview, asking the participants to confirm what was recorded in the transcript" (p. 203).

Member reflections can also involve inviting participants to review preliminary analysis and comment on the salience (or lack thereof) of themes that the researcher has identified. For instance, one of the authors of this book, Shaw, has typically included a question such as the following in interviews scheduled late in a research process:

> During this project, I identified various themes that seem important to [describe the central phenomenon]. As I describe these themes, please comment on their importance from your vantage point as [describe participant's role]:
>
> a. Theme a
> b. Theme b
> c. Theme c [specific themes are inserted once identified]

Some researchers invite participants to review drafts of articles they intend to submit for publication or applications to present at professional conferences. Opportunities for member reflection therefore range from reviewing raw data to reviewing disseminable products.

Prolonged Engagement in the Field

In any study, researchers will be engaged in a number of processes that require time to unfold: developing detailed understanding of the research context, building rapport with participants that encourages disclosure, making decisions about emergent design elements, and even identifying which phenomena are truly at the center of the inquiry. Accordingly, prolonged engagement in the field is considered one hallmark of a well-conducted study. Fetterman (2010), a noted expert on ethnography, emphasizes that "participant observation requires close, long-term contact with the people under study" (p. 39). In recommending an approach to phenomenological interviewing, Seidman (2019) warns, "Interviewers who propose to explore their topic by arranging a one-shot meeting with an 'interviewee' whom they have never met may tread on thin contextual ice" (p. 21). Stauffer (2014) concurs, warning that "one-time encounters are flimsy grounds for narrative work" (p. 177).

To bolster claims that one's engagement has been "prolonged," it is instructive to provide details that allow readers to appreciate the extent to which this was the case. Authors might detail the timeframe for fieldwork, the number of hours invested in various types of data generation, and the resulting quantities of data (e.g., hours of recorded interviews, pages of field notes or transcripts). The following passage illustrates this strategy:

> I attended all 3-hour Monday evening rehearsals and 1 hour of each Wednesday evening rehearsal, resulting in more than 150 hours of formal observations. I also spent more than 200 hours as a participant observer, interacting with younger choristers as the conductor of the Allegra choir . . . and as a teacher of beginning-level theory and sight-singing classes. Although many of my observations were conducted during weekly rehearsals, I also was present at other SGC [Seattle Girls' Choir] events, including performances, board meetings, summer camps, and faculty meetings. (Bartolome, 2013, p. 400)

Details provided in this passage demonstrate the extent of the researcher's sustained engagement, as opposed to merely mentioning "prolonged engagement" as a validation strategy used in the study. Another option is to present similar details in tabular form. When the researcher has used an innovative approach such as a strategically planned rotation of individual interviews, group interviews, and observations, a table summarizing the data generation schedule can highlight its novel features while also illustrating the extensiveness of data generation (e.g., Kelly-McHale, 2011, p. 129).

Collaboration With Participants

This validation strategy is "based on the idea (and ever-growing body of research) that the study is more likely to be supported and findings used when participants are involved" (Creswell & Poth, 2018, p. 262). Possibilities for close collaboration with participants exist at every stage of the research, from initially shaping the research questions and data generation protocols to taking an active role in disseminating the findings (e.g., co-authoring or co-presenting). The extent to which participants are engaged in these ways can vary from minimal to extensive according to the project's goals and the researcher's theoretical, methodological, epistemological, and ethical commitments. Community-based participatory practices are an example of an approach that maximizes collaborative aspects of research, often to the extent that participants are engaged as co-researchers (see, e.g., Hacker, 2013).

Nichols's (2013) study "Rie's Story, Ryan's Journey," which was highlighted in Chapter 10, exemplifies extensive collaboration between researcher and participant. Both within the 2013 research report and a subsequent autoethnography (2016) about her engagement in this research process, Nichols detailed her approach to redressing researcher-participant power differentials and navigating the myriad ethical considerations involved in co-constructing this narrative account. One goal of their collaboration was to ensure that "Ryan's voice and his expertise in his own life narrative" (Nichols, 2013, p. 264) were honored:

> Ryan . . . reviewed the interview transcripts; read, corrected, and discussed multiple drafts of the manuscript; monitored the proposal and abstract submission process for conference presentations and journal publication; and discussed the reviewer responses with me as I prepared revisions. . . . Ryan retained control over how he is represented in the text and how his story is used. (p. 265)

Such an approach "moves far beyond the qualitative practice of 'member checking' and strives for the holistic inclusion and empowerment of the participant as a valued partner in the research endeavor" (p. 265).

Validation Strategies That Engage Reviewers or Readers

Thick Description

"Thick description" is that which captures rich detail, contextual nuance, and layer upon layer of locally informed meanings (see Geertz, 1973). According to Stake (2010), "a description is rich if it provides abundant, interconnected details" about the research context and participants (p. 49). Researchers may develop thick descriptions by describing physical locations and atmospheric details, using strong action verbs, establishing connections between details, and embedding verbatim quotes (Creswell & Poth, 2018). Porcello's (1996) study of technological and discursive practices in a contemporary sound recording studio offers abundant examples of thick description, including the following:

> [W]hen you enter the studio proper and the control and cutting rooms from either the front or back entrance, heavy wooden doors thunk shut behind you, accompanied by the quiet squish of air being expelled as the thick rubber weather stripping on the door frame is compressed by the weight of the door. If you tap the sheet rock walls with your knuckles, the sound seems to get swallowed up, due to the heavy insulation and/or sand poured into the space where conventional walls are hollow between studs. Look closely at the control room and you'll notice that the ceiling has several different heights and slopes, that the walls have crazy recesses built into them, are partially carpeted, and meet at odd angles. . . . Soon you'll become of aware that, attached to every door, are Sonex pads, that dark brown, extremely dense but porous foam textured in alternating rows of protruding and receding pyramid shapes. . . . If there is no one around or no music playing, the room seems "dead." . . .

> When the heavy studio doors go thunk and seal off the noises of the outside world, they simultaneously mark a boundary between the physical space of the everyday and this new physical space. . . . Twelve-hour work days, food ordered and eaten in, the lack of windows, the dim lighting, the unnatural quietness, and, perhaps above all, the constant immersion in musical time, often draw session participants further into this creative space . . . and the external flow of time seems drastically altered. People look at their watches and shake their heads, startled. Or you step out onto the fire escape . . . and are shocked that it is pitch black outside. The isolation in the studio can at times be so complete that such commonplace events as the phone ringing or the thunk of the studio door are jolting intrusions of an outside world temporarily forgotten. (pp. 127–130)

The vivid description and plethora of sensory details offered in this passage transport readers to the recording studio. A key function of thick description is to describe a context or situation in sufficient detail that readers can make determinations about the potential "transferability" of findings to settings that share important contextual similarities (Lincoln & Guba, 1985).

However, thick description is not without its potential challenges and disadvantages. One issue of *Research Studies in Music Education* (volume 31) offered balanced treatment of both possibilities for and pitfalls associated with thick description. In that issue, Jorgensen (2007) offered a critical appraisal prompting readers to consider the "dark side" of thick description, such as the potential for a researcher's descriptions to contribute to essentialist, stereotypical, or racist portrayals of research participants. She cautioned that "although [thick description] constitutes an important way of investigating social events, there are limits to its use and value as an investigative tool" (p. 76). In light of these cautions, researchers might use thick description in consort with additional validation strategies, particularly those oriented toward managing researcher subjectivity.

Establishing an Audit Trail

Researchers might engage an external auditor who has no connection to the study to evaluate the extent to which the study's analysis, interpretations, and conclusions are warranted in light of supporting data. To facilitate this process, Silver and Lewins (2014) recommend maintaining "a log of all the processes followed, describing the small analytic leaps contributing to the analysis as a whole" in a document called an "audit trail" (p. 140). In their research reports, researchers who have engaged in an audit might detail the auditor's key observations and recommendations as well as how these were accounted for in the research process.

Peer Debriefing

This strategy also entails a review of the research process, but from the perspective of "someone who is familiar with the research or the phenomenon explored"

(Creswell & Miller, 2000, p. 129). Peer reviewers often serve as a "devil's advocate" by asking challenging questions about methods, meanings, and interpretations and "keeping the inquirer honest" (Lincoln & Guba, 1985, p. 308). Beyond merely mentioning that one has participated in peer debriefing, discussing specific ways the researcher has accounted for debriefers' feedback can lend credibility to a report. For procedural advice about peer debriefing, readers are encouraged to consult Spall (1998).

Ankney (2014) consulted with both an external reviewer and a panel of peer reviewers as part of her case study investigating jazz pedagogues' responses to student thinking during improvisation. Highlighted in Chapter 8 for its innovative approach to data generation, this study equipped participants with point-of-view cameras that recorded lessons they taught from the teacher's perspective. While teaching, participants could press a button to create a timestamp for moments in which they noticed something about their students' improvisations. These "tagged moments" then served as prompting material for stimulated recall interviews. Ankney developed a coding scheme for categorizing data according to "what teachers noticed" and "how and why they responded to the noticed event" (p. 100). Early in the analysis process, she had a panel of "knowledgeable peers" code selected video excerpts and suggest refinements to her coding scheme (p. 101). She then revised the codes in light of reviewers' suggestions and used the refined coding scheme to analyze the data corpus. Once coding was complete, an expert jazz educator who was not connected to the study independently coded a random selection of 15% of each teacher's tagged moments. Ankney reported the interrater reliability to be "Kappa = .807 ($p < .001$) indicating very strong agreement" (p. 103). That she engaged both a panel of peer reviewers and an external reviewer to audit her analysis and constructively critique her interpretive sensemaking enhances the credibility of her analysis.

Guiding Questions for Discerning Quality Inspired by Tracy's (2010) "Big Tent Criteria"

Just as considerable debate has surrounded appropriate terms for describing excellence or quality in qualitative research, the prospect of developing evaluation criteria for discerning these qualities in published research has sparked controversy within the field. Some authors have argued that the field's obsession with formulating such criteria is ultimately unproductive given the diversity of aims and approaches embraced by qualitative researchers. See, for example, Schwandt's (1996) "Farewell to Criteriology" and Bochner's (2000) "Criteria Against Ourselves." In light of these swirling controversies, Denzin (2008) asserted:

> We cannot afford to fight with one another.... We need to find new strategic and tactical ways to work with one another.... We must expand the size of our tent, indeed we need a bigger tent! (p. 321)

In response to this charge, Tracy (2010) advanced a set of eight "big tent criteria" for evaluating the "goodness" of qualitative research that are intended to be applicable to researchers who conduct their work from differing perspectives and through varying approaches (p. 839).

In the following section, we summarize Tracy's (2010) criteria and suggest questions that can guide readers' considerations of each as they review research reports with an eye toward discerning their quality. The list of questions is not intended to be exhaustive, and while they point to positive features that well-conducted studies may exhibit, not every report will incorporate all of these. Other authors have put forth evaluation criteria that readers are encouraged to consult, including Creswell and Poth (2018), who provide criteria specific to each of the five primary qualitative research designs.

Worthy Topic

Producing a quality study begins with pursuing a worthy topic, a decision that might be informed by priorities within a scholarly discipline, constructs that are theoretically interesting, or societal events that are timely and relevant. Topics chosen merely for their convenience are "likely to be pursued in a shallow way, with less care devoted to design and data collection" (Miles & Huberman, 1994, p. 290). Tracy (2010, p. 840) further cautioned, "When research merely confirms existing assumptions, people will deny its worth while acknowledging its truth. In short, audiences will think, 'that's obvious' rather than the more coveted 'that's interesting'!" In contrast, a worthy topic will "shake readers from their common-sense assumptions and practices" (p. 840).

When reviewing a study, readers might consider questions such as the following:

- For what reasons, beyond mere convenience, has the topic been chosen?
- In what ways do the research questions probe topics beyond those that have already been thoroughly addressed in extant literature?
- For what reasons, if any, does the topic seem worthy of researchers' time, effort, and resources?

Rich Rigor

This criterion pertains to the rigor with which the author has approached the study's theoretical framing, sampling, data generation, and analysis. Tracy (2010) offered the following questions to prompt reviewers' considerations of rigor:

- Are there enough data to support significant claims?
- Did the researcher spend enough time to gather interesting and significant data?
- Is the context or sample appropriate given the goals of the study?
- Did the researcher use appropriate procedures in terms of field note style, interviewing practices, and analysis procedures? (p. 841)

To these, we might add:

- Has the author described the study's focal point and the reasons it was selected (e.g., why cases were selected for a case study, why a culture-sharing group was selected for an ethnography)?
- Are the data sources well-suited for exploring the phenomenon of interest?
- Are data generation techniques described in sufficient detail that readers can gauge the extent to which they have been used competently?
- Is the researcher's approach to interviewing well-aligned with their theoretical perspective (e.g., a constructivist approach to interviewing, a decolonizing orientation toward interviewing)? See Roulston (2010) for detailed treatment of this ideal.
- Has the author described procedures for coding the data, provided examples of codes generated during analysis, or shared the coding scheme in whole or in part?
- Is sufficient raw data presented in support of analysis and interpretations?
- Is the author's interpretive commentary persuasive?
- "Has the writer made sound assertions, neither over- nor misinterpreting" (Stake, 1995, p. 131)?

Sincerity

The next criterion, sincerity, refers to the way that research "is marked by honesty and transparency about the researcher's biases, goals, and foibles as well as about how these played a role in the methods, joys, and mistakes of the research" (Tracy, 2010, p. 841). Engaging in reflexive practices and managing researcher subjectivity are therefore keys to establishing sincerity. Richardson (2000a) posed two relevant guiding questions:

- How did the author come to write this text?
- Is there adequate self-awareness and self-exposure for the reader to make judgments about the point of view? (p. 254)

To these, the following questions might be added:

- To what extent has the researcher illuminated relevant subject positions they occupy and how these have shaped the perspective from which they write?
- Has the researcher gone beyond listing subject positions they occupy to explain how these have informed and influenced the research process?
- Does the researcher describe reflexive practices in which they have engaged in order to navigate the participant-researcher relationship in ways that are aligned with their theoretical, methodological, and ethical commitments?
- Through what efforts has the researcher managed their subjectivity?

o Have they described their use of strategies such as writing autobiographical notes, maintaining a researcher's journal, participating in a bracketing interview, composing a written epoche, or analyzing their own contributions to data generation?
o In addition to describing ways they have managed subjectivity, do they provide evidence of their use of these strategies within the reports? (For example, are excerpts from autobiographical notes or a researcher's journal embedded throughout the report? Does the author provide examples of how they filtered observations through lenses other than that of researcher and explain how they adjusted their approach accordingly?)
- To what extent does the researcher describe how they have positioned their role for the purposes of the study?
- Does the researcher describe their preconceptions about and prior experiences with the phenomenon being investigated to the extent that the reader can understand the vantage point from which they write?

Credibility

Credibility "refers to the trustworthiness, verisimilitude, and plausibility of the research findings" (Tracy, 2010, p. 842). Practices that serve to enhance a study's credibility include some of Creswell and Poth's (2018) aforementioned validation strategies: triangulation or crystallization, thick description, member reflections, and collaboration with participants. To these, Tracy (2010) adds multivocality, which involves representing a diversity of perspectives within a study, including views that diverge from the researcher's own or from those held by a majority of participants. Intense collaboration with participants offers one pathway toward achieving multivocality. Engaging participants as more equal collaborators or co-researchers may require relinquishing editorial control, but it opens possibilities for presenting "more nuanced analyses with deeper meanings to members at hand" (p. 844). The following questions may guide readers' considerations of the credibility of reports they review:

- Are the findings of this research "trustworthy enough to act on and make decisions in line with" (p. 843)?
- Has the researcher consulted multiple sources of data, types of data, researchers, or theoretical frameworks to explore whether and how they corroborate one another? (Does the research design include triangulation?)
- Has the author gone beyond conventional notions of triangulation to represent multiple possible meanings of the study, or to illustrate how the meaning of the study depends upon the angle from which it is viewed? (Does the research exemplify crystallization?)
- Has the author described the research context, participants, and events in the field in rich, vivid detail to such an extent that readers can consider

the potential transferability of findings? (Has the researcher provided thick description?)
- Has the author achieved multivocality in the report by representing multiple and various perspectives, including those that diverge from their own views and those held by a majority of participants?
- Has the author discussed or accounted for ways that facets of identity such as race, ethnicity, class, gender, age, sexual orientation, and exceptionality informed the process of meaning-making in the study?

Resonance

Tracy's (2010) next criterion, resonance, refers to "research's ability to meaningfully reverberate and affect an audience" (p. 844). Pertinent research practices include those that enhance a report's aesthetic merit as well as those that promote transferability (Lincoln & Guba, 1985) or naturalistic generalization (Stake & Trumbull, 1982). With regard to aesthetic merit, research reports might exhibit qualities of artful writing, such as colorful word choices, vivid description, and literary devices, including symbolism, plot, foreshadowing, and denouement. Porcello's (1996) dissertation, referenced earlier as an example of thick description, is an informative example of artful writing. One noteworthy feature is the author's innovative use of terms associated with the study's central phenomenon, audio recording, to describe its methodological approach and findings. For example, the report is organized into chapters that correspond to phases of an audio-recording process: "Preproduction," "Arrival, Setup, Soundcheck," "Tracking and Overdubbing," "Break," and "Mix and Playback" (p. ix). The report goes beyond being clearly written and methodologically sound, representing a product with aesthetic merit.

Tracy (2010) further points to transferability and naturalistic generalization, concepts that were introduced in Chapter 9, as features that contribute to a report's resonance. "Transferability" occurs when "readers feel as though the story of the research overlaps with their own situation" (p. 845). Naturalistic generalization provides readers with vicarious experience of a phenomenon that may prompt them to reconsider their prior conceptions (Stake & Trumbull, 1982). Questions helpful for considering the resonance of a research report might then include the following:

- In what ways does the report exemplify qualities of artful writing?
- In what ways does the research report's structure and style align with its purpose and goals to demonstrate "aesthetic merit"?
- Has the author provided thick description to such an extent that the reader can determine whether "the story of the research overlaps with their own situation" (p. 845)?
- What aspects of the writing, if any, promote readers' vicarious experience with a phenomenon?

Significant Contribution

The next criterion considers the significance of a study' contribution, whether theoretically, heuristically, practically, or methodologically (Tracy, 2010). The following questions can guide readers' consideration of a research contribution's significance:

- In what ways does the study contribute toward a profession's knowledge base?
- In what ways does the study illuminate a contemporary issue?
- How, if at all, does the study have implications for pedagogical practice in K–12 settings?
- How, if at all, does the study have implications for music teacher education?
- In what ways does this study suggest possibilities for ongoing research?
- In what ways, if any, does the study break new ground in terms of methodological approach?
  o Does the study introduce a novel approach to data generation or analysis?
  o Does the research incorporate new, innovative design elements?
- Has the researcher offered an answer to the "So what?" question (Creswell & Poth, 2018, p. 262)?

Ethical Conduct

The next criterion considers the extent to which the research has been conducted ethically. Pertinent guiding questions include:

- Has the researcher obtained the approval of an IRB? Do they indicate that they have obtained participants' informed consent? While these details can sometimes be implied, their explicit treatment can be an indicator of an ethically conducted study.
- Has the researcher discussed procedures for maintaining participants' privacy and confidentiality?
- Has the researcher discussed the possibility of unintended negative consequences that could arise from disseminating findings? Have they described efforts they have made to preclude these possibilities?
- Have data been presented in a way that clearly aligns with the research purpose (as opposed to introducing irrelevant details for the purpose of sharing a salacious story)?
- Does the report respectfully give primacy to participants' views, or does it appear to contribute toward silencing or marginalizing particular individuals or groups?
- "Does it appear that individuals were put at risk?" (Stake, 1995, p. 131).
- In what ways has the researcher detailed their efforts to approach the participant-researcher relationship ethically?

Meaningful Coherence

A final criterion considers whether a research report exhibits "meaningful coherence" in the way that its purpose, theoretical framework, research design, data collection, and analysis procedures align with and complement one another. In short, this criterion considers whether these various elements "hang together." Tracy (2010) described meaningfully coherent studies as those that

(a) achieve their stated purpose; (b) accomplish what they espouse to be about; (c) use methods and representation practices that partner well with espoused theories and paradigms; and (d) attentively interconnect literature reviewed with research foci, methods, and findings. (p. 848)

The following questions may be useful for considering the extent to which a research report exhibits meaningful coherence:

- Does the author provide a strong rationale for why the chosen research design affords an appropriate fit for the study's purpose and questions?
- To what extent are methodological decisions aligned with the researcher's paradigmatic or theoretical perspective?
- Have the findings been situated in relation to pertinent extant literature?
- To what extent are the conclusions and implications supported by the data that have been presented?
- To what extent do the reported findings answer the stated research questions?

Summary

This chapter has considered how qualities such as "quality," "excellence," "credibility," and "trustworthiness" can be demonstrated in qualitative research, and how consumers can discern these characteristics in research reports that they review. Strategic actions that researchers can take include pursuing triangulation or crystallization, presenting negative case analysis, engaging in reflexive practices, and taking steps to recognize and manage their own subjectivity. Participants can be actively engaged in validation through member reflections, by interacting with the researcher in the field over a prolonged period of time, or through more intense collaboration with researchers in various phases of the research. Additional validation strategies call for a reviewer to audit the research process and products, whether an external reviewer with no direct connection to the study or a peer reviewer with knowledge of the scholarly discipline or phenomenon being investigated. Thick description engages readers in a validation process as they determine the potential transferability of findings to settings and situations beyond the original research context. Ultimately, well-conducted qualitative research exhibits characteristics such as the following: "worthy topic, rich rigor, sincerity, credibility, resonance, significant contribution, ethical [conduct], and meaningful coherence" (Tracy, 2010, p. 837).

The following questions will assist you with reviewing and applying content presented in this chapter:

1. Identify a research topic that is of interest to you (perhaps one you explored for additional review exercises suggested in Chapters 7–10) and write a journal entry exploring your subjectivity in relation to that research topic. Reflect on questions such as the following:
    a. What experiences have led to your interest in this topic?
    b. What motivates you to conduct research in this area?
    c. Why do you believe this topic is important and worthy of study?
    d. What positions do you occupy with respect to age, (dis)ability, gender, ethnicity, linguistic background, race, religion, sexual orientation, and additional facets of identity that relate to the topic of your study?
        i. How might these positions present advantages if you were to conduct a study on this topic?
        ii. What potential challenges might arise related to the positions you occupy? How might you strategically navigate these?
    e. What is your relationship to people who might serve as participants in this study?
    f. What personal or professional roles do you occupy that might interact with your role as researcher?
    g. Describe any potential "blind spots" that your relationship to this topic might present if you were to undertake a research analysis.
2. Review qualitative exemplar studies that are cited in this volume, that are recommended by your instructor, or that you have identified as strong contributions in order to review the authors' approaches to enhancing credibility. Compile a list of validation strategies you found to be most effective, citing the sources in which you located them. Consider sharing or compiling lists collaboratively with colleagues to create a list of recommended validation techniques for possible future use.
3. Review Creswell and Poth's (2018) nine validation strategies and consider which would be most directly applicable to a qualitative research project that you would like to undertake. Write a one- to two-page memo detailing your plans for enhancing the credibility of your study with reference to these nine strategies.
4. Select a qualitative research report to review and develop a critical appraisal of the professional contribution the study makes. (In this case, "critical" means "thoughtfully reflective" as opposed to "negative.") Use Tracy's (2010) "big tent criteria" and the questions presented in this chapter to guide your thinking.

For this exercise, a dissertation-length report might be most instructive to review as it will offer more detailed information about the researcher's methodological approach than an article-length report will have space to provide.

Important Terms for Review

An *audit trail* is a written document that tracks methodological decisions that have been made over the course of conducting a study, enabling an external reviewer to audit the research process and findings (Silver & Lewins, 2014).

Member reflection is a process through which participants are invited to provide input about whether data, interpretations, or disseminable products accurately and faithfully represent their contributions to the research. While some authors use the term *member checking* to refer to such practices, the term *reflection* avoids the implication that a single, purportedly objective truth can be "checked" or definitively verified (Tracy, 2010).

Multivocality refers to the inclusion of multiple and differing perspectives in a research report, including those that diverge from the researcher's views or those held by a majority of participants (Tracy, 2010).

Negative case analysis is a process through which a researcher presents evidence that disconfirms or is contrary to codes, themes, or theories that develop during a research process (Lincoln & Guba, 1985).

Peer debriefing is a process through which a peer with knowledge of the scholarly discipline or phenomenon under investigation reviews the research process and findings in order to raise questions, serve as a "devil's advocate" (Lincoln & Guba, 1985, p. 308), and productively challenge the researcher's interpretive sensemaking (Spall, 1998).

Reflexivity describes "thoughtful, self-aware analysis of the intersubjective dynamics between researcher and the researched" (Finlay & Gough, 2003, p. ix).

Subjectivity refers to "a researcher's personal assumptions and presuppositions" (Roulston, 2010, p. 58).

In *subjectivity statements,* researchers describe the social locations that they occupy in relation to their research topic and participants, discuss potential advantages and liabilities associated with these positions, and describe practices in which they have engaged to manage their subjectivity (Preissle, 2008).

Thick description is that which captures rich detail, contextual nuance, and layer upon layer of locally informed meanings (Geertz, 1973).

Triangulation refers to a process of corroborating evidence from multiple data sources, methods of generating data, investigators, or theories to enhance a study's credibility (Denzin, 1978; Patton, 1999).

References

Angen, M. J. (2000). Evaluating interpretive inquiry: Reviewing the validity debate and opening the dialogue. *Qualitative Health Research, 10,* 378–395. https://doi.org/10.1177/104973230010 00308

Ankney, K. L. (2014). *Master jazz teachers' noticing and responses to students during improvisation activities* (Publication No. 3669190) [Doctoral dissertation, Northwestern University]. ProQuest Dissertations & Theses Global.

Bartolome, S. J. (2013). "It's like a whole bunch of me!": The perceived values and benefits of the Seattle Girls' Choir experience. *Journal of Research in Music Education, 60*(4), 395–418. https://doi.org/10.1177/0022429412464054

Bloor, M. (2001). Techniques of validation in qualitative research: A critical commentary. In R. M. Emerson (Ed.), *Contemporary field research* (pp. 383–396). Waveland Press.

Bochner, A. (2000). Criteria against ourselves. *Qualitative Inquiry, 6,* 266–272. https://doi.org/10.1177/107780040000600209

Cape, J., & Nichols, J. (2012). Engaging stories: Constructing narratives of women's military band members. In M. S. Barrett & S. L. Stauffer (Eds.), *Narrative soundings: An anthology of narrative inquiry in music education* (pp. 23–35). Springer.

Creswell, J. W., & Miller, D. L. (2000). Determining validity in qualitative inquiry. *Theory into Practice, 39*(3), 124–130. https://doi.org/10.1207/s15430421tip3903_2

Creswell, J. W., & Poth, C. N. (2018). *Qualitative inquiry and research design: Choosing among five approaches* (4th ed.). Sage.

Denzin, N. K. (1978). *Sociological methods: A sourcebook.* McGraw-Hill.

Denzin, N. K. (2008). The new paradigm dialogs and qualitative inquiry. *International Journal of Qualitative Studies in Education, 21,* 315–325. https://doi.org/10.1080/09518390802136995

Eisner, E. W. (1991). *The enlightened eye: Qualitative inquiry and the enhancement of educational practice.* Macmillan.

Fetterman, D. M. (2010). *Ethnography: Step-by-step* (3rd ed.). Sage.

Finlay, L., & Gough, B. (Eds.). (2003). *Reflexivity: A practical guide for researchers in health and social sciences.* Blackwell Science.

Geertz, C. (1973). Thick description: Toward an interpretive theory of culture. In C. Geertz (Ed.), *The interpretation of cultures* (pp. 3–30). Basic Books.

Glesne, C. (2006). *Becoming qualitative researchers: An introduction* (3rd ed.). Pearson Education.

Guba, E. G., & Lincoln, Y. S. (2005). Paradigmatic controversies, contradictions, and emerging confluences. In N. K. Denzin & Y. S. Lincoln (Eds.), *The Sage handbook of qualitative research* (3rd ed., pp. 191–215). Sage.

Hacker, K. (2013). *Community-based participatory research.* Sage.

Harding, S. (2007). Feminist standpoints. In S. N. Hesse-Biber (Ed.), *Handbook of feminist research: Theory and praxis* (pp. 45–70). Sage.

Jorgensen, E. R. (2007). Concerning justice and music education. *Music Education Research, 9*(2), 169–189. https://doi.org/10.1080/14613800701411731

Kelly-McHale, J. (2011). *The relationship between children's musical identities and music teacher beliefs and practices in an elementary general music classroom* (Publication No. 3456672) [Doctoral dissertation, Northwestern University]. ProQuest Dissertations & Theses Global.

Kelly-McHale, J. (2013). The influence of music teacher beliefs and practices on the expression of musical identity in an elementary general music classroom. *Journal of Research in Music Education, 61*(2), 195–216. https://doi.org/10.1177/0022429413485439

Lather, P. (1991). *Getting smart: Feminist research and pedagogy with/in the postmodern.* Routledge.

Lather, P. (1993). Fertile obsession: Validity after poststructuralism. *Sociological Quarterly, 34,* 673–693. https://doi.org/10.1111/j.1533-8525.1993.tb00112.x

LeCompte, M. D., & Goetz, J. P. (1982). Problems of reliability and validity in ethnographic research. *Review of Educational Research, 51*, 31–60. https://doi.org/10.3102/0034654305 2001031

Lincoln, Y. S., & Guba, E. G. (1985). *Naturalistic inquiry*. Sage.

Merriam, S. B., & Tisdell, E. J. (2015). *Qualitative research: A guide to design and implementation* (4th ed.). Jossey-Bass.

Miles, M. B., & Huberman, A. M. (1994). *Qualitative data analysis: An expanded sourcebook*. Sage.

Nichols, J. (2013). Rie's story, Ryan's journey: Music in the life of a transgender student. *Journal of Research in Music Education, 61*(3), 262–279. https://doi.org/10.1177/0022429413498259

Nichols, J. (2016). Sharing the stage: Ethical dimensions of narrative inquiry in music education. *Journal of Research in Music Education, 63*(4), 439–454. https://doi.org/10.1177/002242941 5617745

Patton, M. Q. (1999). Enhancing the quality and credibility of qualitative analysis. *Health Sciences Research, 34*, 1189–1208.

Patton, M. Q. (2002). Two decades of developments in qualitative inquiry: A personal, experiential perspective. *Qualitative Social Work, 1*, 261–283. https://doi.org/10.1177/147332500200 1003636

Porcello, T. G. (1996). *Sonic artistry: Music, discourse, and technology in the sound recording studio* (Publication No. 9719458) [Doctoral dissertation, The University of Texas at Austin]. ProQuest Dissertations & Theses Global.

Preissle, J. (2008). Subjectivity statement. In L. M. Given (Ed.), *The Sage encyclopedia of qualitative research methods* (Vol. 2, pp. 844–845). Sage.

Richardson, L. (2000a). Evaluating ethnography. *Qualitative Inquiry, 6*, 253–256. https://doi.org/10.1177/107780040000600207

Richardson, L. (2000b). Writing: A method of inquiry. In N. K. Denzin & Y. S. Lincoln (Eds.), *Handbook of qualitative research* (2nd ed., pp. 923–948). Sage.

Robinson, M. (2014). Changing the conversation: Considering quality in music education qualitative research. In C. M. Conway (Ed.), *The Oxford handbook of qualitative research in American music education* (pp. 94–100). Oxford University Press.

Roulston, K. (2010). *Reflective interviewing: A guide to theory and practice*. Sage.

Roulston, K., & Shelton, S. A. (2015). Reconceptualizing bias in teaching qualitative research methods. *Qualitative Inquiry, 21*(4), 332–342. https://doi.org/10.1177/1077800414563803

Schwandt, T. A. (1996). Farewell to criteriology. *Qualitative Inquiry, 2*, 58–72. https://doi.org/10.1177/107780049600200109

Seidman, I. (2019). *Interviewing as qualitative research: A guide for researchers in education and the social sciences* (5th ed.). Teachers College Press.

Silver, C., & Lewins, A. (2014). *Using software in qualitative research: A step-by-step guide* (2nd ed.). Sage.

Sindberg, L. K. (2006). *Comprehensive Musicianship through Performance (CMP) in the lived experience of students* (Publication No. 3221852) [Doctoral dissertation, Northwestern University]. ProQuest Dissertations & Theses Global.

Spall, S. (1998). Peer debriefing in qualitative research: Emerging operational models. *Qualitative Inquiry, 4*(2), 280–292. https://doi.org/10.1177/107780049800400208

Stake, R. E. (1995). *The art of case study research* (2nd ed.). Sage.

Stake, R. E. (2010). *Qualitative research: Studying how things work*. Guilford Press.

Stake, R. E., & Trumbull, D. (1982). Naturalistic generalizations. *Review Journal of Philosophy and Social Science, 7*(1), 1–12.

Stauffer, S. L. (2014). Narrative inquiry and the uses of narrative in music education research. In C. M. Conway (Ed.), *The Oxford handbook of qualitative research in American music education* (pp. 163–185). Oxford University Press.

Sweet, B. (2015). The adolescent female changing voice: A phenomenological investigation. *Journal of Research in Music Education, 63*(1), 70–88. https://doi.org/10.1177/002242941 5570755

Tracy, S. J. (2010). Qualitative inquiry: Eight "big tent" criteria for excellent qualitative research. *Qualitative Inquiry, 16*(10), 837–851. https://doi.org/10.1177/1077800410383121

Tsugawa, S. (2009). *Senior adult music learning, motivation, and meaning construction in two new horizons ensembles* (Publication No. 3392131) [Doctoral dissertation, Arizona State University]. Retrieved from ProQuest Dissertations & Theses Global.

Wolcott, H. F. (1990). On seeking—and rejecting—validity in qualitative research. In E. W. Eisner & A. Peshkin (Eds.), *Qualitative inquiry in education: The continuing debate* (pp. 121–152). Teachers College Press.

12
Quantitative Descriptive and Correlational Research

Chapter Preview

In this chapter, you will have an opportunity to learn about research designs for descriptive and correlational quantitative research. Descriptive research designs are used to address the question "What is x?" Correlational research designs are used to address the question "How are things related?" In contrast to some experimental research designs, in these design types the primary area of interest under investigation is not manipulated by the researcher. Researchers investigating descriptive or correlational research questions commonly use surveys or observational methods to gather data. Surveys are an efficient method for gathering large amounts of information about such things as individuals' experiences, beliefs, and attitudes. When designing a survey, researchers must consider how long it will be, what it will cover, and so on. Observation is an important means of gathering data, as when researchers observe video recordings of teachers or students in various situations. Another approach to observational research is the experience sampling method (ESM). In ESM, participants are interrupted at random times throughout the day and asked to respond to questions concerning their experiences in real time. In other words, researchers ask participants what they are doing at the moment they are contacted.

Introduction

Fundamentally, there are three general categories of questions that quantitative researchers ask: questions of description, questions of association, and questions of cause and effect. In this chapter, we will discuss the research approaches for investigating questions of description and association; in the next two chapters we will discuss approaches for investigating questions of cause and effect. See Box 12.1 for brief examples of how these research approaches can inform music teaching and learning practices. In descriptive research, the primary area of interest under investigation is not controlled or manipulated by the researcher. Rather, researchers engage in systematic data collection to determine the status of a phenomenon or how a phenomenon exists under various circumstances. For example, a survey of principals' opinions (e.g., Abril & Gault, 2008) and a study of expert studio teachers'

Box 12.1 Research to Practice: Quantitative Research

Research conducted via quantitative designs has much to offer for those concerned with the practical matters of music education.

Descriptive Research

Drawing from data gathered in the U.S. National Center for Education Statistics' High School Longitudinal Study of 2009 (Ingels et al., 2007), Elpus and Abril (2011, 2019) have revealed how African American and Latino students are underrepresented in high school band and orchestra classes in the United States. Their findings highlight a troubling systemic issue that music teachers should consider when reflecting on enrollments in their courses, as well as, perhaps, the courses that comprise the curricular offerings at their schools.

Correlational Research

Ilari et al. (2020) conducted a study of the associations among young children's (i.e., three- and four-year-olds) prosocial skills and participation in music in both formal programs and their homes. These researchers found moderate relationships between the children's music participation and skills involving helping and sharing such that those children with relatively more time participating in music also tended to display more of each of the prosocial skills. Although a causal link cannot be determined in a study incorporating a correlational design, Ilari et al.'s findings raise interesting questions about the myriad ways early childhood music educators may be able to impact children's development.

Experimental Research

Mornell and Wulf (2019) sought to determine whether adopting an internal or external focus of attention would cause more accurate and expressive musical performances. Participants in their studies were asked to either (a) focus on playing for an imagined audience and for the sake of expression—an external focus experimental condition, (b) focus on attending to finger movements or lip movements (e.g., for singers)—an internal focus experimental condition, or (c) play the way they normally did—a control condition. Overall, those in the external condition produced performances rated by judges as more musically expressive than those in the other conditions. However, those in the internal condition produced more technically proficient performances than those in the other conditions. These results have important implications for the sorts of instructions teachers could use when coaching students to achieve musical performance skills.

teaching behaviors (e.g., Blackwell, 2020) are both examples of research topics wherein the primary purpose is to systematically describe a phenomenon.

Correlational research designs are used to explore relationships among various aspects of music teaching and learning phenomena. Again, as with descriptive research, researchers do not intervene when conducting correlational research. Instead, they investigate whether associations are present among variables as they are observed without any form of manipulation. For instance, Schmidt (2005) explored relationships between high school instrumental music students' various motivational beliefs and their teachers' ratings of their performance ability and effort, and Miksza (2006) investigated associations between high school instrumentalists' use of selected practice behaviors and their performance ability. Neither researcher intervened with the high school students in their studies; they simply observed the students' attributes and assessed whether there were associations among them. Given that both of these studies are examples of correlational research, claims about cause and effect could not be derived from either of them, only conclusions of association. Generally speaking, claims of cause and effect can be derived only from experimental research. The difference between correlation and causation is discussed in more detail in Chapter 13.

The kinds of scientific inquiry carried out via quantitative research designs will tend to emphasize relatively inductive or deductive processes. Inductive approaches to research involve scholars working from particular observations to generate general theoretical principles. For example, a researcher who begins a program of inquiry by systematically observing how students cooperate (or not) in chamber music rehearsals and ultimately derives a general theory of chamber music cooperation would be engaging in an inductively driven process (i.e., specific observations of students → general theoretical hypothesis). In contrast, a deductive approach occurs when scholars work from general theoretical principles to derive hypotheses and make predictions about the ways that particular observations will turn out.[1] For example, should the same researcher design a study to test the hypotheses stated in their general theory of chamber music cooperation among additional chamber music students, then one would describe that research as deductively driven (i.e., general theoretical hypotheses → specific observations of students to test them).

Descriptive research designs are most often employed for relatively exploratory and inductive purposes since researchers do not typically state specific hypotheses or predictions about their data prior to conducting descriptive research. When conducting descriptive research, scholars generally aim to collect a large amount of information (i.e., particular observations) from which they can build general models, theories, and hypotheses. In contrast, experimental designs (which will be discussed in Chapters 13 and 14) are most often employed for relatively deductive

[1] "Deductive" and "inductive" are terms that denote quite general concepts. However, when these terms are applied in the context of the scientific method, they typically refer to the narrow usages included in this chapter. It's important to recognize that scientists' use of these terms involves one type of inductive process among many and one type of deductive process among many. For example, see Chapter 5 to learn how the terms "deductive reasoning" and "inductive reasoning" operate in other ways when conducting philosophical research.

purposes since researchers conducting experiments will always have a hypothesis to test—whether or not they explicitly state it. When conducting experiments, scholars work from a general assumption about the effects of an experimental treatment (i.e., general theoretical principals/hypotheses) and test whether the effects they anticipate will appear among the observations they make. Compared to descriptive and experimental designs, correlational research is less likely to be strictly inductive or deductive in nature. For example, sometimes researchers aim to explore associations among variables to see whether or not the associations exist, without hypotheses about the nature of those potential relationships (i.e., relatively inductive aims). However, it is perhaps more common for researchers to have at least some sort of hypothesis about the nature of the associations they investigate. One typically wouldn't choose to look for an association unless one were working from some general theoretical reason as to why variables might be related in the first place (i.e., relatively deductive aims).

Quantitative descriptive and correlational research includes scientific investigations wherein observations are made via measurements. These measurements yield numerical data that are subjected to statistical analyses to derive meaningful conclusions. Surveys and observational research designs are the most common methods quantitative researchers use when investigating questions of description and association. Given the prominence of survey research in the literature and its accessibility as a method for emerging scholars to employ, the majority of this chapter is devoted to explaining the basic issues researchers consider when conducting survey research. However, we also discuss examples of both observational and survey research from the literature. In addition, we encourage you to explore the methodological texts we have listed in Box 12.2 for more information about descriptive research design. Qualitative approaches to research questions that might be used to explore issues of description or association from a variety of ontological and epistemological perspectives are covered in Chapters 9 and 10.

Survey Methods

A survey is a very commonly used descriptive research technique and an efficient method for gathering a large amount of information. Researchers often conduct surveys to collect information about individuals' experiences, beliefs, and attitudes. Surveys can be administered in person, via phone, via paper methods, and via online methods. There are advantages and disadvantages of each administration form, major considerations being time and costs involved in delivering the survey and collecting data. Given the low cost, quick response time, and automatic data collation possible, online survey administration has become by far the most common form used today.

Surveys administered to a group only once are called "cross-sectional." They take a snapshot of what people are thinking at a given point in time, and the responses from categories of participants can be compared. Surveys given to people at two or

> **Box 12.2 Additional Methodological Readings: Descriptive and Correlational Research**
>
> **General Approaches to Quantitative Research Design**
>
> Cozby, P., & Bates, S. (2020). *Methods in behavioral research* (14th ed.). McGraw Hill.
>
> Gall, M. D., Gall, J. P., & Borg, W. R. (2007). *Educational research: An introduction* (8th ed.). Pearson.
>
> **Observational Research**
>
> Bakeman, R., & Gottman, J. M. (2009). *Observing interaction: An introduction to sequential analysis* (2nd ed.). Cambridge University Press.
>
> Kerlinger, F. N., & Lee, H. B. (2000). *Foundations of behavioral research* (4th ed.). Cengage Learning.
>
> **Survey Research**
>
> Dillman, D. A., Smyth, J. D., & Christian, L. M. (2014). *Internet, phone, mail, and mixed-mode surveys: The tailored design method* (4th ed.). Wiley.
>
> Groves, R. M., Fowler, F. J., Jr., Couper, M. P., Lepkowski, J. M., Singer, E., & Tourangeau, R. (2009). *Survey methodology* (2nd ed.). John Wiley & Sons.
>
> Rea, L. M., & Parker, R. A. (2014). *Designing and conducting survey research: A comprehensive guide* (4th ed.). Jossey-Bass.
>
> **Correlational Research**
>
> Cresswell, J. W., & Guetterman, T. C. (2019). *Educational research: Planning, conducting, and evaluating quantitative and qualitative research* (6th ed.). Pearson.
>
> Kerlinger, F. N., & Lee, H. B. (2000). *Foundations of behavioral research* (4th ed.). Cengage Learning.

more different points in time are called "longitudinal." They allow the researcher to see how opinions or attitudes may change over time. Suppose, for example, that you were interested in the development of students' preferences for various musical genres over three years of secondary school. You could survey 10th-, 11th-, and 12th-grade students all at once; this would be a cross-sectional survey allowing you to compare responses across the age groups. You could also survey a group of 10th graders, survey them again the next year as 11th graders, and again the next year as 12th graders. This would be a longitudinal study showing how students' attitudes persisted or changed over three years.

There are a number of steps to be taken when developing a survey study. First, as described in Chapter 2, a quantitative research study must (a) be grounded with a robust rationale and justification, (b) be conceived with respect to what's been learned from previous literature on the topic, and (c) have a specific purpose and research questions and/or hypotheses. Once these elements are established, you will determine the population you want to study. Who are the people who could best answer your questions? Who has the most informed opinion about these issues? And so on. Next, you will determine the best means of surveying this population. Will you survey the entire population (i.e., a census), use random sampling or a stratified random sampling technique to choose a representative sample, or will you be reliant on a convenience sample of volunteers?

Sampling

Researchers conduct surveys to learn about a specific population—all the members of a specific group of people. For example, researchers might be interested in learning about the job satisfaction of all music teachers in the nation or middle school students' attitudes toward course offerings in a particular state or the ways that parents interact musically with their infant children. Each group of people described in the previous sentence could be considered a population. However, it is most often neither possible nor cost effective to survey an entire population of individuals. As a result, researchers will choose members of a population to survey with the aim of generalizing the responses they get from those selected members to the entire population of interest. This is called "sampling."

A sample is a selection of members from a given population meant to represent the entire population. Researchers must identify a sampling frame in order to select individuals. A sampling frame is a list of people who can actually be contacted as potential participants in the study. Researchers often use lists of individuals from governmental records or membership lists from professional organizations as sampling frames. When conducting a survey, it is important to argue convincingly that the chosen sampling frame is a reasonable approximation of the population and to attain a sample that is large and varied enough that the results you obtain can be generalized to the larger population. In general, relatively larger samples will more likely yield responses representative of a population than relatively smaller samples. However, it is also possible to compute the relative size of a sample you need for generalizability given certain tolerances for error using long-established formulas (see Miksza & Elpus, 2018, Figure 3.1, p. 26). The representativeness of a sample will also depend on the *response rate* of the survey: the proportion of individuals sampled that actually complete the survey. Surveys with high response rates, say, greater than 60%, are much more likely to yield representative information than those with low response rates. However, surveys with low response rates can still be representative of a population if the characteristics of the respondents are similar to those of the broader population and if it can be argued that nonresponse bias is not present.

The best way to safeguard that a sample will be varied enough to be representative of a population is to use probability sampling techniques such as *simple random sampling*. In this case, every member of the population has an equal and independent opportunity (i.e., probability) of being selected. This can be done through various means but generally involves numbering the individuals listed in a sampling frame and then using random numbers to select potential participants. Assuming that the sample is large enough with respect to the target population, the probability that the diversity of the population will be represented in the sample is strong.

Other sampling techniques are *systematic sampling*, *cluster sampling*, and *stratified sampling*. Systematic sampling involves randomly picking an individual from a sampling frame and then choosing every nth individual on the list, (e.g., beginning with random selection of participant 52, then with $n = 10$, choose 62, then 72, then 82, and so on). Cluster sampling is carried out when subgroups of individuals are chosen systematically, and then participants are randomly selected from within the subgroups. Large-scale educational surveys conducted by the U.S. government often employ multistage cluster sampling processes. For example, clusters of districts could be selected, followed by clusters of schools, and then teachers could be randomly sampled within schools. *Stratified random sampling* involves breaking the population down into strata of individual characteristics (e.g., by education level attained, age groups, race/ethnicity) and then drawing random samples proportionately from each stratum. These individual characteristics should represent important variables related to the topic of the study.

In contrast to the probability sampling techniques described above, samples consisting of volunteers recruited via a nonprobability sampling approach are *convenience samples*. For example, a high school choir taught by the researcher's personal contact is not necessarily representative of high school choirs at large. As you might imagine, convenience samples are more likely to yield biased findings that are not representative of a population. Unfortunately, convenience samples are quite common in music education research, given the limited resources typically available to researchers (e.g., lack of funds for incentives to participate or data collection assistance).

As an example of probability sampling, suppose a researcher is interested in gathering information about the kinds of professional development activities that music teachers from a particular state engage in and how valuable the teachers perceive them to be. In this case the population of interest is all music teachers in the state. In regard to identifying a sampling frame, the state's music education association member list would be a convenient and expedient means for identifying a large number of teachers. Since such a list would not necessarily include every music teacher in the state, it would be important to acknowledge that the survey findings may not generalize to music teachers who are not interested in joining or who are unable to join the professional organization. However, once the list is attained, it would simply be a matter of randomly selecting enough potential respondents to achieve a sample of participants large enough to be representative of the population.

Table 12.1 Fictitious data for a stratified sample of music teachers from a single state

	General Music		Instrumental Music		Choral Music		Other Emphasis	
	n	%	n	%	n	%	n	%
< 5 years	150	15%	65	6.5%	60	6%	5	0.5%
6 to 10 years	150	15%	65	6.5%	50	5%	10	1%
11 to 15 years	100	10%	45	4.5%	30	3%	20	2%
> 16 years	100	10%	25	2.5%	10	1%	15	1.5%
Total	500	50%	200	20%	150	15%	50	5%

If a researcher were particularly interested in comparing subgroups of the population of music teachers, for example, according to years of teaching experience and area of teaching emphasis, then they could use a stratified sampling approach. As a hypothetical case, let's assume there are 1,000 music teachers in the state and the breakdown of these teachers according to the strata you are interested in exploring is as depicted in Table 12.1. If you use established formulas (Miksza & Elpus, 2018), you would find that you need a sample of about 280 people to be representative of the population. With that known, you could then randomly select participants from each combination of strata such that 50% of the 280 (i.e., 190) are general music teachers, and 20% of the 280 (i.e., 56) are instrumental music teachers, and so on, until your sample is proportionately representative of the population.

Developing a Questionnaire

After determining a sampling approach, practical issues regarding the development of the questionnaire must be considered. Seeking out ideas from questionnaires that have been used to address the same or similar topics in previous research can be a good way to begin. Adapting existing questionnaires or items from existing questionnaires to serve your research purposes can save time and make findings from multiple studies on the same topic more easily comparable. However, it can also be necessary or preferable to develop an original questionnaire if previously used tools are not suitable for addressing the particular research questions you seek to ask. What follows is a list of specific points to consider when designing your questionnaire:

- *Length and duration:* In general, the shorter a questionnaire can be, the better. Questionnaires that are brief and focused on an issue relevant to a population are much more likely to yield higher response rates than those that are relatively longer. Therefore, a questionnaire should contain only items that are absolutely necessary for addressing the specific purpose and research questions set forth in your study. It is also important to consider the developmental maturity of your population; for example, children will have more difficulty than adults maintaining concentration.

- *Formatting:* The visual appearance of the questionnaire is important. It must be organized and include instructions that are clear and easy to follow. All instructions and items must be written at a reading level that the potential respondents can easily comprehend. Whether it is a web-based or paper questionnaire, the items should be organized across pages in a logical way and not require participants to flip or click back and forth to answer questions.

- *Aligning content with research questions and consulting experts:* Always and continually consider the research questions of the study, that is, the objectives of the questionnaire. It can be helpful to create an outline on which you indicate which questionnaire items are for gathering information for each research question. This will help to establish the content validity of the questionnaire and will help make sure that you are gathering enough information to address the purpose of the research. Asking content area experts to review your items and offer feedback is another way to bolster the validity of your questionnaire.

- *Item ordering:* For relatively longer questionnaires, arrange the presentation of items such that the most critical information is gathered first. That way, if respondents choose to stop participating you will more likely have gathered information you can use. Grouping items according to similar content areas is helpful for respondents. However, if you are concerned that the order of a particular collection of items will bias responses, then it could be beneficial to use a web-based service that randomizes the ordering of items within a section of a questionnaire across respondents.

- *Item design:* Consider the relative benefits of both close-ended items (i.e., participants choose among provided response options; checkbox, yes/no, rating scales) and open-ended items (i.e., participants supply a response; text boxes). Close-ended items require relatively less time for respondents to respond to and less time for researchers to code and analyze than open-ended items. However, open-ended items can yield highly detailed information and offer participants opportunities to provide important information you may not have anticipated. Items can be phrased as statements for respondents to respond to or as questions for respondents to select/provide an answer. Regardless of type, items should address one idea (rather than several), be clearly worded, be written at a reading level appropriate for the population of interest, and be free from bias (e.g., no leading language, skewed response options, or offensive language). Using succinct, unambiguous, objective terminology is helpful when aiming for clarity. Ultimately, the reliability of your questionnaire will depend on the degree to which your item design allows participants to interpret and respond to the items accurately.

- *Response options:* There are a wide variety of response option formats that can be paired with questionnaire items. Examples of several common formats are provided below:

  Numerical or short text response
  Example: Indicate the number of full-time teachers in each arts area in your school district:

  _____ Music _____ Visual Art _____ Dance _____ Theater

  Checkbox for a single response
  Example: How many elementary schools are in your district?

  ☐ one ☐ two ☐ three ☐ four ☐ five or more

  Checkbox for multiple possible responses
  Example: Check those items that best describe your choir director. Choose as many as are relevant.

  ☐ kind ☐ harsh ☐ dictator ☐ understanding ☐ fun ☐ lazy

  Provide rankings
  Example: Rank your preference for the following composers from most (1) to least preferred (5):

  __ Bach __ Mozart __ Beethoven __ Wagner __ Shostakovich

  Likert-type rating scales: Rating scale item types can be paired with statements or questions. The number of response choices provided for a rating scale can vary, as well as whether an odd or even set of response choices are provided. For most purposes somewhere between four and nine response options is suitable. Fewer than four makes it difficult to capture potential variability in participants' responses, whereas it becomes difficult for respondents to discriminate among more than nine choices. For some rating scale options, an odd number of choices will be offered to allow a respondent to choose a middle or neutral response, whereas an even number of choices will force respondents to commit to an opinion since there will be no neutral position available to select. In some cases, it can also be valuable to offer a "not applicable" response option following the rating scale options to avoid forcing responses from participants who do not have the relevant experience to provide an answer.

  Example: I am an excellent singer. [The odd number of options includes a neutral option]

☐	☐	☐	☐	☐
strongly agree	agree	neither agree nor disagree	disagree	strongly disagree

Example: I am an excellent singer. [The even number of options forces the respondent to commit to an opinion]

☐	☐	☐	☐
strongly agree	agree	disagree	strongly disagree

There is a great deal of flexibility possible when designing labels used in a Likert-type scale. Here are a few more examples:

How do you rate yourself as a musician?

☐	☐	☐	☐	☐
very poor	below average	average	above average	excellent

I enjoy practicing my instrument.

☐	☐	☐	☐
always	sometimes	rarely	never

How do you feel about the recent decision to add additional arts graduation requirements for high school students in your state?

☐	☐	☐	☐	☐
strongly approve	somewhat approve	neutral/ no opinion	somewhat disapprove	strongly disapprove

How important is the inclusion of popular music in the music education curriculum for secondary school students?

☐	☐	☐	☐	☐
not important	somewhat important	not sure/ no opinion	important	very important

Open-ended response with text box
Example: Please describe any curricular changes that you have influenced in your school district in the past five years.

- *Pilot testing and revision:* Once a draft of the questionnaire has been created, it is important to pilot-test the tool and complete any necessary revisions indicated from the pilot test results. A pilot test can consist of administering the questionnaire to a relatively small group of people with characteristics similar to your proposed respondents. In addition to providing their responses to the items, the pilot test respondents should be able to provide you with written and/or verbal comments on all aspects of the questionnaire. All concerns raised by the pilot test respondents should inform your revisions and, depending upon the magnitude of the revision necessary, it may be necessary to pilot-test it again.

Administering the Questionnaire

Once the questionnaire is complete, it is important to think carefully about the steps you will take when collecting data. There is much to consider when choosing how to administer your survey. For example:

- What is the timeframe during which you want to obtain your responses?
- When surveying teachers and students, the academic calendar must be considered; sending a survey during times when your population of interest has particularly heavy commitments will almost guarantee poor response rates (e.g., competition seasons for high school music directors).
- Will you conduct the survey via phone, in person, or via paper copies in the mail, or create an online questionnaire through a web service (e.g., Qualtrics)? If you do use a website, will your target population have online access?
- How will you contact your potential participants prior to administering the survey?
- Are there incentives you can offer that may increase the chances that people will participate?
- Do you have funds to include postage for participants to return completed paper surveys?
- How will you keep track of who has responded and who has not?
- In what ways and how often will you follow up with those who do not respond to the first solicitation?
- What procedures will you follow to ensure participants' anonymity?

Each of these concerns has implications for the response rate that you might achieve. Recall that the higher the response rate, the greater chance you have of obtaining findings representative of the population. Try to think through as many practical issues as you can before you launch into a survey project.

In most cases, it would be valuable to contact potential participants of your survey study prior to administering the actual questionnaire in order to draw their attention to the study and let them know they will shortly be receiving an invitation to participate. This is referred to as a precontact notice and could consist of something as simple as a postcard or short email. Participants may be less likely to perceive the actual survey invitation as spam or junk mail if they receive a prenotification.

A cover letter should accompany the main invitation to participate in the survey. The cover letter is an opportunity to persuade potential participants to complete your questionnaire. Upon reading the cover letter, the potential participant should have a sense that the research is important and relevant to them and that it will be helpful for them and the profession. Being succinct and clear when writing a cover letter is important, since people will not typically want to devote too much time to reading a lengthy letter. Some important topics to address in cover letters include:

- The purpose of your study (in clear and straightforward terms).
- Why the recipient's particular perspective is valuable for the research.
- The purpose for which the data will be used and how the knowledge gained could benefit respondents or the field.
- Whether there are any incentives for participating in the research (e.g., money, prizes).
- How participants might learn of the results of the study.
- Definitions of any special terms used in the questionnaire.
- Instructions for completing the questionnaire.
- The approximate time it will take to complete the questionnaire.
- Where to send the completed questionnaire (if using mail-in forms).
- The deadline for completing/returning the questionnaire.
- Assurances that respondents' identity will be protected.

Offering incentives to potential participants can help to increase response rates. Even small amounts of money or minor tokens of appreciation can be powerful motivators. If funds are limited (and they usually are), offering participants a chance to win a prize via a lottery can be cost effective. In contrast to material rewards, offering to share results of the study with potential respondents can also encourage people to participate. This might especially be the case if the participants find the topic intrinsically meaningful.

Planning a follow-up strategy for those who don't initially respond is also critical. Follow-up reminders to participate in the survey can consist of remailing/resending the entire cover letter or reminding the respondent via a simple, brief note that they have been contacted recently. Either way, participants should be able to access and complete the questionnaire from the reminder, for example, either via a link to an electronic survey in the reminder message or via an additional copy of the paper questionnaire accompanying the reminder mailing. If a respondent has any intention to complete or interest in completing the questionnaire, two or three follow-up reminders will typically be sufficient. Any more than that and you are at risk of offending or at least annoying the target population. If it is possible to do so, send follow-up reminders only to nonrespondents, not the entire sample. Participants do not appreciate being asked again to complete a questionnaire if they have already done so.

As final steps prior to administering your survey, it would be valuable to reexamine the questionnaire in terms of your original research topic. Does the revised version still seek information that can serve to answer your research questions? Also, if it is to be mailed, check all aspects of the procedures: bulk mailing, return envelopes, address, size of envelopes, return postage, delivery, and return time. If an online questionnaire is used, proofread the online version carefully. Make certain all the buttons and links work correctly. Also make certain the reporting mechanism (e.g., exporting answers to a spreadsheet) works correctly. Once the questionnaire is sent, it cannot be recalled for a correction of errors. Therefore, it can also be beneficial to first release the survey to only a small portion of the sample; that way, if an error is present, it can be corrected prior to administering the survey to the rest of the potential respondents.

It is possible that your response rate will be poor even after several follow-up reminders. Data from surveys with low response rates are more likely to be susceptible to nonresponse bias; however, there are mitigation efforts that you can make to try to demonstrate that the data are not biased despite the low response rate. The most robust method is to resample from the pool of nonrespondents and then compare the findings from that specific group of people to those from the original respondents. If the findings are similar, that would suggest response bias may not be present. Another approach is to compare the data from a group of respondents who were the latest to respond to those who were the earliest to respond. The reasoning underlying this method is that late responders may be similar to nonresponders. Again, if the data from both groups are similar, a case could be made that nonresponse bias may be minimal. It is also always important to describe the characteristics of your respondents with as much detail as possible. By doing so, you can demonstrate the degree to which the characteristics of your respondents match that of the population. If their characteristics are similar, it is easier to argue that your data may be representative of the population despite a poor response rate.

The final steps of conducting survey research are to analyze and interpret the data as well as fashion a report to disseminate to the scientific community and any other relevant stakeholders. As described in Chapter 21, the dissemination of research is usually done through an article or a presentation. However, it could be a report to administrators or other means of communication. We will restrict our discussion of how to analyze and interpret data yielded from descriptive and correlational research to the chapters in this book devoted to statistical methods.

Examples of Survey Methods in Music Education Research

Survey Methods and Descriptive Aims

Buonviri and Paney (2015, p. 226) conducted a survey study to "identify pedagogical approaches to melodic dictation employed by AP [Advanced Placement] music theory teachers across the United States." The research questions articulated for this study highlight the authors' explicit descriptive aims:

1. What pedagogical approaches to rhythm and pitch do teachers use to build dictation skills?
2. Which resources (texts, music, software, and websites) do teachers employ in melodic dictation teaching?
3. What strategies do teachers recommend students use during dictation?
4. Do teachers address test-taking skills as part of their dictation instruction? (p. 227)

The population Buonviri and Paney (2015) were interested in learning about was all AP music theory teachers in the United States. As a sampling frame, they chose a list of 2,269 schools from the AP Course Ledger, which is maintained by the College Board—the publisher and administrator of AP exams. The AP Course Ledger includes all schools authorized to include AP course designations in their students' transcripts. Buonviri and Paney calculated that a sample size of between 330 and 340 randomly selected participants would be necessary to generalize their findings to the entire population of teachers. However, anticipating a lower than optimal response rate, they decided to select a random sample of 894 teachers in the hopes of achieving adequate size.

The questionnaire for this study included two sections: a section that included 24 items pertaining to pedagogical approaches for melodic dictation and a section that included 4 items pertaining to the teachers' background characteristics and teaching context. Buonviri and Paney (2015) chose to conduct their survey via the internet using Qualtrics software and included close-ended items (i.e., choose a single response, check all that apply, rating scale) as well as open-ended items (i.e., fill in answers). Four music theory instructors were asked to evaluate the content of the survey to provide evidence of validity, that is, to confirm that the dictation pedagogy topics included in the questionnaire were relevant to the population and fairly exhaustive as far as coverage goes.

The authors did not report sending a precontact notification, but instead sent their invitation to participate via teachers' email addresses or through contact forms provided by school websites. The email invitation included the cover letter and a link to participate in the survey. Three follow-up reminders were sent at two, three, and six weeks from the initial mailing. Ultimately, they achieved a 44% response rate (393 out of 894 potential respondents).

Among several interesting findings, Buonviri and Paney (2015) learned that teachers preferred pitch and rhythm dictation pedagogy that involved systems emphasizing scale degrees and meter, respectively. In addition, the results suggested that the content of the AP music theory exam itself influenced the teaching approaches the teachers used.

Survey Methods and Correlational Aims

In another example, Schmidt et al. (2006) surveyed public-school music programs in Indiana with the intention of addressing both descriptive and correlational aims. In order to create a snapshot of the status of public-school music at the time, they collected information on the following topics: "curricular offerings, instructional time, student participation, teaching loads, ensemble performance activity and achievement, and teachers' experience and licensing" (p. 26). They also wanted to explore whether these topics might vary as a function of school enrollment, percentage of minority students, and socioeconomic status.

The population of interest in Schmidt et al.'s (2006) study was all music teachers in Indiana, and they used a directory of music teachers in the state furnished by Indiana University as their sampling frame. The researchers used a two-stage, cluster sampling process wherein they first sampled 33% of the 98 public school districts in Indiana and then the 619 music teachers employed within those districts.

Schmidt et al. (2006) developed separate paper questionnaires for different teaching emphasis areas (e.g., general music, choral, instrumental band, instrumental strings). The participants were asked to complete questionnaires for each of the emphasis areas they taught. The questionnaires included a variety of close- and open-ended items pertaining to each of the topic areas described in the paragraph above. No additional information is provided regarding the specific content or validation of the questionnaires; however, this is likely due to the authors' desire to save space in their article for reporting findings as opposed to reflecting a less than rigorous approach to questionnaire design. The initial mailing of the paper questionnaires was followed by two reminders that were conducted via mail, email, or phone. The response rate for the teachers was 65%, although 100% of the school districts sampled were represented among the responses.

Many notable findings emerged from the data, one of the most compelling being the degree of variability "in program characteristics, enrollment, participation rate, and performance activity" (Schmidt et al., 2006, p. 25). As an example of correlational results, the size of general music teachers' teaching loads was associated with the amount of time they devoted to various types of instructional activities in which they engaged their students. For example, general music teachers who were responsible for relatively more students per week were also somewhat less likely to engage students in listening and music reading activities, but somewhat more likely to engage students in movement, singing, and performance preparation activities.

Examples of Observational Methods in Music Education Research

Observational Methods and Descriptive Aims

Key elements of observational research are (a) choosing a salient setting and context in which the phenomenon of interest is likely to occur in a compelling and authentic manner, (b) specifying clear definitions of the behaviors to be observed, (c) establishing a clear protocol for how to record the behaviors to be observed (e.g., frequency, duration, interval recording), and (e) determining a method for demonstrating the reliability of the observations made (i.e., interrater agreement). Orman (2002) conducted a descriptive observational study to investigate how elementary music specialists used their instructional time. She collected video recordings of "typical" instruction from 30 teachers, which included five classes from each teacher working with students in grades 1 through 6. She created a scheme by which she coded the duration of teachers' and students' behaviors as belonging to one of the following categories: getting ready, talking, singing, playing, singing and moving, singing and playing, verbal rhythm, movement, listen to music, listen to student, combination of categories, and other. She also coded the duration of classroom events as being focused on the following kinds of activities (these areas reflect several of the National Standards for Music Education at the time she conducted the study): improvising; composing/arranging; reading/notating; listening/analyzing/describing; evaluating; understanding relationships between music, the other arts, and disciplines outside the arts; and understanding music in relation to history and culture. Orman also enlisted an independent observer to code 30% of the video recordings to establish evidence for the reliability of the observations she made. Overall, she found that the teachers spent the majority of class time talking, and accordingly, students spent the majority of class time in passive roles. In regard to types of activities, the largest percentages of class time were devoted to reading and notating music and listening and analyzing music, whereas the smallest percentages of class time were devoted to evaluating music and composing and arranging music.

Observational Methods and Correlational Aims

Miksza et al. (2012) investigated the degree of self-regulation that middle school band students demonstrated when practicing on their own. Their study had both descriptive and correlational goals. The researchers sought to describe (a) the way students organize their practice time, (b) the kinds of musical objectives they emphasize, and (c) the strategies they would use to achieve their objectives. However, they were also curious to determine whether the frequency with which students used certain practice behaviors would be associated with ratings of the students' overall degree of self-regulation during practice.

Miksza et al. (2012) recruited 30 middle school band students from a summer band clinic and video-recorded them practicing their band repertoire by themselves for 20 minutes. The students were asked to practice their band music as if they were working on it at home. The researchers developed an observation scheme with which they segmented the participants' practice videos according to apparent shifts in their practice goals; that is, they documented a new "practice frame" each time a participant "stopped playing a passage and jumped to a section of the same piece that was at least four measures from the last spot he or she played or shifted to another piece of music altogether" (p. 258). They then measured the duration of each practice frame and coded each of the practice frames according to (a) the length of the musical passage being practiced, (b) the musical objective the participant appeared to be focusing on, and (c) the particular practice strategies that were evident (counting aloud, silent fingering, varying articulation, playing rhythm on a single pitch, whole-part repetition, chunking, etc.). In addition, two independent raters were recruited to watch the video recordings and rate the students for the degree of self-regulation observed in their practice (e.g., whether they were thoughtfully engaged in practice, managing their time, and able to evaluate their own progress).

The descriptive data revealed that, on average, the participants' practice sessions consisted of around eight practice frames lasting between two and three minutes each. The participants most frequently focused on relatively large chunks of music (i.e., nine measures in length or more) and tended to address simple objectives such as note accuracy. The most frequently used strategies were varying tempo and repetition. The correlational findings indicated that the students who exhibited the greatest degree of self-regulation also tended to be more likely to write on their music, vary tempo, and repeat chunks of music consisting of four or more measures.

Experience Sampling Methods and Descriptive Aims

A special type of observational research that has particular usefulness for music education research is that which employs experience sampling methods (ESM). In ESM, participants are interrupted at random times throughout the day and asked to respond to questions concerning their experiences in real time. What are they doing at the moment they are contacted? There are different ways to contact individuals; one is to use specialized software that contacts participants on their smartphones. In the following example, researchers used ESM to study musical imagery.

Beaty and colleagues (2013) were interested in the frequency and nature of music that people hear in their minds in the absence of actual physical sounds. In the first phase of the experiment, a cross-sectional approach was used. People were asked to remember how often they reported hearing inner music and the extent to which they enjoyed it. Based on responses from 190 undergraduate students, music imagery was found to be a common experience and people generally enjoyed it. In the second phase, responses from 26 music majors were compared to responses from 78 undergraduates who were not music majors. Participants were contacted on their cell phones at random intervals up to 10 times a day for seven days. When participants answered their phones, they responded to a series of questions related to music imagery. Overall, participants reported hearing inner music 17% of the time. These musical experiences were positive and frequently involved music that was personally meaningful. Music majors tended to hear inner music more often than non-music majors.

Summary

Descriptive research is concerned with "what is." Researchers want to describe a current situation by gathering data about a phenomenon. There is enormous variety in descriptive research designs, but two prominent approaches are survey and observational methods. Correlational research is concerned with whether phenomena are related to each other. As we've shown in the examples above, correlational research questions can also be addressed with data gathered from survey and observational designs. A significant limitation of descriptive and correlational research is that it does not allow us to draw cause-and-effect conclusions. In the next chapter, on experimental research, we will discuss ways to manipulate the structure of an experiment such that we can gain insights into casual relationships. In the meantime, it is important to note that descriptive and correlational research often precedes experimental research. That is, exploratory descriptive and correlational research may yield findings that inform how a researcher could construct an experiment to determine a cause-and-effect relationship.

Before we come to that in the next chapter, here are some prompts that you can respond to with your newfound knowledge of quantitative descriptive research:

1. What is descriptive research, and what is correlational research? Can you think of research questions that illustrate each approach?
2. What are some topics you would like to address via survey methods? Who would be your target population?
3. What is the difference between a sample and a population? What is the purpose of identifying a sampling frame?
4. Why is random sampling desirable? What are the benefits of using stratified random sampling?
5. Describe some of the steps necessary to develop a questionnaire.
6. Give some examples of questionnaire items that would be most appropriately paired with the following response types: (a) check box, (b) ranking, (c) Likert-type scale, and (d) open-ended text box.
7. There are nearly endless possibilities of observational methods. Give at least three examples of music education phenomena you could learn about

via systematic observation. Describe how you might quantify the particular aspects of the phenomena you would like to study.
8. Write a brief summary of a quantitative descriptive research study that you would like to conduct. Write a short purpose statement and a set of research questions. Briefly describe how you would approach attaining a sample as well as some aspects of a questionnaire or observational scheme that you would develop.

Important Terms for Review

Quantitative research includes scientific investigations wherein observations are made via measurements. These measurements yield numerical data that are subjected to statistical analyses to derive meaningful conclusions.

Descriptive research is the systematic investigation of the status of a phenomenon or how a phenomenon exists under various circumstances.

Correlational research is the systematic investigation of whether and how aspects of a phenomenon or phenomena are related to each other.

An *inductive* research approach it taken when one works from specific observations to develop general theoretical principles.

A *deductive* research approach is taken when one begins with general theoretical principles and then creates hypotheses that predict how specific observations will turn out.

Observational designs typically involve the systematic quantification of participants' behaviors in particular settings.

Survey designs involve collecting responses to a series of questions (via phone, questionnaire, in-person, etc.) from a large group of people. *Cross-sectional* surveys are given to a group only once to determine responses across categories of participants at a given time. *Longitudinal* surveys are given to the same participants two or more times to allow the researcher to compare responses across time.

A *population* is the group of people who are the main focus of a study.

A *sampling frame* is a list of people that serves as an approximation of the population and from which researchers can choose a sample.

A *sample* is a smaller group of persons chosen from the sampling frame to represent the larger population.

Simple random sampling is a technique of choosing a sample in such a way that every member of the population has an equal and independent chance (i.e., equal probability) of being selected.

Response rate refers to the proportion of individuals from the sample that actually responded to the survey.

Convenience sampling is a nonprobability sampling technique in which volunteers choose to respond or participate in a research study rather than being chosen at random to respond.

References

Abril, C. R., & Gault, B. M. (2008). The state of music in secondary schools: The principal's perspective. *Journal of Research in Music Education, 56*(1), 68–81. https://doi.org/10.1177/0022429408317516

Bakeman, R., & Gottman, J. M. (2009). *Observing interaction: An introduction to sequential analysis* (2nd ed.). Cambridge University Press.

Beaty, R., Burgin, C., Nusbaum, E., Kwapil, T., Hodges, D., & Silvia, P. (2013). Music to the inner ears: Exploring individual differences in musical imagery. *Consciousness and Cognition, 22*, 1163–1173. https://doi.org/10.1016/j.concog.2013.07.006

Blackwell, J. (2020). Expertise in applied studio teaching: Teachers working with multiple levels of learners. *International Journal of Music Education, 38*(2), 283–298. https://doi.org/10.1177/0255761419898312

Buonviri, N. O., & Paney, A. S. (2015). Melodic dictation instruction: A survey of advanced placement music theory teachers. *Journal of Research in Music Education, 63*(2), 224–237. https://doi.org/10.1177/0022429413508411

Cozby, P., & Bates, S. (2020). *Methods in behavioral research* (14th ed.). McGraw Hill.

Cresswell, J. W., & Guetterman, T. C. (2019). *Educational research: Planning, conducting, and evaluating quantitative and qualitative research* (6th ed.). Pearson.

Dillman, D. A., Smyth, J. D., & Christian, L. M. (2014). *Internet, phone, mail, and mixed-mode surveys: The tailored design method* (4th ed.). Wiley.

Elpus, K., & Abril, C. R. (2011). High school music ensemble students in the United States: A demographic profile. *Journal of Research in Music Education, 59*(2), 128–145. https://doi.org/10.1177/0022429411405207

Elpus, K., & Abril, C. R. (2019). Who enrolls in high school music? A national profile of US students, 2009–2013. *Journal of Research in Music Education, 67*(3), 323–338.

Gall, M. D., Gall, J. P., & Borg, W. R. (2007). *Educational research: An introduction* (8th ed.). Pearson.

Groves, R. M., Fowler, F. J., Jr., Couper, M. P., Lepkowski, J. M., Singer, E., & Tourangeau, R. (2009). *Survey methodology* (2nd ed.). John Wiley & Sons.

Ilari, B., Helfter, S., & Huynh, T. (2020). Associations between musical participation and young children's prosocial behaviors. *Journal of Research in Music Education, 67*(4), 399–412. https://doi.org/10.1177/0022429419878169

Ingels, S. J., Pratt, D. J., Wilson, D., Burns, L. J., Currivan, D., Rogers, J. E., & Hubbard-Bednasz, S. (2007). *Education Longitudinal Study of 2002 (ELS:2002): Base year to second follow-up data file documentation (NCES 2008-347)*. National Center for Education Statistics.

Kerlinger, F. N., & Lee, H. B. (2000). *Foundations of behavioral research* (4th ed.). Cengage Learning.

Miksza, P. (2006). Relationships among impulsiveness, locus of control, sex, and music practice. *Journal of Research in Music Education, 54*(4), 308–323. https://doi.org/10.1177/002242940605400404

Miksza, P., & Elpus, K. (2018). *Design and analysis for quantitative research in music education*. Oxford University Press.

Miksza, P., Prichard, S., & Sorbo, D. (2012). An observational study of intermediate band students' self-regulated practice behaviors. *Journal of Research in Music Education, 60*(3), 254–266. https://doi.org/10.1177/0022429412455201

Mornell, A., & Wulf, G. (2019). Adopting an external focus of attention enhances musical performance. *Journal of Research in Music Education, 66*(4), 375–391. https://doi.org/10.1177/0022429418801573

Orman, E. K. (2002). Comparison of the national standards for music education and elementary music specialists' use of class time. *Journal of Research in Music Education, 50*(2), 155–164. https://doi.org/10.2307/3345819

Rea, L. M., & Parker, R. A. (2014). *Designing and conducting survey research: A comprehensive guide* (4th ed.). Jossey-Bass.

Schmidt, C. P. (2005). Relations among motivation, performance achievement, and music experience variables in secondary instrumental music students. *Journal of Research in Music Education, 53*(2), 134–147. https://doi.org/10.1177/002242940505300204

Schmidt, C. P., Baker, R., Hayes, B., & Kwan, E. (2006). A descriptive study of public school music programs in Indiana. *Bulletin of the Council for Research in Music Education, 169,* 25–37. https://www.jstor.org/stable/40319308

13
Experimental Research

Chapter Preview

Experimental research designs are used to address questions of cause and effect, such as "What can be?" and "What if?" A simple definition of experimental research is that a primary independent variable (e.g., a new teaching method) is manipulated by the researcher to determine its effect on a dependent variable (the outcome). Researchers conducting experiments generally set out to test a particular theory and/or hypothesis about some aspect of music teaching or learning. As first steps, you will need to clarify the problem under consideration, provide a rationale or the need for your study, and conduct a thorough review of literature related to your problem. After you clearly define your research problem, you will write a statement of purpose, followed by research questions and/or hypotheses. The method section typically includes detailed descriptions of how the study was organized and conducted, including information on the participants; measures of the outcome, equipment, and materials; and procedures. After analyzing the data you have collected, you will present the results by answering each of your research questions. In the final section of a research report, you will describe the conclusions you have reached based on the results of your study. Another type of experimental research is ex post facto research, which is conducted after a treatment has already occurred.

Introduction

In experimental research, we try to determine cause-and-effect relationships. For example, what are the effects of putting tape on the fingerboards of beginning violin students; will they learn to play in tune better? What effect will adding movement have on the expressiveness of a secondary school choir? Both these hypothetical questions imply a desire to find out whether a change in a pedagogical approach will *cause* a change in some performance outcome.

Suppose we are interested in improving the pitch accuracy of seven-year-old children when they sing. We might begin by testing their ability to sing melodies accurately (the *pretest*). Then we could divide them into two groups. Group 1 can be a "control condition" that involves continuing with regular music instruction; Group 2 can be the "experimental" or "treatment" condition which entails learning to sing melodies using solfege syllables (do, re, mi, fa, sol, la, ti, do). Following six weeks of instruction, we could retest their ability to sing pitches accurately in selected melodies (the *posttest*). If there is no difference at the end, we might say that the use of solfege syllables does not help. However, if Group 2 improves more than Group 1, we can say that using solfege syllables is an effective way to improve pitch accuracy in young singers. In other words, we would infer that the solfege syllables caused an improvement in the young singers' pitch accuracy.

Causation vs. Correlation

Experimental research designs are the only quantitative designs from which causal claims can be made. It is important to recognize that causal claims cannot be derived from correlational research. Although correlational methods can reveal systematic associations among variables, inferences about cause and effect cannot be drawn from associations found through correlational research designs. In other words, as the saying goes, correlation does not equal causation.

Consider a correlational study in which a researcher measured singers' pitch perception ability as well as their intonation while singing and found a positive association between the two measures; that is, those who tended to sing more accurately also tended to have the strongest pitch perception abilities, and those who tended to sing less accurately also tended to have the weakest pitch perception abilities. It would be tempting to interpret this finding in terms of cause and effect—that pitch perception abilities caused intonation performance while singing. However, it would be wrong to do so. There are two issues that must be acknowledged when evaluating an association between two variables: (a) that it is not possible to determine the *direction* of the relationship between the two measures, that is, whether X causes Y or Y causes X, and (b) it is not possible to rule out that there may be a third, yet to be observed variable (e.g., years of singing experience, variable Z) that serves as an underlying cause of both variables and, therefore, confounds the possibility of a causal relationship between X and Y (see Figure 13.1).

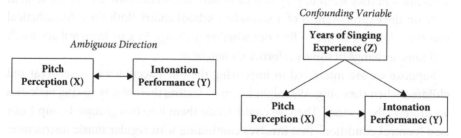

Figure 13.1 Illustrations of the issues of directionality and third variable confounds in correlational research.

In order to make causal inferences, that is, to conclude that a cause-and-effect relationship actually occurred, we must meet the three conditions put forth by philosopher John Stuart Mill (Shadish et al., 2002, p. 6):

1. The hypothesized cause must precede the hypothesized effect in time.
2. The hypothesized cause must be associated, that is, correlated with the effect.
3. There can be no plausible alternative explanations for the effect other than the purported cause.

Conditions 1 and 2 are fairly obvious; however, condition 3 is trickier to satisfy. Much of the art and craft involved in designing an experiment has to do with creating a situation where condition 3 can be satisfied.

Theoretically, the "effect" is the difference between what we observe in the presence of a potential "cause" (i.e., an experimental condition) in contrast to what we would have observed simultaneously for the same participants if the cause were not present. This latter condition, in which we would have observed the same participants without the cause present, is called a "counterfactual condition." As you might have intuited, we cannot physically observe people having two different experiences at one point in time—well, not without the ability to bend the spacetime continuum! Fortunately, we do not need mystical sci-fi powers since, instead, we can simulate a counterfactual condition with established experimental designs. Shadish et al. (2002, p. 5) summarize these points as follows:

> A counterfactual is something that is contrary to fact. In an experiment, we observe what did happen when people received a treatment. The counterfactual is knowledge of *what would have happened* to those same people if they simultaneously had not received treatment. [The] effect is the difference between what did happen and what would have happened. We cannot actually observe a counterfactual. . . . So, a central task for all cause-probing research is to create reasonable approximations to this physically impossible counterfactual.

When dealing with human participants, the simplest and clearest way to simulate a counterfactual condition is to design an experiment in which we randomly assign people to two groups, one group that receives an experimental treatment and the other—a control group—that does not. Then we compare the outcome between the groups to see if the treatment caused an effect. In so doing, the outcome we observe from the participants in the control group becomes our best guess at what we would have observed simultaneously for the participants in the treatment group if the cause were not present.

Let's return to the example presented at the start of this chapter, of improving the pitch accuracy of seven-year-old children when they sing. In that example, we imagined dividing the children into two groups, an experimental treatment group that used a solfege system for six weeks and a control group that went along with regular class instruction. The ability of the children in the control group to sing with pitch accuracy at the end of the six-week experiment would be our best guess at what we would have observed simultaneously for the children in the solfege instruction group if we had mystical time-bending abilities such that we could also observe them after not experiencing six weeks of solfege instruction. In other words, the control condition in this experiment is a simulation of the counterfactual condition for those in the experimental treatment group.

Designs in which participants are randomly assigned to either a treatment or a control condition are referred to as "true experimental designs." This category of experimental designs is the best for making causal inferences because it does the best job of satisfying Mill's three criteria. Other designs are less robust because they are less likely to satisfy Mill's criteria, particularly criteria 3: There can be no plausible alternative explanations for the effect other than the cause. These other, less robust designs include pre-experimental designs and quasi-experimental designs. The differences between these different types of designs are discussed in Chapter 14.

Conducting an Experimental Study

The study example that follows makes it look fairly easy to conduct an experimental research study. However, there are many details we would need to consider to ensure that our results could be trusted. The purpose of this chapter is to introduce you to experimental research in music education. Before we delve into details, let us read a brief summary of a published experimental study. We will return to this study throughout this chapter to provide illustrations of various concepts. Additional examples will be used to illustrate topics not covered by this particular study.

Example 1. Stephanie Prichard (2021) designed an experiment to examine the effect of a specific music practice instruction approach on middle school band students' knowledge and execution of practice strategies. Although all teachers would agree that practicing is important, formal instruction on how to practice can often be lacking. This study provided evidence that strategic practicing can indeed be taught to novice musicians. Specifically, at the end of the study, the participants who received three weeks of focused practice instruction were more knowledgeable of strategic practice strategies and, accordingly, more strategic in their actual practice behavior than those who did not receive focused practice instruction. Prichard's work is an example of how a specific pedagogical intervention can be put to an empirical test.

Many aspects of experimental research have been covered in previous chapters. Here, we will review relevant topics, expand coverage of aspects particular to experimental research, offer additional details, and use Prichard's (2021) and others' studies for illustrations.

Choosing a Theoretical Framework and Reviewing the Related Literature

In contrast to descriptive and correlational research, experimental research is less likely to be exploratory or inductive in nature. Instead, researchers conducting experiments are more likely to set out to test a particular theory and/or hypothesis about some aspect of music teaching and learning. In other words, experimental research is most often deductive by nature. As such, it is especially important to be aware of the previous research on the topic and to present a clear theoretical framework when proposing an experiment. This is not to say that good topics could not arise inductively from your own experiences and observations; instead we wish to emphasize (a) that it is important to have a theoretical explanation for why you believe your experimental intervention might cause a difference in a potential outcome and (b) that you can refine your study ideas a great deal by consulting and applying ideas from previous research.

Prichard (2021) began her article by providing research-based evidence demonstrating that novice musicians are not typically good at practicing and that, instead, they often waste time and effort when left to their own devices. Her positioning of these previous findings helped to establish the need for her work. She then presented a social psychological theory of self-regulated learning as a framework for describing what it takes for a student to be a self-sufficient learner and for explaining how various motivational, behavioral, and cognitive elements underlie effective practicing. This clear theoretical perspective (i.e., self-regulated learning) was well-suited for deductively generating research questions as well as informing what should be emphasized in a pedagogical intervention for practicing. To close the introduction to her article, Prichard summarized previous research that has led to generalizations about effective practice strategies. By doing so, she established an evidence-based rationale for selecting the specific strategies she decided to include in the pedagogical intervention. As you can see, it is valuable to have an informative theoretical framework to work from and a broad knowledge of the previous research in your area of concern. Not only is it important for you to have this knowledge, but you must also share it with your readers so that they will understand your study in the proper context.

Problem, Purpose, Research Questions, and Hypotheses

Once your problem is clearly defined, you will write a statement of purpose: "The purpose of this study is to. . . ." This will be followed by research questions and/or hypotheses. Although this sounds like a linear process, in reality you will likely go back and forth among the problem, purpose, and questions, as well as other aspects of your study (e.g., research design), before everything is organized just the way you want it. Recall the "upside-down pyramid" in Figure 2.1. Notice how Prichard (2021) started very broadly by reviewing related literature in specific areas. Throughout the introduction of the article, she refined the problem and then made a very clear statement of purpose, along with specific research questions. Although Prichard did not specify hypotheses in this particular study, hypotheses are sometimes presented in addition to or in lieu of research questions in experimental research.

Prichard's (2021) article provides a very good model to follow:

- *Research Problem*: Prichard noted that novice musicians are often not effective practicers. "Despite its ubiquity, however, independent practice time has proved to be challenging for most young musicians whose musical knowledge, skills, and ability to manage time may not be refined enough to effectively structure their practice sessions" (p. 420).
- *Rationale and Literature Review*: In the following statements, Prichard drew from previous research to support the need for her study. "Music practice research has demonstrated that novice instrumentalists are typically unsure of how to budget practice time and may also be unable to select appropriate music practice strategies (Austin & Berg, 2006; Hallam, 1997; McPherson & Renwick, 2001; Miksza et al., 2012; Prichard, 2017)" (p. 420). "The quality of practice time, not just the time itself, is what contributes to musical proficiency (Hallam et al., 2012; Nielsen, 2001)" (p. 421).
- *Research Framework*: "The social cognitive perspective of self-regulation can be a useful framework within which to explore independent music practice" (p. 420).
- *Purpose Statement*: "The purpose of this study was to investigate the impact of music practice instruction on middle school band students' ability to articulate and incorporate practice strategies. A secondary purpose of this study was to explore the possible impact of music practice instruction on middle school band students' self-regulated practice behaviors" (p. 422).
- *Research Questions*: Prichard specified four research questions; research question 3 is most relevant to our discussion of experimental research since it deals with whether a cause-and-effect relationship can be found. In contrast, research questions 1 and 2 address descriptive aims, and research question 4 addresses a correlational aim.
  1. Given a challenging and unfamiliar musical excerpt, what strategies do middle school band students identify for use in independent music practice?
  2. How do middle school band students approach their practice sessions with respect to time allocation, musical objective, and practice strategies?
  3. What, if any, impact does a unit of music practice instruction have on middle school band students' identification of practice strategies,

allocation of time, musical objective, and use of practice strategies within their independent music practice time?
4. What relationships are evident between middle school band students' independent music practice and an observational assessment of their self-regulation while practicing? (p. 422).

- *Hypotheses:* If Prichard had specified her research questions as hypotheses instead, they might have been presented as either *null hypotheses* or *directional hypotheses*. A null hypothesis would entail a prediction that there will be no significant differences between the treatment and control conditions in her study, for example, "There will be no significant difference in identification of practice strategies, allocation of time, musical objective, and use of practice strategies between students in the treatment and control conditions." A directional hypothesis would entail a prediction of one experimental condition being particularly advantageous compared to the other, for example, "The students in the treatment condition will identify more practice strategies, allocate time more strategically, choose more specific musical objectives, and use more practice strategies compared to the students in the control condition." Note that generally you would not use directional hypotheses unless you had compelling research evidence that these outcomes were likely. Otherwise, using directional hypotheses might appear to be prejudicing the outcome.

Dependent and Independent Variables

An important aspect of the shaping of your problem when conducting quantitative research is the identification of key variables. A simple definition of experimental research is that a primary independent variable is manipulated to determine its effect on the dependent variable. A *dependent variable* is the outcome variable you will measure. *Independent variables* are all of the things that you hypothesize will influence the outcome, that is, the dependent variable. The independent variable is most often a categorical variable that indicates exposure to treatment or control conditions, that is, the manipulations the researcher includes in the experiment.

Consider the variables in Prichard's (2021) study. The independent variable is the categorical indicator of whether the students were in the treatment condition (i.e., were exposed to the music practice instruction intervention) or the control condition (i.e., were *not* exposed to the music practice instruction intervention). The treatment condition was administered across three weeks, with practice instruction occurring during a 10-minute warm-up period on three days per week (i.e., 30 minutes per week total). It included instruction in how to identify challenging excerpts of music, teacher demonstrations of practice strategies, and group instruction of how to apply practice strategies. To answer her research questions, Prichard needed to measure several dependent variables before and after the music practice instruction. The dependent variables included (a) counting practice strategies students reported being knowledgeable of; (b) variables derived from observations of video recordings of students' actual practice, such as time usage, the length of passages the students selected to practice, the musical objective they emphasized when practicing each passage, and the strategy they employed when practicing each passage; and (c) ratings of the students' self-regulated learning behavior made by independent observers. To have a successful experiment, it is important that the dependent variable is measured accurately and that the independent variables have been adequately controlled (e.g., that no other extraneous variables influence the outcome or confound the effect of the treatment).

Method

The method section of an experimental study must include detailed descriptions of how the study was organized and conducted. This section is often organized in three primary sections that provide information about the study participants; any measures, equipment, and materials used; and the procedures for carrying out the steps of the experiment, sometimes referred to as the "experimental protocol."

Participants

In this section of the method, you describe the characteristics of the participants in the study as well as how were they were selected. We introduced the terms "population" and "sample" and discussed various approaches for selecting a sample and the reasons for providing a detailed description of a sample in the previous chapter. The same information and sampling methods we discussed when introducing quantitative descriptive and correlational research applies to experimental research as well. However, it is also important to make a clear distinction between two concepts that, despite sounding similar, are quite different: random sampling of participants from a population and random assignment of participants to groups (e.g., treatment vs. control conditions).

Whether or not a researcher has randomly assigned the participants to groups is a key factor as to whether an experiment qualifies as a true experiment or a quasi-experiment. (This distinction will be explained in detail in Chapter 14.) Briefly, a true experiment always entails participants being assigned randomly to treatment or control conditions. If a researcher instead works with groups of participants that have been formed previously (e.g., students from classroom A vs. students from classroom B), then they would describe their groups as "intact," and their study would be considered a quasi-experiment.

Random assignment to groups is advantageous when conducting a study to determine cause and effect. One of the most challenging issues to contend with when designing an experiment is the need to control for any extraneous factors that could impact the outcome (i.e., dependent variable) other than the independent variable (i.e., the difference between treatment and control conditions). Many such extraneous factors could emerge if the participants in the treatment and control groups differ in some systematic way. For example, if students in the treatment group are wealthier than those in the control group, then any differences found between the groups could be due to disparities in wealth and the access and opportunity that comes with it, as opposed to the conditions imposed by the treatment and control conditions. By randomly assigning participants to groups and assuming the groups are relatively large (e.g., roughly ≥ 20 participants), researchers can rely on probability to result in groups that are similar.

Unfortunately, true experimental designs are rarely used in music education research because it is often very difficult to individually assign students to groups within schools. For example, school administrators are not typically willing to move students from class to class for the sake of a research project. More on the distinction between true and quasi-experiment designs and the variety of design choices researchers have at their disposal will be discussed in Chapter 14.

In her study, Prichard (2021) randomly assigned 105 participants to the treatment or control group using a random number generator. By doing so, she decreased the likelihood that the students in the control and treatment groups would differ systematically on some characteristic that could invalidate her experiment. However, she notes that despite being individually assigned to groups, the participants remained in their previously scheduled band classes for the duration of the study. As such, her procedure of assigning students was slightly different from that found in most true experiments, and even though she didn't technically use intact groups in her study she described her experiment as a quasi-experiment.

Prichard (2021, p. 423) also described in detail the characteristics of her participants, which provides the reader with important information about which contexts and types of students her findings may be generalizable to:

> Participants were seventh- and eighth-grade band students at Eastwood Middle School (EMS; pseudonym). Located in a densely populated suburb of a major city, EMS has a total enrollment of 1,260 students (64.4% White, 14.4% Hispanic, 10.5% Black, 5.5% Asian, 4.8% two or more ethnicities). Eleven percent of students receive free or reduced-price meals, 7% of students are limited English proficient, and 9% of students receive special education services (school district data in 2016). I obtained consent and assent forms from 105 of the 121 seventh and eighth graders enrolled in band (87%), with relatively even representation from both grades (seventh grade = 49%; eighth grade = 51%). Woodwind (54.3%), brass (41.0%), and percussion (4.7%) instruments were included within the sample.

Measures, Equipment, and Materials

Whenever possible, researchers prefer to use preexisting measures that have been determined to be both reliable and valid, referring to the degree of consistency and accuracy of a measure, respectively. These terms as well as how to demonstrate evidence of the reliability and validity of a measure for a particular use are discussed in detail in Chapter 15. When suitable measures or are not available, researchers need to create their own. Either way, researchers must provide evidence of the reliability and validity of their measures.

Prichard (2021, p. 423) measured the participants' practice strategies knowledge by having the students respond to the following prompt and then coding and counting their response:

> Look over the musical excerpt in front of you. If you were asked to go home and learn how to play this excerpt by practicing it on your own, what kinds of things would you do in order to be able to play it? After you've taken a moment to look through the music, make a list of all of the strategies you would use to practice this excerpt.

She measured the participants' practice behavior by analyzing videos using an observation protocol established by previous research. Two experienced instrumental music teachers completed the observations, and Prichard (2021) established the reliability of these measurements by noting that the observers reached a high degree of agreement (96%–100%) in their coding. Here is a description of the basics of her observational scheme:

> Based in part on Duke's (1999/2000) concept of rehearsal frames and Maynard's (2006) adaptation of practice frames, the protocol facilitated collection of data regarding participants' use of practice time, length of musical passage practiced (≤ 4 measures, 5–8 measures, ≥ 9 measures), and musical objective (note accuracy, rhythmic accuracy, and a third category encompassing stylistic elements, musical accuracy), as well as the occurrence of specific practice behaviors. A new practice frame was documented each time a participant jumped ahead or behind in their music by four or more measures or switched pieces entirely. (p. 424)

Last, Prichard (2021) measured the participants' degree of self-regulated learning tendencies while practicing by having independent observers evaluate the practice videos. The independent observers rated the participants' practice with a preestablished rating scale. The reliability of these measurements was demonstrated via correlation coefficients (see Chapters 15 and 17 for more detail about such procedures):

> To rate the participants' degree of self-regulation within their independent practice time, I used a scale created for the purpose of evaluating self-regulated practice behaviors (Miksza, 2012). Composed of 12 Likert-type items, the scale included McPherson and Zimmerman's (2002) dimensions of method, behavior, and time

use. Interrater reliability for the scale was strong ($r = .92$), as was internal consistency for both independent observers (α's = .97 and .95). (pp. 424–425)

Prichard (2021) required no special equipment for her study except a recording device, which is so commonly used that she did not report the make or model. She described the selection of musical materials that the participants made as follows:

> During pretesting and posttesting, participants were presented with an unfamiliar musical excerpt. Excerpts, which were selected in consultation with the participants' band teacher, differed among instrument groups based on range and instrument-specific challenges. I began by selecting a series of 16-measure excerpts, each of which were approximately Grade 3 difficulty. After reviewing excerpts with the participants' teacher, we opted to provide an appropriate challenge for each instrument group. (p. 423)

Procedures/Experimental Protocol

It is important to provide exact details on how you carried out your experiment. The reader should have sufficient information such that they could replicate your experiment. Prichard (2021) reported the procedures of her study in excellent detail. Consider the following text pertaining to the design of the music practice intervention:

> The practice instruction protocol was developed based on Bandura's (1986) principles of observational learning with the inclusion of recommendations from prior research in this area (Miksza et al., 2012; Prichard, 2017). To create the most naturalistic context for data collection, musical excerpts used throughout the practice strategy intervention included passages from concert music and method book exercises selected by the participants' band teacher. Together, the band teacher and I wrote a brief script to ensure that each day of practice instruction would follow an identical format. Each practice instruction session therefore included (a) identification of a challenging excerpt, (b) cognitive and live modeling (Bandura, 1986), and (c) group practice of one or more appropriate practice strategies. The teacher first modeled an applicable thought process (i.e., "I see that this passage includes a challenging rhythm, so I've decided to play the rhythm by itself on a single pitch"). The teacher then modeled the use of the strategy by applying it to a specific excerpt of music. Finally, the teacher guided students through practicing the strategy as a group. (p. 424)

Prichard's descriptions of the protocols for video-recording the participants' practice are similarly detailed. Moreover, she provided an outline of the practice instruction intervention as a supplemental document in the online version of her article that researchers who might wish to replicate her work could consult.

Results

In this section, you will provide details about the data analyses and their results. The presentation of results should be organized in such a way that the answer to each of the research questions is clear. Although this is the section of a research paper that contains the statistical analysis, that will not be covered here. Instead, we refer you to Chapters 16, 17, and 18 for more information about the types of statistical tools quantitative researchers use. It is also important to note that this is not the portion of an article in which authors make comments about or interpretations of their findings. In this section, researchers tend to keep the focus on objective answers to the questions based on the results of their data analyses.

Prichard (2021, p. 422) conducted several different types of analyses with several different data sources (i.e., students' self-reported practice knowledge, behavioral observations of practice, self-regulated learning ratings of practice) to determine the answer to the question most critical to her experiment: "What, if any, impact does a unit of music practice instruction have on middle school band students' identification of practice strategies, allocation of time, musical objective, and use of practice strategies within their independent music practice time?"

She found that participants in the treatment group reported significantly more practice strategies at posttest than the control group participants. Prichard (2021) also found that several aspects of the treatment group participants' observed practice behavior had changed significantly from pretest to posttest, whereas no change was found among the control group participants. Compared to their practicing at pretest, the treatment group participants organized their time into fewer, longer practice frames at posttest and used more practice strategies at posttest. However, no differences were found between the groups for the self-regulated learning tendency ratings.

Conclusions

In some papers, the final section is entitled "Discussion" or "Discussion and Conclusions," and sometimes discussion and conclusion sections are presented separately. No matter how it is titled, this portion of the paper generally begins with a brief overview of the purpose of the study as well as brief summaries of the answers to the research questions. Although this may seem somewhat redundant with the information presented in the results section, it is actually quite different. The material presented in a discussion and/or conclusion section does not usually include references to data or statistical jargon. Instead, in these sections, authors will explain their findings using plain language. Generally, your goal in this section of the manuscript is to consider the following question: Now that you have completed your experiment, what do you conclude? Prichard (2021, p. 433), who titled this portion of her paper "Discussion," drew this conclusion in the last two sentences of the article:

> It is important to consider young musicians' abilities within the formative middle school years, particularly in light of findings in this study suggesting that music practice instruction may be a productive use of large ensemble instructional time. With careful consideration of many interrelated factors surrounding the challenge of independent music practice, music teachers can support students' growth and development through practice strategy instruction, thereby encouraging productive independent practice time.

Also, and in contrast to the results section, the discussion and/or conclusion sections are where authors will offer interpretations of their findings and conclusions with respect to the previous literature. Generally, it is important to describe how the findings of your experiment extend our collective knowledge of the topic in question. More specifically, an author should discuss whether their findings support or contradict those from previous research. For example, Prichard (2021, pp. 430–431) made this statement:

> Prior research has indicated that young musicians tend to be ineffective in time organization within independent practice sessions and/or have a tendency to become fatigued or distracted over time (McPherson & Davidson, 2002; McPherson & Renwick, 2001; Miksza et al., 2012; Oare, 2012). However, results of the present study as well as other research involving practice instruction as an educational intervention indicate that it may be possible to encourage middle school musicians to manage time more effectively and perhaps work in a more focused manner (Prichard, 2017).

The discussion is also the place to bring up any limitations in the study or provide informal observations that were not formally part of the study. Accordingly, Prichard (2021, p. 432) offers the following:

> Although the inclusion of a control group within this study is an important step in this line of research, it is important to consider the limitations of this design as well as possible improvements for future studies. The comparison of the MPI [music practice instruction] group to the control group's untouched rehearsal procedures gives rise to additional questions: Would simply allowing for unstructured individual practice time facilitate improvement in students' practice behaviors? Is it

necessary to model practice strategies, or would providing a list with definitions suffice?

The discussion section is also the place to suggest implications of the findings for music teaching and learning or to provide suggestions for future research. Prichard (2021) did both, as is evident in the following passages:

> Therefore, teachers who wish to support students' individual practice efforts may consider devoting a portion of large ensemble rehearsal time to teach students how to identify, select, and apply various practice strategies. (p. 431)
>
> [T]he incorporation of a self-reflection element such as follow-up interviews, participant review of practice videos, or responding to written reflection prompts could provide important insight regarding participants' capabilities to plan, execute, reflect, and revise their approach to independent music practice. (p. 432)

Following is another example of an experimental study; although the participants and setting are very different, this study illustrates many of the same features that were found in Prichard's (2021) experiment.

Example 2. Siu and Cheung (2016) were interested in finding out whether emotional experiences induced by music influence an infant's developing understanding of the social world. Based on previous research, they predicted "an early effect of music-making in relation to emotion learning on infants' general understanding of how emotion and behavior are related" (p. 3). To find out, they randomly assigned 15-month-old infants to either a music training treatment condition ($n = 40$) or a control group ($n = 36$). Both groups received three months of training in the communication of emotions through facial, bodily, and vocal expressions. In addition, the music-training group participated in musical activities such as singing, playing toy percussion instruments, and dancing to action songs and lullabies. No musical activities were used with the control group.

Siu and Cheung (2016) measured sensitivity to expressive features in music by presenting happy or sad music that was paired with emotionally consistent displays (happy faces with happy music and sad faces with sad music) or inconsistent displays (happy music with sad faces and sad music with happy faces). An actress portrayed the happy and sad faces. The amount of looking time was measured as an indicator of emotional sensitivity. Longer looking time was associated with surprise at the inconsistent matches between music and faces. A second procedure involved the actress interacting with two toy bears; the bears were identical except for their color. Consistent events occurred when the actress interacted positively or negatively with the same color bear in both a pretrial familiarization episode and the test episode; in inconsistent trials the actress responded to each colored bear in the opposite way from the familiarization episode.

A pretest was given, followed by three months of training at the Centre for Developmental Psychology at the Chinese University of Hong Kong. A posttest concluded the experiment. Results of the pretest analysis demonstrated that there were no significant differences in looking times between consistent and inconsistent trials for either the music treatment or control group. However, in the posttest, infants in the music group looked significantly longer during inconsistent trials (i.e., they were surprised) than during consistent trials. Based on these results, the researchers concluded that the music training was effective in fostering infants' sensitivity to expressive features in music and on their understanding of the general relationship between emotions and actions in a social context. Because of the design of the study, the authors were able to argue that the music training *caused* a change in the infants' behavior.

Ex Post Facto Research

The Latin phrase *ex post facto* means "after the fact." In most experimental research, a researcher intervenes in some way to manipulate an independent variable (e.g., music or no music) to determine what effect this will have on the dependent variable. In ex post facto research, the study is conducted after the treatment has already occurred. Two main types of ex post facto research are causal comparative and correlation studies. Correlational research was discussed in Chapter 12 and will not be dealt with again in this chapter.

Causal Comparative

In a causal comparative study, two or more groups are compared on an independent variable that is categorical or fixed in nature and that doesn't involve a researcher assigning participants to a group. For example, we could divide participants according to some preexisting grouping, such as whether they are in a morning music class or an afternoon music class if we wanted to explore the effect of class offering time on students' attitudes about singing. In other words, we would want to know whether taking music class in the morning vs. the afternoon *caused* a difference in attitude. A primary weakness of causal comparative research is that it is difficult to establish a cause-and-effect relationship if the analysis takes place after the cause has already occurred, violating one of Mill's criteria for causal inference. Perhaps there are other explanations. In our simple example, the assignment of a student to the morning or afternoon class session may have been predicated on some particular circumstance; for example, those on the honor track might have to schedule the morning class, whereas other students would have to take the class in the afternoon. Even if we were to find a difference between the two classes in attitudes toward singing, we wouldn't know whether it was due to class offering time or the differences in the students' academic ability. Following is an example of a published ex post facto, causal comparative study regarding the relative effectiveness of different ways to organize choir rehearsals.

Example 3. Cox (1989) wanted to know what effect different ways of organizing choral rehearsals would have on student attitudes. High school choir directors were placed into one of three groups based on their own self-assessment of how they organized their rehearsals: (a) rehearsals beginning and ending with a fast pace and a slower pace in the middle ($n = 31$); (b) rehearsals beginning and ending with a fast pace and a slower pace in the middle that built to a fast-paced climax ($n = 13$); or (c) rehearsals that fluctuated frequently between a fast and a slow pace ($n = 15$). Selected students from each of the choirs completed a questionnaire designed to determine their attitudes toward chorus. Although the fast-slow-fast rehearsal organization plan was used most frequently, students had a predominantly positive attitude toward choir regardless of the rehearsal structure used. In this study, Cox did not control or manipulate the primary independent variable (i.e., rehearsal organization) and did not assign the students to various rehearsal organization conditions. Rather, he investigated its effects on the dependent variable (i.e., student attitudes) after the fact, or ex post facto.

Summary

Experimental research addresses curiosities such as "What can be?" and "What if?" Experiments are conducted in an attempt to determine cause-and-effect relationships. In experimental research, a primary independent variable is controlled and manipulated to determine the effect on the dependent variable. If one group of beginning piano students observes a teacher performing the students' piece, while a control group does not get to observe the teacher performing, what will be the effect on the students' ability to perform the piece? In this case, we would measure student piano performance achievement (the dependent variable) to determine what effect the primary independent variable (observing the teacher or not observing the teacher) had.

Conducting an experimental research study involves (a) developing a problem, (b) providing an overview of related literature, (c) identifying a theoretical framework, (d) stating a purpose, and (e) proposing specific research questions and/or hypotheses. Reporting experimental research requires a careful description of the participants, measures, equipment, materials, and exact procedures that were followed. Once data are gathered and analyzed, the research questions are answered in the results section and broad conclusions are presented in the discussion section. If the researcher has designed their experiment carefully, they may be able to state whether the treatment did or did not have a particular effect.

Ex post facto research, sometimes characterized as a type of quasi-experimental research, involves an examination of treatments after they have already been given. One example of ex post facto research is the causal-comparative study, in which a researcher examines the relationship between independent and dependent variables after the purported cause has occurred (i.e., ex post facto). In this type of study, the researcher does not manipulate the independent variable, nor do they assign participants to groups.

Experimental design is a broad topic with a deep history. Indeed, conducting studies that yield robust causal inferences is quite difficult given the myriad potential confounds that could arise. Because of the intricate nature of this issue, we cover it in the next chapter, which is solely dedicated to experimental design methods. However, in addition to the materials presented in Chapter 14, readers are encouraged to seek out supplementary information from materials such as those presented in Box 13.1. The Shadish et al. (2002) text is perhaps the most authoritative volume on this issue today. For additional discussions of experimental research published in music education, see Phillips's (2008) text, designed for music education and music therapy students. In the meantime, here are some questions that will allow you to test your understanding of experimental research:

1. How is experimental research different from descriptive research?
2. What aspects of the research process do experimental and descriptive studies share?
3. What is the difference between an independent and a dependent variable? Give some examples.
4. Why is it important to provide specific details in the method section on participants, equipment, materials, and procedures?
5. What is the main difference between the results section and the conclusions section?

Box 13.1 Additional Methodological Readings: Experimental Research

---

Busch, J. C., & Sherbon, J. W. (1992). Experimental research methodology. In R. Colwell (Ed.), *Handbook of research on music teaching and learning: A project of the Music Educators National Conference* (pp. 124-140). Schirmer Books.

Cohen, L., Manion, L, & Morrison, K. (2017). *Research methods in education.* New York: Routledge.

Cresswell, J. W., & Guetterman, T. C. (2019). *Educational research: Planning, conducting, and evaluating quantitative and qualitative research* (6th ed.). Pearson.

Gall, M. D., Gall, J. P., & Borg, W. R. (2007). *Educational research: An introduction* (8th ed.). Pearson.

Kerlinger, F. N., & Lee, H. B. (2000). *Foundations of behavioral research* (4th ed.). Cengage Learning.

Shadish, W., Cook, T., & Campbell, T. (2002). *Experimental and quasi-experimental designs for generalized causal inference.* Wadsworth Cengage Learning.

Important Terms for Review

Causal inference is a formal term that researchers use to describe claims of cause and effect.

A *dependent variable* is the outcome variable that is being measured in a study, so called because the outcome *depends* on one or more additional factors, called "independent variables."

Independent variables are those factors that might have an effect on the outcome, that is, the dependent variable. In an experiment, one or more independent variables are manipulated (changed) to determine what effect they might have on the dependent variable. Independent variables in an experiment are most often categorical variables that simply signal whether participants experience treatment or control conditions.

Treatment condition(s) is a term used to describe the various situations experienced by participants who are assigned to an experimental group. The experimental group receives an experience the researcher designs that is different from or that involves adding something to what they would otherwise typically experience.

Control condition is a term used to describe the situation experienced by participants who are not assigned to an experimental group. The researcher does not intervene with the control group's experience or does so only for the sake of making it comparable to the experimental group's experience. At the conclusion of an experiment, the control condition serves as a point of reference when evaluating any observed effects of the treatment condition.

Counterfactual generally refers to something that is counter to a fact or something that has not happened. In experimental research, the counterfactual condition is what would have happened to participants had they not received an experimental treatment experience. This counterfactual condition is most often simulated with the creation of a control group.

Random assignment of participants to conditions is a critical element of true experimental designs. Random assignment to groups increases the chance that the participants in both groups will have similar characteristics and, therefore, that any differences between the groups will be due to the treatment. Note that random assignment to groups is not the same thing as random selection of participants from a population.

A *null hypothesis* is a prediction that there will be no significant differences between two or more conditions (e.g., there will be no significant effect of the independent variable[s]).

A *directional hypothesis* is a prediction of a certain outcome of an experiment (e.g., that the participants in the treatment condition will score higher or lower in their performance than those in the control group).

Ex post facto research is a type of research that is conducted after a treatment has already occurred. Two types are *causal comparative* and *correlation studies*.

Causal comparative research involves two or more groups that are compared on a dependent variable that is categorical or not able to be changed by a researcher (e.g., enrolled at school A vs. school B) rather than continuous (e.g., test scores).

References

Austin, J. R., & Berg, M. H. (2006). Exploring music practice among 6th grade band and orchestra students. *Psychology of Music, 34*(4), 535–558. http://doi.org.10.1177/0305735606067170

Bandura, A. (1986). *Social foundations of thought and action: A social cognitive theory.* Prentice-Hall.

Busch, J. C., & Sherbon, J. W. (1992). Experimental research methodology. In R. Colwell (Ed.), *Handbook of research on music teaching and learning: A project of the Music Educators National Conference* (pp. 124–140). Schirmer Books.

Cohen, L., Manion, L, & Morrison, K. (2017). *Research methods in education.* New York: Routledge.

Cox, J. (1989). Rehearsal organizational structures used by successful high school choral directors. *Journal of Research in Music Education, 37*(3), 201–218. https://doi.org/10.2307/3344670

Cresswell, J. W., & Guetterman, T. C. (2019). *Educational research: Planning, conducting, and evaluating quantitative and qualitative research* (6th ed.). Pearson.

Duke, R. A. (1999/2000). Measures of instructional effectiveness in music research. *Bulletin of the Council for Research in Music Education, 143,* 1–48. https://www.jstor.org/stable/40319011

Gall, M. D., Gall, J. P., & Borg, W. R. (2007). *Educational research: An introduction* (8th ed.). Pearson.

Hallam, S. (1997). Approaches to the instrumental music practice of experts and novices: Implications for education. In H. Jorgensen & A. C. Lehman (Eds.), *Does practice make perfect? Current theory and research on instrumental music practice* (pp. 89–108). Norges Musikkhogskole.

Hallam, S., Rinta, T., Varvarigou, M., Creech, A., Papageorgi, I., Gomes, T., & Lanipekun, J. (2012). The development of practising strategies in young people. *Psychology of Music, 40*(5), 652–680. http://doi.org.10.1177/0305735612443868

Kerlinger, F. N., & Lee, H. B. (2000). *Foundations of behavioral research* (4th ed.). Cengage Learning.

Maynard, L. M. (2006). The role of repetition in the practice sessions of artist teachers and their students. *Bulletin for the Council of Research in Music Education, 167,* 61–72. https://www.jstor.org/stable/40319290

McPherson, G. E., & Davidson, J. W. (2002). Musical practice: Mother and child interactions during the first year of learning an instrument. *Music Education Research, 4,* 141–156. http://doi.org.10.1080/14613800220119822

McPherson, G. E., & Renwick, J. M. (2001). A longitudinal study of self-regulation in children's musical practice. *Music Education Research, 3*(2), 169–186. http://doi.org.10.1080/14613800120089232

McPherson, G. E., & Zimmerman, B. J. (2002). Self-regulation of musical learning: A social cognitive perspective. In R. Colwell & C. Richardson (Eds.), *The new handbook of research on music teaching and learning* (pp. 327–347). Oxford University Press.

Miksza, P. (2012). The development of a measure of self-regulated practice behavior for beginning and intermediate instrumental music students. *Journal of Research in Music Education, 59*(4), 321–338. http://doi.org.10.1177/0022429411414716.

Miksza, P., Prichard, S., & Sorbo, D. (2012). An observational study of intermediate band students' self-regulated practice behaviors. *Journal of Research in Music Education, 60*(3), 254–266. http://doi.org.10.1177/0022429412455201

Nielsen, S. (2001). Self-regulating learning strategies in instrumental music practice. *Music Education Research, 3*(2), 155–167. http://dx.doi.org.10.1080/14613800112008922

Oare, S. (2012). Decisions made in the practice room: A qualitative study of middle school students' thought processes while practicing. *Update: Applications of Research in Music Education, 30*(2), 63–70. http://doi.org.10.1177/8755123312437051

Phillips, K. (2008). *Exploring research in music education and music therapy.* Oxford University Press.

Prichard, S. (2017). Music practice instruction in middle school instrumental ensembles: An exploratory analysis. *Bulletin of the Council for Research in Music Education, 213,* 73–86. http://doi.org.10.5406/bulcouresmusedu.213.0073

Prichard, S. (2021). The impact of music practice instruction on middle band students' independent practice behaviors. *Journal of Research in Music Education, 68*(4), 419–435. https://doi.org/10.1177/0022429420947132

Shadish, W., Cook, T., & Campbell, T. (2002). *Experimental and quasi-experimental designs for generalized causal inference.* Wadsworth Cengage Learning.

Siu, T. S. C., & Cheung, H. (2016). Emotional experience in music fosters 18-month-olds' emotion-action understanding: A training study. *Developmental Science, 19*(6), 933–946. https://doi.org/10.1111/desc.12348

14
Designing Experimental Research

Chapter Preview

The focus in this chapter is on experimental research design, or the way an experiment is organized. One must critically consider methods for reducing or eliminating threats to internal and external validity. "Internal validity" refers to a concern about whether an experimental treatment did, in fact, make a difference in the outcome of an experiment. "External validity" refers to generalizability, whether the results of an experiment can be applied broadly or only to a specific population and the situations circumscribed by the experimental procedures. Threats to external validity are more difficult to resolve with experimental design features. One approach is to conduct a delimited experiment with reasonable controls of the threats to internal validity that represents one population, one treatment approach, one compelling outcome, and one setting, then—should that experiment yield promising results—conduct more research to systematically expand the generalizability of the findings by varying the population, treatment, outcome, or setting one step at a time. We will also discuss pre-experimental and quasi-experimental designs. Pre-experimental designs lack controls over threats to internal validity and should rarely be used. True experimental designs are the strongest designs since they are the most resilient to threats of internal validity. Quasi-experimental designs are not quite as strong as true experimental designs, but they do offer many useful possibilities.

Introduction

Researchers who wish to test claims about cause and effect must be rigorous in their approach to experimental design. In this chapter, we focus on the myriad ways that an experiment could be organized. In particular, we discuss the reasons why certain design elements and types are more likely than others to lead to strong causal inferences. As was discussed in the previous chapter, experimental research is the only type of research from which causal claims can be derived, and in order for causal claims to be valid, researchers must design their experiment such that it can satisfy Mill's three conditions for causal inferences:

1. The hypothesized cause must precede the hypothesized effect in time.
2. The hypothesized cause must be associated (i.e., correlated) with the effect.

3. There can be no plausible alternative explanations for the effect other than the cause.

Before we delve into research design, it is important to understand the specific reasons why researchers must control for any variables that might invalidate their experiment. We begin by considering the most common issues that can confound or limit the conclusions of any particular experiment; these are referred to as threats to internal and external validity, respectively. Much of the information presented in this chapter builds upon the foundational work of Campbell and Stanley (1972), who revolutionized the discussion of experimental design, as well as the more recent updates of that original work from Shadish et al. (2002).[1]

Threats to Internal and External Validity

Internal validity refers to a concern about whether an experimental treatment did, in fact, make a difference in the outcome of an experiment. In other words, the degree to which an experiment is internally valid is directly related to the degree to which we can have confidence in any cause-and-effect conclusions drawn from the study. A critical question to ask concerning internal validity is: How do we know that the results we obtained were due to the experimental treatment and not to some other factor?

External validity refers to generalizability; whether the results of this experiment can be applied broadly, or if they apply only to a specific population and the situations circumscribed by the experimental procedures. Obviously, the results of an experiment are more useful to the music education profession if they can be applied to a variety of groups of students in different places. The ideal goal is to have very strong evidence for both the internal and external validity of an experiment. However, increasing internal validity—tightening the control one has over independent variables—almost always results in decreases in external validity, and vice versa. This point will become clearer after we review some threats to internal and external validity.

Factors Relevant to Internal Validity

A researcher's goal is to design an experiment in such a way that the outcome is due to the effectiveness or ineffectiveness of the experimental treatment and not to some extraneous variable. The more control over independent variables a researcher has,

---

[1] Aside from issues of internal and external validity, there are other, more nuanced considerations that one could take into account when evaluating an experiment. Shadish et al. (2002) describe how issues of "statistical conclusion validity" and "construct validity" can play a role in experimental design as well. However, a thorough discussion of those categories of validity requires a more in-depth understanding of measurement principles and statistical tests, which is beyond the scope of this book. We encourage you to seek out this information once you are familiar with the more traditionally foundational topics presented in this chapter.

the higher the internal validity. Factors 1–8 listed below are considered threats to internal validity. Each of these factors can compromise the validity of an experiment unless it is controlled. A major way to control these factors is through research design, which will be discussed subsequently.

1. *History.* Sometimes events in addition to the experimental treatment take place across the duration of an experiment (e.g., between the administration of the pretest and posttest) that will affect the outcome. Suppose, for example, an experiment was being conducted with a particular teacher delivering the treatment and/or control conditions. Should the original teacher become ill during the experiment and be replaced by a new teacher, it could be that the change of teachers caused differences in a posttest measure, not the experimental treatment.

2. *Maturation.* Changes within participants or their behaviors can occur as a result of time, not the experimental treatment. For example, if we gave a pretest at the beginning of first grade and a posttest at the end of first grade, students will have matured during that time simply by becoming older. Other events that affect participants' lives can also interfere with a causal inference. Suppose you were studying a high school choir for six weeks and during the second week of the experiment one popular student leader within the choir had to move out of town suddenly. This might affect all the members of the choir.

    One particular circumstance that can influence the outcome of an experiment is something called the *Hawthorne effect*. This refers to a situation in which participants alter their behavior in response to their awareness of being observed. For example, students may try harder to please the teacher if they know that the results of the experiment are important to the teacher. Conversely, some students could intentionally misbehave or do poorly as a reaction against being observed.

3. *Testing.* Simply taking a pretest may give participants some experience with the questions and procedures that allow them to do better on the posttest. Other aspects of the testing procedures themselves may bias the outcome of the experiment.

4. *Instrumentation.* Changes in the way the dependent variable is measured could affect the outcome. This is particularly true when human observers are used. For example, in an experiment in which graduate students were trained by the researcher to observe and make records of student behaviors, the observers will have gained more experience by the time of the posttest and may observe the participants differently at the end than at the beginning. This specific measurement phenomenon is sometimes also referred to as observer drift.

5. *Statistical regression.* An extremely high pretest score is likely to be lower on the posttest, and an extremely low pretest score is likely to be higher on the posttest. In an experiment in which participants scored at the extremes (very high or very low) on the pretest, they are likely to move toward a middle score (regression toward the mean). Suppose, for example, several participants

gained a perfect score on the pretest; since they cannot score any higher on the posttest, any change in their scores would have to be lower (i.e., move in the direction of the mean).
6. *Selection biases.* Any bias in assigning participants to the different comparison groups can affect the outcome. If students who are selected for an experimental group actually volunteered and the students in a control group were placed there because they were not available at a time the experimental treatment was to be given, this would be considered a possible source of selection bias.
7. *Experimental mortality.* Sometimes participants have to leave an experiment while it is in progress; this might be caused by illness, moving to a different community or school, simply opting out of participation after the study began, and so on. If 8 out of 15 participants in the experimental group dropped out and none of the 15 participants in the control group dropped out, the outcome of the experiment would be severely compromised—especially if the drop out was precipitated by some feature of the experimental conditions.
8. *Interaction effects.* The effects of interactions between various aspects of an experiment may be mistaken for the effect of the experimental treatment. For example, aspects of the selection process may be affected by maturation.

Researchers always strive to design experiments that are as resilient as possible to these threats to internal validity discussed above. To reiterate an important point, the more we control for threats to internal validity, the more confident we can be that any effect we observe is actually due to the independent variable (e.g., the treatment vs. control conditions) rather than some other extraneous factors. The various experimental design types discussed below—following our descriptions of the threats to the external validity of an experiment—are approaches that can be used for creating experiments that are more or less robust to such threats.

However, no matter how well it is designed, a single experiment is only the beginning of confirming a causal inference. In other words, it is necessary to conduct several studies on a particular topic to have true confidence in the findings. As such, researchers should conduct *replication* studies to determine whether their findings can be reliably reproduced. Replications are studies conducted to attempt to confirm or contradict results from previous experiments. Replicating an experiment involves designing a study that incorporates participant groups, methods, and procedures that match the original as closely as possible. Unfortunately, replication studies are quite rare in many fields, including music education. There are many possible reasons why replications are rare; for example, research journal editors and members of editorial review boards have historically been more welcoming of studies that present novel results rather than those that tread established ground. Despite how rare they are, it's important to recognize that replications are critical for furthering our knowledge about music teaching and learning.

Factors Relevant to External Validity

Research findings are most useful when they can be applied to many different circumstances. Unfortunately, tight control over an experiment (internal validity) may make it more difficult to generalize the results to other contexts (external validity). Suppose, for example, you were investigating the effects of practice time on performance achievement. If you set up an experiment in which you monitored students as they practiced at school, you would be able to control the amount of their practice time to a great degree. You could also ask the participants to practice the same étude or materials so that their performance achievement could be more easily compared. However, such precisely controlled conditions do not necessarily represent the sorts of practice students would do naturally on their own—by themselves at home, for example. In addition, most schools do not have the resources of both physical facilities and supervisory personnel to monitor or supervise individual students' practicing at school. Therefore, the results of the experiment may not transfer very readily to other, more naturalistic situations or school contexts. Factors 9–13 below outline the common threats to the external validity of an experiment.

9. *Interaction of the causal relationship with units.* The effects found in experiments are necessarily delimited to the population that the sample represents. In other words, one must acknowledge that any significant (or nonsignificant) differences found between experimental conditions are potentially generalizable only to the population represented by the participants in their particular study.

10. *Interaction of the causal relationship with treatment variations.* The effects found in experiments are necessarily delimited to the specific experiences included in the treatment and control conditions included in a given study. Any variation in that treatment could lead to different results. For example, if a researcher tests the effect of a particular music reading treatment in their experiment and then a teacher adapts a variation of that music reading approach for their classroom, the effects may not generalize as a result of any changes the teacher made to the music reading approach.

11. *Interactions of the causal relationship with outcomes.* The effects of an experiment are bound to the particular outcomes that were studied and may not generalize to other outcomes, even if they are similar. Consider an experiment that indicated that a particular movement activity was beneficial for establishing elementary school students' understanding of duple meter. It is possible that the treatment conditions for that experiment would not be effective for helping students' understanding of triple meter.

12. *Interactions of the causal relationships with settings.* Similar to the threat to external validity regarding units, the effect of an experiment is necessarily delimited to the type of setting in which it was conducted. For example, an

experimental instructional feedback system that leads to increased intrinsic motivation among students in a rural setting may not generalize to students in urban or suburban settings due to the differences that abound among settings.

13. *Context-dependent mediation.* Sometimes in an experiment the intervention (i.e., the independent variable) impacts a third or mediating variable, which then ultimately impacts the outcome (i.e., the dependent variable). Consider a study in which the independent variable consists of a treatment condition where free musical instruments are offered to students from a number of randomly selected schools, whereas schools in a control condition are not offered instruments. It's possible that such an intervention could impact a number of compelling outcomes (i.e., dependent variables), such as greater enrollment and interest in school music. It's possible that this could be successful among low-income schools because the financial burden of procuring an instrument (i.e., a mediating effect) was no longer a barrier to school music instruction, whereas it might not make a difference among high-income schools because a financial burden was never an issue in the first place. As a result, the effects of the experiment would generalize only to other situations where the mediating effect of reduction in financial burden would occur.

As opposed to the common threats to internal validity, these five threats to external validity are more difficult to resolve with experimental design features. This is especially so when considering the limited resources that music education researchers often have at their disposal. For example, one way to increase generalizability of an experiment would be to design a broad enough study that several populations, treatment variations, outcomes, and/or settings are represented. However, conducting research at such a scale would require an incredible amount of time, the involvement of a very large quantity of participants, and huge sums of money. The more reasonable approach is to first conduct a carefully delimited and well-designed experiment with reasonable controls of the threats to internal validity that represents one population, one treatment approach, one compelling outcome, and one setting, then—should that experiment yield promising results—conduct more research to systematically expand the generalizability of the findings by varying the population, treatment, outcome, or setting one step at a time.

Research Designs

In the discussion of research designs that follows, we incorporate several shorthand conventions which were established by Campbell and Stanley (1972) and more recently described by Shadish et al. (2002).

- X stands for the exposure of a group to an experimental condition. Subscripts are attached to the X to indicate different conditions. For example, X_a and X_b can be used to symbolize treatment (i.e., X_a) and control (i.e., X_b) conditions.
- O stands for an observation or measurement of the primary dependent variable. When there are multiple measurement occasions, the Os are placed from left to right to indicate time order.
- Reading from left to right implies time. Thus, O X O stands for a pretest, followed by a treatment and a posttest.
- Xs and Os that appear above/below one another indicate that these events happen at the same time to different groups.
- Xs and Os in a single row imply that measurements and treatments are given to the same participants.
- R indicates random assignment of participants to treatment groups.
- M stands for materials.

Pre-experimental Designs

Some research designs do not rise to the rigor of true experimental research (see next section). Such designs are referred to as "quasi-experimental," and particularly weak quasi-experimental designs are referred to as "pre-experimental." As indicated in Table 14.1, these pre-experimental designs are quite weak due to their vulnerability to many threats to internal validity. The use of pre-experimental designs should be limited to early exploratory work and pilot testing of intervention

Table 14.1 Threats to internal validity for pre-experimental designs

	History	Maturation	Testing	Instrumentation	Regression	Selection	Mortality	Interaction of Selection, etc.
One-shot case study X O	–	–				–		
One-group pretest-posttest design O X O	–	–	–	–	?	+	+	–
Static-group comparison X O O	+	?	+	+	+	–	–	–

Note: This table has been amended from Campbell and Stanley (1972, p. 8). A plus (+) indicates that the source has been controlled. A question mark (?) indicates a possible source of concern. A dash (–) indicates a weakness because the source is not well controlled in the given design. A blank space means that the source is irrelevant for the given design. X = treatment, O = observation or measurement.

approaches for use later with the more robust designs we explain in the following sections. Although there may be circumstances in which the use of one of these designs is better than doing nothing at all, in general these are not the best designs to use if we wish to gather evidence to support effective practices in music education.

One-Shot Case Study

X O

In this pre-experimental design, an intact group is given an experimental treatment and a posttest at the end of the treatment period. An intact group is a preexisting group, such as a particular high school choir. Sometimes intact groups are called "convenience samples," since they are generally made up of groups that are readily available. As can been seen in Table 14.1, history, maturation, selection, and mortality are all threats to internal validity. To take the factor of selection as only one example, if the researcher simply takes an intact group of students as participants, there is no assurance that this group is not biased towards one particular outcome or another in some fashion. For example, they might include a group that has a great deal of prior musical experience, or a group that has a very poor attitude about school music, and so on. Because a one-shot case study fails to control for any threats to internal validity, it is weak and should be avoided if at all possible.

One-Group Pretest-Posttest Design

O X O

A one-group pretest-posttest design is similar to a one-shot case study design except for the addition of a pretest. As shown in Table 14.1, there are considerable weaknesses to this design. It is not strong in either internal or external validity. Suppose, for example, that the results of the posttest show considerable improvement over the pretest. While we might be inclined to claim that the higher scores are the result of the experimental treatment, the reality is that we cannot know whether that is the reason because there are many other ways we could account for the results.

Sometimes it is appropriate to conduct a study with a single group of participants who serve as their own controls in a criterion-referenced design. In this case, a single group is used (e.g., a high school choir) and participants serve as their own controls. This design is most effective when criterion levels can be established for the dependent variable. For example, suppose you state that the desired outcome is for students to reach 90% pitch accuracy on a singing test. Students could be pretested, the number of incorrect pitches noted, the students given a treatment, and then posttested to determine whether they were successful in achieving the stated criterion level.

An alternative to the above is to set sliding criterion levels: 100%, 90%, 80%, and so on. Sometimes you cannot adequately specify what the criterion level should be before the experiment starts. Also, using multiple criterion levels allows you to determine at what point the treatment becomes effective, if at all. In this situation, you can reanalyze the data at each criterion level.

Static-Group Comparison

X   O

O

According to Table 14.1, the static-group comparison design is the strongest of the pre-experimental designs. In this case, two intact groups are selected. We can imagine, for example, two high school choirs. One is given an experimental treatment, and both groups are posttested. Although this is the strongest of the pre-experimental designs, it is not as strong as the posttest-only control group design. As we will see, the posttest-only control group design is similar to the static-group comparison design but has the addition of random assignment of participants to the two groups. This added factor increases internal validity substantially.

Although they can be useful for exploratory purposes, pre-experimental designs should generally not be used in music education research because they fail to control for most of the threats to internal and external validity. The strongest designs, and the ones most highly recommended, are the true experimental designs.

True Experimental Designs

Three true experimental designs are most highly recommended because they are resilient to many of the threats to internal validity. The primary difference between true experimental designs and pre-experimental or quasi-experimental designs is the random assignment of participants to groups. In school settings, it is often difficult or even impossible to assign students randomly to treatment groups. In such cases, other designs, especially quasi-experimental designs (described later in this chapter), can be utilized. However, whenever possible, it is highly desirable to randomly assign participants to different treatment groups.

Threats to internal validity are shown in Table 14.2. As a reminder, R indicates that participants were randomly assigned. The same pretest is given to the two groups at the same time. X_a and X_b refer to two different conditions. Often, these are called the experimental or treatment group (X_a) and the control group (X_b).

Table 14.2 Threats to internal validity for true experimental designs

	History	Maturation	Testing	Instrumentation	Regression	Selection	Mortality	Interaction of Selection, etc.
Pretest-posttest control group design R O X$_a$ O R O X$_b$ O	+	+	–	+	+	+	+	+
Solomon four-group design R O X$_a$ O R O X$_b$ O R X$_a$ O R X$_b$ O	+	+	+	+	+	+	+	+
Posttest-only control group design R X$_a$ O R X$_b$ O	+	+	+	+	+	+	+	+

Note: This table has been amended from Campbell and Stanley (1972, p. 8). A plus (+) indicates that the source has been controlled. A question mark (?) indicates a possible source of concern. A dash (–) indicates a weakness because the source is not well controlled in the given design. A blank space means that the source is irrelevant for the given design. R = random assignment of participants, X = treatment, O = observation or measurement.

Sometimes a control group does not receive any special treatment and the design could have a blank instead of X$_b$. However, it is important to remember that the control group is not uninvolved. Rather, it is normally the case that both groups are engaged in the same activities, with the experimental group getting an extra treatment in addition to what the control group receives. For example, suppose we want to know whether Kodály hand signs are useful in helping young children learn to sing pitches. Third-grade students might be assigned randomly to two groups. Both groups engage in the same musical activities with the same teacher at different times. However, the experimental group also uses hand signs, while the control group does not. Then they are given a posttest at the end of the experiment to determine whether the "extra" or experimental treatment made a significant difference.

The Pretest-Posttest Control Group Design

R O X$_a$ O

R O X$_b$ O

In the pretest-posttest control group design, participants from a specified population are randomly assigned to two different groups. Both groups are then given a pretest.

The experimental group receives treatment X_a, while the control group does not and is labeled X_b. As stated previously, in most circumstances the experiences for the two groups are alike in every regard except one. The one difference is the experimental treatment, or the key element of the primary independent variable. Following the treatment period, both groups are given a posttest.

Random assignment of participants to the two groups reduces nearly all of the threats to internal validity. Because participants were assigned on a random basis, there is no reason to believe that one group would mature faster than the other, or that one group would react differently to the testing situation, and so on. However, since the participants all experience a pretest, it is not possible to rule out that their behavior on the posttest could have been affected by their exposure to the pretest. Thus, although not perfect, the pretest-posttest control group design has very high internal validity. This means that whatever the outcome, we can be relatively sure that the results are due to the effectiveness or ineffectiveness of the experimental treatment and not to any other cause. A significant amount of music education research has employed this design to good effect.

Example 1. Liao and Davidson (2016) wanted to know what effects using gestures and movement would have on intonation in children's singing. They used the pretest-posttest control group design, only in this case there were three groups instead of two:

$$R \quad O \quad X_a \quad O$$
$$R \quad O \quad X_b \quad O$$
$$R \quad O \quad X_c \quad O$$

Liao and Davidson randomly assigned 53 fifth-grade students (10–11 years old) from a primary school in Taiwan into three groups: Experimental Group 1 ($n = 18$) received gesture training, Experimental Group 2 ($n = 18$) received gesture and movement training, and Control Group 3 ($n = 17$) received neither gesture nor movement training. All three groups were taught by the same teacher (the first author) and received the same choral training, with the addition of gesture and movement training for Groups 1 and 2. The special training procedures were used only during the choral warm-up; all other instruction was the same. Students received two 40-minute training sessions per week for 12 weeks (24 sessions). Gesture and movement training were described in the following manner:

1. *Gesture training*: static movement on the spot using primarily upper body gesture, including hands, arms, and knee bends. The main function of the gesture technique was to reinforce motor images to promote vocal technique. However, the function of the gestures did not show pitch levels.

2. *Movement training*: including movement activities and exercises by moving in space to develop the sensation of pictures of sound, travelling through time, space, and energy, and controlling one's body weight. The fundamental aim of movement training is to develop a general awareness of the body in balance, coordination and control, alignment, and rooting posture. (p. 7)

Students were pretested and posttested individually. Each child sang five melodic patterns and was videotaped while doing so. Three experienced choral teachers viewed the recordings and scored each child on a 9-point rating scale ranging from "1 = This child does not sing, but chants the vocal pattern" to "9 = This child sings varied melodies of steps and skips with accuracy and exhibits use of extended singing range." Special training sessions for the judges were implemented to ensure reliability. Reliability analyses indicated that the judges were very consistent; all of the reliability coefficients were .80 or above, with only one below that level, and most were above .90. (Methods for demonstrating evidence of the reliability and validity of a measure for a particular use are discussed in detail in Chapter 15.)

Intonation improvement was highest for the gesture and movement group, next highest for the gesture group, and lowest for the control group. Liao and Davidson (2016) used a strong design, including random assignment of students to treatment groups, that controlled for many threats to internal validity. In addition, they employed effective strategies such as using the same teacher for all three groups and training the judges. Therefore, we may have a great deal of confidence that the results they obtained are valid and that causal inferences are justified. This is an excellent example of what is called evidence-based pedagogy. The value of using gesture and movement does not rely on opinion or guesswork, but rather on carefully conducted, objective research.

Solomon Four-Group Design

$$R \quad O \quad X_a \quad O$$
$$R \quad O \quad X_b \quad O$$
$$R \quad \quad \quad X_a \quad O$$
$$R \quad \quad \quad X_b \quad O$$

In the Solomon four-group design, the previous design is doubled, using four groups instead of two. However, in this instance, the second experimental and control groups do not receive a pretest. In effect, this design is a combination of the pretest-posttest control group design and the posttest-only control group design. One reason not to use a pretest is to avoid the internal validity threat of testing that the pretest-posttest control group design is vulnerable to. In other words, if one suspects that merely taking the pretest might bias the results of the posttest—perhaps because the students learned from the pretest or gained a negative or positive attitude toward the treatment—these interactions can be avoided by not giving a pretest. If the outcomes of the groups that did not receive a pretest are similar to the outcomes for the groups that did receive the pretest, then the researcher can be assured that testing was not a threat to the internal validity of the study. Another reason not to give a pretest is that in some cases, a pretest is not possible because students do not have any experience with the material. Suppose we were interested in teaching five-year-olds how to read traditional Western music notation. If the children had not previously been exposed to musical notation, there is no point in asking them to take a pretest on it.

The Solomon four-group design retains all of the strengths of pretest-posttest control group design for controlling threats to internal validity. Notice in Table 14.2, however, that the minus under testing has turned into a plus in the Solomon four-group design.

Posttest-Only Control Group Design

R   X   O

R   X   O

As indicated in the previous discussion, there are times when a pretest is not warranted. Perhaps we suspect that by taking the pretest, students will perform differently on the posttest because they are now familiar with the material or become excited about learning the material or the reverse, develop a poor attitude about the material. Or it could be that we cannot give a pretest because students have insufficient background and cannot do the task. For example, if we have a group of students who do not know how to read music, a pretest on music notation would be meaningless because any score a student achieved would likely be due to guessing. As can be seen in Table 14.2, the posttest-only control group design is a strong one, controlling for all the threats to internal validity.

Quasi-Experimental Designs

True experimental designs are the ideal. They are the strongest designs, controlling for nearly all the threats to internal validity. Unfortunately, there are many circumstances in educational settings in which it is not possible to randomly assign students to different treatment groups or to manipulate the schedule in such a way as to conduct a true experiment. In these cases, quasi-experimental designs (Table 14.3) allow

Table 14.3 Threats to internal validity for quasi-experimental designs

	Threats to Internal Validity							
	History	Maturation	Testing	Instrumentation	Regression	Selection	Mortality	Interaction of Selection, etc.
Within-subjects design (counterbalanced) R X_a O X_b O R X_b O X_a O	+	+	−	?	+	+	+	+
Time series $O_1 O_2 O_3 X O_4 O_5 O_6$	−	+	+	?	+	+	+	+
Equivalent time samples design $X_a O_1 X_b O_2 X_a O_3 X_b O_4$	+	+	−	+	+	+	+	+
Equivalent materials samples design $M_a X_1 O\, M_b X_0 O\, M_c X_1 O\, M_d X_0 O$	+	+	−	+	+	+	+	+
Nonequivalent control group design O X O O O	+	+	−	+	−	−	+	−

Note: This table has been amended from Campbell and Stanley (1972, p. 40). A plus (+) indicates that the source has been controlled. A question mark (?) indicates a possible source of concern. A dash (−) indicates a weakness because the source is not well controlled in the given design. A blank space means that the source is irrelevant for the given design. R = random assignment of participants, X = treatment, O = observation or measurement, M = materials.

us to conduct research that has many controls—not so many as true experimental designs, but far more than pre-experimental designs. As Campbell and Stanley (1972, p. 34) point out, "every experiment is imperfect." Thus, while we should use true experimental designs whenever possible, when it is not possible, quasi-experimental designs can and should be used.

In educational settings where random assignment is not possible and even when it is not possible to arrange for more than one group, there are several designs to accommodate a single sample. The within-subjects design, time series design, equivalent time samples, and equivalent materials samples design are each single-sample designs. These designs are an improvement over pre-experimental designs.

Within-Subjects Design (Counterbalanced)

R X_a O X_b O

R X_b O X_a O

In the within-subjects design, all participants experience all experimental conditions, and the dependent variable is measured following their exposure to each condition. Designing an experiment in which all participants receive each experimental condition removes the potential threats to internal validity that might arise due to differences between different groups of participants. In this design, the participants serve as their own controls since any comparisons made between measurements following the experimental conditions is, in actuality, just comparisons made of the participants with themselves on different occasions. The within-subjects design is often perceived as an efficient design since it requires recruiting only one group of participants for a study.

However, there are problems that arise in within-subjects designs that are not relevant to designs with multiple groups of participants, namely, order and carryover effects. Since the participants are experiencing more than one condition, it is possible that the results of the experiment could be due to the order in which they experience the conditions rather than the differences in the conditions themselves. Therefore, the order in which the conditions are presented must be counterbalanced across the participants. This is fairly simple to do if you have an experimental design with two treatment conditions (i.e., condition A and condition B). In that case, you'd simply randomly assign half of the participants to receive condition A first and condition B second, and the other half would receive condition B first and condition A second. Once the experiment is complete, you could examine the results to determine whether the findings varied as a function of the order in which the conditions were presented.

As you might have intuited, the number of orderings that are possible with more than two conditions can quickly become unwieldy; for example, four conditions can be arranged in 24 different ways (i.e., $4! = 4 \times 3 \times 2 \times 1 = 24$). As such, researchers sometimes employ what are called Latin Square counterbalancing approaches to try to mitigate order effects. Rather than consider every possible order, the Latin Square approach involves creating enough orders such that each condition appears in each sequential spot in the order once. If we extend this to our hypothetical example of four conditions (i.e., conditions A, B, C, D), we would arrive at the four orders presented in Figure 14.1 and randomly assign an equal number of participants to each. Notice that each condition appears only once in each row and column in Figure 14.1.

Order 1	A	B	C	D
Order 2	B	A	D	C
Order 3	C	D	A	B
Order 4	D	C	B	A

Figure 14.1 Latin Square arrangement of four hypothetical experimental conditions (i.e., conditions A, B, C, D).

Potential carryover effects are more difficult to deal with. No matter what order the conditions are presented in, it is always possible that the condition the participants experienced first could have some effect on their experiences in subsequent condition(s) as well as subsequent measurements. As a result, researchers must think very carefully as to whether a within-subjects design is a feasible method for studying their topic of interest. For example, employing a within-subjects design to study various learning methods could be quite problematic. Even if conditions in such an experiment were counterbalanced, the learning that may have occurred during the first condition the participants experience would inevitably be carried over to their experience in the next condition(s) they experience as well as any subsequent measures of learning gains.

Example 2. Klinger et al. (1998, p. 25) wanted to compare the effectiveness of two rote teaching approaches commonly used to teach songs to young children: (a) an immersion approach in which the teacher sings the whole song repeatedly and the children gradually learn the words, rhythm, and pitches; and (b) a phrase-by-phrase approach in which the teacher models song fragments sequentially, and the children gradually "chunk" them together. They employed a within-subjects experimental design to determine if one of these approaches would be more effective for teaching two intact classes of second-grade children ($N = 39$) two traditional songs, "Let Us Chase the Squirrel" and "All around the Buttercup." The independent variable in this experiment was instruction method (i.e., immersion vs. chunking), and the dependent variable was singing accuracy. Because this was a within-subjects design with an inherent potential confound of order of presentation, the researchers counterbalanced the presentation of the two treatment conditions (i.e., immersion and chunking) across the second-grade classes. In addition, the researchers chose to use two different songs when evaluating the children's singing accuracy to avoid potential practice effects. In other words, if they had the children sing the same song twice—once after experiencing each condition—it would be very likely that their second performance of the song would be influenced by both conditions, thus confounding the experiment. As such, the researchers chose two songs they believed to be equivalent in characteristics and difficulty and they actually include the sheet music for each song in their article so that readers can judge that for themselves as well. Their design can be depicted as:

Class One $X_{immersion}$ $O_{Let\ us\ chase\ the\ squirrel}$ $X_{chunking}$ $O_{All\ around\ the\ buttercup}$

Class Two $X_{chunking}$ $O_{Let\ us\ chase\ the\ squirrel}$ $X_{immersion}$ $O_{All\ around\ the\ buttercup}$

The treatment conditions were presented to the students by the same teacher in separate single class meetings, one week apart from each other. To their credit, the researchers include a figure that describes the procedures the teacher used to teach using the immersion and chunking methods (see Klinger et al., 1998, p. 29). The children were individually recorded singing the songs after each of the treatment conditions. Two judges rated the recordings of the children's singing by tallying errors within four possible categories: melodic contour, rhythmic accuracy, text, and pitch. The reliability of the judges' ratings was good (Kendall's Tau = .89).

The researchers first analyzed their data to determine if the children's singing varied as a function of treatment order (i.e., chunk/immersion vs. immersion/chunk) or song (i.e., squirrel vs. buttercup), since both could function as confounds in a within-subjects design. The singing performance ratings did not vary by either order or song. However, the researchers did find that the children's singing performance varied significantly according to instructional method. The children learned to sing their respective songs better when taught via the immersion method.

Time-Series Design

$$\underline{O_1 O_2 O_3 O_4 X O_5 O_6 O_7 O_8}$$

A time-series experiment involves only one group. For example, this could be an intact classroom, such as a third-grade class, a beginning violin class, or a high school band. In this situation, you would identify the dependent variable, that is, what you want to measure, and find a reliable and valid way to do so. Then you would observe or measure the group on this dependent variable periodically, perhaps every two weeks. After you have made the observation or given the test a specified number of times—as depicted above it is four times—you would introduce the experimental treatment, the primary independent variable. Following the treatment, you would observe or measure the dependent variable the same number of times you did before the treatment. It is important to measure the dependent variable enough times, both prior to and after the treatment, that a relatively stable measurement of the outcome can be achieved. That way, you can be more certain that any change in the outcome that is observed after the introduction of the treatment is not just a fluke.

Let us create a fictitious example involving a beginning violin class. Our research question is: Will singing selected pitch patterns for two weeks have an effect on intonation among beginning violin students? We will use the format for the time series design depicted in Table 14.3. Note, however, that the unit of time we choose to use should be thoughtfully considered. For example, we could record every week, every three weeks, or at any predetermined period. We could also continue the experiment for six weeks, eight weeks, or as long as we desire.

Our primary dependent variable is intonation in violin performance. The experimental treatment is singing pitch patterns. We would record the violin class performing selected pitch patterns once every two weeks. After eight weeks, we introduce singing into the violin class. Students vocalize each pitch pattern as they are learning to play it. They do this for two weeks and are then recorded performing pitch patterns. After the two weeks of singing during class, students continue to learn new pitch patterns but do not sing them in class any longer. They are recorded every two weeks for an additional six weeks. The total experiment takes 16 weeks.

Let us now imagine several possible outcomes. In one scenario (Figure 14.2), we can see that the beginning violinists did not improve their intonation over the eight measurements. In this case, we would conclude that singing pitch patterns during violin class did not help.

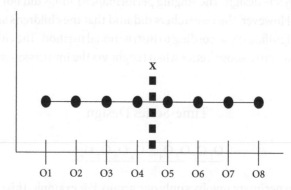

Figure 14.2 O1–O8 = eight measurements of intonation among beginning violin students. X = the introduction of the experimental treatment, singing pitch patterns during violin class.

If the data turned out as depicted in Figure 14.3, we can see that the beginning violinists made no improvements in their intonation for the first eight weeks. Following the experimental treatment, a significant improvement was made at measurement 5, and this remained steady for the duration of the experiment. From these data, we would conclude that singing pitch patterns caused a dramatic improvement in violin intonation. Furthermore, the effect was persistent.

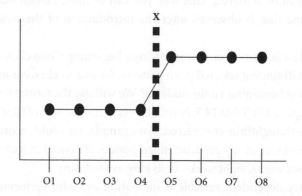

Figure 14.3 The introduction of the experimental treatment, singing pitch patterns during violin class, made a dramatic improvement in violin intonation that persisted for the remainder of the experiment.

Another possible outcome is depicted in Figure 14.4. Here, we see that beginning violin students made steady improvement in intonation throughout the 16 weeks of the experiment. The experimental treatment had no discernible effect on the outcome.

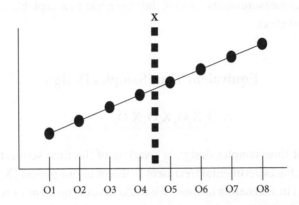

Figure 14.4 Violin students made steady improvement in intonation throughout the 16 weeks of the experiment. Singing pitch patterns, the experimental treatment, had no discernible effect.

A fourth possibility is shown in Figure 14.5. Beginning violin students made steady gains in intonation for the first eight weeks. Following the introduction of the experimental treatment, students improved dramatically. At the next measurement (O6) they declined, but then regained their steady improvement. In this case, we could conclude that singing pitch patterns had a positive effect and that even afterward, when they did not continue singing patterns, the students continued to improve.

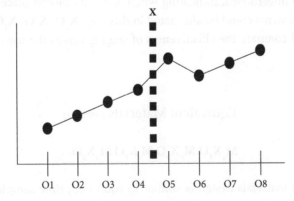

Figure 14.5 Violin students made small but steady improvements in intonation for the first eight weeks of the experiment. Singing pitch patterns, the experimental treatment, caused a dramatic increase in intonation scores. At the next measurement, there was a decline followed by a return to steady improvement.

These four possible outcomes demonstrate how a time series experiment with a single intact group can provide useful information. As shown in Table 14.3, time series designs can control for many of the threats to internal validity. It does not control for history—other things than singing may occur during the length of the experiment to affect the outcome—nor for interactions between each measurement and subsequent measurements. Overall, however, it is an acceptable design that can be used to good effect.

Equivalent Time Samples Design

$$\underline{X_0 O_1\ X_1 O_2\ X_0 O_3\ X_1 O_4}$$

The equivalent time samples design is a variant of the time series design. In this case, however, the experimental treatment is absent in one period (X_0) and present in the next (X_1) in alternating fashion. We could have designed our previous experiment this way. Beginning violin students have violin classes for two weeks, and then their ability to play pitch patterns in tune is measured (O_1). For the next two weeks, students sing the pitch patterns they are learning; again, they are measured (O_2). Another two-week period follows in which students do not sing, and so on. This continues for as many iterations as the researcher deems necessary. Comparing intonation following no treatment with intonation following the experimental treatment should give us an idea of whether singing pitch patterns is an aid to improving intonation or not.

Instead of alternating an experimental treatment with no treatment, we could alternate two different treatments. Suppose, for example, that X_1 represents singing pitch patterns, as in the previous examples. Then suppose that X_2 represents the use of tape on the fingerboard, indicating where students should place their fingers. These two treatments could be alternated in this way: $X_1 O_1\ X_2 O_2\ X_1 O_3\ X_2 O_4$. Data analysis would compare the effectiveness of singing versus the use of tape on the fingerboard.

Equivalent Materials Design

$$\underline{M_a X_1 O\ M_b X_0 O\ M_c X_1 O\ M_d X_0 O}$$

The equivalent materials design is similar to equivalent time samples design, the main difference being the use of equivalent materials as well as the experimental treatment. $M_{a\text{-}d}$ represents four different but equivalent sets of materials. In our example of the beginning violin students, this could be four equivalent sets of pitch patterns. In the discussion of the previous two designs, if the pitch patterns became increasingly more difficult over the 16 weeks of the experiment, that might cause invalid results. We would not be able to measure the effect of singing or using tape on the finger board in the light of increasingly difficult pitch patterns. In the case of equivalent materials design, the difficulty level of the pitch patterns remains constant, although changing with four equivalent sets of pitch patterns. This provides a fair and unbiased test of the experimental treatment.

Nonequivalent Control Group Design

O   X   O

O   O

The nonequivalent control group design is similar to the pretest-posttest control group true experimental design, with one very critical difference: participants are not randomly assigned to groups. As discussed previously, random assignment is the strongest deterrent against threats to internal validity. Unfortunately, random assignment of participants is often extremely difficult or even impossible in school settings. Students are already assigned to regular classes, and the freedom to move them randomly to different treatment groups rarely exists. As described earlier, any comparisons of intact, nonequivalent groups would be compromised by threats such as selection.

However, there are additional strategies researchers could use to try to mitigate the limitations of this design. For example, researchers sometimes try to identify variables that could contribute to any nonequivalence between groups and adjust the participants' scores on the dependent variable according to participants' scores on these additional variables. When used in this way, these variables are referred to as "covariates." For example, imagine a situation in which a researcher would like to conduct an experiment to test a musical intervention of some kind in a school using a nonequivalent control group design with one fourth-grade class assigned to the experimental condition and another fourth-grade class assigned to the control condition. In order to reduce the initial discrepancies between these two intact groups of fourth-graders, the researchers could try to identify how the groups may differ and measure those differences. Perhaps the students in one of the classes score higher than the other on academic achievement, or maybe indicators of socioeconomic status show that one class is, on average, wealthier than another. The researcher could treat academic achievement and socioeconomic status as covariates in their design; that is, they could use statistical procedures to adjust the participants' scores on the dependent variable of interest according to how the groups differ on academic achievement and socioeconomic status. Limitations of using covariates in lieu of randomization include (a) that one can never know what all of the relevant covariates are (although clear theoretical guidance regarding causal mechanisms can help), and (b) measuring covariates will consume resources such as time and statistical power.

Example 3. Kang and Yoo (2016) investigated the effects of Westernized versions of traditional Korean folk songs on collegiate elementary education students' familiarity with and preferences for the traditional versions of the same songs. One intact group of students was taught lessons that included active listening activities with traditional versions of the Korean songs. This group was also taught by an instructor with expertise in Korean music. Another intact group of students was taught lessons that included active listening activities with versions of the same Korean songs but arranged in a Western style. This group was taught by an instructor with expertise in Western music. Last, an additional group of students did not have any listening components to their lessons at all. These conditions were carried out across eight weeks in the students' typical classroom settings. This quasi-experiment involved a pretest-posttest, nonequivalent control group design with two treatment conditions and can be notated as follows:

$$O \quad X_{traditional} \quad O$$
$$O \quad X_{Westernized} \quad O$$
$$O \quad \quad \quad \quad O$$

For the pretest and posttest measures, the participants listened to 12 musical excerpts (4 Western popular music songs, 4 Western classical pieces, and the 4 traditional Korean folk songs) and rated them on two scales: a 3-point familiarity scale and a 7-point preference scale. As expected, familiarity ratings for the traditional Korean folk songs increased the most from pre- to posttest for the participants in the instructional condition that included listening to the traditional Korean folk songs. More interesting, the preference ratings for the traditional Korean folk songs also increased the most from pre- to posttest for the participants in the instructional condition that included listening to the traditional Korean folk songs. We have focused on the researchers' analyses of the participants' ratings of the traditional Korean folk songs in this summary; however, there are more nuanced findings as well. Kang and Yoo (2016) included an extensive discussion of several issues that would be important for teachers to consider when introducing non-Western musical styles to Western listeners.

Summary

Pre-experimental designs (Table 14.1) lack controls over threats to internal validity and should be used only for exploratory or pilot-testing purposes. True experimental designs (Table 14.2) are the strongest designs since they are the most resilient to threats of internal validity. Quasi-experimental designs (Table 14.3) are not quite as strong as the true experimental designs, but they do offer many useful possibilities. Review the section in the previous chapter on ex post facto research for additional design possibilities. Experimental research designs beyond those discussed in this chapter are possible, but they are not frequently used in music education research and so are not covered here. Readers interested in more options are encouraged to read Shadish et al. (2002) and Kirk (2012). Answering the following questions will provide a good review for the material covered in this chapter:

1. What are some examples of threats to internal validity and external validity?
2. Discuss the concepts of internal and external validity as they relate to experimental research. Why is it that increasing internal validity—tightening the control one has over independent variables—almost always results in decreases in external validity, and vice versa?
3. Why are pre-experimental designs weak in controlling threats to validity?
4. Why are true experimental designs considered the strongest and most desirable?
5. Under what circumstances would it be advisable to avoid giving a pretest?
6. Under what circumstances would it be advisable to use a within-subjects counterbalanced design?
7. What weaknesses keep quasi-experimental designs from being as strong as true experimental designs, and what factors make them better to use than pre-experimental designs?

Important Terms for Review

Pre-experimental designs are suitable for exploratory or pilot work, but are otherwise inferior designs that do not rise to the level of control that is desirable for causal inferences.

True experimental designs are the most desirable because they have the most control over internal and external validity. Random assignment of participants to treatment groups is an essential feature of true experimental designs.

Quasi-experimental designs are weaker than true experimental designs but stronger than pre-experimental designs. They are useful when true experimental designs are not possible.

A *replication* is an experiment that is a repetition of a previous study. Researchers most often replicate experiments to determine whether previous findings are reliable or a fluke.

Factors Relevant to Internal Validity

Internal validity is concerned with the extent to which an experimental treatment, rather than some other factor, actually caused a difference in the outcome.

History as a factor in internal validity refers to events that may occur over time that could influence the outcome of the experiment.

Maturation refers to the possibility that the outcome of an experiment was influenced by the growth and development of participants rather than the experimental treatment.

The *Hawthorne effect* occurs when participants in an experiment change their behaviors as a result of being observed.

Testing itself can sometimes affect the outcome of an experiment.

Instrumentation refers to changes in measurement of the dependent variable (e.g., human observers) that might affect the outcome of the experiment.

Statistical regression is the probability that those who scored extremely high or low on a pretest are likely to move toward the mean on the posttest.

Selection biases are factors that create imbalances in comparison groups.

Experimental mortality refers to participants who leave an experiment before it is over.

Interaction effects occur when one aspect of the experiment influences another, and therefore the effects observed can be mistakenly attributed to the experimental treatment.

Factors Relevant to External Validity

Interaction of the causal relationship with units occurs when the outcome of the experiment is generalizable only to the specific population represented in an experiment.

Interaction of the causal relationship with treatment variations occurs when the outcome of the experiment is generalizable only to the specific treatment conditions incorporated in an experiment.

Interactions of the causal relationship with outcomes occurs when the outcome of the experiment is generalizable only to the specific methods of measuring the outcome included in an experiment.

Interactions of the causal relationships with settings occurs when the outcome of the experiment is generalizable only to settings similar to those represented in an experiment.

Context-dependent mediation is when the intervention (i.e., the independent variable) is effective only when it impacts a specific third or mediating variable, which then ultimately impacts the outcome (i.e., the dependent variable).

References

Campbell, D., & Stanley, J. (1972). *Experimental and quasi-experimental designs for research*. Rand McNally.

Kang, S., & Yoo, H. (2016). Effects of a westernized Korean folk music selection on students' music familiarity and preference for its traditional version. *Journal of Research in Music Education*, 63(4), 469–486. https://doi.org/10.1177/0022429415620195

Kirk, R. E. (2012). *Experimental design: Procedures for the behavioral sciences* (4th ed.). Sage.

Klinger, R., Campbell, P. S., & Goolsby, T. (1998). Approaches to children's song acquisition: Immersion and phrase-by-phrase. *Journal of Research in Music Education*, 46(1), 24–34. https://doi.org/10.2307/3345757

Liao, M.-Y., & Davidson, J. (2016). The effects of gesture and movement training on the intonation of children's singing in vocal warm-up sessions. *International Journal of Music Education*, 34(1), 4–18. https://doi.org/10.1177/0255761415614798

Shadish, W. R., Cook, T. D., & Campbell, D. T. (2002). *Experimental and quasi-experimental designs for generalized causal inference*. Wadsworth.

15
Measurement

Chapter Preview

The focus of this chapter is measurement, the assignment of numbers to variables. Applying measurement scales to information creates a way to quantify phenomena, such as attitudes or behaviors, objectively. Four levels of measurement are nominal, ordinal, interval, and ratio. Nominal data represent names or labels of categories; even when numbers are assigned, they have no quantitative meaning (e.g., 1 = pianists and 2 = singers). Ordinal data can be ranked, but the distance separating one value from another on a scale is not necessarily consistent (e.g., first chair, second chair). Interval data communicate both order and quantity, and the intervals between data points are assumed to be equal along a scale. With interval data (e.g., many test scores), it is possible to perform mathematical operations and there are many suitable statistical analyses. Ratio-level data are assumed to be from a scale that has a true absolute zero. Reliability and validity are critical to measurement. "Reliability" refers to the consistency of measurement. "Validity" generally refers to the extent to which a measurement tool measures what it is supposed to. If a measurement tool is unreliable (i.e., inconsistent), we have no confidence that scores represent true values. If a measurement tool does not measure what it is supposed to (i.e., is inaccurate), it is invalid.

Introduction

In this chapter, we consider measurement and the criteria researchers use to determine whether measurement tools are robust. Measurement is a critical component of quantitative research in particular. Generally speaking, measurement is the quantification of information. By applying measurement scales to information, we create a way to objectively quantify phenomena such as attitudes, performance qualities, behaviors, and so on. Without measurement it would not be possible to conduct statistical analyses of data, which are covered in subsequent chapters. We begin by describing what measurement is and the various kinds of data that are obtained from measurement tools. Next, we briefly distinguish among terms that are often colloquially confused: "assessment," "tests," "measurement," and "evaluation." To close the chapter, we discuss how researchers demonstrate evidence for the reliability and validity of the measurement tools they use. Readers seeking

> **Box 15.1 Additional Methodological Readings: Measurement**
>
> Boyle, J. D., & Radocy, R. E. (1987). *Measurement and evaluation of musical experiences*. Schirmer Books.
> Furr, R. M. (2021). *Psychometrics: An introduction*. Sage.
> Miller, D. M., Miller, M. D., Linn, R. L., & Gronlund, N. E. (2021). *Measurement assessment in teaching* (11th ed.). Pearson.
> Robinson Kurplus, S. E., & Stafford, M. E. (2005). *Testing and measurement: A user-friendly guide*. Sage.

information regarding measurement principles beyond that offered in this chapter could consult the resources presented in Box 15.1.

Measurement

Measurement is the process of quantifying things. Measurement of physical objects or phenomena can be done with fairly straightforward tools. For example, if we wanted to measure the physical distance between soloists and accompanists, we could use a tape measure; if we wanted to measure the loudness level of an ensemble performing in a rehearsal room, we could use a decibel meter. However, we can also develop tools to measure more complex or less easily observed phenomena. For example, it is also possible to measure knowledge, dispositions, opinions, attitudes, preferences, psychological attributes, and so on. The term "psychometrics" refers to the design and implementation of tools for measuring psychological attributes.

Levels of Measurement

Measurement tools can be designed to yield four different types of data: nominal, ordinal, interval, and ratio. These four types of data are more formally referred to as levels of measurement.

Nominal

The term "nominal" comes from the Latin root word *nomen*, for "name." Accordingly, nominal data represent names or labels of categories. For example, if a researcher were to ask participants to report whether they are a guitarist, pianist, singer, brass player, woodwind player, or percussionist, they would be collecting nominal data. The researcher might assign numbers to represent these categories to help them organize the responses and count them up (1 = guitarist, 2 = pianist, 3 = singer, etc.), but the numbers would have no quantitative meaning (e.g., it would be nonsensical to add them up or perform any mathematical operation upon them), and the numbers could be interchangeable. For example, the researcher could just as well choose to use different numbers as indicators for the categories (1 = pianist, 2 = singer, 3 = guitarist, etc.) without any consequence, since the numbers are only labels. As such, nominal data are simply categorical data that do not imply any order or quantity. Nominal data communicate the least amount of information among all levels of measurement. Again, mathematical operations with nominal data are quite limited.

Ordinal

Ordinal data are also a form of categorical data. However, true to its name, the numbers applied in ordinal data have intrinsic meaning in that they can be ordered. In other words, in contrast to nominal measurement, ordinal data can be ranked. A limitation of ordinal data is that the distance separating one value from another on an ordinal scale is not necessarily consistent. For example, suppose 10 students competed in a singing contest. If judges arranged them from best to worst, but did not assign point values, we could rank them but could not say how much better the best singer was than the next best singer, and so on. Also, the difference between singers 3 and 4 would not necessarily be the same as the difference between singers 7 and 8. As another example, suppose a researcher asked students to place musical genres in order of preference, and two participants responded with the same ranking: 1. hip-hop, 2. alternative, 3. Western classical music, 4. jazz, and so on. From this, we know only that hip-hop music is the most preferred, but we do not know how much more preferred it is than the others. Regarding potential differences between the participants, one might like both genres nearly the same, while the other might love hip-hop music but not care for alternative music hardly at all. Ordinal measurement provides information only about order or ranking; it does not communicate anything about quantity. Like nominal data, it is not appropriate to perform mathematical operations upon ordinal-level data. Similar to nominal levels of measurement, basic mathematical operations cannot be performed with ordinal data.

Interval

In contrast to ordinal data, interval data communicate both order and quantity. Consistent with its name, the intervals between score points can be assumed to be equal along a scale when data are at the interval level. For example, suppose we collected data with a measurement tool in which the scores could range from 1 to 100 and every number in between. The difference in scores between participants who scored 30 and 40 (i.e., the interval between 30 and 40) would be the same as the distance between participants who scored 80 and 90 (i.e., the interval between 80 and 90). Accordingly, interval measurement provides more information than nominal or ordinal data. In contrast to nominal and ordinal data, it is possible to perform mathematical operations upon interval data.

Ratio

Ratio-level data contain all the properties of interval-level measurements but are also assumed to be from a scale that has a true absolute zero. The key difference between interval- and ratio-level data is that, with ratio-level data, ratios of scores are preserved as well as intervals between score points. Measurements of physical properties can serve as good examples of ratio-level data. For instance, imagine a researcher were to measure the duration of time that children spend listening to music at a classroom workstation. The measurements could be recorded in seconds, and in this case, a measurement of 0 seconds literally means no time spent listening. The phenomenon that distinguishes interval and ratio data is that the ratio between durational measurements would be preserved due to this absolute zero. For example, a duration of 30 seconds would literally be three times as long as 10 seconds, a 3:1 ratio, and a duration of 90 seconds would be three times as long as 30 seconds, also a 3:1 ratio. Like interval data, it is possible to perform mathematical operations upon ratio data. Ratio measurement occurs infrequently in music education research.

As you have learned, data at nominal and ordinal levels of measurement represent only categorical information, whereas data at the interval and ratio levels of measurement have actual quantitative properties. Whether you are reading research or conducting your own studies, it is important to be aware of the level of measurement of data that are gathered. As discussed in the following chapters, one's choice of statistical procedures depend on the level of data one has to work with.

Assessment, Tests, Measurement, and Evaluation

"Assessment"—a term relevant to both teaching and research contexts—refers to a process of gathering information from which one can make analytical judgments. There are several additional terms that are used to describe more specific aspects of an assessment process that are also important to clarify. The term "test" is often used in research contexts to describe a data gathering tool, which can also be referred to as an "instrument." Tests come in many forms, some of which are quite familiar to us as teachers (e.g., written exams, performance tests). However, in research, tests—or data gathering instruments more generally—can come in many, many forms (e.g., attitude questionnaires, surveys, observation protocols, personality measures, performance tasks, tests of cognitive abilities). Consistent with our discussion above, "measurement" refers to the application of a quantitative scale to the information we gather. Finally, "evaluation" is used to describe the process of making judgments based on our measurements.

Suppose we'd like to assess the loudness level of a rehearsal space. We could use a dosimeter as a data gathering tool (i.e., testing device, instrument) for such a task. A dosimeter can gather information about the sound levels of a space and report that information via a number representing a decibel level (dB) (i.e., a measurement). Then we can use standards for room acoustics to determine whether the loudness level is too high and might damage the hearing of ensemble members who rehearse there. Audiologists generally consider that a loudness level of 85 dB experienced for 8 hours is safe (Kardous et al., 2016). For each 3-dB increase, the amount of exposure time that is considered safe is cut in half. Levels above these are considered unsafe; that is, a person is at risk of permanent hearing loss. Additional markers for risk of hearing loss are 88 dB for 4 hours, 91 dB for 2 hours, 94 dB for 1 hour, and so on. Suppose we measured the loudness level of a rehearsal room with an ensemble rehearsing for one hour and got a reading of 95 dB. Our evaluation would be that this is an unsafe environment as it places ensemble members and the conductor at risk of hearing loss.

We can also apply these terms to assessment processes as they might typically unfold in a traditional school context. A teacher might assess students' knowledge via a written exam. The students' performance on the test would then be placed on a measurement scale. For example, suppose the teacher gave a test with a possible 100 points and used the following grading scale: 90–100 = A, 80–89 = B, 70–79 = C, 60–69 = D, 59 and below = F. Thus, a student who earned 83 points would be assessed a B. We would use this information to form an analytical judgement. In other words, if a student was assessed a B for earning 83 points on their exam, we could evaluate whether the student did well or poorly. If the student had received A's on all their previous exams, receiving a B would be a weaker performance for them. On the other hand, if they had received C's and D's on previous exams, earning a B would be a significant improvement and we would evaluate their performance as successful.

Overall, then, an assessment process can entail gathering information with tests (i.e., data gathering tools), measuring quantities, and evaluating the results by placing a value on the measured quantity according to some known standard.

Reliability and Validity

Two key aspects of measurement are the reliability and validity of measurement tools. "Reliability" refers to the consistency of measurement; an inconsistent measurement tool produces unreliable data. "Validity" generally refers to the extent to which a measurement tool measures what it is supposed to. More specifically, validity can be described as the degree to which evidence and theory support using the scores of a measurement tool the way a researcher intends to. A measurement tool can be reliable but invalid, but it cannot be valid and unreliable. That is, an unreliable tool cannot be a valid measurement.

A researcher must provide evidence that the measurement tools (e.g., tests) they have chosen or designed for their study are sufficiently reliable and valid. Reliability and validity are qualities of measurement tools that are demonstrated by degree rather than as being a "yes or no" proposition. As described below, there are several ways that researchers can gather evidence of the reliability and validity of their measures. Furthermore, reliability and validity are not necessarily static properties that accompany a measurement tool from study to study. Instead, researchers must convincingly demonstrate that the measurement tools they employ are reliable and valid within the context of their particular study, for example, suitable for use with their participants, in the particular context of their research, and for their research purposes.

It is also important to draw a clear conceptual distinction between the internal and external validity of an experiment and the validity of a measurement tool. These are "slippery" ideas that beginning researchers can often conflate. It would be understandable to do so since both concepts involve the degree to which accurate inferences could be made. However, in the case of the internal and external validity of an experiment, one is concerned with the validity of a causal inference (i.e., whether the independent variable caused some change in the dependent variable) and the degree to which one could generalize the results of the experiment to other types of people and circumstances. In contrast, in the case of the validity of a measure one is concerned with the validity of inferences that could be made from the scores of a test (i.e., whether the test scores actually represent variation on the phenomenon the researcher believes they do).

The Relationship between Reliability and Validity

One useful analogy for thinking about the relationship between reliability and validity, and especially how reliability is a necessary condition for validity to occur, is to consider the precision and accuracy that are possible to achieve when playing darts. First, let's create an analogy for a situation in which a measurement tool is shown to be reliable but not valid. Imagine a situation in which someone throws several darts and they all cluster together—except they don't cluster together near the target in the center of the board. This is depicted in Panel a of Figure 15.1, in which each arrow represents an individual dart. You could describe the collection of throws in Panel a as being precise or consistent but not accurate, which is not

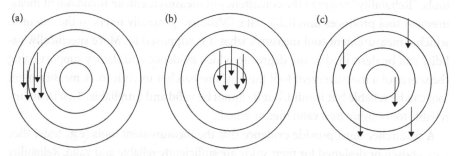

Figure 15.1 Illustration of the relationship between reliability and validity.

Note: Panel a appears to evidence reliability as the scores (arrows) land closely (consistently) together; however, validity is not evident as the target (bullseye) was not *hit*. Panel b appears to evidence reliability because the scores are landing close together and validity because the scores are landing at the target. Panel c appears to have low reliability (score inconsistency) and, therefore, does not evidence validity (scores do not land at the target).

Source: Waldon (2016, p. 147). Used by permission.

the most desirable outcome. To continue the analogy, now imagine instead that the arrows are a participant's scores from a measurement tool and suspend your disbelief so that you can imagine the participant being tested several times over again. The fact that the scores are all similar (i.e., the arrows are near each other) suggests that the measurement tool is consistent, or in other words, reliable. However, since the scores are off the mark in terms of not being on target, they are not accurate. This inaccuracy is analogous to a test not measuring what it purports to measure, or in other words, that the measurements are not valid.

Next, Panel b of Figure 15.1 depicts a series of throws that indicate the dart player is both precise and accurate. This is evident in the tight clustering of the arrows (i.e., consistency) and the fact that the darts are all within the bullseye (i.e., accuracy). This is the most desirable outcome when playing darts. To continue the analogy between darts and measurement, this is indicative of a situation where the scores are very similar (e.g., consistent) across multiple test administrations and the scores are also on target in regard to measuring what the research purports that they measure (e.g., accuracy). This is the only situation in which it is possible to gain meaningful information from a measurement tool—when evidence for both reliability and validity are clear.

Last, let's consider a situation where a measurement tool is neither reliable nor valid for use. The pattern of dart throws in Panel c of Figure 15.1 depicts this scenario, since the darts have been thrown with neither precision nor accuracy. To complete our set of analogous measurement examples, you can see it is not possible to achieve measurement validity if you cannot demonstrate test reliability. In other words, if a measurement tool yields scores that are unreliable (i.e., inconsistent), it is impossible to assess whether it is valid to use the measurement tool.

Reliability and validity are critical to measurement. If a measurement tool is unreliable (i.e., inconsistent), we have no confidence that scores represent true values. If a measurement tool does not measure what it is supposed to (i.e., is inaccurate), it is invalid. Clearly, administering a measure that is unreliable and invalid is a fatal flaw in the research process.

Reliability Evidence

There are four traditional ways of providing evidence of the reliability (i.e., consistency) of a measurement tool:

- *Consistency over time*: Sometimes referred to as test-retest reliability, this is when a measurement tool is administered more than once to the same group of participants and the results of the two administrations are compared. Factors to consider are the length of time between administrations and the possibility that the first administration will affect the outcome of the second. If there is too much time between administrations, learning may occur; if there is too

little time between administrations, participants may simply respond the same way from memory. Also, the act of measurement itself (e.g., simply taking a test) may introduce students to new information in such a way that the second measurement is affected.
- *Internal consistency*: This approach involves assessing the degree to which individual items (e.g., questions, ratings) within a measure contribute consistently to a total score yielded from the measure. A classic approach to demonstrating internal consistency is the split-halves method. In this method, the scores on the odd-numbered items are compared with scores on the even-numbered items and then adjusted to account for the "halving" of the items to give a measure of internal consistency. Other statistical approaches for assessing internal consistency are Cronbach's alpha and omega.
- *Consistency across forms*: This approach is also described as parallel forms reliability (or equivalent forms). It involves comparing one group of participants' scores from two different versions of a test. Both versions would need to be designed to cover equivalent material regarding a topic or domain. The major difficulty here is in creating two equivalent versions of the same test. In research, it can be particularly useful to have two equivalent forms of a test since it would allow you to conduct pretest and posttest measurements—you could use one form as a pretest measure and the other form as a posttest measure—while reducing the likelihood that the participants' posttest performance would be impacted by their exposure to the pretest.
- *Consistency across raters*: This method is also called "interrater" or "interjudge" reliability." In this approach, multiple raters (or judges) are recruited to make observations or score performances, and then their scores are compared. There are two concerns researchers attend to when it comes to interrater reliability: consistency among judges and agreement among judges. The consistency of the judges' scores is present when their pattern of scoring across participants is generally similar; for example, the participants that judge 1 scored relatively high were also scored relatively high by judge 2. In contrast, the agreement of judges' scores is present when the judges are using similar absolute scoring scales; for example, agreement would be achieved if the values of the judges' scores were similar, in other words, when judges are neither more severe nor more lenient than each other. When scores are being used for high-stakes decisions, fairly exact agreement among judges is important. However, for other exploratory research purposes, approximate agreement can be sufficient evidence for interjudge reliability.

The various comparisons described above are often reported via correlation coefficients and other similar statistical methods. A correlation coefficient summarizes the direction and strength of the relationship between two sets of scores. Correlation coefficients can take numbers ranging from −1 (i.e., a perfect inverse relationship) to +1 (i.e., a perfect positive relationship), with a coefficient of

0 representing no relationship. A thorough explanation of correlation as a general concept and correlation coefficients, specifically, is presented in Chapter 17. For the purposes of this chapter, it is sufficient to state that correlation coefficients indicative of measurement reliability should be positive, and that the closer they are to +1, the more consistent or reliable the test scores are thought to be.

Correlation coefficients used as indicators of reliability evidence are referred to as "reliability coefficients." For example, evidence of consistency over time could be reported via the correlation between the participants' scores at time 1 with their scores at time 2. Consistency across two raters could be reported via a correlation of one rater's scores with the other rater's scores. Regardless of the statistical methods used, when correlation coefficients are used to report reliability, they can be interpreted using the following rules of thumb:

- Coefficients greater than or equal to .9 indicate that reliability is excellent.
- Coefficients greater than or equal to .8 but less than .9 are indicative of good reliability.
- Coefficients greater than or equal to .7 but less than .8 suggest acceptable reliability.
- Coefficients greater than or equal to .6 but less than .7 suggest questionable reliability.
- Coefficients less than .6 reflect unacceptable reliability.

Descriptions of the Reliability of Measures in Research

Bergee (2003) conducted a study of the reliability of end-of-semester applied performance evaluations made by faculty panels at a large midwestern university. He reported reliability coefficients that indicate the degree of interjudge reliability achieved among a number of faculty panels of various sizes. The faculty panels were also varied in regard to primary instrument, with separate panels for brass, percussion, woodwind, voice, piano, and string faculty groups. The coefficients Bergee found among the full faculty panels were extremely varied as well, ranging from a low of .70 for the voice panel, indicating acceptable reliability, to a high of .93 for the percussion panel, indicating excellent reliability. Overall, Bergee recommended erring on the side of having more judges on evaluation panels since the reliability evidence documented with larger panels tended to be somewhat stronger than that with smaller panels.

Validity Evidence

As stated previously, validity has to do with whether a measurement tool measures what it is supposed to measure, that is, whether evidence and theory support using the scores of a measurement tool the way a researcher intends to. The methods for establishing the validity of a measure are more diverse than those for gathering evidence of reliability. Whereas reliability is often illustrated via correlation coefficients that result from comparisons of sets of scores, validity is often established via reasoned argumentation as well as through statistical analyses. There are five primary methods researchers use to gather evidence of the validity of their measures, and these are often used in combination with each other:

- *Face validity* is a subjective judgment of whether an instrument appears to address the content it purports to measure. Evidence for face validity can be acquired by simply examining the tool to look for problems that might cause it to appear inappropriate. Researchers often attain face validity by asking others to review the measurement tool.
- *Content validity* refers to whether the items of a measurement tool capture a representative sampling of the domain being measured. For example, when designing a questionnaire for a survey, a researcher could analyze the items on the survey according to whether the items could sufficiently capture all of the information that is needed to fulfill the purpose of the research and the research questions. Researchers will often create test blueprints to visually map out how the items of a measure capture the domain of interest. Another common method of gathering evidence of content validity is to have experts confirm that the content covered in the measurement tool is a match to the domain it purports to measure. For example, should a researcher wish to design a survey tool for gathering information about culturally responsive teaching practices, it would be valuable to check with an expert that the content of the survey was truly representative of the principles underlying culturally responsive pedagogy.
- *Criterion validity* refers to comparison of scores of the measurement tool in question with scores from some other measurement tool (e.g., other tests) of a related variable that could serve as an external criterion. The term "concurrent criterion validity" refers to situations in which a researcher administers their measure along with another measure at roughly the same time. For example, a researcher developing a measure of sight-reading ability for intermediate students might also ask the students' teacher to rate the students according to how well they generally perform as sight-readers. The researcher could then correlate the scores yielded from their measure with the ratings of the teacher. If the two are positively related, then the researcher would have criterion validity evidence for their new sight-reading ability measure.

Sometimes measurement tools are intended to forecast future performance. In that case it would be appropriate to examine the *predictive validity* of the measure: whether the scores from the measure accurately predict future performance on a relevant external criterion. For example, a researcher might develop a measure of the degree to which students are likely to enroll in music courses in the future. Administering such a measure and comparing the results to students' actual enrollment choices in the future could be a way to gather evidence of predictive criterion validity. The degree to which the students' scores on the intention-to-enroll measure correlate with their actual enrollment choices would be indicative of the extent of the predictive validity of the intention-to-enroll measure.

- *Construct validity* refers to the extent to which scores from a measurement tool can be interpreted in terms of some latent theoretical construct. Consider the development of a tool to measure performance anxiety. There are numerous explanatory theories of performance anxiety, and each can be quite complex (see Kenny, 2011). Should a researcher wish to measure musicians' feelings of performance anxiety, they need to demonstrate how the measurement tool they create or choose is aligned with the particular theoretical perspective they are taking when framing their study of performance anxiety. In this case, evidence for construct validity could take the form of theoretical argumentation. In other words, the researcher would describe in detail how their measure captures the relevant theoretical aspects of performance anxiety. If the measure fails to capture all theoretically relevant aspects of the phenomenon, then it could be said that the validity of the measure suffers from construct underrepresentation. If the measure inadvertently captures aspects of performers' beliefs unrelated to performance anxiety, then it could be said that the validity of the measure suffers from construct-irrelevant variance (i.e., the differences between the scores represent something other than differences in performance anxiety). There are also statistical methods that can be used to evaluate the construct validity of certain kinds of measurement tools (e.g., factor analysis, multitrait multimethod analysis); however, those are beyond the scope of this book.
- *Consequential validity* refers to consideration of the implications, positive or negative, of using a particular test for a particular purpose. For example, an unintended negative consequence of using a commercial standardized test to determine which students should be awarded scholarships could be to perpetuate socioeconomic bias if those who tend to score better on such tests are also shown to be more likely to be able to afford extra test preparation training and materials. This aspect of measurement validity is somewhat more likely to be highlighted with reference to the development of school-related tests and educational policy than in research studies.

As implied in the discussion of methods for demonstrating validity above, correlation coefficients are sometimes used for illustrating criterion validity evidence. When that's the case, the correlation coefficients are referred to as "validity coefficients." However, in contrast to reliability coefficients, there is no clear rule of thumb for evaluating validity coefficients. That said, convincing validity coefficients tend to be much lower than reliability coefficients. For example, should a researcher wish to design a new measurement tool and then choose to demonstrate criterion validity by comparing the scores from the new tool to a preexisting measurement tool, one would not expect the two sets of scores to correlate very strongly with coefficients approaching 1.0. If that were the case, then the information yielded from the new measure would nearly duplicate the information one could gain from the old measure, and therefore the new measure would not be worth designing. Instead, and in contrast to reliability coefficients, validity coefficients that range less than even .50 or .40 can be encouraging.

Descriptions of Validity in Research

Williams (1996) investigated the validity of Edwin Gordon's (1984) Instrument Timbre Preference Test (ITPT). Gordon designed the test to be used by teachers when helping students choose an appropriate instrument to play. The general rationale underlying the use of the test was that students would ultimately be more satisfied with their choice of instrument and more successful in learning if they chose an instrument to learn based on its timbral quality. The test involves students listening to pairings of seven different synthesized sounds that are intended to represent 14 different instruments and indicating which of each pair they prefer. The students' preference for a particular timbre and, therefore, the instrument they presumably should choose is essentially determined by identifying the synthesized timbre they preferred the most.

Throughout the article Williams (1996) presented arguments as well as data to refute the validity of the test for such uses. Regarding content validity, he highlighted that artificial-sounding synthesized tones are used as stimuli for test items rather than recordings of actual instruments, that the melodies presented through the synthesized tones have no sense of musical expression, and that some synthesized tones are supposed to be representative of more than one instrument. However, the main thrust of his study is a critique of the criterion validity of the test. Williams administered the ITPT to 128 high school and college wind instrument music students. He also asked the participants to write which instrument they thought each synthesized sound was supposed to represent. In this case, the external criteria to which the test scores were compared were the actual instruments the students chose to play and their assessment of which synthesized sounds matched with which actual instruments. Overall, Williams found that the timbre preference indicated by the participants' performance on the ITPT was often not indicative of the actual instrument they played and that the participants often labeled the various synthesized timbres as representative of instruments other than what Gordon intended. Ultimately, Williams concluded that the validity of using the ITPT to inform students' instrument choices was suspect.

Summary

Measurement is a very important part of the research process. Measuring something involves using a tool (e.g., test, observation protocol, questionnaire, judges' rating protocol) to gather information about/observations of a phenomenon and then assigning a numerical scale to the observations. Measurement scales applied to phenomena include nominal, placing information into categories and assigning each category a number; ordinal, assigning numbers to information that communicates rank or order; interval, arranging scores along a continuous, equal interval scale; and ratio, measurement with an absolute zero. Interval and ratio levels of measurement can communicate more information than nominal or ordinal levels and allow for the most variety of mathematical operations.

Reliability, the consistency of measurement, and validity, the accuracy of measurement, are two critical aspects to consider when evaluating the measurement tools and data used in quantitative research. Often reliability, and less frequently validity, are expressed via correlation coefficients. Correlation coefficients indicate the direction and degree of a relationship among sets of scores. Researchers present evidence for test reliability by demonstrating the (a) consistency of scores over time (test-retest reliability), (b) internal consistency of test items (e.g., via split-half reliability, Cronbach's alpha, omega), (c) consistency of scores across equivalent versions of a test administered to the same group (parallel forms reliability), or (d) consistency and agreement of scores among raters or judges (interrater reliability). The validity of a measure for use in any particular study is determined by evaluating (a) face validity, (b) content validity, (c) criterion validity (i.e., concurrent validity, predictive validity), (d) construct validity, and/or (e) consequential validity. A measurement tool cannot be valid if it is not reliable. To familiarize yourself with the concepts of measurement, read through examples of quantitative research. As you read, pay particular attention to how reliability and validity were determined, what forms of measurement were used, and how the researcher presents evidence for the reliability and validity of their measurement tools.

As you may have gathered, developing useful, reliable, and valid measurement tools for research can be quite an intensive process. Demonstrating evidence for the reliability and validity of a new measure can entail conducting many studies devoted to that purpose alone. In fact, some music education researchers have focused a good deal of their research activities on the development of measurement tools. See, for example, the work Bergee (1995, 2015) and colleagues (Bergee & Rossin, 2019; Rossin & Bergee, 2021) have done toward developing a concert band rating scale or Wesolowski (2016, 2017) and colleagues' (Wesolowski et al., 2017) many studies of various rubrics and ratings scales that could be used to assess music learning. Generally speaking, beginning researchers often do not develop their own measures. Instead, it is much more common for researchers to search the literature for tools suitable to adopt for their own research or for tools that they can adapt for their research via minor alterations. However, it is important to reiterate that the reliability and validity of a measure are not static properties that accompany a tool from study to study. Therefore, all researchers are required to provide evidence for the reliability and validity of the measures they choose to use for the particular contexts and purposes of their studies.

Here are a few prompts that may be helpful for reviewing the main points of this chapter:

1. Give examples of how the terms "measurement," "test," "evaluation," and "assessment" can be used.
2. Give an example of data representing something relevant to music education for each of the four levels of measurement: nominal, ordinal, interval, and ratio.
3. Describe reliability and validity. Why are they important for evaluating and conducting research?
4. A correlation coefficient is often used to indicate reliability and validity. Although correlation coefficients are numbers, we must use words to describe them. How would you categorize a measurement tool if a researcher reported the following reliability coefficients: .49, .93, .72, .67, .88?
5. Choose a phenomenon that you would be interested in developing a measurement tool for. For your proposed tool:
   a. Describe a form of reliability evidence from among the common types that would be suitable for your measure: (a) consistency of scores over time, (b) internal consistency of test items, (c) consistency of scores across equivalent versions of a test administered to the same group, or (d) consistency and agreement of scores among raters or judges.
   b. Describe how you could provide two or three sources of validity evidence from the common types: (a) face validity, (b) content validity, (c) criterion validity (i.e., concurrent validity, predictive validity), (d) construct validity, and/or (e) consequential validity.

Important Terms for Review

Measurement is the process of quantifying information.

Nominal measurement is the labeling of categories with numbers that do not imply order or quantity (e.g., brass vs. woodwinds).

Ordinal measurement yields data that can be ordered but that do not communicate quantity (e.g., from first chair to last chair).

Interval measurement results in data in which distances are equal between points along the scale and which, therefore, communicate order and quantity (e.g., test scores).

Ratio measurement requires a scale with a true absolute zero value. It yields data in which distances are equal between points along the scale and ratios between values on the scale are preserved (e.g., duration in seconds).

Assessment is a data gathering process that appears in similar ways in both school and research settings.

Evaluation is the process of placing a value on a measurement or assessment.

Reliability refers to the consistency of measurement.

Validity is the degree to which a measurement tool measures what it claims to measure and whether the intended use of the scores yielded from the tool is appropriate.

References

Bergee, M. J. (1995). Primary and higher-order factors in a scale assessing concert band performance. *Bulletin of the Council for Research in Music Education, 126*, 1–14. https://www.jstor.org/stable/40318730

Bergee, M. J. (2003). Faculty interjudge reliability of music performance evaluation. *Journal of Research in Music Education, 51*(2), 137–150. https://doi.org/10.2307/3345847

Bergee, M. J. (2015). A theoretical structure of high school concert band performance. *Journal of Research in Music Education, 63*(2), 145–161. https://doi.org/10.1177/0022429415585959

Bergee, M. J., & Rossin, E. G. (2019). Development and validation of a scale assessing midlevel band performance: A mixed methods study. *Journal of Research in Music Education, 67*(2), 214–232. https://doi.org/10.1177/0022429418825144

Boyle, J. D., & Radocy, R. E. (1987). *Measurement and evaluation of musical experiences.* Schirmer Books.

Furr, R. M. (2021). *Psychometrics: An introduction.* Sage.

Gordon, E. E. (1984). *Instrument timbre preference test.* GIA Publishers.

Kardous, C., Themann, C., Morata, T., & Lotz, G. (2016). Understanding noise exposure limits: Occupational vs. general environmental noise. National Institute for Occupational Safety and Health (NIOSH) Science Blog. https://blogs.cdc.gov/niosh-science-blog/2016/02/08/noise/

Kenny, D. (2011). *The psychology of music performance anxiety.* Oxford University Press.

Miller, D. M., Miller, M. D., Linn, R. L., & Gronlund, N. E. (2021). *Measurement assessment in teaching* (11th ed.). Pearson.

Robinson Kurplus, S. E., & Stafford, M. E. (2005). *Testing and measurement: A user-friendly guide.* Sage.

Rossin, E. G., & Bergee, M. J. (2021). Cross-validation and application of a scale assessing school band performance. *Journal of Research in Music Education, 69*(1), 24–42. https://doi.org/10.1177/0022429420951789

Waldon, E. G. (2016). Measurement issues in objectivist research. In B. L. Wheeler & K. M Murphy (Eds.), *Music therapy research* (3rd ed., pp. 142–152). Barcelona Publishers.

Wesolowski, B. C. (2016). Assessing jazz big band performance: The development, validation, and application of a facet-factorial rating scale. *Psychology of Music, 44*(3), 324–339. https://doi.org/10.1177/0305735614567700

Wesolowski, B. C. (2017). A facet-factorial approach towards the development and validation of a jazz rhythm section performance rating scale. *International Journal of Music Education, 35*(1), 17–30. https://doi.org/10.1177/0255761415590524

Wesolowski, B. C., Amend, R. M., Barnstead, T. S., Edwards, A. S., Everhart, M., Goins, Q. R., Grogan, R. J., Herceg, A. M., Jenkins, S. I., Johns, P. M., McCarver, C. J., Schaps, R. E., Sorrell, G. W., & Williams, J. D. (2017). The development of a secondary-level solo wind instrument performance rubric using the multifaceted Rasch partial credit measurement model. *Journal of Research in Music Education, 65*(1), 95–119. https://doi.org/10.1177/0022429417694873

Williams, D. A. (1996). A study of the internal validity of the instrument timbre preference test. *Journal of Research in Music Education, 44*(3), 268–277. https://doi.org/10.2307/3345599

16
Descriptive Statistics

Chapter Preview

The purpose of this chapter is to learn about descriptive statistics, that is, how numbers are used to summarize and describe data gathered in quantitative research. Prior to analysis, it's important to look at the values in your database (i.e., spreadsheet) and examine it for data entry errors or anomalies. Next, you should always visualize your data via plots and summarize the data by calculating measures of frequency, central tendency, and variability. For interval-/ratio-level data, you can also create histograms and box plots to visualize frequency distributions. The mean, median, and mode are measures of central tendency that will help you understand the most "representative" or "typical" single value. In a normal distribution (i.e., bell curve), the mean, median, and mode are the same. Interval-/ratio-level data are also often described according to the degree to which the values follow the shape of normal distribution properties. Measures of variability provide the degree of spread among values in a distribution. These include minimum/maximum values, range, variance, standard deviation, and quartiles. When data do not conform to a normal distribution, indices other than the mean and standard deviation, such as the median, mode, minimum, maximum, range, and quartiles, should be used to describe the central tendency and variability of that variable. Frequency counts and percentages are often used to summarize ordinal- and nominal-level data, and bar plots are used to visualize such data.

Introduction

Descriptive statistics are used to summarize and describe numerical data gathered in quantitative research. Numerical data in research can come from many sources: numbers of participants in a particular category, questionnaire responses, observed behaviors, test scores, judges' ratings, acoustical features of a musical performance, and so on. When analyzing and reporting quantitative data, we can use descriptive statistics to highlight important features and/or patterns in our data so that they can be easily understood by others. Sometimes the most impactful way to summarize and present data is with graphic visualizations rather than numbers. Ultimately, descriptive statistics and graphs are tools we can use to communicate the salient features of our data to others. In this chapter we introduce methods for visualizing and summarizing data yielded from scalar (i.e., interval- or ratio-level), ordinal, and nominal variables. However, prior to embarking on an analysis, it is important to "get to know" your data and screen them for any errors.

Data Screening

A first step toward screening your data for errors or anomalies is to simply examine the raw values in a database, in other words, a spreadsheet. The most typical way to arrange data in a spreadsheet is with columns representing variables (e.g., age or grade level) and rows representing cases (i.e., participants). (See Appendix B for a description of how to arrange data in a spreadsheet and examples of how to code data from various sources.) It is important to identify any miscoded or mislabeled values or any values that are out of the possible range of the measurement tools used (e.g., a value of 6 erroneously inputted for a questionnaire item that has response options ranging only from 1 to 5). Cases with extreme values for a variable (i.e., outliers) are also important to note. Although extreme values are certainly possible and not necessarily problematic, they could also reflect a mistake in measurement, scoring, or coding. It is necessary to note any missing values or duplicate values which could be the result of a case whose data were entered twice. If missing values can be assumed to have occurred at random, then they can generally be ignored. However, often missing values occur for systematic reasons (e.g., segments of a population being unwilling to reveal information or being more likely to drop out of a study for some reason), and therefore they should be reported and dealt with by some other means.[1] Examining the data set could also reveal unusual cases, such as those in which the same response was recorded for all items within a particular set (e.g., all ratings of 1) or response patterns that indicate a participant zigzagged back and forth across items in a questionnaire, both of which would suggest disingenuous responses. Although looking at raw values in a spreadsheet can be dizzying if your data set includes many cases and/or many variables, it's important to screen them for potential problems.

Data for the Examples in This Chapter

The data used in this chapter are a slightly altered portion of those gathered in a research study by Miksza and Tan (2015, p. 165), the purpose of which was

> to examine whether students' reports of practice efficiency, flow during practicing, and self-efficacy for practicing self-regulation varied as a function of reports of (1) their own tendencies toward self-evaluation, (2) their knowledge of practice strategies, (3) their tendencies to exhibit grit, (4) their self-regulatory tendencies to be self-reflective when practicing, and (5) their teachers' methods of instruction in practicing.

---

[1] A discussion of sophisticated methods for dealing with substantive issues of missing data is beyond the scope of this text. Please see Little and Rubin (2019) for an in-depth presentation of the most current methods for dealing with missing data.

Table 16.1 Variables adapted from Miksza & Tan (2015) for use in the examples in this chapter

Variable Name (*Label*)	Numerical Values Possible (*Measurement Level*)
1. age (*Participant's current age*)	Participants were free to enter their age (*scalar, ratio level*)
2. flow_scale (*Flow while practicing scale score*)	A score derived from the average of ratings to 9 items regarding how often participants experienced flow (e.g., a state of effortless absorption and intense concentration) while practicing, with a possible range of 1, indicating infrequent flow, to 5, indicating very frequent flow (*scalar, interval level*)
3. practice_efficiency_rating (*Practice efficiency rating item*)	A rating of how much participants felt their practicing was efficient, with a possible range of 1, not at all efficient, to 7, extremely efficient (*ordinal level*)
4. degree (*Participant's degree program*)	Eight category codes created from participants' open-ended response: BA, BM, BME, MA, MM, DMA, PhD, and non-music (*nominal level*)
5. graduate_undergraduate_status (*Whether participant is an undergraduate or graduate student*)	Two category codes to indicate graduate or undergraduate student status (*nominal level*)

The data are from 170 of the college/university musicians who took part in Miksza and Tan's (2015) research and are available as an online supplement to this chapter (see item 4, Chapter 16 on the Companion website ▶). We will refer to several variables from this data set to illustrate how descriptive statistics and graphs can be used to summarize and describe scalar (i.e., interval or ratio), ordinal, and nominal data (see Table 16.1). Video demonstrations for conducting the analyses described in this chapter using the Statistical Package for the Social Sciences (SPSS) are also available as online supplements (see items 2 and 3, Chapter 16 on the Companion website ▶).[2]

Summarizing Ratio- or Interval-Level Data (Scalar Data)

Frequency

A very simple way to summarize the data of any variable, which also happens to be an additional method for screening data, is to arrange the data according to a frequency distribution. A frequency distribution is a depiction, either in a table or

---

[2] SPSS is a proprietary software package that is often available to students via a college or university site license. Those looking for an alternative could try the free open-source programs Jamovi (www.jamovi.org) or JASP (www.jasp-stats.org) instead. These free alternatives have many of the same features as SPSS, although not all analysis tasks are as convenient to execute and the graphing functions are a bit more difficult to manipulate.

in a graph, of how many instances (i.e., the frequency) of each value are present in the data. When presented in a table, a frequency distribution is essentially an ordered listing of observed data values for a variable and how many of each were present in the data. For example, a frequency distribution of the flow_scale variable values is presented in Table 16.2. In this table you can see each of the distinct values of the participants' flow_scale results in the data set (i.e., "Value" column), how many of each value was present (i.e., "Frequency" column), the percentage of the values each distinct value represents (i.e., "Percentage"), and the cumulative percentage that falls at or below each distinct value (i.e., "Cumulative Percentage"

Table 16.2 Frequency distribution of flow_scale values

Value	Frequency	Percentage	Cumulative Percentage
1.67	1	0.6	0.6
2.22	1	0.6	1.2
2.56	1	0.6	1.8
2.67	3	1.8	3.5
2.78	2	1.2	4.7
2.89	3	1.8	6.5
3.00	2	1.2	7.6
3.11	8	4.7	12.4
3.22	8	4.7	17.1
3.33	18	10.6	27.6
3.44	15	8.8	36.5
3.56	12	7.1	43.5
3.67	14	8.2	51.8
3.78	15	8.8	60.6
3.89	13	7.6	68.2
4.00	15	8.8	77.1
4.11	11	6.5	83.5
4.22	4	2.4	85.9
4.33	8	4.7	90.6
4.44	4	2.4	92.9
4.56	6	3.5	96.5
4.67	2	1.2	97.6
4.78	1	0.6	98.2
5.00	3	1.8	100.0
Total	**170**	**100**	**100.0**

Value: an average of 9 item ratings of how often participants experienced flow during a practice session. **Frequency**: the number of participants who had the same value. **Percentage**: the percentage each frequency represents of all the scores. **Cumulative Percentage**: the total percentage of all the frequencies to this point. **Example**: On average, participants rated their experience of flow as a 3.33 (out of 5). Eighteen participants obtained this same score, which represented a total of 10.6% of all the reported scores; 27.6% of all the scores were 3.33 or below.

column). By looking at the table, we can see that the most common value (though not by far) was 3.33, with 18 different people having that score, and that this value represented 10.6% of the 170 values. Interestingly, we can also see that only 7.6% of the values were at the magnitude of 3 or less, suggesting that it was relatively rare for participants not to experience flow while practicing—given that the possible range of the flow_scale variable was 1, indicating infrequent flow, to 5, indicating very frequent flow.

Visualization

Visualizing data is an essential step in any quantitative research project since there are things that can become apparent in data when viewed on a graph that could otherwise be obscured when looking just at raw values or summary statistics. Scalar data can be effectively visualized via histograms and box plots. A histogram is like a simple bar graph, except that the bars in the plot can represent how many instances there are of a range of values—referred to as bins of values. In Figure 16.1, Panel a is a histogram of the flow_scale variable values and Panel b is a histogram of the age variable values. A histogram can help to identify extreme values and provide a sense of where values seem to bunch together (i.e., the sections with the highest

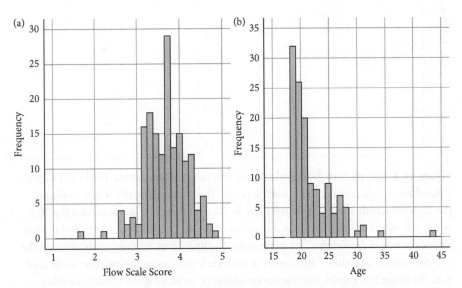

Figure 16.1 Histograms of flow_scale values and age distributions of participants. a. A histogram showing the distribution of flow_scale values. Most values fall between 3 and 4.5; few values were found at the lowest and highest extremes of the range. b. A histogram indicating the distribution of ages of participants. Most of the participants were 18–21 years of age. Note that bars are called "bins of value" and represent how many instances there are of a range of values, not specific, discrete values.

bins). Compare the two histograms and notice how different the distributions of the flow_scale and age variables appear. It's clear that there is much more bunching of values in the lower end of the range of the age variable, whereas there the values of the flow_scale variable are slightly bunched toward the higher end of its range. We will discuss how skewness and kurtosis statistics can be used to summarize various distribution shapes in the sections below.

In Figure 16.2, Panel a is a box plot (sometimes called a "box and whiskers" plot) of the flow_scale variable values and Panel b is a box plot of the age variable values. A box plot depicts scalar variables according to ranges of the values that comprise certain percentiles, which themselves refer to the percentage of values in a distribution that fall at or below a given value. The features of the box plot in Figure 16.2 are markers (sometimes called "whiskers") for the minimum and maximum values and markers for the values that fall at the 25th, 50th (i.e., median), and 75th percentile, which are indicated via a box. The span of values between the 25th and 75th percentiles is the interquartile range. Some statistics programs produce box

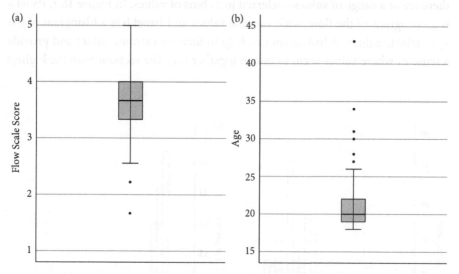

Figure 16.2 Box plots of flow_scale values and range of age values. The box (i.e., gray-shaded area) indicates the interquartile range. The bottom line of the box indicates the 25th percentile value; the heavier line in the middle of the box indicates the 50th percentile or the median (half the scores fall above and below this point); and the top line of the box indicates the 75th percentile. The line extending vertically through the box connects the top line (the marker or whisker), indicating the maximum value of 5, to the lower line (again, the marker or whisker), indicating the minimum value. Because there are outliers, the lower marker is not the literal observed minimum flow_scale value but the smallest value within 1.5 times the interquartile range below the 25th percentile. a. The two black dots below the box are outlier values. b. Given the range of age values, the span of values between the 25th and 75th percentile is fairly narrow. Also, there are several outliers at the higher end of the range, indicating that six participants were older than most of the other participants.

plots that also highlight outlier values, which are then plotted as points beyond the markers for the minimum and maximum values—meaning that those markers no longer represent the actual observed minimum and maximum values (as is the case in Figure 16.2).[3] Once again, notice the differences in the distributions of the flow_scale and age variables that become apparent when comparing the two plots.

Central Tendency

It is helpful to summarize distributions of scalar variable values according to what could be considered the most "representative" or most "typical" single value. Researchers use what are referred to as measures of central tendency to do this, in other words, the mean, median, and mode of a distribution. The mean is simply the arithmetic average of the values of a variable. Researchers sometimes indicate the mean with the symbols M or $\bar{X}$ in an article text, tables, and/or printed formulas. You can calculate the mean by adding up all the values you have and dividing the total by the number of values. The mean of the flow_scale variable is 3.70. It's important to interpret the mean in relation to the possible range of values for a given variable. For example, the value 3.70 doesn't mean anything in particular without a point of reference. However, when considered in the context of a possible flow_scale range of 1 to 5, then 3.70 is indicative of a relatively frequent experience of flow.

The median is the middle point in a range of values, the point in a range of values at which 50% of the values fall below and 50% of the values fall above. When there is an odd number of values in a distribution, the middle score will be the median. If there is an even number of values, we interpolate the median by finding a score halfway between the two middle scores (i.e., we take the average of the two middle scores). The distribution of flow_scale scores is comprised of an even number of values (i.e., 170 values). As such we would arrange our 170 values in order from least to greatest, identify the middle two values (from position 85 and 86 out of 170), and average them together to find that the median is 3.66.

The mode is simply the most common score in a distribution. The mode of the flow_scale variable is 3.33 with 18 occurrences. There can be more than one mode or no mode at all. If no score appears more frequently than another score in a distribution, there is no mode. Distributions can also have more than one mode. Multimodal distributions are those in which no single value is the most frequently occurring. For example, in a bimodal distribution, two values are the most frequently occurring. If there were three more instances of the value 3.48 in the flow_scale scores, then 3.33 and 3.48 would both have 18 occurrences, and the distribution could be described as bimodal.

---

[3] Outliers are often calculated as any value that falls beyond 1.5 times the interquartile range below the 25th percentile or above the 75th percentile. When outliers are present in a box plot, the markers at the ends of the plot typically indicate the smallest and largest values within 1.5 times the interquartile range below the 25th percentile or above the 75th percentile.

Variability

Although a single estimate of the most representative or typical value in a distribution can be helpful for summarizing the data, it is critical to have a sense of the degree of spread among values in a distribution. The descriptive statistics commonly used by researchers as measures of variability or dispersion include minimum/maximum values, the range, the variance, and the standard deviation. The minimum and maximum values are, literally, the smallest and greatest observed value in a distribution, respectively, whereas the *range* of a distribution is the difference between the maximum and minimum values. The maximum observed value of the flow_scale variable is 5.00 and the minimum value is 1.67, therefore, the range is 3.33 (i.e., 5.00–1.67). These three measures—minimum, maximum, and range—provide a simple and clear sense of how widely the data are distributed by characterizing the spread of the data with the lowest and highest values. However, these statistics do not provide much detail regarding the nature of the spread throughout the observed range of the values.

In contrast, the variance and the standard deviation are measures of the average amount of deviation from the mean within a distribution. As such, these statistics can be more informative than the minimum, maximum, and range. For example, it is possible that two variables could have very similar ranges but still have very different degrees of variability that would not be evident in minimum, maximum, or range values. Compare Panels a and b in Figure 16.3 and note how there is clearly

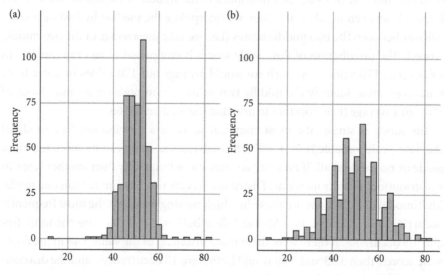

Figure 16.3 These two histograms, based on fictitious data, demonstrate contrasting score distributions that have the same range of values but different degrees of variability. The scores in Panel **a** are more closely grouped around the middle (i.e., relatively less variability), while the scores in Panel **b** are more widely dispersed (i.e., relatively more variability).

more variability about the mean among the values in Panel b when compared to Panel a despite the two distributions having identical ranges. Also, as will be described below, when a distribution is relatively normal in shape, the standard deviation can be used to estimate approximate proportions of the values that fall within certain distances from the mean (see Figure 16.4, Panel a).

The formula for calculating variance involves subtracting each value in a distribution from the mean, squaring the differences that result, summing those squared differences, and then dividing by the number of values in the distribution minus 1. In other words, the variance is the adjusted average squared difference between each value and the mean. The variances of distributions of values measured on the same scale can be compared; larger variance numbers indicate more variability and vice versa. However, the variance values will be based on the "squared" deviation from the mean, so the number itself will not be interpretable with respect to the scale of the original value. Because of this interpretational issue, variance values are rarely discussed except as values in the context of other, more advanced statistical procedures (see, for example, the discussion of analysis of variance in Chapter 18).

Fortunately, and in contrast to variance, the standard deviation is a number that is expressed within the units of the original values (as opposed to squared units). The steps for calculating the standard deviation are the same as for calculating the variance, except once you finish the steps and arrive at a value for the variance, you then take the square root of that value to arrive at the standard deviation. More simply put, the standard deviation is the square root of the variance. By taking the square root of the variance, you solve the problem of interpretation and arrive at a measure of variability in a distribution that can be interpreted in terms of units of the scale the values are in. For example, the standard deviation of the flow_scale variable is 0.52, which can be interpreted as roughly half a point on the possible flow_scale measure that has a possible range of 1.00 to 5.00. The standard deviation provides a much more sensible number to deal with when describing the variability within a distribution of values; more on how to use the standard deviation will be presented shortly.

An additional method for examining the variability of a distribution is to examine quartile values. As described above when discussing the features of a box plot, quartiles are the values at the 25th, 50th, and 75th percentiles (see Figure 16.2). The quartiles are the values at or below which each respective percentage of the distribution falls. For example, the 25th, 50th, and 75th percentiles of the flow_scale variable distribution are 3.33, 3.67, and 4.00, respectively. We also know from the earlier discussion that the minimum value is 1.67 and the maximum value is 5.00. Therefore, we can say that the lowest 25% of values in the distribution fall between 1.67 and 3.33, 50% of the values in the distribution fall between 1.67 and 3.67, 75% of the values in the distribution fall between 1.67 and 4.00, and 100% of the values fall at or below 5.00. We could also reference the interquartile range—the span of values between the 25th and 75th percentiles—when describing the variability of

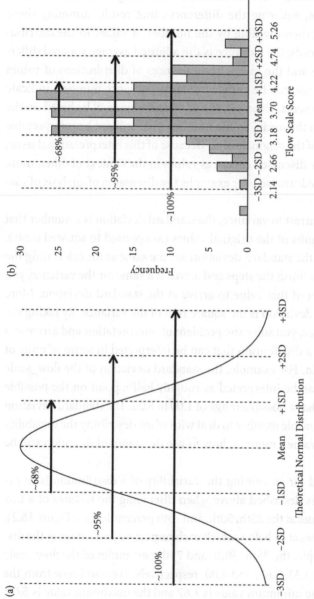

Figure 16.4 Panel a presents a theoretical normal distribution in which the mean, median, and mode are all the same value. At the bottom of the distribution we can see that the vertical dashed lines indicate 1, 2, and 3 standard deviations above and below the mean. The black arrows indicate that approximately (shown by the tilde, or ~) 100% of the scores fall between ± (plus or minus) 3 SDs; approximately 95% of the scores fall between ± 2 SDs; and approximately 68% of the scores fall between ± 1 SD. Panel b presents a histogram of the flow_scale scores. The SD scores given below are based on a SD of 0.52, which you can obtain by subtracting the mean (3.70) from +1 SD (4.22), or any SD from the one above. Knowing this, you can determine the range of approximately 100%, 95%, or 68% of the scores, as shown by the black arrows.

the distribution. In other words, the "middle" half (i.e., 50%) of the values in the distribution falls between 3.33 and 4.00.

Distributional Properties

Scalar data values are often described according to the degree to which the values follow the shape and exhibit the properties of a normal distribution. A normal distribution is sometimes called a bell curve, because the shape of a histogram representing a normal distribution is similar to that of a bell (see Figure 16.4, Panel a). Technically, a normal distribution is derived from a specific mathematical function. Because discussion of this formula is beyond the scope of this book, we will restrict our discussion of the normal distribution to its practical use for describing scalar data. In a theoretical normal distribution, the mean, median, and mode are all the same value, and exactly 50% of the values fall within each half of the distribution. Moreover, the standard deviation value can be used for very specific interpretations when a distribution is roughly normal. For example, in a normal distribution approximately 68% of the values will fall within 1 standard deviation above and below the mean, approximately 95% of the values will fall within 2 standard deviations above and below the mean, and approximately 99% of the values will fall within 3 standard deviations above and below the mean. Therefore, if you find that a distribution of scalar values is normal, you can find out a great deal about the variability of the values with knowledge of the mean and standard deviation.

For example, we know that the mean of the flow_scale variable is 3.70 and the standard deviation 0.52. Also, if we look at a histogram for this variable (Figure 16.4, Panel b), we can see that there is somewhat of a bell shape to the distribution, suggesting that, although not perfectly, it resembles a normal distribution. Therefore, we can estimate that (a) roughly 68% of the values will fall between 1 standard deviation below and above the mean, that is, 3.70 − 0.52 = 3.18 and 3.70 + 0.52 = 4.22; (b) roughly 95% of the values will fall between 2 standard deviations below and above the mean, that is, 3.70 − 0.52 − 0.52 = 2.66 and 3.70 + 0.52 + 0.52 = 4.74, and (c) roughly 99% of the values will fall between 3 standard deviations below and above the mean, that is, 3.70 − 0.52 − 0.52 − 0.52 = 2.14 and 3.70 + 0.52 + 0.52 + 0.52 = 5.26. Notice that the value of 5.26—3 standard deviations above the mean—is beyond the possible range of the flow_scale, which is 5. This occurs because, as we noted, the distribution is not perfectly normal but only approximately normal. Although the proportions of values falling within certain standard deviations from the mean aren't theoretically exact, the estimates that are possible to make with a mean and standard deviation when a distribution is nearly normal are still useful for describing the data.

However, if a distribution is not roughly normal in shape, then the interpretive benefits of the mean and standard deviation no longer apply since the mean may not be the best indicator of the most representative or typical value and the values will no longer be distributed in such predictable ways (i.e., 68% within 1 SD, 95% within 2 SDs, 99% within 3 SDs). Therefore, it would be more appropriate to use indices such as the median, mode, minimum, maximum, range, and quartiles when describing the central tendency and variability of a nonnormal distribution of scalar variables.

The terms "skewness" and "kurtosis" are used by researchers to describe how distributions of scalar values depart from relatively normal, bell curve shapes. Skewness refers to an excessive bunching of cases in a relatively low range of the values (i.e., positive skewness) or a high range of values (i.e., negative skewness) such that the shape of the distribution is not normal or bell-shaped (see Figure 16.5). When used with reference to skewness, the positive and negative adjectives refer to the "tail" of the distribution, that is, the longer, flatter part of the shape. For example, a bunching of scores in the low range of a distribution leaves a long flat "tail" of the distribution in the "positive" (i.e., high) end of the range; thus, it is described as positive skewness. In contrast, a bunching of scores in the high range of a distribution leaves a long flat "tail" of the distribution in the "negative" (i.e., low) end of the range; thus, it is described as negative skewness. The mean, median, and mode are not equal when a distribution is skewed. When a distribution is positively skewed and scores are bunched at the low end of a distribution, the mode and median will be less than the mean, whereas when a distribution is negatively skewed and scores are bunched at the high end of a distribution, the mode and median will be greater than the mean. Kurtosis refers the "peakedness" of a distribution; positive kurtosis is indicative of distributions that have a more exaggerated peak than the normal distribution shape (technically called a "leptokurtic" distribution), whereas negative kurtosis is indicative of a distribution that is relatively flatter (technically called "platykurtic") or even inverted with respect to the shape of the normal distribution (see Figure 16.5).

Skewness and kurtosis values can be used to determine whether or not a distribution can be considered approximately normal when interpreting scalar data. The statistics themselves involve very complicated calculations, but we do not need to discuss that here. Fortunately, statistics programs can produce them with a click of a button, and they are quite simple to interpret. Skewness and kurtosis values of 0 indicate the complete absence of each and, therefore, that a distribution is perfectly normal.[4] As you might imagine, real data gathered in the world (as opposed to data generated with mathematical models) are practically never perfectly normal. However, skewness and kurtosis values that are within the range of −1.00 to +1.00 suggest that a distribution can generally be interpreted as

---

[4] Technically, the value that statistical programs compute is referred to as "excess kurtosis." The literal kurtosis value of the normal distribution is actually +3.00. However, we refer to excess kurtosis with the single term "kurtosis" to avoid confusion and so that readers can ultimately interpret the values that statistical programs compute accurately.

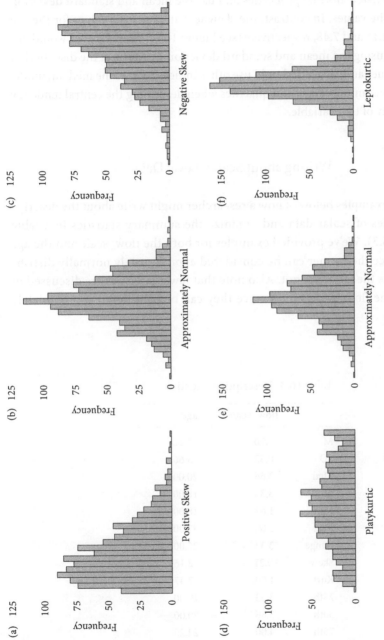

Figure 16.5 Panel a. This histogram has a positive skew because the mode and median are less distributed more on the low end than the high. Panel c is the opposite; it has a negative skew, with scores bunched at the high end and the mode and median higher than the mean. Panel d is platykurtic, meaning that scores are distributed more equally than in a normal distribution. Panel f is leptokurtic, meaning that scores have an exaggerated peak compared to a normal curve. Panels b and e are approximately normal distributions.

approximately normal; values that exceed that range (i.e., less than −1.00 or greater than +1.00) should not be considered even approximately normal. For example, the skewness and kurtosis values of the flow_scale variable are −0.27 and 1.00, respectively. As such, we can consider the distribution of flow_scale variables to have approximately normal properties and use the mean and standard deviation to interpret the values. In contrast, the skewness and kurtosis values for the age variable are 2.16 and 7.48, respectively (see Figure 16.1). Therefore, we would not benefit from using the mean and standard deviation to interpret the distribution of the age values and, instead, should use other indices such as the median, mode, minimum, maximum, range, and quartiles when describing the central tendency and variability of that variable.

Writing about Scalar-Level Data

We provide examples below of how a researcher might write about the descriptive properties of scalar data and organize the summary statistics in a table (see Table 16.3). We've provided examples for both the flow_scale and the age variables since the former can be considered approximately normally distributed, whereas the latter cannot. Also note that fewer statistics are discussed in relation to the flow_scale values since they can be considered approximately normal.

Table 16.3 Descriptive statistics

	flow_scale	age
M	3.70	21.12
SD	0.52	3.66
Med	3.66	20.00
Mode	3.33	18.00
Min	1.67	18.00
Max	5.00	43.00
Range	3.33	25.00
Skew	−0.21	2.16
Kurt	1.00	7.47
25th	3.33	19.00
50th	3.66	20.00
75th	4.00	22.25

Note: M = mean, SD = standard deviation, Med = median, Min = minimum, Max = maximum, $Skew$ = skewness, $Kurt$ = kurtosis, $25th$ = 25th percentile, $50th$ = 50th percentile, and $75th$ = 75th percentile.

The participants' mean age was 21.12 years and the most frequently reported age was 18 years. There was a moderate amount of variation across participants given the standard deviation value of 3.66 and the 25th percentile, median, and 75th percentile of 19.00, 20.00, and 22.23, respectively. However, the range of responses was somewhat large with 18 years being the youngest participant's age and 43 years being the oldest participant's age. The distribution of participants' ages was positively skewed (2.16) with a great deal of kurtosis (7.47).

The mean of the participants' flow_scale reports was 3.70, suggesting that flow was experienced relatively often given that the possible range of values on the scale was 1.00 to 5.00. The scores were moderately varied with a standard deviation of 0.52 and an observed range of values of 3.33. The skewness and kurtosis values fall within the range of −1 and +1, and therefore do not suggest extreme departures from normality.

Summarizing Ordinal-Level and Nominal-Level Data

In comparison to scalar (i.e., interval- and ratio-level) variables, ordinal- and nominal-level variables are much simpler to summarize. Since equivalent distances cannot be assumed between scale points for ordinal data and since nominal values have no quantitative properties whatsoever, we are generally restricted in how we can summarize these types of data. Consider the ordinal variable practice_efficiency_rating and the nominal variable degree among our example variables described in Table 16.2. The practice_efficiency_rating variable represents a single rating scale item with possible response options ranging from 1, *not at all efficient*, to 7, *extremely efficient*. To summarize this variable, we could display the frequencies and percentages of participants' responses according to each possible scale point, as is displayed in Table 16.4. We could also describe the variability of an ordinal variable according to the minimum, maximum, and range of response options that were chosen.

The degree variable consists of eight possible category codes created from participants' open-ended response: BA, BM, BME, MA, MM, DMA, PhD, and non-music. To summarize this variable, our only options are to display the frequencies and percentages of participants' responses according to each category,

Table 16.4 Practice efficiency rating responses

	\multicolumn{7}{c}{Practice Efficiency Rating}
	1	2	3	4	5	6	7
Frequency	2	6	10	32	52	45	19
Percentage	1.2	3.6	6.0	19.3	31.3	27.1	11.4

Table 16.5 Degree type responses

	\multicolumn{8}{c}{Degree Types}
	BA	BM	BME	MA	MM	DMA	PhD	NonMusic
Frequency	8	62	58	1	15	20	2	4
Percentage	4.7	36.5	34.1	0.6	8.8	11.8	1.2	2.4

as is displayed in Table 16.5. Reporting the proportions of the participants who responded with each response option for either of these variables would simply involve transforming the percentages for each response type to proportions by dividing each by 100.

Cross-Tabulation

It can be informative to cross-tabulate multiple ordinal- or nominal-level variables. For example, it might be interesting to summarize how the responses to the practice_efficiency_rating item vary as a function of whether the participants were undergraduate or graduate students, which is also a variable in our example data set (i.e., graduate_undergraduate_status). To do so, a researcher would create a table that depicts every possible combination of the seven rating options for the practice_efficiency_rating item and the two categories of the graduate_undergraduate_ status variable, as we have done in Table 16.6, and then examine the frequencies, percentages, and/or proportions for each combination of responses.

Table 16.6 Cross-tabulation of practice efficiency ratings and undergraduate vs. graduate student status

	\multicolumn{7}{c}{Practice Efficiency Rating}
	1	2	3	4	5	6	7
Undergraduate	1 (.8)	6 (4.7)	8 (6.3)	25 (19.5)	42 (32.8)	31 (24.2)	15 (11.7)
Graduate	1 (2.6)	0 (0)	2 (5.3)	7 (18.4)	10 (26.3)	14 (36.8)	4 (10.5)
Total	2 (1.2)	6 (3.6)	10 (6.0)	32 (19.3)	52 (31.3)	45 (27.1)	19 (11.4)

Note: Values outside parentheses are frequencies and values inside parentheses are percentages.

Visualization

Visualizing ordinal- and nominal-level data is also fairly straightforward. Both variable types are often visualized with bar plots. A bar plot depicts the frequency of each category or value that is present in a nominal or ordinal variable, respectively (see Figure 16.6, Panels a and b). In contrast to a histogram, in which the bars represent bins of a range of values, each bar in a bar plot represents a discrete value, and the height of each bar represents the frequency for each value. Nominal-level variables are also sometimes visualized with pie charts; however, it can be difficult to intuit quantities from pie charts since they rely on an individual comparing relevant amounts of area occupied by each slice of the pie to each other rather than to a numerical axis, as is the case with a bar plot. Cross-tabulations of ordinal and/or nominal variables can be visualized effectively with clustered bar charts (see Figure 16.7).

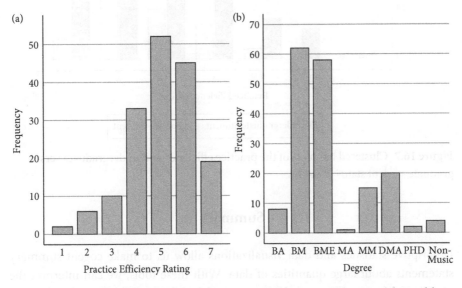

Figure 16.6 Bar plots of the practice efficiency and degree variables. Note that unlike a histogram, bar graphs indicate the number of instances or frequency of specific numbers or categories.

Writing about Ordinal- and Nominal-Level Data

We provide examples below of how a researcher might summarize and visualize the descriptive properties of ordinal- and nominal-level data with a written excerpt drawing from the values generated by cross-tabulating the practice_efficiency_rating and graduate_undergraduate_status variables depicted in Table 16.6 and Figure 16.7.

> Overall, most participants reported relatively efficient practicing with nearly 70% responding with a rating of 5, 6, or 7 on the scale of 1, *not at all efficient,* to 7, *extremely efficient*. Accordingly, very few (i.e., only 2, 1.2%) participants reported being not at all efficient in their practicing. These trends were apparent for both undergraduate and graduate student participants, although a slightly greater percentage of graduate students (73.6%) responded with a rating of 5, 6, or 7 than undergraduate students (68.7%).

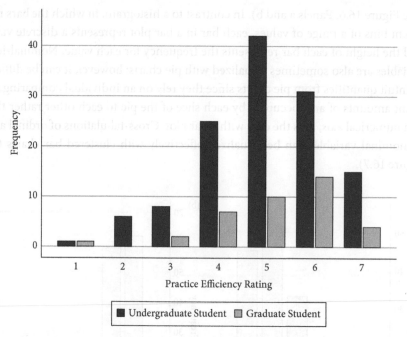

Figure 16.7 Clustered bar plots of the practice efficiency and undergraduate versus graduate student status variables.

Summary

Descriptive statistics and data visualizations allow us to make cogent summary statements about large quantities of data. With these tools, we can interpret the meaningful features (e.g., trends, patterns) of data distributions. It is important to use the descriptive statistics and types of plots that best fit the type of data that your variables represent. Scalar data can be summarized according to frequencies, several indices of central tendency (i.e., mean, median, mode), several indices of variability (i.e., minimum, maximum, range, variance, standard deviation, quartiles), and distribution shape (e.g., skewness and kurtosis). Ordinal data can be summarized according to frequencies, percentages, and proportions of response options, as well as via basic indices of variability such as minimum, maximum, and range. However, nominal data values do not represent quantities in any way and, therefore, should be summarized according to frequencies, percentages, and proportions of participants within each category. Readers interested in more information about descriptive statistical analyses could consult any number of introductory statistics textbooks. Miksza and Elpus's (2018) book on foundational and advanced concepts for quantitative research in music education is a particularly relevant source. Field's (2016) text *An Adventure in Statistics* includes an approachable introduction to statistical analysis in general. In addition, Jaeger's (1990) book *Statistics: A Spectator Sport* presents many of the statistical methods discussed in this book in a clear manner with minimal reference to computation.

Working through the following questions will give you a good way to determine your level of understanding of descriptive statistics:

1. How can descriptive statistics be of use to researchers?
2. Explain the measures of central tendency: the mean, median, and mode.
3. Explain the measures of variability: the range, minimum and maximum score, variance, standard deviation, and quartiles.
4. Why is it important to know both the measures of central tendency and the measures of variability? What could happen if you knew only one and not the other?
5. Draw pictures of histograms that illustrate skewness and kurtosis and explain what they mean to someone who has not heard of these terms before.
6. Generate a fictitious set of data with the online application that is linked in the online supplement associated with this chapter (see the link titled "Supplemental Web Apps for Exploring Statistical Concepts", Chapter 16 on the Companion website ▶). Consult the videos on how to use SPSS for descriptive analyses that is linked in the online supplement associated with this chapter and conduct the following analyses (see items 2, 3, and 4, Chapter 16 on the Companion website ▶):
   a. For the scalar variables: mean, median, mode, minimum, maximum, range, standard deviation, skewness, kurtosis, quartiles.
   b. For the ordinal variables: frequencies.
   c. For the nominal variables: frequencies.

   Also consult the videos on how to use SPSS for visualizing data linked in the online supplement associated with this chapter and create the following plots (see items 2, 3, and 4, Chapter 16 on the Companion website ▶):
   a. For the scalar variables: histogram, box plot.
   b. For the ordinal variables: bar plot.
   c. For the nominal variables: bar plot, pie chart.
7. Identify a table with descriptive statistics in a quantitative research article of your choosing. Practice summarizing the findings in your own words and compare your summary to that of the article's author.

Important Terms for Review

A *frequency distribution* is an ordered depiction, either in a table or in a graph, of how many instances (i.e., the frequency) of each value are present in the data.

Percentile refers to the percentage of values in a distribution that fall at or below a given value.

A *histogram* depicts the frequencies of values for interval- and ratio-level data (e.g., "scalar" data). In contrast to a bar plot, the bars in a histogram represent how many instances there are of a range of values—referred to as "bins of values."

A *box plot* can also be used to depict the frequencies of values for interval- and ratio-level data (e.g., "scalar" data). The features of a box plot are markers (sometimes called "whiskers") for the minimum and maximum values and markers for the values that fall at the 25th, 50th (i.e., median), and 75th percentiles, which are indicated via a box. The span of values between the 25th and 75th percentiles is referred to as the *interquartile range*.

A *bar plot* depicts the frequency of each category or value that is present in a nominal or ordinal variable, respectively. Each bar represents a discrete value, and the height of each bar represents the frequency for each value.

A *pie chart* is typically used to depict the frequency of each category present in a nominal variable. The frequency of each value is represented by the proportion, that is, a "slice of the pie," assigned to it.

Measures of central tendency are summary statistics that are used to get a sense of a most typical value that could best represent a distribution of values, such as the mean, median, and mode.

A *mean* is the arithmetic average of all the values in a distribution.

The *median* is the exact midpoint of all the values in a distribution, that is, the point at which 50% of the values fall below and 50% of the values fall above.

The *mode* is the most common value in a distribution, that is, the most frequently occurring value.

Measures of variability provide information about the variability within a distribution of values, that is, the degree of spread among the values. Indices for variability include minimum/maximum values, range, variance, standard deviation, and quartiles.

Minimum and *maximum values* are, literally, the smallest and greatest observed value in a distribution, respectively.

The *range* of a distribution is the difference between the maximum and minimum values.

Variance is a measure of how the values are dispersed from the mean. Mathematically, it is the adjusted average squared difference between each value and the mean.

The *standard deviation* is a measure of how the values are dispersed from the mean. In contrast to *variance*, the standard deviation is a number that is expressed within the units of the original values (as opposed to squared units). The standard deviation is calculated as the square root of the variance.

A *normal distribution*, sometimes called a bell curve, is a distribution derived from a particular mathematical function in which the mean, median, and mode are all the same value.

Skewness refers to an excessive bunching of cases in a relatively low range of the values (i.e., positive skewness) or a high range of values (i.e., negative skewness) such that the shape of the distribution is not "normal." The mean, median, and mode are not equal when a distribution is skewed.

Kurtosis refers to the "peakedness" of a distribution; positive kurtosis is indicative of distributions that have more of an exaggerated peak than the normal distribution shape (i.e., a leptokurtic distribution), whereas negative kurtosis is indicative of a distribution that is relatively flatter (i.e., platykurtic) or even inverted with respect to the shape of the normal distribution.

References

Field, A. (2016). *An adventure in statistics: The reality enigma*. Sage.
Jaeger, R. M. (1990). *Statistics: A spectator sport* (2nd ed.). Sage.
Little, R. J. A., & Rubin, D. B. (2019). *Statistical analysis with missing data* (3rd ed.). Wiley.
Miksza, P., & Elpus, K. (2018). *Design and analysis for quantitative research in music education*. Oxford University Press.
Miksza, P., & Tan, L. (2015). Predicting collegiate wind players' practice efficiency, flow, and self-efficacy for self-regulation: An exploratory study of relationships between teachers' instruction and students' practicing. *Journal of Research in Music Education, 63*(2), 162–179. https://doi.org/10.1177/0022429415583474

17
Correlational Statistics

Chapter Preview

The purpose of this chapter is to learn how correlational statistics are used to summarize and describe associations between variables. Although identifying correlations among variables can yield important insights, it is important to remember that correlation does not equal causation. That is, just because two variables are related does not mean that one necessarily caused the other. Much can be learned about the nature of a relationship between interval- and/or ratio-level variables by creating a scatterplot. The most common statistical tool used for investigating correlation (i.e., the direction and degree of a relationship) between two interval- or ratio-level variables is the Pearson Product Moment Coefficient (Pearson coefficient or Pearson's r). The coefficient can range from –1 to +1, with negative coefficients (i.e., less than 0) indicative of an inverse relationship and positive coefficients (i.e., greater than 0) indicative of a positive relationship. Common ranges are –.30 to 0 or 0 to .30, described as weak relationship; –.70 to –.30 or .30 to .70, described as moderate; and –1.0 to –.70 or .70 to 1.0, described as strong. Information about the visualization and statistical analysis of relationships using ordinal and nominal data is also given.

Introduction

Seeking patterns and associations among phenomena in the world is a natural human proclivity, and teachers and scholars are often curious about how various phenomena relevant to music teaching and learning may be related to each other. Such questions of association often make for very compelling research topics. As introduced in Chapter 12, quantitative correlational research is the systematic investigation of whether and how aspects of a phenomenon or phenomena are related to each other. Whereas descriptive analysis tools help us summarize the variability that may exist across a set of values, correlational analysis tools are used to explore the extent to which two or more sets of values are related to each other. For example, when collecting data from people, correlational statistics can be used to summarize whether the group's values on one variable vary in a way that is similar to how the group's values vary on another variable—in other words, whether a relationship exists between the variables. This straightforward case involving two variables is generally called a "bivariate relationship." Many techniques are available for simultaneously analyzing whether relationships exist among multiple variables; however, such techniques are beyond the scope of this book.[1]

Prior to moving ahead, it is important that we once again emphasize the fact that correlation does not equal causation. Even though it is often exciting to find a statistical correlation and tempting to interpret it as an indication of cause and effect, it is not reasonable to do so. In fact, now would be a good time to revisit Chapter 13 to review the criteria that must be in place before causal inferences can be drawn. That said, conducting correlational research is often a good step toward exploring causal mechanisms, since in order for a cause to yield an effect, the cause must at least be related to the effect. For example, researching what sorts of variables might be correlated with greater degrees of student retention in elective music courses would be an important precursor to designing an experiment that could determine whether certain teacher interventions could increase retention. After all, scholars and teachers alike need to be selective when choosing how they devote their time and resources. Preliminary correlational evidence that indicates which variables may influence retention and which may not would be very helpful to have prior to designing a rigorous experiment and/or enacting a pedagogical intervention.

In this chapter, we discuss the statistical tools that are most commonly used to describe the degree and direction of a relationship between two variables. We begin with methods appropriate for variables measured with interval or ratio (e.g., scalar) measurement scales and then move on to methods for ordinal and nominal variable types. The chapter concludes with a brief discussion of how inferential tests can be applied to correlation coefficients.

Please note that there are many statistical tools available for (a) investigating relationships among more than two variables (e.g., regression analyses), (b) identifying patterns of relationships among many variables (e.g., factor analysis), and (c) modeling complex systems of directional relationships among many variables (i.e., path analysis, structural equation modeling). In fact, researchers conducting correlational studies will almost always explore relationships that go beyond two variables. However, explanations of the techniques for such complex analyses are beyond the scope of this introductory text. Please consult the books referenced in Box 17.1 for more information about correlation in general and more advanced correlational techniques specifically.

Data for the Examples in This Chapter

The data used in this chapter are a slightly altered portion of those gathered in a research study by Miksza and Hime (2015, p. 178), the purpose of which was "to examine undergraduate music education and performance alumni's career path,

---

[1] See Miksza and Elpus (2018) for an explanation of how multivariate correlational methods can be applied in music education research.

> **Box 17.1 Additional Methodological Readings: Correlation Analysis**
>
> **Foundational and Advanced Methods**
>
> Field, A. (2016). *An adventure in statistics: The reality enigma*. Sage.
> Jaeger, R. M. (1990). *Statistics: A spectator sport* (2nd ed.). Sage.
> Miksza, P., & Elpus, K. (2018). *Design and analysis for quantitative research in music education*. Oxford University Press.
> Russell, J. A. (2018). *Statistics in music education research*. Oxford University Press.
> Tabachnik, B. G., & Fidell, L. S. (2019). *Using multivariate statistics* (7th ed.). Pearson.
>
> **Advanced Methods: Regression**
>
> Fox, J. (2008). *Applied regression analysis and generalized linear models*. Sage.
> Raudenbush, S. W., & Bryk, A. S. (2001). *Hierarchical linear models: Applications and data analysis methods* (2nd ed.). Sage.
>
> **Advanced Methods: Factor Analysis, Path Analysis, and Structural Equation Modeling**
>
> Gorsuch, R. L. (1983). *Factor analysis* (2nd ed.). Laurence Erlbaum Associates.
> Kline, R. B. (2015). *Principles and practices of structural equation modeling* (2nd ed.). Guilford Press.
> Loehlin, J. C. (2004). *Latent variable models: An introduction to factor, path, and structural equation modeling* (4th ed.). Erlbaum.

retrospective institutional satisfaction, and financial status." The data are from 584 individuals who responded to a nationwide, multi-institutional online survey conducted by the Strategic National Arts Alumni Project and are available as an online supplement to this chapter (see item 7, Chapter 17 on the Companion website ⓑ). We will refer to several variables from this data set to illustrate how to interpret graphs and correlation coefficients that can be used to describe relationships between scalar- (i.e., interval- or ratio-level), ordinal-, or nominal-level variables (see Table 17.1). Video demonstrations for conducting the analyses described in this chapter using the SPSS are also available as online supplements (see item 6, Chapter 17 on the Companion website ⓑ).[2]

---

[2] SPSS is a proprietary software package that is often available to students via a college or university site license. Those looking for an alternative could try the free open-source programs Jamovi (www.jamovi.org), JASP (www.jasp-stats.org), or VassarStats (http://vassarstats.net) instead. These free alternatives have many of the same features as SPSS, although not all analysis tasks are as convenient to execute and the graphing functions are a bit more difficult to manipulate.

Table 17.1 Variables adapted from Miksza & Hime (2015) for use in the examples in this chapter

Variable Name (*Label*)	Numerical Values Possible (*Measurement Level*)
1. participant_number (*A number as a label for each participant*)	A numerical code assigned to each participant (*nominal level*)
2. degree_program (*Participant's degree program*)	Two category codes to indicate whether a participant was a music education or a music performance major (*nominal level*)
3. institution_type (*Attended a public or private institution*)	Two category codes to indicate whether a participant attended a public or private institution (*nominal level*)
4. job_match (*Match between first job and kind of work participant wanted*)	A rating of how well the participants felt their first job or work experience after completing their degree was a match with what they wanted: *1, not at all what I wanted; 2, not very close match; 3, fairly close match; 4, very close match; 5, perfect match* (*ordinal level*)
5. time_to_job (*Time it took to get a job after completing degree*)	An indication of how quickly the participants obtained their first job or work experience after completing their degree: *1, prior to leaving institution; 2, less than 4 months; 3, four to 12 months; 4, more than 1 year* (*ordinal level*)
6. intrinsic_job_sat (*Degree of intrinsic job satisfaction*)	A score derived from a composite of items regarding participants' relatively intrinsic reasons for feeling satisfied at their jobs: it matches their interests and values, it allows them to contribute to a greater good, and it allows them to be creative. It has a possible range of 0, indicating little intrinsic satisfaction, to 75, indicating strong intrinsic job satisfaction. (*scalar, interval level*)
7. extrinsic_job_sat (*Degree of extrinsic job satisfaction*)	A score derived from a composite of items regarding participants' relatively extrinsic reasons for feeling satisfied at their jobs, such as opportunities for career advancement, income, and job security. It has a possible range of 0, indicating little extrinsic satisfaction, to 75, indicating strong extrinsic job satisfaction. (*scalar, interval level*)

Correlation with Interval- or Ratio-Level Data (Scalar Data): Visualization, Interpretation, and the Pearson Coefficient

Much can be learned about the nature of a relationship between interval- and/or ratio-level variables by creating a scatterplot. A scatterplot is a graph in which participants' values from two measures are used as x and y coordinates. A participant's score from one variable is plotted according to the x-axis and the same participant's score from the other variable is plotted according to the y-axis. A scatterplot of the participants' pairs of scores (n = 584 pairs, one pair per participant) on the intrinsic_job_sat and extrinsic_job_sat variables is presented in Figure 17.1. Several of the dots on this graph are labeled according to the participants' set of scores that they represent. For example, if you locate participant 1 on the graph you could estimate that they scored around 11 or 12 on the intrinsic_job_sat variable and around 25 on the extrinsic_job_sat variable. Similarly, if you locate participant 5 on the graph you could estimate that they scored just less than 20 on the intrinsic_job_sat variable and just greater than 50 on the extrinsic_job_sat variable.

In Figure 17.1, notice that the dots that are further to the right on the x-axis also tend to be higher on the y-axis—indicating that people who scored higher on intrinsic_job_sat also tended to score higher on extrinsic_job_sat. Accordingly, the dots that are further to the left on the x-axis also tend to be lower on the y-axis—indicating that people who scored lower on intrinsic_job_sat also tended to score lower on extrinsic_job_sat. This kind of trend, where relatively high scores on one variable are associated with high scores on the other, and vice versa for low scores, is referred to as a "positive relationship." If the trend showed the opposite pattern, such that relatively high scores on one variable were associated with relatively low scores on the other and so on, then that would be described as an "inverse" or "negative relationship."

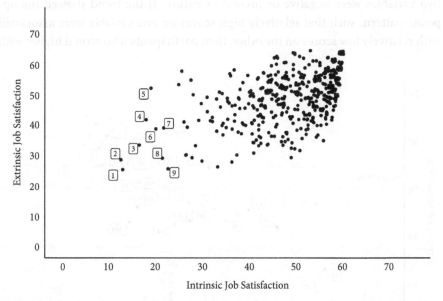

Figure 17.1 A scatterplot of the participants' pairs of scores (n = 584 pairs, one pair per participant) on the intrinsic_job_sat and extrinsic_job_sat variables. Several of the dots on this graph are labeled according to the participants' set of scores that they represent. This scatterplot depicts a positive relationship of moderate strength; that is, participants who tended to report relatively higher degrees of intrinsic job satisfaction also tended to report relatively higher degrees of extrinsic job satisfaction and vice versa.

A zoomed-in scatterplot of only 30 of the participants' values for intrinsic_job_sat and extrinsic_job_sat is presented in Figure 17.2. All of the dots on this graph are labeled according to the participants' set of scores that they represent. In addition, dotted lines have been annotated on the plot to indicate where the mean of each variable lies with respect to the observed range of each: the vertical dotted line indicates the mean of the intrinsic_job_sat variable and the horizontal dotted line indicates the mean of the extrinsic_job_sat variable. Notice the relative positions of the participants' values for the variables with respect to the means of each. For example, look at the data point representing participant 584; their score on intrinsic_job_sat is much greater than the mean (e.g., to the right of the vertical line) for that variable, and their score on extrinsic_job_sat is also much greater than the mean (e.g., above the horizontal line) for that variable. Similar patterns can be observed for participants 531, 548, 489, and others. In contrast, participant 19's data point indicates that they scored well below the mean on each variable (e.g., to the left of the vertical line and below the horizontal line). Similar patterns can be observed for participants 21, 39, 79, and others. This pattern of participants tending to score in similar relative positions to the mean is the key to the "positive direction" of the relationship between these two variables.

You can also imagine how this would be different if the relationship for the two variables were negative or inverse in nature. If the trend showed the opposite pattern, such that relatively high scores on one variable were associated with relatively low scores on the other, then participants who scored higher with

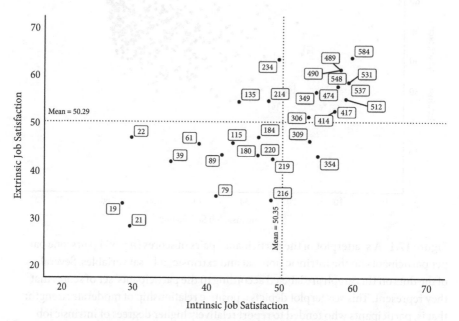

Figure 17.2 A zoomed-in scatterplot of only 30 of the participants' values for intrinsic_job_sat and extrinsic_job_sat.

respect to the mean on one variable would also tend to score lower with respect to the mean on the other variable. We've created plots out of hypothetical data to illustrate positive and negative/inverse relationships of various strengths and present them in Figure 17.3. Panels a, b, and c of Figure 17.3 show plots of positive relationships, whereas Panels d, e, and f, show plots of negative or inverse relationships. Imagine that each of the dots in each of these plots represents a participant's pair of scores on two variables, and notice the inverse nature of the relationship in Panels d, e, and f. Generally speaking—and scanning the plots in each panel from left to right—scatterplots of positive relationships will appear as a trend in which the dots are scattered from the lower left-hand corner across to the upper right-hand corner, whereas negative relationships will appear as a trend in which the dots are scattered from the upper left-hand corner across to the lower right-hand corner.

If the pattern of how the participants varied from the mean of each variable is key to the direction of the relationship between two variables, then the degree to which that pattern is consistent across participants is key to the strength of the relationship. Panels a and d of Figure 17.3 are indicative of "weak" relationships, whereas Panels b and e depict "moderate strength" relationships, and Panels c and f show "strong" relationships. The positive relationship depicted in Figure 17.3, Panel a is weak because, although there seems to be a pattern wherein participants who tend to score relatively high with respect to mean on the X variable also tend to score relatively high with respect to the mean on the Y variable and vice versa, the distance each data point is from each mean is not consistent. In other words, there are data points where the distance from the mean of the X could be relatively small, but the distance from the mean of the Y is quite large and vice versa. For example, consider the dots just below the label of $r = .35$ (which we will explain shortly) and how those dots represent hypothetical individuals whose scores on the X variable would be near the middle of the X variable range, whereas their scores on the Y variable would be near the top of the Y variable range. If you then compare Panel a to Panel b, you can see that the scoring pattern—distance from mean on X and distance from mean on Y—is more consistent. Finally, if you compare Panel b to Panel c, it is apparent that the pattern is nearly perfect in Panel c in the sense that the data points seem to be in nearly identical locations with respect to the range of the X variable and the range of the Y variable.

The most common statistical tool used for investigating correlation between two interval- or ratio-level variables is the Pearson Product Moment Coefficient, often simply described as the Pearson coefficient or Pearson's r, where r stands for "correlation coefficient." The mathematical formula for the Pearson coefficient yields a single number representing the direction and strength of the relationship between the two variables. The coefficient can range from -1 to $+1$, with negative coefficients (i.e., less than 0) indicative of an inverse relationship and positive coefficients (i.e., greater than 0) indicative of a positive relationship. The language used to describe the strength of correlations is somewhat subjective, but consistent with the

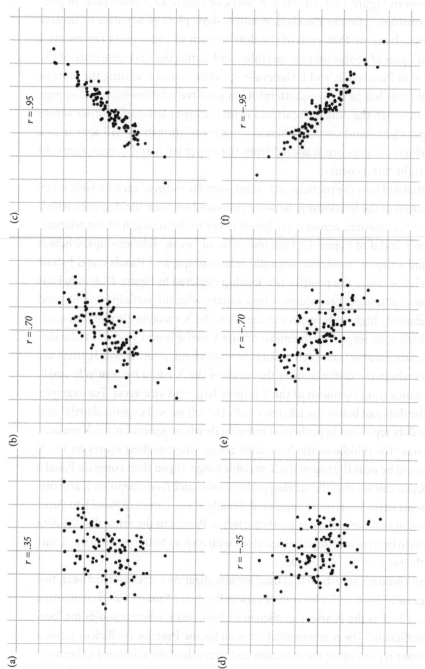

Figure 17.3 Plots demonstrating positive and negative/inverse relationships. When scanning the plots in each panel from left to right—those depicting positive relationships (a, b, c) will reveal a trend in which the dots are scattered from the lower left-hand corner across to the upper right-hand corner, whereas negative relationships (d, e, f) will appear as a trend in which the dots are scattered from the upper left-hand corner to the lower right-hand corner. Also, the degree to which that pattern is consistent across participants (e.g., the density of the dots along a line) is key to interpreting the strength of the relationship.

depictions in Figure 17.3, the following rough conventions apply in music education research:

- Coefficients ranging from about –.30 to 0 or 0 to .30 are described as weak.
- Coefficients ranging from about –.70 to –.30 or .30 to .70 are described as moderate.
- Coefficients ranging from about –1.0 to –.70 or .70 to 1.0 are described as strong.

A coefficient of –1 indicates a "perfect" inverse relationship, and a coefficient of +1 indicates a "perfect" positive relationship—although such relationships are rarely seen when dealing with real-world data. If there's no relationship between variables, then the Pearson's coefficient will be approximately 0 and the data points will appear as randomly scattered with no detectable trend, as is the case in Figure 17.4, Panel a. The Pearson coefficient for the relationship between the intrinsic_job_sat and extrinsic_job_sat variables is $r = .54$, indicating that the correlation is positive and moderate in strength. Revisit the plot of these two variables in Figure 17.1 and compare it to positive relationships depicted with hypothetical data in Figure 17.3, Panels a, b, and c. Although Figure 17.1 is not identical to any of those in Figure 17.3, it's pretty safe to say that the relationship between the intrinsic_job_sat and extrinsic_job_sat is most similar to the moderate-strength relationship in Figure 17.3, Panel b.

The Pearson coefficient should be applied only to interval- or ratio-level data, and it is best used when each of the variables demonstrates a relatively normal distribution and when there is an absence of outliers. If the interval- or ratio-level data you have do not conform to these characteristics, then it is better to use a different statistical tool, such as the Spearman coefficient, described in the next section. Moreover, it is important to recognize that most bivariate statistical techniques for interval- or ratio-level data, such as the Pearson coefficient we have used in this section, are designed to detect positive or negative linear relationships. However, it is also possible for other shapes to occur in a scatterplot, which could indicate systematic relationships between variables besides linear trends.

Among the possibilities that could occur, a curvilinear relationship is a relatively clear nonlinear pattern to consider. Note in Figure 17.4, Panel b how the pattern between the variables shows that those who scored relatively low with respect to the mean on the variable represented by the x-axis sometimes scored relatively low with respect to the mean on the variable represented by the y-axis, but also sometimes scored relatively high with respect to the mean on the variable represented by the y-axis. As such, the trend between the X and Y variable looks like an upside-down U. This type of curvilinear relationship can be modeled as a quadratic mathematical function (e.g., as a function of the square of a variable, x^2). However, relationships between variables can be quite complicated and reveal trends even more difficult to interpret. See, for example, Figure 17.4, Panel c, in which there are two inflections

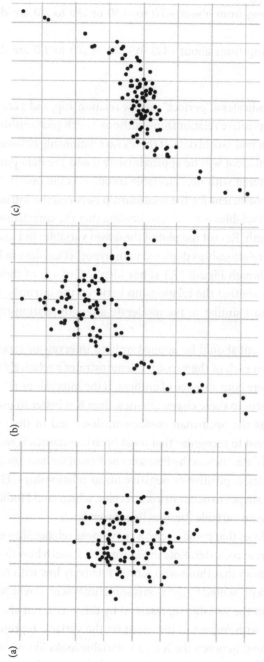

Figure 17.4 Scatterplots depicting virtually no correlation (a), a curvilinear relationship with one inflection (i.e., bend) in the shape of an upside-down U (e.g., a quadratic function) (b), and a more complex curvilinear relationship with two inflections (e.g., a cubic function) (c).

in the curve depicted by the trend between the X and Y variables. This type of curvilinear relation is a mathematical function that includes a cubic term (e.g., as a function of a variable raised to the power of 3, x^3). Although, the statistical techniques that would be necessary to describe these nonlinear trends are beyond the scope of this book, we include examples of them to alert you to the possibility of such relationships (and other nonlinear trends) and to underscore how important it is to visualize your data prior to interpreting a statistical summary. Always visualize your data.

Correlation with Ordinal Data: Visualization, Interpretation, and the Spearman Coefficient

Relationships between ordinal and nominal variables are most commonly visualized with clustered bar charts. A clustered bar chart of the relationship between job_match and time_to_job variables is presented in Figure 17.5. Look at the four bars above the *Very close match* and the *Perfect match* options on the x-axis, and for each option notice the differences in the relative sizes of the two bars representing those who got their first job prior to graduating and those who got their first job less than four months after graduation compared to the two bars representing those who got their first job between four months and a year or more than a year after graduating. Now make the same sort of comparison for the bars above the *Not very close match* and *Not at all what I wanted* options on the x-axis. You can see that participants who indicated that their first job was a *Very close match* or a *Perfect match* were somewhat more likely to have gotten their first job prior to or within four months of graduating. This is the sort of disproportionality that suggests there may be a systematic relationship between two ordinal or nominal variables.

The Spearman rank correlation coefficient is a statistical tool designed to describe the direction and strength of a relationship between ordinal variables. It is sometimes referred to as the Spearman coefficient or Spearman's *rho*, where *rho* stands for "correlation coefficient." Fortunately, although it is derived from a mathematical formula that takes into account the properties of ordinal data, interpreting the Spearman coefficient is nearly the same as interpreting a Pearson coefficient. The coefficient can range from −1 to +1, with negative coefficients indicative of an inverse relationship, positive coefficients indicative of a positive relationship, and the same ranges of coefficients referring to the strength of a relationship as those we discussed with reference to the Pearson coefficient. The Spearman coefficient for the relationship between the job_match and time_to_job variables is *rho* = −.10, which indicates a very weak correlation such that there is only a slight tendency for participants who report a relatively better match between their first job and what they wanted also reporting that they got their first job relatively soon after graduation.

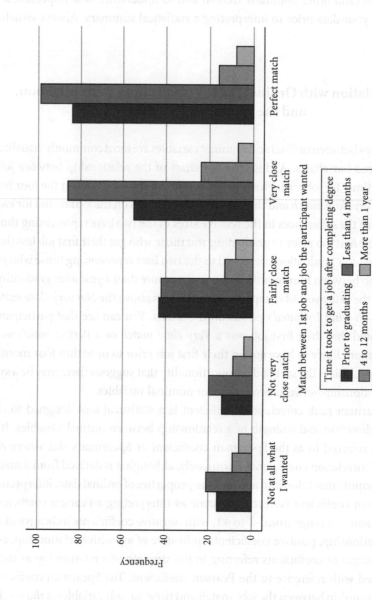

Figure 17.5 Clustered bar charts of the relationships between job_match and time_to_job variables.

You might wonder why we don't suggest using a scatterplot to visualize a relationship between ordinal variables since the values represent a quantitative sense of order. Scatterplots are often less informative when examining such associations because the possible values that an ordinal variable can take on are typically limited. For example, look at the scatterplot of the job_match and time_to_job in Figure 17.6, Panel a and notice how the limited number of possible values for both variables (i.e., five possible values for job_match and four possible values for time_ to _job) make it impossible to interpret the direction and strength of any possible correlation (or lack thereof) due to overplotting. Overplotting occurs when many participants have the same values for both variables—in other words, each dot in Figure 17.6, Panel a represents many duplicate points. Overplotting can be mitigated and therefore the plot made more interpretable by adding a third dimension such as "point size," representing the number of data points for any possible combination of X and Y values, as has been done in Figure 17.6, Panel b (the "n" in the legend title stands for the number of participants represented by each dot size). It is now possible to see a slight inverse trend between the variables that the Spearman coefficient revealed, such that those who reported a *Very close match* or a *Perfect match* tended to report getting their first job sooner rather than later (i.e., *Prior to graduation* or *Less than 4 months* after graduating). However, it's usually simpler to create and easier to interpret a more straightforward, two-dimensional clustered bar chart.

Correlation with Nominal Data: Visualization, Interpretation, and the Phi and Cramer's V Correlation Coefficients

A clustered bar chart depicting the relationship between the nominal variables degree_program and institution_type is presented in Figure 17.7. Scatterplots are never appropriate for nominal variables since the categories of a nominal measurement scale have no inherent order or quantitative meaning. As described in the previous section, the key to interpreting correlation in a clustered bar chart is identifying where disproportionalities lie. For example, the proportion of music education to performance degree students who went to public institutions appears to be different from the proportion of music education to performance degree students who went to private institutions. The Phi coefficient is a statistical tool designed to describe strength of a relationship between two nominal variables when each has only two categories, as is the case with the degree_program and institution_type variables. The Cramer's V coefficient can be used if one or both of the nominal variables in question have more than two categories, and the coefficients for Phi and Cramer's V are interpreted in the same way.

Recall that the differences between categories in a nominal variable are only differences in labels and, therefore, that nominal variables are not truly quantitative variables. As such, there is no real meaning in interpreting a relationship between

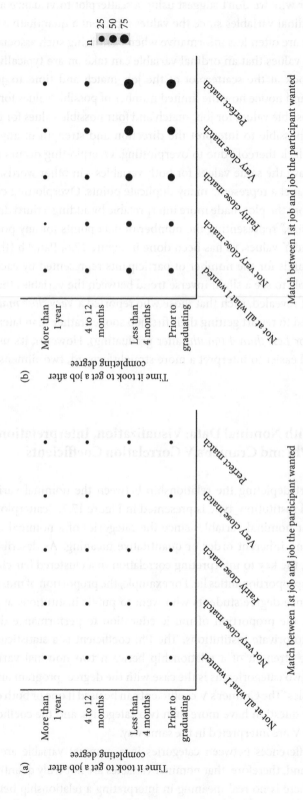

Figure 17.6 Scatterplot of the job_match and time_to_job. Note how the overplotting in Panel a obscures the relationship between the two variables. This is due to the limited number of values for each ordinal variable. In contrast, the relationship becomes more clear when a third dimension of "point size" is added to the plot, as depicted in Panel b — in this instance, "point size" refers to the number of participants with each possible pair of values.

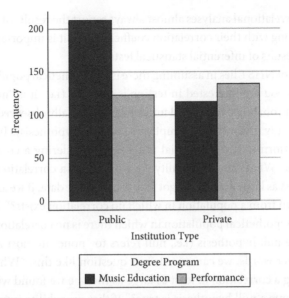

Figure 17.7 Clustered bar chart depicting the relationship between the nominal variables degree_program and institution_type. Note the disproportionality of "music education to music performance majors" attending public and private institutions.

nominal variables as positive or negative in direction. Instead, it's best to restrict the interpretation of the Phi and Cramer's V coefficients to characteristics of strength. Again, the ranges of coefficients that can be interpreted as indicating weak, moderate, or strong correlations for the Phi and Cramer's V coefficients are roughly the same as for Pearson and Spearman coefficients. The Phi coefficient for the correlation between degree_program and institution_type is .17, suggesting a weak relationship. Authors sometimes use the Greek symbol for Phi (ϕ) when reporting this coefficient.

Correlation and Inferential Analyses

Consistent with the general principles of science, quantitative researchers evaluate their hypotheses by testing whether the data they gather would refute or corroborate their theories. The tools that music education researchers most commonly use to test hypotheses in quantitative research are called "inferential statistical techniques." Although there are several ways to conduct inferential statistical tests, the method that is pervasive in music education research is null hypothesis significance testing (NHST). The logical steps involved in using the NHST approach are somewhat counterintuitive, and an in-depth discussion of the logical and mathematical underpinnings of it is beyond the scope of this book.[3] However, researchers

---

[3] See Miksza and Elpus (2018) for a detailed description of the conceptual underpinnings of null hypothesis significance testing as an inferential analysis method.

conducting correlational analyses almost always report the results of inferential statistical tests along with their correlation coefficients, so it is important to be able to interpret the results of inferential statistical tests.

The essence of NHST lies in assuming there is a hypothetical population in which the hypothesis you are interested in testing is not true (i.e., it is "null"), and then evaluating the probability you would find what you actually observed from the data in your own study given that assumption (i.e., null hypothesis). In other words, researchers performing an inferential test when considering a correlation would ask themselves "What's the probability we would find a correlation between two variables at least as large as what we got from our sample data, if we assume that our data were drawn from a population in which no correlation exists?" The conjecture that there is a hypothetical population in which there is no correlation between two variables is the null hypothesis (i.e., null refers to "none" in most applications of NHST). In other words, we can rewrite our question like this: "What's the probability of finding a correlation at least as large as the one we found with our sample data, if we assume a null hypothesis is true?" If that probability is very small, then we can reject the null hypothesis and declare that the correlation we found among our sample's data is "statistically significant." A typical cutoff for the probability being small enough to reject the null hypothesis and declare statistical significance is .05.[4] If that probability is not very small, that is, greater than .05, then we would find ourselves in a position where we fail to reject the null hypothesis and should not declare statistical significance.

The technical term for the criterion for rejecting a null hypothesis and declaring statistical significance is "alpha level." As implied in the paragraph above, a traditional alpha level that researchers employ is .05. Technically, when researchers declare an alpha level, they are expressing the degree to which they are willing to reject a null hypothesis when they shouldn't. For example, if a researcher chooses an alpha level of .05 when conducting an inferential test of a correlation, the researcher is willing to reject a null hypothesis and declare statistical significance even though there is a 5% (i.e., .05 = 5/100 = 5%) chance that a correlation between two variables at least as large as what they found from their sample data would occur if they assumed that their data were drawn from a population in which no correlation exists. As such, it is possible that researchers sometimes reject the null hypothesis when it is indeed true. In NHST, this is referred to as a Type I error.

The statistical probability that a researcher would get the finding they observed from their sample data if they assumed the null hypothesis was true is referred to as a "probability value" or "p value." Although it is possible to compute inferential statistical tests and arrive at p values by hand, modern statistical software has made it

---

[4] The choice of .05 as a cutoff criterion for statistical significance is largely based on tradition. There could be many valid reasons for choosing smaller values, such as .01 or .001, or larger values, such as .10 or .15, depending on the context of a given study. However, the discussion of why, how, or when to choose a different criterion for statistical significance is beyond the scope of this book. Again, see Miksza and Elpus (2018) for more on this topic.

unnecessary to do so. Assuming we choose the correct options, statistics programs can perform inferential tests on our data and let us know the p values resulting from such tests immediately. We have provided videos demonstrating how to conduct correlational analyses using statistical software among the online supplemental materials for this chapter.

Scientifically, a statistically significant finding is considered valuable and interesting because such a finding was resilient when put to a formal and fairly standard test of refutation. However, it's important to recognize that statistical significance does not equate to the importance of a research finding. In other words, statistical significance and practical significance are not necessarily the same thing. For example, in some circumstances, statistically significant findings can still be trivial findings. Most of the time this is because the underlying mathematics of NHST processes mean that the likelihood of arriving at a statistically significant finding (i.e., the likelihood of being able to reject a null hypothesis) is directly related to the sample size of a study. The probability of being able to reject a null hypothesis if it is indeed false is referred to as "statistical power." For example, with very large samples, even very weak correlation coefficients can be declared statistically significant. In other words, very large samples lead to studies with a great deal of statistical power, such that even weak or trivial effects can be large enough to reject a null hypothesis and declare statistical significance. As a result, researchers also must report on the magnitude of a finding and discuss whether it is meaningful in a practical sense. When conducting inferential tests with correlation coefficients, the correlation coefficient itself is an indicator of effect size. Therefore, it is critical to describe whether a correlation coefficient is indicative of a weak, moderate, or strong relationship, in addition to describing whether the coefficient is statistically significant.

One interesting dilemma that can occur is when a researcher finds a correlation coefficient that indicates a substantially strong relationship but fails to reject the null hypothesis and declare statistical significance. The most likely cause for such a dilemma is a lack of statistical power, and in many cases the solution to this problem is to conduct a study with a larger sample size. Failing to reject a null hypothesis when it is indeed false is referred to as a Type II error.

At this point we have established that researchers will seek to determine whether a correlation coefficient they calculated from their data could be declared statistically significant and that they could also describe the coefficient with regard to the magnitude of the effect. Although the binary decision of "statistically significant" (i.e., reject the null hypothesis) or "not statistically significant" (i.e., fail to reject the null hypothesis) is important, it is also valuable to report some expression of the degree of certainty one could have in one's findings. The most common way researchers do this is by reporting the "confidence interval" surrounding their coefficient. A confidence interval describes the range of possible values one would not reject as possible hypothetical population values that could have generated the sample coefficient within a given level of precision. For example, researchers commonly report 95% confidence intervals, which are indicative of a range of values one would *not* reject as plausible hypothetical population values given an alpha criterion of statistical significance of .05. The precision of one's statistical estimate in terms of how narrow or wide a confidence interval might be can depend on several things relative to the statistical parameter in question (e.g., correlation coefficient, mean, difference between means, variance). All else being equal, relatively larger samples sizes will always result in narrower confidence intervals—that is, relatively less uncertainty and more precise estimates.

Reporting Correlations in Research

Correlation Matrices

In this section, we present examples of how correlation analyses might typically be presented in quantitative research reports. Statistical analyses will most typically appear in the results section of an article or the results chapter of a thesis or dissertation. Correlations are sometimes presented one at a time in the text of the results. Sometimes several correlations between a set of variables are presented together in a table, in which case it is referred to as a "correlation matrix," meaning an arrangement of data into columns and rows.

An excerpt of a table of Pearson correlation coefficients from Miksza et al.'s (2021) study of the wellness of collegiate music students is presented in Table 17.2. As you can see, a correlation matrix is simply a convenient way of displaying the coefficients for each possible pairing of a set of variables. For example, Table 17.2 indicates that a moderate, inverse relationship was found between collegiate music students' reports of stress and vitality (e.g., subjective feeling of energy and being alive), since the coefficient corresponding to that pair of variables is $r = -0.41$. This suggests that students who tended to report more stress also tended to report feeling less vital. In contrast, the coefficient of $r = 0.50$ describing the relationship between students' reports of adaptability and vitality is indicative of a moderate, positive

Table 17.2 Excerpt of a table published in Miksza et al.'s (2021) report of a study on collegiate music students' wellness

	Pearson Correlations among Wellness Variables		
	Stress	Perfectionism	Adaptability
Vitality	−0.41***	−0.11	0.50***
Stress		0.21***	−0.42***
Perfectionism			−0.08

Note: The coefficients in the table correspond to the relationships between each respective variable pair. The asterisk marks next to certain coefficients are indications that those are statistically significant—that a null hypothesis of zero correlation could be rejected. *$p < .05$, **$p < .01$, ***$p < .001$.

relationship. In other words, students who tended to report being more adaptable also tended to report feeling more vital. In addition, it is common for researchers to denote statistically significant findings with asterisk marks. In Table 17.2, four of the correlations the researchers found in their study were large enough that they were able to reject the null hypothesis. In other words, in those four correlation coefficients the probability of finding a coefficient at least as large as those Miksza et al. (2021) found in their data, if we assume a "null hypothesis" of 0 correlation is true, is very, very small—literally less than 1 in 1,000, that is, $p < .001$.

Writing about Correlations

Here we present samples of how authors might write about correlations, using correlations we calculated with the example data described in Table 17.1. At least four items should be addressed: (a) the direction of the correlation—positive or negative for ordinal-, interval-, and ratio-level data; (b) the strength of the correlation—weak, moderate, or strong; (c) whether the correlation can be declared statistically significant; and (d) what the correlation means with respect to the variables in the analysis. When reporting statistical significance, it is helpful for readers if you report the exact p value your software returns for your analysis. If a p value is exceedingly small, less than .001, then simply indicating $p < .001$ will suffice. Reporting the confidence interval is typically done via the simple notations included in the examples below.

- Pearson coefficient (r) for interval- or ratio-level data.

A significant, moderate, positive correlation was found between participants' reports of intrinsic job satisfaction and extrinsic job satisfaction, $r = 0.54$, $p < .001$, 95% CI [0.49, 0.60]. Participants who tended to report greater degrees of intrinsic job satisfaction also tended to report greater degrees of extrinsic job satisfaction and vice versa.

- Spearman coefficient (*rho*) for ordinal data.

A weak, yet statistically significant, negative correlation was found between participants' reports of the match between their first job and the kind of work they wanted and the time it took for them to get their first job after completing their degree, *rho* = –0.10, $p = .009$, 95% CI [–0.21, –0.05]. There was a slight tendency for participants who reported a better match between their job and their interests to also report getting their first job relatively sooner after graduation.

- Phi coefficient for nominal data.

A weak, statistically significant correlation was found between participants' degree program (i.e., music education or music performance) and the type of institution they attended (i.e., public or private), ϕ = .17, $p < .001$, 95% CI [0.09, 0.25]. The proportion of music education students in public schools was somewhat greater than the proportion of music education students in private schools.

Summary

Bivariate correlation coefficients are tools we can use to summarize and describe whether and how two variables may be related. It is important to choose the correlation coefficient that is most appropriate for the type of data your variables represent. The Pearson coefficient is suitable for interval- or ratio-level data, assuming the relationship between the variables is linear, that the data are approximately normally distributed, and that there are no substantial outliers. If either of those conditions is not met, then another procedure may be more appropriate. The Spearman coefficient can be used if analyzing correlations with ordinal-level data or interval- or ratio-level data that do not conform to the characteristics described in the previous sentence. For nominal-level data in which each variable has two categories, the Phi coefficient is appropriate. However, if either or both variables include more than two categories, the Cramer's V coefficient can be used. Researchers also subject their correlational analyses to inferential tests and seek to refute their hypotheses via NHST. If researchers are able to reject a null hypothesis, then they can declare their finding to be statistically significant. However, researchers must always describe the magnitude of their statistical findings along with statistical significance, since it is possible that trivial findings could be declared statistically significant.

Work through the following questions to help yourself get comfortable discussing and interpreting correlation:

1. How can correlation coefficients be of use to researchers?
2. Explain what a scatterplot is and how positive and negative relationships appear on such plots.
3. Explain how the strength of a relationship between interval- or ratio-level variables can be observed in a scatterplot.
4. Why is only one half of a correlation matrix typically presented in a table of correlation coefficients?
5. Explain what it means if a correlation coefficient is found to be "statistically significant"?
6. Generate Pearson, Spearman, and Phi correlation coefficients with the online application in the online supplement associated with this chapter (see the link titled "Supplemental Web Apps for Exploring Statistical Concepts", Chapter 17 on the Companion website ▶). Experiment with the application by changing the input parameters for each type of coefficient and observing the differences in the visualizations that result.

7. Consult the video on how to use SPSS for correlation analyses that is linked in the online supplement associated with this chapter and conduct the following analyses (see items 6 and 6, Chapter 17 on the Companion website ▶):
   a. A scatterplot and Pearson correlation coefficient describing the relationship between the intrinsic_job_sat and extrinsic_job_sat variables.
   b. A clustered bar chart and Spearman correlation coefficient describing the relationship between the job_match and time_to_job variables.
   c. A scatterplot and Spearman correlation coefficient describing the relationship between the job_match and intrinsic_job_sat variables.
   d. A clustered bar chart and Phi correlation coefficient describing the relationship between the degree_program and institution_type variables.
8. Identify a correlation matrix in a quantitative research article of your choosing. Practice summarizing the findings in your own words and compare your summary to that of the article's author.

Important Terms for Review

A *scatterplot* is a graph used to visualize the relationship between two scalar (i.e., interval- or ratio-level) variables. In this type of plot, participants' values from two measures are used as x and y coordinates. A participant's score from one variable is plotted according to the x-axis, and the same participant's score from the other variable is plotted according to the y-axis.

A *Pearson coefficient* is used to describe the direction and strength of a relationship between two scalar (i.e., interval- or ratio-level) variables. A positive coefficient indicates that participants with relatively higher values on one variable will also tend to have relatively higher values on the other; a negative coefficient indicates the inverse—that participants with relatively higher values on one variable will also tend to have relatively lower values on the other. Such patterns of association will be more consistent if the coefficient is relatively large, and less if the coefficient is relatively small. A Pearson coefficient can range from −1 to +1. Coefficients with absolute values (i.e., positive or negative) between 0 and .30 can be considered weak, between .30 and .70 can be considered moderate, and between .70 and 1.00 can be considered strong.

A *clustered bar chart* is often used to visualize the relationship between two ordinal or two nominal variables or a combination of ordinal and nominal variables. The plot depicts the frequency of each category or value that is present in a nominal or ordinal variable, respectively. Each bar represents a discrete value, and the height of each bar represents the frequency for each value.

A *Spearman coefficient* is a statistic used to describe the direction and strength of a relationship that exists between two ordinal variables. Although the underlying mathematics of the statistic are different, the value of the coefficient that results from the procedure is interpreted in roughly the same way as for a Pearson correlation coefficient.

A *Phi coefficient* is used to describe the strength of a relationship that exists between two nominal variables that each has only two possible categories (e.g., brass/woodwind, private lesson/no private lesson). Given that values for nominal variables do not have any quantitative meaning, the Phi coefficient is always presented as a positive value. However, the strength of the relationship is interpreted in roughly the same way as for a Pearson correlation coefficient.

Cramer's V coefficient is used to describe the strength of a relationship that exists between two nominal variables and that allows for the variables to have any number of categories (e.g., brass/woodwind/percussion/strings/piano, freshman/sophomore/junior/senior). Given that values for nominal variables do not have any quantitative meaning, the Cramer's V coefficient is always presented as a positive value. However, the strength of the relationship is interpreted in roughly the same way as for a Pearson correlation coefficient.

Null hypothesis significance testing (NHST) is a method of statistical inference that researchers use when attempting to refute their hypotheses. When using NHST a researcher will assume there is a hypothetical population in which the hypothesis they are interested in testing is not true (i.e., it is "null"), and then will determine the probability of getting the finding they observed from their sample data under that assumption. If the probability of getting the finding they observed from their sample data is sufficiently small (traditionally < .05), then they reject the null hypothesis and can declare statistical significance. If the probability of getting the finding they observed from their sample data is *not* sufficiently small (traditionally > .05), then they fail to reject the null hypothesis and cannot declare statistical significance.

Alpha level is the criterion for rejecting a null hypothesis and declaring statistical significance, which is traditionally a probability of .05.

A *probability value* or *p value* is the statistical probability that a researcher would get a result at least as extreme as that which they observed from their sample data if they assumed the null hypothesis was true.

Effect size is an indication of the magnitude of an effect irrespective of statistical significance. It is important to report an indicator of effect size along with statistical significance because a statistically significant finding is not necessarily a meaningful finding in any practical sense. When conducting inferential tests with correlation coefficients, the relative strength of the correlation coefficient itself (e.g., weak, moderate, strong) is an indicator of effect size.

Statistical power refers to the likelihood a researcher will be able to reject a null hypothesis if it is indeed false. The most direct method of increasing statistical power is by increasing the sample size (i.e., the number of participants) in a study.

Type I error occurs when a null hypothesis is mistakenly rejected when it is true. Given the probabilistic nature of NHST, Type I error is more likely to occur when many statistical tests are run on the same data set.

Type II error occurs when one fails to reject a null hypothesis even though it is false. A common reason that Type II error occurs is a lack of statistical power.

A *confidence interval* is an expression of the uncertainty in one's statistical findings. Confidence intervals indicate the range of possible values one would not reject as possible hypothetical population values that could have generated the sample data within a given level of precision.

References

Field, A. (2016). *An adventure in statistics: The reality enigma*. Sage.
Fox, J. (2008). *Applied regression analysis and generalized linear models*. Sage.
Gorsuch, R. L. (1983). *Factor analysis* (2nd ed.). Laurence Erlbaum Associates.
Jaeger, R. M. (1990). *Statistics: A spectator sport* (2nd ed.). Sage.
Kline, R. B. (2015). *Principles and practices of structural equation modeling* (2nd ed.). Guilford Press.
Loehlin, J. C. (2004). *Latent variable models: An introduction to factor, path, and structural equation modeling* (4th ed.). Erlbaum.
Miksza, P., & Elpus, K. (2018). *Design and analysis for quantitative research in music education*. Oxford University Press.
Miksza, P., Evans, P., & McPherson, G. E. (2021). Wellness among university-level music students: A study of the predictors of subjective vitality. *Musicae Scientiae, 25*(2), 143–160. https://doi.org/10.1177/1029864919860554
Miksza, P., & Hime, L. (2015). Undergraduate music program alumni's career path, retrospective institutional satisfaction, and financial status. *Arts Education Policy Review, 116*(4), 1–13. https://doi.org/10.1080/10632913.2014.945628
Raudenbush, S. W., & Bryk, A. S. (2001). *Hierarchical linear models: Applications and data analysis methods* (2nd ed.). Sage.
Russell, J. A. (2018). *Statistics in music education research*. Oxford University Press.
Tabachnik, B. G., & Fidell, L. S. (2019). *Using multivariate statistics* (7th ed.). Pearson.

18
Determining Differences with Inferential Statistics

Chapter Preview

The purpose of this chapter is to learn about inferential tests that could be used to analyze differences between groups. Quantitative researchers typically rely on inferential statistical procedures for testing hypotheses pertaining to differences between sets of scores. Although researchers nearly always find mathematical differences in scores from different groups, determining whether these differences are statistically significant requires inferential tests. Before deciding on a particular test, you must consider whether your data are nominal-, ordinal-, interval-, or ratio-level since different tests are suitable for each level. Also, you need to consider whether your data come from independent or dependent samples. Independent samples generally are gathered from groups that consist of different individuals. Dependent samples are gathered from the same group of individuals on multiple occasions. Specific details are provided for a variety of statistical procedures. For determining differences with interval- or ratio-level outcome data researchers typically use independent samples t-test, dependent samples t-test, one-way analysis of variance (ANOVA), repeated-measures ANOVA, and post-hoc analyses (e.g., Tukey HSD test, Bonferroni method). For ordinal data researchers may use the Mann-Whitney U test, the Wilcoxon test for paired samples, the Kruskal-Wallis test, and Friedman's tests. For nominal-level data the Chi square test of independence and McNemar's tests can be used.

Introduction

In Chapter 16, we covered descriptive statistics, which are used to summarize and describe numerical data gathered in quantitative research. Here, we cover inferential statistics, which are used to make inferences about situations that extend beyond the data of a particular study. Quantitative researchers typically rely on inferential statistical procedures for testing hypotheses pertaining to differences between sets of scores. For example, a researcher who has designed an experiment with a treatment group and a control group will want to determine whether a statistically significant difference can be declared between the groups on some outcome measure following an intervention of some sort. That is, the researcher would wish to evaluate their hypothesis that the experimental intervention would have some effect by testing whether the data they gathered would refute a null hypothesis of no significant difference between the groups. Alternatively, a researcher could be interested in examining whether scores from a single group of individuals that is measured on multiple occasions differ significantly from each other. In this case, this researcher would also want to be able to evaluate whether they could refute a null hypothesis of no significant difference between the measurements made on different occasions.

Researchers will nearly always find some mathematical difference when comparing the scores of different groups of research participants or comparing multiple measurements of the same group of participants. However, determining whether such a difference could be scientifically valuable requires subjecting our data to formal inferential tests of refutation. Thus, researchers seek to test whether their observed differences are, in fact, statistically significant differences.

When choosing an inferential statistical tool for examining differences, it is important to consider (a) the level of measurement of your data (i.e., nominal, ordinal, interval, ratio) and (b) whether the sets of scores you wish to compare come from independent or dependent samples. Inferential tests are often categorized as being either a parametric or nonparametric test. Parametric inferential tests include specific mathematical assumptions about the hypothetical population distributions involved in null hypothesis significance testing (NHST), whereas nonparametric tests involve fewer assumptions or none at all. Although a discussion of the nature of such assumptions is beyond the scope of this book, it is valuable at this point to have a general sense of what these categories refer to, since these terms will appear in the research literature. The tests we describe for interval- or ratio-level outcome variables in this chapter are parametric tests, whereas those we describe for nominal- and ordinal-level outcome variables are nonparametric tests. Parametric tests are more precise and more powerful than nonparametric tests when analyzing interval- or ratio-level data that meet the necessary assumptions; however, nonparametric tests will be more robust when the data fail to meet such assumptions. What is important is to choose the correct statistical procedures that match the data gathered in your study.

Independent samples are gathered from groups that consist of different individuals when the individuals in one group are not systematically related to those in the other group in any way. Therefore, the scores gathered from such groups represent samples of individuals that are independent of the other. Data gathered from two groups that were formed by randomly assigning individuals to a treatment or control group is a prototypical example of independent samples. Dependent samples are gathered from groups where the individuals in each group are systematically related to each other in some way. One of the most common types of dependent samples in music education research occurs when data are gathered from the same group of individuals on multiple occasions. In that case, the scores from the first group are as related as can be to the scores from the second group, since they literally come from the same people.

Consider how inferential statistical tests of differences could be used to test hypotheses implied by each of the following research questions:

- What is the effect of a dance-infused curricular approach as compared to a traditional approach on elementary children's rhythmic perception?
- Do preservice music educators' perceptions of their ability to effectively manage a classroom differ from their perceptions of their ability to assess students?
- Are high school auditionees accepted into all-state choir more or less likely to come from relatively lower socioeconomic circumstances?

In each case, the researchers would test the data they gathered in their respective studies to determine whether they could reject a null hypothesis of no significant difference and, therefore, declare the observed differences between the sets of scores on the outcome measure of interest to be statistically significant. In this chapter, we first review some general principles of statistical inference, and then describe the foundational statistical tools that are most commonly used to test for differences. We describe methods appropriate for variables measured with interval or ratio (e.g., scalar) measurement scales first, and then move on to methods for ordinal and nominal variable types. There are many statistical tests available to researchers who wish to test for more complex patterns of differences among variables. Readers are encouraged to consult the books in Box 18.1 for extensions of the techniques discussed in this chapter as well as other techniques that may be used for more complex research designs.

Box 18.1 Additional Methodological Readings: Determining Differences

Foundational and Advanced Methods

Field, A. (2016). *An adventure in statistics: The reality enigma*. Sage.
Miksza, P., & Elpus, K. (2018). *Design and analysis for quantitative research in music education*. Oxford University Press.
Russell, J. A. (2018). *Statistics in music education research*. Oxford University Press.
Tabachnik, B. G., & Fidell, L. S. (2019). *Using multivariate statistics* (7th ed.). Pearson.

Nonparametric Statistical Tests

Siegel, S., & Castellan, J. (1988). *Nonparametric statistics for the behavioral sciences* (2nd ed.). McGraw-Hill.

A Review of Concepts Central to Statistical Inference

Recall from the previous chapter, dealing with correlation, that scientists typically use NHST inferential methods when attempting to refute their hypotheses. The same is true when music education researchers conduct inferential tests to investigate differences. Although, as we explained in Chapter 2, researchers often ask questions instead of posing hypotheses, in reality they are variants of the same thing. For instance, one of the examples given in Chapter 2 came from Stambaugh's (2011) study on blocked versus random practice conditions:

- Stambaugh writes, "Students in the blocked condition will perform more accurately, faster, and more steadily than students in the random condition at the end of practice (acquisition)" (p. 370). This is considered a directional hypothesis because it predicts an outcome.
- Here is one way you could rewrite this as a null hypothesis, that is, as a prediction of no difference: "There will be no significant difference in performance accuracy, speed, and steadiness between students in the blocked condition and students in the random condition at the end of practice (acquisition)."
- Posed as a research question, it could be written: "Will there be a significant difference in performance accuracy, speed, and steadiness between students in the blocked condition and students in the random condition at the end of practice (acquisition)?"

In the following examples, we focus on the use of NHST to determine whether the differences researchers observe between sets of scores can be declared statistically significant.

The logic of using NHST when investigating differences is similar to that described in the previous chapter. Generally speaking, a researcher will adopt the posture of assuming that there will be no difference between the sets of scores; that is, they will assume that a null hypothesis of no difference is true. Then they will assess the probability of arriving at a difference as large as they actually observed between their sets of scores, assuming their data were derived from a hypothetical population in which no true difference exists. To phrase this another way, the researcher would essentially be using NHST to evaluate the following question: "What's the probability we would find a difference as large as we did with our sample data if we assume that our data were drawn from a population in which no difference exists?" If the probability is sufficiently small, then they would *reject the null hypothesis* of no difference and declare the differences they observed to be statistically significant. If the probability is not sufficiently small, then they would *fail to reject the null hypothesis* and not be able to declare statistical significance.

All inferential statistical tests for investigating differences—whether they are designed for independent or dependent samples or for nominal, ordinal, or interval/ratio data—result in a specific value for the probability of arriving at an observed difference at least as large as they found given an assumption of no difference (i.e., assuming a null hypothesis is true). This value is called a "*p* value," where *p* stands for "probability." Consistent with our discussion in the previous chapter, the level of probability that is sufficiently small such that a null hypothesis can be rejected and statistical significance can be declared is referred to as the "alpha criterion." Researchers traditionally employ an alpha criterion of .05. In other words, traditionally, the *p* value that results from a statistical test must be less than .05 in order for the researcher to declare statistical significance. When choosing an alpha criterion of .05, a researcher is essentially accepting the risk of a 5% (i.e., .05 = 5/100 = 5%) chance that they could mistakenly reject a null hypothesis when it is actually true. Mistakenly rejecting a null hypothesis when it is true is a Type I error and is sometimes colloquially called a "false positive."

Determining whether a difference is statistically significant is valuable. However, it is also important to examine the magnitude of a difference in order to interpret whether it is meaningful in a practical sense. Fortunately, there are established statistical tools, or measures of effect size, that yield numbers that can be interpreted as being indicative of small, moderate, or large differences. Moderate and large differences are those that are most often interpreted as having practical significance. We will discuss appropriate measures of effect size that can be paired with each of the inferential tests we present throughout this chapter.

To reiterate a point made in the previous chapter and to further underscore the importance of examining effect size, statistical significance does not automatically imply practical significance. In fact, it is entirely possible for a statistically significant difference to be a trivial difference. In a manner similar to any inferential statistical test conducted within the framework of NHST, if the sample size of a study is large enough, it is possible to reject a null hypothesis with even very small observed differences between sets of scores. As such, the sample size of a study is directly related to the statistical power of a test, which is defined as the probability of being able to reject a null hypothesis if it is indeed false. However, this also means that the opposite is true: If the sample size of a study is too small, then a researcher may not be able to reject a null hypothesis even if the difference between sets of scores is meaningful and large. This is a Type II error, sometimes colloquially described as a "false negative." In other words, the researcher failed to reject a null hypothesis when the null hypothesis was indeed false.

As with our discussion of correlation in the previous chapter, it is also valuable to report some expression of the degree of certainty one could have regarding the difference that was found in the sample data by reporting a "confidence interval." A confidence interval is the range of possible differences one would not reject as possible hypothetical population values that could have generated the sample data within a given level of precision. To review from the previous chapter, we remind the reader that researchers will commonly report 95% confidence intervals, which are indicative of a range of values one would *not* reject as plausible hypothetical population values given an alpha criterion of statistical significance of .05. Although dependent on several factors, all else being equal, relatively larger samples sizes will always result in narrower confidence intervals for differences—that is, relatively less uncertainty and more precise estimates.

A Note on Statistical Fluency

Please note that the information dealing with approaches to inferential analysis presented in this book are intended to serve only as an introduction to the topic. Similar to nearly all of the topics addressed in this book, there is much more that could be covered before anything approaching a complete treatment would be achieved. For example, there are many other statistical tools that music education researchers find useful. Moreover, NHST is only one of the possible methods for conducting inferential analyses in general. We hope that by working through the materials in this book, you will begin to feel comfortable discussing and interpreting some of the basic statistical analyses that commonly appear in music education research. To reiterate our suggestion above, please see Box 18.1 for further information about inferential statistical analyses.

As with any subject, acquiring mastery over foundational concepts and skills requires a good deal of time and much practice. At this point in your research career, it is not critical that you acquire an in-depth understanding of technical aspects, such as the mathematical formulas that result in the particular test statistics that each procedure yields (i.e., the t statistic for the *t*-tests, the F statistic for the ANOVA tests, the U statistic for the Mann-Whitney U test, etc.). Instead, consider that although the mathematical underpinnings for the variety of inferential tests described in this book can be complex and can vary a great deal, at a basic level interpreting the results of the tests is roughly the same. For example, all of the inferential analyses discussed in this chapter as well as the previous chapter result in a *p* value that is then compared to an alpha criterion for the purpose of deciding whether or not to reject a null hypothesis. If the *p* value is sufficiently low, traditionally less than .05, then the null hypothesis can be rejected. If the *p* value is not sufficiently low, then the researcher fails to reject the null hypothesis. Should the result of the test indicate statistical significance, then it is incumbent upon the researcher to go a step further and also interpret the result in terms of its effect size or magnitude.

Although there is much more that can be said about the procedures described in this book, we believe that the knowledge you will construct when working through the statistical material we did choose to present will serve as a good "jumping-off point" for delving into these concepts more deeply and branching out to other statistical techniques. Should you wish to conduct statistical analyses for a research project of your own, we recommend working closely with a mentor, a more knowledgeable peer, or a statistical consultant who can serve as a resource by guiding and checking your work.

Data for the Examples in This Chapter

Hypothetical data have been generated to use as examples in this chapter. The data are suitable for demonstrating inferential tests of differences with interval/ratio-, ordinal-, or nominal-level outcome measurements (i.e., dependent variables) gathered from either independent or dependent samples. Brief descriptions of several research scenarios and variables relevant to each are presented in Tables 18.1, 18.3, and 18.4. Data files and video demonstrations for conducting the analyses described in this chapter using the SPSS are available as an online supplement to this chapter (see items 9 and 10, 12 and 13, and 15 and 16, Chapter 18 on the Companion website ▶. for videos and data files corresponding to the interval/ratio-, ordinal-, and nominal-level outcome data analyses in this chapter, respectively.).[1]

Writing about Inferential Tests for Determining Differences

Throughout the chapter, we present samples of how authors might write about inferential tests for determining differences. We include writing excerpts for each of the analyses we conducted with the various hypothetical data sets presented in the following sections. At least five items may be addressed when writing about inferential tests of differences: (a) the direction of any observed differences—which groups of scores appear relatively lower or higher than which others; (b) whether the difference can be declared statistically significant; (c) the effect size of the difference in terms of being relatively small, moderate, or large; (d) the measure of uncertainty for the finding (e.g., confidence interval); and (e) if there are more than two sets of scores being compared, the results of any post-hoc comparisons. When reporting statistical significance, it is best to report the exact p value your software returns for your analysis. If a p value is exceedingly small, less than .001, then simply indicating $p < .001$ will suffice. There are idiosyncratic conventions for reporting inferential tests that we include in the examples below, even though we have not discussed them. For example, explanations regarding test statistic values, values indicating degrees of freedom, and elements of ANOVA tables are only briefly commented on and in-depth treatments of these topics are beyond the scope of this book. We included these additional elements in our write-ups to conform to the guidelines for reporting from the American Psychological Association (2019) and because they will often appear in the research articles you read.[2]

---

[1] SPSS is a proprietary software package and can be quite expensive without a college or university site license. Those looking for an alternative could try the free open-source programs Jamovi (www.jamovi.org), JASP (www.jasp-stats.org), or VassarStats (http://vassarstats.net) instead. These free alternatives have many of the same features as SPSS, although not all analysis tasks are as convenient to execute and the graphing functions are a bit more difficult to manipulate.

[2] There are, of course, additional issues that could be addressed when writing about inferential tests for differences. Some statistical tests rely on assumptions about the data that are to be analyzed. For example, the independent samples t-test and one-way ANOVA assume that the data within the groups being compared are from a population in which the sampling distribution of the mean is normal and that the variances of the groups are equal, whereas the repeated-measures ANOVA assumes that the data conform to a statistical concept called "sphericity." There are additional statistical tests for evaluating these assumptions, such as

Determining Differences with Interval- or Ratio-Level Outcome Data

Independent Samples *t*-Test

An independent samples *t*-test can be used to compare the means of two independent samples with interval- or ratio-level data, such as when individuals are assigned to one group or another (e.g., control vs. treatment) or are already grouped via some preexisting method (e.g., classroom A vs. classroom B). For example, imagine a study in which a researcher would like to examine the effect of a dance-infused elementary music approach on children's rhythmic perception. The researcher could first (a) randomly assign children to either a control group that involved a traditional pedagogical approach without dance activities or a treatment group that involved a traditional pedagogical approach infused with dance activities throughout, then (b) deliver the instruction, and finally (c) measure the students' rhythmic perception ability at the conclusion of the study. The researcher could use an independent samples t-test to determine whether there is a significant difference between the groups on rhythmic perception ability. The data in Table 18.1 have been constructed to illustrate these analyses.

As with any statistical analysis, we first visualize and summarize our data with plots and descriptive analyses. A plot of the rhythm_perception_post_test data according to the control versus dance groups is presented in the first two sets of dots that appear in Figure 18.1. In this figure, each gray dot represents a participant's score, and the mean of each group is marked with a black star symbol. This type of dot plot can be useful for getting a sense of the variability among the scores within each group and is also helpful for emphasizing the fact that while means of groups can be different, the individuals' scores within each group can range such that they overlap with the individuals' scores in another group. For example, even though the mean of the children in the dance group is higher than those in the control group, there are several children in the control group with scores much higher than some of those in the dance group. Therefore, when discussing group differences, researchers typically speak in terms of differences "on average." The descriptive analyses of the data show that the rhythm_perception_post_test mean for the dance group ($M = 60.48$, $SD = 12.21$) is quite a bit higher than that for the control group ($M = 47.95$, $SD = 9.53$) but that the variability is similar, and both sets of scores are approximately normally distributed (e.g., skewness and kurtosis values are not too extreme).

---

the Shapiro Wilk test, the Levene's test, and Bartlett's test, respectively. The normality and equality of variance assumptions were met for the analyses in this chapter; the sphericity assumption was not. Therefore, a common correction for the failure to meet the sphericity assumption was applied. It is also important to report additional information about the precision of an inferential test (e.g., by presenting confidence intervals). However, discussing these additional issues would distract from the core ideas you need to consider when interpreting the inferential tests discussed in this chapter. Therefore, we refer you to other texts for such information (e.g., Miksza & Elpus, 2018; Russell, 2018).

Table 18.1 Description of the data generated for use in the scalar outcome data examples in this chapter: Investigating the effect of dance on children's rhythm perception

Research Scenario 1: Scalar Outcome Data
A researcher has designed an experiment to determine the effect of a dance-infused curricular approach on children's rhythm perception. Children have been randomly assigned to different groups, whose rhythm perception ability was measured at three points in time: once immediately at the conclusion of the experiment, once six months following the conclusion of the experiment, and once one year following the conclusion of the experiment. Variable names and labels refer to the coding of the variables as they appear in the corresponding SPSS data file provided in the supplemental materials for this chapter.

Variable Name (*Label*)	Numerical Values Possible (*Measurement Level*)
1. participant_code_sca (*A number as a label for each participant*)	A numerical code assigned to each participant (*nominal level*)
2. experimental_group_two_cat (*Two-category experimental group designation*)	Two category codes to indicate whether a participant was in a no movement–control group or a dance-infused curriculum treatment group (*nominal level*)
3. experimental_group_three_cat (*Three-category experimental group designation*)	Three category codes to indicate whether a participant was in a no movement–control group or a dance-infused treatment group or a free-movement treatment group (*nominal level*)
4. rhythm_perception_post_test (*Rhythm perception score at conclusion of the experiment*)	A score derived from a measure of participants' rhythmic perception ability at the conclusion of the experiment (i.e., posttest), possible range of 0, indicating poor rhythm perception, to 10, indicating excellent rhythm perception (*scalar, interval level*)
5. rhythm_perception_six_mo_follow_up (*Rhythm perception score six months following the conclusion of the experiment*)	A score for the same measure as the one described in 4, except administered six months after the experiment concluded (*scalar, interval level*)
6. rhythm_perception_year_follow_up (*Rhythm perception score a year following the conclusion of the experiment*)	A score for the same measure as the one described in 4, except administered one year after the experiment concluded (*scalar, interval level*)

Upon conducting an independent samples *t*-test with experimental_group_cat_two as the independent variable (i.e., whether students were in the control or dance group) and rhythm_perception_post_test as the dependent variable (i.e., the outcome), we find out that the difference is statistically significant, since the *p* value resulting from the analysis is well below .05 (i.e., $p = .0009$, which would traditionally be presented as $p < .001$). In other words, the probability of observing a difference between groups at least as large as what we observed in our sample data if we assumed a null hypothesis of "0" difference was true was 9 out of 10,000—a very small probability.

Since we are able to reject a null hypothesis and declare statistical significance, the next step is to examine the effect size of the difference. Cohen's *d* is the typical

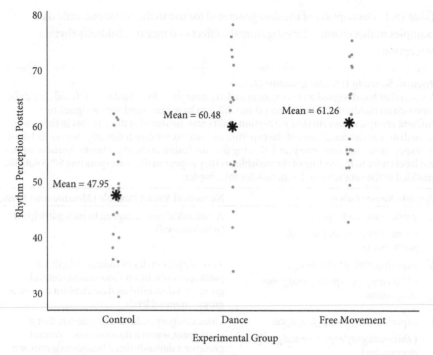

Figure 18.1 A dot plot depicting children's rhythm perception ability posttest scores according to experimental grouping. Each dot represents an individual child's score; black stars represent the means of each group of scores.

measure of effect size used for determining the magnitude of a significant difference between two means. Cohen's *d* values between .20 and .50 are considered small; values between .50 and .80 are considered medium; and those greater than .80 are considered large. Generally speaking, each unit of a Cohen's *d* value is indicative of a standard deviation unit. In other words, a Cohen's *d* value of .50 indicates that the means are one-half of a standard deviation apart from each other; a difference with a value of 1.0 is indicative of 1 standard deviation apart; and so on. The Cohen's *d* value for this difference is 1.14, which is indicative of a very large effect.

Here is an example of how to write for publication about an independent samples *t*-test for interval- or ratio-level data:

> A significant difference was found between the mean of the posttest rhythm perception scores for the control group ($M = 47.95$, $SD = 9.53$) and that of the dance-infused instruction group ($M = 60.48$, $SD = 12.21$), $t(38) = 3.62$, $p < .001$, 95% CI [5.51, 19.54].[3] On average, the dance-infused instruction group performed better than the control group, and the difference represented a large effect (Cohen's $d = 1.14$).

---

[3] The notation $t(38) = 3.62$, $p < .001$, includes two items not discussed in this chapter: the "degrees of freedom" of the analysis (38 degrees of freedom) and the t-statistic generated from the data ($t = 3.62$). Degrees

Dependent Samples *t*-Test

True to its name, a dependent samples *t*-test can be used to compare means gathered from dependent samples, such as when a single group of individuals is measured on more than one occasion (e.g., across time or on multiple variables using the same measurement scale). Let's imagine that the researcher conducting the dance-infused curriculum example was also interested in whether *all* of the children's rhythm perception scores increased over time, regardless of whether they were in the control or dance groups. For example, a dependent samples *t*-test could be used to compare the mean of rhythm perception scores of all the children at the end of the study to the mean of their scores if they were measured again six months after the conclusion of the study. We will use the rhythm_perception_post_test and rhythm_perception_six_mo_follow_up variables to demonstrate this analysis. Visualizing the data and conducting descriptive analyses of the variables show that the mean of the children's scores at the six-month follow-up ($M = 66.30$, $SD = 8.76$) was higher than that at posttest ($M = 56.56$, $SD = 11.90$) and that the scores were somewhat less varied at the six-month follow-up as well (Figure 18.2). Both sets of scores were approximately normally distributed.

When conducting a dependent samples *t*-test to compare the children's scores at posttest (rhythm_perception_post_test) to their score at the six-month follow-up (rhythm_perception_six_mo_follow_up), we can think of the rhythm perception scores as the dependent variable and time (or occasion of measurement) as the independent variable. The test results indicate that the difference between the two occasions is statistically significant, since the *p* value resulting from the analysis is well below .05 (i.e., $p < .001$). In other words, the probability of observing a difference between measurement occasions at least as large as what we observed in our data if we assumed a null hypothesis of "0" difference was true was less than 1 in 1,000—a very small probability. Again, we can reject the null hypothesis of no difference and examine the effect size. The Cohen's *d* value is 0.84, suggesting that the magnitude of this difference is also large.

Here is one way you might write about a dependent samples *t*-test for interval- or ratio-level data:

> A significant difference was found between the children's posttest rhythm perception scores ($M = 56.56$, $SD = 11.90$) and their rhythm perception scores from the

of freedom are the number of independent objects free to vary in an inferential analysis. For example, in this analysis we began with 40 independent values, that is, one rhythm perception posttest score from each independent participant. Then, to test the difference between the groups, we first had to calculate the mean for each group. Calculating the mean removed 1 degree of freedom from each group, leaving us with 19 independent values in each group rather than 20 and, therefore, 38 degrees of freedom in total. Test statistics result from transformations of sample data into a single value that can be compared to a particular distribution for the purposes of NHST. For this example, the sample data are transformed into a *t* statistic, which is then compared to a *t* distribution. Many inferential statistical tests within the NHST tradition will involve degrees of freedom, and all will involve a test statistic. These values are provided by statistical computing packages as a matter of routine. Please see the texts in Box 18.1 for more information about these items.

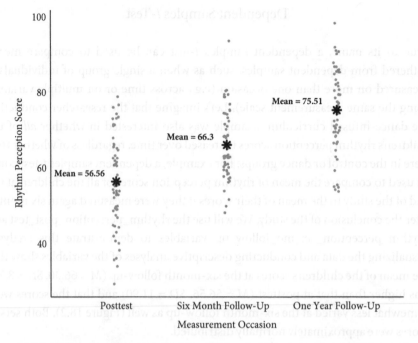

Figure 18.2 A dot plot depicting all of the children's rhythm perception ability scores at posttest, at a six-month follow-up, and at a one-year follow-up. Each dot represents an individual child's score; black stars represent the means of each group of scores.

six-month follow-up ($M = 66.30$, $SD = 8.76$), $t(59) = 6.56$, $p < .001$, 95% CI [6.76, 12.70].[4] On average, the rhythm perception scores were higher at the six-month follow-up than at posttest. Cohen's d indicates that the difference represented a large effect ($d = .84$).

One-Way ANOVA

Researchers who wish to conduct tests of differences with an interval- or ratio-level outcome variable across more than two independent or dependent samples must look beyond the t-test for doing so. A family of inferential statistical tests that can be used to compare more than two groups are various versions of the ANOVA. The mathematical procedures of the ANOVA are quite different from those of the t-test; however, recall our note on inferential statistical tests, wherein we suggested that even though the mathematical underpinnings of procedures will vary, the results of the tests can be interpreted in very similar ways. As such, we will not delve into the

---

[4] See note 3 regarding the custom of reporting degrees of freedom and test statistic values. Also note that the calculation of degrees of freedom for different tests will vary. See the texts in Box 18.1 for further information.

particularities of the computations for ANOVA and, instead, will focus on issues central to interpretation.

Imagine that our hypothetical researcher investigating children's rhythm perception abilities included three groups in their experimental design rather than two: (a) control, (b) a dance treatment group, and (c) a free-movement treatment group (i.e., movement, but not dance specifically). Comparing all three sets of scores in Figure 18.1, it seems that while the means for the dance (M = 60.48, SD = 12.21) and free-movement (M = 61.26, SD = 9.06) groups were quite similar, the means for both of those groups were higher than the mean for the control group (M = 47.95, SD = 9.53). The version of ANOVA applicable to comparing more than two independent samples is a one-way ANOVA; the "one" refers to the fact that an outcome (i.e., a dependent variable) is being compared as a function of one independent variable.

Conducting a one-way ANOVA with these data results in a p value of p = .0001, which is again much less than .05 (i.e., $p < .001$). That is, the probability of observing differences due to grouping at least as large as the differences we found in our data if we assumed a null hypothesis of "0" was true was less than 1 out of 1000—which is very small. Therefore, we can reject the null hypothesis of no difference among the three groups and declare statistical significance. When conducting an ANOVA, the initial test comparing all of the groups is referred to as an "omnibus test," derived from the Latin *omni* for "all," since the differences among all the groups is being evaluated with a single result.

Given that there are more than two groups involved in this analysis (i.e., control, dance, free-movement), the Cohen's d statistic is not appropriate for calculating effect size. Calculating effect size following a significant ANOVA test involves determining how much of the total variation among outcome variable scores is explained by the grouping. Recall from our chapter on descriptive statistics that variance is, roughly speaking, the average amount of variation in a set of scores relative to the mean. When determining the effect size for ANOVA, researchers report the proportion of the variation around a "grand" mean (i.e., the mean of all 60 of the scores regardless of grouping) that can be explained by the groupings. The statistic representing the proportion of the variance in the outcome due to the grouping variable is called "eta squared" (symbolized with the Greek letter: η^2). The eta squared value for the test of differences in rhythm_perception_post_test scores among the control, dance, and free-movement groups is .26, which means that approximately 26% of the variation in rhythm perception scores is explained by the grouping variable (i.e., experimental conditions). Eta squared values between .01 and .06 are indicative of a small effect, whereas those between .06 and .14 are considered medium-size effects, and those greater than .14 are interpreted as large effects. Therefore, the statistically significant difference we found across the experimental groups on rhythm_perception_post_test can be considered a large effect. The 95% confidence interval for this effect size is 95% CI [.08, .42].

Post-Hoc Analyses of One-Way ANOVA

As you have likely intuited, a significant result for an omnibus test of an ANOVA still leaves several questions for the researcher to pursue. For example, although we know that there is a difference in rhythm perception as a function of the three experimental groups, we don't know between which groups those differences lie. Consequently, researchers need to conduct additional follow-up tests to compare pairs of groups. These follow-up tests are called "post-hoc" tests, from the Latin meaning "after this."[5] At this point, you might be wondering, what's the point of using an ANOVA for examining differences between more than two groups if researchers will just turn around and compare pairs anyway? This is a good question, and if the result of the ANOVA is nonsignificant (i.e., there are no significant differences between the means of the three groups), we don't need to run the separate follow-up comparisons. However, a more complete answer requires a discussion of the phenomenon of "family-wise error."

Every time you conduct an inferential analysis in the framework of NHST you are also taking a risk—"rolling the dice," so to speak—and accepting the fact that you may reject the null hypothesis when you shouldn't have, that is, you may be committing a Type I error. For example, recall that if we apply the traditional alpha criterion of .05, then we are accepting the risk of committing a Type I error 5% of the time in the long run; that is, that 1 out of every 20 times we reject a null hypothesis we will have done so mistakenly. Theoretically, the more tests we run, the greater that risk becomes. The degree to which that risk increases is the family-wise error rate, and a simple formula for calculating how much it increases for each additional test you wish to run is:

$$\textit{Family-wise error rate} = 1 - (1 - \textit{alpha criterion})^{(\text{\# of tests})}$$

We have three groups that can be paired with each other in our example for a maximum of three possible pairings, that is, three possible tests: (a) control versus dance, (b) control versus free-movement, and (c) dance versus free-movement. If we substitute .05 for "alpha criterion" and "3" for "# of tests" in the formula, we have:

$$\textit{Family-wise error rate} = 1 - (1 - .05)^3 = .1426$$

Computing the formula with our values results in a family-wise error rate of .1426. This means that if we conduct the three possible pairwise inferential tests,

---

[5] In some circumstances, researchers hypothesize that particular pairs of groups will be different prior to conducting their ANOVA test. In these cases, the tests used for such pair-wise comparisons are called "a priori tests" or "a priori contrasts," stemming from the Latin for "from before." However, compared to post-hoc tests, these are much less common in the music education literature, and so we will not focus on them in this book.

each with an alpha criterion of .05, our risk of committing a Type I error rises from .05 to .1426. In other words, in the long run we would be likely to commit a Type I error 14.26% of the time rather than 5% of the time. That's a substantial increase in making an error! Although running a single ANOVA test as opposed to multiple t-tests for each possible pair of groups in the first place avoids this inflation of risk, conducting post-hoc analyses that ultimately involve pairwise comparisons of the groups does not. Therefore, we need a particular kind of post-hoc test that will allow us to test differences among pairs without inflating the risk of committing a Type I error.

Fortunately, there are many formulas for conducting post-hoc analyses that account for the problem of family-wise error rate in many different ways. Such procedures mathematically adjust the results of tests to compensate for increased risk due to family-wise error. For example, a commonly used post-hoc procedure that does this is Tukey's tests of honest significant differences (Tukey HSD). Applying Tukey HSD tests to the three possible pairings of groups in our example reveals that, as you may have guessed, the mean of the control group is significantly lower than the means of the dance ($p < .001$) and free-movement ($p < .001$) groups, but that the means of the dance and free-movement groups are not significantly different from each other ($p = .96$). Having used the Tukey HSD tests, we can rest assured that the chance of committing a Type I error is indeed only 5% (i.e., alpha criterion = .05), since the procedure is designed to automatically adjust the analyses to compensate for any inflation in risk due to family-wise error rate.

Here is an example of writing about one-way ANOVA for two or more independent groups and interval- or ratio-level data:

A one-way ANOVA was performed with posttest rhythm perception scores serving as the dependent variable and experimental condition (i.e., control vs. dance vs. free-movement) as the independent variable. Rhythm perception ability scores varied significantly as a function of experimental condition, $F(2, 57) = 10.39, p < .001$[6] (see Table 18.2). The eta squared value of .26 indicated that this was a large effect, 95% CI [.08, .42]. Post-hoc Tukey HSD tests showed that the control group ($M = 47.95, SD = 9.53$) scored significantly ($p < .001$) lower than the dance-infused ($M = 60.48, SD = 12.21$) or free-movement ($M = 61.26, SD = 9.06$) treatment groups. However, the dance-infused and free-movement treatment groups means were not significantly different from each other.[7]

---

[6] ANOVA findings are reported with two degrees-of-freedom values. In the one-way ANOVA, one is related to the variation due to the grouping of the participants (between group variation) and another references the variation not due to the grouping or, in other words, the variation left among the participants within each of the groups (within-group or residual variation). In this analysis the degrees of freedom are 2, representing 3 groups in the analysis minus 1, and 57, representing 60 participants minus 2 degrees of freedom for the grouping minus 1. The F statistic is the test statistic used in ANOVA procedures. As described in the previous note, this statistic results from transformations of the sample data into a single value that can be compared to a particular distribution for the purposes of NHST—in this case, the F distribution.

[7] Confidence intervals can also be reported for each difference examined in post-hoc tests; however, we do not include them here.

Table 18.2 ANOVA summary table for the effects of experimental treatment on rhythm perception

Source	df	SS	MS	F	p	η^2
Experimental group	2	2231.86	1115.93	10.39	< .001	.26
Residual	57	6120.10	107.37			
Total	59	8351.96				

Note: The "SS" and "MS" columns refer to "sums of squares" and "mean squares," respectively. Briefly, the SS column represents that variation due to each of the "sources" listed in the table, i.e., variation due to Experimental group and variation not due to Experimental group, i.e., residual variation. The MS column is the result of dividing the SS column by the degrees of freedom for each "source." The MS of the Experimental group source is then divided by the MS of the residual source to arrive at the *F* statistic. These values are also provided by statistical computing packages as a matter of routine. Further discussion of the derivation and calculation of these values is beyond the scope of this book, and the reader is directed to the texts in Box 18.1.

Repeated-Measures ANOVA

Researchers who wish to conduct tests of differences on some interval- or ratio-level variable across more than two dependent samples must also look beyond the *t*-test for doing so. Imagine that our hypothetical researcher investigating children's rhythm perception abilities measured the children at three points in time rather than two: (a) at the conclusion of the study (i.e., posttest), (b) six months following the conclusion of the study, and (c) one year following the conclusion of the study. The children's rhythm perception scores for these three time points are plotted in Figure 18.2. If we were to compute descriptive analyses of the rhythm perception scores on each occasion for all the children regardless of experimental grouping, we would find that their scores increased from the posttest measurement at the conclusion of the study ($M = 56.56$, $SD = 11.90$) to the six-month follow-up ($M = 66.30$, $SD = 8.76$), and then again to the one-year follow-up ($M = 75.51$, $SD = 10.33$). A version of ANOVA applicable to comparing more than two dependent samples is the repeated-measures ANOVA; the term "repeated" refers to the fact that the sets of scores being compared come from multiple measurements of the same group of people (as opposed to different groups of people).

Conducting a repeated-measures ANOVA with these data results in a *p* value that is, yet again, well below .05 (i.e., $p < .001$). The probability of observing a difference due to measurement occasion at least as large as that which we found in our data if we assumed a null hypothesis of "0" difference was true was, again, very small. Therefore, we can reject the null hypothesis of no difference among the sets of scores from the three measurement occasions and declare statistical significance. As with our previous example, this initial test comparing across all the measurement occasions is referred to as an "omnibus test" since the differences among the three measurement occasions are being evaluated with a single test. The effect size indicator for a result from a repeated-measures ANOVA is also an eta squared value, although in this case it is a "partial" eta squared value (η_p^2), the reason for which is beyond the scope of this book. Suffice it to say that partial eta squared is also interpreted as the proportion of variance across all 180 of the scores (i.e., 60 children measured three times each) that is due to the grouping of the scores—except, in this case, the groupings are measurement occasions. The partial eta squared value for this repeated-measures ANOVA result is .36, indicating that 36% of the variation among all of the children's scores across all time points is explained by the grouping of the scores within each time point. Like our previous ANOVA example, this is indicative of a large effect size.

Post-Hoc Analyses of Repeated-Measures ANOVA

At this point we are in a situation similar to our previous ANOVA analyses in that we have found a significant and substantial difference among the rhythm perception scores across measurement occasions, but we have yet to determine what differences may exist between measurement occasion pairs. However, again, we would not want to simply conduct multiple pairs of t-tests since that would increase our chances of committing Type I error due to the family-wise error rate phenomenon. As such, we need to follow our omnibus result with a post-hoc analysis procedure that compensates for the potential for increased Type I error.

Another common way to control for Type I error is the Bonferroni method, which involves lowering the traditional alpha criterion of .05 according to the number of tests you wish to conduct and then applying that as your decision rule for declaring statistical significance. The formula for the Bonferroni correction is simply:

$$Bonferroni\ corrected\ alpha\ criterion = \frac{original\ alpha\ criterion}{\#\ of\ tests}$$

If we begin with an alpha criterion of .05 and wish to run three tests, one for each possible pairing of measurement occasions (i.e., posttest vs. six-month follow-up, posttest vs. one-year follow-up, six-month follow-up vs. one-year follow-up), we would compute the following:

$$Bonferroni\ corrected\ alpha\ criterion = \frac{.05}{3} = .016$$

Our Bonferroni procedure–corrected alpha criterion is .016, meaning that the p values from our pairwise post-hoc tests must be less than .016 in order for us to declare a statistically significant difference between any of the pairs. When actually applying this procedure to the data for this example, we find that the differences for all possible pairings of measurement occasions are indeed statistically significant, since dependent samples t-tests results in p values much lower than .016 for each pairing.

Table 18.3 Repeated-measures ANOVA examining the differences among flexibility routines

Source	df	SS	MS	F	p	η_p^2
Time	2	10767.72	6294.64	56.50	< .001	.36
Residual	100.93	11244.18	111.41			

Note: The "SS" and "MS" columns refer to "sums of squares" and "mean squares," respectively.

This is one way to write up the results of a repeated-measures ANOVA for two or more dependent groups and interval- or ratio-level data:

A repeated-measures ANOVA with measurement occasion (i.e., posttest, six-month follow-up, one-year follow-up) serving as the independent variable and rhythm perception ability scores serving as the dependent variable was conducted. The assumption of sphericity was not met, and therefore the Greenhouse-Geisser correction was applied, revealing a significant difference among conditions, $F(2, 100.93) = 56.50, p < .001, \eta_p^2 = .36$[8] (see Table 18.3). The partial eta squared value indicated this was a large effect. We conducted follow-up pairwise comparisons with the Bonferroni correction for Type I error applied. These analyses showed rhythm perception abilities increased significantly across time. More specifically, the posttest mean ($M = 56.56, SD = 11.90$) was significantly lower than the six-month follow-up mean ($M = 66.30, SD = 8.76$) ($p < .001$), and the mean for the six-month follow-up scores was significantly lower than the mean for one-year follow-up scores ($M = 75.51, SD = 10.33$) ($p < .001$).

Determining Differences with Ordinal-Level Outcome Data

Inferential tests for determining differences between sets of scores consisting of ordinal-level data are not based on the comparisons of means or ANOVA among scores. This is because, in contrast to interval- or ratio-level data, the quantitative nature of ordinal data is such that computations of means, standard deviations, variances, and so on are not typically meaningful. Instead, the tests suitable for ordinal data that we are going to present in this section are based on computations involving ranks. However—to once again reiterate our earlier point—even though

---

[8] The data for this analysis did not meet the assumption of sphericity, which is a common occurrence when conducting repeated-measures ANOVA. Sphericity is a complicated concept, and, at this point, it is not critical to understand for interpreting the inferential test results. Fortunately, correcting for this failed assumption is a simple matter of choosing to report the Greenhouse-Geisser test statistic that is automatically returned by many statistical software programs, which is what we have done with this example. Confidence intervals could be reported for elements of these analyses as well. However, some of them are not as easily attainable from software, and we do not report them here.

the mathematical methods for conducting the inferential tests for ordinal-level data are different from those for tests with interval- or ratio-level data, the results of both categories of tests can be interpreted in very similar ways.

Mann-Whitney U Test

A Mann-Whitney U test can be used to compare the means of two independent samples with ordinal-level data. For example, imagine a study in which a researcher would like to explore whether preservice music teachers' perceptions of their ability to execute effective instructional sequences varies as a function of the type of degree program that they are in. The hypothetical data set described in Table 18.4 includes variables we can use to illustrate this scenario. For example, the variable teacher_

Table 18.4 Description of the data generated for use in the ordinal outcome data examples in this chapter: Exploring preservice teacher efficacy

Research Scenario 2
Among a host of other issues, a team of researchers is investigating the teaching efficacy beliefs of preservice music educators. They are interested in whether their participants' sense of efficacy differs according to whether they are considering their ability to execute effective instructional sequences, their ability to manage the classroom environment, or their ability to assess students. Variable names and labels refer to the coding of the variables as they appear in the corresponding SPSS data file provided in the supplemental materials for this chapter.

Variable Name (*Label*)	Numerical Values Possible (*Measurement Level*)
1. participant_code_ord (*A number as a label for each participant*)	A numerical code assigned to each participant (*nominal level*)
2. major_emphasis_two_cat (*Two-category major emphasis area indicator*)	Two category codes to indicate whether a participant was in an instrumental-emphasis degree program or a choral/general music–emphasis degree program (*nominal level*)
3. major_emphasis_three_cat (*Three-category major emphasis area indicator*)	Three category codes to indicate whether a participant was in an instrumental-emphasis, a choral-emphasis, or a general music–emphasis degree program (*nominal level*)
4. teacher_sequence_efficacy_item (*A rating of one's perception of teaching efficacy regarding ability to execute effective instructional sequences*)	A rating of participants' efficacy regarding their ability to execute effective instructional sequences, with a range of 1, not at all efficacious, to 7, extremely efficacious (*ordinal level*)
5. teacher_management_efficacy_item (*A rating of one's perception of teaching efficacy regarding classroom management abilities*)	A rating of participants' efficacy regarding their ability to successfully manage their classroom, with a range of 1, not at all efficacious, to 7, extremely efficacious (*ordinal level*)
6. teacher_assessment_efficacy_item (*A rating of one's perception of teaching efficacy regarding assessment abilities*)	A rating of participants' efficacy regarding their ability to assess student learning, with a range of 1, not at all efficacious, to 7, extremely efficacious (*ordinal level*)

sequence_efficacy_item represents a group of preservice music teachers' ratings of efficacy beliefs regarding executing instructional sequences on a single questionnaire item that could range from a score of 1 to 7 (i.e., an ordinal rating scale item from lowest to highest efficacy) and the major_emphasis_two_cat variable is an indicator of whether the preservice music teacher was in an instrumental- or choral/general-emphasis program.

The researcher could visualize this data with a clustered bar chart to get a sense of how the preservice music teachers responded on the rating scale as well as whether their ratings seem to vary as a function of degree emphasis types. Figure 18.3 is a plot of the major_emphasis_two_cat and teacher_sequence_efficacy_item variables from our hypothetical data set. Looking at Figure 18.3, it is apparent that the choral/general degree–emphasis students tended to rate themselves higher than the instrumental degree–emphasis students. Conducting a Mann-Whitney U test on these data shows that the difference in the ratings between the groups is statistically significant with a p value much below the threshold of .05 (i.e., $p < .001$). The probability we would observe a difference as large as we did in our data if we assumed a

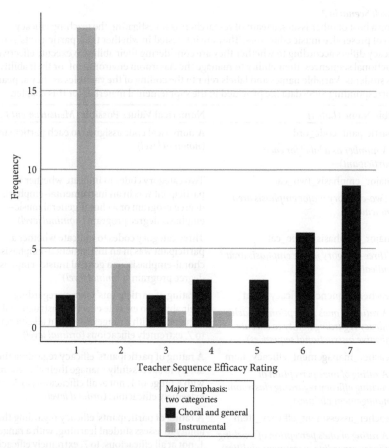

Figure 18.3 A clustered bar chart depicting the preservice music teachers' ratings of their instructional sequencing efficacy beliefs.

null hypothesis of "0" difference was true is, once again, very small. Therefore, we can reject a null hypothesis of no difference between the groups of preservice music teachers on their perceptions of instructional sequence efficacy.

Like the examples described in the sections above, it is also important to report a measure of effective size to depict the magnitude of this difference. The statistic for communicating the effect size of a difference when analyzing ordinal-level data with two independent samples is abbreviated r—although be careful to note the context that surrounds any presentation of r in the literature, since it is easy to confuse it with the r that is used as a symbol for the Pearson correlation coefficient. When reporting effect size with r, values ranging from .10 to .30 are considered indicative of small effects; values from .30 to .50 are considered moderate effects; and those greater than .50 are considered large effects. The effect size for this example is .79, indicating that the difference in ratings between the instrumental-emphasis and choral/general-emphasis students is large. Confidence intervals can be calculated for this effect size, but they are rarely reported.

Using these data, here is how you could write up the details of a Mann-Whitney U test for ordinal data:

> A significant difference between the instrumental- and choral/general degree–emphasis group's ratings of instructional sequence efficacy was found, Mann-Whitney U = 589.50, $p < .001$. Choral and general music degree–emphasis participants tended to report stronger instructional sequencing efficacy beliefs than instrumental-emphasis participants, and this represented a large difference, $r = .79$.

Wilcoxon Test for Paired Samples

An inferential test that is commonly used for comparing two dependent samples on an ordinal-level outcome variable is the Wilcoxon test for paired samples. Let's extend the example from the previous section and imagine that the researcher also wished to compare the preservice music teachers' efficacy beliefs regarding their instructional sequencing ability with their efficacy beliefs regarding their ability to manage a classroom. In this case, the researcher would be comparing the same set of individuals on two variables which are measured on the same ordinal scale; that is, both variables are represented by the participants' ratings on scales with a possible range of 1 to 7. However, since the scores for the instructional sequencing ability ratings and the classroom management ability ratings are coming from the same group of people, these data are considered dependent samples. Note that it's possible to compare these scores only because they are measured on the same scale. If these variables were represented by different measurement scales, such as one being rated on a scale of 1 to 5 and the other being rated on a scale of 1 to 7, then any differences found between them could be a function of the scales themselves rather than differences in the phenomena we were most interested in measuring.

Figure 18.4 is a clustered bar chart of the teacher_sequence_efficacy_item and teacher_management_efficacy_item variables from the 50 preservice music teachers in our hypothetical data set (see Table 18.4). It is difficult to see a clear contrast between the ratings of the two items in this particular plot. Although it seems there is some tendency for the preservice educators to rate their classroom management efficacy greater than their instructional sequencing efficacy, no clear difference is apparent. Conducting the Wilcoxon test for paired samples results in a p value of .20, which is not below the alpha criterion threshold of .05. Therefore, in this case we fail to reject the null hypothesis and cannot declare the difference between these variables to be statistically significant. As such, our analyses are essentially complete. Since there is no statistically significant difference, there is no need to conduct an analysis of the effect size of this difference. (Although, if we did, we would use the same r statistic as we did with the Mann-Whitney U test and judge the effect according to the same criteria for small, medium, and large differences—in fact, the effect size of this particular nonsignificant difference is $r = .17$, which is,

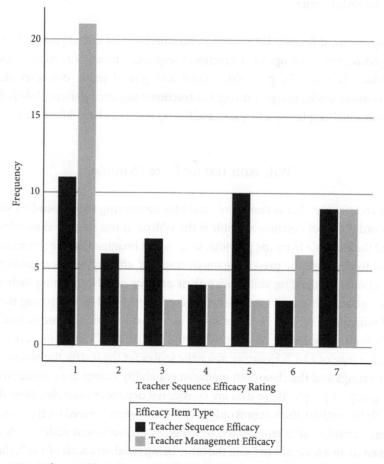

Figure 18.4 A clustered bar chart depicting the preservice music teachers' ratings of their instructional sequencing efficacy and classroom management beliefs.

logically, very small. Confidence intervals can be calculated for this effect size as well, but they are rarely reported.)

A Wilcoxon test for grouped pairs for ordinal data could be written up in this fashion:

> We used a Wilcoxon paired-samples test to investigate the difference between the participants' efficacy ratings for instructional sequencing and classroom management. A significant difference was not found, $Z = 458.00$, $p = .20$. Therefore, preservice music education majors did not rate themselves as more able to provide effective instructional sequences than to manage a classroom.

Tests for Comparing Ordinal Data across More Than Two Samples

There are inferential tests for comparing more than two samples on ordinal-level outcome variables. The Kruskal-Wallis test is commonly used for comparing more than two independent samples, and Friedman's test is typically used for comparing more than two dependent samples. As with the ANOVA tests we described above, the Kruskal-Wallis and Friedman's tests would yield an omnibus test result indicating whether it is possible to reject the null hypothesis of a difference among the two or more samples. Should the omnibus test result in a p value sufficiently small to reject the null hypothesis, the researcher could then follow up this result with post-hoc analyses that incorporate some method of correction for Type I error inflation due to family-wise error.

Although we will not present an example of the Kruskal-Wallis and Friedman's tests in this chapter, there are variables in the hypothetical data set we have created that will allow you to do these analyses. For example, for the Kruskal-Wallis test, you could compare the preservice music teachers' instructional sequence efficacy as a function of three (rather than two) groups, with instrumental, choral, and general each serving as distinct categories of degree emphases. For the Friedman test, you could compare the preservice music teachers' ratings of instructional sequencing, classroom management, and assessment efficacy since all three variables are measured on the same ordinal scale of 1 to 7.

Determining Differences with Nominal-Level Outcome Data

The Chi square test of independence and McNemar's test are inferential tests for determining differences between groups with nominal-level data consisting of independent or dependent samples, respectively. In comparison to the tests for ordinal- or interval/ratio-level outcomes described above, the mathematics underlying these two tests involves comparing the observed frequencies for the various categories of the nominal variables to what might be expected by chance. That said,

394 MUSIC EDUCATION RESEARCH

Table 18.5 Description of the data generated for use in the nominal outcome data examples in this chapter: Exploring differences in the socioeconomic status of all-state choir participants

Research Scenario 3
A researcher is curious to know whether students who audition successfully for elite honor ensembles such as all-state choir are also more or less likely to come from relatively lower socioeconomic status. They've acquired a list of all who auditioned for all-state choir in a given year and matched the students listed to records identifying eligibility for free and reduced lunch in school. They also acquired the same information for the following year's all-state choir audition process.

Variable Name (*Label*)	Numerical Values Possible (*Measurement Level*)
1. participant_code_nom (*A number as a label for each participant*)	A numerical code assigned to each participant (*nominal level*)
2. all_state_status_year_one (*Two-category all-state choir audition result status*)	Two category codes to indicate whether a participant was or was not accepted to all-state choir (*nominal level*)
3. frl_eligible (*Two-category free and reduced lunch eligibility status*)	Two category codes to indicate whether or not a participant was eligible for free and reduced lunch in school (*nominal level*)
4. all_state_status_year_two (*Two-category all-state choir audition result status in the following year*)	Two category codes to indicate whether a participant who was or was not accepted to all-state choir in year 1 of the study was accepted or not into all-state choir the following year (*nominal level*)

like all of the other tests discussed above, the Chi square and McNemar tests will also return a *p* value which can be used to determine whether a null hypothesis of no difference can be rejected. As was the case in the previous sections, we've created a hypothetical data set to illustrate both of these analyses (see Table 18.5).

Chi Square Test of Independence

For this example, we propose that a researcher may be interested in determining whether students who are accepted to all-state choir vary according to their socioeconomic status. In order to conduct this study, a researcher could acquire a list of all who auditioned for all-state choir in a given year and match the students listed to records identifying whether or not they were eligible for federal free and reduced lunch in school. The variables in the hypothetical data set named all_state_status_year_one and frl_eligibility can be used to illustrate how the researcher could conduct a Chi square test of independence to answer their research question.

Figure 18.5 depicts the relative frequencies of students who were or were not accepted into all-state choir according to whether they were eligible for free and reduced lunch. Given the discrepancies evident in the figure, it appears that the proportion of students who were accepted into all-state choir who were eligible for free

DETERMINING DIFFERENCES WITH INFERENTIAL STATISTICS 395

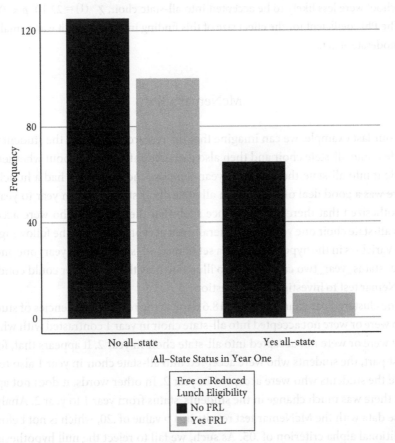

Figure 18.5 A clustered bar chart depicting the quantities of students who were or were not accepted into all-state choir according to whether or not they were eligible for free and reduced lunch (FRL).

and reduced lunch was smaller than that for students who were not accepted into all-state choir. Conducting a Chi square test of independence on these data results in a p value well below the traditional alpha criterion of .05 ($p < .001$). As such, we can reject the null hypothesis of no difference. The results indicate that the students who were accepted into all-state choir differed as a function of whether they were eligible for free and reduced lunch. The Phi correlation coefficient described in Chapter 17 is a statistic that is often used as an indicator of effect size when conducting Chi square tests. The Phi coefficient for the relationship between the all_state_status_year_one and frl_eligibility variables is .27, which, in this context, is indicative of a small to moderate effect. Confidence intervals are not reported along with Chi square tests.

This is an example of how you might write about the results of a Chi square test of independence for nominal data:

> Whether or not students were accepted into all-state choir varied as a function of their socioeconomic status. Students who qualified for free and reduced lunch at

school were less likely to be accepted into all-state choir, χ^2 (1) = 22.10, $p < .001$. The Phi coefficient for the effect size of this finding indicated that it was a small to moderate effect.

McNemar's Test

For our last example, we can imagine that the researcher tracked the students who made it into all-state choir and then also gathered information about whether they made it into all-state the following year. Suppose the researcher had a hunch that there was a good deal of turnover in all-state choir students from year to year and hypothesized that there is a difference such that the students who were accepted into all-state choir one year were generally not accepted again in the following year. The variables in the hypothetical data set named all_state_status_year_one and all_state_status_year_two can be used to illustrate how the researcher could conduct a McNemar test to investigate this question.

The clustered bar chart in Figure 18.6 depicts the relative frequencies of students who were or were not accepted into all-state choir in year 1 contrasted with whether they were or were not accepted into all-state choir in year 2. It appears that, for the most part, the students who were accepted into all-state choir in year 1 also tended to be the students who were accepted in year 2. In other words, it does not appear that there was much change in the students' status from year 1 to year 2. Analyzing these data with the McNemar test results in a p value of .20, which is not below the traditional alpha criterion of .05. As such, we fail to reject the null hypothesis and it seems that our informal analysis based on the bar chart is correct. Confidence intervals are also not reported along with McNemar tests.

You could write up the results of the McNemar's test for nominal data in this manner:

> Generally, students who were accepted into all-state choir in year 1 were also accepted in year 2. Although several students who were not accepted into all-state choir the first year were subsequently accepted in the second year, no significant difference in the consistency of whether the students were accepted into all-state choir was found across years. McNemar's $\chi^2 = 1.62$, $p > .20$, and thus we fail to reject the null hypothesis (i.e., there was no significant difference in all-state acceptance from year 1 to year 2).

Summary

Quantitative researchers often use inferential statistical procedures to test hypotheses pertaining to differences between sets of scores. Questions regarding differences can emerge from many different research designs, such as surveys,

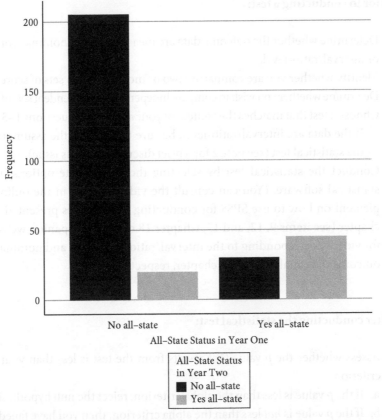

Figure 18.6 A clustered bar chart depicting the quantities of students who were or were not accepted into all-state choir at year 1 according to whether they were or were not accepted into all-state choir at year 2.

observational research, and—of course—experimental studies. In this chapter, we emphasized the importance of choosing an inferential test that is suited for the level of measurement of your outcome variable. We also emphasized the need to identify whether the sets of scores you wish to compare are from independent or dependent samples. Despite the multitude of different inferential statistical tests that exist, it is important to remember that there are commonalities when it comes to interpreting their results. For example, all statistical tests within the framework of NHST will return a *p* value, and if a test result indicates statistical significance, then that result should also be interpreted with regard to some measure of effect size. Also, recognize that there is always more to be learned when it comes to analytical tools applicable for research. We hope that you will work from the introductions presented in this book and seek out more information to expand your knowledge and skills. When embarking on your first quantitative research study, we recommend working with others who can serve as mentors and guides. In the meantime, we offer the following series of steps to consider should you have the opportunity to conduct tests with your own data:

Prior to conducting a test:

1. Determine whether the outcome data are measured at the nominal-, ordinal-, or interval/ratio-level.
2. Identify whether you are comparing two or more than two sets of scores.
3. Determine whether you wish to compare independent or dependent sets of scores.
4. Choose a test that matches the context of your answers to questions 1–3 above.
    a. If the data are interval/ratio-level, be sure to examine the assumptions of the statistical test (see note 2 for a brief discussion of this issue).
5. Conduct the statistical test by selecting the appropriate options in your statistical software. (You can consult the videos linked in the online supplement on how to use SPSS for conducting the analyses presented in this chapter (see items 9, 12, and 15, Chapter 18 on the Companion website ⏵. for videos corresponding to the interval/ratio-, ordinal-, and nominal-level outcome data analyses in this chapter, respectively.).)

After conducting the statistical test:

6. Assess whether the p value that results from the test is less than your alpha criterion.
    a. If the p value is less than the alpha criterion, reject the null hypothesis.
    b. If the p value is *not* less than the alpha criterion, then you have failed to reject the null hypothesis. If this is the case, then your analyses are more or less done.
7. If the test indicates that you can reject the null hypotheses, then you should consider the following:
    a. Report the nature of the differences between the sets of scores.
    b. Report the magnitude of the difference as indicated by an effect size metric.
    c. Report estimates of certainty via confidence intervals, as appropriate.
    d. For statistical tests that are used to investigate differences across more than two groups, conduct additional tests (i.e., post-hoc tests) to examine pairwise differences between groups.

Working through the following questions will give you a good way to determine your level of understanding of the inferential concepts and tests presented in this chapter:

1. Explain the differences between nominal-, ordinal-, and interval/ratio-level measurement scales to someone who hasn't learned about them yet.
2. Explain the difference between independent samples and dependent samples and describe situations that could include examples of each.
3. Explain what it means if a difference is declared statistically significant.
4. Explain why it is important to report the effect size of a statistically significant finding.

5. Explain the difference between Type I and Type II error.
6. Consult the videos included in the online supplement on how to use SPSS for conducting the inferential tests discussed in this chapter and follow along, conducting the analyses with the software yourself as well (see items 9, 12, and 15, Chapter 18 on the Companion website ⏵. for videos corresponding to the interval/ratio-, ordinal-, and nominal-level outcome data analyses in this chapter, respectively.).
7. Identify inferential tests for differences in a quantitative research article of your choosing. Practice summarizing the findings in your own words and compare your summary to that of the article's author.
8. Navigate to the online applications that are linked in the online supplement associated with this chapter (see the link titled "Supplemental Web Apps for Exploring Statistical Concepts", Chapter 18 on the Companion website ⏵).
   a. Experiment with the independent samples t-test application by changing the input parameters for the means of each of the groups and examining the changes in the output that occur. Note how much the distributions overlap with each other, even when there are significant differences between their means. Also try the following:
      i. Change the sample sizes to be very small or very large while keeping the means and standard deviations the same, and observe how the p values for the analyses change.
      ii. Change the standard deviations while keeping the means and the sample sizes the same, and observe how the p values as well as the Cohen's d effect sizes for the analyses change.
   b. Experiment with the one-way ANOVA application by changing the input parameters for the means of each of the groups and examining the changes in the output that occur.
      i. Notice how the variation around the "grand mean" (i.e., the red dots) matches up with the variation around each of the group means (i.e., the blue dots) as you change the parameters.
      ii. Also notice how the eta squared value (printed as eta.2 in the application) decreases or increases according to how little or how much the variation across the blue dots within each does or does not match up/align across groups.
      iii. Change the sample sizes to be very small or very large while keeping the means and standard deviations the same, and observe how the p values for the analyses change.
      iv. Change the standard deviations while keeping the means and the sample sizes the same, and observe how the p values as well as the Cohen's d effect sizes for the analyses change.
   c. Experiment with the Chi square application by changing the input parameters for the frequencies of each of the cells in the cross-tabulation. Notice how the p value changes as the distribution of frequencies across cells become less and less even.

Important Terms for Review

Independent samples are gathered from groups that consist of different individuals and when the individuals in one group are not systematically related to those in the other group in any way. Therefore, the scores gathered from such groups represent samples of individuals that are independent of the other.

Dependent samples are gathered from groups where the individuals in each group are systematically related to each other in some way. One of the most common types of dependent samples in music education research occurs when data are gathered from the same group of individuals on multiple occasions. In that case, the scores from the first group are as related as can be to the scores from the second group, since they literally come from the same people.

Inferential tests for examining differences: It's important to choose the test that is a match to the data you wish to analyze.

Null hypothesis significance testing (NHST) is a method of statistical inference that researchers use when attempting to refute their hypotheses. When using NHST, researchers will assume there is a hypothetical population in which the hypothesis they are interested in testing is not true (i.e., it is "null"), and then determine the probability of getting the finding they observed from their sample data if that assumption were true. If the probability of getting the finding they observed from their sample data is sufficiently small (traditionally $< .05$), then they reject the null hypothesis and can declare statistical significance. If the probability of getting the finding they observed from their sample data is *not* sufficiently small (traditionally $> .05$), then they fail to reject the null hypothesis and cannot declare statistical significance.

Inferential tests are often categorized as being either *parametric* or *nonparametric*. Parametric inferential tests include specific mathematical assumptions about the hypothetical population distributions involved in NHST, whereas nonparametric tests involve fewer assumptions or none at all. The tests we describe for interval- or ratio-level outcome variables in this chapter are parametric tests; those we describe for nominal- and ordinal-level outcome variables are nonparametric tests.

Alpha level is the term used to describe the criterion for rejecting a null hypothesis and declaring statistical significance, which is traditionally a probability of .05.

A *probability value* or *p value* is the statistical probability that a researcher would find a result at least as extreme as that which they observed from their sample data if they assumed the null hypothesis were true.

Effect size is an indication of the magnitude of an effect irrespective of statistical significance. It is important to report an indicator of effect size along with statistical significance because a statistically significant finding is not necessarily a meaningful finding in a practical sense.

Statistical power refers to the likelihood a researcher will be able to reject a null hypothesis if it is indeed false. The most direct method of increasing statistical power is by increasing the sample size (i.e., the number of participants) in a study.

Type I error occurs when a null hypothesis is mistakenly rejected when it is true. Given the probabilistic nature of NHST, Type I error is more likely to occur when many statistical tests are run on the same data set.

Family-wise error is the term used to describe the increased likelihood Type I error due to conducting multiple inferential tests.

Type II error occurs when one fails to reject a null hypothesis even though it is false. A common reason that Type II error occurs is a lack of statistical power.

A *confidence interval* is an expression of the uncertainty in one's statistical findings. Confidence intervals indicate the range of possible values one would not reject as possible hypothetical population values that could have generated the sample data within a given level of precision.

References

American Psychological Association. (2019). *Publication manual of the American Psychological Association* (7th ed.). American Psychological Association.

Field, A. (2016). *An adventure in statistics: The reality enigma*. Sage.

Miksza, P., & Elpus, K. (2018). *Design and analysis for quantitative research in music education*. Oxford University Press.

Russell, J. A. (2018). *Statistics in music education research*. Oxford University Press.

Siegel, S., & Castellan, J. (1988). *Nonparametric statistics for the behavioral sciences* (2nd ed.). McGraw-Hill.

Stambaugh, L. A. (2011). When repetition isn't the best practice strategy: Effects of blocked and random practice schedules. *Journal of Research in Music Education, 58*(4), 368–383. https://doi.org/10.1177/0022429410385945

Tabachnik, B. G., & Fidell, L. S. (2019). *Using multivariate statistics* (7th ed.). Pearson.

19
Action Research

Chapter Preview

The purpose of this chapter is to learn the aims and history, explain key features, and look closely at published examples of action research. Action research includes a diverse family of inquiry approaches that teachers use to study practice. Action researchers study what is going on now and make plans for or take action within their inquiries. In addition to the reflection that practitioners engage in every day, action researchers *intentionally* and *systematically* look at issues with the aim of making a difference in specific ways. Action researchers may utilize either qualitative or quantitative approaches; what distinguishes action research is the *spiral* of action that includes multiple cycles of look-think-act to systematically study and build sustainable change in the communities under study. Three epistemological beliefs connect various approaches. First, individuals working and living in the setting participate in the research process as participants or co-researchers. Second, one's professional context is the site for inquiry (e.g., a classroom). Third, through successive cycles of thought, action, and reflection, participants provide recommendations, address issues, and make improvements themselves. Action researchers rarely work alone; many developed their projects in partnership with co-researchers who offered staying power when the realities of overfull teaching schedules made the work challenging.

Introduction

Action research encompasses multiple ways of studying teacher practice, focusing on issues among individuals, schools and organizations, institutions, or broader society. Teachers may apply action research to investigate topics alone or with students, other teachers, staff members, administrators, or community members. Following Herr and Anderson (2015), we use the term "action research" to include a diverse family of inquiry approaches that teachers can use to examine their practice. First, at the heart of action research is *action* or dynamic movement within and among individuals and their communities. Action researchers study the present and make plans for future action. Second, using the term "action research"—as opposed to "teacher research" or "practitioner research"—broadens the notion of *who* conducts the research and makes space for a variety of persons to become involved.

Researchers might include all members of a community or specific individuals, depending on the research context and topic under study.

Various action research approaches may be distinguished by their foundations and aims. For example, some approaches focus on groups, such as participatory action research in which participants engage as co-researchers working to enact social change (Reason & Bradbury, 2001). Other approaches focus on individuals, such as self-study, which may combine pieces of history and biography, and involve examining one's practice in relation to the self (Bullough & Pinnegar, 2001). Still others might engage in reflective practice to improve teaching and learning interactions (Schön, 1983). For instance, individual teachers or collaborative action study groups might study their instruction as a form of professional development. Important to note is that those conducting action research might have different relationships to the school setting, such as PreK–12 teachers who have insider status or university faculty who have PreK–12 experience but are not insiders to the specific school environment. At this point, you may be wondering what distinguishes action research from the reflection that practitioners engage in every day. Action researchers *intentionally* and *systematically* look at issues with the aim of making a difference in specific ways (Stringer & Ortiz Aragon, 2021).

As you read this chapter, you may note intersections among qualitative, quantitative, and action research approaches. Indeed, action researchers may decide to collect and analyze different types of data to address the issue under study. For example, researchers who seek individual perspectives from participants for action research projects may collect interview data and analyze them inductively using qualitative approaches. Researchers who seek descriptive data to inform curricular decisions may choose a survey design and analyze their data using quantitative methods. However, a distinguishing feature of action research is the *spiral* of action or intervention that occurs during the research itself. Action researchers include multiple look-think-act cycles to systematically study and build sustainable change within their communities (see Figure 19.1; Stringer & Ortiz Aragon, 2021). Action researchers *look* through regular observation, gather data from stakeholders, and describe what is going on. Action researchers *think* as they question, study, and

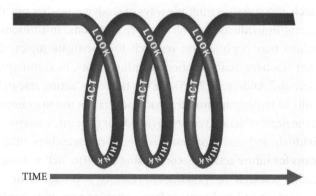

Figure 19.1 Action research spiral.
Source: Stringer and Ortiz Aragon (2021).

theorize about why things are the way they are. Then action researchers make plans, implement those plans, and evaluate. Their look-think-act cycle continues as they base subsequent decisions and actions on what they have learned.

Beginnings of Action Research

Action research began with a call to develop theory inside of practice. German physician, philosopher, and poet Jacob Moreno (1872–1974) focused on interactive social processes, which led him to argue for mixing theory, research, and practice (Gunz, 1996). At the University of Berlin, Moreno worked with social psychologist Kurt Lewin, who later emigrated to the United States. With a focus on how individuals' environments impacted their behavior, Lewin (1946) called on social scientists to generate theory in practice settings, citing concerns of studying social problems in controlled environments. Lewin believed change might more readily occur through studying complex phenomena in natural environments.

Fast-forward to the 1960s and 1970s, when teachers in the United States began recognizing students as active agents in the classroom and revisiting the work of progressive educator and philosopher John Dewey (Kemmis et al., 2014). Arguing that teachers hold contextual knowledge and need both theoretical and practical understandings to be effective, Dewey (1904) suggested that universities value the experiences that preservice teachers have had as students and professionals. The goals of teacher preparation should include reflecting on one's own experience and becoming a keen observer of others' actions in schools. This knowledge, in addition to teaching experiences, would inform future teacher practice. In Latin America during the same time period, Paulo Freire (1970) and colleagues began projects focused on social change which ultimately led to the development of participatory action research approaches. In these contexts, projects had a dual purpose: to help adults build literacy skills and engage in social action. Freire's aim was to include all voices in research to realize change and see one another's humanity.

In the 1980s, philosopher and professor of urban studies Donald Schön focused on how individuals make visible existing knowledge as well as how they create new knowledge. Schön (1983) believed that practitioners exercise a kind of artistry as they respond to challenging situations. In difficult moments, practitioners create remedies and solutions through improvisation, thus demonstrating knowledge in context. Calling educators' responses "reflection-in-action," Schön worked to connect professional and practitioner knowledge, or tacit responses of thinking while doing. In contrast, reflection-on-action includes how teachers analyze their work to gather knowledge and make changes in future practice. One of Schön's missions was to advocate for teachers as professionals since teachers are constantly making decisions and reflecting on choices; they are not just delivering others' knowledge. More recently Ken Zeichner and colleagues sought to build teacher education programs that foreground action research to foster preservice teachers' examinations of personal experiences and their reexamination of assumptions about schools and schooling (Liston & Zeichner, 1991).

At this point, you might wonder when action research took hold in music education. Early rumblings of action research began in the 1960s with publications advocating for teachers as researchers, and action research as scientific research (e.g., Haack, 1968; Pernecky, 1963). Action research studies then gained momentum in the 1990s, and with each successive decade, evidence of action research continued to build as individuals published dissertations and peer-reviewed journal articles, and shared their work from local to international levels (Bresler, 1995; Robbins, 2014).

Even within this brief historical overview, you can see key features of action research taking shape—specifically, how action researchers value context-dependent practitioner knowledge and the inclusion of differing stakeholders to make lasting change in communities.

Key Features of Action Research

Though action research approaches may differ from one another, at least three epistemological beliefs connect them. First, individuals working and living in the setting participate in the research process as participants or co-researchers. Second, one's professional context is the site for inquiry. Inquiry may involve participants with specific roles, such as teachers in a study group, or teacher and students within a classroom. Inquiries may also engage many persons with a variety of roles, for example, a department-, building- or district-wide project with staff, faculty, students, and community. Third, through successive cycles of thought, action, and reflection, participants provide recommendations, address issues, and make improvements themselves (Kemmis et al., 2014). Participants are engaged in the research not only as experts; their expertise frames potential solutions and ways to address the problem. Critical to valuing those who contribute to action research is that the knowledge generated need not be external to one's experience. In action research, experts understand the realities of their context and have the capacity to address change within them. What follows is a description of an experience that led me— the author of this chapter, Elizabeth Parker—to become engaged in action research.

My Personal Connection to Action Research

While teaching in a middle and high school music program in a large northeastern city, I overheard conversations among students describing experiences of social bonding because of their long-term participation and time-intensive experiences in school choir. At the same time as this dialogue emerged, I spoke with a few new students who expressed their experience of feeling on the outside. I wondered what contributed to the experience of belonging in choir and how we might include more members of the classroom community into this experience. Along with the choir students, we decided to engage in an action research study to understand how singers defined belonging to combat adolescents' experiences of isolation. Approximately 45% of the choir chose to participate in small group interviews over several lunch periods to discuss the meanings of belonging in choir and develop future action plans. The result of our work included recommendations to the school administration, changes in our choir schedule, and intentional development of social activities planned within and outside of the classroom. Through the action research process, I came to appreciate my choral students' perspectives and invested in becoming a co-learner alongside them. Conducting research with my students continues to influence the ways that I develop relationships with students, strive to create classroom community, and conduct research (see Parker, 2010 for more details).

Boundary Crossing and Inquiry as Mindset

A consistent theme across action research approaches is that of boundary crossing. Action researchers themselves are boundary crossers, as they assume multiple roles in their practice, including as teachers, community members, and researchers. Boundary crossing can be ethically complex and tense as teachers work to navigate expectations and structures in their schools among such stakeholders as state departments of education, local administrators, community members, families, and students. Boundary crossing may also enliven community creativity and spur innovation, leading to change and heightened engagement.

Action researchers can begin to unpack their role in a setting by engaging in self-examination. Importantly, they should strive to answer *why* the topic or area of concern is important as well as who might benefit from the inquiry. They might consider relationships with participants, especially those situated in power and privilege. In schools, power relationships between teachers and students and/or teachers and administrators must be constantly negotiated. Critical to self-examination is entering into continual dialogue with researchers and participants around values, identities, and power. Researchers might ask themselves whose voices are being included and whose voices are missing. How do participants share power, check their privilege, and make decisions in this research relationship?

Boundary crossing also becomes visible in how communities represent and share their research. Researchers might publish reports in peer-reviewed publications to disseminate to their professional spaces while facilitating dialogues to incite change in the local community. Researchers may choose to present research in professional development sessions or share informally with colleagues. Either way, researchers should consider how they could share projects in ways that resonate with their community (Cochran-Smyth & Lytle, 2007). Reflecting back on the aim of the work and heightening one's awareness of whose voice is being heard and who might be speaking for whom is key. The spirit of action research is to make change; thus researchers should prioritize a sense of responsibility and ethical action.

Practitioners who engage as action researchers can strengthen their sense of researcher identity, further blurring boundaries and roles. In school settings, valuable practitioner knowledge runs deep—because of practitioners' positions as insiders, they might embrace inquiry as stance or inquiry as mindset (Cochran-Smith & Lytle, 2009). Viewing the world through inquiry may also bring one's research into greater alignment with practice. Practitioners may begin to erase the separateness between when one is engaging in research and being a practitioner. In this way, practitioners are always looking critically at issues with opportunities for enacting change.

Research Questions for Which Action Research Is Particularly Well Suited

You may have already begun to note questions, issues, or concerns for which action research may be particularly well suited. In the spirit of action research, we now look at a five examples of action research projects. During review of these studies, we encourage you to note themes of valuing and investing in insider knowledge, striving to reflect on and change practice, and collaborating in learning communities.

Investigating Sensory Development with Children in a Montessori Setting

Dansereau and Wyman (2020) noted that sensory development, specifically sound, is not held in equal regard with visual development in early childhood education. Furthermore, in the Montessori classroom, music interactions may be made available only outside of the primary classroom where children spend much of their time. In response, the researchers chose a critical participatory action research approach to disrupt the classroom and make change. They designed six different works[1] for children to interact with to address sound development. The works afforded children opportunities to explore pitch, pitch direction, melodic direction, and dynamic changes. Participants in the study were 20 children ages three to six and the researchers (one a university faculty member and also a parent at the school and the other the primary teacher). Wyman introduced each work and documented children's responses by collecting quantitative data related to the accuracy of each child's response and qualitative data regarding their interest, whether

---

[1] The term "works" refers to activities that children could choose to do independently, collaboratively, or with teacher assistance in a Montessori classroom setting.

they completed the task, and their comments. After individual sessions, the works were placed on the shelves and Dansereau collected observational data on how children used the items in the classroom.

The researchers noted that the children found the sound tasks unexpectedly challenging. Quantitative data revealed that the children were accurate with pitch direction regardless of what type of tool they used, and qualitative data spoke to children's positive reception of the works. All children chose to use the works in the classroom, and some did so many times. The researchers observed that the children engaged differently than previously in the classroom as they "deeply fixated on the aural stimulus while engaged with the works" (Dansereau & Wyman, 2020, p. 26). Though they acknowledged progress with their approach, they also stated that attention to sound experiences remained out of balance in the curriculum as compared to visual experiences. They suggested including a dedicated music shelf or area for students to engage with sound and developing works that involved sound and movement. More curricular innovations might provide young children a holistic education that better addresses sensory development.

Building Composition Skills by Teaching for Transfer

Strand (2005) investigated how students transfer understanding of musical concepts from listening and performance to composition. More specifically, the researcher was concerned with how composition tasks are often used as summative evaluations when students may not be making such transfers. Strand's goal was to collect data while teaching students to compose over several action research cycles. Eight 9- to 12-year-olds in an urban elementary school summer enrichment class participated in this research.

Strand (2005) first planned eight hours of instruction by synthesizing theories of transfer and research findings pertaining to children's compositional processes. During the instruction cycle, the researcher collected lesson plans, video recordings of classes, field notes, and varied student artifacts and analyzed them by categorizing instructional content and strategies as well as how students engaged with the content. At the end of each cycle of instruction, Strand determined what did and did not work and changed instruction to address emerging issues, repeating the cycle four times.

The researcher found that concepts needed to be introduced in a way that led to practical application, not only for the sake of student understanding. Strand's (2005) data analysis also revealed that composing in front of the students and task order were of critical importance. For example, listening tasks, which allowed students to focus and respond during music listening, were best followed by performance tasks that allowed students to practice their understanding. Guided composition was also useful since it gave students opportunities to practice in incremental steps. Students struggled with new tasks and also sometimes had trouble with revision. Although students found the final concert of their compositions stressful, the presence of a concert heightened their collaboration and engagement. Strand summarized her findings by indicating that direct instruction and guided discovery strategies were both important to student success. In addition, a sense of shared experience helped to develop a community of learners in the classroom.

Using Reflective Practice in Sixth-Grade Concert Band

Reynolds and Beitler (2007) examined reflective practice techniques within a sixth-grade concert band classroom. Citing reflective practice as a means to improving teaching and learning, the researchers sought to understand the challenges and benefits of engaging students in reflective practice. A secondary aim of their project included instituting writing across the curriculum into the instrumental music classroom. Participants were sixth-grade concert band students and the researchers, one of whom was the music teacher of the band class, and the other a university faculty member.

For eight months of one school year, the student participants journaled once weekly for five minutes in response to open-ended reflection questions. During Phase 1 of the study, the music teacher-researcher wrote comments in response to the students' journals and kept a reflective journal of her own. After reading through the students' journal entries, she would reread her own journal. The university researcher gathered documentation of informal communications in the researchers' log. During Phase 2, the researchers met to analyze student reflections and the researcher journal entries and logs by creating a chart to show how the reflection process influenced instruction, informal assessment, and reflective practice.

Data revealed that the teacher-researcher began incorporating changes in her work as early as six weeks after beginning reflective practice. Student responses affected how she approached her planning and choices of objectives. Challenges she experienced included having enough time for reflective writing, adjusting to schedule changes, and writing effective reflective questions. Through reflection, the teacher-researcher was able to hear students' experiences differently, specifically their emotional responses to lessons and performances. The teacher's journal focused on how student responses encouraged re-review of the lesson content or reteaching portions of the lesson. The teacher's journal and the student journals together served as a kind of dialogue between the teacher and students. Hearing their insights in this way helped the teacher-researcher develop new ways to guide them and support their learning.

Even with challenges of time and schedule, the researchers' responsibility to one another helped the project continue. The teacher's journal became an informal emotional outlet, a space for decompression, and helped place her accomplishments in perspective. Moreover, conducting research together with the university music teacher educator helped combat feelings of isolation.

Understanding Why Students Re-enroll in Choir from Middle School to High School

Conway and Borst (2001) sought to understand students' personal motivations for participating in choir. Borst identified most strongly as a middle school choral teacher, yet he was asked to teach a high school ensemble. He noted that the majority of students chose to discontinue choir once they reached high school. Along with Conway, a university faculty member, Borst first interviewed six high school choral students individually to learn about their musical and nonmusical reasons for being in choir. This was followed by a panel interview with all participants at once. The researchers also conducted interviews with some of the parents of the student participants.

The student participants described what they learned in choir and from music in general, which included opportunities for self-expression and enjoyment, social benefits, performance opportunities, and feelings of belonging in the school. Their parents discussed how choir helped build their children's self-esteem and confidence. Based on these findings, the researchers developed a plan of action to foster student involvement and initiate opportunities for students to connect with students from other schools. Implementation plans included creating a buddies mentoring system between middle and high school students, concerts with multiple levels of choirs from within the school district, and prioritizing teamwork and camaraderie as important aims in choir. The researchers suggested that choral teachers across the schools could unify their curriculum to prioritize and strengthen the benefits that student participants cited.

Looking at Student Collaboration through a Teacher Study Group

Collaborative teacher study groups (CTSGs) present valuable opportunities for professional development as they represent spaces of mutual growth and support. Stanley (2012) investigated a CTSG that consisted of three elementary general music teachers who hailed from different teaching contexts and with different backgrounds. In the CTSG, teachers explored how to engage elementary music students in collaborative activities. Stanley wondered how the CTSG might change the teachers' practices and how what they learned together about student collaboration could be shared with others.

The CTSG engaged in seven, once-weekly, two-hour afterschool meetings during which they watched and discussed unedited videos from their classrooms. In addition to the meetings, Stanley (2012) conducted two individual interviews with each participant to learn more about their perspectives on professional development and collaboration. The researcher recorded and analyzed the transcripts of their meetings, looking for ways to understand how the teachers' experiences from the study group influenced their teaching practice. Data revealed that the CTSG helped boost the participants' confidence and draw deeper reflective insights. Watching the videos together allowed the participants to begin seeing their teaching through the eyes of their colleagues. This led to insights whereby participants shifted their focus from an emphasis on the content they were teaching to student learning and methods for facilitating student collaboration. Reflecting on each other's videos also broadened the participants' views on student collaboration in general as each teacher had different ways of facilitating collaboration. The videos shed light on the teaching realities shared among the group, and the weekly structure of meetings moved participants productively forward.

The participants in the CTSG wanted to disseminate what they learned and so they created a document of ideas to share with other teachers. They developed a set of collaborative principles which emphasized (a) the importance of self-expression, independence, and shared goals; (b) the teacher's role as a facilitator of productive collaborative possibilities; and (c) recommendations that teachers provide background skills, optimize student buy-in for the goal, and fade away to allow student ownership. Moreover, the teachers recognized that collaboration is multidirectional, between teachers and students and between students and students.

Summary and Reflection Exercise

Take a moment to reflect on how these five projects bring alive the key features of action research introduced earlier in the chapter, specifically that action research (a) includes multiple voices in communities, (b) embraces professional contexts as sites for inquiry, and (c) empowers those in the research community to make change. Consider how the researchers made visible their boundary crossing as they embraced multiple roles, navigated power and position in their settings, and worked in collaboration with others as co-learners. Whether the researchers focused on students' sensory experiences, composition, reflective practice, collaboration, or motivation, their shared aim was to grow communities of learners. Last, each study used the spiral of action research to look-think-act in systematic ways with a clear intention to transform practice. By committing to action research, the researchers placed value on doing work together, further enriching relationships in their communities.

Action researchers rarely work alone. In several of the examples, the researchers developed their projects in partnership with others who helped keep their research on track when the realities of overfull teaching schedules made the work challenging. For those considering action research projects, locating a partner can make research more feasible. Whether teachers connect with other teachers or members of the school community or a local university, research partnerships offer rich opportunities for individuals to learn from one another.

Lewin (1946) proposed that education, action, and research may be conceived as three points of a triangle (see Figure 19.2). Each point shares a side—thus they are

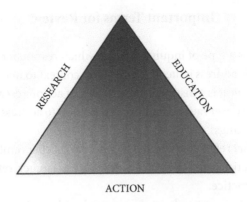

Figure 19.2 Independent research to practice relationships.

interdependent to one another and stronger together. Action research calls on us to develop theory inside of practice. As we look to become part of the change we seek in schools, organizations, and society, we might consider action research as a critical tool to incite the transformation we seek.

We hope that you can see yourself in the examples presented throughout the chapter and that you feel empowered to explore action research in your own context. To get started, we encourage you to take a few moments and complete this reflective exercise:

1. Brainstorm four to five critical issues or questions relevant to your teaching setting. Issues might be in the classroom, the school building, among small or large groups of students, or perhaps in your community.
2. Select one topic from the issues or questions you generated to explore for this exercise.
3. Describe in detail what you know about the issue and the questions you wish to grapple with or answer.
4. List persons who might be involved in the action research project (e.g., students, teachers, administrators, parents/caregivers, and/or community members).
5. Write about ethical issues (e.g., power, representation) with the persons you mentioned above and how you might navigate those issues.
6. Jot down who outside of the work could support the project, such as colleagues inside or outside of the school district, other administrators and staff, or university faculty.
7. Note two to three steps to begin the work. For example, what questions need to be asked, and of whom?
8. Write about your hopes for how this work could inform your practice.
9. Closure: In the coming weeks, strive to locate those stakeholders involved in the issue and those who can partner and support your work. Develop a collective plan of action with others whereby you might begin the action research cycle.

Important Terms for Review

Action research is a type of inquiry through which researchers intentionally and systematically address issues or concerns in context to make change.

Look-think-act spiral is a distinct characteristic of action research involving iterative cycles of observation, planning, and action to address issues or concerns in practice settings.

Inquiry as mindset refers to a worldview whereby teachers embrace intersections between practice and research to develop researcher reflexivity and deep analyses of practice.

Participatory action research is an approach originating with critical theorist Paulo Freire which involves communities enacting social change and in which participants are invited as co-researchers with attention to negotiating power relationships in the research community.

Reflective practice: Valuing context-bound knowledge and expertise, Donald Schön proposed "reflection-in-action," whereby practitioners use reflection in the moment, and "reflection-on-action," whereby practitioners analyze their work to make change in future practice.

Self-study is an action research approach that interweaves autobiography and analysis of one's practice in relation to the self.

Collaborative teacher study groups involve collaborations between practitioners toward professional development, in which teachers select topics to systematically study as a group.

References

Bresler, L. (1995). Ethnography, phenomenology and action research in music education. *Quarterly Journal of Music Teaching and Learning, 6*(3), 4–16.

Bullough, R. V., & Pinnegar, S. (2001). Guidelines for quality in autobiographical forms of self-study research. *Educational Researcher, 30*(3), 13–21. https://doi.org/10.3102/0013189X030003013

Cochran-Smith, M., & Lytle, S. (2007). Everything's ethics: Practitioner inquiry and university culture. In A. Campbell & S. Groundwater-Smith (Eds.), *An ethical approach to practitioner research* (pp. 24–41). Routledge.

Cochran-Smith, M., & Lytle, S. (2009). *Inquiry as stance*. Teachers College Press.

Conway, C., & Borst, J. (2001). Action research in music education. *Update: Applications of Research in Music Education, 19*(2), 3–8. https://doi.org/10.1177/87551233010190020102

Dansereau, D. R., & Wyman, B. (2020). A child-directed music curriculum in the Montessori classroom: Results of a critical participatory action research study. *Journal of Montessori Research, 6*(1), 19–31. https://doi.org/10.17161/jomr.v6i1.10631

Dewey, J. (1904). The relation of theory to practice in education. In C. A. McMurry (Ed.), *The third yearbook of the National Society for the Scientific Study of Education, part I* (pp. 9–30). University of Chicago Press.

Freire, P. (1970). *Pedagogy of the oppressed*. Continuum.

Gunz, J. (1996). Jacob L. Moreno and the origins of action research. *Educational Action Research, 4*(1), 145–148. https://doi.org/10.1080/0965079960040111

Haack, P. (1968). Teachers can be researchers can be teachers. *Music Educators Journal*, *54*(7), 81–83.
Herr, K., & Anderson, G. (2015). *The action research dissertation* (2nd ed.). Sage.
Kemmis, S., McTaggart, R., & Nixon, R. (2014). *The action research planner: Doing critical participatory action research*. Springer.
Lewin, K. (1946). Action research and minority problems. *Journal of Social Issues*, *2*(4), 34–46. https://doi.org/10.1111/j.1540-4560.1946.tb02295.x
Liston, D. P., & Zeichner, K. M. (1991). Reflective teaching and action research in preservice teacher education. *Journal of Education for Teaching*, *16*(3), 235–254. https://doi.org/10.1080/0260747900160304
Parker, E. C. (2010). Exploring student experiences of belonging within an urban high school choral ensemble: An action research study. *Music Education Research*, *12*(4), 339–352. http://dx.doi.org/10.1080/14613808.2010.519379
Pernecky, J. (1963). Action research methodology. *Bulletin of the Council for Research in Music Education*, *1*, 33–37.
Reason, B., & Bradbury, H. (2001). Introduction. In P. Reason & H. Bradbury (Eds.), *Handbook of action research* (pp. 1–15). Sage.
Reynolds, A., & Beitler, N. (2007). Reflective practice in a middle-school instrumental setting. *Bulletin of the Council for Research in Music Education*, *173*, 55–79. https://www.jstor.org/stable/40319470
Robbins, J. (2014). Practitioner inquiry. In C. Conway (Ed.), *The Oxford handbook of qualitative research in American music education* (pp. 186–208). Oxford University Press.
Schön, D. (1983). *The reflective practitioner: How professionals think in action*. Basic Books.
Stanley, A. M. (2012). The experiences of elementary music teachers in a collaborative teacher study group. *Bulletin of the Council for Research in Music Education*, *192*, 53–74. https://www.jstor.org/stable/10.5406/bulcouresmusedu.192.0053
Strand, K. (2005). Nurturing young composers: Exploring the relationship between instruction and transfer in 9–12 year-old students. *Bulletin of the Council for Research in Music Education*, *165*, 17–36. https://www.jstor.org/stable/40319268
Stringer, E., & Ortiz Aragon, A. (2021). *Action research* (5th ed). Sage.

20
Scholarly Writing
Practice, Patience, and Passion

Chapter Preview

Scholarly writing is markedly different from the kinds of writing that might be found in nonresearch venues (e.g., newspapers), requiring precise and often technical language, support from many citations, a nonbiased tone, and the communication of complex ideas in the clearest and most concise manner possible. Developing scholarly writing skills takes patience and dedication over time and is aided by having a committed schedule and a dedicated space free from distractions. Another key component of scholarly writing involves setting clear goals, both large and small. Effective small goals are specific, measurable, and easily achievable within the time that an author allots for them. Keeping their large goal in mind, authors might continually revise their small goals in light of changing circumstances and reward themselves for their accomplishments. Perhaps one of the biggest differences between student writing projects and articles written for submission is the process of revision. Revising and polishing a manuscript before submission to a journal is crucial. Scholarly writing is difficult, and all writers experience days when they feel frustrated with their work. The aims and desires that motivated you to continue engaging in musical tasks that did not yield immediate joy may parallel those that can energize your ongoing commitment to scholarly writing.

Introduction

Writing research papers requires learning how to write in a scholarly manner. As you have likely gleaned from previous chapters, as well as any research works you have read, scholarly writing is markedly different from the kinds of writing that might be found in nonresearch venues (e.g., newspapers, blog sites, letters to parents, notes to administrators). For example, the work you will find in music education research journals will tend to (a) be written with precise and often technical language, (b) include many citations to support the ideas presented, (c) be cast in a tone such that the author is actively working to avoid bias, and (d) be written with the goal of communicating complex ideas in the clearest and most concise manner possible. Moreover, scholars write with an assumption that their audience is composed of specialists with a good deal of prerequisite knowledge at hand. As such, all scholars at some point will have devoted serious amounts of time and effort toward developing a skill set necessary to communicate within these stylistic conventions.

Most music educators find that their first attempts at scholarly writing feel awkward, and at first glance, developing the skills necessary can feel overwhelming. This is only natural since scholarly writing is simply not a regular part of most teachers' lives. While you may have spent years developing the ability to communicate effectively with students, parents, and other education stakeholders, the sorts of writing you need to do as a teacher (e.g., lesson plans, curricular documents, program handbooks, newsletters, advocacy statements) are not likely to have been similar to that which is expected of researchers. However, it is important to recognize that just as it has taken dedicated practice to become the sophisticated and skilled musician that you are, it is similarly possible to become fluent and comfortable with the skills necessary for scholarly writing. For example, at one point in your musical development you likely struggled to read quarter note rhythmic patterns and recognize simple chord progressions. Through training and practice, these initially unfamiliar skills became easier for you and may now feel quite natural. Likewise, researchers develop their scholarly writing skills through practice and patience.

To carry this analogy further, both musicianship and scholarly writing can be developed through the acquisition of general skills and knowledge. Just as developing musicians benefit from method books and étude collections devoted to musical concepts and techniques, writers can benefit from consulting texts and resources devoted to grammar, style, and formatting. More information about such writing elements can be found in texts such as Strunk's (1918/2018) well-known *The Elements of Style* and websites such as the one hosted by the Purdue Writing Lab (https://owl.purdue.edu/). Making music also involves knowledge and skills specific to one's instrument or form of musical engagement, such as understanding jazz music theory or producing a proper clarinet embouchure. Scholarly writing skills specific to one's selected research methodology are described in Chapters 4 through 19 of this text. Additionally, almost any form of musical skill development necessitates certain organizational and self-regulatory skills and dispositions, such as goal-setting and maintaining motivation. Many of the same skills and dispositions are also important for producing high-quality scholarly writing.

Clearly, a full treatment of the mechanics of scholarly writing is beyond the scope of this book; however, we thought it might be useful to offer a few suggestions that could facilitate the process. This chapter offers practical tips that may assist beginning researchers in developing their scholarly writing skills and habits. We begin with the topics of time management and goal setting. Next, we present practices that may assist authors when revising their work. Finally, ideas for rekindling one's passion for writing in the face of frustration or doubt are offered.

Time, Time, Time

Just as learning to sing or to play an instrument takes years of dedicated practice, one's scholarly writing skills develop over time. While two students beginning to learn the same musical instrument may progress at slightly different rates, the amount of time each student devotes to focused practice will typically correlate with their individual achievement over the course of many months and years. Likewise, the rate at which one develops one's scholarly writing skills often correlates with the amount of focused time one devotes to such endeavors. Yet, skill development necessitates not only certain quantities of practice but also practice with certain qualities.

A Committed Schedule

Musical skills are often best developed through daily practice. Setting aside even 20 minutes of practice time per day often produces better results than sporadic, elongated practice sessions. It is difficult, if not impossible, to perfect an audition piece by practicing minimally for weeks and then cramming eight hours of practice into a single day. Similarly, researchers may find that setting aside daily, or at least regular, writing time is the most efficient way to develop their skills.

Researchers can help protect their regular writing time by treating such sessions as required commitments. While one might make a rough plan to write for two hours at a certain time each day, without conceiving of that time as an unbreakable requirement, other competing work and personal needs may easily override such intended commitments. Instead, researchers might schedule scholarly writing time on their calendars just as they would a mandatory school meeting or doctor's appointment. Individuals might break such commitments in the event of an emergency, but they would neither schedule another formal commitment over them nor enable themselves to be drawn into informal conversations or other work during such time. While researchers' friends often get used to the phrase "Sorry, that is my writing time," simply saying "Sorry, I have a commitment" when faced with a potential conflict provides one's scholarly writing the important status that it deserves.

In addition to regularly scheduled writing times, researchers might find themselves surprised by how much they can accomplish just by taking advantage of small down periods throughout the day. Suppose you typically have a 30-minute meeting with your music department colleagues once per week and—by chance— the meeting happens to be canceled for the current week. If you're in the habit of using these moments to further your research, you can immediately switch to writing mode.

When reserving regular amounts of time for scholarly writing, researchers might consider what time of day they write most effectively. Just as some individuals do their most focused music making first thing in the morning, while others prefer midday times, and still others enthusiastically practice well into the night, researchers may find that their productivity will vary based on the time of day. Experimenting with when one feels most alert and focused can save significant amounts of time in the long run. For example, a researcher who works best in the morning but has free time primarily after 8:00 p.m. might find that by waking up an hour earlier each day they accomplish in one hour what would otherwise take them two or three hours in the evening.

Authors may also consider which writing tasks necessitate the most focus. For instance, synthesizing articles for a literature review or constructing part of a philosophical argument may require one's utmost attention, as well as a sustained period of uninterrupted time. Alphabetizing sources or transcribing an interview verbatim may take less concentration; researchers might therefore engage in such tasks when they have shorter periods of time available, such as at the end of a lunch break or between classes or meetings, or during longer periods of time when they feel less alert.

Even when researchers feel focused, long hours of scholarly writing without any break can lead to burnout. Authors who push themselves to work too many hours without sufficient breaks or too many hours in a single day, even with breaks, may experience a sense of exhaustion that inhibits their productivity for days to come. When authors plan to devote multiple consecutive hours to writing, they might tentatively plan to take one 15-minute break following every hour of work. Stretching, going for a short walk, or drinking water can lead to feeling recharged for another hour of work. While sometimes researchers may feel a sense of focused flow that enables them to work for multiple hours absent a break, permitting oneself a break after every hour of work (or whatever time period feels right for you) can encourage greater overall productivity.

Distraction-Free Locations

Additionally, researchers might consider how their location affects their writing quality and quantity. Imagine what conditions make for a good music practice space; while individuals may have varying preferences, ideal spaces are often quiet, have good lighting and air circulation, and contain comfortable (but not too comfortable) chairs. Likewise, authors might consider the best position for a comfortable writing desk or chair within their residence. They might find a local library, study room, or coffee shop that meets their optimal writing space needs.

Importantly, authors might avoid places with frequent distractions. If you live with young children, a significant other, or friendly roommates, it is crucial either to separate your writing space from their locations or to write when they are out of the house or asleep. While it may initially feel cruel to close the door to your writing space while children play or friends socialize in a neighboring room, many writers find it difficult to produce high-quality work when contending with even relatively minor interruptions. If you find it difficult to separate yourself from others in your place of residence, then you might find a different place to call your writing home (e.g., a coffee shop, a library, an office space at work). The advantage of having a designated writing home is not only practical but psychological. Over time, being in your writing home signifies "This is where I get my writing done."

Yet, even an ideal location cannot minimize the digital distractions so pervasive in contemporary life. Many individuals frequently check email and social media on their writing devices, and such actions can become habitual and almost involuntary. These activities can easily eat away at your precious writing time. At the start of your scheduled writing time, consider silencing your phone and closing webpages or apps not directly related to your work. Authors may initially feel an ongoing temptation to open distracting content. However, just as one develops the discipline needed to practice scales and other musical exercises, authors can develop the habit of avoiding digital distractions while writing, and such action often becomes easier over time. Additionally, using part of your planned hourly breaks to engage in favorite distractions may alleviate some of the temptation to do so during your focused writing time. Authors might also use their favorite distractions as a reward at the conclusion of their scheduled writing time. (See more information about rewards in the following section.)

One practical way that researchers might make time for their writing in a relatively distraction-free location is by joining a writing group. Many colleges offer graduate student writing groups, which typically meet a few hours each week. Researchers working in such groups may find that writing alongside their peers encourages them to stay focused and on task. In the absence of such preformed groups, you might consider creating your own regular in-person or virtual writing group with peers at your own or other institutions.

In short, scholarly writing is not an innate gift but a skill learned and developed over time. Just as improving one's musical skills necessitates sustained, consistent practice, there is no shortcut to becoming a clear, thoughtful writer. Maintaining a committed writing schedule, considering the times of day best suited for different writing tasks, taking planned breaks, and finding a writing location with few distractions can assist beginning researchers in developing their scholarly writing skills.

Goals: Large and Small

Another key component of scholarly writing involves setting clear goals, both large and small. As a musician, you have likely set countless goals for yourself. You may have had the large goal of an audition or concert planned for a certain date, and you then needed to consider the small intermediary goals that would prepare you for that event. While researchers may have some large goals imposed upon them, such as a deadline for defending a thesis or dissertation in order to graduate, they often need to set the vast majority of their large and small goals on their own.

Setting large writing goals can give authors a key starting point for more detailed writing plans. Once you have decided on an overall deadline for a particular project, you might work backward to determine the weekly and daily work needed to meet your goal. Absent this attention, researchers may let weeks or even months pass without significant progress, and they may quickly find their large goal out of reach. Keep in mind that your timeline needs to include both the initial writing process and multiple revisions. (See more information about the revision process in the following section.)

The more authors can break down and account for the numerous tasks involved in the research process, the more likely they will be to meet their large goal. Researchers might begin by creating an outline of their overall project. Using that outline, they can then construct a comprehensive list of related small goals. Subsequently, they can determine the ordering of their small writing goals.

Researchers rarely write their documents by moving linearly from the introduction to the conclusion. In many studies, the introduction is one of the last parts to be written. For a quantitative or qualitative article, you might want to begin with the method section, which is often the easiest section to write since it is mostly straightforward. For philosophical research, you may want to begin with the main problem (see Chapter 5) or first main argument. The order in which a researcher plans their small goals is often less important than the clarity and achievability of those goals.

Effective small goal setting often involves three elements. First, small goals should be specific and measurable. For example, a researcher might set the small goal of finding four usable sources for their literature review, or they might aim to write two paragraphs of their findings section. Notice that since both goals contain specific end products, a researcher will know when they have met them. Measurable goals enable authors to evaluate their progress more easily than, for example, the goal of spending two hours working on a literature review.

Second, the small goal should be easily achievable within the planned time. Setting unrealistic goals can encourage frustration, self-doubt, and a sense of defeat. Given the unpredictability of the researching and writing processes, beginning and even established researchers may not have a clear sense of how long it will take to accomplish a specific goal.

Beginning researchers might find that doubling the amount of time that they anticipate each small goal taking enables them to construct more realistic writing plans. For example, if a researcher thinks that finding two usable sources for their literature review will take one hour, they might leave themselves two hours to meet that goal. If finding two usable sources takes only one hour, then they can move on to another goal or end their writing session early. And if finding two usable sources takes significantly longer than the anticipated one hour, the researcher will not feel panicked or immediately overwhelmed. In addition to setting aside time for parts of the research process, such as reading related literature, analyzing data, and forming arguments, researchers solely focused on writing might initially estimate that they will complete one paragraph per hour. While this might be an overestimate for parts of a research document, the careful logic and considered wording needed for much scholarly writing make one hour per paragraph a good rule of thumb.

Third, researchers might constantly reevaluate their small and large goals in light of their present progress. As researchers learn more about their own writing process, including when and where they do their best work and how long specific small goals actually take, they can change their plans accordingly. Adapting one's plan to fit changing needs and information is far more important than getting the plan right in the first place.

Even the best goal setters will encounter moments during the research and writing process when things do not go as planned. As such, researchers may find it helpful to include a few extra open writing days, which they can use for unexpected issues or developments, in their initial plan. Importantly, the process of planning, as well as the scholarly writing process itself, takes practice and generally becomes easier over time.

What about the days when you have a plan but just do not feel like writing? In such moments, authors might try setting a timer for 15 minutes and committing to writing until the timer stops. Often, a researcher will find that they get into a rhythm during those 15 minutes and are able to continue and even complete their allotted writing time. If you work for 15 minutes and still do not feel motivated to keep going, it might mean you simply need a day off.

Just as you have likely had days when you could not bring yourself to practice your instrument or to meet your musical goals, there will be days when you do not accomplish your writing goals. As long as these days are relatively few and far between, it is important to be patient with yourself. Take the time that you need to rest or to do something for yourself and try again the following day.

Hopefully you will often find the writing process itself intrinsically rewarding. (Ideas for how to rekindle your passion for research will be addressed in the final section of this chapter.) However, when you feel uninterested in or defeated by a particular part of your document or unmotivated to begin writing day after day, initiating a reward system may assist you in meeting your writing goals.

Almost any small pleasure that motivates you to write can constitute a reward: buying a cup of coffee, going for a walk, calling a friend, watching a favorite television show or movie, or spending time on social media. Researchers can use these rewards to mark the achievement of a small goal, such as writing a certain number of paragraphs or finishing a section of their document. If you know of peers also striving to achieve their writing goals, you might consider shared rewards, such as a night out or group dinner. But don't consider essential processes like healthy eating, basic exercise, and sleep as rewards. Undermining your physical, psychological, and emotional well-being in order to accomplish small writing goals will ultimately inhibit your large goals and scholarly longevity.

In short, setting large and small goals is a key part of the writing process. Working backward from an overarching deadline, authors might use an outline of their end product to determine small goals. Effective small goals are specific, measurable, and easily achievable within the time an author allots for them. Keeping their large goal in mind, authors might continually revise their small goals in light of changing circumstances and reward themselves for their accomplishments.

The Art of Revision

Recall the first time you thought you had mastered a complex musical endeavor only to have a teacher describe your progress as just the tip of the iceberg. For example, accurately replicating the correct notes and rhythms of a piece does not mean that you are ready to give a public recital; rather, you can now begin intensely focusing on artistry, expressivity, and interpretation. Likewise, the initial draft of a research document is only the first step toward a refined final product. While an author might celebrate reaching the milestone of a completed draft, the revision process may take just as long as the initial writing of the manuscript.

Perhaps one of the biggest differences between student writing projects, such as term papers, and articles written for submission is the process of revision. In a typical term paper scenario, the student submits the paper, the professor grades it, the two may go over the comments together, and that is most often the end of the process. Prior to submitting a document to your graduate research committee or for publication, "Revise, revise, revise" should be your new motto.

In some ways, the process of revising a piece of scholarly writing parallels how you might prepare a piece of music for an audition or performance. You might start by breaking the draft into sections and then refining each section. During this process, you might check that each paragraph has a clear topic sentence and that you have placed the paragraphs in the most logical order. You might also consider the flow and ordering of ideas within paragraphs.

At this point, writers should also examine the specific words that they have selected. When an author has selected an imprecise word or a word with problematic or limiting connotations, they might consider possible synonyms. For example, imagine an author using the word "urban" to describe a particular school. They might ponder whether they intended to emphasize the school's geographic location, in which case "urban" is the appropriate term, or if they selected "urban" as a euphemism for schools with a high proportion of Black students, in which case they might rephrase their description.

Next, just as a musician ensures matching phrasing and stylistic decisions across their performance, authors of quantitative and qualitative studies might consider whether they have achieved optimal alignment across their literature review, problem statement, and research questions. They might also ask whether their findings completely align with their research questions, and if their implications follow directly and specifically from their findings. Authors working in all methodologies might also check for the consistency and clarity of language throughout a document. For instance, writers should ensure that they use terms like "creativity," "informal learning," and "motivation" to denote the same idea or process consistently across their study.

Another way to refine one's research is through reading and copying. Musicians often listen to different recordings of a piece in order to gather ideas about possible interpretations or improvisations. While they may ultimately aim to make their own unique expressive decisions, listening to other music makers' ideas can assist them in not deviating wildly from currently accepted practices. Likewise, an author might examine published research and ensure that, while still asserting their individual voice, they replicate key scholarly conventions.

Once an author has determined to which journal they will submit their work (see more information about this process in Chapter 21 and a list of music education journals in Appendix C), they might find four or more articles published in that journal that utilize their chosen methodology (e.g., historical, quantitative, qualitative, mixed methods, philosophical, action). Authors might then go section by section within those articles and compare them to their current document. For example, if an author of a quantitative study observes that their literature review or discussion sections are markedly longer or shorter than those of quantitative articles from the journal in which they aim to publish, they might alter their work accordingly. Spending a significant amount of time engaging in the process of comparing published articles with one's own manuscript can assist in aligning one's work with currently accepted scholarly conventions. While such action does not guarantee publication, it enables reviewers to focus on issues of content and methodology rather than style, which may assist authors in getting more out of the review process.

Two other tactics that authors might find useful in the revision process are reading aloud and stepping away. When you are silently reading work on a computer screen, your brain may automatically fill in missing words or correct grammatical errors. Reading a document aloud can reveal omissions and wording mistakes. It can also alert you to awkwardly constructed phrases or sentences. A variation on this idea is printing out a draft of your paper, particularly with altered line spacing or in a different font than the one you have grown accustomed to seeing on the computer. Working with a pencil on a printed copy can reveal previously missed errors and issues. Still, looking at the same piece of writing day after day in any format can numb writers to both simple errors and flaws in logic. Authors who take a few days or weeks away from specific sections of their work may more readily see mistakes and limitations when they return to them.

One practical suggestion if you are making a series of revisions: Don't keep saving the newest version with the same name that overwrites the previous version. It is possible that several revisions down the line you might decide to return to the original text that has since been amended. Instead, use a system that allows you to keep track of various iterations. For example, you could save them as draft 1, draft 2, draft 3, and so on, or by date as draft 1.17.21, draft 2.19.21, draft 3.8.21, and so on. Sometimes researchers find the need to delete small or large amounts of material for one reason or another. This decision can be difficult, especially if you spent a good deal of time writing what you now must discard. If you happen to delete an entire sentence, paragraph, or section from your draft, cut-and-paste it into a file named "Extra." You can then retrieve that material if you decide to reinsert or revise it at a later time.

Since scholarly writing ultimately involves the clear communication of complex ideas, authors might also seek inspiration from writers outside of academia who engage in such processes. Researchers can learn from how bestselling fiction, nonfiction, short story, and poetry authors communicate ideas as well as through reporting and essays in magazines such as *The Atlantic* and *The New Yorker*. Considering the tactics used in thoughtful podcasts, blogs, or TED Talks can assist authors in developing their communication skills. Authors might also consider reading books about writing, such as Lamott's (1995) *Bird by Bird: Some Instructions on Writing and Life,* Silvia's (2018) *How to Write a Lot: A Guide to Productive Academic Writing,* and Zinsser's (2016) *On Writing Well: A Classic Guide to Writing Nonfiction*.

There are limits to how much one can improve one's own writing in isolation. Before sending a thesis or dissertation to your committee or a manuscript out to a journal for review, ask multiple individuals if they would provide feedback on your work. Begin by asking for input from peers in your cohort or from those pursuing the same degree at a different institution. Thoughtful individuals outside of one's discipline can also provide helpful observations and critiques; in particular, they may illuminate the need for added explanations or clarifications regarding ideas that those close to an author's area of expertise take for granted. Additionally, most collegiate music education faculty members are heavily invested in having students from their institution publish. Do not hesitate to ask a trusted faculty mentor if they might look over your final document prior to submitting it for review.

The revision process does not end when you submit a paper to a journal. Even when you have revised your work multiple times, reviewers often request substantial revisions. A balance must be achieved between taking feedback to heart and doing one's best to improve, while at the same time not becoming devastated to the point of despair over what can be perceived as hurtful comments. Rather than take it personally—after all, in a blind review, commentators do not know to whom their feedback is addressed—make an effort to read and respond to the suggestions carefully. For more information about revising a paper based on reviewers' feedback, see the Review Process section of Chapter 21.

In short, successful researchers spend a significant amount of time revising their work. Using an array of tactics during the revision process can assist an author in producing high-quality scholarly writing. Tactics may include examining the manuscript at the micro and macro levels, comparing it to published articles, and seeking input from peers and mentors.

Recalling and Rekindling Your Passion

Scholarly writing is hard. All writers experience days when they feel frustrated with their work. Think back to all the times you did not enjoy undertaking the precision-oriented tasks needed to improve your musical skills. The aims and desires that motivate you to continue engaging in musical tasks that do not yield immediate joy may parallel those that can energize your ongoing commitment to scholarly writing.

One way that writers can revive their motivation is by considering the curiosities and questions that drove them to want to learn more about their research topic in the first place. Perhaps you had a particularly troubling or exciting teaching experience that you wanted to explore further. Or maybe you encountered the topic through an insightful engagement with a friend, workshop, class, or social media post. Researchers find joy in entertaining and building on those curiosities and seeing them through to a final written product.

Writers might energize their motivation for scholarly writing by considering the impact that their work could have in the field. Diving deeply into scholarly topics can improve one's own teaching practices. Furthermore, the music education profession should evolve continually in response to changing student and community needs and circumstances. Bringing your research insights to colleagues and to the wider music education community through presentations and publications can play an important role in helping the profession improve its practices.

Additionally, authors might consider the external rewards associated with their research achievements. Perhaps you will receive recognition for your work in the form of praise from your collegiate mentor, school, or local music education community. Completing a scholarly writing project may be a prerequisite to obtaining a graduate degree, which is a huge achievement; currently, only 13% of the American population holds a master's or doctoral degree (U.S. Census Bureau, 2019). There is no substitute for the sense of personal accomplishment that comes from attaining a substantial goal, such as completing a high-quality research project.

If you are not currently finding your curiosity piqued by researching and writing, you might reflect on your selected topic and methodology. Just as musicians may find themselves learning a certain piece or style of music that does not retain their interest, sometimes researchers find themselves stuck working on a topic that no longer resonates. While researchers may use different methodologies (historical, quantitative, qualitative, philosophical, action) over the course of their careers, they often find themselves drawn to some more than others. Until a researcher has a chance to engage deeply with different topics and methodologies, they may not realize which ones they prefer.

If a writer experiences a disconnect between their interests and topic or methodology early on in the research process, they may find switching the topic or methodology a worthwhile use of time. Authors who gain awareness of a disconnect much farther along into a research project may find it helpful to keep other topics and methodologies in mind for future endeavors. Just because an author did not enjoy a particular research experience does not mean that they will never enjoy researching and writing.

Another major impediment to scholarly writing may be feeling like an imposter or fraud. You may think, "I'm not a real researcher; I'm just pretending to be a researcher." In a study of early career collegiate music educators, Sims and Cassidy (2019) found that all 54 participants experienced some degree of imposter feelings in relation to research, with 70% falling into the frequent or intense category. While most outsiders would consider these doctorate-holding individuals to be researchers, they struggled to view themselves as such.

When you feel like an imposter rather than a researcher, you may find it helpful to remind yourself that you are not alone. You might also consider that others do not see you as a fraud. Imagine yourself learning a new musical instrument. You might consider yourself a beginner on that instrument, but given your other musical experiences, you would likely not say that you are no longer a musician. Likewise, learning the new skills needed to conduct research and to write in a scholarly manner can feel overwhelming, but that does not mean that you are not a researcher or scholar. Just as music educators hope that the students they teach think of themselves as musicians, understanding and referring to yourself as a researcher may assist you in developing your scholarly identity.

Each researcher is a unique individual who will make scholarly contributions informed by their own life experiences. A final way of rekindling your passion for research may be to remind yourself of the one-of-a-kind perspectives and background that you bring to your work. Just as no one can ever fully replicate another's musical interpretations, expressivity, improvisations, and compositions, no one will ever be able write a scholarly article in the exact same way as you. By bringing your individual insights and voice to scholarly work, you provide a contribution to the music education profession that only you can give.

It is unrealistic to think that reflecting on all these ideas will always cause you to engage happily in the sometimes tedious researching and writing processes. Even highly motivated researchers have moments when they do not enjoy aspects of their work. Ultimately, persistence is a key part of the writing process. No one starts out as a brilliant researcher or writer; those who eventually succeed work through repeated failures. They remain determined, refuse to quit, and occasionally find joy in the ongoing curiosity, rigor, and challenge of the researching and writing processes.

Summary

Scholarly writing is a skill that necessitates sustained, consistent practice. Maintaining a dedicated writing schedule and considering when and where you write most effectively can help you to develop your writing skills. Additionally, you might set both large and small writing goals and constantly reevaluate them in light of your progress and setbacks. Revision constitutes a key part of the writing process; revising a research document can take just as long as authoring an initial draft. Examining a manuscript at the micro and macro levels, comparing it to published articles, and seeking input from peers and mentors can assist writers in the revision process. When you feel frustrated or unmotivated, recall the curiosities that brought you to research in the first place as well as the sense of accomplishment that can come from finalizing a research document. Remind yourself that you are not an imposter but rather a researcher using your unique voice and insights to further the ongoing development of the music education profession.

References

Lamott, A. (1995). *Bird by bird: Some instructions on writing and life*. Anchor.

Silvia, P. (2018) *How to write a lot: A practical guide to productive academic writing* (2nd ed.). American Psychological Association.

Sims, W. L., & Cassidy, J. W. (2019). Imposter phenomenon responses of early career music education faculty. *Journal of Research in Music Education, 67*(1), 45–61. https://doi.org/10.1177/0022429418812464

Strunk, W., Jr. (1918/2018). *The elements of style: Classic edition* (R. De A'Morelli, Ed.). Spectrum Ink USA.

U.S. Census Bureau. (2019). *Number of people with masters and doctoral degrees double since 2000*. https://www.census.gov/library/stories/2019/02/number-of-people-with-masters-and-phd-degrees-double-since-2000.html

Zinsser, W. (2016). *On writing well: The classic guide to writing nonfiction* (30th anniversary ed.). Harper Perennial.

21
Disseminating Research

Chapter Preview

Presenting a poster, giving a talk, and publishing an article are the primary ways of distributing your research. Each has its own advantages and possibilities, and over a period of years, you will likely want to engage in all three activities. Presentations generally include sharing your research during a poster session or in a lecture-type format at state, national, or international conferences. Research poster sessions have specific guidelines, and it is important that you follow directions exactly. Specific ideas for how to prepare and present a research poster are given, along with several examples. The amount of time available to give spoken presentations varies widely, so paying attention to this and other requirements (e.g., technology support available) is critical. Researchers often choose to illustrate a presentation with a computer slide show. We provide many helpful tips for creating an effective presentation. We also discuss preparing handouts and publishing a presentation in a book of proceedings. Publishing a research paper is an important outcome of scholarly work, and this chapter focuses on finding a journal, publication guidelines, editor's response to submission, the revision process, and publication. We also describe important ethical considerations for both publications and presentations.

Introduction

One of the most important things about conducting research is sharing it with others. After all, even the most informative findings will not do much good if no one knows about them. We have divided this chapter into four segments: giving a presentation, creating a slide show, publishing a paper, and ethical considerations. Each of these topics is central to the dissemination of research.

Giving a Presentation

A basic way of disseminating research findings is through some type of presentation. This might involve something as simple as sharing your findings with colleagues at a school in-service meeting or presenting in a more public venue at a state or national music education conference, during a poster session or in a lecture-type format.

Presentations may or may not summarize research that you have documented in a formal paper. Presenting your research at conferences is a good way for you to interact and connect with other scholars in music education. It is an important means of sharing research findings that can influence the profession.

Publications have the advantage of being permanent and widely distributed. In contrast, presentations are immediate and intimate and allow for direct interaction with an audience. Many organizations have state or regional conferences, national conferences, and international conferences. Most conferences have a website where they post information about scheduled events and submission deadlines. The Music Research Nexus Listserv, maintained at the University of Georgia, publicizes calls for presentations from conferences held throughout the world. Anyone interested in music education research can subscribe at http://musicresearchnexus.com/. Most conferences run on a predictable cycle (e.g., every two years). By planning ahead, you can coordinate your research activity with upcoming conferences.

Applying to Present

It is important to consider where and when you should apply to make a presentation at a conference. Conference websites and calls for presentations will include information about the aims and scope of each event (i.e., what topics organizers are apt to consider) and instructions for presentation. Most organizations require potential presenters to submit a proposal. Formats vary, but they usually require an abstract or a summary of 500 to 750 words. A good proposal usually approaches the word count without going over. It should include (a) the background for the study, including numerous citations to related literature; (b) a purpose statement; (c) research questions, or main argument for philosophical research; (d) a summary of the findings; and (e) conclusions and applications of the research for music teaching and learning.

Most conferences will review conference presentation submissions in a manner similar to a publication. That is, a panel of peers will review the submission to determine whether it should be accepted. Read and follow the instructions for the proposal carefully. Sometimes conference organizers share the rubric or categories that they will use to evaluate your proposal. Taking this information into account when writing a proposal will increase your chances of being accepted. A sloppy proposal that is disorganized and contains spelling and grammatical errors or incomplete information rarely gets accepted. Make certain you meet the submission deadline, as conference organizers do not accept late proposals.

Research Poster Presentations

One of the most common ways of presenting research is through a poster session at a state, national, or international conference. Poster sessions allow many authors

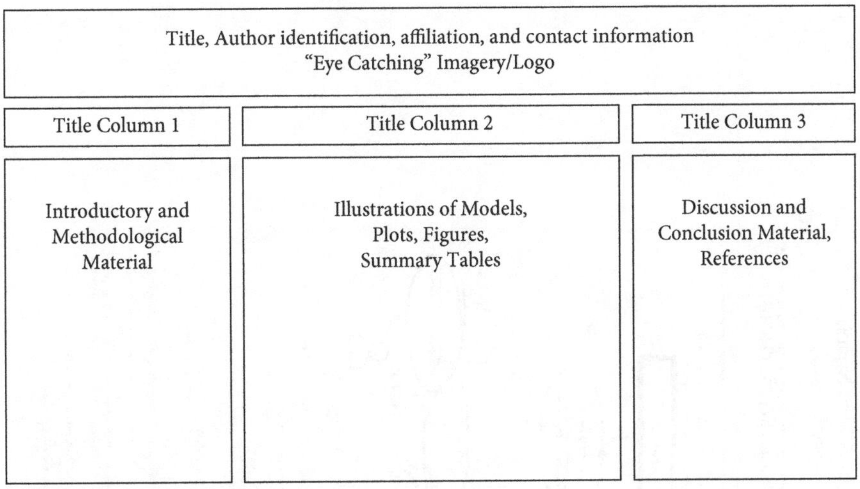

```
┌─────────────────────────────────────────────────────────────┐
│       Title, Author identification, affiliation, and contact information       │
│                    "Eye Catching" Imagery/Logo                │
└─────────────────────────────────────────────────────────────┘
┌──────────────┐  ┌──────────────────┐  ┌──────────────┐
│ Title Column 1│  │  Title Column 2  │  │Title Column 3│
└──────────────┘  └──────────────────┘  └──────────────┘
┌──────────────┐  ┌──────────────────┐  ┌──────────────┐
│Introductory and│ │Illustrations of Models,│ │  Discussion and │
│Methodological │  │   Plots, Figures,    │  │Conclusion Material,│
│   Material   │  │   Summary Tables    │  │   References  │
│              │  │                  │  │              │
│              │  │                  │  │              │
│              │  │                  │  │              │
└──────────────┘  └──────────────────┘  └──────────────┘
```

Figure 21.1 Example of a conference research poster.

to share their findings at one time in an open and informal setting. Posters generally occupy a common space where you are assigned a particular place and time to display your work. In the research poster venue, which might be a separate room or even a hallway, your poster will be displayed on the wall or a special board. Some conferences supply push pins or other means of fastening a poster (e.g., Velcro strips, clips), but you should plan to take your own.

During the allotted time, often an hour, you will stand beside your poster as conference attendees circulate around the room. Some may walk by your poster with barely a glance. Others will stop to look more carefully at your poster and to ask questions. Sometimes attendees will ask for a summary of your research. In preparation, it may be helpful to practice a one-minute talk addressing your purpose and key findings or arguments. You may have a very fruitful exchange in which you gain important insights into your topic or meet new colleagues.

Your poster should present the main points of your study in the clearest form possible. Make certain you include the title of your paper, your name and affiliation, and important components of the research, such as background, aims, method, results, and conclusions. Do not try to cram too much information onto the poster; if your poster is full of text in a small font, other researchers may not be able to read it easily. Try to find creative ways to display your research, through photographs, diagrams, or charts. Remember, viewers can ask you questions and pick up a handout, so you do not need to put *everything* on the poster. Figures 21.1 and 21.2 present two examples. Figure 21.1 is a template for how a typical research poster is usually constructed, with different sections laid out for the title materials, introductory and methodological information, a relatively larger middle section for describing and illustrating findings or main points, and a section for discussion/conclusion materials and references. We have also included examples of posters using this or a very similar format and an editable PowerPoint slide for Figure 21.1

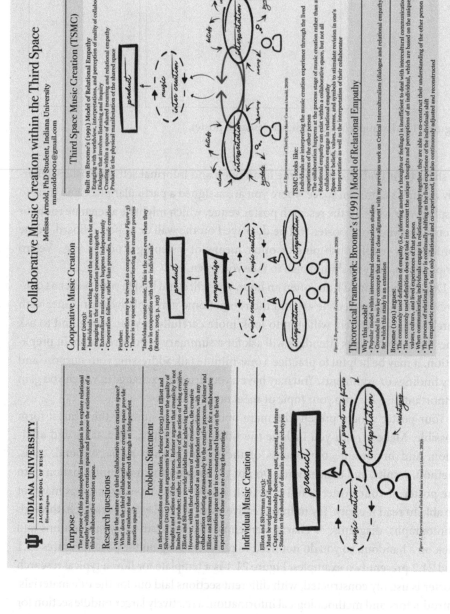

Figure 21.2 Example of a philosophical study conference research poster.

among the supplemental online materials for this book (see items 18, 19, and 20, Chapter 21 on the Companion website ▶). However, not all posters are or need to be formatted in the same way, and there is certainly room for creative license. For example, Figure 21.2 is an example of a poster summarizing a philosophical research study, notice how it incorporates imagery with the text of the poster. Notice also that you can incorporate logos from your university or school unit.

Conference poster dimensions can vary, but common sizes are 91 cm x 122 cm (36" x 48") or 100 cm x 100 cm (40" x 40"). Your acceptance letter from the conference organizer will give you specific instructions on poster dimensions and other pertinent information (time, place, etc.). There are different ways to create a poster, but one of the easiest is to use the same program you use for creating slides. Set the dimensions according to the required specifications. When you are finished, you can have it printed out. Many universities and most office supply companies have facilities to print color posters on one sheet. Some are even printing them on cloth. When you travel to the conference, you can roll up the poster for easy transportation and to avoid creases. If the conference is not far, you can carry the poster in a cardboard tube. For longer trips, such as on a plane, you might want to invest in a sturdy plastic tube that will protect your poster from possible damage.

Spoken Presentations

In addition to presenting a poster, most conferences select studies for presentation in a lecture format. Presenters typically have 20 to 25 minutes to present their research, followed by 5 to 10 minutes for questions and discussion. Conferences specifically designed for philosophical research, such as the MayDay Group Colloquia and International Society for Philosophy of Music Education Symposia, may follow presentations with an assigned formal response and extended time for scholarly discussion. Anticipating potential critiques and questions can assist presenters in preparing for such interactions. Acceptance to present is often quite competitive, especially for larger events such as the National Association for Music Education's (NAfME) Music Research and Teacher Education Conference and the Society for Music Teacher Education's Symposium on Music Teacher Education.

Be well prepared. Make sure you know the time and location of your session, as well as the timeframe for presentation, available technology, and other details. Sufficient preparation will help you feel at ease and communicate your ideas effectively. Here are some additional suggestions for giving a spoken presentation:

- *Rehearse*: Practice your talk frequently, both alone and in front of friends or colleagues who will provide you with feedback. You may even want to video yourself so that you can critique the playback. Doing so will ensure that when the time comes for your presentation, you will have the confidence that your hard work has prepared you well.

- *Be aware of the timing*: Conference presentations range from a brief 15 minutes to an hour. It takes considerable practice to adjust the content and your speaking rate to the required time. A novice speaker may be nervous and talk so quickly that they finish well before the time limit. Or they may wander off topic or become distracted, and the time may run out well before they have finished what they planned to say. You may wish to have a timer running in the background when you practice. Set it to go off five minutes before you are to finish to make certain you have time for a summary. If the conference guidelines indicate that you should include a question-and-answer period in your talk, be certain to account for that time as well.
- *Prepare your speaking style*: Strive for a balance between a formal and conversational speaking style. A formal, scholarly explication of a research project is often far too dense and complicated to be easily understood in an oral presentation. Conversely, speaking in a manner that is too casual is not appropriate for a conference presentation.

    Frequently, though not always, a presentation is based on a written paper. In earlier conferences, such presentations were called "paper reading" sessions and speakers did, in fact, read a written paper. Today, however, many researchers talk directly to their audience using only notes or an outline, or read from a script created especially for the presentation. There are advantages to both approaches. Speaking directly to attendees with limited notes is often more engaging, while a script can ensure smooth delivery and more precise timing. Given the importance of specific word choice in philosophical research and participants' voices in qualitative research, such scholars often still read directly from a paper.
- *Make eye contact*: Along with a pleasant and easily understood speaking style, eye contact is critically important. Try to make certain you engage your audience with direct eye contact as much as possible. If you are speaking before a large audience, make certain you do not fixate on one spot. Move your gaze from side to side and front to back in a controlled and deliberate manner.
- *Take care over dress and stance*: Make certain your dress is professional and appropriate for the circumstances. You should be neat and clean and dressed in a way that presents you as a confident authority on your topic. Likewise, try to adjust your stance so that you are neither stiff and wooden nor too casual and informal. Try to avoid pacing around too much, but do move in a comfortable manner.
- *Use notes*: Unless you have had considerable experience, memorizing a talk may lead to a stiff and awkward recitation. Conversely, as mentioned in the preceding points, reading too much may take your focus away from the audience. Preparing notes in some format can help you remember key points, stay on track, and present in a calm, organized, and sequential manner. Speakers can prepare notes within most slide presentation platforms or use the "old school" approach of preparing a stack of large note cards (e.g., 4" x 6" or 10 cm x 15 cm).

    Create notes in a bullet-point format; rather than writing full sentences, use only a few cues to remind you of the details. Prepare notes similar to those at the

(a)
> Participants included 60 fourth graders divided into three groups: Experimental Group 1 (*n* = 20) learned tonal patterns with hand signs. Experimental Group 2 (*n* = 20) learned tonal patterns with hand signs and body movement. The Control Group (*n* = 20) learned tonal patterns without hand signs or body movement.

(b)
> Participants: 60 4th graders — tonal patterns
> 1. hand signs.
> 2. hand signs **and** body movement.
> 3. **without** hand signs or body movement.

Figure 21.3 Presentation notes. The example at the top is an ineffective way of presenting notes. The example on the bottom is a more effective way of doing so.

bottom of Figure 21.3 rather than those at the top. Print your notes or have them available on a device in a font large enough to read quickly and easily.

- *Using a script*: A script might be useful for novice presenters because it removes the pressure of remembering what to say next and provides more support than using only bullet-point notes. Scripts also allow for precise timing during practice, which might be especially useful in facilitating presentations involving multiple authors and limited rehearsal time.

Authors who choose this approach should create a script especially for the presentation. Do not simply cut and paste from your manuscript; rather, create a new narrative that is conversational and less formal than a research paper. Focus on the most important details for understanding the study. Avoid going too deeply into the nuances of procedure and statistical analysis. A script combined with an elegant slide presentation can be very effective in conveying the findings and implications of studies in any method. Figure 21.4 provides an excerpt from a script used in a presentation on a historical topic.

> The invention of the phonograph in 1877 and the gramophone in 1887 opened the door for the use of recorded music in the school room by the early 20th century. This new technology moved music education away from primarily singing and reading notation to also include movement, listening and appreciation. Classroom teachers unable to play piano or model good singing could rely on recordings to help teach rote songs, introduce instruments of the orchestra, and provide music for marching, dancing, and recreation. Music textbook companies took advantage of audio technology and provided records to accompany their materials.
>
> For many people, especially in rural and remote areas, recorded music provided their first opportunity to hear artist caliber musicianship and large ensembles. How amazing it must have been to hear such sounds for the first time!

Figure 21.4 Script excerpt from a historical presentation.

Creating a Slide Show

Frequently, researchers choose to illustrate a presentation with a computer slide show. Though not mandatory, almost all presentations today involve some type of presentation platform, such as PowerPoint, Google Slides, or Prezi. Features such as graphs, figures, tables, and photographs are shared more easily with an audience as graphical images rather than oral descriptions. The following information may be helpful advice for creating a slide show.

Organizational Features of a Slide Show

- *Title slide*: Include the title of your presentation, your name, and professional affiliation (see Figure 21.5).
- *Appreciation*: If you have people to thank, such as conference organizers or the person who invited you to speak or who made travel arrangements, including a slide something like Figure 21.6 will ensure you do not forget. This can be done at the beginning and/or at the end. This slide may be unnecessary for a typical conference presentation.
- *Organizational outline*: A simple, three-point model is an easy but effective way to organize your presentation. (1) Tell the audience what you are going to tell them. You can do this by listing the major themes you plan to discuss. (2) Tell them. This is the main body of your presentation and will involve several slides. Presenters may find it helpful to emphasize the information unique to their study. For example, while a literature review might take up multiple pages in a published study (see more information about publishing below), a presenter

> **MUSIC INSTRUCTION**
> **AT SELECTED STATE NORMAL SCHOOLS**
> **DURING THE NINETEENTH CENTURY**
>
> Phillip M. Hash
> Illinois State University
> pmhash@ilstu.edu

Figure 21.5 An opening slide that presents the title of the presentation, along with the name and affiliation of the presenter.

DISSEMINATING RESEARCH 439

THANK YOU!
QUESTIONS?

Figure 21.6 A "thank you" slide. Placing a slide like this at either the beginning or the end will ensure that you will not forget to thank people.

may move quickly through the literature review and focus on the study findings. (3) Conclude with a summary (see next point). Figure 21.7 provides a clear statement of the purpose of the presentation, along with images that illustrate the main topic.

- *Conclusions*: Save a few minutes at the end of your talk to summarize your main points. Leave your audience with a take-home message: If you could overhear members of your audience sharing what they heard from you with those who were not at the presentation, what would you want them to say? What are the most important points you want your audience to remember?

Figure 21.7 An organizational slide.

Suggestions for a Successful Slide Show Presentation

- *Preparation*: Plan to spend an adequate amount of time in preparation. Do not make the mistake of thinking that writing the talk takes a long time but that the slides can be thrown together quickly. Preparing an effective slide show can be time-consuming. Start early. You will definitely have a problem if you wait until the last minute.
- *Screen layout*: Don't put too much information on the screen at any one time. Just include a few words or a phrase that you can talk about. This is especially important: if you have too many words on the screen, the audience will be busy reading instead of paying attention to you. Choose images that illustrate the point you are making. Your spoken presentation can amplify what is on the screen. In Figure 21.8, for example, the speaker might highlight research findings; the stars (which are red in the original) indicate that the respective rows pertain to qualities of feedback an instructor could provide.
- *Avoid reading slides*: When possible, talk to the audience about what they are seeing rather than reading directly from the screen. Use different words to amplify what is written on the screen. However, there are times—such as when presenting a dense quotation—when both displaying the text and reading it directly can facilitate the audiences' understanding, particularly in international settings. Use this tactic sparingly.
- *Address your audience*: A common mistake that novice presenters make is to turn and look at the screen while they read what is printed there. This takes

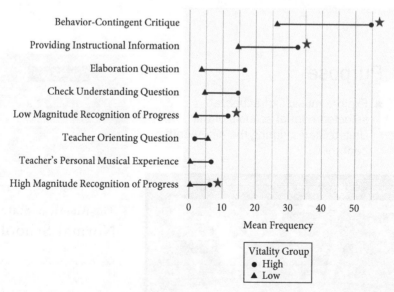

Figure 21.8 Let the images on the slide present the point under discussion in a clear and direct way. Your spoken message can fill in details and provide explanations.

your focus away from the audience and makes them look at your back. In addition, most people can read faster than you can speak, so they have already read what you are saying as you finish the screen. Use your notes to help guide you through your discussion and allow the slides to supplement rather than reproduce your talk.
- *Multimedia examples*: Visual and aural examples will make a strong impact on your audience. Use drawings, photographs, animations, and so on. Since this will not be a published work, you can scan in photographs from journals, take pictures off the web, and so on. Also, you can put in sound clips from web links or audio files. If you do use audio or video examples, plan to keep them brief and focused; make certain the audience knows what they are supposed to be hearing or seeing. It is a good idea to cite various media on a final slide at the end of your presentation, though there is no need to say anything about it.

  Do not let extra elements such as images, audio examples, and video clips take away from the points you want to make. In other words, do not get carried away making a highly entertaining presentation and forget to convey your research in a complete, concise, and clear manner.
- *Equipment*: Save your program on a flash drive and in a cloud storage platform. Be certain to check with the conference organizer about equipment. Some conferences will allow you to use your own computer. If you do take your computer, make certain you have the correct connecting cables. If you must use a computer supplied by the conference, make certain your slide show program will run on the computer they have.

Handouts

At most conferences, it is appropriate to have handouts or to share links to further materials for your colleagues should they wish more information about your study. Different conferences have their own restrictions: sometimes you will be allowed to hand out a one-page abstract; sometimes you can distribute copies of the entire paper. Make certain that your contact information is on the handout. An interested colleague may wish to contact you for further conversation about your research. And you can always email a copy of your paper to interested colleagues.

Conference Proceedings

Some conferences publish a book of proceedings in which they include abstracts and/or full papers. Sometimes you must submit a written paper for consideration; sometimes all papers are included with the consent of the authors. Most conferences will provide detailed instructions for how to prepare your submission if you want your paper to appear in the published proceedings. If you plan to publish your paper in a journal at a later date, you should check the journal website, as some do not print articles that have appeared elsewhere or in other formats. If you are uncertain, contact the editor, as the particular circumstances may alter your decision. See the subsequent discussion of ethical considerations related to publishing later in this chapter.

Publishing a Paper

Some would argue that publications are the most important outcome of scholarly work: (a) publications reach a broader audience than presentations and (b) they are permanent. Years after publication, an article can still be very informative and influential. Even if they are not more important than presentations, publications are critically important not only to the growth of one's career in higher education but also to the growth of the field of music education. Therefore, this section focuses on how to get an article published.

Finding a Journal

One of the first things you will want to do is choose a journal to which you plan to submit your article. Several journals, such as the *Journal of Research in Music Education* and the *Bulletin of the Council for Research in Music Education*, accept a wide variety of topics within all common methods (i.e., quantitative, qualitative, historical, philosophical, mixed methods). Others, such as the *String Research Journal*, the *Journal of Historical Research in Music Education*, and the *Philosophy of Music Education Review*, publish only studies written on specific topics and/or using specific methods. Though perhaps difficult for novice researchers to ascertain, authors should also consider the quality, depth, and scope of their manuscript when selecting a journal. Compare your paper to articles published in the journal you are considering. The *Journal of Research in Music Education* publishes only research at the highest level and accepts approximately 15% to 20% of submissions in any given year. Other journals have higher acceptance rates and might publish articles rejected by other periodicals. A manuscript that does not rise to the level of publication in a top-tier journal might still have much to offer the profession and deserve an audience. See Appendix C for a list of research journals in music education.

If there are several good journal possibilities, you may want to investigate more than one. As noted in the subsequent discussion on ethics, it is inappropriate to submit an article for publication to more than one journal at a time. Therefore, you need to gather pertinent information before you make a choice of where to submit. You will want to know how often a journal publishes, that is, how many times a year a new issue appears. How wide is the distribution; is the journal local, regional, national, or international? Is it published in print, online, or both? Are journal articles available through online indexes and databases such as JSTOR, ProQuest Music Periodicals, RILM, or EBSCO? Once you have decided on one or more journals where you would like to submit, the next step is to peruse their guidelines.

Publication Guidelines

Nearly every journal provides publication guidelines on its website. It is critically important that you follow these guidelines very carefully. Failure to do so may mean a rejection of your submission. What follows are generic topics addressed in many, but not necessarily all, journal guidelines:

- *Aims and scope*: Sometimes this is called "About the Journal." Often, a journal will describe the types of articles they publish. Some have fairly narrow interests; for example, the *Journal of Historical Research in Music Education* states that "it is the only music education journal whose topics focus solely on the diverse international history of music education including biographical, methodological, sociological, historiographical and qualitative studies of music teaching and learning" (https://us.sagepub.com/en-us/nam/journal-of-historical-research-in-music-education/journal202484). Similarly, the *Journal of Band Research* states that it "is the premiere scholarly publication in the world devoted to band music, band history and band methodology" (https://www.journalofbandresearch.org). *Research Studies in Music Education,* on the other hand, states that "the journal covers a wide range of topics across all areas of music education" (https://us.sagepub.com/en-us/nam/research-studies-in-music-education/journal201863#aims-and-scope). You should take considerable time and effort in identifying a journal that is likely to publish an article on your topic of interest. It may be very helpful to read several articles from a journal before you submit to it. This will give you an idea of what they accept for publication.
- *Editorial board*: Professional journals have an editor (sometimes co-editors or assistant/associate editors as well) who has the responsibility for organizing the work of the editorial board; together they maintain the quality of the journal by accepting or rejecting article submissions. In our field, the editor and members, the editor and members of the editorial board are professional music educators who have earned a reputation for successful publication of music education research. Many, but not all, are university professors. Sometimes they are appointed, and other times they are elected. Sometimes they are chosen to represent a geographical region; this is particularly important in boards of international journals. Some members have a place on the editorial board because of their particular research expertise. Regardless, these individuals are unpaid and work as volunteers to review submissions. More details about editorial boards are given in the next point on peer review.

- *Peer review*: One of the most important aspects of publishing research is peer review. When you submit an article to a research journal, an editorial assistant may log it into a cataloguing system. The editor will then read the article and determine whether it is appropriate for review. If the topic of the article does not match the aim and scope of the journal or the quality is very obviously far below the standards of the journal, the editor may inform the author(s) that the article will not be reviewed.

    If the editor deems the article appropriate for the journal, they will send it to (usually) three members of the editorial board. These reviewers are charged with reading the article very carefully and making a recommendation for acceptance or rejection. You should get a message from the editor (or editorial assistant) acknowledging that they received your submission. However, you may wait three months or longer to receive the results of the review committee's deliberations. A simplified version of the decision-making process is for the editor to:
    - Accept your article for publication either as is or with only very minor revisions. This is a rare occurrence, and only very experienced researchers are likely to get this kind of notification.
    - Recommend revisions. This response does not imply acceptance or rejection. Rather, it means that specific aspects of the paper must be addressed before a final decision can be made. For additional details, see the next section.
    - Reject. If the consensus of the editor and the review committee is that the article has inherent problems or limitations that cannot be corrected even with revisions, the author is notified that it will not be accepted for publication in the journal.

    Another aspect of the peer review process is that it is most often a double-blind review. That is, the editor will see your name on the submission, but the review panel most often will not. Furthermore, the author will not know which members of the editorial board reviewed the article. See below for comments about preparing a manuscript with no name or affiliation indicated.
- *Submission guidelines*: Each journal will specify formatting for things like headings, references, and text citations. In English-language music education research journals, the most common reference styles are APA and the Chicago Manual of Style, but there are others.

    Most journals prefer to have tables and figures submitted separately, not embedded in the text. For figures, specifications usually prescribe at least 300 dpi (dots per inch) in a format such as tiff or jpeg. Most journals print only black-and-white graphics; online publications usually allow the use of color. Tables and figures are often sent as a separate file, but might also be included at the end of the manuscript after the reference list or notes. In the text of the manuscript, you will include a note on where the copy editor should eventually insert a particular table or figure in the published article.

Most journals today only accept submissions online. Many use an online platform such as Scholar One, while others simply take submissions through email. Regardless, you may be asked to submit some or all of the following:

- o A cover letter that provides (a) title and author(s), (b) assurance that the manuscript is not under consideration with another journal, (c) notice of any conflicts of interest, (d) details regarding any closely related manuscripts (see below on piecemeal publication), and (e) contact information for the lead author.
- o A cover sheet that includes title, author's name, affiliation, and contact information.
- o An abstract and keywords.
- o The main body of the paper; make certain that all identifying information has been removed so that the reviewers can perform a "blind" review (i.e., they have no idea of the author's identity).
- o References.
- o Tables.
- o Figures.
- o Appendix.
- o Online supplementary files. Many journals allow authors to provide an online supplementary file that they post on their website. The supplementary file allows authors to share large amounts of material such as raw data, additional tables and figures, questionnaires, multiple photographs, audio files, and so on. Many appendixes for journal articles today appear in this form.

Before you submit an article, make certain to proofread it very carefully. Ask friends or a mentor to read it and make comments. Also, you should make certain that in-text citations match the reference list exactly (i.e., names are spelled the same, dates match). Undoubtedly, there is a great deal of work in preparing a manuscript. For students, most, if not all, of the work is done before turning in a paper for a grade. In the case of submission for publication, however, most of the work comes after a draft is completed. Then comes a period of extensive revisions. Revise, revise, revise before submitting for publication. Save multiple copies of your paper (e.g., on backup files or in cloud-based storage). Also, each time you make changes, save it with a different title (e.g., draft 1, draft 2, draft 3, or drafts with dates, as in draft 4.13.21, draft 5.7.21) so that you can easily go back to recover something from a previous version.

Editor's Response to Submission

The editor will contact you regarding the results of the peer review process for your submission. Here are some examples of items that the reviewers consider; sometimes these are rated on a scale from poor to excellent:

- *Relevance to the journal*: Is the topic of the submitted article appropriate for the journal?
- *Writing style*: Is the article written in the appropriate reference style (e.g., APA or Chicago; see below for more details)? Are there excessive mechanical errors (e.g., poor grammar, misspellings, incorrect punctuation)? Is the article well organized and easy to follow? Is the article written so that the ideas are effectively communicated?
- *Content*: Are the various aspects of research design (explanation of the problem, statement of the purpose, review of related literature, methodology, data analysis, results, and conclusions) clearly described and thoroughly discussed? Are the research methods appropriate for the study and effectively executed?
- *Overall evaluation*: Taking all the elements into consideration, the reviewer can, as noted previously, recommend that (a) the article be accepted (either as is or with only very minor corrections), (b) the author(s) revise and resubmit for further consideration, or (c) the article be rejected.

You will receive a detailed list of comments, suggestions, and recommendations separately from each member of the review committee and often from the editor as well. Reviewers will identify each item on these lists by page and line number. It is common to feel overwhelmed or frustrated upon receiving substantial critical feedback on research to which you have devoted much time. In such moments, it can be helpful to imagine the reviewers' perspectives. As Graue (2006) explained, reviewers aim for fairness. They try to use objective, unbiased criteria to ensure that limited journal space is allocated to the highest quality research. While Graue noted that unfortunately some reviewers occasionally act like playground bullies, the vast majority volunteer their time because of their genuine interest in developing professional knowledge and mentoring beginning researchers.

Perhaps the most common reason for rejection is that the manuscript is too confusing. Missing details, contradictions from one portion of the paper to another, and minimal sources cited can lead to a weak paper. Occasional typographical errors are not usually a reason for rejection because they can be easily corrected. However, excessive errors may be an indication of other, more serious problems.

Revision Process

If you receive a response with a recommendation to revise and resubmit, it is important that you pay very close attention to the details. First, note whether there is a deadline for resubmission. Then take each comment in turn and do your best to address the stated concern. After thinking it over, you can choose one of three options: (a) change it exactly as the reviewer has requested (assuming a suggestion for how to correct the problem was included); (b) correct the problem, but in your own way; or (c) decide not to make a change in your manuscript regarding this point. Ignoring the comments of reviewers is not a usual response. However, in some cases reviewers will contradict each other. If you fix a problem according to one, you will be in disagreement with the other. Or you may simply feel so strongly about a position that you are not willing to change it. If you do decide not to abide by a reviewer's suggestion, you must provide an explanation for why you have chosen not to do so. For every item on each reviewer's list, indicate whether you have or have not made a change in the manuscript, and if you did so, describe the change in detail. It is sometimes helpful to include direct quotations from the revised text that demonstrate the changes. You will also need to prepare a clean manuscript that contains all of your revisions. Follow the instructions from the editor regarding how to resubmit your article.

Once you have submitted a revision, you can expect to wait another few months before hearing back from the editor about a final decision. In some cases, there is a second or even third round of revisions. Altogether, it may be several years from the time you start working on a research project to the time it appears in print as a journal article.

Publication

The percentage of submissions accepted for publication varies widely by journal. Factors involved include the number and quality of submissions received, the number of issues per year, and the number of pages a publisher will allow a journal to publish per year. Top-tier journals in the field such as the *Journal of Research in Music Education* and the *Bulletin of the Council for Research in Music Education* usually publish fewer than 25% of the submissions they receive. Other journals may accept as many as 60%.

Once a journal has accepted a submission, it will begin the publication process. The author might be asked to submit a final revision with corrections or changes requested during the final review. From there, the editor will edit a proof and send it to the author for review. Review this proof several times and accept or reject the editor's changes. For the most part, you will want to accept the editorial changes and perhaps make some of your own. Look carefully at every aspect of the paper, including the abstract, tables and figures, and references or notes. Correct any spelling, grammatical, or format issues found by you or the editor. Double-check mathematical calculations and statistical procedures for accuracy. At this stage, it is still possible to make minor revisions to organization or sentence structure. However, you should not need to make changes that involve adding a great deal of content.

Once you return the editor's proof, they will create another clean version and forward it to a copyeditor for production. You will likely receive another proof typeset in the format the article will be published in from this individual, who will ask you to review it again. Do not assume that all errors and edits are complete at this point. Review the final proof very carefully. This will be your final chance to make minor edits and corrections. Take responsibility for your own work. The editor and copyeditor will do all they can. However, they do not know your study or writing as well as you do. Know that it is very frustrating to see your article in print only to find an error or a typo.

The publication process will likely take another several months. Many journals publish the final versions of accepted articles online before they move to publication in print. Articles published online often receive a DOI (digital object identifier) or a stable URL (uniform resource locator) that serves as a permanent link for locating the article. These become part of the article's citation information and are particularly useful for quickly locating an article. If your article is cited by another author, a reader can simply click on the DOI or URL in the reference list to locate your article. You might also use it if you announce the publication of your article on social media platforms such as Facebook or Twitter. The complete article will likely be available only to those with access to the journal through subscription or a library database. However, the abstract and reference list often will be available to all.

It can be daunting and even exhausting to go through the writing, submission, revision, and publication process. However, it is quite rewarding to see your name in print. Even more important is the fact that your ideas have now joined the professional dialogue. You have contributed to the literature, and this is what keeps the music education profession moving forward. The rewards to you and to others are well worth the effort.

Ethical Considerations

Most journals and conferences subscribe to a code of ethics regarding publications and presentations. In the United States, music education journals generally follow the National Association for Music Education's Society for Research in Music Education "Research Publication and Presentation Code of Ethics" (http://www.sagepub.com/upm-data/62972_Code_of_Ethics_SRME.pdf) and the APA Guidelines for Ethical and Legal Standards in Publishing (*Publication Manual of the American Psychological Association*, latest edition). Here are some of the things they proscribe:

- *Multiple submissions*: You should not submit the same article to more than one journal at a time. If you have submitted it to a journal and it is under review, you must wait until you have a final decision from that journal before submitting to another.
- *Duplicate publications*: Once an article has been published, it cannot be published in another journal, in whole or in part, without permission from

the original journal. For example, if a written version of a presentation was published in a conference proceeding, it cannot be submitted for journal publication.
- *Piecemeal publication*: Authors should not publish data from one study in multiple articles. A single study should be published as one article. Possible exceptions include a historical study divided by topic or time period, the use of public data sets used in differing ways for multiple studies, and submissions from a multi-article type of doctoral dissertation. Authors pursuing one of these exceptions, even through different journals, should explicitly state the circumstances of multiple articles from one study in the cover letter to the editor.
- *Conference presentations*: The same presentation or research poster should not be submitted to more than one major conference. If a presentation has been made to a small gathering with a local audience, it may be submitted to a major conference; however, such a submission should include details of the prior presentation. For example, you can present at multiple state music education conferences, but should not present at more than one national or international conference, unless you know the audiences are substantially different.

Other concerns are generally listed on the journal or conference website. If you feel that an exception should be made to any of the posted proscriptions, you should contact the journal editor or conference organizer for a ruling.

Summary

Once you have finished a research project, it is important for you to share your findings with the profession. Of course, you will want to begin thinking about this even before you have completed the study. Presenting a poster or a talk and publishing an article are the primary ways of distributing your research. Each has its own advantages and possibilities. Over a period of years, you will likely want to engage in all three activities.

If you have read all the chapters in this book, and especially if you have answered the questions at the end of each chapter, you should have a basic understanding of research in music education. Of course, there are many advanced courses you can take and books you can read, but at this point the best way to learn to do research is to do it! Be certain to check with an instructor or other authority figures at your institution about proper protocols—especially in filing IRB forms—before you get started. But once you have the appropriate permissions, you should conduct a small-scale study. You are likely to make many mistakes, just as you did when you first started learning to play or sing music, but that is often the best way to learn. If you persist and try again, you will soon be on your way to conducting research that can have a positive impact on the music education profession.

Important Terms for Review

Professional journals have an *editor* and an *editorial board*. The editor is the person who is responsible for the maintaining the quality of the journal by accepting or rejecting article submissions. The editorial board consists of a group of professionals who read and review submitted articles.

Peer review refers to the process of evaluating a submitted article by a panel of professional scholars.

Often at professional conferences, researchers display their research findings in a *research poster*. This is typically a large, printed poster that presents key aspects of a research study in an attractive and engaging manner.

Reference

Graue, B. (2006). The transformative power of reviewing. *Educational Researcher, 35*(9), 36–41. https://doi.org/10.3102/0013189X035009036

APPENDIX A

Selected Online Resources for Primary Source Material on the History of Music Education

Books/Periodicals

1. Google Books

A comprehensive index of full-text books and periodicals.

2. HathiTrust Digital Library

HathiTrust is a partnership of academic and research institutions offering a collection of millions of titles digitized from libraries around the world.

3. International Arcade Museum

Contains a searchable database for full text issues of *Presto Magazine* and *Music Trade Review* back to the 19th century. Excellent source for music industry involvement with music education.

4. Internet Archive

A nonprofit library of millions of free books, movies, software, music, and more. Excellent historical resource for full text publications into the 19th century.

5. ProQuest Historical Newspapers

This database contains several newspapers from the United States and abroad. Access through a university or public library.

6. Saxophone Museum

Includes historical trade publications from C. G. Conn, H. W. White (King), Buescher, and others. Excellent source for industry-related information on instrumental music education. School bands were an important feature of these publications.

Genealogy

1. Ancestry.com

Excellent resource for genealogy, with extras such as newspapers and school yearbooks included. Subscription required.

2. Family Search

Free database with access to over 2,000 historical collections, including the U.S. census and military records. Start here before purchasing a subscription for other sites.

3. HeritageQuest Online

A comprehensive treasury of American genealogical sources, rich in unique primary sources, local and family histories, and finding aids. Access through a public or university library.

Music Scores and Parts

1. Band Music PDF Library

Preserves and shares band music from the Golden Age of the American town band. Over 3,400 public domain selections, including scores and parts, are available for free download.

2. International Music Score Library Project/Petrucci Music Library

The IMSLP database includes thousands of Western art music scores and parts, including music for wind band and tune books from the 18th and 19th centuries. All scores and parts are available for download free of charge.

Newspapers

1. Chronicling America

This free database at the Library of Congress contains full-text U.S. newspapers from 1789 to 1924.

2. Gale's 19th Century U.S. Newspapers

Features full-text articles from a variety of publications, including major newspapers as well as those published by African Americans, Native Americans, women's rights groups, labor groups, the Confederacy, and other groups and interests. Access through a university or public library.

3. GenealogyBank

Excellent source for historical newspapers. Subscription required.

4. Newspapers.com

Source for historical newspapers. Subscription required.

Photographs & Recordings

1. Internet Bandsman's Everything Within

Includes photographs, discography, and histories of bands from the United Kingdom, Australia, Canada, New Zealand, the United States, and elsewhere.

2. Discography of American Historical Recordings

The DAHR includes information and master recordings from American record companies during the 78 rpm era. It is part of the American Discography Project at the University of California, Santa Barbara, and the Packard Humanities Institute.

3. National Jukebox at the Library of Congress

Digital recordings from the collections of the Library of Congress Packard Campus for Audio Visual Conservation and other contributing libraries and archives. Many recordings from the Victor Company, including many labeled as educational.

K–12 and College/University Yearbooks

1. Classmates

Contains thousands of school and university yearbooks from the early 20th century to the present. Fee account required.

2. E-Yearbook

Contains thousands of school annuals from the late 19th century to the present. Although the site requires a subscription, users may search for free to determine if the database meets their needs.

APPENDIX B
Data Entry

Entering Data into a Spreadsheet

Quantitative researchers must enter their data into a spreadsheet prior to performing their analyses. Spreadsheets consist of rows and columns. Most statistical software packages are designed such that each object that has been measured is assigned a row in a spreadsheet, and each attribute the object is measured on is assigned a column. In most music education research, measurements are gathered from people—the participants in a study (e.g., students, teachers, parents, administrators). The participants in the study are the "objects," and therefore are represented in rows. The columns are the attributes the people were measured on, that is, the variables in the study. Data gathered on multiple variables from multiple participants are typically arranged as depicted in Figure B.1.

Wide versus Long Data Formats

Researchers typically choose between two options for entering data when their participants have been measured on the same variable on multiple occasions. They can choose a *wide format*, in which participants appear in only one row and the variables are labeled such that it is clear which measurement occasion each column represents. A wide data format of four participants' measurements on a single variable at two points in time is depicted in Figure B.2 (which is very similar to Figure B.1). This is the format that is most easy to use when conducting analyses of data representing multiple measurement occasions in SPSS.

Alternatively, researchers could choose a *long format*, in which participants' multiple measurement occasions are represented via multiple rows per participant, and there is a separate column that represents the time of the measurement occasion (see Figure B.3).

Figure B.1 An example of a typical participant (row) by variable (column) spreadsheet layout.

	Variable 1	Variable 2	Variable 3
Participant 1	Participant 1's value for variable 1	Participant 1's value for variable 2	Participant 1's value for variable 3
Participant 2	Participant 2's value for variable 1	Participant 2's value for variable 2	Participant 2's value for variable 3
Participant 3	Participant 3's value for variable 1	Participant 3's value for variable 2	Participant 3's value for variable 3
Participant 4	Participant 4's value for variable 1	Participant 4's value for variable 2	Participant 4's value for variable 3

Figure B.2 An example of a wide format spreadsheet that is arranged with participants appearing in one row and the multiple measurement occasions appearing as separately labeled columns.

	Variable 1 Time 1	Variable 1 Time 2
Participant 1	Participant 1's value for variable 1, time 1	Participant 1's value for variable 1, time 2
Participant 2	Participant 2's value for variable 1, time 1	Participant 2's value for variable 1, time 2
Participant 3	Participant 3's value for variable 1, time 1	Participant 3's value for variable 1, time 2
Participant 4	Participant 4's value for variable 1, time 1	Participant 4's value for variable 1, time 2

Going from a Measure to a Spreadsheet

Gathering data from participants and entering it into a spreadsheet can be quite straightforward if the data are in the form of physical measurements of some kind. However, it can be a more complicated process when it involves entering in data for individual test items, judges' ratings, questionnaire responses, and so on. Entering data from these types of measures can require some sort of coding process. It is critical that researchers take an organized approach to data entry.

Coding Judges' Ratings

Consider a scenario in which a researcher measures the performance achievement of string students. The researcher could choose a measure similar to Zdzinski and Barnes's (2002) string performance rating scale. A scale like this would typically be used by judges who are asked to evaluate the degree to which they agree with various statements describing the performance by circling a value along a Likert-type continuum. The response mode Zdzinski and Barnes describe in their study ranges from "5–Strongly Agree" to "1–Strongly Disagree."

Consider the two performance criteria from Zdzinski and Barnes's (2002) measure shown in Figure B.4 (note that there are over 20 performance criteria on the full rating scale).

Notice that the phrasing of the first criterion is *positive*; that is, ratings of "strongly agree" on this criterion would be indicative of "good" performance. However, the phrasing of the second

Figure B.3 An example of a long format spreadsheet that is arranged with participants' multiple measurement occasions spread across rows. Note the additional column that indicates time of measurement.

	Time (i.e., measurement occasion)	Variable 1
Participant 1	Time 1	Participant 1's value for variable 1, time 1
Participant 1	Time 2	Participant 1's value for variable 1, time 2
Participant 2	Time 1	Participant 2's value for variable 1, time 1
Participant 2	Time 2	Participant 2's value for variable 1, time 2
Participant 3	Time 1	Participant 3's value for variable 1, time 1
Participant 3	Time 2	Participant 3's value for variable 1, time 2
Participant 4	Time 1	Participant 4's value for variable 1, time 1
Participant 4	Time 2	Participant 4's value for variable 1, time 2

Figure B.4 Two performance criteria from Zdzinski and Barnes's (2002) string performance rating scale.

Performance Criteria	Ratings				
	Strongly Agree				Strongly Disagree
Clear articulation produced by left hand	5	4	3	2	1
Tempo is not stable	5	4	3	2	1

criterion is *negative*; that is, ratings of "strongly agree" on this criterion would be indicative of "poor" performance. The second criterion, "Tempo is not stable," is an example of what is called a "reverse-scored" item. As such, once the researcher entered data for the judges' ratings of this criterion in their spreadsheet, they would then have to either transform the scores in that column of data to reflect the negative wording, or—and preferably—create an additional column in their spreadsheet with a label indicative of reverse scoring, such as "tempo_reversed," that contains the reversed scores for that criterion. Spreadsheet programs such as Excel and statistical software packages such as SPSS have functionalities that can allow you to automate recoding processes such as these.

Coding Questionnaire Responses

Entering data from questionnaires is another common scenario that requires careful attention to how data are coded. Consider how data from the following hypothetical questionnaire items could be coded for data entry (some of these items were presented in Chapter 2):

Categorical indicator

Is your school a Title I school?
☐ yes   ☐ no
- Create one variable (i.e., 1 column) with data entered via the following codes: yes = 1, no = 0

Categorical indicator

Which best describes the setting of your school?
☐ urban   ☐ suburban   ☐ rural
- Create one variable (i.e., 1 column) with data entered via the following codes: urban = 1, suburban = 2, rural = 3

Numerical or short text response

Indicate the number of full-time teachers in each arts area in your school district:
____ Music ____ Visual Art ____ Dance ____ Theater
- Create separate variables (i.e., 4 columns) for each discipline; that is, this single question is represented in the spreadsheet with four columns, then enter the ACTUAL VALUES the participants entered.

Checkbox for a single response

How many elementary schools are in your district?
☐ one   ☐ two   ☐ three   ☐ four   ☐ five or more
- Create one variable (i.e., 1 column) with data entered via the following codes: one = 1, two = 2, three = 3, four = 4, five or more = 5
  o (Of course, in this case, it is important to remain aware that "5" does not necessarily mean 5 schools.)

Checkbox for multiple possible responses
Check those items that best describe your choir director. Choose as many as are relevant.
☐ kind   ☐ harsh   ☐ dictator   ☐ understanding   ☐ fun   ☐ lazy

- Create separate variables (i.e., 6 columns) for each adjective; that is, each adjective is represented in the spreadsheet with its own column, then enter 1 if the participant checked/clicked the adjective and 0 if they did not.

Code Books

It is important to keep a record of how you have chosen to code your data and what the values you entered mean. Creating a code book with this sort of information can save you time and help you avoid frustration that could occur should you forget how you initially coded your data. A code book usually has the following information:

- Variable name (i.e., column name).
- A longer label of what the variable is (e.g., the full name of a test, the verbiage of a rating criterion, the verbiage of a questionnaire item).
- The labels that have been assigned to each value, for example:
  o 1 = Strongly Agree, 2 = Agree, 3 = Disagree, 4 = Strongly Disagree
  o 1 = Freshman, 2 = Sophomore, 3 = Junior, 4 = Senior
- An obviously noticeable value (i.e., –99) or symbol (i.e., NA) that indicates a value is missing for a particular participant on a particular variable.

You can keep track of this in a Word document or on another sheet in a spreadsheet program. Some statistical software packages have fields associated with their spreadsheets that allow you to enter this information directly into your data set. For example, the "Variable View" of the SPSS data editor will allow you to input information for all of the variable attributes listed above; this is a convenient functionality SPSS offers.

Reference

Zdzinski, S. F., & Barnes, G. V. (2002). Development and validation of a string performance rating scale. *Journal of Research in Music Education, 50*(3), 245–255. https://doi.org/10.2307/3345801

APPENDIX C
Research Journals Related to Music Education

Title	Publisher
*Action, Criticism, and Theory for Music Education**	The Mayday Group
Arts Education Policy Review	Taylor & Francis
Australian Journal of Music Education	Australian Society for Music Education/Informit
British Journal of Music Education	Cambridge University Press
Bulletin of the Council for Research in Music Education	University of Illinois Press
Contributions to Music Education	Ohio Music Education Association
*Finnish Journal of Music Education**	Sibelius Academy–University of the Arts, Helsinki/Finnish Society for Research in Arts Education
*International Journal of Education and the Arts**	Penn State Libraries Open Publishing
International Journal of Music Education	International Society for Music Education/Sage
International Journal of Music in Early Childhood	Early Childhood Music & Movement Association/Intellect
*International Journal of Research in Choral Singing**	American Choral Directors Association
Journal of Aesthetic Education	Project MUSE/University of Illinois Press
Journal of Band Research	American Bandmasters Association
Journal of Historical Research in Music Education	Sage
*Journal of Learning through the Arts**	University of California–Irvine
Journal of Music Teacher Education	National Association for Music Education /Sage
Journal of Music Technology & Education	Association for Technology in Music Education/Intellect
Journal of Music Therapy	National Association for Music Therapy
Journal of Popular Music Education	Association for Popular Music Education/Intellect
Journal of Research in Music Education	National Association for Music Education /Sage
*Missouri Journal of Research in Music Education**	Missouri Music Educators Association
Musicae Scientiae	European Society for the Cognitive Sciences of Music/Sage
Music Education Research	Taylor & Francis
*Nordic Research in Music Education**	Nordic Network of Music Education Research
*Perspectives in Music Education Research**	Florida Music Educators Association/Ingenta
Philosophy of Music Education Review	Project MUS/Indiana University Press
Psychology of Music	Society for Music, Education & Psychology/Sage
Psychomusicology: Music, Mind, and Brain	American Psychological Association
*Research and Issues in Music Education**	James Madison University
Research Studies in Music Education	Sempre/Sage
String Research Journal	American String Teachers Association
*Texas Music Education Research Issues**	Texas Music Education Association
Update: Applications of Research in Music Education	National Association for Music Education /SAGE
*Visions of Research in Music Education**	New Jersey Music Education Association

*Open access online.

Out-of-Print Journals Available Online

Title	Publisher
Gender, Education, Music, and Society (GEMS)*	Gender Research in Music Education
*Music Education Research International**	University of South Florida
*Quarterly Journal of Music Teaching and Learning**	University of Northern Colorado/Reprinted by New Jersey Music Education Association

*Open access online.

Index

For the benefit of digital users, indexed terms that span two pages (e.g., 52–53) may, on occasion, appear on only one of those pages.

Tables, figures, and boxes are indicated by *t*, *f*, and *b* following the page number

abstract, 74–75
action research, boundary crossing, 407–8
action research, features of, 406
action research, history of, 405–6
action research, inquiry as mindset, 408
action research spiral, 404–5, 404*f*
ad hominem. *See* philosophical fallacies
aesthetic. *See* philosophical questions (types of)
alpha criterion. *See* alpha level
alpha level, 362, 374–75
ambiguous argument. *See* philosophical fallacies
analysis of variance (ANOVA)
    one-way analyasis of variance (one-way ANOVA), 371, 382–83
    repeated measures analysis of variance (repeated measures ANOVA), 371, 386–87
analytic frame. *See* theoretical framework
Analytic generalization. *See* case study
anthropology and ethnohistory, 62
APA guidelines for Ethical and Legal Standards in Publishing. *See* journal submission
appeal to authority. *See* philosophical fallacies
archives, 66, 67–69
artifact-elicited interviews. *See* interviews
assessment, 312
axial coding. *See* coding
axiological. *See* philosophical questions (types of)

bandwagon. *See* philosophical fallacies
bar plot, 340–41, 341*f*, 342*f*
begging the question. *See* philosophical fallacies
bell curve. *See* normal distribution
bias, 13–14, 123
"big tent criteria," 229–35
    ethical conduct, 234
    meaningful coherence, 235
    resonance, 233
    rich rigor, 230–31
    significant contribution, 234
    sincerity, 231–32
    worthy topic, 230
biographical. *See* research questions in historical research
Bonferroni method, 371, 387
Boolean search techniques, 42–43, 67
box and whiskers plot. *See* box plot
box plot, 329–30, 330*f*
bracketing, 198, 199, 201, 203–4, 223
bracketing interviews. *See* interviews

carryover effects, 298
case study, 116, 130
    categorical aggregation, 175
    correspondence and pattern, 175
    cross-case analysis, 173
    definitions of case study, 158–61
    direct interpretation, 175
    generalizability in case study, 161–63, 178
        analytic generalization, 162, 178
        case-to-case transfer, 178
        naturalistic generalizability, 162, 175, 178
    key case, 165
    local knowledge case, 165
    outlier case, 165
    types of case study, 164–65, 164*f*
        diachronic case study, 160
        intrinsic case study, 164*f*, 165–66
        instrumental case study, 164*f*, 166
        evaluative case study, 164*f*, 167
        explanatory case study, 164*f*, 166
        exploratory case study, 164*f*, 167
        multiple case study, 164*f*, 171–74, 172*f*
        parallel multiple case study, 173
        retrospective case study, 174
        sequential multiple case study, 173
        single case study, 164*f*
        snapshot case study, 174
    unit of analysis in case study, 176–77
    within-case analysis, 173

case-to-case transfer. *See* case study
categorical aggregation. *See* case study
causal claims, 264–66
causal comparative research, 277–78
central phenomenon, 9, 116–17, 130
central tendency, 325, 331
checkbox for multiple possible responses. *See* questionnaire item types
checkbox for a single response. *See* questionnaire item types
Chicago Manual of Style, 73
Chi square test of independence, 371–73, 394–96
chronological. *See* research questions in historical research
circular reasoning. *See* philosophical fallacies
cluster sampling. *See* sampling in quantitative research
coding, 144–45, 175
   axial coding, 188
   coding paradigm, 188
   inductive coding, 195
   open coding, 188
   selective coding, 188–89
coding paradigm. *See* coding
Cohen's *d*, 379–80, 381
collaborative teacher study groups (CTSGs), 411–12
combination or mixed sampling. *See* sampling strategies in case study
comparative history, 61
complete observer. *See* researcher's role in qualitative research
complete participant. *See* researcher's role in qualitative research
conceptual framework. *See* interpretive framework
concurrent criterion validity, 318
conference proceedings, 441–42
confidence interval, 357, 363–64, 383
confirmability, 218
confirming and disconfirming cases sampling. *See* sampling strategies in case study
consequential validity, 319
consistency across forms reliability. *See* equivalent forms reliability
consistency across raters. *See* interrater reliability
constant comparative method, 142–43
constructivism. *See* interpretive framework
content analysis, 62
content validity, 318, 320
context-dependent mediation, threats to external validity, 288

control condition, 217, 276
control group. *See* control condition
construct validity, 319
convenience sampling, case study. *See* sampling strategies in case study
convenience sampling, quantitative research. *See* sampling in quantitative research
correlation coefficient, 316–17
correlation matrices, 364–65
correlational research, 242*b*, 243, 277–78, 347–48
correlation with interval/ratio (scalar) data, 350–57
correlation with nominal data, 357–59
correlation with ordinal data, 359–61
correspondence and pattern. *See* case study
counterarguments. *See* philosophical argument
counterfactual, 265
Cramer's V coefficient, 359–61
creation. *See* philosophical argument
credibility, 218, 232–33
criterion sampling. *See* sampling strategies in case study
criterion validity, 318–19, 320
critical ethnography. *See* ethnography, types of
critical participatory action research, 408–9
critical storytelling. *See* narrative research
critical theory. *See* interpretive framework; philosophical research, supporting sources
critique. *See* philosophical argument
cross-case analysis. *See* case study
cross-sectional (survey), 244–45
cross-tabulation, 340
crystalization, 220–21
curvilinear relationship, 355–57, 356*f*

data analysis in qualitative research, 120–21, 142–45
  in case study, 175
  in ethnography, 208–9, 211–12
  in grounded theory, 188–89, 190
  in narrative research, 195
  in phenomenology, 201–2, 203–4
data analysis spiral, qualitative research, 143
data generation in qualitative research, 9, 120, 134–42
  in case study, 174–75
  in ethnography, 207–8, 211
  in grounded theory, 187–88
  in narrative research, 194
  in phenomenology, 200–1

INDEX   463

data presentation in qualitative research
    in case study, 176
    in ethnography, 209–10
    in grounded theory, 189
    in narrative research, 195–96
    in phenomenology, 202–3
data reduction. *See* coding
deduction. *See* deductive reasoning
deductive reasoning
    in philosophical research, 104–5
    in qualitative research, 120–21, 142
    in quantitative research, 243–44, 267
defining terms. *See* philosophical argument
delimitations, 26–27
dependability, 218
dependent samples, 372
dependent samples *t* test. *See t* test
dependent variable, 263, 269–70
diachronic case study. *See* Case study
direct interpretation. *See* Case study
directional hypothesis, 269, 374
disabled theory. *See* interpretive framework
discriminant sampling, 183–84
dispersion. *See* variability

editorial board. *See* journal submission
effect size, 363–64, 375, 379–80, 381, 383, 386–87, 391
elements of Style, Strunk, 418
emic views, 209
endnotes, 73
epistemological. *See* philosophical questions (types of)
epoche, 198, 199, 201, 203–4, 223
equivalent forms reliability, 316
equivalent materials design. *See* experimental research designs
equivalent time samples design. *See* experimental research designs
equivocation. *See* philosophical fallacies
eta squared, 383
ethical. *See* philosophical questions (types of)
ethical considerations for narrative research. *See* narrative research
ethical considerations for publication. *See* journal submission
ethnography, 116, 130
ethnography, types of, 205–6
    critical ethnography, 206
    realist ethnography, 205–6
ethnohistory. *See* anthropology and ethnohistory
etic views, 209
evaluative case study. *See* case study

evaluation in quantitative research, 312
excerpt-commentary units, 150–51
experience sampling. *See* sampling in quantitative research
experimental condition. *See* treatment condition
experimental mortality, internal validity, 286
experimental protocol, 273–74
experimental research design, 288–303
    experimental research design shorthand, 288–89
    pre-experimental designs, 289–91
        one group pretest posttest design, 290–91
        one-shot case study, 290
        static group comparison, 290–91
    quasi experimental design, 270, 295–302
        equivalent materials design, 302–3
        equivalent time samples design, 323
        nonequivalent control group design, 303–4
        time-series design, 299–302
        within-subjects design (counterbalanced), 296–99
    true experimental design, 270, 291–95
        posttest-only control group design, 295
explanatory case study. *See* case study
exploratory case study. *See* case study
ex post facto research, 277–78
extension. *See* philosophical argument
external criticism, 70–71
external validity, 283, 284, 314
    threats to external validity, 287–88
extreme or deviant case sampling. *See* sampling strategies in case study

face validity, 318
false dichotomy. *See* philosophical fallacies
false dilemma. *See* philosophical fallacies
familywise error, 384–85, 387
feminist theory. *See* interpretive framework
fieldnotes, 120, 139–40
field jottings, 139
field observations, 138–40
    structured observations, 138–39
    unstrcutured observations, 138–39
finding aid, 67–68
findings in case study. *See* case study
focus group. *See* interviews
footnotes, 73
frequency, 325, 327–29, 328*t*
Friedman's test, 371, 393
functional. *See* research questions in historical research

gender history, 62–63
geographical. *See* research questions in historical research
grounded theory, 116, 130, 185
   constructivist approach to grounded theory, 186
   data analysis in grounded theory (*see* data analysis in qualitative research)
   data presentation in grounded theory, 189
   restorying data, 195
   systemic approach to grounded theory, 186
group interviews. *See* interviews

hasty generalization. *See* philosophical fallacies
Hawthorne effect, 285
histogram, 329–30, 329f
historical sociology, 62
history, internal validity, 285
homogeneous critical case sampling. *See* sampling strategies in case study
horizonalization, 201–2
How to Write a Lot: A Guide to Productive Academic Writing, 426
hypothesis, 24–26. *See* directional hypothesis; null hypothesis; null hypothesis significance testing (NHST)

immersion in historical research, 66
imposter syndrome, scholarly writing, 428
independent samples, 372
independent samples *t* test. *See t* test
independent variable, 263, 269–70
induction. *See* inductive reasoning
inductive reasoning
   in philosophical research, 105
   in qualitative research, 120–21, 142
   in quantitative research, 243–44
inferential tests for determining differences, 361–62, 377
informed consent, 32
inquiry as mindset. *See* action research, inquiry as mindset
institutional review board (IRB), 31–33
instrument, 312
instrumental case study. *See* case study
instrumentation, internal validity, 285
intensity sampling. *See* sampling strategies in case study
interactive effects, internal validity, 286
interjudge reliability. *See* interrater reliability
internal consistency, 316
internal criticism, 70–71, 72
internal validity, 283, 284–86, 314
   threats to internal validity, 284–86

interpretive framework, 121–22, 130
   critical theory, 121
   disabled theory, 121
   feminist theory, 121
   postmodernism, 121
   postpositivism, 121
   pragmatism, 121
   social constructivism, 121
   queer theory, 121
interpretation of qualitative data, 145
interrater reliability, 316
interval level data, 309, 311
interviews, 120, 135–38
   artifact-elicited interviews, 141–42
   bracketing interviews, 222–23
   focus group, 138
   group interviews, 137–38
   Seidman's approach to phenomenological interviews, 201
   semi-structured interviews, 137
   stimulated recall interviews, 142
   sturctured interviews, 136
   unstructured interviews, 136–37
intrinsic case study. *See* Case study
introductory section. *See* writing, article organization
invariant meaning units, 202

journal submission
   abstract, 445
   aims and scope, 443
   APA guidelines for Ethical and Legal Standards in Publishing, 448
   COVER letter, 445
   editorial board, 443
   ethical considerations for publication, 448–49
   keywords, 74–75, 445
   online supplemental files, 445
   peer review, 444
   publication guidelines, 443–45
   publication process, 442–49
   references, 445
   reviewer evaluation criteria, 445–46
   revision process, 446–47
   submission guidelines, 444–45

keywords. *See* journal submission
Kruskal-Wallis test, 371, 393
kurtosis, 336–38, 337f

large-scale humanistic historical study, 60
Latin Square, 297, 297f
lecture presentation, 435–37, 437f

lecture presentation handouts, 441
leptokurtic, 336, 337f
levels of measurement, 309, 310–12, 372
libraries, 66
Likert-type rating scale. *See* questionnaire item types
limitations in qualitative research, 148–50
literature review
   finding relevant sources, 41–44
   formatting sources, 22–23
   organizing sources, 40–41
   strategies for summarizing and synthesizing sources, 47–54
lived experience descriptions (LEDs), 200–1
longitudinal (survey), 244–45

Mann-Whitney U test, 371, 389–91
maturation, internal validity, 285
maximum variation sampling. *See* sampling strategies in case study
McNemar's test, 371, 396
mean, 325, 331
meaning clusters, 202
median, 325, 331
member checking, 224–25
member reflection, 224–25
memo in qualitative research, 144
methods for answering questions, 2–3
Mills' conditions for causal claims, 265, 266, 283–84
Mills, John Stewart, 265, 277–78
minimum/maximum value, 325, 330–31, 332
mixed-methods research, 10–11
mode, 325, 331
multiple case study. *See* case study
multivocality, 232

narrative history, historical research, 59–61
narrative inquiry, qualitative research. *See* narrative research
narrative research, 116, 130, 191–97
   critical storytelling, 192–93
   ethical considerations for narrative research, 192
   narrative knowing, 192–93
   types of narrative research, 192–93
naturalistic equivalents to quantitatively oriented constructs in qualitative research, 218
naturalistic generalizability. *See* case study
naturalistic research setting, 9, 119
negative case analysis, 221–22
nominal level data, 309, 310–11
nonequivalent control group design. *See* experimental research designs

nonparametric inferential tests, 372
nonparticipant. *See* researcher's role in qualitative research
nonparticipant observer. *See* researcher's role in qualitative research
nonreactive observer. *See* researcher's role in qualitative research
nonresponse bias, 246, 254
normal distribution, 325, 334f, 335
null hypothesis, null hypothesis significance testing (NHST), 269, 361–64, 371–72, 374–75
numerical/short text responses. *See* questionnaire item types

objectivity, 123–24, 218
observational research designs, 257
omnibus test, 383, 386–87
one group pretest posttest design. *See* experimental research designs
one-shot case study. *See* experimental research designs
one-way analysis of variance (one-way ANOVA). *See* analysis of variance (ANOVA)
online archives, 66–67
online supplemental files. *See* journal submission
ontological. *See* Philosophical questions (types of)
open coding. *See* coding
open-ended response text box. *See* questionnaire item types
operational definition, 26–27
opportunistic sampling. *See* sampling strategies in case study
oral history, 69–70
oral history interview protocols, 70
ordinal level data, 309, 311
outcome variable. *See* independent variable

parallel forms reliability. *See* equivalent forms reliability
parallel multiple case study. *See* case study
parametric inferential tests, 372
partial eta squared, 386–87
participatory action research, 404, 405
Pearson's coefficient. *See* Pearson product moment coefficient
Pearson product moment coefficient, 347, 353–55
Pearson's r. *See* Pearson product moment coefficient
peer debriefing, 228–29

peer review. *See* journal submission
Performing Arts Library at the University of Maryland, College Park, 70
phenomenological reduction, 121, 198, 199, 223
phenomenological reflection, 202
phenomenology, 116, 130, 197–99
    hermeneutical phenomenology, 198–99
    transcendental phenomenology, 199
Phi coefficient, 359–61, 394–95
philosophical argument, 90–91
    counterarguments, 105
    creation, 83, 90–91
    critique, 83, 90
    defining terms, 83, 91
    extension, 83, 90
    synthesis, 83, 90
philosophical fallacies, 106–9
    ad hominem, 106
    ambiguous argument, 107
    appeal to authority, 107
    appeal to the people, 107
    bandwagon, 107
    begging the question, 107–8
    circular reasoning, 107–8
    equivocation, 107
    false dichotomy, 108
    false dilemma, 108
    hasty generalization, 108
    red herring, 108
    slippery slope, 108–9
    straw man, 109
philosophical problem (characteristics of), 86–87
    realistic, 86
    significant, 86–87
    sufficiently narrow, 86
philosophical questions (types of), 98–100
    aesthetic, 97, 99
    axiological, 97, 98–99
    epistemological, 7–8, 97, 98
    ethical, 97, 99
    ontological, 8, 97, 98
    political, 97, 99–100
philosophical research, supporting sources, 100–4
    critical theory, supporting sources 102–3
        Adorno, Theodor, 102–3
        Frankfurt School, 102–3
        Freire, Paulo, 102–3, 405
        Said, Edward, 102–3
        Spivak, Gayatri, 102–3
    eastern philosophies, supporting sources, 103–4
        Buddhism, 103–4
        Confucianism, 103–4
        Daoism, 103–4
    education philosophy, supporting sources, 102
        Bildung, 61, 102
        Dewey, John, 102, 405
        Greene, Maxine, 102
        hooks, bell, 102
        Noddings, Nel, 102
    empirical and historical research, supporting sources, 104
    feminist philosophy, supporting sources, 103
        Ahmed, Sara, 103
        Braidotti, Rosi, 103
        Butler, Judith, 103
        Haraway, Donna, 103
    political philosophy, supporting sources, 103
        Arendt, Hannah, 103
        capitalism, 103
        class antagonisms, 103
        democracy, 103
        globalization, 103
        Marx, Karl, 103
        neoliberalism, 103
        Rancière, Jacques, 103
    poststructuralist philosophy, supporting sources, 103
        Deleuze, Gilles, 103
        Derrida, Jacques, 103
        différence, 103
        Foucault, Michel, 103
    Western music philosophy, supporting sources, 101–2
        Aristotle, 101
        Boethius, 101
        Concise Survey of Music Philosophy by Donald Hodges, 101–2
        Davies, Stephen, 102
        Gurney, Edmund, 101–2
        Hanslick, Eduard, 101–2
        Hegel, Wilhelm Friedrich, 101–2
        Husserl, Edmund, 102
        Johnson, Mark, 102
        Kant, Immanuel, 101–2
        Kivy, Peter, 102
        Langer, Susanne, 102
        Luther, Martin 101
        MacIntyre, Alasdair, 101
        Merleau-Ponty, Maurice, 102
        Meyer, Leonard, 101–2
    Music education philosophical literature, 100–1

Robinson, Jenefer, 102
Schiller, Friedrich 101–2
Schopenhauer, Arthur, 101–2
platykurtic, 336, 337f
political. *See* philosophical questions (types of)
politically important sampling. *See* sampling strategies in case study
population, 246, 270
positionality, 122, 147–48
poster presentation, 432–35, 433f, 434f
post-hoc analyses, 371, 384–85, 387–88
postmodernism. *See* Interpretive framework
postpositivism. *See* Interpretive framework
posttest, 217, 277
pragmatism. *See* Interpretive framework
predictive validity, 318–19
pretest, 263–64, 277
primary sources, 11–12, 64–66, 67
probability sampling. *See* sampling in quantitative research
probability value. *See* P value
publication guidelines. *See* journal submission
public history, 63
publishing a paper. *See* journal submission
Purdue Writing Lab, 418
purpose statement, 23–24
  action research, 24
  historical research, 24
  philosophical research, 24
  qualitative research, 24
    in case study, 163
    in ethnography, 206–7
    in experimental research, 267–68
    in grounded theory, 186, 189
    in narrative research, 193–94
    in phenomenology, 199–200
purpose statement, quantitative research, 24
purposeful sampling. *See* sampling strategies in case study
p value, probability value, 362–63, 374–75, 379, 381, 383

quantitative history, historical research, 61–62
quartiles, 241, 333–35
quasi-experimental design. *See* experimental design
queer theory. *See* interpretive framework
questionnaire development, 248–52
questionnaire formatting, 249
questionnaire item ordering, 249
questionnaire item types, 249–51
  checkbox for multiple possible responses, 250
  checkbox for a single response, 250

Likert-type rating scale, 250–51
  numerical/short text responses, 250
  open-ended response text box, 251
  ranking, 250
questionnaire length and duration, 248–49
questionnaire pilot testing, 252

random assignment, 270–71, 276
random purposeful sampling. *See* sampling strategies for case study
range, 325, 332
ranking. *See* questionnaire item types
ratio level data, 309, 312
readily accessible identity, 147
realist ethnography. *See* ethnography, types of
red herring. *See* philosophical fallacies
references. *See* journal submission
reflective practice in action research, 404, 410
reflexivity, 123–24, 223, 238
reliability, 271–72, 309, 313–20, 314f
repeated measures analysis of variance (repeated measures ANOVA). *See* analysis of variance (ANOVA)
replication studies, 286
repositories, 66
research methodological paradigms, 7–13
research poster presentation. *See* poster presentation
research/practice relationship, 5–6
researcher's role in qualitative research, 146–47
  complete participant, 146
  complete observer, 146
  nonparticipant, 146
  nonparticipant observer, 146
  nonreactive observer, 146–47
researcher subjectivity. *See* subjectivity
research questions in action research, 408–10
research questions in case study, 164
research questions in ethnography, 206–7
research questions in experimental research, 267–68, 274
research questions in grounded theory, 186, 190
research questions in historical research, 64
  biographical, 64
  chronological, 64
  functional, 64
  geographical, 64
research questions in narrative research, 193–94
research questions in phenomenology, 199–200
research questions in philosophical research, 12
response rate, 246, 254

restorying data. *See* grounded theory
retrospective case study. *See* case study
r statistic, 391, 392–93
reviewer evaluation criteria. *See* journal submission
revision process. *See* journal submission

sample definition, quantitative research, 246, 270
sample size in qualitative research, 131–33
sampling bias, 29–30
sampling strategies in case study, 133, 134*t*
   combination or mixed sampling, 134*t*
   confirming and disconfirming cases sampling, 134*t*
   convenience sampling, case study 134*t*
   criterion sampling, 134*t*
   extreme or deviant case sampling, 134*t*
   homogeneous critical case sampling, 134*t*
   intensity sampling, 134*t*
   maximum variation sampling, 134*t*
   opportunistic sampling, 134*t*
   politically important sampling, 134*t*
   purposeful sampling, 131
   random purposeful sampling, 134*t*
   stratified purposeful sampling, 134*t*
   theory-based sampling, 134*t*
   typical case sampling, 134*t*
sampling frame, 246, 255
sampling in quantitative research, 246, 257
   cluster sampling, 247
   convenience sampling, quantitative research, 247
   experience sampling, 258
   probability sampling, 247
   simple random sampling, 247
   stratified random sampling, 247
   stratified sampling, 247
   systematic sampling, 247
sampling strategies in grounded theory, 186–87
sampling strategies in ethnography, 207
sampling strategies in narrative research, 194
sampling strategies in phenomenology, 200
saturation in historical research, 66
scalar data, 350–57
scatterplot, 347, 350–53, 351*f*, 352*f*, 354*f*, 359
secondary sources, 65–66, 67
Seidman's approach to phenomenological interviews. *See* interviews
selection bias, internal validity, 286
selecting a journal to submit research, 442–43
selective coding. *See* coding
self-study in action research, 404

semi-structured interviews. *See* interviews
sequential multiple case study. *See* case study
simple random sampling. *See* sampling in quantitative research
single case study. *See* case study
skewness, 336–38, 337*f*
slide show, lecture presentation, 438–41
slippery slope. *See* philosophical fallacies
small-scale humanistic historical study, 60
snapshot case study. *See* case study
social constructivism. *See* interpretive framework
Spearman coefficient. *See* Spearman rank correlation coefficient
Spearman rank correlation coefficient, 357
Spearman's *rho*. *See* Spearman rank correlation coefficient
spoken presentation. *See* lecture presentation
standard deviation, 325, 332–33, 334*f*, 335
static group comparison. *See* experimental research designs
statistical power, 363
statistical regression, internal validity, 285–86
statistical significance, 362, 363, 372
stimulated recall interviews. *See* Interviews
stratified sampling. *See* sampling in quantitative research
stratified purposeful sampling. *See* sampling strategies in case study
stratified random sampling. *See* sampling in quantitative research
straw man. *See* philosophical fallacies
structural description, 202–3
structured interviews. *See* interviews
structured observations. *See* field observations
subjectivity, 122–24, 145, 147–48, 223, 238
subjectivity statement, 147–48, 222
submission guidelines. *See* journal submission
survey study, recruiting participants, 253–54
synthesis. *See* philosophical argument
systematic sampling. *See* sampling in quantitative research

t test
   dependent samples *t* test, 381–82
   independant samples *t* test, 378–80
test. *See* instrument
testing, internal validity, 285
test-retest reliability, 315–16
textural description, 202–3
thematic analysis, 121, 175
themes in qualitative research, 145
theoretical framework, 20–21, 121–22, 168, 177, 267

theoretical sampling, 186–87
theory-based sampling. *See* sampling strategies in case study
thick description, 209, 227–28
threats to external validity. *See* external validity
threats to internal validity. *See* internal validity
threats to internal validity for quasi-experimental designs, 296*t*
time-series design. *See* experimental research designs
transferability, 218
treatment condition, 217, 276
triangulation, 71, 72, 120, 141, 220
true experimental design. *See* experimental research
Tukey HSD test, 371, 385
Type I error, 362, 374–75, 387
Type II error, 363, 375
typical case sampling. *See* sampling strategies in case study

unit of analysis in case study. *See* case study
unstructured interviews. *See* interviews
unstructured observations. *See* field observations

validity, 271–72, 283, 284–88, 309, 313–20, 314*f*
validity coefficients, 319–20
variability, 325, 332–35, 332*f*
variance, 332–33

Wilcox test for paired samples, 371, 391–93
within-case analysis. *See* case study
within-subjects design (counterbalanced). *See* experimental research designs
writing environment, 420–21
writing goals, 421–24
writing group, 421
writing motivation, 423, 427
writing, revisions, 424–26
writing schedule, 419–20

Printed in the USA/Agawam, MA
January 24, 2023

804870.071